Frommer's®
Chicago

WRIGLEY FIELD
HOME OF
CHICAGO CUBS

My Chicago
by Elizabeth Canning Blackwell

FOR ME, CHICAGO IS ALL ABOUT ATTITUDE—AND NOT THE IN-YOUR-FACE

kind. The city and many of its citizens buzz with positive energy. It's easy to define Chicago by what it's not—not high-pressure like New York, not edgy like San Francisco or Seattle; not blessed with beautiful weather like L.A. But what Chicago does have is all the adrenaline rush and diverse charms of a big city without the accompanying pressure.

I can stroll through the Loop and feel sufficiently awed by the towering high-rises; then a few minutes later I can get a nature fix by walking along the shores of Lake Michigan. There's enough culture to keep my mind sharp, but no one's competitive about snagging tickets to the latest exhibit or theater performance. I can find pretty much any designer look I covet, but most people aren't caught up in fashion and fads.

Chicago may be big and bustling, but it still has a self-effacing, Midwestern reticence. It's the kind of place that seduces you with comfort rather than flashiness. When I came here for college, I didn't plan on staying. But Chicago sucked me in. I was drawn to the down-to-earth people, the bike paths along the lakefront, the great restaurants, and most of all the welcoming aura the city exudes that made me feel I belonged. I hope you have the same experience. These photos offer a glimpse of the Chicago I love.

© Tim Turner/Charlie Trotter's

Chicago restaurants run the gamut from gourmet showplaces to neighborhood dives to virtually every ethnic cuisine you can imagine. If you want to splurge, **CHARLIE TROTTER'S (left)** is the place to do it. The food (such as this turbot ceviche wrapped in smoked salmon with razor clam vinaigrette) is beautifully presented, painstakingly prepared, and always dazzlingly original.

Though Chicago has more than its fair share of fancy, pricey restaurants, on an average evening, I'm more likely to head to **LOU MALNATI'S (above)** for deep-dish pizza. There are plenty of other pizza joints in this town known for its pizza—all of them fine—but Malnati's is my favorite: not too much cheese, generous toppings, and a fantastic cornmeal crust.

Serious shoppers can spend days scouting for deals around Chicago. But the massive **MACY'S DEPARTMENT STORE (above)** on State Street has a special place in most Chicagoans' hearts. Built in the mid–19th century as Marshall Field's, the grand building harks back to a time when shopping downtown was an event; highlights include the massive **TIFFANY GLASS DOME (right)** that towers over a multi-story atrium. Although locals mourn the loss of the Field's name, New York–based Macy's has kept the store's mix of designer mini-boutiques and more affordable brands.

Walk through downtown Chicago and you'll get a capsule history of modern urban architecture. One of the city's earliest high-rises, **THE ROOKERY** (designed by some of Chicago's best-known architects: Burnham & Root and Frank Lloyd Wright), looks gloomy and imposing from the outside, with thick, fortress-like walls. But step inside, and you'll find yourself entering a bright, two-story atrium filled with natural light and artfully-twisting staircases curving overhead (far more open and welcoming than your standard office lobby). Take an architectural walking tour around Chicago to glimpse more of the city's hidden treasures.

What I love most about Chicago's theater scene is the variety: You can see everything from flashy, Broadway-bound musicals to in-your-face storefront shows where the performers on stage outnumber the people in the audience. Two of the best theater companies in town are particularly visitor-friendly, since they're within easy reach of downtown hotels. The **LOOKINGGLASS THEATRE COMPANY** (above) usually takes inspiration from works of literature to create thought-provoking and visually-arresting shows (this photo is from a performance of George Orwell's *1984*). On Navy Pier, the **CHICAGO SHAKESPEARE THEATRE** (right) presents the classics in a lovely courtyard-style theater that brings the actors up close and personal.

It seems like every movie set in Chicago features an elevated train zipping along in the background of a crucial scene. **THE EL (right)** is more than just a symbol of the city; it's also a great way to experience the town. Take a ride on my favorite route, the Brown Line, to see what I mean.

Whether you're headed to the monkey house, the polar bear pool, or the elaborate African habitat, the **LINCOLN PARK ZOO (below)** takes you worlds away. Because it's free, families wander in and out, stopping to watch whatever catches their fancy or take a break on the zoo's welcoming lawns; this zoo feels like an extension of the park rather than a special excursion.

© Pierre Tremblay/Masterfile

© Linda Matlow/Pix International/Alamy

Millennium Park covers only a few blocks in the northwest corner of downtown's Grant Park, but that compact space is home to some stunning works of art—pieces meant to be experienced up close rather than admired from afar. The **CROWN FOUNTAIN (left)** projects massive photos of ordinary Chicagoans; water pours out of their mouths every few minutes, splashing giggling children below.

Another highlight of Millennium Park is sculptor Anish Kapoor's ***CLOUD GATE*** (above, at left), which reflects the city skyline and the figures of people walking around and underneath it. A few steps away, dramatic curves of steel seem to billow over the **PRITZKER MUSIC PAVILION (above, at right)**, designed by Frank Gehry, where the Grant Park Music Festival performs free summer concerts.

The **FIELD MUSEUM OF NATURAL HISTORY** **(left)** is one of those massive institutions that seem to have everything: mummies, precious gems, dusty dioramas, and modern interactive exhibits. But it's "Sue," the most complete *Tyrannosaurus rex* fossil ever discovered, that makes a dramatic first impression.

If you've only got time for one trip out of Chicago, head to Oak Park. Home to Frank Lloyd Wright in the years he began transforming American architecture, the town's juxtaposition of traditional wood-frame Victorian houses and low-slung, Prairie-style homes show exactly why Wright's work was so revolutionary. One of Wright's Oak Park masterpieces is **UNITY TEMPLE (below)**, a building that subverts traditional church architecture to create a new kind of sacred space.

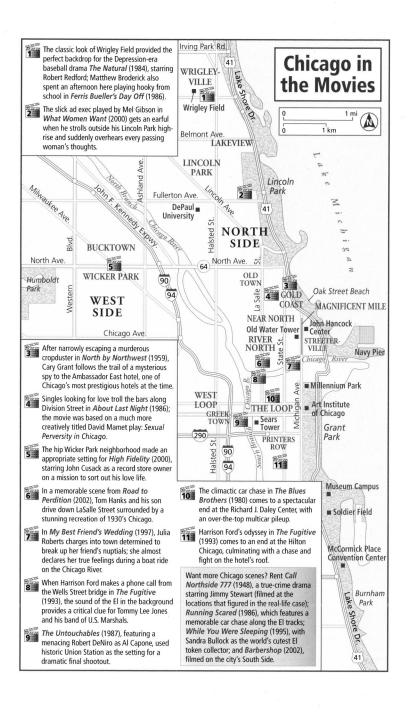

Chicago in the Movies

0   1 mi

0   1 km

1 The classic look of Wrigley Field provided the perfect backdrop for the Depression-era baseball drama *The Natural* (1984), starring Robert Redford; Matthew Broderick also spent an afternoon here playing hooky from school in *Ferris Bueller's Day Off* (1986).

2 The slick ad exec played by Mel Gibson in *What Women Want* (2000) gets an earful when he strolls outside his Lincoln Park high-rise and suddenly overhears every passing woman's thoughts.

3 After narrowly escaping a murderous cropduster in *North by Northwest* (1959), Cary Grant follows the trail of a mysterious spy to the Ambassador East hotel, one of Chicago's most prestigious hotels at the time.

4 Singles looking for love troll the bars along Division Street in *About Last Night* (1986); the movie was based on a much more creatively titled David Mamet play: *Sexual Perversity in Chicago*.

5 The hip Wicker Park neighborhood made an appropriate setting for *High Fidelity* (2000), starring John Cusack as a record store owner on a mission to sort out his love life.

6 In a memorable scene from *Road to Perdition* (2002), Tom Hanks and his son drive down LaSalle Street surrounded by a stunning recreation of 1930's Chicago.

7 In *My Best Friend's Wedding* (1997), Julia Roberts charges into town determined to break up her friend's nuptials; she almost declares her true feelings during a boat ride on the Chicago River.

8 When Harrison Ford makes a phone call from the Wells Street bridge in *The Fugitive* (1993), the sound of the El in the background provides a critical clue for Tommy Lee Jones and his band of U.S. Marshals.

9 *The Untouchables* (1987), featuring a menacing Robert DeNiro as Al Capone, used historic Union Station as the setting for a dramatic final shootout.

10 The climactic car chase in *The Blues Brothers* (1980) comes to a spectacular end at the Richard J. Daley Center, with an over-the-top multicar pileup.

11 Harrison Ford's odyssey in *The Fugitive* (1993) comes to an end at the Hilton Chicago, culminating with a chase and fight on the hotel's roof.

Want more Chicago scenes? Rent *Call Northside 777* (1948), a true-crime drama starring Jimmy Stewart (filmed at the locations that figured in the real-life case); *Running Scared* (1986), which features a memorable car chase along the El tracks; *While You Were Sleeping* (1995), with Sandra Bullock as the world's cutest El token collector; and *Barbershop* (2002), filmed on the city's South Side.

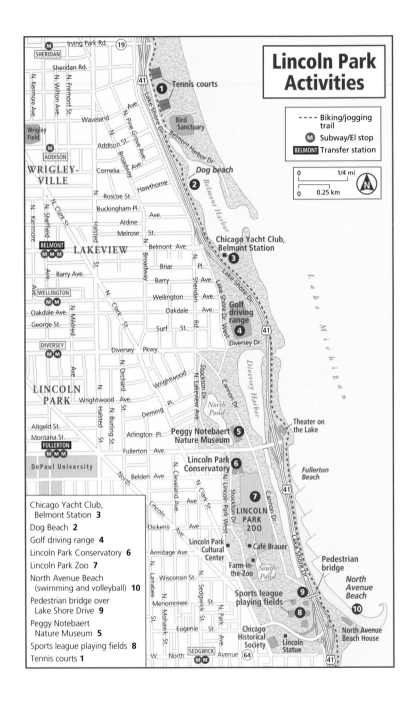

Lincoln Park Activities

- - - - Biking/jogging trail
Ⓜ Subway/El stop
BELMONT Transfer station

| 0 | | 1/4 mi |
| 0 | 0.25 km | |

Irving Park Rd. ⑲
SHERIDAN
Sheridan Rd.
N. Kenmore Ave.
N. Wilton Ave.
N. Fremont St.
Waveland
N. Pine Grove Ave.
Lake Shore Dr.
㊶ ❶ **Tennis courts**
Wrigley Field
ADDISON
Addison St.
Broadway
Cornelia
Hawthorne
Bird Sanctuary
Belmont Harbor Dr.
Dog beach
❷
Belmont Harbor
WRIGLEY-VILLE
Roscoe St.
Buckingham Pl.
Ave.
Aldine
Melrose
St.
Broadway
BELMONT
Ⓜ Ⓜ Ⓜ
LAKEVIEW
Belmont Ave.
N. Clark St.
N. Sheffield
N. Kenmore
Halsted
St.
Briar
Pl.
Chicago Yacht Club, Belmont Station
❸
Barry Ave.
WELLINGTON
Ⓜ Ⓜ
Barry
Ave.
Sheridan
Wellington Ave.
Lake Shore Dr.
N. Mildred
N. Clark St.
Oakdale Ave.
Oakdale Ave.
George St.
Surf St.
Rd.
Golf driving range
❹
DIVERSEY
Ⓜ Ⓜ
Diversey Pkwy.
Diversey Dr.
㊶
Lake Michigan
N. Orchard
N. Burling St.
Halsted St.
Wrightwood
LINCOLN PARK
Wrightwood Ave.
Pl.
Deming
N. Lakeview Ave.
Stockton Dr.
Cannon Dr.
North Pond
Diversey Harbor
Altgeld St.
Montana St.
FULLERTON
Ⓜ Ⓜ Ⓜ
Arlington Pl.
Fullerton Ave.
Peggy Notebaert Nature Museum ❺
Theater on the Lake
DePaul University
Belden Ave.
North
N. Cleveland Ave.
N. Clark St.
N. Lincoln Park West
Stockton Dr.
Lincoln Park Conservatory ❻
Fullerton Beach
❼
Lincoln Ave.
Dickens Ave.
LINCOLN PARK ZOO
Lake Shore Dr.
㊶
Lincoln Park Cultural Center
Armitage Ave.
Café Brauer
Pedestrian bridge
N. Larrabee
Wisconsin St.
Farm-in-the-Zoo
South Pond
North Avenue Beach
Sedgwick
N. Park
Sports league playing fields
❾
❽
❿
Menomonee St.
Mohawk St.
Eugenie St.
Chicago Historical Society
Lincoln Statue
North Avenue Beach House
SEDGWICK
Ⓜ Ⓜ
W. North Avenue ㉔
㊶

Chicago Yacht Club, Belmont Station **3**
Dog Beach **2**
Golf driving range **4**
Lincoln Park Conservatory **6**
Lincoln Park Zoo **7**
North Avenue Beach (swimming and volleyball) **10**
Pedestrian bridge over Lake Shore Drive **9**
Peggy Notebaert Nature Museum **5**
Sports league playing fields **8**
Tennis courts **1**

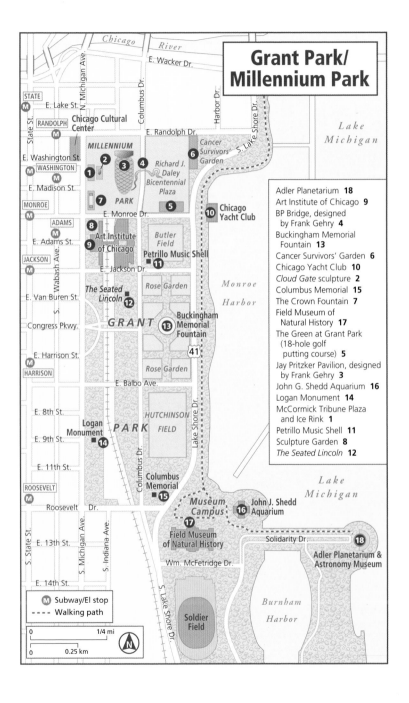

Grant Park/ Millennium Park

Chicago River

E. Wacker Dr.

STATE

E. Lake St.

N. Michigan Ave.

Columbus Dr.

Harbor Dr.

S. Lake Shore Dr.

Lake Michigan

RANDOLPH

Chicago Cultural Center

E. Randolph Dr.

E. Washington St.

WASHINGTON

MILLENNIUM

Cancer Survivors' Garden

E. Madison St.

Richard J. Daley Bicentennial Plaza

MONROE

PARK

E. Monroe Dr.

Chicago Yacht Club

ADAMS

E. Adams St.

Art Institute of Chicago

Butler Field

JACKSON

Petrillo Music Shell

E. Jackson Dr.

Monroe Harbor

E. Van Buren St.

The Seated Lincoln

Rose Garden

Congress Pkwy.

GRANT

Buckingham Memorial Fountain

S. Wabash Ave.

E. Harrison St.

41

HARRISON

Rose Garden

E. Balbo Ave.

E. 8th St.

Logan Monument

PARK

HUTCHINSON FIELD

E. 9th St.

S. Lake Shore Dr.

Columbus Dr.

E. 11th St.

ROOSEVELT

Columbus Memorial

Lake Michigan

Roosevelt Dr.

Museum Campus

John J. Shedd Aquarium

S. State St.

S. Michigan Ave.

S. Indiana Ave.

E. 13th St.

Field Museum of Natural History

Solidarity Dr.

Adler Planetarium & Astronomy Museum

Wm. McFetridge Dr.

E. 14th St.

Subway/El stop

Walking path

0   1/4 mi

0   0.25 km

N

Soldier Field

Burnham Harbor

S. Lake Shore Dr.

Adler Planetarium **18**

Art Institute of Chicago **9**

BP Bridge, designed by Frank Gehry **4**

Buckingham Memorial Fountain **13**

Cancer Survivors' Garden **6**

Chicago Yacht Club **10**

Cloud Gate sculpture **2**

Columbus Memorial **15**

The Crown Fountain **7**

Field Museum of Natural History **17**

The Green at Grant Park (18-hole golf putting course) **5**

Jay Pritzker Pavilion, designed by Frank Gehry **3**

John G. Shedd Aquarium **16**

Logan Monument **14**

McCormick Tribune Plaza and Ice Rink **1**

Petrillo Music Shell **11**

Sculpture Garden **8**

The Seated Lincoln **12**

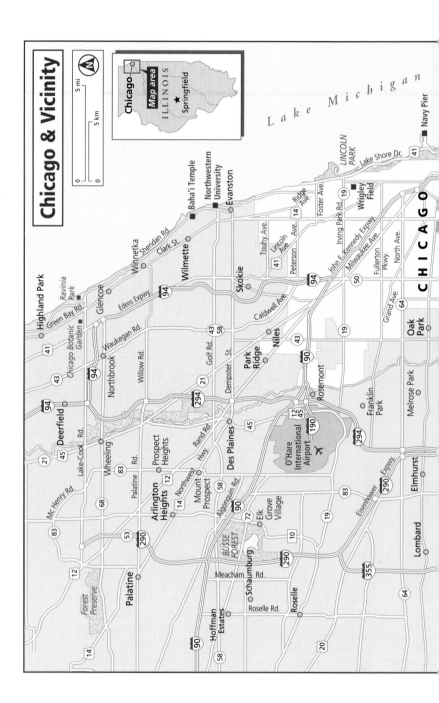

Chicago & Vicinity

5 mi

5 km

Map area

ILLINOIS

Chicago

Springfield

Lake Michigan

Navy Pier

Lake Shore Dr.

LINCOLN PARK

Baha'i Temple

Northwestern University

Evanston

Highland Park

Ravinia Park

Green Bay Rd.

Glencoe

Winnetka

Sheridan Rd.

Clark St.

Wilmette

Chicago Botanic Garden

Waukegan Rd.

Willow Rd.

Edens Expwy.

Skokie

Foster Ave.

Ridge Ave.

Wrigley Field

Touhy Ave.

Lincoln Ave.

Peterson Ave.

Irving Park Rd.

John F. Kennedy Expwy.

Milwaukee Ave.

Fullerton Ave.

North Ave.

Grand Ave.

Golf Rd.

Dempster St.

Caldwell Ave.

Niles

Park Ridge

Northbrook

Deerfield

Lake-Cook Rd.

Wheeling

Palatine Rd.

Prospect Heights

Rand Rd.

Des Plaines

Rosemont

Franklin Park

Melrose Park

Oak Park

CHICAGO

McHenry Rd.

Northwest Hwy.

Arlington Heights

Mount Prospect

Algonquin Rd.

Elk Grove Village

O'Hare International Airport

Eisenhower Expwy.

Elmhurst

Lombard

BUSSE FOREST

Palatine

Meacham Rd.

Schaumburg

Roselle Rd.

Roselle

Hoffman Estates

Forest Preserve

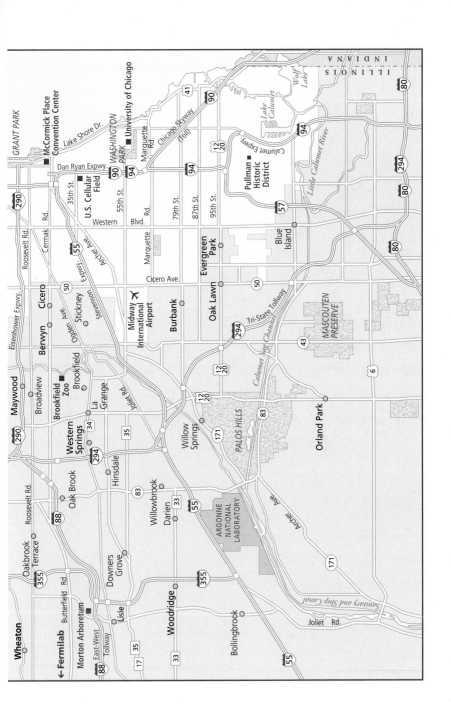

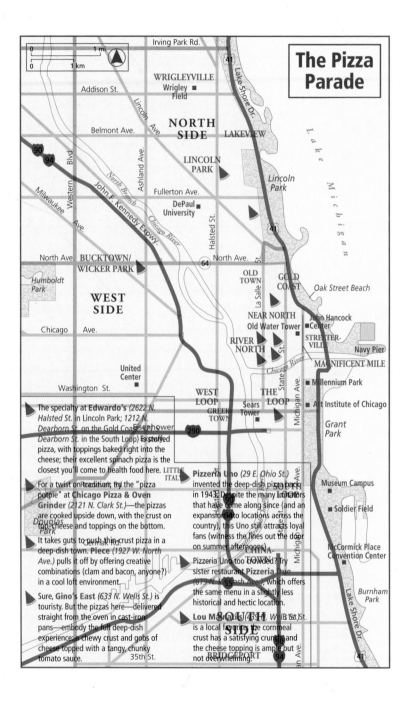

The Pizza Parade

The specialty at **Edwardo's** *(2622 N. Halsted St.* in Lincoln Park; *1212 N. Dearborn St.* on the Gold Coast; *521 S. Dearborn St.* in the South Loop) is stuffed pizza, with toppings baked right into the cheese; their excellent spinach pizza is the closest you'll come to health food here.

For a twist on tradition, try the "pizza potpie" at **Chicago Pizza & Oven Grinder** *(2121 N. Clark St.)*—the pizzas are cooked upside down, with the crust on top, cheese and toppings on the bottom.

It takes guts to push thin-crust pizza in a deep-dish town. **Piece** *(1927 W. North Ave.)* pulls it off by offering creative combinations (clam and bacon, anyone?) in a cool loft environment.

Sure, **Gino's East** *(633 N. Wells St.)* is touristy. But the pizzas here—delivered straight from the oven in cast-iron pans—embody the full deep-dish experience: a chewy crust and gobs of cheese topped with a tangy, chunky tomato sauce.

Pizzeria Uno *(29 E. Ohio St.)* invented the deep-dish pizza back in 1943. Despite the many imitators that have come along since (and an expansion to 94 locations across the country), this Uno still attracts loyal fans (witness the lines out the door on summer afternoons).

Pizzeria Uno too crowded? Try sister restaurant **Pizzeria Due** *(619 N. Wabash Ave.)*, which offers the same menu in a slightly less historical and hectic location.

Lou Malnati's *(439 N. Wells St.)* is a local favorite: the cornmeal crust has a satisfying crunch and the cheese topping is ample but not overwhelming.

Frommer's®

Chicago 2010

by Elizabeth Canning Blackwell

WILEY
Wiley Publishing, Inc.

Published by:

WILEY PUBLISHING, INC.

111 River St.
Hoboken, NJ 07030-5774

ISBN 978-0-470-50468-0

Editor: Hilary Achauer with Anuja Madar
Production Editor: M. Faunette Johnston
Cartographer: Elizabeth Puhl
Photo Editor: Richard Fox
Production by Wiley Indianapolis Composition Services

Front cover photo: The Wrigley Building, Chicago, Illinois, © Walter Bibikow / AGE Fotostock, Inc. / Photolibrary

Back cover photo: Chicago night game at Wrigley Field, view of stands and field with fans clapping and cheering, © Kim Karpeles / Alamy Images

For information on our other products and services or to obtain technical support, please contact our Customer Care Department within the U.S. at 877/762-2974, outside the U.S. at 317/572-3993 or fax 317/572-4002.

Wiley also publishes its books in a variety of electronic formats. Some content that appears in print may not be available in electronic formats.

Manufactured in the United States of America

5   4   3   2   1

CONTENTS

4 SUGGESTED CHICAGO ITINERARIES 54

5 WHERE TO STAY 66

6 WHERE TO DINE 90

7 EXPLORING CHICAGO 149

8 CHICAGO STROLLS   205

9 SHOPPING   217

10 CHICAGO AFTER DARK   246

11 FAST FACTS, TOLL-FREE NUMBERS & WEBSITES   287

INDEX   296

LIST OF MAPS

ABOUT THE AUTHOR

Elizabeth Canning Blackwell began life on the East Coast, but 4 years at Northwestern University transformed her into a Midwesterner. She has worked as a writer and editor at *Encyclopedia Britannica*, Northwestern University Medical School, the *Chicago Tribune*, and *North Shore*, a lifestyle magazine for the Chicago suburbs. She has also written for national magazines on everything from planning the perfect wedding to fighting a duel. She lives just outside the city with her husband, three kids, and an extensive collection of long underwear.

HOW TO CONTACT US

In researching this book, we discovered many wonderful places—hotels, restaurants, shops, and more. We're sure you'll find others. Please tell us about them, so we can share the information with your fellow travelers in upcoming editions. If you were disappointed with a recommendation, we'd love to know that, too. Please write to:

Frommer's Chicago 2010
Wiley Publishing, Inc. • 111 River St. • Hoboken, NJ 07030-5774

AN ADDITIONAL NOTE

Please be advised that travel information is subject to change at any time—and this is especially true of prices. We therefore suggest that you write or call ahead for confirmation when making your travel plans. The authors, editors, and publisher cannot be held responsible for the experiences of readers while traveling. Your safety is important to us, however, so we encourage you to stay alert and be aware of your surroundings. Keep a close eye on cameras, purses, and wallets, all favorite targets of thieves and pickpockets.

FROMMER'S STAR RATINGS, ICONS & ABBREVIATIONS

Every hotel, restaurant, and attraction listing in this guide has been ranked for quality, value, service, amenities, and special features using a **star-rating system.** In country, state, and regional guides, we also rate towns and regions to help you narrow down your choices and budget your time accordingly. Hotels and restaurants are rated on a scale of zero (recommended) to three stars (exceptional). Attractions, shopping, nightlife, towns, and regions are rated according to the following scale: zero stars (recommended), one star (highly recommended), two stars (very highly recommended), and three stars (must-see).

In addition to the star-rating system, we also use **seven feature icons** that point you to the great deals, in-the-know advice, and unique experiences that separate travelers from tourists. Throughout the book, look for:

Finds	Special finds—those places only insiders know about
Fun Facts	Fun facts—details that make travelers more informed and their trips more fun
Kids	Best bets for kids and advice for the whole family
Moments	Special moments—those experiences that memories are made of
Overrated	Places or experiences not worth your time or money
Tips	Insider tips—great ways to save time and money
Value	Great values—where to get the best deals

The following **abbreviations** are used for credit cards:

AE	American Express	**DISC**	Discover	**V**	Visa
DC	Diners Club	**MC**	MasterCard		

TRAVEL RESOURCES AT FROMMERS.COM

Frommer's travel resources don't end with this guide. Frommer's website, **www.frommers. com**, has travel information on more than 4,000 destinations. We update features regularly, giving you access to the most current trip-planning information and the best airfare, lodging, and car-rental bargains. You can also listen to podcasts, connect with other Frommers.com members through our active-reader forums, share your travel photos, read blogs from guide-book editors and fellow travelers, and much more.

The Best of Chicago

Like any great city, Chicago's got something for everyone, whether your tastes run toward world-famous museums and blow-your-budget luxury hotels or family-friendly lodgings and low-key neighborhood restaurants. Narrowing down your choices may seem daunting, but never fear: Here's your cheat sheet to the very best of the city, the places where I send out-of-town friends and relatives when they want to experience the "real" Chicago. Some are well-known tourist attractions, others insider secrets, but all are places and experiences that truly sum up this town. Happy exploring!

1 THE MOST UNFORGETTABLE TRAVEL EXPERIENCES

- **Studying the Skyline:** The birthplace of the modern skyscraper, Chicago is the perfect place to learn about—and appreciate—these dramatic buildings. If you're only in town for a short time, get a quick skyscraper fix by strolling through the heart of downtown, known as the Loop, where you'll be surrounded by canyons of stone, concrete, and glass. (To get the full urban experience, visit on a weekday, when the streets are bustling.) If you have more time, take an architectural tour by foot, bus, bike, or boat. See "Sightseeing Tours," p. 193.

- **Chilling Out on the Lakefront:** It really is cooler by the lake (both meteorologically and metaphorically), and we Chicagoans treat the Lake Michigan waterfront as our personal playground. Miles of parkland hug the shoreline; walk to Monroe Harbor for picture-perfect views of downtown or join active Lincoln Park singles for biking or jogging farther north. For an even better look at the city, get out on the water. At Navy Pier, you can board a vessel that's just your speed, from a powerboat to a tall-masted schooner. See "Staying Active," p. 199.

- **Riding the Rails:** Find out why the Loop is so named by hopping a Brown Line elevated train (or "the El," for short). Watch the city unfold as the train crosses the Chicago River and screeches past downtown high-rises. Half the fun is peeping into the windows of offices and homes as you speed by. (Don't feel guilty—we all do it!) See "Getting Around," p. 41, and "Sightseeing Tours," p. 193.

- **Escaping Downtown:** Local politicians like to refer to Chicago as "a city of neighborhoods"—and in this case, they're telling the truth. You won't really experience Chicago unless you leave downtown and explore some residential areas, whether it's the historic wood-framed homes in Old Town or the eclectic boutiques of Wicker Park. It's one of the best ways to get a feeling for how the people here actually live, from Latino families in Pilsen to gay couples on Halsted Street. See "Neighborhoods in Brief," p. 56.

- **Four Seasons** (120 E. Delaware Place; ℂ 800/332-3442; www.fourseasons. com): Appropriately enough in this skyscraper-packed city, some of the best hotels perch far above the sidewalk. The Four Seasons (as well as the Ritz-Carlton; see below) is tucked above a high-rise shopping mall on Michigan Avenue. A favorite among camera-shy celebrities who want to keep a low profile, the hotel exudes understated luxury. Expect discretion, not a lively lobby scene. Where the Four Seasons really shines is its service—the concierges might be the best in town. The clubby full-service spa provides on-site pampering, for a price. See p. 76.

- **Park Hyatt** (800 N. Michigan Ave.; ℂ 800/233-1234; www.parkchicago. hyatt.com): If the thought of over-stuffed couches and thick brocade curtains makes you wince, this is the hotel for you. With its focus on modern design and clean lines, the Park Hyatt feels like one of those cool urban spaces featured in *Architectural Digest.* Reproductions of Eames and Mies furniture fill the guest rooms, and the in-room electronics are similarly sleek. The coolest feature? Moveable bathroom walls that allow you to soak in the view while you lounge in the tub. See p. 76.

- **Peninsula** (108 E. Superior St.; ℂ 866/288-8889; www.chicago.peninsula. com): Inspired by the elegance of 1920s Shanghai and Hong Kong, the Chicago outpost of this Asian chain is a seamless blend of classic and modern. The grand public spaces may be a throwback to the past, but the hotel's amenities are ultramodern. Bedrooms and bathrooms feature "command stations" that allow you to adjust lights, temperature, and TVs without getting up. The top-notch gym, spa, and indoor swimming pool (filled with natural light) make the Peninsula a must for fitness fanatics. See p. 78.

- **The Ritz-Carlton Chicago** (160 E. Pearson St.; ℂ 800/621-6906; www. fourseasons.com/chicagorc): Located above the Water Tower Place shopping center, the Ritz has one of the most welcoming lobbies in town, with light streaming through the windows, masses of fresh flowers, and bird's-eye views of the city. The guest rooms, decorated in warm shades of yellow and blue, have European-style elegance, and the staff prides itself on granting every wish. See p. 78.

- **W Chicago Lakeshore** (644 N. Lake Shore Dr.; ℂ 877/W-HOTELS or 877/946-8357; www.whotels.com): The city's only hotel with a lakefront address may try a little too hard to be hip, but it offers a nightclubby vibe that sets it apart from the many cookie-cutter convention-friendly hotels in town. (The rates are substantially lower than those at the hotels listed above, but the W is still a splurge for thrifty travelers.) The color scheme in the rooms—shades of gray, black, and deep red—is a refreshing change from the chain hotel look (although they won't appeal to guests who like things light and airy). The top-floor Whiskey Sky bar is cramped, but good for people-watching, and the outpost of New York's trendy Bliss spa is a must-visit for beauty junkies. See p. 80.

3 THE BEST MODERATELY PRICED HOTELS

- **Hotel Allegro Chicago** (171 W. Randolph St.; ℂ **800/643-1500;** www. allegrochicago.com): Its prime Loop location and stylish decor make the Allegro an appealing home base for visitors in search of an urban getaway. Rooms are compact but cheerful, and you can mingle with other guests at the complimentary evening wine reception in the lobby. See p. 74.

- **Hampton Inn & Suites Chicago Downtown** (33 W. Illinois St.; ℂ **800/ HAMPTON** or 800/426-7866; www. hamptoninn.com): Located in a busy neighborhood full of restaurants and nightlife, the Hampton Inn feels more expensive than it is. The rooms have an upscale urban look, and the indoor pool is a draw for families. The hotel's hot breakfast buffet, included in the room rates and served in an attractive second-floor lounge, puts the standard coffee-and-doughnut spread at other motels to shame. See p. 86.

- **Red Roof Inn** (162 E. Ontario St.; ℂ **800/733-7663;** www.redroof-chicago-downtown.com): This high-rise version of the roadside motel is your best bet for the cheapest rates downtown. The rooms don't have much in the way of style (or natural light), and the bathrooms, though spotless, are a little cramped, but it fits the bill if you want a central location and plan on using your hotel as a place to sleep rather than hang out. See p. 83.

- **Majestic Hotel** (528 W. Brompton St.; ℂ **800/727-5108;** www.cityinns.com): A bit off the beaten path, this neighborhood hotel is tucked away on a residential street just a short walk from Wrigley Field and the lakefront. You won't find lots of fancy amenities, but the atmosphere here has the personal touch of a B&B. Rates include continental breakfast and afternoon tea in the lobby. See p. 89.

4 THE MOST UNFORGETTABLE DINING EXPERIENCES

- **Charlie Trotter's** (816 W. Armitage Ave.; ℂ 773/248-6228): Charlie Trotter is the city's original celebrity chef, and his intimate restaurant, inside a town house, is a must for foodie visitors. The formula may be rigid (tasting menus only), but the food is anything but: Fresh-as-can-be ingredients in dazzling combinations. The service lives up to Trotter's legendary perfectionism; the chef himself has been known to come out of the kitchen and ask diners why they didn't finish a certain dish. See p. 136.

Impressions

We were on one of the most glamorous corners of Chicago. I dwelt on the setting. The lakeshore view was stupendous. I couldn't see it but I knew it well and felt its effect—the shining road beside the shining gold vacancy of Lake Michigan. Man had overcome the emptiness of this land. But the emptiness had given him a few good licks in return.

—Saul Bellow, *Humboldt's Gift*, 1975

• **Alinea** (1723 N. Halsted St.; ✆ **312/ 867-0110**): Widely considered the town's top restaurant of the moment, Alinea has gotten national press for chef Grant Achatz's revolutionary twist on contemporary dining. Each course of the ever-changing prix-fixe menu showcases Achatz's creativity, whether it's duck served on a scented "pillow" of juniper or a complete reinvention of wine and cheese (frozen grape juice rolled in grated bleu cheese and served with red wine gelée). An added bonus: Service that's friendly, not snobby. See p. 136.

• **Gibsons Bar & Steakhouse** (1028 N. Rush St.; ✆ **312/266-8999**): Chicago has no shortage of great steakhouses, but Gibsons has a great scene, too—a mix of moneyed Gold Coast singles, expense-account-fueled business travelers, and the occasional celebrity. This is the kind of place to live large (literally). The portions are enormous, so you're encouraged to share, which only adds to the party atmosphere. See p. 114.

• **foodlife** (Water Tower Place, 835 N. Michigan Ave.; ✆ **312/335-3663**): This is my top pick for a quick, affordable, family-friendly meal downtown. Leaps and bounds beyond the standard mall food court, foodlife offers a wide range of non-chain food stations at affordable prices. Get everything from Asian noodles and vegetarian fare to more standard options such as pizza and burgers. See p. 119.

• **The Italian Village** (71 W. Monroe St.; ✆ **312/332-7005**): The old-school fettuccine alfredo won't win any culinary awards, but eating at this Chicago landmark is like taking a trip back in time, from the so-tacky-they're-cool twinkling stars on the ceiling to the vintage waiters (some of whom look like they've been working here since the place opened in 1927). See p. 104.

5 THE BEST MUSEUMS

• **Art Institute of Chicago** (111 S. Michigan Ave.; ✆ **312/443-3600**): A mustsee for art lovers, the Art Institute manages to combine blockbuster exhibits with smaller, uncrowded spaces for private meditation. Internationally known for its French Impressionist collection, the Art Institute can also transport you to Renaissance Italy, ancient China, or the world of the Old Masters. The dazzling, light-filled Modern Wing, added in 2009, has also given the museum's 20th-century modern art collection the setting it deserves. See p. 152.

• **Field Museum of Natural History** (Roosevelt Rd. and Lake Shore Dr.; ✆ **312/922-9410**): The grand neoclassical entrance hall will make you feel as if you've entered somewhere important, a sense of drama only enhanced by the towering figure of Sue, the largest *Tyrannosaurus rex* skeleton ever uncovered. The Field can easily entertain for an entire day. Exhibits include ancient Egyptian mummies, a full-size Maori Meeting House, and stuffed figures of the notorious man-eating lions of Tsavo. See p. 163.

• **John G. Shedd Aquarium** (1200 S. Lake Shore Dr.; ✆ **312/939-2438**): Sure, you'll find plenty of tanks filled with exotic fish, but the Shedd is also home to some wonderful large-scale recreations of natural habitats. Stroll through Wild Reef, and you'll see sharks swim overhead. The lovely Oceanarium (renovated in 2009 with a Polar Play Zone for the kids), where you can watch a dolphin show, features floor-to-ceiling windows; you'll feel as if you're sitting outdoors, even on the chilliest Chicago day. See p. 164.

- **Museum of Science and Industry** (57th St. and Lake Shore Dr.; © **800/468-6674**): You can come here year after year and still not see it all. Although the exhibits promote scientific knowledge, most have an interactive element that makes them especially fun for families. But it's not all computers and technology. Some of the classic exhibits—the underground re-creation of the coal mine and the World War II German U-boat—have been attracting crowds for generations. See p. 175.

- **Frank Lloyd Wright Home and Studio** (951 Chicago Ave., Oak Park; © **708/848-1976**): The Midwest's greatest architect started out in the Chicago suburb of Oak Park, and his house—now a museum with guided tours—gives a first-hand look at his genius and influence. The surrounding neighborhood, where Wright's Prairie-style homes sit side by side with rambling Victorian villas, is an eye-opening lesson in architectural history. See p. 184.

6 THE BEST NIGHTLIFE EXPERIENCES

- **Getting the Blues:** Here, in the world capital of the blues, you've got your pick of places to feel them, from the touristy but lively atmosphere of Kingston Mines in Lincoln Park, where musicians perform continuously on two stages, to the roadhouse feel of Buddy Guy's Legends, where musicians in town while on tour have been known to play impromptu sets. See "The Music Scene," p. 262.

- **Taking in a Show:** The stage lights rarely go dark on one of the country's busiest theater scenes. Chicago is home to a downtown Broadway-style district anchored by beautifully restored historic theaters, the nationally known Goodman Theatre, and the city's resident Shakespeare troupe. Beyond downtown, you'll find a number of innovative independent companies, where future stars get their big breaks

and the pure love of theater makes up for the low budgets. See "The Performing Arts," p. 246.

- **Taking in Some Cool Jazz at the Green Mill:** This atmospheric Uptown jazz club is the place to go to soak up smooth sounds from some of the hottest up-and-coming performers on the jazz scene, while the club itself is a living museum of 1930s Chicago. The Sunday night "Poetry Slam" is a big crowd-pleaser. See p. 262.

- **Watching Improv Come Alive:** Chicago is a comedy breeding ground, having launched the careers of John Belushi, Bill Murray, Mike Myers, and Tina Fey through improv hot spots such as Second City and iO. The shows may soar or crash, but you just might catch one of comedy's newest stars. See p. 259.

7 THE BEST PLACES TO HANG WITH THE LOCALS

- **Shopping the Town:** Michigan Avenue is often touted as a shopper's paradise,

and I'll admit it has a great lineup of big-name designer boutiques and multilevel high-end shopping malls. But that's all stuff you can find in any other big city. For more distinctive items, head to Chicago's residential districts, where trendy independent clothing boutiques sit next to eclectic home design stores filled with one-of-a-kind treasures. The home decor shops along Armitage Avenue cater to stylish young families with plenty of spending money, while Wicker Park and Bucktown attract edgy fashionistas with a range of funky clothing shops. Southport Avenue (near Wrigley Field) and West Division Street (south of Wicker Park) are the newest up-and-coming shopping meccas—with no nametag-wearing conventioneers in sight. See chapter 9.

- **Soaking Up Sun at Wrigley Field:** It's a Chicago tradition to play hooky for an afternoon, sit in the bleachers at this historic baseball park, and watch the Cubbies try to hit 'em onto Waveland Avenue. Despite being perennial losers, the Cubs sell out almost every game; your best bet is to buy tickets for a weekday afternoon (although you'll often find season ticket holders selling seats at face value in front of Wrigley right before a game). Even if you can't get in, you can still soak in the atmosphere at one of the neighborhood's many watering holes. See "In the Grandstand: Watching Chicago's Athletic Events," p. 202.

- **Playing in the Sand:** If you're staying at a downtown hotel, you can hit the sands of Chicago's urban beaches almost

as quickly as your elevator gets you to the lobby. Oak Street Beach (at Michigan Ave. and Lake Shore Dr.) is mostly for posing. North Avenue Beach, a little farther north along the lakefront path, is home to weekend volleyball games, family beach outings, and a whole lot of eye candy. You probably won't do any swimming (even in the middle of summer, the water's frigid), but either beach makes a great place to hang out with a picnic and a book on a warm afternoon. See "Beaches," p. 199.

- **Raising a Glass (or a Coffee Cup):** Chicago has its share of trendy lounges that serve overpriced specialty martinis, but the heart of the city's nightlife remains the neighborhood taverns. These are the places you can soak in a convivial atmosphere without attitude or self-consciously flashy decor, but also have a conversation without being drowned out by the hoots and hollers of drunken frat boys (although there are plenty of bars catering to that particular demographic). My favorites include **Celtic Crossings** (751 N. Clark St.; ✆ **312/337-1005**) in River North, **Miller's Pub** (134 S. Wabash Ave.; ✆ **312/645-5377**) in the Loop, and the **Map Room** (1949 N. Hoyne Ave.; ✆ **773/252-7636**) in Bucktown. If you prefer to keep things nonalcoholic, grab coffee and dessert at either of my two favorite cafes: **Third Coast** (1260 N. Dearborn St.; ✆ **312/649-0730**), on the Gold Coast, or **Uncommon Ground** (1214 W. Grace St.; ✆ **773/929-3680**) in Wrigleyville. See chapter 10.

8 THE BEST FREE (OR ALMOST FREE) THINGS TO DO

- **Exploring Millennium Park:** This downtown park, carved out of the northwest corner of Grant Park, has become one of the city's best spots for

strolling, hanging out, and people-watching (*Bonus:* It's an easy walk from downtown hotels). While the Pritzker Music Pavilion, designed by Frank

Gehry, is the highest-profile attraction, the park's two main sculptures have quickly become local favorites. *Cloud Gate,* by British sculptor Anish Kapoor, looks like a giant silver kidney bean; watch your reflection bend and distort as you walk around and underneath. The *Crown Fountain,* designed by Spanish sculptor Jaume Plensa, is framed by two giant video screens that project faces of ordinary Chicagoans. It looks a little creepy at first, but watch the kids splashing in the shallow water and you'll soon realize that this is public art at its best. See p. 156.

- **Bonding with the Animals at Lincoln Park Zoo:** You have no excuse not to visit: Lincoln Park Zoo is open 365 days a year and—astonishingly—remains completely free, despite many recent upgrades. Occupying a prime spot of Lincoln Park close to the lakefront, the zoo is small enough to explore in an afternoon, and varied enough to make you feel as though you've traveled around the world. For families, this is a don't-miss stop. See p. 170.

- **Listening to Music Under the Stars:** Summer is prime time for live music—

and often you won't have to pay a dime. The Grant Park Music Festival presents free classical concerts from June through August in Millennium Park. A few blocks south, you'll find the outdoor dance floor that's home to Chicago SummerDance, where you can learn new dance moves and swing to a variety of live acts on Thursday through Sunday nights. The summer also brings a range of large-scale music festivals—from Blues Fest to a rock-'n'-roll-themed Fourth of July concert—but the Grant Park classical concerts are considerably less crowded (and far more civilized). See "Classical Music," p. 248.

- **Discovering Future Masterpieces:** Chicago's vibrant contemporary art scene is divided between two different neighborhoods. The original, River North, is still home to many of the city's best-known galleries and is within walking distance from downtown hotels. The West Loop houses newer galleries—with, overall, a younger perspective—in freshly renovated lofts. You don't need to be a serious collector to browse; just bring an open mind. See "Art Galleries" in chapter 9.

9 THE BEST ONE-OF-A-KIND SHOPS

- **ArchiCenter Shop** (224 S. Michigan Ave.; ✆ **312/922-3432**): Looking for unique, well-designed souvenirs? This store, run by the Chicago Architecture Foundation, should be your first stop. You'll find Frank Lloyd Wright bookmarks, puzzles of the Chicago skyline, picture frames with patterns designed by famed local architect Louis Sullivan, and a great selection of Chicago history books. See p. 242.

- **Uncle Fun** (1338 W. Belmont Ave.; ✆ **773/477-8223**): No other place lives up to its name like Uncle Fun, one of the quirkiest shops in town. This

old-fashioned storefront is crammed with a random assortment of classic dime-store gadgets (hand buzzers, Pez dispensers, rubber chickens), along with an equally eclectic selection of retro bargain-bin items. (Where else can you pick up a Mr. T keychain?). See p. 235.

- **The T-Shirt Deli** (1739 N. Damen Ave.; ✆ **773/276-6266**): Got a soft spot for those cheesy 1970s "Foxy Lady" T-shirts? Head to the T-Shirt Deli, where the staff will customize shirts while you wait. Come up with your own message, or browse the hundreds of

Impressions

He glances at the new Civic Center, a tower of russet steel and glass, fronted by a gracious plaza with a fountain and a genuine Picasso-designed metalwork sculpture almost fifty feet high. He put it all there, the Civic Center, the plaza, the Picasso. And the judges and county officials who work in the Civic Center, he put most of them there, too.

Wherever he looks as he marches, there are new skyscrapers up or going up. The city has become an architect's delight, except when the architects see the great Louis Sullivan's landmark buildings being ripped down for parking garages or allowed to degenerate into slums.

—Mike Royko, *Boss: Richard J. Daley of Chicago,* 1971

in-stock iron-on decals (everything from Gary Coleman to Hello Kitty). And just like at a real deli, your purchase is wrapped in white paper and served with a bag of potato chips. See p. 235.

- **Architectural Artifacts, Inc.** (4325 N. Ravenswood Ave.; ✆ 773/348-0622): This vast warehouse of material salvaged from historic buildings is a home renovator's dream. Although it's far off the usual tourist route, design buffs will find it well worth the trip—the enormous inventory includes fireplace mantels, stained glass windows, and garden sculptures. The owners display pieces of particular historic value in an attached museum. See p. 228.

10 THE BEST CHICAGO WEBSITES

- **Metromix** (www.chicago.metromix. com): Operated by the *Chicago Tribune,* this site features expanded versions of the newspaper's entertainment and restaurant coverage. It's a good place to check reviews and get an early look at new bars and nightclubs.
- **The Chicago Reader** (www.chicago reader.com): The site of the city's alternative weekly paper is the place to find extensive coverage of the local music scene and reviews of smaller theater productions.
- **Chicago Landmarks** (www.cityof chicago.org/Landmarks/index.html): This site, part of the city government's official website, includes definitions of Chicago architectural styles, tour information, and maps.
- **Chicago Office of Tourism** (www. explorechicago.org): This local government site gives a good overview of festivals, parades, and other upcoming events in town.
- **Chicagoist** (www.chicagoist.com): Want to see what issues have Chicagoans riled up? Check out this sounding board for local news (an offshoot of the New York-centric site Gothamist.com), which covers everything from government corruption scandals to the latest celebrity sightings. You'll find a similar roundup of news, local gossip, and opinion pieces at the online magazine *Gapers Block* (www.gapersblock.com).
- **LTH Forum** (www.lthforum.com/bb/ index.php): Local foodies come to this

bulletin board to get the scoop on hot new restaurant openings. The site also keeps a running list of "Great Neighborhood Restaurants," if you're looking for places with character rather than buzz.

- **League of Chicago Theatres** (www. chicagoplays.com): If you're planning to catch a show while in town, visit this comprehensive theater site, where you can search specific dates to see what's playing.

Chicago in Depth

Chicago has been in the national media spotlight recently, for reasons both inspiring and embarrassing. On the one hand, it's the adopted hometown of President Barack Obama, the place he got his start in politics and where he still maintains his Hyde Park home as the first family's vacation getaway. His victory rally in downtown's Grant Park signaled Chicago's vitality and influence to the whole world (many of his top presidential advisors were local business and philanthropic leaders before they moved to Washington). Not long after the cheers died down, however, news broke that the state governor, Rod Blagojevich, was being indicted on federal fraud charges. "Blago," a product of the city's shady Democratic political machine, stunned even cynical Chicagoans with his blatant moneygrubbing and attempts to sell Obama's former Senate seat to the highest bidder. Obama may have promised to usher in a new era of hope and honesty in politics, but Blagojevich proved that the old ways of doing business aren't so easily erased.

In this chapter, you'll get an overview of the issues facing the city today, as well as a quick primer on Chicago's history. Because architecture plays such an important role in the look of the city—and so many influential architects have worked here—you'll also find a guide to the major styles of buildings you'll pass by during your visit. But you won't get a full sense of the city's spirit unless you understand the city's role in popular culture, too. Chicago has been home to many great writers and has served as a setting for dozens of films, so this chapter includes a section on recommended books and movies. Check out a few of these books or movies before your trip to put you in a Chicago state of mind.

---

1 CHICAGO TODAY

Like other major American cities, Chicago has benefited from a renewed interest in urban living during the last decade or so, as former suburbanites flock to luxury high-rise condos downtown. Where the Loop used to shut down after dark and on weekends, it's now buzzing all week long, with a busy theater district and lively restaurants. Massive new condo buildings have sprung up along the lakefront south of the Loop, while the West Loop—once a no-man's-land of industrial buildings— has become another hot residential neighborhood.

In many ways, this building boom has erased the physical legacy of Chicago's past. The stockyards that built the city's fortune have disappeared; the industrial factories that pumped smoke into the sky south of the city now sit vacant. While no one misses the stench of the stockyards or the pollution that came with being an industrial center, the city's character has become muted along the way. Living here no longer requires the toughness that was once a hallmark of the native Chicagoan.

And yet, a certain brashness remains. While some people may still have a "Second City" chip on their shoulders, most don't even bother about competing with New York or Los Angeles. We know our museums, restaurants, and entertainment options are as good as any other city's in the country; we just wish everyone else knew it, too. That's why Chicagoans took such pride when the city was chosen as one of the finalists for the 2016 Summer Olympics: It showed the world Chicago can compete on an international level.

Relatively affordable compared to New York, Chicago is a destination for ambitious young people from throughout the Midwest. The city also draws immigrants from other countries (as it has for more than 100 years). Latinos (mostly of Mexican origin) now make up about one-third of the city's population. Immigration from Eastern Europe is also common, especially from countries such as Poland, Russia, and Romania. This constant influx of new blood keeps the city vibrant.

That's not to say the city doesn't have problems. With roughly 2.8 million people total, Chicago has nearly equal numbers of black and white residents—a rarity among today's urban areas—but the residential districts continue to be some of the most segregated in the country. The South Side is overwhelmingly black; the North Side remains mostly white. As in other major cities, the public school system seems to constantly teeter on the edge of disaster. While fine schools are scattered throughout the city, many families are forced to send their children to substandard local schools with high dropout rates.

However, the waves of gentrification sweeping the city have transformed many neighborhoods for the better. For years, the city's public housing was a particular disgrace, epitomized by decrepit 1960s high-rises that had degenerated into isolated bastions of violence and hopelessness. The largest and worst complexes have been torn down in the past few years, and are gradually being replaced with low-rise, mixed-income housing. Some streets I would have avoided after dark 10 years ago are now lined with brand new supermarkets, parks, and—inevitably—a Starbucks or two.

The city's crime problem has been more intractable. Despite a murder rate that's one of the highest in the country, Chicago

doesn't strike visitors as a dangerous place, because most of the violence is contained within neighborhoods where gangs congregate and tourists rarely go. But gang-instigated shootings are still shockingly common on the South Side, and children are often innocent victims caught in the cross fire. It's something we've gotten far too blasé about, and it continues to be a blot on Chicago's reputation.

Another continuing embarrassment is our local politics. Time and again, our aldermen and other city officials reward our cynicism with yet another scandal involving insider payoffs and corrupt city contracts. Our current "mayor for life," Richard M. Daley, has been in office since 1989, and he wins every election by an overwhelming margin, with no serious opponents. There's no question he's helped the city blossom (often literally, since he's ordered thousands of trees and flowers planted downtown). A proponent of bike travel, he added bike lanes to city streets and has spearheaded an effort to make the city more energy efficient. (Under his direction, the top of City Hall was covered with low-maintenance plants to make a "green" roof.)

But we can never quite forget that Richard M. is the son of Richard J. Daley, the longtime mayor who ran a patronage machine that has kept the Democrats in power in local office to this day. Every few months or so, another minor scandal involving the mayor hits the news. It's never quite enough to bring Daley down—he always claims he knows nothing about the current affair, whatever it is—but the ongoing disgraces do little to change the general air of seediness pervading our local government. Yet in spite of the local politicians, we Chicagoans passionately defend and boast about our city. Ever since the stockyards were our main source of wealth, we've become masters at overlooking the unsavory. As long as Chicago thrives, we don't seem to really care how it happens.

2 LOOKING BACK AT CHICAGO

FIRST SETTLEMENT

Chicago owes its existence to its strategic position: The patch of land where it stands straddles a key point along an inland water route linking Canada to the Gulf of Mexico.

In 1673, Jacques Marquette, a French Jesuit missionary, and Louis Joliet, an explorer, found a short portage between two critically placed rivers, one connected to the Mississippi, and the other, via the Chicago River, to Lake Michigan. Although Native Americans had blazed this trail centuries beforehand, its discovery by the French was the first step in Chicago's founding—although no permanent settlement was built there for another 100 years.

By then, the British controlled the territory, having defeated the French over 70 years of intermittent warfare. After the Revolutionary War, the land around the mouth of the Chicago River passed to the United States. The Native American inhabitants, however, wouldn't give up their land without a fight, which is why the first building erected here—between 1803 and 1808—was the military outpost Fort Dearborn. (It sat on the south side of what is now the Michigan Avenue Bridge, on the site of the current McCormick Tribune Bridgehouse & Chicago River Museum; p. 157.) Skirmishes with local Native American tribes continued until 1832. A year later, the settlement of 300-plus inhabitants was officially incorporated under the name "Chicago." (A French version of a Native American word

believed to mean "wild onion," it may also have referred to the equally non-aromatic local skunks.)

COMMERCE & INDUSTRY

Land speculation began immediately, and Chicago was carved piecemeal and sold off to finance the Illinois and Michigan Canal, which eliminated the narrow land portage and fulfilled the long-standing vision of connecting the two great waterways. Commercial activity quickly followed. Chicago grew in size and wealth, shipping grain and livestock to the Eastern markets and lumber to the prairies of the West. Ironically, by the time the Illinois and Michigan Canal was completed in 1848, the railroad had arrived, and the water route that gave Chicago its raison d'être was rapidly becoming obsolete. Boxcars, not boats, became the principal mode of transportation throughout the region. The combination of the railroad, the emergence of local manufacturing, and, later, the Civil War, caused Chicago to grow wildly.

The most revolutionary product of the era sprang from the mind of Chicago inventor Cyrus McCormick, whose reaper filled in for the farmhands laboring on the nation's battlefields. Local merchants not only thrived on the contraband trade in cotton during the war, but also secured lucrative contracts from the federal government to provide the army with tents, uniforms, saddles, harnesses, lumber, bread, and meat. By 1870, Chicago's

---

Speaking of Chicago . . .

"Chicago is a facade of skyscrapers facing a lake, and behind the facade every type of dubiousness."

–E.M. Forster, British author

Speaking of Chicago . . .

"Chicago is not the most corrupt American city, it's the most theatrically corrupt."
—Studs Terkel, Chicago writer

population had grown to 300,000, a thousand times greater than its original population, in just 37 years since incorporation.

THE GREAT FIRE

A year later, the city lay in ashes. The Great Chicago Fire of 1871 began on the southwest side of the city on October 8. Legend places its exact origin in the O'Leary shed on DeKoven Street, although most historians have exonerated the poor cow that supposedly started the blaze by kicking over a lantern. The fire jumped the river and continued north through the night and the following day, fizzling out only when it started to rain. The fire took 300 lives—a relatively low number, considering its size—but destroyed 18,000 buildings and left 90,000 people homeless.

The city began to rebuild as soon as the rubble was cleared. By 1873, the city's downtown business and financial district was up and running again, and 2 decades later Chicago had sufficiently recovered to stage the 1893 World's Columbian Exposition commemorating the 400th anniversary of the discovery of America. The Exposition was, in effect, Chicago's grand coming-out party, a chance to show millions of visitors that this was a modern, progressive city. Chicago already had a reputation as a brash business center; now, it proved it could also be beautiful. *Harper's Magazine* described the "White City," the collection of formal buildings constructed for the Exposition, as "a Venus that arose from Lake Michigan."

The Great Fire gave an unprecedented boost to the professional and artistic development of the nation's architects. Drawn by the unlimited opportunities to build, they gravitated to the city in droves, and

the city raised a homegrown crop of architects. Chicago's reputation as an American Athens, packed with monumental and decorative buildings, is a direct byproduct of the disastrous fire that nearly brought the city to ruin.

In the meantime, the city's labor pool continued to grow, as many immigrants decided to stay rather than head for the prairie. Chicago still shipped meat and agricultural commodities around the nation and the world, and the city was rapidly becoming a mighty industrial center, creating finished goods, particularly for the markets of the ever-expanding Western settlements.

THE CRADLE OF TRADE UNIONISM

Chicago never seemed to outgrow its frontier rawness. Greed, profiteering, exploitation, and corruption were as critical to its growth as hard work, ingenuity, and civic pride. The spirit of reform arose most powerfully from the working classes, people whose lives were plagued by poverty and disease despite the city's prosperity. When the labor movement awoke in Chicago, it did so with a militancy and commitment that would inspire unions throughout the nation.

The fear and mistrust between workers and the local captains of industry came to a head during the Haymarket Riot in 1886. On May 1, tens of thousands of workers went on strike to demand an 8-hour workday. (Eventually, that date would be immortalized as a national workers' holiday around the world—although never, ironically, in the United States.) A few days later, toward the end of a rally held by a group of anarchist labor activists

6 The Great Chicago Fire of 1871 starts in the barn behind the O'Leary house—although Mrs. O'Leary's cow was never proven as the culprit. What's on the site today? The Chicago Fire Department's training academy.

7 Demonstrators and Chicago police clash in front of the Chicago Hilton during the 1968 **Democratic Convention.** Reflecting on the events a few days later, Mayor Richard J. Daley utters the unfortunate malapropism: "The policeman isn't there to create disorder, the policeman is there to preserve disorder."

1 Seven men are shot in a garage on North Clark Street in what becomes known as the **St. Valentine's Day Massacre,** in 1929. Al Capone—suspected of masterminding the killings—becomes an international celebrity, much to the dismay of embarrassed Chicagoans.

2 1959 was a big year for Chicago: the improv-comedy troupe **Second City** sets up on Wells Street, and a few blocks away, Hugh Hefner establishes the original **Playboy Mansion** in the swanky Gold Coast neighborhood (a sign over the doorbell reads: "If You Don't Swing, Don't Ring"). Hef moves to California in the 1970s, and Chicago—unfortunately—becomes considerably less swingin'.

3 Fort Dearborn, the first permanent settlement in what would become Chicago, is completed in 1803. Although the site occupies prime real estate today, at the time it over-looked swampy marshland and was filled with the not-so-fragrant scent of wild onions.

Subway/El stop

1/4 mi
0.25 km

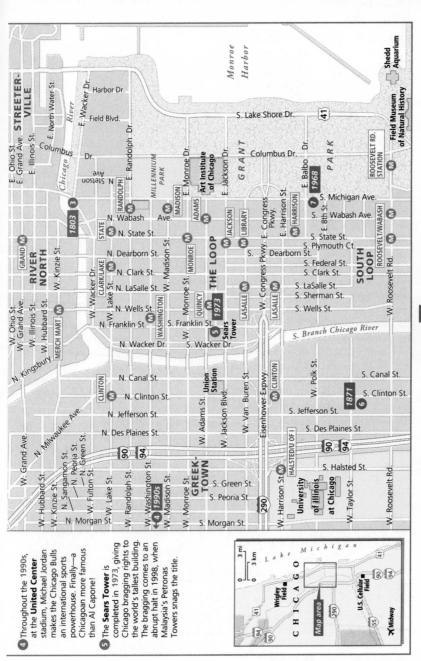

4 Throughout the 1990s, at the **United Center** stadium, Michael Jordan makes the Chicago Bulls an international sports powerhouse. Finally—a Chicagoan more famous than Al Capone!

5 The **Sears Tower** is completed in 1973, giving Chicago bragging rights to the world's tallest building. The bragging comes to an abrupt halt in 1998, when Malaysia's Petronas Towers snags the title.

Speaking of Chicago . . .

"Loving Chicago is like loving a woman with a broken nose. You may find lovelier lovelies, but never a lovely so real."

–Nelson Algren, Chicago novelist

CHICAGO IN DEPTH

2

LOOKING BACK AT CHICAGO

in Haymarket Square, a bomb exploded near the line of policemen standing guard. The police fired into the crowd, and seven policemen and four workers were killed.

Although the 5-minute incident was in no sense a riot, it seemed to justify fears about the radicalism of the labor movement, and eight rally leaders were soon arrested. After a speedy and by no means impartial trial, five of the men—none of whom were ever proven to have a connection to the bombing—were sentenced to death. The bomber was never found. Haymarket Square itself no longer exists, but a plaque commemorates the spot, on a fairly desolate stretch of Des Plaines Street, just north of Randolph Street.

The city's labor movement fought on. By the 1890s, many of Chicago's workers were organized into the American Federation of Labor. The Pullman Strike of 1894 united black and white railway workers for the first time in a common struggle for higher wages and workplace rights. The Industrial Workers of the World, or the Wobblies, which embraced for a time so many great voices of American labor— Eugene V. Debs, Big Bill Haywood, and Helen Gurley Flynn—was founded in Chicago in 1905.

THE GANGSTER ERA

During the 1920s, the combination of Prohibition and a corrupt city administration happy to accept kickbacks from mobsters allowed organized crime to thrive. The most notorious local gangster of the era was a New York transplant named Al Capone, who muscled his way into control of the so-called Chicago Outfit. During his heyday, in the mid-1920s, Capone's

operations included bootlegging, speakeasies, gambling joints, brothels, and pretty much every other unsavory-but-profitable business; the Outfit's take was reportedly $100 million a year.

Capone liked to promote himself as a humble, selfless business man—and he did set up soup kitchens at the start of the Great Depression—but he was also a ruthless thug who orchestrated gangland killings while always giving himself an alibi. The most notorious of these hits was the Valentine's Day Massacre of 1929, when four of Capone's men killed seven members of a rival gang in a North Side garage. To gain access to the building, two of Capone's gang dressed as policemen. Thinking it was a raid, the intended victims dropped their guns and put their hands up against the wall, only to be gunned down. The execution-style murder became national news, reinforcing Chicago's already bloody reputation.

In the end, Capone and the Outfit were brought down by a combination of growing public outrage and federal government intervention. With the repeal of Prohibition, the gangsters' main source of income was erased. At around the same time, an agent of the Internal Revenue Service put together evidence that Capone—who had never filed a tax return and claimed to have no income—was in fact earning plenty of cash. He was found guilty of tax evasion and served 7 years in prison, including a stint at Alcatraz in San Francisco. After his release, he retired to Florida and died of a heart attack in 1947, at the age of 48. Although the Chicago Outfit continued its shady dealings after Capone's fall—using Las Vegas casinos for massive money-laundering operations—the city was no longer the site of vicious turf battles.

THE CHICAGO MACHINE

While Chicago was becoming a center of industry, transportation, and finance, and a beacon of labor reform, it was also becoming a powerhouse in national politics. Between 1860 and 1968, Chicago was the site of 14 Republican and 10 Democratic presidential nominating conventions. (Some even point to the conventions as the source of Chicago's "Windy City" nickname, laying the blame on politicians who were full of hot air.) The first of the conventions gave the country Abraham Lincoln; the 1968 convention saw the so-called Days of Rage, a series of increasingly violent confrontations between demonstrators protesting the Vietnam War and Chicago police officers. The simmering tension culminated in a riot in Grant Park, outside what's now the Chicago Hilton; as police began beating protestors and bystanders with clubs and fists, TV cameras rolled, and demonstrators chanted, "The whole world is watching."

And it was. The strong-arm tactics of Mayor Richard J. Daley—a supporter of eventual nominee Hubert Humphrey—made Humphrey look bad by association and may have contributed to Humphrey's defeat in the general election. (Maybe it was a wash; some also say that Daley stole the 1960 election for Kennedy.) A national inquiry later declared the event a police-instigated riot, while the city's own mayor-approved investigation blamed out-of-town extremists and provocateurs.

The supposed ringleaders of the uprising included Black Panther leader Bobby Seale; Tom Hayden, co-founder of Students for a Democratic Society; and Abbie Hoffman and Jerry Rubin, founders of the Youth International Party, or Yippies. They were charged with conspiracy and incitement to riot in the trial of the so-called Chicago 8 (later the Chicago 7, after charges in one case were dropped). Five were sentenced to prison terms, but their sentences were soon reversed after it was revealed that the FBI had bugged the offices of the defense lawyers.

The reversal was a setback for Mayor Daley, but his local power base held firm. The Democratic machine that he put in place during his years in office, from 1955 to 1976, was based on a practical sharing of the spoils: As long as the leaders of every ethnic and special interest group in town were guaranteed a certain number of government jobs, their leaders would bring in the votes.

His reach extended well beyond Chicago's borders; he controlled members of Congress, and every 4 years he delivered a solid Democratic vote in the November elections. But he also helped build Chicago into a modern business powerhouse, promoting the construction of O'Hare Airport, the McCormick Place Convention Center, and the Sears Tower, as well as expanding the city's highway and subway systems. Since his death in 1976, the machine has never wielded such national power, but it still remains almost impossible for a Republican to be voted into local office.

Speaking of Chicago . . .

"Come and show me another city with lifted head singing, so proud to be alive and coarse and strong and cunning."

–From the poem "Chicago," by Carl Sandburg

Chicago Stories: The Great Black Migration

From 1915 to 1960, hundreds of thousands of black Southerners poured into Chicago, trying to escape segregation and seeking economic freedom and opportunity. The "Great Black Migration" radically transformed Chicago, both politically and culturally, from an Irish-run city of recent European immigrants into one in which no group had a majority and no politician—white or black— could ever take the black vote for granted. Unfortunately, the sudden change gave rise to many of the disparities that still plague the city, but it also promoted an environment in which many black men and women could rise from poverty to prominence.

While jobs in the factories, steel mills, and stockyards paid much better than those in the cotton fields, Chicago was not the paradise that many blacks envisioned. Segregation was almost as bad here as it was down South, and most blacks were confined to a narrow "Black Belt" of overcrowded apartment buildings on the South Side. But the new migrants made the best of their situation, and for a time in the 1930s and '40s, the Black Belt—dubbed "Bronzeville" or the "Black Metropolis" by the community's boosters—thrived as a cultural, musical, religious, and educational mecca. As journalist Nicholas Lemann writes in The Promised Land: The Great Black Migration and How It Changed America, "Chicago was a city where a black person could be somebody."

Some of the Southern migrants who made names for themselves in Chicago included black separatist and Nation of Islam founder Elijah Muhammed; Robert S. Abbott, publisher of the powerful Chicago Defender newspaper, who launched a "Great Northern Drive" to bring blacks to the city in 1917; Ida B. Wells, the crusading journalist who headed an antilynching campaign; William Dawson, for many years the only black congressman; New Orleans–born jazz pioneers "Jelly Roll" Morton, King Oliver, and Louis Armstrong; Native Son author Richard Wright; John H. Johnson, publisher of Ebony and Jet magazines and one of Chicago's wealthiest residents; blues musicians Willie Dixon, Muddy Waters, and Howlin' Wolf; Thomas A. Dorsey, the "father of gospel music," and his greatest disciple, singer Mahalia Jackson; and Ralph Metcalfe, the Olympic

3 CHICAGO'S ARCHITECTURE

Although the Great Chicago Fire leveled almost 3 square miles of the downtown area in 1871, it did clear the stage for Chicago's emergence as a breeding ground for innovative architecture. Some of the field's biggest names, Fank Lloyd Wright, Louis Sullivan, and Ludwig van der Rohe, made their mark on the city. And today, Chicago's skyline is home to iconic buildings including the John Hancock center and the (former) Sears Tower.

EARLY SKYSCRAPERS (1880–1920)

In the late 19th century, important technical innovations—including safety elevators, fireproofing, and telecommunications— combined with advances in skeletal gold medalist sprinter who turned to politics once he got to Chicago, eventually succeeding Dawson in Congress.

When a 1948 Supreme Court decision declared it unconstitutional to restrict blacks to certain neighborhoods, the flight of many Bronzeville residents to less crowded areas took a toll on the community. Through the 1950s, almost a third of the housing became vacant, and by the 1960s, the great social experiment of urban renewal through wholesale land clearance and the creation of large tracts of public housing gutted the once-thriving neighborhood.

Community and civic leaders now appear committed to restoring the neighborhood to a semblance of its former glory. Landmark status has been secured for several historic buildings in Bronzeville, including the Liberty Life/Supreme Insurance Company, 3501 S. King Dr., the first African-American-owned insurance company in the northern United States, and the Eighth Regiment Armory, which, when completed in 1915, was the only armory in the U.S. controlled by an African-American regiment. The former home of the legendary Chess Records at 2120 S. Michigan Ave.—where Howlin' Wolf, Chuck Berry, and Bo Diddley gave birth to the blues and helped define rock 'n' roll—now houses a museum and music education center. Willie Dixon's widow, Marie Dixon, set up the **Blues Heaven Foundation** (✆ 312/808-1286; www.bluesheaven.com) with financial assistance from rock musician John Mellencamp. Along Dr. Martin Luther King, Jr. Drive, between 24th and 35th streets, several public art installations celebrate Bronzeville's heritage. The most poignant is sculptor Alison Saar's Monument to the Great Northern Migration, at King Drive and 26th Street, depicting a suitcase-toting African-American traveler standing atop a mound of worn shoe soles.

For tours of Bronzeville, contact the Chicago Office of Tourism's **Chicago Neighborhood Tours** (✆ 312/742-1190; www.chicagoneighborhoodtours.com); **Tour Black Chicago** (✆ 312/332-2323; www.tourblackchicago.com); or the **Bronzeville Visitor Information Center** (✆ 773/373-2842).

construction to create a new building type: The skyscraper. These buildings were spacious, cost-effective, efficient, and quick to build—in short, the perfect architectural solution for Chicago's growing downtown. Architect Louis Sullivan (1865–1924) was the first to formalize a vision of a tall building based on the parts of a classical column. His theories inspired the Chicago school of architecture, examples of which still fill the city's downtown. Features of Chicago school buildings include a rectangular shape with a

flat roof; large windows (made possible by the development of load-bearing interior skeletons); and the use of terra cotta, a light, fireproof material that could be cast in any shape and attached to the exterior, often for decoration.

A good example of the development of the skyscraper is the Monadnock Building, 53 W. Jackson Blvd. (Holabird & Root, 1889–91; Holabird & Roche, 1893). The northern section has 6-foot-thick walls at its base to support the building's 17 stories; the

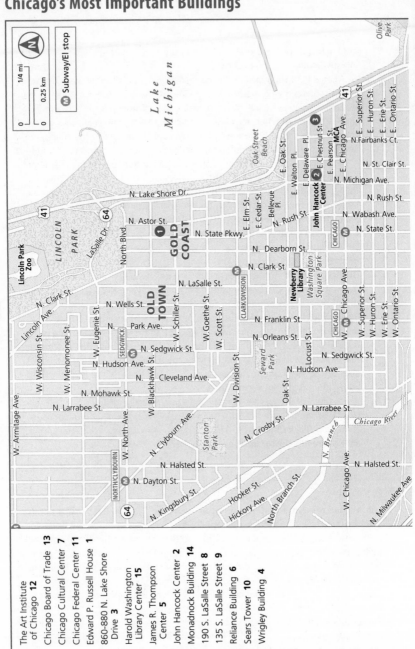

The Art Institute
of Chicago **12**

Chicago Board of Trade **13**

Chicago Cultural Center **7**

Chicago Federal Center **11**

Edward P. Russell House **1**

860–880 N. Lake Shore
Drive **3**

Harold Washington
Library Center **15**

James R. Thompson
Center **5**

John Hancock Center **2**

Monadnock Building **14**

190 S. LaSalle Street **8**

135 S. LaSalle Street **9**

Reliance Building **6**

Sears Tower **10**

Wrigley Building **4**

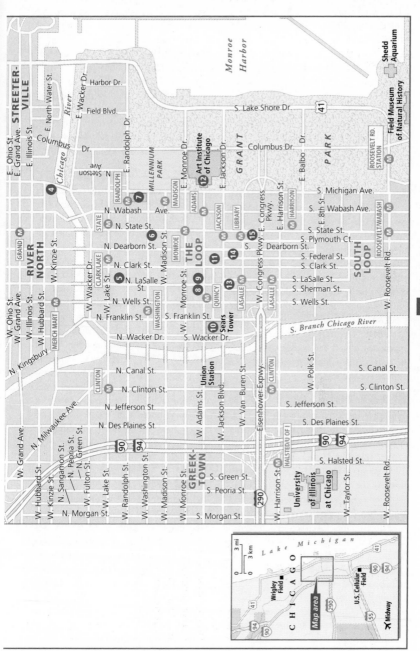

newer, southern half has a steel frame clad in terra cotta (allowing the walls to be much thinner). The Reliance Building, now the Hotel Burnham (p. 70.), 1 W. Washington St. (Burnham & Root and Burnham & Co., 1891–95), was influential for its use of glass and decorative spandrels (the horizontal panel below a window).

SECOND RENAISSANCE REVIVAL (1890–1920)

The grand buildings of the Second Renaissance Revival, with their textural richness, suited the tastes of the wealthy Gilded Age. Typical features include a cubelike structure with a massive, imposing look; a symmetrical facade, including distinct horizontal divisions; and a different stylistic treatment for each floor, with different column capitals, finishes, and window treatments on each level. A fine example of this style is the **Chicago Cultural Center,** 78 E. Washington St. (Shepley, Rutan & Coolidge, 1897), originally built as a public library. This tasteful edifice, with its sumptuous decor, was constructed in part to help secure Chicago's reputation as a culture-conscious city.

BEAUX ARTS (1890–1920)

This style takes its name from the Ecole des Beaux-Arts in Paris, where a number of prominent American architects received their training, beginning around the mid–19th century. In 1893, Chicago played host to the World's Columbian Exposition, attended by 21 million people at a time when Chicago's population was just over one million. Overseen by Chicagoan Daniel H. Burnham (1846–1912), the fairgrounds in Hyde Park were laid out in Beaux Arts style, with broad boulevards, fountains, and temporary ornate, white buildings, mostly by New York–based architects. (One of the few permanent structures is now the Museum of Science and Industry, p. 175.)

Grandiose compositions, exuberance of detail, and a variety of stone finishes typify most Beaux Arts structures. Chicago has several Beaux Arts buildings that exhibit the style's main features. The oldest part of the Art Institute of Chicago, Michigan Avenue at Adams Street (Shepley, Rutan & Coolidge, 1893), was built for the World's Columbian Exposition. A later example of yet another skyscraper is the gleaming white Wrigley Building, 400–410 N. Michigan Ave. (Graham, Anderson, Probst & White, 1919–24), which serves as a gateway to North Michigan Avenue.

ART DECO (1925–33)

Art Deco buildings are characterized by a linear, hard edge or angular composition, often with a vertical emphasis and highlighted with stylized decoration. The Chicago Board of Trade, 141 W. Jackson Blvd. (Holabird & Root, 1930), punctuates LaSalle Street with its dramatic Art Deco facade. High atop the pyramidal roof, an aluminum statue of Ceres, the Roman goddess of agriculture, gazes down over the building. 135 S. LaSalle St. (originally the Field Building; Graham, Anderson, Probst & White, 1934), the last major construction project in Chicago before the Great Depression deepened, has a magnificent Art Deco lobby. A fine example of an Art Deco town house is the Edward P. Russell House, 1444 N. Astor St. (Holabird & Root, 1929), in the city's Gold Coast.

INTERNATIONAL STYLE (1932–45)

The International Style was popularized in the United States through the teachings and designs of **Ludwig Mies van der Rohe** (1886–1969), a German émigré who taught and practiced architecture in Chicago after leaving Germany's influential Bauhaus school of design. In the 1950s, erecting a "Miesian" office building made companies appear progressive. Features of the style include a rectangular shape; the frequent use of glass; an absence of ornamentation; and a clear expression of the building's form and function. (The

Only in Chicago: The Master Builders

Visitors from around the world flock to Chicago to see the groundbreaking work of three major architects: Sullivan, Wright, and Mies. They all lived and worked in the Windy City, leaving behind a legacy of innovative structures that still inspire architects today. Here's the rundown on each of them:

Louis Sullivan (1865–1924)
- **Quote:** "Form ever follows function."
- **Iconic Chicago building:** Auditorium Building, 430 S. Michigan Ave. (1887–89).
- **Innovations:** Father of the Chicago school, Sullivan was perhaps at his most original in the creation of his intricate, nature-inspired ornamentation.

Frank Lloyd Wright (1867–1959)
- **Quote:** "Nature is my manifestation of God."
- **Iconic Chicago building:** Frederick C. Robie House, 5757 S. Woodlawn Ave., Hyde Park (1909).
- **Innovations:** While in Chicago, Wright developed the architecture of the Prairie School, a largely residential style combining natural materials, communication between interior and exterior spaces, and the sweeping horizontals of the Midwestern landscape. (For tours of Wright's home and studio, see "Exploring the 'Burbs," p. 182.)

Ludwig Mies van der Rohe (1886–1969)
- **Quote:** "Less is more."
- **Iconic Chicago building:** Chicago Federal Center, Dearborn Street between Adams Street and Jackson Boulevard (1959–74).
- **Innovations:** Mies van der Rohe brought the office tower of steel and glass to the United States. His stark facades don't immediately reveal his careful attention to details and materials.

interior structure of stacked office floors is clearly visible, as are the locations of mechanical systems, such as elevator shafts and air-conditioning units).

Some famous Mies van der Rohe designs are the Chicago Federal Center, Dearborn Street between Adams Street and Jackson Boulevard (1959–74), and 860–880 N. Lake Shore Dr. (1949–51). Interesting interpretations of the style by Skidmore, Owings & Merrill, a Chicago firm that helped make the International Style a corporate staple, are the Sears Tower (1968–74) and the John Hancock Center (1969)—impressive engineering feats that rise 110 and 100 stories, respectively.

POSTMODERN (1975–90)

As a reaction against the stark International Style, postmodernists began to incorporate classical details and recognizable forms into their designs—often applied in outrageous proportions. 190 S. LaSalle St. (John Burgee Architects with Philip Johnson, 1987) brings the shape of a famous Chicago building back to the skyline. The overall design is that of the 1892 Masonic Temple (now razed), complete with the tripartite divisions of the Chicago school. Another amalgam of historical precedents is the Harold Washington Library Center, 400 S. State St.

(Hammond, Beeby & Babka, 1991). An extremely modern interpretation of a three-part skyscraper—but you have to look for the divisions to find them—is 333 Wacker Dr. (Kohn Pedersen Fox, 1979–83), an elegant green-glass structure that curves along a bend in the Chicago River. Unlike this harmonious juxtaposition, the James R. Thompson Center, 100 W. Randolph St. (Murphy/Jahn, 1979–85), inventively clashes with everything around it.

4 CHICAGO IN POPULAR CULTURE

BOOKS

So many great American writers have come from Chicago, lived here, or set their work in the city that it's impossible to recommend a single book that says all there is to say about the city. But I won't let that stop me from suggesting a few works to get you started.

Upton Sinclair's enormously influential *The Jungle* tells the tale of a young immigrant encountering the brutal, filthy city (see box, "Jungle Fever," below). James T. Farrell's trilogy *Studs Lonigan,* published in the 1930s, explores the power of ethnic and neighborhood identity in Chicago. Other novels set in Chicago include Saul Bellow's *The Adventures of Augie March* and *Humboldt's Gift,* and Richard Wright's *Native Son. The Time Traveler's Wife,* by local author Audrey Niffenegger, unfolds amid recognizable Chicago backdrops such as the Newberry Library. (The movie version, alas, filmed only a few scenes here.)

For an entertaining overview of the city's history, read *City of the Century* by Donald Miller (an excellent PBS special based on the book is also available on DVD). **Erik Larson's** *Devil in the White City,* a history book that reads like a thriller, tells the engrossing story of the 1893 World's Columbian Exposition and the serial killer who preyed on young women who visited from out of town. For another look at the seamy underside of Chicago's history, try *Sin in the Second City* by Karen Abbott, which focuses on the city's most notorious—and expensive—brothel.

Two books give a human face to the city's shameful public housing history: Daniel Coyle's *Hardball: A Season in the Projects,* the true story of youngsters on a Little League baseball team; and Alex Kotlowitz's *There Are No Children Here,* a portrait of children growing up in one of the city's most dangerous projects. Kotlowitz also wrote *Never A City So Real: A Walk in Chicago,* which tells the stories of everyday Chicagoans, from a retired steelworker to a public defender to the owner of a soul-food restaurant.

But no one has given a voice to the people of Chicago like Studs Terkel, whose books **Division Street: America, Working,** and **Chicago,** are based on interviews with Chicagoans from every neighborhood and income level; and the late newspaper columnist **Mike Royko,** author of perhaps the definitive account of Chicago machine politics, *Boss.* His columns have been collected in *One More Time: The Best of Mike Royko* and *For the Love of Mike: More of the Best of Mike Royko.*

FILM

Chicago became a popular setting for feature films in the 1980s and '90s. For a look at Chicago on the silver screen, check out *Ferris Bueller's Day Off* (1985), the ultimate teenage wish-fulfillment fantasy, which includes scenes filmed at Wrigley Field and the city's annual St. Patrick's Day Parade; *The Fugitive* (1993), which used the city's El trains as an effective backdrop; and *My Best Friend's Wedding* (1996). For many Chicagoans, the quintessential

Jungle Fever

"It's hard to get a man to understand something if his salary depends on him not understanding it."

–Upton Sinclair

The most influential work of Chicago-based literature may also be the most disturbing. Upton Sinclair's *The Jungle,* an exposé of the city's meatpacking industry, caused a sensation when it was published in 1906. Although the book was a novel, following the tragic life of a poorly paid Lithuanian immigrant, it was based on Sinclair's firsthand observations at the Union Stockyards; many of its most gruesome scenes, such as when a man falls into a processing tank and is ground up along with the rest of the meat, were based on fact. After *The Jungle* became an international bestseller, U.S. meat exports plummeted and panicked meat packing companies practically begged for government inspections to prove their products were safe. A Food and Drug Act was passed soon after, which made it a crime to sell food that had been adulterated or produced using "decomposed or putrid" substances; eventually, that led to the founding of the Food and Drug Administration (FDA).

hometown movie scene is the finale of *The Blues Brothers* (1979), which features a multi-car pileup in the center of downtown Daley Plaza.

Sometimes, locally born actors choose to shoot movies in their hometown. A film that fueled a thousand paparazzi photographs was *The Break-Up* (2006), starring local-boy-made-good Vince Vaughn and Jennifer Aniston and filmed on location throughout the city. Another hometown actor, John Cusack, starred in *High Fidelity* (2000), where hip Wicker Park makes an appropriate backdrop for the tale of a music-obsessed record store owner. Director Michael Mann, a Chicago native, filmed part of the gangster movie *Public Enemies* (2009) in town—appropriately enough, since this was the place where bank robber John Dillinger (played by Johnny Depp in the movie) was caught and killed by federal agents.

Though it technically takes place in Gotham City, the setting of the Batman blockbuster *The Dark Knight* is clearly recognizable as Chicago. Although I have to reassure you—the real city isn't nearly as dark as the movie version!

MUSIC

If Chicagoans were asked to pick one musical style to represent their city, most of us would start singing the blues. Thanks in part to the presence of the influential **Chess Records,** Chicago became a hub of blues activity after World War II, with musicians such as Muddy Waters, Howlin' Wolf, and Buddy Guy recording and performing here. (For a glimpse of what the music studio was like in its glory days, rent the 2008 movie *Cadillac Records,* starring Jeffrey Wright as Muddy Waters and Beyoncé Knowles as Etta James.) Buddy Guy is still active on the local scene, making regular appearances at his eponymous downtown blues club, one of the best live music venues in the city (p. 263).

In the '60s and '70s, Chicago helped usher in the era of "electric blues"—low-tech, soulful singing melded with the rock sensibility of electric guitars. Blues-influenced rock musicians, including the

A Chicago Playlist

The classic swingin' anthem of the city is Frank Sinatra's rendition of **"Chicago"** ("That toddlin' town…free and easy town, brassy, breezy town"), overblown versions of which show up regularly at local karaoke bars. Sinatra also sang his praises to the city in **"My Kind of Town (Chicago Is),"** which mentions the Wrigley Building and the Union Stockyards. But an even better pick for official city theme song is Robert Johnson's **"Sweet Home Chicago,"** with its appropriately bluesy riff ("Come on, baby don't you want to go, to the same old place, Sweet Home Chicago"). 1970s pop-lite group Chicago didn't sing specifically about the city (probably because they moved to L.A. as soon as they hit it big), but their cheery **"Saturday in the Park"** captures the spirit of Grant Park and Lincoln Park in the summertime. Fast-forwarding a few decades, the blistering **"Cherub Rock"** by Smashing Pumpkins is a harsh take on the city's 1990s-era music scene (opening with the line: "Freak out, give in, doesn't matter what you believe in…"); more mellow is the elegiac **"Via Chicago"** by current indie darlings Wilco. And no survey of Chicago music would be complete without mentioning the maestros of hip-hop, Common and Kanye West, who name-check their hometown in the songs **"Southside"** and **"Homecoming,"** respectively.

Rolling Stones, Led Zeppelin, and Eric Clapton, made Chicago a regular pilgrimage spot.

Today, the blues has become yet another tourist attraction, especially for international visitors, but the quality and variety of blues acts is still impressive. Hard-core blues fans shouldn't miss the annual (free) **Blues Fest,** held along the lakefront in Grant Park in early June. For a listing of the city's best blues clubs, see chapter 10.

5 EATING & DRINKING IN CHICAGO

Joke all you want about bratwurst and deep-dish pizza; Chicago is a genuine culinary hot spot. One of the city's most creative dining spots, **Alinea,** was even named the top restaurant in the United States by *Gourmet* magazine in 2007 (take that, New York and San Francisco!). What makes eating out in Chicago fun is the variety. We've got it all: Stylish see-and-be-seen spots, an amazing array of steakhouses, chef-owned temples to fine dining, and every kind of ethnic cuisine you could possibly crave. Plus—yes—some not-to-be-missed deep-dish pizza places.

Fueled in part by expense-account-wielding business travelers, high-end dining is a growth industry here. What makes Chicago's top restaurants unique, however, is their inclusive, low-key attitude. This isn't the kind of city where snooty waiters show off their foodie expertise or stare in horror if you have no idea what wine to order. By and large, hospitality is more than just a buzzword here, and as long as you can afford the eye-popping bill, the city's top chefs will welcome you. If you want to splurge on a one-of-a-kind meal—the kind you'll be describing to friends

Obama's Chicago

For years, Chicago's biggest hometown celebrity was Oprah Winfrey (despite the fact that she's rarely seen out and about, preferring to spend all her free time at her sprawling California estate). These days, she's been replaced by another big O—President Barack Obama. Though his primary residence is now a certain White House in Washington, D.C., his family returns to their South Side home for regular visits, and he and his wife still hit local restaurants for occasional date nights (albeit with the Secret Service tagging along).

Tourists from around the world make pilgrimages to the Obama's house at 5046 S. Greenwood Ave. on the city's South Side. You can get a glimpse of the home from a distance, but you won't see much; the whole block is closed to passers-by for security reasons. However, the surrounding neighborhood of Kenwood—with its lovingly restored historic mansions—as well as adjacent Hyde Park are well worth a stroll (see "Exploring Hyde Park," p. 172). After visiting the campus of the University of Chicago—where President Obama once taught constitutional law—you can browse the stacks at the Seminary Co-op Bookstore (p. 232), where he was a regular.

A couple of Chicago-based fashion mavens have been instrumental in cultivating Michelle Obama's sense of style. Craving a First Lady–worthy makeover? Head to designer boutique Ikram (p. 234), where owner Ikram Goldman stocks pieces by up-and-coming and off-the-radar designers; or the store of Chicago designer Maria Pinto (p. 234), who crafts couture-level coats and dresses.

For dinners out, the Obamas have often eaten at the upscale Mexican restaurant Topolobampo (p. 123). Another favorite for special occasions is Spiaggia (p. 114), one of the best Italian restaurants in the country—and among the most expensive. To celebrate their first Valentine's Day as first couple, the Obamas chose Table Fifty-Two (p. 116), an unassuming spot that gives classic Southern dishes an upscale twist. Not only is the restaurant's chef-owner, Art Smith, a friend and former South Side neighbor, he also happens to be Oprah's former personal chef.

For more casual meals in Hyde Park, the Obamas were regulars at **Italian Fiesta Pizzeria,** 1400 E. 47th St. (© **773/684-2222**), a family-owned restaurant that was also a favorite of Michelle and her parents when she was growing up. Barack has also mentioned the **Valois Cafeteria,** 1518 E. 53rd St. (© **773/667-0647**), a no-frills, old-school neighborhood landmark, as his top breakfast spot in the city. For family outings on the North Side, the Obamas liked to stop in at **R.J. Grunts,** 2056 N. Lincoln Park West (© **773/929-5363**), known for its all-American lineup of burgers and Tex-Mex specialties, as well as its enormous salad bar. An added bonus for kids: It's right across the street from Lincoln Park Zoo.

weeks later—Chicago is the place to do it. (See chapter 6, "Where to Dine.")

That said, ever-increasing restaurant prices are one of my pet peeves; eating out downtown has become more and more of a luxury. While finding bargains in the Loop or around the Magnificent Mile isn't easy, you can still fill up without going broke by stopping at one of the food courts inside the malls along Michigan Avenue (as many locals on their lunch break do). Ethnic restaurants also tend to be less expensive, whether you're sampling *spanakopita* in Greektown (p. 111) or a noodle dish at a Thai restaurant (see box, "A Taste of Thai," on p. 140).

And about that pizza: Yes, Chicagoans hate to be stereotyped as cheese-and-sausage-devouring slobs, but we really do eat deep-dish pizza, which was created in the 1940s at the original **Pizzeria Uno** restaurant (p. 133). If you've never had this decadent, cholesterol-raising delicacy, you should definitely try it while you're here (especially on a chilly day—it's not as appealing during a summer heat wave). I give a rundown of the best pizza spots on p. 118.

Planning Your Trip to Chicago

As a major American city, Chicago is easy to reach by air, with two major airports (O'Hare and Midway) and hundreds of flights arriving each day. Once you arrive in town, it's fairly simple to get to the major tourist attractions using public transportation, including buses and the "El," a system of subways and elevated trains. Taxis are easy to flag down on any busy street. If you're staying downtown, you won't need to rent a car while you're here.

When planning your trip, book your hotel as early as possible, especially during the busy summer tourist season. The more affordable a hotel, the more likely it is to be sold out in June, July, and August, especially on weekends. It's also worth checking if a major convention will be in town during the dates you hope to travel (see the "Major Convention Dates" box, later). It's not unusual for every major downtown hotel to be sold out during the Housewares Show in late March or the Restaurant Show in mid-May.

If you're planning on catching a show while you're here (and I highly recommend you do), it's a good idea to buy tickets before you arrive. You can browse a list of what's showing at the League of Chicago Theaters website, **www.chicagoplays.com**, then visit individual theater websites to buy tickets online. The day before you leave, be sure to check Chicago's local weather forecast (see "The Climate" under "When to Go," below). The temperatures here can be unpredictable, so you'll find packing a lot easier if you know whether to expect snow, rain, or sweltering heat. (That said, bring a range of clothes if you're going to be in town for awhile—you should be prepared for anything!)

This chapter covers the basics of getting here and getting around. For additional help in planning your trip and for more on-the-ground resources in Chicago, please turn to "Fast Facts," in chapter 11.

1 WHEN TO GO

THE WEATHER

When I tell people from more temperate climates that I live in Chicago, their first question is how I handle the winters. Actually, winters here are no worse than in other northern cities, but it still isn't exactly prime tourist season. I encourage my own friends and family to visit during the summer or in the fall. Summer offers a nonstop selection of special events and outdoor activities; the only downside is that you'll be dealing with the biggest crowds and periods of hot, muggy weather.

Autumn days are generally sunny, and the crowds at major tourist attractions grow thinner—you don't have to worry about snow until late November at the earliest. Spring is extremely unpredictable, with dramatic fluctuations of cold and warm weather, and usually lots of rain. If your top priority is indoor cultural sights, winter's not such a bad time to visit: No lines at museums, the cheapest rates at hotels, and the pride that comes with slogging through the slush with the natives.

Chicagoans like to joke that if you don't like the weather, just wait an hour—it will change. (In spring and autumn, I've been known to use my car's heat in the morning and the air-conditioning in the afternoon.) The key is to be prepared for a wide range of weather with clothing that can take you from a sunny morning to a chilly, drizzly evening. As close to your departure as possible, check the local weather forecast at the websites of the *Chicago Tribune* newspaper (www.chicagotribune.com) or the **Weather Channel** (www.weather.com).

Chicago's Average Temperatures & Precipitation

	Jan	Feb	Mar	Apr	May	June	July	Aug	Sept	Oct	Nov	Dec
High °F	29	34	45	58	70	80	84	82	75	63	48	35
Low °F	13	18	28	39	48	57	63	62	54	42	31	20
High °C	−1	1	7	14	21	26	28	27	23	17	9	2
Low °C	−10	−7	−2	3	8	13	17	16	12	5	−1	−7
Rainfall (in.)	1.7	1.4	2.7	3.6	3.2	3.8	3.6	4.1	3.5	2.6	2.9	2.2

CHICAGO CALENDAR OF EVENTS

The best way to stay on top of the city's current crop of special events is to check in with the **Chicago Convention & Tourism Bureau** (© **877/CHICAGO** or 877/244-2246; www.choosechicago.com). Visit their website to browse the *Chicago Visitor's Guide,* a quarterly publication that surveys special events, including parades, street festivals, concerts, theatrical productions, and museum exhibitions (you can also get a copy mailed to you). The **Mayor's Office of Special Events** (© 312/744-3315) lets you search for upcoming festivals, parades, and concerts on its website, www.explorechicago.org).

For an exhaustive list of events beyond those listed here, check http://events.frommers.com, where you'll find a searchable, up-to-the-minute roster of what's happening in cities all over the world.

JANUARY

Chicago Boat, RV & Outdoor Show, McCormick Place, 23rd Street and Lake Shore Drive (© **312/946-6200;** www.chicagoboatshow.com). All the latest boats and recreational vehicles are on display, plus trout fishing, a climbing wall, boating safety seminars, and big-time entertainment. January 13 to January 17.

Winter Delights. Throughout January and February, the city's Office of Tourism (© **877/CHICAGO** or 877/244-2246; www.choosechicago.com) offers special travel deals to lure visitors during tourism's low season. Incentives include bargain-priced hotel packages, affordable prix-fixe dinners at downtown restaurants, and special music and theater performances. Early January through February.

FEBRUARY

Chicago Auto Show, McCormick Place, 23rd Street and Lake Shore Drive (© **630/495-2282;** www.chicagoautoshow.com). More than 1,000 cars and trucks, domestic and foreign, current and futuristic, are on display. The event draws nearly a million visitors. Look for special weekend packages at area hotels that include show tickets. February 12 to February 21.

Chinese New Year Parade, Wentworth and Cermak streets (© **312/326-5320;** www.chicagochinatown.org). Join in as the sacred dragon whirls down the boulevard and restaurateurs pass out small envelopes of money to their regular customers. In 2010, Chinese New Year begins on February 14; call to verify the date of the parade.

MARCH

St. Patrick's Day Parade. In a city with a strong Irish heritage (and a mayor of Irish descent), this holiday is a big deal. The Chicago River is even dyed green for the occasion. The parade route is along Columbus Drive from Balbo Drive to Monroe Street. A second, more neighborhood-like parade is held on the South Side the day after the Dearborn Street parade, on Western Avenue from 103rd to 115th streets. Visit www.chicagostpatsparade.com for information. The Saturday before March 17.

APRIL

Opening Day. For the **Cubs,** call ✆ **773/404-CUBS** or 773/404-2827, or visit **www.cubs.mlb.com**; for the **White Sox,** call ✆ **312/674-1000** or go to **www.whitesox.mlb.com**. Make your plans early to get tickets for this eagerly awaited day. The calendar may say spring, but be warned: Opening Day is usually freezing in Chi-town. (The first Cubs and Sox home games have occasionally been postponed because of snow.) Early April.

Chicago Improv Festival. Chicago's improv comedy scene is known as a training ground for performers who have gone on to shows such as *Saturday Night Live* or *MADtv*. Big names and lesser-known (but talented) comedians converge for a celebration of silliness, with large main-stage shows and smaller, more experimental pieces. Most performances are at the Lakeshore Theater on the North Side (3175 N. Broadway; ✆ **773/472-3492;** www. chicagoimprovfestival.org). Second week in April.

Buckingham Fountain Color Light Show, Grant Park, Congress Parkway and Lake Shore Drive. The water and ever-changing colored lights put on a show in the landmark fountain daily from May 1 to October 1 until 11pm.

The Ferris Wheel and Carousel begin spinning again at Navy Pier, 600 E. Grand Ave. (✆ **312/595-PIER** or 312/595-7437; www.navypier.com). The rides operate through October. From Memorial Day through Labor Day, Navy Pier also hosts twice-weekly fireworks shows Wednesday nights at 9:30pm and Saturday nights at 10:15pm.

Wright Plus Tour, Frank Lloyd Wright Home and Studio, Oak Park (✆ **708/848-1976;** www.wrightplus.org). This annual tour of 10 buildings, including Frank Lloyd Wright's home and studio, the Unity Temple, and several other notable buildings in both Prairie and Victorian styles, can sell out within 6 weeks. Tickets go on sale March 1. Third Saturday in May.

JUNE

Printers Row Lit Fest, Dearborn Street from Congress Parkway to Polk Street (✆ **312/222-3986;** www.printersrow litfest.org). One of the largest free outdoor book fairs in the country, this weekend event celebrates the written word with everything from readings and signings by big-name authors to panel discussions on penning your first novel. Located within walking distance of the Loop, the fair also features more than 150 booksellers with new, used, and antiquarian books; a poetry tent; and special activities for children. First weekend in June.

Chicago Gospel Festival, Petrillo Music Shell, Jackson Drive and Columbus Drive, Grant Park (✆ **312/744-3315**). Blues may be the city's most famous musical export, but Chicago is also the birthplace of gospel music: Thomas Dorsey, the "father of gospel," and the greatest gospel singer, Mahalia Jackson, were Southsiders. This 3-day festival—the largest outdoor, free-admission event of its kind—offers music on three stages with more than 40 performances. First weekend in June.

Chicago Blues Festival, Petrillo Music Shell, Randolph Street and Columbus Drive, Millennium Park (© **312/744-3315**). Muddy Waters would scratch his noggin over the sea of suburbanites who flood into Grant Park every summer to quaff Budweisers and accompany local legends Buddy Guy and Lonnie Brooks on air guitar. Truth be told, you can hear the same great jams and wails virtually any night of the week in one of the city's many blues clubs. Still, a thousand-voice chorus of "Sweet Home Chicago" under the stars has a rousing appeal. Blues Fest is free, with dozens of acts performing over 4 days, but get there in the afternoon to get a good spot on the lawn for the evening show. Second weekend in June.

Ravinia Festival, Ravinia Park, Highland Park (© **847/266-5100;** www.ravinia.com). This suburban location is the open-air summer home of the Chicago Symphony Orchestra and the venue of many first-rate visiting orchestras, chamber ensembles, pop artists, and dance companies. See also "Exploring the 'Burbs," in chapter 7. June through September.

Puerto Rican Fest, Humboldt Park, Division Street and Sacramento Boulevard (© **773/292-1414**). One of the city's largest festivals, this celebration includes 5 days of live music, theater, games, food, and beverages. It peaks with a parade that winds its way from Wacker Drive and Dearborn Street to the West Side Puerto Rican enclave of Humboldt Park. Mid-June.

Old Town Art Fair, Lincoln Park West and Wisconsin Street, Old Town (© **312/337-1938;** www.oldtown triangle.com). This juried fine arts fair has drawn crowds to this historic neighborhood for more than 50 years with the work of more than 250 painters, sculptors, and jewelry designers from the Midwest and around the country on display. It also features an art auction, garden walk, concessions, and children's art activities. Second weekend in June.

Wells Street Art Festival, Wells Street from North Avenue to Division Street (© **312/951-6106;** www.oldtown chicago.org). Held on the same weekend as the more prestigious Old Town Art Fair, this event is lots of fun, with 200 arts and crafts vendors, food, music, and carnival rides. Second weekend in June.

Grant Park Music Festival, Pritzker Music Pavilion, Randolph Street and Columbus Drive, Millennium Park (© **312/742-7638;** www.grantpark musicfestival.com). One of the city's greatest bargains, this classical music series presents free concerts in picture-perfect Millennium Park. Many of the musicians are members of the Chicago Symphony Orchestra, and the shows often feature internationally known singers and performers. Concerts begin the last week in June and continue through August.

Chicago Country Music Festival, Petrillo Music Shell, Jackson Drive and Columbus Drive, in Grant Park (© **312/744-3315**). Chicago may be a long way from Dixie, but country music still has a loyal Midwest fan base. This popular event features free concerts from big-name entertainers. Last weekend in June.

Taste of Chicago, Grant Park (© **312/744-3315**). The city claims that this is the largest free outdoor food fest in the nation. Three and a half million rib and pizza lovers feeding at this colossal alfresco trough say they're right. Over 10 days of feasting in the streets, scores of Chicago restaurants cart their fare to food stands set up throughout the park. To avoid the heaviest crowds, try going on weekdays earlier in the day. *Claustrophobics, take note:* If you're here the evening of July 3 for the Independence Day fireworks, pick out a vantage point farther north on the lakefront—unless dodging sweaty limbs, spilled beer, and the occasional bottle rocket sounds fun. Admission is free; you pay for the sampling. June 27 through July 6.

Gay and Lesbian Pride Parade, Halsted Street, from Belmont Avenue to Broadway, south to Diversey Parkway, and east to Lincoln Park, where a rally and music festival are held (✆ 773/348-8243; www.chicagopridecalendar.org). This parade is the colorful culmination of a month of activities by Chicago's gay and lesbian communities. Halsted Street is usually mobbed; pick a spot on Broadway for a better view. Last Sunday in June.

JULY

Independence Day Celebration (✆ 312/744-3315). Chicago celebrates the holiday on July 3 with a free concert in Grant Park in the evening, followed by fireworks over the lake. Expect huge crowds. July 3.

Old St. Patrick's World's Largest Block Party, 700 W. Adams St., at Des Plaines Avenue (✆ 312/648-1021; www.oldstpats.org). This hugely popular blowout is hosted by the city's oldest church, an Irish Catholic landmark in the West Loop area. It can get pretty crowded, but Old St. Pat's always lands some major acts. Six bands perform over 2 nights on two stages and attract a young, lively crowd. Second weekend in July.

Chicago Yacht Club's Race to Mackinac Island, starting line at the Monroe Street Harbor (✆ 312/861-7777; www.chicagoyachtclub.org). This 3-day competition is the grandest of the inland water races. The public is welcome at a Friday-night party. On Saturday, jockey for a good place to watch the boats set sail. Mid-July.

Sheffield Garden Walk, starting at Sheffield and Webster avenues (✆ 773/929-9255; www.sheffieldfestivals.org). Here's your chance to snoop in the lush backyards of Lincoln Park homeowners. The walk isn't just for garden nuts; the bands, children's activities, and food and drink tents attract lots of singles and young families. Third weekend in July.

Dearborn Garden Walk & Heritage Festival, North Dearborn and Astor streets (✆ 312/632-1241; www.dearborngardenwalk.com). A more upscale affair than the Sheffield Garden Walk, this event allows regular folks to peer into private gardens on the Gold Coast, one of the most expensive and exclusive neighborhoods in the city. As you'd expect, many yards are the work of the best landscape architects, designers, and art world luminaries that old money can buy. There's also live music, a marketplace, and a few architectural tours. Third Sunday in July.

Chicago SummerDance, east side of South Michigan Avenue between Balbo and Harrison streets (✆ 312/742-4007; www.cityofchicago.org/summerdance). From July through late August, the city's Department of Cultural Affairs transforms a patch of Grant Park into a lighted outdoor dance venue on Thursday, Friday, and Saturday from 6 to 9:30pm, and Sunday from 4 to 7pm. The 4,600-square-foot dance floor provides ample room for throwing down moves while live bands play music—from ballroom and klezmer to samba and zydeco. One-hour lessons are offered from 6 to 7pm. Free admission.

Venetian Night, Monroe Harbor to the Adler Planetarium (© **312/744-3315**). This carnival of illuminated boats on the lake is complete with fireworks and synchronized music by the Grant Park Symphony Orchestra. Shoreline viewing is fine, but you'll have to get there early to snag a prime viewing spot. The best way to take it in, if you can swing it, is from another boat nearby. This is a fine time to woo your sweetie with a dinner cruise. (See "Sightseeing Tours," in chapter 7.) Last Saturday in July.

Taste of Lincoln Avenue, Lincoln Park, between Fullerton Avenue and Wellington Street (© **773/868-3010;** www.wrightwoodneighbors.org). This is one of the largest and most popular of Chicago's many neighborhood street fairs; it features 50 bands performing music on five stages. Neighborhood restaurants staff the food stands, and there's also a kids' carnival. Last weekend in July.

Newberry Library Book Fair & Bughouse Square Debates, 69 W. Walton St. and Washington Square Park (© **312/255-3501;** www.newberry. org). Over 4 days, the esteemed Newberry Library invites the masses to rifle through bins stuffed with tens of thousands of used books, most of which go for less than $2 a pop. Better than the book fair is what happens across the street in Washington Square Park: Soapbox orators re-creating the days when left-wing agitators came here to make their case. Late July.

AUGUST

Northalsted Market Days, Halsted Street between Belmont Avenue and Addison Street (© **773/883-0500;** www. northalsted.com). The largest of the city's street festivals, held in the heart of this gay neighborhood, Northalsted Market Days offers music on three stages, lots of food and offbeat merchandise, and the best people-watching of the summer. First weekend in August.

Bud Billiken Parade and Picnic, starting at 39th Street and King Drive and ending at 55th Street and Washington Park (© **773/536-3710;** www.bud billikenparade.com). This annual African-American celebration, which celebrated its 80th anniversary in 2009, is one of the oldest parades of its kind in the nation. It's named for the mythical figure Bud Billiken, reputedly the patron saint of "the little guy," and features the standard floats, bands, marching and military units, drill teams, and glad-handing politicians. Second Saturday in August.

Chicago Air & Water Show, North Avenue Beach (© **312/744-3315**). The U.S. Air Force Thunderbirds and Navy Seals usually make an appearance at this hugely popular aquatic and aerial spectacular. (Even if you don't plan to watch it, you can't help but experience it with jets screaming overhead all weekend.) Expect huge crowds, so arrive early if you want a spot along the water, or park yourself on the grass along the east edge of Lincoln Park Zoo, where you'll get good views (and some elbow room). Free admission. Third weekend in August.

Viva! Chicago Latin Music Festival, Petrillo Music Shell, Jackson and Columbus drives, Grant Park (© **312/ 744-3315**). This free musical celebration features salsa, mambo, and the hottest Latin rock outfits. Free admission. Last weekend in August.

SEPTEMBER

Chicago Jazz Festival, Petrillo Music Shell, Jackson and Columbus drives, Grant Park (© **312/744-3315**). Several national headliners are always on hand

Major Convention Dates

Listed below are Chicago's major (30,000 visitors or more) conventions for 2010, with projected attendance figures. Plan ahead because hotel rooms and restaurant reservations can be hard to come by when the big shows are in town—and even if you snag a room, you'll be paying top price. Contact the **Chicago Convention and Tourism Bureau** (✆ **877/CHICAGO** or 877/244-2246; www.choosechicago.com) to double-check the latest info before you commit to your travel dates, as convention schedules can change.

Event	2010 Dates	Projected Attendance
Chicago Dental Society	Feb 25–27	30,000
International Home and Housewares Show	Mar 14–16	60,000
Kitchen/Bath Industry Show	April 16–18	60,000
National Restaurant Association Show	May 22–25	75,000
American Society of Clinical Oncology	June 4–8	35,000
Neo-Con—World's Trade Fair	June 14–16	40,000
International Manufacturing Tech Show	Sept 13–18	95,000
Graph Expo	Oct 3–6	50,000
Pack Expo	Oct 31–Nov 4	75,000
American Heart Association	Nov 14–17	35,000
Radiological Society of North America	Nov 28–Dec 3	55,000

at this steamy gathering, which provides a swell end-of-summer bookend opposite to the gospel and blues fests in June. The event is free; come early and stay late. First weekend in September.

The art season, in conjunction with the annual Visions series of art gallery programs for the general public, begins with galleries holding their season openers in the Loop, River North, River West, and Wicker Park/Bucktown gallery districts. Contact the **Chicago Art Dealers Association** (✆ **312/649-0065;** www.chicagoartdealers.org) for details. First Friday after Labor Day.

Boulevard Lakefront Bike Tour (Chicagoland Bicycle Federation; ✆ **312/427-3325;** www.boulevardtour.org). This 35-mile leisurely bicycle excursion is a great way to explore the city, from the neighborhoods to the historic link of parks and boulevards. There's also a 10-mile tour for children and families. The Sunday morning event starts and ends at the University of Chicago in Hyde Park, which plays host to vendors and entertainment at the annual Bike Expo. Mid-September.

Mexican Independence Day Parade, Dearborn Street between Wacker Drive and Van Buren Street (② **312/744-3315**). This parade is on Saturday; another takes place the next day on 26th Street in the Little Village neighborhood (② **773/521-5387**). Second Saturday in September.

Celtic Fest Chicago, Petrillo Music Shell, Jackson and Columbus drives, Grant Park (② **312/744-3315**). This festival celebrates the music and dance of global Celtic traditions. Second weekend in September.

OCTOBER

Chicago International Film Festival (② **312/683-0121**; www.chicagofilm festival.org). The oldest U.S. festival of its kind screens films from around the world, as well as a few high-profile American independent films. It's a great way to catch foreign movies that may never be released in the U.S. Screenings take place over 2 weeks, with most held at downtown movie theaters that are easily accessible to visitors. First 2 weeks of October.

Chicago Marathon (② **312/904-9800**; www.chicagomarathon.com). Sponsored by Bank of America, Chicago's marathon is a major event on the international long-distance running circuit. It begins and ends in Grant Park, but can be viewed from any number of vantage points along the route. Second Sunday in October.

NOVEMBER

The **Chicago Humanities Festival** takes over locations throughout downtown, from libraries to concert halls (② **312/661-1028**; www.chfestival.org). Over a 2-week period, the festival presents cultural performances, readings, and symposiums tied to an annual theme (recent themes included "Brains & Beauty" and "Crime & Punishment"). Expect appearances by major authors, scholars, and policymakers, all

at a very reasonable cost (usually $5 per event). Early November.

Dance Chicago (② **773/989-0698**; www.dancechicago.com). All of the city's best-known dance troupes (including Hubbard Street and Joffrey Ballet) and many smaller companies participate in this month-long celebration of dance, with performances and workshops at the **Athenaeum Theatre,** 2936 N. Southport Ave., on the city's North Side. It's a great chance to check out the range of local dance talent.

Magnificent Mile Lights Festival (② **312/642-3570**; www.magnificent milelightsfestival.com). Beginning at dusk, a colorful parade of Disney characters makes its way south along Michigan Avenue, from Oak Street to the Chicago River. Thousands of lights are entwined around trees, and street lights switch on as the procession passes. Carolers, elves, and minstrels appear with Santa along the avenue throughout the day and into the evening, and many retailers offer hot chocolate and other treats. Saturday before Thanksgiving.

Christmas Tree Lighting, Daley Plaza, in the Loop (② **312/744-3315**). The arrival of the city's official tree signals the beginning of the Christmas season. The switch is flipped the day after Thanksgiving, around dusk.

DECEMBER

Christkindlmarket, Daley Plaza, in the Loop (② **312/644-2662**; www. christkindlmarket.com). This annual holiday event is inspired by traditional German Christmas festivals. A mini European village springs up in downtown's Daley Plaza, where German-speaking vendors showcase handcrafted ornaments and other seasonal decorations. Of course, it wouldn't be a German celebration without beer, sausages, and hot spiced wine, too. The fair is open from Thanksgiving Day until Christmas Eve.

A Christmas Carol, Goodman Theatre, 170 N. Dearborn St. (*C* 312/443-3800; www.goodman-theatre.org). This seasonal favorite, performed for more than 2 decades, runs from about Thanksgiving to the end of December.

The *Nutcracker* ballet, Joffrey Ballet of Chicago, Auditorium Theatre, 50 E. Congress Pkwy. For tickets, call *C* 312/559-1212 (Ticketmaster), or contact the Joffrey office (*C* 312/739-0120; www.joffrey.com). The esteemed company performs its Victorian-American twist on the holiday classic. Late November to mid-December.

2 ENTRY REQUIREMENTS

PASSPORTS

Virtually every air traveler entering the U.S. is required to show a passport. All persons, including U.S. citizens, traveling by air between the United States and Canada, Mexico, Central and South America, the Caribbean, and Bermuda are required to present a valid passport. U.S. and Canadian citizens entering the U. S. at land and sea ports of entry from within the Western Hemisphere will need to present government-issued proof of citizenship, such as a birth certificate, along with a government issued photo ID, such as a driver's license. A passport is not required for U.S. or Canadian citizens entering by land or sea, but it is highly encouraged to carry one.

VISAS

The U.S. State Department has a **Visa Waiver Program (VWP)** allowing citizens of the following countries to enter the United States without a visa for stays of up to 90 days: Andorra, Australia, Austria, Belgium, Brunei, Denmark, Finland, France, Germany, Iceland, Ireland, Italy, Japan, Liechtenstein, Luxembourg, Monaco, the Netherlands, New Zealand, Norway, Portugal, San Marino, Singapore, Slovenia, Spain, Sweden, Switzerland, and the United Kingdom. Citizens of Czech Republic, Estonia, Hungary, Latvia, Lithuania, Malta, Republic of Korea, and Slovakia are soon to be admitted to the VWP. (*Note:* This list was accurate at press time;

for the most up-to-date list of countries in the VWP, consult http://travel.state.gov/visa.) Even though a visa isn't necessary, in an effort to help U.S. officials check travelers against terror watch lists before they arrive at U.S. borders, visitors from VWP countries must register online through the Electronic System for Travel Authorization (ESTA) before boarding a plane or a boat to the U.S. Travelers will complete an electronic application providing basic personal and travel eligibility information. The Department of Homeland Security recommends filling out the form at least three days before traveling. Authorizations will be valid for up to 2 years or until the traveler's passport expires, whichever comes first. Currently, there is no fee for the online application. *Note:* Any passport issued on or after October 26, 2006, by a VWP country must be an **e-Passport** for VWP travelers to be eligible to enter the U.S. without a visa. Citizens of these nations also need to present a round-trip air or cruise ticket upon arrival. E-Passports contain computer chips capable of storing biometric information, such as the required digital photograph of the holder. If your passport doesn't have this feature, you can still travel without a visa if it is a valid passport issued before October 26, 2005, and includes a machine-readable zone, or between October 26, 2005, and October 25, 2006, and includes a digital photograph. For more information, go to

http://travel.state.gov/visa. Canadian citizens may enter the United States without visas; they will need to show passports (if traveling by air) and proof of residence, however.

Citizens of all other countries must have (1) a valid passport that expires at least 6 months later than the scheduled end of their visit to the U.S., and (2) a tourist visa.

CUSTOMS
What You Can Bring Into the U.S.
Every visitor more than 21 years of age may bring in, free of duty, the following: (1) 1 liter of wine or hard liquor; (2) 200 cigarettes, 100 cigars (but not from Cuba), or 3 pounds of smoking tobacco; and (3) $100 worth of gifts. These exemptions are offered to travelers who spend at least 72 hours in the United States and who have not claimed them within the preceding 6 months. It is forbidden to bring into the country almost any meat products (including canned, fresh, and dried meat products such as bouillon, soup mixes, and so forth). Generally, condiments including vinegars, oils, spices, coffee, tea, and some cheeses and baked goods are permitted. Avoid rice products, as rice can often harbor insects. Bringing fruits and vegetables is not advised, though not prohibited. Customs will allow produce depending on where you got it and where you're going after you arrive in the U.S. International visitors may carry in or out up to $10,000 in U.S. or foreign currency with no formalities; larger sums must be declared to U.S. Customs on entering or leaving, which includes filing form CM 4790. For details regarding U.S. Customs and Border Protection, consult your nearest U.S. embassy or consulate, or **U.S. Customs** (www.customs.gov).

What You Can Take Home from Chicago
For information on what you're allowed to bring home, contact one of the following agencies:

U.S. Citizens: U.S. Customs & Border Protection (CBP), 1300 Pennsylvania Ave., NW, Washington, DC 20229 (© **877/ 287-8667;** www.cbp.gov).

Canadian Citizens: Canada Border Services Agency (© **800/461-9999** in Canada, or 204/983-3500; www.cbsa-asfc. gc.ca).

U.K. Citizens: HM Customs & Excise (© **0845/010-9000;** from outside the U.K., dial 020/8929-0152; or consult their website at www.hmce.gov.uk).

Australian Citizens: Australian Customs Service (© **1300/363-263;** www. customs.gov.au).

New Zealand Citizens: New Zealand Customs, The Customhouse, 17–21 Whitmore St., Box 2218, Wellington (© **04/473-6099** or 0800/428-786; www. customs.govt.nz).

MEDICAL REQUIREMENTS
Unless you're arriving from an area known to be suffering from an epidemic (particularly cholera or yellow fever), inoculations or vaccinations are not required for entry into the United States.

---

3 GETTING THERE & GETTING AROUND

GETTING TO CHICAGO
By Plane
Chicago's **O'Hare International Airport** (© **773/686-2200;** www.flychicago.com; online airport code ORD) has long battled Atlanta's Hartsfield-Jackson Airport for the title of the world's busiest airport. O'Hare is about 15 miles northwest of downtown Chicago. Depending on traffic, the drive to or from the city center can

take anywhere from 30 minutes to more than an hour.

O'Hare has information booths in all five terminals; most are on the baggage level. The multilingual employees, who wear red jackets, can assist travelers with everything from arranging ground transportation to getting information about local hotels. The booths, labeled "Airport Information," are open daily from 9am to 8pm.

Most major U.S. and international airlines fly in to O'Hare. You'll find the widest range of choices on United Airlines (which is headquartered in Chicago) and American Airlines (which has a hub at O'Hare).

At the opposite end of the city, on the southwest side, is Chicago's other major airport, **Midway International Airport** (© 773/838-0600; www.flychicago.com; online airport code MDW). Although it's smaller than O'Hare and handles fewer airlines, Midway is closer to the Loop and attracts more discount airlines, so you may be able to get a cheaper fare flying into here. (Always check fares to both airports if you want to find the best deal.) A cab ride from Midway to the Loop usually takes between 20 and 30 minutes. You can find the latest information on both airports at the city's Department of Aviation website: www.flychicago.com.

To find out which other airlines travel to Chicago, please see "Airline, Hotel & Car Rental Websites," p. 293.

Getting into Town from O'Hare and Midway

Taxis are plentiful at both O'Hare and Midway, but you can get downtown relatively easily by public transportation as well. A cab ride into the city will cost about $35 from O'Hare and $25 from Midway. *One warning:* Rush-hour traffic can be horrendous, especially around O'Hare, and the longer you sit in the traffic, the higher the fare will be.

If you're not carting enormous amounts of luggage and want to save money, I highly recommend taking public transportation, which is convenient from both airports. For $2, you can take the El (elevated train) straight into downtown.

O'Hare is on the Blue Line; a trip to downtown takes about 40 minutes. (If you're staying on or near Michigan Avenue, you'll probably want to switch to the Red Line, which will add another 10 or 15 minutes to your trip.) Trains leave every 6 to 10 minutes during the day, and every half-hour in the evening and overnight.

Getting downtown from Midway is even faster; the ride on the Orange Line takes 20 to 30 minutes. (The Orange Line stops operating each night at about 11:30pm and resumes service by 5am.) Trains leave the station every 6 to 15 minutes. The train station is a fair walk from the terminal—without the benefit of O'Hare's moving sidewalks—so be prepared if you have heavy bags.

Both airports also have outposts for every major car rental company.

(Value) Insider Tours—Free!

Want a personalized view of the city—aside from your trusted Frommer's guidebook? A program called **Chicago Greeter** matches tourists with local Chicagoans who serve as volunteer guides. Visitors can request a specific neighborhood or theme (everything from Polish heritage sites to Chicago movie locations), and a greeter gives them a free 2- to 4-hour tour. (Greeters won't escort groups of more than six people.) Specific requests should be made at least a week in advance, but "InstaGreeters" are also available on a first-come, first-served basis at the Chicago Cultural Center, 77 E. Randolph St., from Friday through Sunday. For details, call (℃) **312/744-8000,** or visit **www.chicagogreeter.com**.

GO Airport Express (℃ **888/2-THE-VAN** or 888/284-3826; www.airport express.com) serves most first-class hotels in Chicago with its green-and-white vans; ticket counters are at both airports near baggage claim (outside Customs at the international terminal at O'Hare). For transportation to the airport, reserve a spot through one of the hotels (check with the bell captain). The cost is $27 one-way ($49 round-trip) to or from O'Hare, and $22 one-way ($39 round-trip) to or from Midway. Group rates for two or more people traveling together are less expensive than sharing a cab, and children ages 6 to 12 ride for $15 each. The shuttles operate from 4am to 11:30pm.

For limo service from O'Hare or Midway, call **Carey Limousine of Chicago** (℃ **773/763-0009;** www.ecarey.com) or **Chicago Limousine Services** (℃ **312/726-1035**). Depending on the number of passengers and whether you opt for a sedan or a stretch limo, the service will cost about $100 to $150 from Midway and $150 to $200 from O'Hare, excluding gratuity and tax.

By Car

Interstate highways from all major points on the compass serve Chicago. I-80 and I-90 approach from the east, crossing the northern sector of Illinois, with I-90 splitting off and emptying into Chicago on the

Skyway and the Dan Ryan Expressway. From here, I-90 runs through Wisconsin, following a northern route to Seattle. I-55 snakes up the Mississippi Valley from the vicinity of New Orleans and enters Chicago from the west along the Stevenson Expressway; in the opposite direction, it provides an outlet to the Southwest. I-57 originates in southern Illinois and forms part of the interstate linkage to Florida and the South, connecting within Chicago on the west leg of the Dan Ryan. I-94 links Detroit with Chicago, arriving on the Calumet Expressway and leaving the city on the Kennedy Expressway en route to the Northwest.

Here are approximate driving distances in miles to Chicago: From **Milwaukee,** 92; from **St. Louis,** 297; from **Detroit,** 286; from **Denver,** 1,011; from **Atlanta,** 716; from **Washington, D.C.,** 715; from **New York City,** 821; and from **Los Angeles,** 2,034.

For listings of the major car rental agencies in Chicago, please see "Airline, Hotel & Car Rental Websites," p. 293.

International visitors should note that insurance and taxes are almost never included in quoted rental car rates in the U.S. Be sure to ask your rental agency about additional fees for these. They can add a significant cost to your car rental.

> **ⓘ Tips   Free Ride**
>
> During the summer, the city of Chicago operates free trolleys daily between Michigan Avenue and the Museum Campus (site of the Adler Planetarium, the Field Museum of Natural History, and the Shedd Aquarium); the trolleys run only on weekends in the fall and spring. Free trolleys also run year-round between Navy Pier and the Grand/State El station on the Red Line. While the trolleys are supposed to make stops every 30 minutes, waits can be longer during peak tourist season—and the trolleys aren't air-conditioned. If you get tired of waiting, remember that CTA public buses travel the same routes for only $2 per person.

By Train

Traveling great distances by train is certainly not the quickest way to go, nor always the most convenient, but some travelers still prefer it to flying or driving.

For tickets, consult your travel agent or call **Amtrak** (*ⓒ* **800/USA-RAIL** or 800/872-7245; www.amtrak.com). Ask the reservations agent to send you Amtrak's travel planner, with useful information on train accommodations and package tours.

When you arrive in Chicago, the train will pull into **Union Station,** 210 S. Canal St., between Adams and Jackson streets (*ⓒ* **312/655-2385**). Bus nos. 1, 60, 125, 151, and 156 all stop at the station, which is just west across the river from the Loop. The nearest El stop is at Clinton Street and Congress Parkway (on the Blue Line), which is a fair walk away, especially when you're carrying luggage.

By Bus

Bus travel is often the most economical form of public transit for short hops between U.S. cities, but it's certainly not an option for everyone (particularly when Amtrak, which is far more luxurious, offers similar rates). **Greyhound** (*ⓒ* **800/ 231-2222;** www.greyhound.com) is the sole nationwide bus line. International visitors can obtain information about the **Greyhound North American Discovery Pass** from foreign travel agents or through www.discoverypass.com. The ticket allows

for unlimited travel and stopovers in the U.S. and Canada.

If you're planning on traveling elsewhere in the Midwest, **Megabus** (*ⓒ* **877/ GO2-MEGA** or 877/462-6342; www. megabus.com) offers low-cost trips to cities such as Milwaukee, Minneapolis, and St. Louis. The well-kept double-decker buses—which come equipped with free Wi-Fi—are a popular option for students. Buses leave from the city's main train station, Union Station.

GETTING AROUND

The best way to savor Chicago is by walking its streets. Walking isn't always practical, however, particularly when moving between distant neighborhoods and on harsh winter days. In those situations, Chicago's public train and bus systems can get you almost anywhere you want to go.

By Train (the El)

The **Chicago Transit Authority,** better known as the **CTA** (*ⓒ* **836-7000** or TTY 836-4949 from any area code in the city and suburbs; **www.transitchicago.com**) operates an extensive system of trains throughout the city of Chicago; both the below-ground subway lines and above-ground elevated trains are know collectively as the El. The system is generally safe and reliable, although I'd avoid long rides through unfamiliar neighborhoods late at night.

Tips **Ticket to Ride**

Visitors who plan on taking a lot of train or bus trips should consider buying a **Visitor Pass,** which works like a fare card and allows individual users unlimited rides on the El and CTA buses over a 24-hour period. The cards cost $5 and are sold at airports, hotels, museums, Hot Tix outlets, transportation hubs, and Chicago Office of Tourism visitor information centers (you can also buy them in advance online at www.transitchicago.com or by calling ℂ **888/YOUR-CTA** or 888/968-7282). You can also buy 2-, 3-, and 5-day passes. While the passes save you the trouble of feeding the fare machines yourself, they're economical only if you plan to make at least three distinct trips at least 2 or more hours apart (remember that you get two additional transfers within 2 hrs. for an additional 25¢ on a regular fare).

Fares are $2 per ride, regardless of how far you go. For an additional 25¢, you can transfer to the bus or take a different El ride within 2 hours. Children 6 and under ride free, and those between the ages of 7 and 11 pay $1. Seniors can also receive the reduced fare if they have the appropriate reduced-fare permit (call ℂ **312/836-7000** for details on how to obtain one, although this is probably not a realistic option for a short-term visitor).

The CTA uses credit card–size fare cards that automatically deduct the exact fare each time you take a ride. The reusable cards can be purchased with a preset value already stored, or riders can obtain cards at vending machines located at all CTA train stations and charge them with whatever amount they choose (a minimum of $2 and up to $100). If within 2 hours of your first ride you transfer to a bus or the El, the turnstiles at the El stations and the fare boxes on buses will automatically deduct from your card just the cost of a transfer (25¢). If you make a second transfer within 2 hours, it's free. The same card can be recharged continuously.

The CTA operates seven major train lines, identified by color: The **Red Line,** which runs north-south, is most likely the only one you'll need, since it runs parallel to the lakefront and past many tourist attractions. The **Green Line** runs west-south; the **Blue Line** runs through Wicker Park/Bucktown west-northwest to O'Hare Airport; the **Pink Line** branches off from the Blue Line and serves the southwest side of the city; the **Brown Line** runs in a northern zigzag route; and the **Orange Line** runs southwest, serving Midway airport. The **Purple Line,** which runs on the same Loop elevated tracks as the Orange and Green lines, serves north-suburban Evanston and runs only during rush hour.

I highly recommend taking at least one El ride while you're here—you'll get a whole different perspective on the city (not to mention fascinating views inside downtown office buildings and North Side homes as you zip past their windows). While the Red Line is the most efficient for traveling between the Magnificent Mile and points south, your only views along this underground stretch will be of dingy stations. For sightseers, I recommend taking the aboveground Brown Line, which runs around the downtown Loop and then north through residential neighborhoods. You can ride all the way to the end of the line at Kimball (about a 45-min. ride from downtown), or hop off at Belmont to wander the Lakeview neighborhood. Avoid this scenic ride during

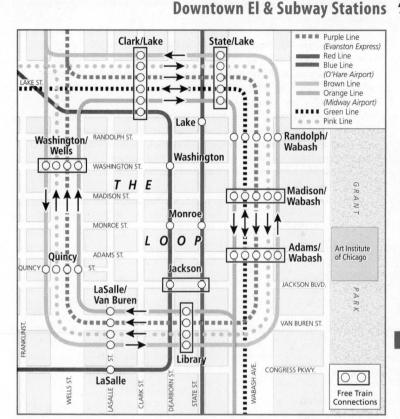

rush hour (before about 9am and 3:30–6:30pm), when your only view will be of tired commuters.

Study your CTA map carefully (there's one printed on the inside back cover of this guide) before boarding any train. Most trains run every 5 to 20 minutes, decreasing in frequency in the off-peak and overnight hours. The Orange Line train does not operate from about 11:30pm to 5am, the Brown Line operates only north of Belmont after about 9:30pm, the Blue Line's Cermak branch doesn't run overnight and on weekends, and the Purple Line operates only during the morning and afternoon rush hours on weekdays.

By Bus

The best way to get around neighborhoods along the lakefront—where the trains don't run—is by public bus. Look for the **blue-and-white signs to locate bus stops,** which are spaced about 2 blocks apart. Each bus route is identified by a number and the name of the main street it runs along; the bus that follows Grand Avenue, for example, is the no. 65 Grand.

Buses accept the same fare cards used for the El, but you can't buy a card onboard. That means you have to stop by a train station to buy a card in advance, or pay $2 cash when you board. The bus drivers cannot make change, so make sure that you've got the right amount in coins or dollar bills before hopping on.

A few buses that are particularly handy for visitors are the **no. 146 Marine/ Michigan,** an express bus from Belmont Avenue on the North Side that cruises down North Lake Shore Drive (and through Lincoln Park during non-peak times) to North Michigan Avenue, State Street, and the Grant Park museum campus; the **no. 151 Sheridan,** which passes through Lincoln Park en route to inner Lake Shore Drive and then travels along Michigan Avenue as far south as Adams Street, where it turns west into the Loop (and stops at Union Station); and the **no. 156 LaSalle,** which goes through Lincoln Park and then into the Loop's financial district on LaSalle Street.

PACE buses (*C* **836-7000** from any Chicago area code or 847/364-7223; Mon–Fri 8am–5pm; www.pacebus.com) cover the suburban zones that surround Chicago. They run every 20 to 30 minutes during rush hour, operating until mid-evening Monday through Friday and early evening on weekends. Suburban bus routes are marked with nos. 208 and above, and vehicles may be flagged down at intersections where stops aren't marked.

By Commuter Train

The **Metra** commuter railroad (*C* **312/ 322-6777** or TTY 312/322-6774; Mon–Fri 8am–5pm; at other times call the **Transit Information Center** at *C* **312/ 836-7000** or TTY 312/836-4949; www. metrarail.com) serves the six-county suburban area around Chicago with 12 train lines. Several terminals are located downtown, including **Union Station** at Adams and Canal streets, **LaSalle Street Station** at LaSalle and Van Buren streets, **North Western Station** at Madison and Canal streets, and **Randolph Street Station** at Randolph Street and Michigan Avenue.

To view the leafy streets of Chicago's northern suburbs, take the **Union Pacific North Line,** which departs from the North Western Station, and get off at one of the following scenic towns: Kenilworth, Winnetka, Glencoe, Highland Park, and Lake Forest.

The **Metra Electric** (once known as the Illinois Central–Gulf Railroad, or the IC), running close to Lake Michigan on a track that occupies some of the most valuable real estate in Chicago, will take you to Hyde Park. (See "Exploring Hyde Park: The Museum of Science and Industry & More," in chapter 7.) You can catch the Metra Electric in the Loop at the Randolph Street Station and at the Van Buren Street Station at Van Buren Street and Michigan Avenue. (Both these stations are underground, so they're not immediately obvious to visitors.)

Commuter trains have graduated fare schedules based on the distance you ride. On weekends, holidays and during the summer, Metra offers a family discount that allows up to three children 11 and under to ride free when accompanying a paid adult. The commuter railroad also offers a $5 weekend pass for unlimited rides on Saturday and Sunday.

By Taxi

Taxis are a convenient way to get around the Loop and to reach restaurants and theaters beyond downtown, in residential neighborhoods such as Old Town, Lincoln Park, Bucktown and Wicker Park.

Taxis are easy to hail in the Loop, on the Magnificent Mile and the Gold Coast, in River North, and in Lincoln Park, but if you go far beyond these key areas, you might need to call. Cab companies include **Flash Cab** (*C* **773/561-4444), Yellow Cab** (*C* **312/TAXI-CAB** or 312/829-4222), and **Checker Cab** (*C* **312/CHECKER** or 312/243-2537).

The meter in Chicago cabs currently starts at $2.25 for the first mile and costs $1.80 for each additional mile, with a $1 surcharge for the first additional rider and 50¢ for each person after that. You will also have to pay an additional $1 fuel

Fun Facts **Sky Train: Chicago's El**

Watch any Hollywood film or TV series set in Chicago, and chances are they'll feature at least one scene set against our screeching elevated train system, more commonly known as the **"El"** (witness *The Fugitive, ER,* and others). The trains symbolize Chicago's gritty, "city-that-works" attitude, but they actually began as cutting-edge technology.

After the Great Fire of 1871, Chicago made a remarkable recovery; within 20 years, the downtown district was swarming with people, streetcars, and horses (but no stoplights). To help relieve congestion, the city took to the sky, building a system of elevated trains 15 feet above all the madness. The first El trains were steam-powered, but by the end of the century, all the lines—run by separate companies—used electricity. In 1895, the three El companies collaborated to build a set of tracks into and around the central business district that all the lines would then share. By 1897, the "Loop" was up and running.

Chicago's El wasn't the nation's first. That honor belongs to New York City, which started running its elevated trains in 1867, 25 years before Chicago. But the New York El has almost disappeared, moving underground and turning into a subway early last century. With 289 miles of track, Chicago has the biggest El and the second-largest public transportation system in the country.

surcharge whenever gas prices are above $3/gallon.

By Car

One of the great things about visiting Chicago is that you don't need to rent a car to get around: Most of the main tourist attractions are within walking distance of downtown hotels or public transportation. If you do drive here, Chicago is laid out so logically that it's relatively easy for visitors to get around the city by car. Although rush-hour traffic jams are just as frustrating as they are in other large cities, traffic runs fairly smoothly at most times of the day. Chicagoans have learned to be prepared for unexpected delays; it seems that at least one major highway and several downtown streets are under repair throughout the spring and summer months. (Some say we have two seasons: Winter and construction.)

Great diagonal corridors—such as Lincoln Avenue, Clark Street, and Milwaukee Avenue—slice through the grid pattern at key points in the city and shorten many a trip that would otherwise be tedious on the checkerboard surface of the Chicago streets. On scenic **Lake Shore Drive** (also known as Outer Dr.), you can travel the length of the city (and beyond), never far from the great lake that is Chicago's most awesome natural feature. If you're driving here, make sure you take one spin along what we call LSD; the stretch between the Museum Campus and North Avenue is especially stunning.

DRIVING RULES Unless otherwise posted, a right turn on red is allowed after stopping and signaling. As in any big city with its share of frustrating rush-hour traffic, be prepared for aggressive drivers and the occasional taxi to cut in front of you or make sudden, unexpected turns without signaling. Chicago drivers almost universally speed up at the sight of a yellow light; you'll most likely hear some honking if you don't make that mad dash before the light turns red.

PARKING Parking regulations are vigorously enforced throughout the city. Read signs carefully: The streets around Michigan Avenue have parking restrictions during rush hour—and I know from bitter firsthand experience that your car will be towed immediately. Many neighborhoods have adopted resident-only parking that prohibits others from parking on their streets, usually after 6pm each day (even all day in a few areas, such as Old Town). The neighborhood around Wrigley Field is off-limits during Cubs night games, so look for yellow sidewalk signs alerting drivers about the dozen-and-a-half times the Cubs play under lights. You can park in permit zones if you're visiting a friend who can provide you with a pass to stick on your windshield. Beware of tow zones, and, if visiting in winter, make note of curbside warnings regarding snow plowing.

A safe bet is valet parking, which most restaurants provide for $10 to $12. Downtown you might also opt for a public garage, but you'll have to pay premium prices. Several garages connected with malls or other major attractions offer discounted parking with a validated ticket.

If you'll be spending an entire day downtown, the best parking deal in the Loop is the city-run **Millennium Park** garage (℗ 312/742-7644), which charges $17 for up to 8 hours (enter on Columbus Dr., 1 block east of Michigan Ave., between Monroe and Randolph sts.). A little farther south are two municipal lots underneath **Grant Park,** with one entrance at Michigan Avenue and Van Buren Street and the other at Michigan Avenue and Madison Street (℗ **312/616-0600**). Parking costs $14 for the first hour and $22 for 2 to 8 hours. Other downtown lots (where prices are comparable or even higher) include **Midcontinental Plaza Garage,**

55 E. Monroe St. (℗ **312/986-6821**), and **Navy Pier Parking,** 600 E. Grand Ave. (℗ **312/595-7437**). There's also a large lot next to the **McCormick Place Convention Center,** 2301 S. Lake Shore Dr. (℗ **312/791-7000**).

CAR RENTAL All the major car-rental companies have offices at O'Hare and Midway, as well as locations downtown. See "Airline, Hotel & Car Rental Websites," p. 293, for more information.

If you're visiting from abroad and plan to rent a car in the United States, keep in mind that foreign driver's licenses are usually recognized in the U.S., but you may want to consider obtaining an international driver's license.

By Bicycle

The city of Chicago has earned kudos for its efforts to improve conditions for bicycling (designated bike lanes have been installed on stretches of Wells St., Roosevelt Rd., Elston Ave., and Halsted St.), but it can still be a tough prospect trying to compete with cars and their drivers, who aren't always so willing to share the road.

The **Chicagoland Bicycle Federation** (℗ **312/427-3325;** www.chibikefed.org), a nonprofit advocacy group, publishes several bicycling maps with tips on recommended on-street routes and parkland routes, as well as a guide to safe cycling in the city.

Bike Chicago rents all sorts of bikes, including tandems and four-seater "quad-cycles," as well as in-line skates, from three locations: North Avenue Beach, Millennium Park, and Navy Pier (℗ **888/BIKE-WAY** or 888/245-3929; www.bikechicago.com). Bike rentals start at $8.75 an hour or $30 a day. Helmets, pads, and locks are provided free of charge. The shops are open daily from 9am to 7pm, weather permitting.

The Value of the Dollar vs. Other Popular Currencies

US$	Can$	UK£	Euro€	Aus$	NZ$
$1	C$1.10	£0.61	0.70€	A$1.19	NZ$1.47

Frommer's lists exact prices in the local currency. The currency conversions quoted above were correct at press time. However, rates fluctuate, so before departing consult a currency exchange website such as **www.oanda.com/convert/classic** to check up-to-the-minute rates.

While not as expensive as New York, Chicago's hotel and restaurant prices are near the high end compared to other American cities. It's hard to find a hotel room for less than $200 a night in the summer (prime tourist season) and entrees at the city's best restaurants can set you back around $30.

Credit cards are accepted just about everywhere, aside from a few hole-in-the-wall restaurants. You should have no trouble using traveler's checks at most hotels and downtown restaurants (places that are used to accommodating international visitors), but they may not be accepted at smaller businesses in the city's residential neighborhoods.

ATMs are easy to find throughout the city. (Most Chicagoans refer to them as "cash stations".) Most ATMs belong to one of two networks: **Cirrus** (© 800/424-7787; www.mastercard.com) or **PLUS** (© 800/843-7587; www.visa.com). Go to your bank card's website to find convenient ATM locations before you leave, and be sure you know your daily withdrawal limit before you depart.

Visitors from outside the U.S. should find out whether their bank assesses a 1% to 3% fee on charges incurred abroad. In the U.S., the most common bills are the $1 (a "buck"), $5, $10, and $20 denominations. There are also $2 bills (seldom encountered), $50 bills, and $100 bills (the last two are usually not welcome as payment for small purchases). Coins come in eight denominations: 1¢ (1 cent, or a penny); 5¢ (5 cents, or a nickel); 10¢ (10 cents, or a dime); 25¢ (25 cents, or a quarter); 50¢ (50 cents, or a half dollar); the gold-colored Sacagawea coin, worth $1; the rare silver dollar; and the new presidential dollar coins.

5 HEALTH

Most Chicago hotels have doctors on call, so get in touch with your concierge or hotel's front desk if you need medical assistance. In case of emergency, head for the ER at **Northwestern Memorial Hospital,** 251 E. Huron St. (© **312/926-2000;** www.nmh.org). One of the city's best hospitals, it's located only a few blocks off Michigan Avenue and is easy to get to from all downtown hotels.

If you need to see a doctor for a non-emergency visit, Northwestern has a **Physician Referral Service** (© **877/926-4664**).

We list **additional emergency numbers** under "Fast Facts" in chapter 11.

6 SAFETY

Although Chicago has one of the highest murder rates in the United States, the vast majority of those crimes are tied to drug dealing or gang activity and take place in areas visitors are unlikely to be walking around. In all my years of living here, I've yet to hear of a violent crime targeted at a tourist.

That said, Chicago has the same problems with theft and muggings as any other major American city, so use your common sense and stay cautious and alert. After dark, stick to well-lit streets along the Magnificent Mile, River North, Gold Coast, and Lincoln Park, which are all high-traffic areas late into the night.

Late at night, avoid wandering dark residential streets on the fringes of Hyde Park and Pilsen, which border areas where gangs are active. You can also ask your hotel concierge or an agent at the tourist visitor center about the safety of a particular area.

The El is generally quite safe, even at night, although some of the downtown stations can feel eerily deserted late in the evening. Buses are a safe option, too, especially nos. 146 and 151, which pick up along North Michigan Avenue and State Street and connect to the North Side via Lincoln Park.

Blue-and-white police cars are a common sight, and officers also patrol by bicycle downtown and along the lakefront and by horseback at special events and parades. There are police stations in busy nightlife areas, such as the 18th District station at Chicago Avenue and LaSalle Street in River North and the 24th District station (known as Town Hall) at Addison and Halsted streets.

7 SPECIALIZED TRAVEL RESOURCES

In addition to the destination-specific resources listed below, please visit Frommers.com for additional specialized travel resources.

GAY & LESBIAN TRAVELERS

While it's not quite San Francisco, Chicago is a very gay-friendly city. The neighborhood commonly referred to as "Boys Town" (roughly from Belmont Ave. north to Irving Park Ave., and from Halsted St. east to the lakefront) is the center of gay nightlife—and plenty of daytime action too. **Gay and Lesbian Pride Week** (© 773/348-8243; www.chicagopride calendar.org), highlighted by a lively parade on the North Side, is a major event each June.

You might also want to stop by **Unabridged Books,** 3251 N. Broadway (© 773/883-9119), an excellent independent bookseller with a large lesbian and gay selection. Here, and elsewhere in the Lakeview neighborhood, you can pick up several gay publications, including the weekly *Chicago Free Press* (www.chicago freepress.com) which covers local news and entertainment. The **Center on Halsted,** 3656 N. Halsted St. (© 773/472-6469, www.centeronhalsted.org), is a gay social service agency and community center that's become an informal gathering place for Boys Town residents. Inside, you'll find an organic grocery store, cafe, and plenty of couches for hanging out and taking advantage of the center's free Wi-Fi.

TRAVELERS WITH DISABILITIES

Thanks to provisions in the Americans with Disabilities Act, most public places in Chicago comply with disability-friendly regulations. Almost all public establishments, including restaurants, hotels, and museums provide accessible entrances and other facilities for those with disabilities.

Pace, the company that runs bus routes between Chicago and its suburbs, offers paratransit services throughout the area for travelers with disabilities. Visitors must be registered with a similar program in their home city. For information, call ✆ **800/606-1282** or visit **www.pacebus.com**.

Several **Chicago Transit Authority (CTA)** El stations on each line have elevators. Call the CTA at ✆ **312/836-7000** for a list of accessible stations. All city buses are equipped to accommodate wheelchairs.

For specific information on facilities for people with disabilities, contact the **Mayor's Office for People with Disabilities,** 121 N. LaSalle St., Room 1104, Chicago, IL 60602 (✆ **312/744-7050** for voice, or 312/744-4964 for TTY; www.cityof chicago.org/disabilities). The office is staffed from 8:30am to 4:30pm Monday through Friday.

Horizons for the Blind, 2 N. Williams St., Crystal Lake, IL 60014 (✆ **815/444-8800**), is a social service agency that provides information about local hotels equipped with Braille signage and cultural attractions that offer Braille signage and special tours. The **Illinois Relay Center** enables hearing- and speech-impaired TTY callers to call individuals or businesses without TTYs 24 hours a day. Calls are confidential and billed at regular phone rates. Call TTY at ✆ **800/526-0844** or voice 800/526-0857. The city of Chicago operates a 24-hour information service for hearing-impaired callers with TTY equipment; call ✆ **312/744-8599.**

FAMILY TRAVEL

Chicago is full of sightseeing opportunities and special activities geared toward children. To locate those accommodations, restaurants, and attractions that are particularly kid-friendly, refer to the "Kids" icon throughout this guide. Also see "Kid Stuff" in chapter 7 for information on family-oriented attractions. Chapter 5 includes a list of the best hotel deals for families, and chapter 6 lists kid-friendly restaurants. The guidebook *Frommer's Chicago with Kids* (Wiley Publishing, Inc.) highlights the many family-friendly activities available in the city.

For information on finding a babysitter, see "Fast Facts" in chapter 11.

MULTICULTURAL TRAVELERS

Chicago is a cosmopolitan city with a population that's about 36% African American, 30% white, and 26% Latino. (Chicago has the second-largest Mexican population in the U.S. after Los Angeles.) Visitors of all racial and ethnic groups shouldn't expect to encounter any discrimination, especially in the downtown area. We're used to welcoming tourists and businesspeople from around the world.

Still, Chicago is extremely divided residentially along racial lines. The South Side is overwhelmingly African American, the North Side is mostly white, and Latino residents tend to settle in neighborhoods such as Pilsen, just southwest of downtown.

Travelers can explore the city's rich black heritage with a specialized tour (see "Neighborhood Tours," p. 198). Visitors with an interest in Latin-American art might want to stop by the vibrant National Museum of Mexican Art and explore the surrounding neighborhood of Pilsen (p. 181).

SENIOR TRAVEL

Traveling as a senior can definitely save you money in Chicago; people 60 and older qualify for reduced admission to most major museums and theaters. Although the local public transportation system recently announced that rides on bus and train lines are now free for seniors, you must be a resident of the Chicago area to qualify. Visitors, alas, must pay full fare, regardless of age.

STUDENT TRAVEL

The best resource for students in Chicago is **STA Travel** (www.statravel.com), one of the biggest student-travel agencies in the world, which can set you up with an ID card and get you discounts on plane tickets and rail travel. There is an STA office in the suburb of Evanston, near Northwestern University, at 900 Church St. (© 847/475-5070).

Chicago also has several hostels offering students and other travelers inexpensive, no-frills lodging. The best is **Hosteling International Chicago,** 24 E. Congress Pkwy., in the Loop (© **312/360-0300;** fax 312/360-0313; www.hichicago.org). It features many amenities (including a free buffet breakfast) and can help set up

activities throughout the city. Another hostel open year-round is the more basic **Arlington House International Hostel,** 616 W. Arlington Place, Chicago, IL 60614 (© **800/HOSTEL-5** or 800/467-8355, or 773/929-5380; fax 773/665-5485; www.arlingtonhouse.com), in Lincoln Park.

Check out the **International Student Travel Confederation (ISTC)** (www.istc.org) website for comprehensive travel services information and details on how to get an **International Student Identity Card (ISIC),** which qualifies students for substantial savings on rail passes, plane tickets, entrance fees, and more. It also provides students with basic health and life insurance and a 24-hour helpline. The card is valid for a maximum of 18 months. If you're no longer a student but are still 25 and under, you can get an **International Youth Travel Card (IYTC)** which entitles you to some discounts. **Travel CUTS** (© **800/592-2887;** www.travelcuts.com) offers similar services for both Canadians and U.S. residents. Irish students may prefer to turn to **USIT** (© **01/602-1904;** www.usit.ie), an Ireland-based specialist in student, youth, and independent travel.

---

8 SUSTAINABLE TOURISM

Thanks to our environmentally minded mayor, Richard M. Daley, Chicago has become a breeding ground for urban green initiatives. The latest addition to the city's massive McCormick Place Convention Center is the largest new construction building in the country to receive LEED (Leadership in Energy and Environmental Design) certification from the U.S. Green Building Council for its environmentally friendly design. More and more bike lanes are being wedged into the city's streets, and Millennium Park provides secured bike parking and showers for two-wheeled

commuters. Daley even appointed the city's first Chief Environmental Officer and oversaw the installation of a green roof on top of downtown's City Hall.

Some major Chicago hotels have also made a serious commitment to minimizing their impact on the environment. The **Hotel Allegro** (p. 74), **Hotel Burnham** (p. 70), **InterContinental Chicago** (p. 79), **Hotel Monaco** (p. 72), and **Talbott Hotel** (p. 80) have all received certification from the nonprofit organization Green Seal, which acknowledges their role

General Resources for Green Travel

The following websites provide valuable wide-ranging information on sustainable travel. For a list of even more sustainable resources, as well as tips and explanations on how to travel greener, visit www.frommers.com/planning.

- **Responsible Travel** (www.responsibletravel.com) is a great source of sustainable travel ideas; the site is run by a spokesperson for ethical tourism in the travel industry. **Sustainable Travel International** (www.sustainable travelinternational.org) promotes ethical tourism practices, and manages an extensive directory of sustainable properties and tour operators around the world.
- The **Internation Ecotourism Society** (TIES; www.ecotourism.org) lists touring companies and associations — listed by destination under "Travel Choice" — as well as provides eco-frendly travel tips and statistics.
- In the U.K., **Tourism Concern** (www.tourismconcern.org.uk) works to reduce social and environmental problems connected to tourism. The **Association of Independent Tour Operators (AITO)** (www.aito.co.uk) is a group of specialist operators leading the field in making holidays sustainable.
- In Canada, **www.greenlivingonline.com** offers extensive content on how to travel sustainably, including a travel and transport section.
- In Australia, the national body that sets guidelines and standards for ecotourism is **Ecotourism Australia** (www.ecotourism.org.au). **The Green Directory** (www.thegreendirectory.com.au), **Green Pages** (www.thegreen pages.com.au), and **Eco Directory** (www.ecodirectory.com.au) offer sustainable travel tips and directories of green businesses.
- **Carbonfund** (www.carbonfund.org), **TerraPass** (www.terrapass.org), **Be green now** (www.begreennow.com), and **Carbon Neutral** (www.carbon neutral.org) provide info on "carbon offsetting," or offsetting the greenhouse gas emitted during flights.
- **Greenhotels** (www.greenhotels.com) recommends green-rated member hotels around the world that fulfill the company's stringent environmental requirements. **Environmentally Friendly Hotels** (www.environmentally friendlyhotels.com) offers more green accommodation ratings. The **Hotel Association of Canada** (www.hacgreenhotels.com) has a Green Key Eco-Rating Program, which audits the environmental performance of Canadian hotels, motels, and resorts.
- **Sustain Lane** (www.sustainlane.com) lists sustainable eating and drinking choices around the U.S.; also visit **www.eatwellguide.org** for tips on eating sustainably in the U.S.
- For information on animal-friendly issues throughout the world, visit **Tread Lightly** (www.treadlightly.org).
- **Volunteer International** (www.volunteerinternational.org) has a list of questions to help you determine the intentions and the nature of a volunteer program. For general info on volunteer travel, visit **www.volunteer abroad.org** and **www.idealist.org**.

in minimizing waste, conserving water and promoting energy efficiency.

A focus on locally produced, organic ingredients has become a hallmark of the city's top chefs. Following the lead of well-known chefs such as **Charlie Trotter** (p. 136), Bruce Sherman of **North Pond** (p. 137),

and Paul Kahan of **Blackbird** (p. 106), more and more local restaurateurs are highlighting seasonal ingredients on their menus, and the **Green City Market** (p. 92) has become a popular shopping destination for both culinary professionals and local foodies.

9 STAYING CONNECTED

Generally, Chicago hotel surcharges on long-distance and local calls are astronomical, so you're better off using your **cellphone** or a **public pay telephone** to make calls. Many convenience groceries and packaging services sell **pre-paid calling cards** in denominations up to $50; for international visitors these can be the least expensive way to call home. Many public pay phones at airports now accept American Express, MasterCard, and Visa credit cards. **Local calls** made from pay phones in Chicago cost 35¢ (pennies aren't accepted).

Most long-distance and international calls can be dialed directly from any phone. **For calls within the United States and to Canada,** dial 1 followed by the area code and the 7-digit number. **For other international calls,** dial 011 followed by the country code, city code, and the number you are calling.

Calls to area codes **800, 888, 877,** and **866** are toll-free. However, calls to area codes **700** and **900** (chat lines, bulletin boards, "dating" services, and so on) can be very expensive—usually a charge of 95¢ to $3 or more per minute, and they sometimes have minimum charges that can run as high as $15 or more.

For **reversed-charge or collect calls,** and for person-to-person calls, dial the number 0 then the area code and number; an operator will come on the line, and you should specify whether you are calling

collect, person-to-person, or both. If your operator-assisted call is international, ask for the overseas operator.

For **local directory assistance** ("information"), dial ☎ **411;** for long-distance information, dial 1, then the appropriate area code and ☎ **555-1212.**

CELLPHONES

As with all large American cities, Chicago is covered by the major national cellphone networks, including AT&T, Sprint, Nextel, and T-Mobile. If you're traveling from elsewhere in the U.S., chances are good that your phone will work here—although you may be hit with roaming charges that make your per-minute costs much higher. If you'd like to rent a cellphone while you're in town, you can get one through **InTouch USA** (☎ **800/872-7626;** www.intouchglobal.com) or most rental car locations, but beware that you'll pay $1 a minute or more for airtime.

If you're not from the U.S., you'll be appalled at the poor reach of the **GSM (Global System for Mobile Communications) wireless network,** which is used by much of the rest of the world. Your phone should work in Chicago, but it definitely won't in many rural areas. To see where GSM phones work in the U.S., check out www.t-mobile.com/coverage. And you may or may not be able to send SMS (text messaging) home.

INTERNET & E-MAIL
With Your Own Computer

Hotels, resorts, airports, cafes, and retailers throughout the Chicago area have gone Wi-Fi, becoming "hotspots" that offer free high-speed access or charge a small fee for usage.

In the Loop, **Millennium Park, Daley Plaza** (along Washington St. btw. Dearborn and Clark sts.), the **Chicago Cultural Center,** 78 E. Washington St., and the **Harold Washington Library Center,** 400 S. State St., all have wireless access. Elsewhere in downtown Chicago, Starbucks, the sandwich chain Cosí, and McDonald's have numerous locations with Wi-Fi access. Wireless hotspots in Lincoln Park include **Panera Bread,** 616 W. Diversey Pkwy. (© **773/528-4556**), and **Argo Tea,** 958 W. Armitage Ave. (© **773/388-1880**).

To find more public Wi-Fi hotspots in Chicago, go to **www.jiwire.com**; its Hotspot Finder holds the world's largest directory of public wireless hotspots.

For dial-up access, almost every hotel in town offers dataports for laptop modems; many also offer free high-speed Internet access.

Without Your Own Computer

Almost every hotel in Chicago has a business center with Internet access for guests (although you usually have to pay extra to use it). Most youth hostels and public libraries also offer Internet access.

Most major airports have **Internet kiosks** that provide basic Web access for a per-minute fee that's usually higher than cybercafe prices. Check out copy shops like FedEx Office (formerly Kinko's), which offers computer stations with fully loaded software (as well as Wi-Fi).

For help locating cybercafes and other establishments where you can go for Internet access, please see "Internet Access" under "Fast Facts" in chapter 11.

Suggested Chicago Itineraries

Downtown Chicago is relatively compact, so it's possible to get a general sense of the city in 1 day (although, of course, you really should spend more than 24 hours here). How you spend your time depends in part on your interests and the weather; you could easily spend 3 days exploring Chicago's museums, and if you're here in the winter, that's probably a lot more appealing than a daylong walking tour. On a sunny summer day, though, you might be tempted to spend an afternoon wandering along the lakefront without any particular destination. Ideally, you should experience both *indoors* and *outdoors*. In this spirit, I've composed the following itineraries, which contain a mix of cultural institutions and scenic walks.

1 ORIENTATION

Chicago proper has about three million inhabitants living in an area about two-thirds the size of New York City; another five million make the suburbs their home. The **Chicago River** forms a Y that divides the city into its three geographic zones: North Side, South Side, and West Side. (Lake Michigan is where the East Side would be.) The downtown financial district is called **the Loop.** The city's key shopping street is **North Michigan Avenue,** also known as the **Magnificent Mile.** In addition to department stores and vertical malls, this stretch of property north of the river houses many of the city's most elegant hotels. North and south of this downtown zone, Chicago stretches along 29 miles of Lake Michigan shoreline that is, by and large, free of commercial development, reserved for public use as green space and parkland from one end of town to the other.

FINDING AN ADDRESS

Chicago is laid out in a **grid system,** with the streets neatly lined up as if on a giant piece of graph paper. Because the city itself isn't rectangular (it's rather elongated), the shape is a bit irregular, but the perpendicular pattern remains. A half-dozen or so major diagonal thoroughfares make moving through the city relatively easy.

Point zero is located at the downtown intersection of State and Madison streets. **State Street** divides east and west addresses, and **Madison Street** divides north and south addresses. From here, Chicago's highly predictable addressing system begins. Making use of this grid, it's easy to plot the distance in miles between any two points in the city.

Virtually all of Chicago's principal north-south and east-west arteries are spaced by increments of 400 in the addressing system—regardless of the number of smaller streets nestled between them—and each addition or subtraction of the number 400 to an address is equivalent to a half-mile. Thus, starting at point zero on Madison Street and traveling north along State Street for 1 mile, you will come to 800 N. State St., which intersects Chicago Avenue. Continue uptown for another half-mile and you arrive at the

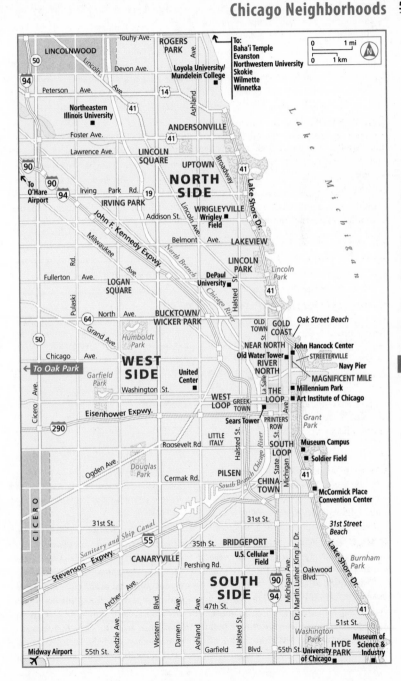

1200 block of North State Street at Division Street. And so it goes, right to the city line, with suburban Evanston located at the 7600 block north, 9½ miles from point zero.

The same rule applies when you're traveling south, or east to west. Thus, starting at point zero and heading west from State Street along Madison and Halsted streets, the address of 800 W. Madison St. would be the distance of 1 mile, while Racine Avenue, at the intersection of the 1200 block of West Madison Street, is 1½ miles from point zero. Madison Street then continues westward to Chicago's boundary with the nearby suburb of Oak Park along Austin Avenue, which, at 6000 W. Madison, is approximately 7½ miles from point zero.

Once you've got the grid figured out, you can look at a map and estimate about how long it will take to walk around any given neighborhood. The other convenient aspect of the grid is that every major road uses the same numerical system. In other words, the cross street (Division St.) at 1200 N. Lake Shore Dr. is the same as at 1200 N. Clark St. and 1200 N. LaSalle St.

STREET MAPS

Free maps are available at the city's official visitor information centers at the **Chicago Cultural Center** and the **Chicago Water Works Visitor Center.** (See "Visitor Information," under "Fast Facts" in chapter 11.) You can also print out maps before your trip by visiting the Chicago Convention and Tourism Bureau's website, **www.choosechicago.com**.

NEIGHBORHOODS IN BRIEF

DOWNTOWN

The Loop   The Loop refers literally to a core of high-rises surrounded by a rectangular "loop" of elevated train tracks. But when Chicagoans use the term, they're referring to the city's downtown, bounded by the Chicago River to the north and west, by Michigan Avenue to the east, and by Roosevelt Avenue to the south. For the most part, the Loop is strictly business, filled with office buildings rather than residential developments. For a suggested walking tour of the Loop, see p. 205.

THE NORTH SIDE

Magnificent Mile   North Michigan Avenue from the bridge spanning the Chicago River to its northern tip at Oak Street is known as the Magnificent Mile (or, simply, "Michigan Avenue," although the street itself stretches much further). Many of the city's best hotels and most concentrated shopping are to be found here. The area stretching east of Michigan Avenue to the lake is some-

times referred to as "Streeterville"—the legacy of George Wellington "Cap" Streeter. Streeter was an eccentric, bankrupt showman who lived in Chicago in the mid-1880s. Looking for a new way to make money, Streeter bought a steamship with a plan to become a gun runner in Honduras. The steamship ran aground during a test cruise in Lake Michigan, and Streeter left the ship where it was, staking out 200 acres of self-created landfill. He then declared himself "governor" of the "District of Lake Michigan." True story.

River North   Just to the west of the Mag Mile is an old warehouse district called River North. These formerly industrial buildings have been transformed into one of the city's most vital commercial districts, with many of the city's hottest restaurants and nightspots; you'll also find the city's highest concentration of art galleries here. In the past 2 decades, large-scale residential loft developments have sprouted on its western and southwestern fringes.

The Gold Coast Some of Chicago's most desirable real estate and historic architecture are found along Lake Shore Drive, between Oak Street and North Avenue and along the adjacent side streets. Despite trendy pockets of real estate that have popped up elsewhere, the moneyed class still prefers to live by the lake. On the neighborhood's southwestern edge, around Division and Rush streets, a string of raucous bars and late-night eateries contrasts sharply with the rest of the area's sedate mood. For a suggested walking tour of the neighborhood, see p. 209.

Old Town West of LaSalle Street, principally on North Wells Street between Division Street and North Avenue, is the residential district of Old Town, which boasts some of the city's best-preserved historic homes (a few even survived the Great Chicago Fire of 1871). This area was a hippie haven in the 1960s and '70s; now the neighborhood is one of the most expensive residential areas in the city. A major transformation is taking place just southwest of Old Town, as Cabrini Green, a massive and once-notorious housing project, is gradually being demolished to make way for mixed-income housing. Old Town's biggest claim to fame, the legendary Second City comedy club, has served up the lighter side of life to Chicagoans for more than 30 years.

Lincoln Park Chicago's most popular residential neighborhood for young singles and urban-minded families is Lincoln Park. Stretching from North Avenue to Diversey Parkway, it's bordered on the east by the huge park of the same name, which is home to one of the nation's oldest zoos (established in 1868). The trapezoid formed by Clark Street, Armitage Avenue, Halsted Street, and Diversey Parkway also contains many of Chicago's liveliest bars, restaurants, retail stores, music clubs, and off-Loop theaters—including the nationally acclaimed Steppenwolf Theatre Company.

Lakeview & Wrigleyville Midway up the city's North Side is a one-time blue-collar, now mainstream middle-class quarter called Lakeview. It has become the neighborhood of choice for many gays and lesbians, recent college graduates, and residents priced out of Lincoln Park. The main thoroughfare is Belmont Avenue, between Broadway and Sheffield Avenue. Wrigleyville is the name given to the neighborhood in the vicinity of Wrigley Field—home of the Chicago Cubs—at Sheffield Avenue and Addison Street. Not surprisingly, the ball field is surrounded by sports bars and memorabilia shops.

Uptown & Andersonville Uptown, which runs along the lakefront as far north as Foster Avenue, has traditionally attracted waves of immigrants. While crime was a major problem for decades, the area has stabilized, with formerly decrepit buildings being converted into—you guessed it—condominiums. Vietnamese and Chinese immigrants have transformed Argyle Street between Broadway and Sheridan Road into a teeming market for fresh meat, fish, and all kinds of exotic vegetables. Slightly to the north and west is the old Scandinavian neighborhood of Andersonville, whose main drag is Clark Street, between Foster and Bryn Mawr avenues. The area has an eclectic mix of Middle Eastern restaurants, a distinct cluster of women-owned businesses, and a burgeoning colony of gays and lesbians.

Lincoln Square West of Andersonville and slightly to the south, where

Lincoln, Western, and Lawrence avenues intersect, is Lincoln Square, the only identifiable remains of Chicago's once-vast German-American community. The surrounding leafy residential streets have attracted many families, who flock to the Old Town School of Folk Music's theater and education center, a beautiful restoration of a former library building.

Rogers Park Rogers Park, which begins at Devon Avenue, is located on the northern fringes of the city bordering suburban Evanston. Its western half has been a Jewish neighborhood for decades. The eastern half, dominated by Loyola University's lakefront campus, has become the most cosmopolitan enclave in the entire city: African Americans, Asians, East Indians, German Americans, and Russian Jews live side by side with the ethnically mixed student population drawn to the Catholic university. The western stretch of Devon Avenue is a Midwestern slice of Calcutta, colonized by Indians who've transformed the street into a veritable restaurant row serving tandoori chicken and curry-flavored dishes.

THE WEST SIDE

West Loop Also known as the Near West Side, the neighborhood just across the Chicago River from the Loop is the city's newest gentrification target, as old warehouses and once-vacant lots are transformed into trendy condos and stylish restaurants. Chicago's old Greektown, still the Greek culinary center of the city, runs along Halsted Street between Adams and Monroe streets. Much of the old Italian neighborhood in this vicinity was the victim of urban renewal, but remnants still survive on Taylor Street. The same is true for a few old delis and shops on Maxwell Street, dating from the turn of the 20th century when a large Jewish community lived in the area.

Bucktown/Wicker Park Centered near the intersection of North, Damen, and Milwaukee avenues, this resurgent area has hosted waves of German, Polish, and, most recently, Spanish-speaking immigrants (not to mention writer Nelson Algren). In recent years, it has morphed into a bastion of hot new restaurants, alternative culture, and loft-dwelling yuppies, although the neighborhood still feels somewhat gritty. The terms Bucktown and Wicker Park are often used interchangeably, but Bucktown is technically the neighborhood north of North Avenue, while Wicker Park is to the south. For a walking tour of the area, see p. 213.

THE SOUTH SIDE

South Loop The generically rechristened South Loop area was Chicago's original "Gold Coast" in the late 19th century, with Prairie Avenue (now a historic district) as its most exclusive address. But in the wake of the 1893 World's Columbian Exposition in Hyde Park, and continuing through the Prohibition era of the 1920s, the area was infamous for its Levee vice district, home to gambling and prostitution, some of the most corrupt politicians in Chicago history, and Al Capone's headquarters at the old Lexington Hotel. However, in recent years, its prospects have turned around. The South Loop—stretching from Harrison Street's historic Printers Row south to Cermak Road (where Chinatown begins), and from Lake Shore Drive west to the south branch of the Chicago River—is now one of the fastest-growing residential neighborhoods in the city.

Pilsen Originally home to the nation's largest settlement of Bohemian-Americans, Pilsen (named for a city in what's now the Czech Republic) was for decades the principal entry point in Chicago for immigrants of every ethnic background. Centered at Halsted and 18th streets just southwest of the Loop, Pilsen now contains one of the largest Mexican-American communities in the U.S. This vibrant and colorful neighborhood, which was happily invaded by the outdoor mural movement launched years earlier in Mexico, boasts a profusion of authentic taquerías and bakeries. The artistic spirit that permeates the community isn't confined to Latin American art. In recent years, artists of every stripe, drawn partly by the availability of loft space in Pilsen, have nurtured a small but thriving artists' colony here.

Hyde Park Hyde Park is like an independent village within the confines of Chicago, right off L... roughly a 30-minute... Loop. Fifty-seventh S... drag, and the Unive... with all its attendant... rants—is the neighb... tenant. The most successful racially integrated community in the city, Hyde Park is an oasis of furious intellectual activity and liberalism that, ironically, is hemmed in on all sides by neighborhoods suffering some of the highest crime rates in Chicago. Its main attraction is the world-famous Museum of Science and Industry.

2 THE BEST OF CHICAGO IN 1 DAY

The day begins with a walking tour of the Loop, which I think is the best way to get your bearings (and understand why Chicago's architecture is world-famous). Then you can squeeze in a quick visit to one of the city's preeminent museums before strolling along Michigan Avenue, Chicago's most famous thoroughfare, which takes you to the ritzy Gold Coast neighborhood. If possible, I'd recommend following this itinerary on a weekday, when downtown offices are open and the sidewalks buzz with energy. This route works fine on weekends as well, but you won't experience quite the same big-city rush. Start: Green, Orange, Brown, or Purple line to Adams, or Red Line to Jackson.

❶ Chicago ArchiCenter

Start your day with the Chicago Architecture Foundation's "Historic Downtown: Rise of the Skyscraper" tour, which begins daily at 10am year-round. The 2-hour walking tour takes you to the oldest high-rises in the Loop, and the docents explain why these early office buildings were revolutionary. Sure, you'll get a basic architecture education, but this is also a great way to get a sense of the Loop's layout and dramatic canyonlike vistas. (Another popular tour, "Modern Skyscrapers," starts daily at 1pm.) See p. 196.

❷ The Art Institute ★★★

Across the street from the Chicago Architecture Foundation stands one of the city's most prestigious cultural institutions; if you have time for only one museum while you're here, this is the one to visit. Since you've got limited time, head right for the two must-see exhibits: First, the world-famous Impressionist collection, followed by the 20th-century American modern art gallery, which houses masterpieces such as Edward Hopper's *Nighthawks*. See p. 152.

❸ Millennium Park ★★★

Just north of the Art Institute is one of the city's most popular gathering spots. Check out the massive video-screen faces on the Crown Fountain, then take a walk around (and under) Anish Kapoor's bean-shaped sculpture **Cloud Gate.** The Pritzker Music Pavilion, designed by Frank Gehry, features

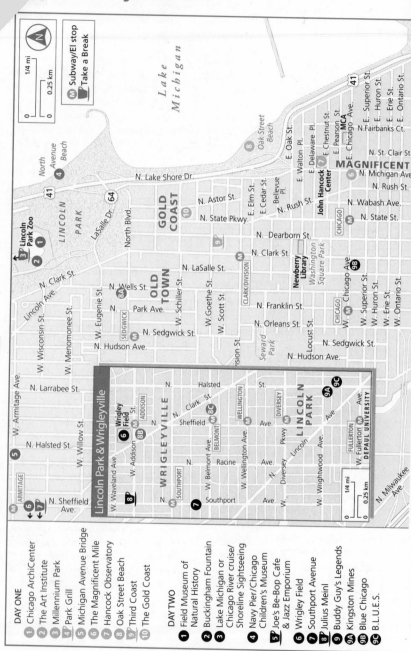

DAY ONE

1. Chicago ArchiCenter
2. The Art Institute
3. Millennium Park
4. Park Grill
5. Michigan Avenue Bridge
6. The Magnificent Mile
7. Hancock Observatory
8. Oak Street Beach
9. Third Coast
10. The Gold Coast

DAY TWO

1. Field Museum of Natural History
2. Buckingham Fountain
3. Lake Michigan or Chicago River cruise/Shoreline Sightseeing
4. Navy Pier/Chicago Children's Museum
5. Joe's Be-Bop Cafe & Jazz Emporium
6. Wrigley Field
7. Southport Avenue
8. Julius Meinl
9. Buddy Guy's Legends
9A. Kingston Mines
9B. Blue Chicago
9C. B.L.U.E.S.

Lincoln Park & Wrigleyville

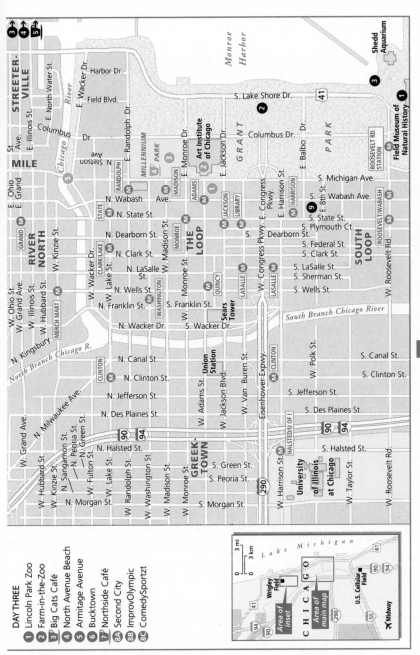

Shedd
Aquarium

Monroe
Harbor

S. Lake Shore Dr. **41**

2

Field Blvd.

Harbor Dr.

E. Wacker Dr.

River

E. North Water St.

E. Illinois St.

Columbus

Dr.

**STREETER-
VILLE**

3
4
5

Columbus Dr.

Art Institute of Chicago

E. Monroe Dr.

E. Jackson Dr.

E. Balbo   Dr.

GRANT

PARK

ROOSEVELT RD.
STATION

Field Museum of
Natural History

1

3

E. Randolph Dr.

N. Stetson Ave.

**MILLENNIUM
PARK**

RANDOLPH

MADISON

ADAMS

JACKSON

LIBRARY

2

3

1

E. Ohio
E. Grand

St.

Ave.

E. Illinois St.

Chicago

MILE

GRAND

5

**RIVER
NORTH**

N. Wabash   Ave.

N. State St.

N. Dearborn St.

N. Clark St.

N. Madison St.

N. LaSalle
St.

N. Wells St.

N. Franklin St.

STATE

MONROE

WASHINGTON

CLARK/LAKE

**THE
LOOP**

S. Michigan Ave.

S. Wabash Ave.

S. State St.

S. Plymouth Ct.

S. Dearborn St.

S. Federal St.

S. Clark St.

S. LaSalle St.

S. Sherman St.

S. Wells St.

9

ROOSEVELT/WABASH

**SOUTH
LOOP**

W. Congress Pkwy.

E. Congress Pkwy.

E. Harrison St.

W. Ohio St.

W. Grand Ave.

W. Illinois St.

W. Hubbard St.

N. Wacker Dr.

W. Wacker Dr.

N. Kinzie St.

MERCH MART

W. Lake St.

S. Monroe St.

W. Washington

S. Franklin St.

**Sears
Tower**

N. Wacker Dr.

S. Wacker Dr.

QUINCY

LASALLE

LASALLE

E. Monroe

E. Randolph

S. Dearborn St.

South Branch Chicago River

W. Roosevelt Rd.

S. Canal St.

S. Clinton St.

N. Kingsbury

North Branch Chicago R.

N. Canal St.

N. Clinton St.

N. Jefferson St.

N. Des Plaines St.

CLINTON

**Union
Station**

W. Adams St.

W. Jackson Blvd.

W. Van Buren St.

Eisenhower Expwy.

CLINTON

W. Polk St.

S. Jefferson St.

S. Des Plaines St.

W. Grand Ave.

N. Milwaukee Ave.

W. Hubbard St.

W. Kinzie St.

N. Sangamon St.

N. Peoria St.

N. Green St.

N. Halsted St.

N. Lake St.

N. Morgan St.

W. Randolph St.

W. Washington St.

W. Madison St.

W. Monroe St.

90
94

**GREEK-
TOWN**

S. Green St.

S. Peoria St.

S. Morgan St.

HALSTED/U OF I

290

W. Harrison St.

**University
of Illinois
at Chicago**

S. Halsted St.

W. Taylor St.

90
94

W. Roosevelt Rd.

S. Halsted St.

DAY THREE
1 Lincoln Park Zoo
2 Farm-in-the-Zoo
3 Big Cats Café
4 North Avenue Beach
5 Armitage Avenue
6 Bucktown
7 Northside Café
8A Second City
8B ImprovOlympic
8C ComedySportzt

Lake Michigan

3 mi

3 km

41

**Wrigley
Field**

Area of
inset

C H I C A G O

Area of
main map

90
94

**U.S. Cellular
Field**

290

55

✈ Midway

94

the architect's signature ribbons of silver steel; Gehry also designed the adjoining serpentine bridge. See p. 156.

> ### 🍴 PARK GRILL ★★
> In the winter, this restaurant overlooks Millennium Park's ice-skating rink; come summer, the rink transforms into an outdoor cafe, perfect for sipping a drink and admiring the skyline. Stay for a full meal or grab a sandwich to go. 11 N. Michigan Ave. 📞 **312/521-PARK** or 312/521-7275. See p. 102.

❺ Michigan Avenue Bridge
Walk north along Michigan Avenue and you'll come to this bridge, which spans the Chicago River. Stop here for a great photo op—on a nice day, you'll be joined by plenty of other visitors doing the exact same thing.

❻ The Magnificent Mile
The 14-block stretch of Michigan Avenue from the river to Oak Street, known as the "Magnificent Mile," is shopping central, a dense concentration of high-rise malls, designer boutiques, and practically every mass-market clothing brand. Even if you're not a shopper, it's worth a stroll; busy at almost all hours, it's great for people-watching. Some Chicagoans dismiss the Mag Mile as too touristy, but I think walking here makes you feel like you're part of a vibrant metropolis. See p. 217.

❼ Hancock Observatory ★★
This may only be Chicago's third-tallest building, but the view from the top is spectacular: In the right weather conditions, you can see all the way to three other states (Wisconsin, Indiana, and Michigan). The "talking telescopes" help you get your bearings by pointing out landmarks in each direction. See p. 166.

❽ Oak Street Beach
Where Michigan Avenue merges into Lake Shore Drive at Oak Street, head down the underpass to get to Oak Street Beach, a curved stretch of sand that's a summertime hot spot and a great background for photos. Bikers, skaters, and joggers fill the paths, while kids play in the sand. Think of it as Chicago's own miniresort getaway—just don't plan on swimming in the frigid water. See p. 199.

> ### ☕ THIRD COAST ★
> If you're tired of generic chain coffeehouses (of which Chicago has plenty), stop by this somewhat shabby, lower-level cafe that welcomes both well-heeled locals and the occasional starving artist. In addition to the usual lattes and muffins, there's a full lunch and dinner menu, and wine and beer are available. 1260 N. Dearborn St. 📞 **312/649-0730.** See p. 284.

❿ The Gold Coast
To get an idea of how Chicago's wealthiest live, take a stroll through this neighborhood of historic town homes (including the original Playboy Mansion, at 1340 N. State Pkwy.). The tranquil, tree-lined streets are only a few blocks away from Michigan Avenue, but they feel like a different city. (For a suggested walking tour, see p. 209.) Finish up the night with dinner at one of the many restaurants in River North, or catch a show and discover Chicago's vibrant theater scene. See p. 252.

---

3 THE BEST OF CHICAGO IN 2 DAYS

After Day 1, you should be familiar with downtown Chicago. Now it's time to explore at least part of the Museum Campus, home to three major museums. Although I recommend the Field Museum for this itinerary, you could certainly substitute the nearby

Shedd Aquarium (p. 164) or Adler Planetarium (p. 162), depending on your interests. **63**
The first part of this day keeps you firmly in tourist territory, but you'll journey off the
beaten track later in the day when you wander through Wrigleyville and get a sense of
how real Chicagoans live. *Start:* Bus no. 6, 10, 12, 130, or 146 to *Roosevelt Road and
Lake Shore Drive.*

❶ Field Museum of Natural History ★★★

You'll feel as though you've entered a truly
grand place when you walk into the
museum's massive Stanley Field Hall and
come face-to-face with Sue, the largest
Tyrannosaurus rex fossil ever discovered.
The Field Museum is one of those classic,
something-for-everyone institutions where
you can wander for hours. The *Inside
Ancient Egypt* exhibit is more than just
mummies: It's a complete re-creation of
ancient daily life, including a marketplace,
royal barge, and religious shrines (with lots
of hands-on activities for kids). The second-floor African and South Pacific exhibits are also worth a stop, with beautifully
designed interactive displays. I have to
admit I still have a soft spot for the old-
fashioned animals-of-the-world dioramas,
which have been here for decades. See
p. 163.

❷ Buckingham Fountain ★

This grand, stone fountain is one of the
city's iconic structures. (If you're a sitcom
fan, you might recognize it from the opening credits of *Married with Children.*) Try
to get here on the hour, when jets of water
spurt dramatically into the sky. The fountain blazes with colored lights at night, so
if you're staying downtown, it's also worth
a stop after dark. (*Note:* The fountain is
closed Nov–Mar.) See p. 156.

❸ Lake Michigan or Chicago River cruise

Departing from a dock at the nearby Shedd
Aquarium, **Shoreline Sightseeing** ★ runs
water taxis that cruise north to Navy Pier
(daily from Memorial Day to Labor Day).
From the pier, you can also catch boats

that cruise along the Chicago River all the
way to the Sears Tower. See p. 195.

❹ Navy Pier ★

Yes, it's touristy and crowded, but Navy
Pier is also full of energy—and if you stroll
all the way to the end, you'll be rewarded
with great views of downtown. If you're
traveling with kids, stopping at Navy Pier
is pretty much mandatory; it has a carousel and other carnival-type rides, lots of
boats to admire, and the **Chicago Children's Museum.** See p. 192.

❺ CHARLIE'S ALE HOUSE

Head to the outdoor patio of this casual
saloon for a front-row look at Navy Pier's
busy waterfront. Cool off with a drink, or
fill up on comfort food classics like burgers or chicken pot pie. 700 E. Grand Ave.
℃ **312/595-1440.** See p. 130.

From Navy Pier, take the free Navy Pier shuttle to the
Grand El station (Red Line), and ride north to the
Addison Street stop.

❻ Wrigley Field ★★

If you're a baseball fan, Wrigley is hallowed
ground: The second-oldest stadium in the
major leagues, home to the perennially
jinxed **Chicago Cubs.** The surrounding
blocks are a good place to stock up on Cubs
souvenirs. If you want to catch a game,
tickets can be tough to come by (the entire
season tends to be sold out by Opening
Day). Show up an hour or so before a game,
and you can sometimes find a season ticket
holder trying to sell unused seats (and ticket
brokers always have seats available—for a
price). See p. 202.

If you're not staying for a game and would rather explore a residential neighborhood, walk west on Addison Street for 5 blocks until you get to:

❼ Southport Avenue

This area is well into the gentrified stage (witness the number of trendy clothing boutiques), but it's still very much a neighborhood. Wander Southport between Belmont Avenue and Grace Street, and you'll see young moms pushing designer strollers, singles walking their dogs, and hardly any other tourists. If you're here in the early evening, you'll find plenty of low-key, affordable restaurants for dinner. When you're ready to head back downtown, you can hop on the Brown Line at the Southport stop. See p. 226.

> ☕ JULIUS MEINL ★
> Run by an Austrian coffee company, this cafe is a mix of Old World and New. Large picture windows make it feel bright and inviting, while the European pastries and

coffee (served elegantly on silver trays) are a welcome change from standard chain coffeehouses. 3601 N. Southport Ave. ☎ 773/868-1857. See p. 284.

❾ Buddy Guy's Legends ★★

Chicago is the birthplace of "electric blues," that rocking blend of soulful singing and wailing electric guitars. To experience the city's most famous form of music, my top pick is Buddy Guy's Legends in the South Loop, which has the honky-tonk feel of a Southern roadhouse. The owner, blues guitarist and Rock and Roll Hall of Famer Buddy Guy, makes regular appearances; even if he's not on the bill, the talent level is always top-notch. (If you're staying on the North Side of the city and would rather stick close to home, try **Kingston Mines, Blue Chicago,** or **B.L.U.E.S..**) See p. 263.

4 THE BEST OF CHICAGO IN 3 DAYS

For this itinerary, it's time to escape downtown completely and spend the day on the North Side of the city. You'll start out in Lincoln Park, which is both an actual park and the name of a popular residential neighborhood, where singles and young families can be seen strolling or jogging along the lakefront paths during nice weather. You'll also visit two major cultural institutions, both suitable for kids, and then head into a residential neighborhood for some shopping. *Start: Bus no. 151 or 156 to North Cannon Drive and Fullerton Parkway.*

❶ Lincoln Park Zoo ★★★

A beloved local institution, this zoo won't dazzle you a la San Diego, but it does a good job of covering all the bases, with a mix of indoor habitats and naturalistic outdoor environments (plus, did I mention it's *free?*). Don't miss the *Regenstein African Journey* exhibit (which re-creates both a tropical jungle and a dusty African savanna), and the internationally renowned Great Ape House. If you have

kids, stop at the **Children's Zoo,** where a unique climbing structure gives little ones 2 and older a chance to release some energy. See p. 170.

❷ Farm-in-the-Zoo ★

Just south of the zoo, this re-creation of a working farm gets children in touch (literally) with animals. The highlight for many little ones is the giant John Deere tractor; you'll usually find a line of kids waiting for their turn to sit behind the massive steering wheel (along with parents waiting to snap a picture). See p. 192.

See p. 192.

🍵3 BIG CATS CAFÉ

This cafe, located on the roof of the zoo's gift shop, has outdoor seating and panoramic views over the zoo. You can order the usual hot dogs and fries, but there's also a selection of more health-conscious wraps. 2200 N. Cannon Dr. ✆ **312/742-2000.**

---

❹ North Avenue Beach

Come summer, this is Lincoln Park's prime playground—a place to jog, play volleyball, build sandcastles, or simply pose. Even in August, the water is usually icy, but if you want to at least dip your feet in Lake Michigan, this wide stretch of sand is the place to do it. Just south of the beach, a grassy stretch of park offers picture-perfect views of downtown. See p. 199.

Take a taxi to the corner of Halsted Street and Armitage Avenue.

❺ Armitage Avenue

To call this the city's chicest shopping strip isn't meant as a put-down to Michigan Avenue; while the Mag Mile goes for big and showy, the boutiques along Armitage tend to be smaller and more personal (most are independently owned rather than chain stores). You'll find an especially appealing selection of home decor stores and gift shops with eclectic selections of well-designed merchandise. Wander the

surrounding side streets to see the neighborhood's eclectic mix of historic homes and modern mansions. See p. 225.

If you're ready to wind down, you'll find plenty of restaurants nearby or in adjacent Old Town. But if you'd like to explore one more neighborhood, take a taxi to the corner of North Avenue and Damen Avenue, then walk north along Damen.

❻ Bucktown

If you're not shopped out yet, finish up the day with a walk through Bucktown, home to the city's highest concentration of edgy clothing boutiques. It feels grittier than Armitage Avenue, and that's part of the appeal for the cool kids who live here. See p. 227.

🍵7 NORTHSIDE CAFÉ

Bucktown's unofficial neighborhood hangout, this low-key cafe is a sandwich spot by day and a bustling bar by night. When the weather's nice, grab a seat on the outdoor patio and people-watch with everyone else. 1635 N. Damen Ave. ✆ **773/384-3555.** See p. 146.

---

❽ Improv Comedy

Although it's best known for **Second City,** Chicago is home to a number of excellent improv comedy troupes. You can catch rising stars before they land their own sitcom deals. Second City is the big man on campus, while **iO** is the slightly scrappier and more creative bunch. If you're here with older kids or teens, catch the family-friendly **ComedySportz.** See p. 259.

Where to Stay

Downtown Chicago is packed with hotels, thanks to the city's booming convention trade. The competition among luxury hotels is especially intense, with the Ritz-Carlton and Four Seasons winning international awards even as newer properties (such as the James and the Felix) get in on the action. The bad news: Low-price lodgings are hard to find. Average room rates aren't as high as New York, but Chicago hotels are still among the most expensive in the country (especially during peak convention season in late spring and during the busy summer months). Since Chicago is not exactly a budget destination, that's all the more reason to do your research before booking.

Many Chicago hotels offer a quintessential urban experience: Rooms come with views of surrounding skyscrapers, and the bustle of city life hits you as soon as you step outside the lobby doors. Although every property listed here caters to business travelers, Chicago attracts lots of tourists as well, and you won't have a problem finding family-friendly hotels in the most convenient neighborhoods; this is not a city where luxury hotels have dibs on all the prime real estate.

Although Chicago has its share of places that tout themselves as "boutique" hotels (Hotel Burnham, Hotel Monaco, W Chicago Lakeshore), these aren't quite the same as their New York, Miami, or Los Angeles counterparts—the so-called beautiful people who frequent these spots on the coasts aren't likely to stop off in Chicago. No matter where you stay in town, you'll likely find that your fellow guests are business travelers or vacationing families, but the boutiques usually attract business travelers who are a little more adventurous.

Hotel rates can vary enormously throughout the year, but I've divided hotels into four categories based on their average rates. "Very Expensive" hotels are luxury properties where rooms cost an average of $400 and up (and are seldom discounted). At "Expensive" hotels, rooms are at least $200 per night, with an upper price limit of $350 to $400. At a "Moderate" hotel, you can usually find a room for $200 or less per night; "Inexpensive" hotels are usually $150 or less per night. The rates given in this chapter are per night and do not include taxes, which are quite steep at 14.9%, nor do they take into account corporate or other discounts. Prices are always subject to availability and vary according to the time of week and season.

Because Chicago's hospitality industry caters first and foremost to the business traveler, rates tend to be higher during the week. The city's slow season is from January to March, when outsiders steer clear of the cold and the threat of being snowed in at O'Hare. (If you'd like to watch your pennies but don't want to sightsee in a heavy down coat, another option is to stay in an outlying neighborhood during the week and then move into downtown for the weekend.)

You never know when some huge convention will gobble up all the desirable rooms in the city (even on the weekends), so it pays to book a room well in advance at any time of year. To find out if an upcoming convention coincides with your trip, check the "Major Convention Dates" calendar in chapter 3 (p. 35). You can also contact the **Chicago Convention & Tourism Bureau** (© **312/567-8500;** www.choosechicago.com).

RESERVATIONS While the following listings give the national toll-free numbers for most of the hotels in this book (as well as their local numbers), the best rates tend to show up on the hotels' websites, which often tout special deals. If you book online, follow up with a call to the hotel to discuss the type of room you want—otherwise you might get stuck with a view of an alley rather than Lake Michigan.

Most hotels have check-in times between 3 and 6pm; if you are going to be delayed, call ahead and reconfirm your reservation to prevent cancellation.

CORPORATE DISCOUNTS Most hotels offer discounts of roughly 10% to individuals who are visiting Chicago on business. To qualify for this rate, your company usually must have an account on file at the hotel. In some cases, however, you may be required only to present some perfunctory proof of your commercial status, such as a business card or an official letterhead, to receive the discount. It never hurts to ask.

RESERVATION SERVICES For discounted rooms at more than 30 downtown hotels, try **Hot Rooms** (© 800/ 468-3500 or 773/468-7666; www.hotrooms.com). Expect to get anywhere from 25% to 50% off standard rates. (The rates here aren't always cheaper than the hotels' own websites, but it's worth checking out.) The 24-hour service is free, but if you cancel a reservation, you're assessed a $25 fee. For a free copy of the annual *Illinois Hotel-Motel Directory*, which also provides information about weekend packages, call the **Illinois Bureau of Tourism** at © 800/ 2-CONNECT or 800/2-266-6328.

The **Chicago Convention & Tourism Bureau**'s website (www.choosechicago. com) allows you to book hotels as well as complete travel packages. Check out the "Immersion Weekends," trips planned around a particular theme (such as fashion or museums) that include behind-the-scenes tours and meals at distinctive local restaurants.

BED & BREAKFAST RESERVATIONS A centralized reservations service called **At Home Inn Chicago,** P.O. Box 14088, Chicago, IL 60614 (© **800/375-7084** or 312/640-1050; fax 312/640-1012; www. athomeinnchicago.com), lists more than 70 accommodations in Chicago. Options range from high-rise and loft apartments to guest rooms carved from a former private club on the 40th floor of a Loop office building. Most lie within 3 miles of downtown (many are located in the Gold Coast, Old Town, and Lincoln Park neighborhoods) and will run you about $150 to $300 per night for apartments, and as low as $105 for guest rooms in private homes. Most require a minimum stay of 2 or 3 nights.

A group of local B&B owners has formed the **Chicago Bed and Breakfast Association,** with a website that links to various properties throughout the city: **www.chicago-bed-breakfast.com**.

ACCESSIBILITY Most hotels are prepared to accommodate travelers with physical disabilities, but you should always inquire when making reservations to make sure that the hotel can meet your particular needs. Older properties, in particular, may not meet current requirements or may only have limited numbers of specially equipped rooms.

AIR-CONDITIONING Air-conditioning is a standard amenity in every hotel reviewed here, so air-conditioning is not listed under the amenities section for each property.

A WORD ABOUT SMOKING A number of Chicago hotels, such as the Renaissance Chicago and the Drake, are completely nonsmoking, and you may be subject to a cleaning fee if you don't comply. If you want to make sure you can light up in your room, check the hotel's policy when making your reservation; most hotels offer specific rooms or floors for smokers.

1 THE BEST HOTEL BETS

- **Best Historic Hotel: The Drake Hotel,** 140 E. Walton Place (𝒞 **800/55-DRAKE** or 800/553-7253), is a master at combining the feel of a grand old hotel with every modern convenience. See p. 79.

- **Best Rehab of a Historic Structure:** The Loop's **Hotel Burnham,** 1 W. Washington St. (𝒞 **866/690-1986**), is a complete rehab of the revered Reliance Building, one of the world's first glass-walled skyscrapers. See p. 70.

- **Best for Business Travelers:** Virtually every hotel in Chicago qualifies, but the **Swissôtel Chicago,** 323 E. Wacker Dr. (𝒞 **888/737-9477**), combines extensive business services with stunning city views from all rooms. See p. 73.

- **Best Service:** The attention to detail, regal pampering, and well-connected concierges at both the ultraluxe **Ritz-Carlton,** 160 E. Pearson St. (𝒞 **800/621-6906**), and the **Four Seasons,** 120 E. Delaware Place (𝒞 **800/332-3442**), make them the hotels of choice for travelers who want to feel like royalty. See p. 78 and 76, respectively.

- **Best for a Romantic Getaway:** For a splurge, the **Peninsula,** 108 E. Superior St. (𝒞 **866/288-8889**), or the **Park Hyatt,** 800 N. Michigan Ave. (𝒞 **800/233-1234**), will pamper you with luxurious rooms and top-notch amenities (p. 78 and 76, respectively). For a cozier getaway, try the **Talbott Hotel,** 20 E. Delaware Place (𝒞 **800/TALBOTT** or 800/825-2688), which is centrally located but tucked away from the crowds. See p. 80.

- **Best Trendy Hotel:** The **W Chicago Lakeshore,** 644 N. Lake Shore Dr. (𝒞 **877/ W-HOTELS** or 877/946-8357), brings the hip W sensibility to a prime location overlooking Lake Michigan (p. 80).

- **Best Views:** This isn't an easy call. Consider several hotels for their mix of lake and city views: the **Swissôtel;** the **Four Seasons;** the **Drake Hotel;** the **Ritz-Carlton;** the **Park Hyatt Chicago;** and the **Doubletree Hotel Chicago Magnificent Mile** (p. 70, 76, 79, 78, 76, and 81, respectively). Peering over the elevated tracks, the **Silversmith Hotel & Suites,** 10 S. Wabash Ave. (𝒞 **800/979-0084** or 312/372-7696), in the Loop, offers a distinctly urban vista (p. 73).

- **Best for Families:** With every room a suite, the **Embassy Suites,** 600 N. State St. (𝒞 **800/362-2779**), and **Homewood Suites,** 40 E. Grand Ave. (𝒞 **800/CALL-HOME** or 800/2-255-4663), are ideal for families looking for a little more space than the typical hotel room provides (p. 86 and 82, respectively). Both also have indoor pools, so the kids can splash around no matter what the weather.

- **Best Off-the-Beaten-Path Hotels:** The **City Suites Hotel,** 933 W. Belmont Ave. (𝒞 **800/248-9108**); the **Majestic Hotel,** 528 W. Brompton St. (𝒞 **800/727-5108**); and the **Best Western Hawthorne Terrace,** 3434 N. Broadway Ave. (𝒞 **888/401-8781**), located in residential North Side neighborhoods, have a more personal feel than many downtown hotels. They're also convenient to public transportation. See p. 88, 89, and 88, respectively.

- **Best Location:** Most visitors will be more than happy with the location of any hotel on the Magnificent Mile of North Michigan Avenue. See the "Near North & the Magnificent Mile" section beginning on p. 76.

- **Best Hotel Dining Experience:** Almost every luxury hotel in town has a first-class restaurant—usually with eye-popping prices. The Atwood Café at the **Hotel Burnham,**

Living the Luxe Life: Condo Hotels

Want to live the life of a wealthy out-of-towner with a downtown pied-a-terre? Book a room at one of the city's condominium-hotels, properties where apartment owners can rent out their units as they wish. The buildings tend to be luxurious (and expensive), with per-night room rates above $300. At 92 stories, the **Trump International Hotel & Tower,** 330 N. Wabash Ave. (© **312/644-0900;** www.trumpchicagohotel.com), is the second-tallest building in the city (after the Sears Tower), and has gorgeous views from its curved facade overlooking the Chicago River. Tastefully elegant—with none of New York's Trump Tower *nouveau-riche* flash—it has all the necessary high-end amenities, including a spa, heated indoor swimming pool with city views, and a pricey restaurant, Sixteen. Other downtown condo hotels include the boutique-style **Amalfi Hotel,** 20 W. Kinzie St. (© **312/395-9000;** www.amalfihotelchicago.com), where the concierges are called "Experience Designers," and the **Elysian,** 11 E. Walton St. (© **312/664-9500;** www.elysianhotels.com), which goes for a more retro, 19th-century-Paris look.

1 W. Washington St. (© **877/294-9712**), offers accessible, modern American dishes in a dining room with real character. See p. 70.

- **Best Health Club:** The fitness center and spa at the **Peninsula,** 108 E. Superior St. (© **866/288-8889**), offer the latest workout equipment and skin treatments in a sparkling, airy setting. Plus, afterward, you can relax on the outdoor sun deck or take a dip in the pool with stunning city views. See p. 78.
- **Best Hotel Pool:** With its dazzling all-tile, junior Olympic-size pool constructed in 1929, the **InterContinental Chicago,** 505 N. Michigan Ave. (© **800/327-0200**), takes this title easily. See p. 79.
- **Best for Travelers with Disabilities:** The **Four Seasons,** 120 E. Delaware Place (© **800/332-3442**), and the **Fairmont Hotel,** 200 N. Columbus Dr. (© **800/526-2008**), go the extra mile for guests with special needs, also providing high-tech accessories for those who are hearing- or vision-impaired. See p. 76 and 70, respectively.

2 THE LOOP

Strictly speaking, "downtown" in Chicago means the Loop—the central business district, a 6×8-block rectangle enveloped by elevated tracks on all four sides. Within these confines are the city's financial institutions, trading markets, and municipal government buildings, making for a lot of hustle and bustle Monday through Friday. The Art Institute of Chicago sits on the Loop's edge, and the Museum Campus, home to the Field Museum of Natural History and John G. Shedd Aquarium, is an easy walk to the south on a nice day. For visitors who want a real "city" experience, the Loop offers dramatic urban vistas of skyscrapers and the feeling that you're at the heart of the action—on weekdays. Come Saturday and Sunday, however, the Loop is pretty dead; on Sunday, almost all the stores are closed. If nightlife is a priority, you won't find much here, but you do have some good dining options.

Fairmont Hotel ★★ The Fairmont is convenient to Millennium Park and Michigan Avenue, but its tucked-away location among anonymous office towers makes it feel somewhat cut off from the life of the city. The grand circular lobby sets the hotel's tone: Upscale and lavish rather than cozy and personal (you might wander awhile before finding the elevators). Still, the rooms—renovated in 2008—are large and bright, with contemporary wood furniture and plush bedding. Though the hotel technically offers views of Millennium Park and Lake Michigan, be aware that you'll often be looking into surrounding high-rises, too. For in-house pampering, visit the tranquil spa, adjacent to a good-sized fitness center. Visiting in winter? The Fairmont is connected to the city's underground "pedway" system, through which you can walk all the way to Macy's on State Street.

200 N. Columbus Dr. (at Lake St.), Chicago, IL 60601. ℂ **800/526-2008** or 312/565-8000. Fax 312/856-1032. www.fairmont.com/chicago. 692 units. $229–$349 double; suites from $399. AE, DC, DISC, MC, V. Valet parking $49 with in-out privileges. Subway/El: Red, Green, Orange, Brown, or Blue line to State/Lake. Small pets accepted for a $25 fee. **Amenities:** Restaurant; lounge; babysitting; concierge; executive-level rooms; health club and spa; room service; free Wi-Fi in lobby. *In room:* TV, hair dryer, high-speed Internet access ($15 per day), minibar, MP3 docking station.

Hard Rock Hotel Chicago ★ The overall theme here is music: Pop tunes echo throughout the lobby, TV monitors show videos, and glass cases display pop-star memorabilia. But the mix of old and new can be somewhat jarring—the black-and-gray lobby feels like a nightclub, while the marble-and-gold-trimmed elevator bank still feels like the office building this once was. Despite the name, you'll pass more business travelers than rock stars in the hallways, but the eclectic decor does give the place a certain edge. Guest rooms go for a neutral, modern look, with larger-than-average windows that let in plenty of natural light. The so-called Hard Rock Rooms on the corners of each floor are larger than the standard double rooms and feature chaise lounges for stretching out. The lobby starts swinging after dark, when the music gets going at the street-level bar, Base ('til 4am, it hosts live music and DJs most nights).

230 N. Michigan Ave. (at Lake St.), Chicago, IL 60601. ℂ **866/966-5166** or 312/345-1000. Fax 312/345-1012. www.hardrockhotelchicago.com. 387 units. $149–$249 double; suites from $299. AE, DC, DISC, MC, V. Valet parking $39 with in-out privileges. Subway/El: Red or Blue line to State/Lake. **Amenities:** Restaurant; bar; concierge; exercise room; room service. *In room:* TV w/DVD player, CD player, hair dryer, minibar, free Wi-Fi.

Hotel Burnham ★★★ If you're looking for a spot with a sense of history, this is it. Formerly known as the Reliance Building (and named for its architect, Daniel Burnham), this was one of the first skyscrapers ever built. The building retains a number of vintage elements, but the rooms have gotten a luxurious modern makeover, with plush gold-and-blue upholstery, mahogany writing desks, and chaise lounges. For views of both the city and lakefront, ask for a room on a high floor in the northeast corner. Don't come to the Burnham if you're looking for extensive amenities—the lobby is tiny, as is the exercise room—but the on-site Atwood Café (p. 100) serves creative comfort food against a Gilded Age backdrop. There's also complimentary Starbucks coffee in the lobby every morning and a wine reception each afternoon from 5 to 6pm.

1 W. Washington St. (at State St.), Chicago, IL 60602. ℂ **866/690-1986** or 312/782-1111. Fax 312/782-0899. www.burnhamhotel.com. 122 units. $199–$299 double; $229–$399 suite. AE, DC, DISC, MC, V. Valet parking $45 with in-out privileges. Subway/El: Red or Blue line to Washington. Pets allowed. **Amenities:** Restaurant; exercise room and access to nearby health club; concierge; room service. *In room:* TV, hair dryer, minibar, Wi-Fi ($10/day, free for hotel loyalty-program members).

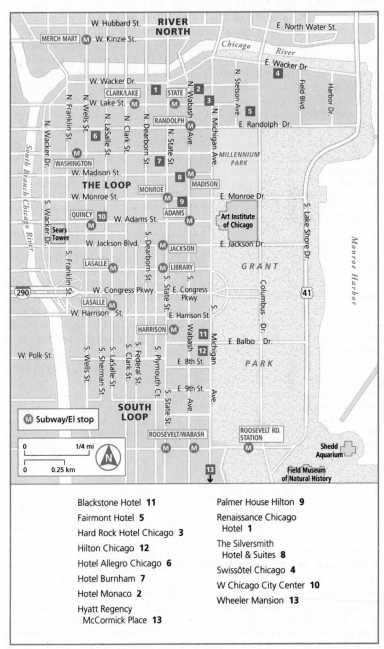

Blackstone Hotel **11**

Fairmont Hotel **5**

Hard Rock Hotel Chicago **3**

Hilton Chicago **12**

Hotel Allegro Chicago **6**

Hotel Burnham **7**

Hotel Monaco **2**

Hyatt Regency
  McCormick Place **13**

Palmer House Hilton **9**

Renaissance Chicago
  Hotel **1**

The Silversmith
  Hotel & Suites **8**

Swissôtel Chicago **4**

W Chicago City Center **10**

Wheeler Mansion **13**

Hotel Monaco ★★★ This boutique hotel deftly manages to straddle the line between fun and conservative. Unlike many other Loop hotels, views at the Monaco are relatively unobstructed by surrounding buildings, especially if you request a room overlooking the Chicago River. Guest rooms feature dramatic deep-red headboards and green-striped walls, and the eclectic furniture includes mahogany writing desks and ergonomic chairs. Despite the funky look, the Monaco overall feels rather subdued; it's a place to relax, not pose. All rooms include "meditation stations"—comfy seats tucked into the larger-than-average windows, which are perfect for taking in the cityscape outside. Suites come with a two-person whirlpool spa and pull-out queen-size sofa bed. (If you're taller than average, you can request a Tall Room, with longer beds.) Given the hotel's playful spirit, it attracts a younger clientele, with an overall vibe that is laid-back and friendly rather than so-hip-it-hurts (this is Chicago, not New York).

225 N. Wabash Ave. (at Wacker Dr.), Chicago, IL 60601. © **800/397-7661** or 312/960-8500. Fax 312/960-1883. www.monaco-chicago.com. 192 units. $169–$329 double; $279–$429 suite. AE, DC, DISC, MC, V. Valet parking $40 with in-out privileges. Subway/El: Brown, Green, or Orange line to Randolph, or Red Line to Washington. Small pets allowed. **Amenities:** Restaurant; concierge; small exercise room and access to nearby health club; room service. *In room:* TV, CD player, hair dryer, minibar, free Wi-Fi ($10/day, free for hotel loyalty-program members).

Palmer House Hilton The longest continually operating hotel in North America (since 1871), the Palmer House retains a Gilded Age aura in its grand lobby (which is worth a look even if you're not staying here). But otherwise, the place often feels like an extension of the McCormick Place Convention Center. Standard double rooms are quite spacious, if somewhat Spartan, with only two uncomfortable chairs to sit in; some come with two bathrooms, a plus for families. No matter where your room is located, don't expect grand views of surrounding skyscrapers; most rooms look out into offices across the street. Executive Level rooms on the top two floors come with DVD players, a dedicated concierge and complimentary breakfast and afternoon hors d'oeuvres. The Palmer House caters overwhelmingly to business travelers, but because it's so big, you can snag good deals here when there are no conventions in town.

17 E. Monroe St. (at State St.), Chicago, IL 60603. © **800/HILTONS** or 800/445-8667, or 312/726-7500. Fax 312/917-1797. www.hiltonchicagosales.com. 1,639 units. $199–$309 double; suites from $349. AE, DC, DISC, MC, V. Valet parking $51 with in-out privileges. Subway/El: Red Line to Monroe. **Amenities:** Restaurant; lounge; concierge; executive-level rooms; health club and spa w/indoor pool and Jacuzzi for $10/day or $20/entire stay; room service. *In room:* A/C, TV, hair dryer, high-speed Internet access, minibar, MP3 docking station.

Fun Facts **Did You Know?**

Merriel Abbott, the dance choreographer who booked all the acts at the Palmer House's famed Empire Room—one of the nation's leading supper clubs from the 1930s to the 1950s—gave Liberace and Bob Fosse their first breaks. Liberace, a cocktail pianist at the club, was "discovered" in Milwaukee by Abbott, who is credited with dressing up the flamboyant entertainer's piano with a candelabra to lend his act some pizzazz. Fosse, a native Chicagoan, made his debut at age 18 as part of a dance team. He and his partner made $500 a month in 1947; Liberace was paid $1,100 for 5 weeks in 1946.

Renaissance Chicago Hotel ★★ A hotel without much of a personality, the 73 Renaissance Chicago is tasteful and understated—perfectly suited to the business travelers who are the hotel's bread and butter. Standard rooms include a small sitting area with an armchair and desk; Club-level rooms, located on the top four floors, are half a room larger and have their own concierge and private lounge, where complimentary continental breakfast and evening hors d'oeuvres are served. Request a river view for the best cityscape (corner suites also have excellent views of both the Chicago River and Lake Michigan). This large operation offers all your standard high-end amenities but is indistinguishable from any number of executive-style hotels elsewhere in the country. Still, this is a good bet for high-end service if you want a Loop location.

1 W. Wacker Dr. (at State St.), Chicago, IL 60601. ℂ **800/HOTELS-1** or 800/468-3577, or 312/372-7200. Fax 312/372-0093. www.marriott.com. 553 units. $199–$399 double; $249–$399 club-level double; suites from $500. AE, DC, DISC, MC, V. Valet parking $49 with in-out privileges. Subway/El: Brown Line to State/Lake or Red Line to Washington. Small pets accepted for a $45 fee. **Amenities:** Restaurant; lounge; concierge; executive-level rooms; health club and spa; indoor pool; room service. *In room:* TV, CD player, hair dryer, minibar, Wi-Fi ($15 per day).

The Silversmith Hotel & Suites ★★ (Finds) This landmark building was built in 1897 to serve the jewelry and silver trade on Wabash Avenue. Fittingly, the Silversmith is a hidden gem, so rooms don't book up as quickly as other, more high-profile spots. The downside is that this very urban hotel is surrounded by other buildings, so natural light is limited; rooms on the main corridor tend to be quite dark. For a quintessentially Chicago view, request a room at the front on the fifth floor or higher, overlooking the El tracks along Wabash Avenue. Yes, the windows are extra thick to muffle the noise of the rumbling trains, but you'll want to avoid the lower-level floors if you like things quiet. Eschewing the usual chain-hotel conformity, the Silversmith has a Frank Lloyd Wright-inspired look, with 12-foot-high ceilings, wrought-iron fixtures, and armoires in the guest rooms. Complimentary desserts—including the city's famous Eli's cheesecake—are served weeknights from 9 to 10pm.

10 S. Wabash Ave. (at Madison St.), Chicago, IL 60603. ℂ **800/979-0084** or 312/372-7696. Fax 312/372-7320. www.silversmithchicagohotel.com. 143 units. $179–$259 double; from $229 suite. AE, DC, DISC, MC, V. Valet parking $42 with in-out privileges. Subway/El: Brown, Green, or Orange line to Madison, or Red Line to Washington. **Amenities:** Restaurant (deli); lounge; concierge; executive-level rooms; exercise room; room service; free Wi-Fi in lobby. *In room:* TV, CD player, fridge, hair dryer, free high-speed Internet access, minibar.

Swissôtel Chicago ★★ (Kids) This sleek, modern hotel may look a bit icy, but its no-nonsense aura makes it especially attractive to business travelers in search of tranquility. The hotel's triangular design gives every room a panoramic vista of Lake Michigan, Grant Park, and/or the Chicago River. The bright, spacious rooms, remodeled in 2008, have separate sitting areas and contemporary wood furnishings. Business travelers will appreciate the oversize desks (convertible to dining tables), ergonomic chairs, and—in upgraded executive rooms—complimentary breakfast and personal concierge service. Active guests will want to break a sweat in the lofty environs of the Penthouse Health Club, perched on the 42nd floor—just make sure the views don't distract you from your workout. In a bid to attract more families, the hotel has also introduced rooms with Kids' Suites, separate but adjoining rooms complete with junior-sized furniture and age-appropriate toys.

323 E. Wacker Dr., Chicago, IL 60601. ℂ **888/737-9477** or 312/565-0565. Fax 312/565-0540. www. swissotelchicago.com. 632 units. $199–$359 double; from $395 suite. AE, DC, DISC, MC, V. Valet parking

$45 with in-out privileges. Subway/El: Red, Brown, Orange, or Green line to Randolph. **Amenities:** 2 restaurants; lounge; concierge; executive-level rooms; health club; indoor pool; room service; sauna. *In room:* High-definition TV, hair dryer, minibar, MP3 docking station, Wi-Fi ($9.95/day).

W Chicago City Center ★   One of two Chicago properties in the hip W hotel chain (the other is the W Chicago Lakeshore, p. 80), this is an oasis of cool in the button-down Loop. The rooms tend toward the small and dark (most look out into a central courtyard), and the W color scheme—deep purple and gray—doesn't do much to brighten the spaces. But if you're the loll-around-in-bed type, this is a great place to do it; the super-comfy beds feature cushiony pillow-top mattresses, soft duvets, and mounds of pillows. The lobby bar is a stylish spot to sit and pose amid dance music and cocktail waitresses who look like models. Given its location, this W is foremost a business hotel—although one that's definitely geared toward younger workers rather than crusty old executives.

172 W. Adams St. (at LaSalle St.), Chicago, IL 60603. ☎ **877/W-HOTELS** or 877/946-8357, or 312/332-1200. Fax 312/332-5909. www.whotels.com. 368 units. $219–$329 double; $399–$1,500 suite. AE, DC, DISC, MC, V. Valet parking $42 with in-out privileges. Subway/El: Brown Line to Quincy. Pets allowed for a $25 fee. **Amenities:** Restaurant; lounge; concierge; exercise room; room service. *In room:* TV/DVD w/ movie library, CD player, hair dryer, free high-speed Internet access, minibar.

MODERATE

Hotel Allegro Chicago ★ (Value)   The Allegro's laid-back vibe makes it a better bet for families and couples than other, more business-focused Loop hotels. The only downside is that you won't have room to spread out: The compact guest rooms don't have much space beyond the bed, an armoire, and an armchair. Still, the bright white-and-blue color scheme is cheery, and the compact bathrooms have built-in marble shelves for ample storage. Befitting a place where the doorman hums along to the tunes playing on speakers out front, the Allegro appeals to younger travelers, many of whom can be found at the complimentary evening wine hour. The hotel's restaurant, 312 Chicago (p. 103), attracts nonguests in search of seasonal Italian cuisine. *A note to theater fans:* The Allegro has access to exclusive seats for many high-profile downtown shows and often promotes special theater packages.

171 W. Randolph St. (at LaSalle St.), Chicago, IL 60601. ☎ **800/643-1500** or 312/236-0123. Fax 312/236-0917. www.allegrochicago.com. 483 units. $149–$299 double; $225–$399 suite. AE, DC, DISC, MC, V. Valet parking $49 with in-out privileges; self-parking $45. Subway/El: All lines to Washington. Pets allowed. **Amenities:** Restaurant; lounge; concierge; exercise room; room service. *In room:* High-definition TV, hair dryer, minibar, MP3 docking station, Wi-Fi ($10/day, free for hotel loyalty-program members).

3 SOUTH LOOP

EXPENSIVE

The Blackstone, A Renaissance Hotel ★★   The Blackstone was once one of Chicago's top hotels; in 1920, when Republican leaders gathered there to pick Warren G. Harding as their presidential candidate, the term "smoke-filled room" was born. Reopened in 2008, it may no longer be the height of luxury, but you'll get a glimpse of the hotel's original glamour in the wood-lined lobby. (The multicolored carpeting and dance-tune soundtrack, unfortunately, detract a bit from the experience.) The rooms, decorated in understated cream, red, and wood tones, are quite spacious, and the large modern bathrooms have marble vanities and glass-enclosed shower stalls (only 20% of

Family-Friendly Hotels

Chicago has plenty of options for families on the go. At the south end of the Loop, the **Hilton Chicago** (p. 75) has lots of public space for wandering, and many of the rooms come with two bathrooms. Another bonus: Both the Field Museum and Shedd Aquarium are within walking distance. At the north end of the Loop near the intersection of Lake Michigan and the Chicago River, the **Swissôtel Chicago** offers Kids' Suites filled with kid-sized furniture, DVDs, stuffed animals, and coloring books (p. 73).

In River North, the **Hampton Inn & Suites** (p. 86) keeps the kids in a good mood with a pool, Nintendo, free breakfast, and proximity to the Hard Rock Cafe and the Rainforest Cafe. The **Best Western River North Hotel** (p. 86) won't win any prizes for its no-frills decor, but it's close to both Michigan Avenue and a dozen family-friendly restaurants. The indoor pool and outdoor deck—with great city views—are other big draws.

When you want a little extra room to spread out, both **Homewood Suites** (p. 82) and **Embassy Suites** (p. 86) make traveling en masse a little easier with separate bedrooms and kitchenettes (so you can save money on food). Both offer free breakfast buffets and have indoor pools.

Of course, luxury hotels can afford to be friendly to all of their guests. At the **Four Seasons Hotel** (p. 76), kids are indulged with little robes, balloon animals, Nintendo, and milk and cookies; the hotel also has a wonderful pool. The concierge at the **Ritz-Carlton Chicago** (p. 78) keeps a stash of toys and games for younger guests to borrow, and kids' menu items are available 24 hours; the hotel even provides a special gift pack just for teenage guests. The upscale **Westin Chicago River North** (p. 85) also caters to families with baby accessories and programs for older kids, respectively.

the bathrooms have tubs). For a great view, book a (more expensive) lakefront room; the well-stocked fitness room also looks out over Lake Michigan. When you've worked up an appetite, head for the Starbucks off the lobby or grab dinner at Mercat a la Planxa (p. 101), a stylish, airy tapas restaurant.

636 S. Michigan Ave. (at Balbo St.), Chicago, IL 60605. ☎ **800/468-3571** or 312/447-0955. Fax 312/765-0545. www.blackstonerenaissance.com. 332 units. $185–$389 double; $3,000 suite. AE, DC, DISC, MC, V. Valet parking $45 with in-out privileges. Subway/El: Red Line to Harrison. **Amenities:** Restaurant; concierge; executive rooms; exercise room; room service. *In room:* TV, hair dryer, minibar, Wi-Fi ($13/day).

Hilton Chicago ★★ (Kids) The colorful history of the Hilton—open since 1927—includes visits by every president since FDR, as well as riots outside its front door during the 1968 Democratic Convention. The classical-rococo public spaces—including the Versailles-inspired Grand Ballroom and Grand Stair Lobby—are magnificent, but the rest of the hotel falls into the chain-hotel mold: Comfortable and well-run, but fairly impersonal. Some rooms are on the small side, but all feel homey thanks to the warm cherry furniture, and many have two bathrooms. Rooms facing Michigan Avenue offer sweeping views of Grant Park and the lake (and, no surprise, you'll pay more for them).

The Hilton is a great choice for families thanks to its indoor pool, proximity to major museums and Grant Park (where kids can run around), and policy of children 17 and under staying free in their parent's room.

720 S. Michigan Ave. (at Balbo Dr.), Chicago, IL 60605. ☎ **800/HILTONS** or 800/445-8667, or 312/922-4400. Fax 312/922-5240. www.hiltonchicagosales.com. 1,544 units. $199–$399 double; suites from $299. AE, DC, DISC, MC, V. Valet parking $55; self-parking $45. Subway/El: Red Line to Harrison. **Amenities:** 2 restaurants; 2 lounges; concierge; executive-level rooms; health club w/indoor track, hot tubs, sauna, and indoor pool; room service. *In room:* TV, hair dryer, minibar, MP3 docking station, Wi-Fi ($20 per day).

Wheeler Mansion ★ (Finds)   Want to feel like you've gone back in time without giving up modern amenities such as cable TV? This grand Italianate building has been restored and transformed into a bed-and-breakfast that combines the best of old and new. The mosaic tile floor in the vestibule and some of the dark walnut woodwork and fixtures are original to the house; welcome additions include good-sized private bathrooms (some have only shower stalls rather than bathtubs). The rooms—spacious enough to include armoires and armchairs—feel even larger thanks to the high ceilings. Antique European furniture fills the house, and guests sleep on goose-down feather beds with high-end linens. Adding to the homey ambience is the courtyard garden, where you can relax with a glass of wine after a day of sightseeing. A full gourmet breakfast—served on elegant bone china—is included in the daily room rate.

2020 S. Calumet Ave., Chicago, IL 60616. ☎ **312/945-2020.** Fax 312/945-2021. www.wheelermansion. com. 11 units. $230–$285 double; $265–$365 suite. AE, DC, DISC, MC, V. Free parking. Bus: 62 from State St. downtown. **Amenities:** Laundry service; computer rental available. *In room:* A/C, TV, hair dryer, high-speed Internet access.

4 NEAR NORTH & THE MAGNIFICENT MILE

VERY EXPENSIVE

Four Seasons Hotel ★★★ (Kids)   Consistently voted one of the top hotels in the world by frequent travelers, the Four Seasons offers an understated luxury that appeals to publicity-shy Hollywood stars and wealthy families. The hotel's location—hidden between the 30th and 46th floors of the 900 N. Michigan Ave. mall—epitomizes the hotel's discretion. The elegant rooms feature contemporary furnishings, subdued colors, and modern artworks. The largest rooms overlook the lake (and therefore cost more), but because the hotel is so high up, even city-facing rooms have relatively unobstructed views. Despite the sophisticated setting, families are positively welcomed here; kid-friendly services include child-size robes and bathtub amenities, board and video games, a special room service menu, and even a dedicated "Teen Concierge" during the summer. The hotel's elegant fitness center exudes upscale exclusivity. (The pool, surrounded by Roman columns, looks like it could be part of an aristocratic private club.)

120 E. Delaware Place (at Michigan Ave.), Chicago, IL 60611. ☎ **800/332-3442** or 312/280-8800. Fax 312/280-1748. www.fourseasons.com. 343 units. $395–$495 double; suites from $695. AE, DC, DISC, MC, V. Valet parking $46 with in-out privileges; self-parking $34. Subway/El: Red Line to Chicago. Pets accepted. **Amenities:** 2 restaurants; lounge; concierge; health club and spa w/indoor pool; room service. *In room:* TV/DVD player, CD player, hair dryer, minibar, free Wi-Fi.

Park Hyatt Chicago ★★★   Searching for chic modern luxury? Then the Park Hyatt is the coolest hotel in town (as long as money is no object). The building occupies one of the most desirable spots on Michigan Avenue, and the best rooms are those that face

Affinia Chicago **16**
The Allerton Hotel **15**
Amalfi Hotel Chicago **30**
Ambassador East **1**
Best Western River North Hotel **25**
Conrad Chicago **27**
Dana Hotel and Spa **18**
Doubletree Hotel Chicago Magnificent Mile **24**
The Drake Hotel **5**
The Elysian **4**
Embassy Suites Chicago–Downtown **19**

Flemish House of Chicago **3**
Four Seasons Hotel **7**
Hampton Inn & Suites Downtown **29**
Homewood Suites **26**
Hotel Cass **20**
Hotel Felix **17**
Hotel Indigo **2**
Hotel Sax Chicago **32**
InterContinental Chicago **28**
The James Hotel **21**
Millennium Knickerbocker Hotel **6**

Park Hyatt Chicago **13**
The Peninsula Chicago **14**
Red Roof Inn **22**
Ritz-Carlton Chicago **12**
Sofitel Chicago Water Tower **9**
Talbott Hotel **8**
Tremont Hotel **11**
Trump International Hotel & Tower **33**
W Chicago Lakeshore **23**
Westin Chicago River North **31**
Whitehall Hotel **10**

east, overlooking the bustling Mag Mile and the lake. The lobby looks like a sleek modern art gallery, with German painter Gerhard Richter's *Piazza del Duomo Milan* as the centerpiece. Rooms feature Eames and Mies van der Rohe reproduction furniture and window banquettes with city views (another plus: The windows actually open). The comfortable beds are well appointed with masses of plush pillows. The spa-like bathrooms are especially wonderful: Slide back the cherrywood wall for views of the city while you soak in the oversized tub. You'll also get great views while sipping cocktails at the outdoor terrace lounge.

800 N. Michigan Ave., Chicago, IL 60611. ✆ **800/233-1234** or 312/335-1234. Fax 312/239-4000. www. parkchicago.hyatt.com. 198 units. $385–$495 double; suites from $695. AE, DC, DISC, MC, V. Valet parking $45 with in-out privileges. Subway/El: Red Line to Chicago. **Amenities:** Restaurant; lounge; concierge; health club and spa w/Jacuzzi and indoor pool; room service. *In room:* A/C, TV/DVD player w/movie library, CD player, hair dryer, minibar, MP3 docking station, Wi-Fi.

Peninsula Chicago ★★★   The Peninsula Chicago mixes an Art Deco sensibility with modern, top-of-the-line amenities. Although the lobby is impressively grand, most rooms are somewhat small for this price range. What makes them stand out are the high-tech amenities: A small "command station" by every bed allows guests to control all the lights, the TV, heating, or air-conditioning without getting out from under the covers. (You can also check the temperature outside, which is particularly useful during our unpredictable spring months.) Add the flatscreen TVs in the marble-filled bathrooms and you have a classic hotel that's very much attuned to the present. The fitness center is my pick as the best hotel health club in the city; the sleek, light-filled workout rooms and indoor pool have views overlooking Michigan Avenue, and the outdoor deck is a great place to relax after a spa treatment.

108 E. Superior St. (at Michigan Ave.), Chicago, IL 60611. ✆ **866/288-8889** or 312/337-2888. Fax 312/ 751-2888. www.chicago.peninsula.com. 339 units. $475–$650 double; suites from $725. AE, DC, DISC, MC, V. Valet parking $45 with in-out privileges. Subway/El: Red Line to Chicago. Pets accepted. **Amenities:** 3 restaurants; bar; concierge; health club and spa w/indoor pool; room service. *In room:* A/C, TV/DVD player, CD player, fax, hair dryer, minibar, free Wi-Fi.

The Ritz-Carlton Chicago ★★★ **Kids**   Top-notch service and a bright, airy setting make this one of Chicago's most welcoming hotels. Perched high atop the Water Tower Place mall, the Ritz-Carlton's lobby is on the 12th floor, with a large bank of windows to admire the city below. Standard rooms aren't very large, but all were renovated in 2009 in soothing blue-and-white tones. Lake views cost more but are spectacular (although in all the rooms, you're up high enough that you're not staring into surrounding apartment buildings). Families will find this luxury crash pad quite welcoming: Kids can borrow toys and games from a stash kept by the concierge, and the room service menu includes family-friendly food. (You can even arrange for delivery of fresh-baked cookies and milk to your door!) The hotel's excellent Sunday brunch includes a special buffet for children replete with M&Ms, macaroni and cheese, and pizza.

160 E. Pearson St., Chicago, IL 60611. ✆ **800/621-6906** or 312/266-1000. Fax 312/266-1194. www.four seasons.com. 435 units. $335–$495 double; suites from $695. AE, DC, DISC, MC, V. Valet parking $40 with in-out privileges; self-parking $32 with no in-out privileges. Subway/El: Red Line to Chicago. Pets accepted. **Amenities:** 2 restaurants; lounge; concierge; health club w/spa and indoor pool; room service. *In room:* TV, CD player, hair dryer, minibar, free Wi-Fi.

EXPENSIVE

Affinia Chicago ★   A relatively recent addition to the competitive boutique hotel arena, the Affinia stands out for its personal touches more than its contemporary-cool style. The bright, fairly large rooms mix neutral-toned bedding and dark wood furniture with bright splashes of color (orange wallpaper gives the bathrooms an extra jolt). But what sets the Affinia apart is its menu of guest preferences (which you can choose via e-mail before arriving). Pick your favorite from six different pillow types; request a complimentary walking tour kit (complete with iPod, map, and pedometer); even order up a golf club or guitar to be waiting in your room upon arrival. Overall, the hotel's casual vibe attracts younger travelers, as does the rooftop lounge C-View (with both indoor and outdoor seating, it makes a good spot for after-dinner drinks year-round).

166 E. Superior St. (at St. Clair St.), Chicago, IL 60611. © **866/246-2203** or 312/787-6000. Fax 312/787-6133. www.affinia.com. 215 units. $199–$299 double; suites from $259. AE, DC, DISC, MC, V. Valet parking $40 with in-out privileges. Subway/El: Red Line to Chicago. **Amenities:** Restaurant; lounge; concierge; exercise room; room service. *In room:* TV, CD player, hair dryer, high-speed Internet access, MP3 docking station.

Conrad Chicago ★ Tucked into the Westfield North Bridge mall, the Conrad Chicago maintains a low profile. But this property—part of the Hilton hotel group's upscale "boutique" brand—is determined to compete with the city's more established luxury properties (with room rates to match). The vibe here is old-money classiness rather than new-money flashiness, from the dark wood furniture in the lobby to the deep brown curtains in the tranquil guest rooms. Rooms tend to be small (especially the least expensive ones on the north side), but the in-room amenities are top-of-the-line, including Bose sound systems. (Rooms with two double beds come with showers only, no tubs.) High rollers can book one of the Terrace Suites, with views of Michigan Avenue. The Conrad makes a good base for anyone visiting during frigid winter weather; with a mall just a few steps away, you can get out without even putting on your coat.

521 N. Rush St. (at Grand St.), Chicago, IL 60611. © **800/HILTONS** or 800/445-8667, or 312/645-1500. Fax 312/645-1550. http://conradhotels1.hilton.com. 311 units. $195–$305 double; from $345 suite. AE, DC, DISC, MC, V. Valet parking $41 with in-out privileges. Subway/El: Red Line to Chicago. **Amenities:** Restaurant; bar; concierge; large exercise room; room service. *In room:* TV, CD player, hair dryer, fridge, MP3 docking station, free Wi-Fi.

The Drake Hotel ★★★ If ever the term "grande dame" fit a hotel, it's the Drake, which opened in 1920. Fronting East Lake Shore Drive, this landmark building is Chicago's version of New York's Plaza or Paris's Ritz. The public spaces still maintain the regal grandeur of days gone by, but the guest rooms have been modernized with upscale-but-homey furniture. Most rooms include a small sitting area with couch and chairs, making them good places to relax after a day of sightseeing; Family Rooms come with two bathrooms. The lakeview rooms are lovely, and—no surprise—you'll pay more for them. Be forewarned that "city view" rooms on the lower floors look out onto another building, so you'll probably be keeping your drapes shut. The hotel's restaurants include the Cape Cod Room (p. 112), an old-timey seafood spot; and the Coq d'Or (p. 269), one of Chicago's most atmospheric piano bars.

140 E. Walton Place (at Michigan Ave.), Chicago, IL 60611. © **800/55-DRAKE** or 800/553-7253, or 312/787-2200. Fax 312/787-1431. www.thedrakehotel.com. 535 units. $199–$299 double; $279–$495 executive floor; from $545 suite. AE, DC, DISC, MC, V. Valet parking $48 with in-out privileges. Subway/El: Red Line to Chicago. **Amenities:** 3 restaurants; 2 lounges; concierge; executive-level rooms; large exercise room; room service; free Wi-Fi in lobby. *In room:* TV, hair dryer, high-speed Internet access, minibar.

InterContinental Chicago ★★ Built as the Medinah Athletic Club in 1929, the building features truly grand details: marble columns, hand-stenciled ceilings, and historic tapestries. (Architecture buffs can pick up a free audio tour from the concierge.)

Rooms in the Main Building (a 1960s addition) have an elegant, urban look, with dark wood and red velvet banquettes. The Historic Tower (the original building) has a more old-world feel, thanks to the elaborately carved headboards and deep-red-and-cream bedding; the bathrooms are also significantly larger. (You'll pay about $50 more for those rooms.) The InterContinental's main claim to fame is its junior Olympic-size pool on the top floor, a beautiful 1920s gem. Despite its historic pedigree, the InterContinental has been on the cutting edge of environmental awareness and has won awards for its eco-friendly practices. The lobby lounge ENO makes a good stop for afternoon wine tastings or late-night chocolate cravings.

505 N. Michigan Ave. (at Grand Ave.), Chicago, IL 60611. (℃) **800/327-0200** or 312/944-4100. Fax 312/944-1320. www.chicago.intercontinental.com. 790 units. $235–$350 double; from $500 suite. AE, DC, DISC, MC, V. Valet parking $53 with in-out privileges. Subway/El: Red Line to Grand. **Amenities:** Restaurant; 2 lounges; concierge; executive-level rooms; health club w/sauna and indoor pool; room service. *In room:* High-definition TV, hair dryer, high-speed Internet access, minibar.

Sofitel Chicago Water Tower ★★

This soaring, triangular white tower makes an emphatic design statement, but the place doesn't take itself too seriously, as you'll see when you walk in the airy lobby and check out the luminescent floor tiles that change color in a never-ending light show. The overall feel of the hotel is European modern, and you'll hear French accents from some of the front desk staff. The guest rooms have a neutral-toned, contemporary look, with natural beech wood walls and chrome hardware. Standard doubles are fairly compact, but thanks to large picture windows, they don't feel cramped. All the rooms enjoy good views of the city (but the privacy-conscious will want to stay on the upper floors, where they won't be as close to surrounding apartment buildings). While the Sofitel doesn't offer amenities that set it apart from the pack, it's popular with younger travelers and international visitors.

20 E. Chestnut St. (at Wabash St.), Chicago, IL 60611. (℃) **800/SOFITEL** or 800/763-4835, or 312/324-4000. Fax 312/324-4026. www.sofitel.com. 415 units. $240–$555 double; $370–$685 suite. AE, DC, DISC, MC, V. Valet parking $40. Subway/El: Red Line to Chicago. Small pets accepted. **Amenities:** Restaurant; bar; concierge; exercise room; room service. *In room:* TV, hair dryer, minibar, free Wi-Fi.

Talbott Hotel ★★ (Finds)

With the feel of an upscale European inn—and a loyal clientele of regulars—the Talbott is one of the city's best small, independent hotels. The cozy, wood-lined lobby has the secluded feel of a private club, with roaring fireplaces in the winter and leather couches for curling up with a cup of tea. The larger-than-average rooms are decorated in soothing neutral tones, with furniture chosen for its residential feel (such as carved-wood desks and headboards). The upscale bathrooms vary in size; some have separate shower stalls and bathtubs and others only tubs. Perhaps surprising for a property that feels so traditional, the Talbott is also at the forefront of guest-service technology; the lights turn on automatically when guests enter their rooms, and a high-tech sensor system shows housekeeping when a room is occupied—so no one will barge in while you're enjoying a late-morning sleep-in.

20 E. Delaware Place (btw. Rush and State sts.), Chicago, IL 60611. (℃) **800/TALBOTT** or 800/825-2688, or 312/944-4970. Fax 312/944-7241. www.talbotthotel.com. 149 units. $199–$329 double; suites from $349. AE, DC, DISC, MC, V. Valet parking $40 with in-out privileges; self-parking $30. Subway/El: Red Line to Chicago. **Amenities:** Restaurant; lounge; concierge; complimentary access to nearby health club; room service. *In room:* TV, hair dryer, minibar, MP3 docking station, free Wi-Fi.

W Chicago Lakeshore ★★

This property promotes itself as a hip boutique hotel, but sophisticated travelers might feel like it's trying too hard, with dance music in the lobby and black-clad staff members doing their best to be eye candy. But the W has a fun, relaxed vibe that appeals to younger travelers. The compact rooms are decorated in deep red, black, and gray, a color scheme that strikes some visitors as gloomy (though others appreciate the change from the sterile look of other chain hotels). Although the Asian-inspired bathrooms are stylish, the wooden shades that separate them from the bedroom don't make for much privacy—so beware if you're sharing a room with a friend. You'll pay more for lake views, but I actually prefer rooms with city views. The onsite outpost of New York's popular Bliss Spa offers a creative range of treatments, but the verging-on-sterile atmosphere won't be to everyone's taste.

644 N. Lake Shore Dr. (at Ontario St.), Chicago, IL 60611. © 877/W-HOTELS or 877/946-8357, or 312/943-9200. Fax 312/255-4411. www.whotels.com. 520 units. $219–$429 double; from $399 suite. AE, DC, DISC, MC, V. Valet parking $44 with in-out privileges. Subway/El: Red Line to Grand. Pets accepted. **Amenities:** Restaurant; bar; concierge; exercise room w/indoor pool; room service; spa. *In room:* TV/DVD player w/ movie library, CD player, hair dryer, minibar, free Wi-Fi.

Whitehall Hotel ★★   Staying here is like visiting a wealthy, sophisticated aunt's town house: Elegant but understated, welcoming but not effusive. The patrician Whitehall was once Chicago's most exclusive luxury hotel, with rock stars and Hollywood royalty dropping by when in town. Although those glory days have passed, the independently owned Whitehall still attracts a devoted clientele who relish its subdued ambience and highly personalized service. Since this is an older property, the hallways are quite narrow and the bathrooms are small. But the rooms are spacious and bright, with elegant furniture. Rooms on the north side of the building come with a wonderful straight-on view of the Hancock Building, with Lake Michigan sparkling in the background. Don't miss the hotel's dimly lit, clubby bar, which hasn't changed since the hotel opened in 1928. (Ask the staff to point out Katharine Hepburn's favorite seat.)

105 E. Delaware Place (west of Michigan Ave.), Chicago, IL 60611. © 866/753-4081 or 312/944-6300. Fax 312/944-8552. www.thewhitehallhotel.com. 222 units. $199–$289 double; suites from $625. AE, DC, DISC, MC, V. Valet parking $39 with in-out privileges. Subway/El: Red Line to Chicago. **Amenities:** Restaurant; bar; concierge; executive-level rooms; exercise room (and access to nearby health club for $20/day); room service. *In room:* TV, hair dryer, minibar, Wi-Fi.

MODERATE

The Allerton Hotel ★   A historic hotel that's gotten a stylish modern makeover, the Allerton's charm lifts it a notch above the standard business-traveler hangout. Built in 1924 as a "club hotel," providing permanent residences for single men and women, its Italian Renaissance–inspired exterior has been painstakingly restored to its original dark-red brickwork, stone carvings, and limestone base. Inside, the building was completely redone in 2008, and the rooms have a glam, Art Deco-inspired look. As is the case with many older properties in town, rooms tend to be small, with some not much wider than a queen- or king-sized bed (the "Classic" rooms are the tiniest). Request a room overlooking Michigan Avenue to get the best views, or at least stop by the hotel's Renaissance Ballroom for a peek at the Mag Mile.

701 N. Michigan Ave. (at Huron St.), Chicago, IL 60611. © 866/553-5040 outside Illinois or 312/440-1500. Fax 312/440-1819. www.theallertonhotel.com. 443 units. $120–$299 double; suites from $200. AE, DC, DISC, MC, V. Valet parking $51 with in-out privileges. Subway/El: Red Line to Chicago. **Amenities:** Restaurant; lounge; concierge; exercise room (w/excellent city views); room service. *In room:* TV, hair dryer, minibar, MP3 docking station, Wi-Fi ($9.95/day).

Doubletree Hotel Chicago Magnificent Mile ★   Despite the name, this high-rise hotel is actually a few blocks east of Michigan Avenue. But its location and amenities make it a good pick for vacationers with children, especially during the summer.

Although I like the view from the north side of the building, where rooms look toward the John Hancock Center, you'll have unobstructed views no matter where you stay. The rooms, which were completely overhauled in 2009, have an urban look, with dark wood headboards and burgundy accents; all come with either a couch or a window seat for lounging. In the summer, hang out on the spacious sun deck beside the smallish-but-adequate outdoor pool; the adjoining lounge is a popular spot for pre- or post-dinner drinks. (Unfortunately, you won't be able to take advantage of these amenities if you visit in the winter.) Lake Michigan and kid-friendly Navy Pier are a short walk away.

300 E. Ohio St. (at Fairbanks Court), Chicago, IL 60611. ℂ **800/557-2378** or 312/787-6100. Fax 312/787-6259. www.chicagomagnificentmile.doubletree.com. 500 units. $149–$209 double. AE, DC, DISC, MC, V. Self-parking in attached lot $41. Subway/El: Red Line to Grand. **Amenities:** Restaurant; cafe; bar; concierge; exercise room; outdoor pool; room service. *In room:* TV, hair dryer, minibar, Wi-Fi ($9.95/day).

Homewood Suites ★★ (Value) (Kids) An excellent choice for families, this hotel offers some nice little freebies that make it an especially good deal. Housed just off the Mag Mile in a sleek tower above retail shops, offices, and a health club—and adjacent to ESPN Zone—the hotel includes a mix of one- and two-bedroom suites; there are also a handful of double-double suites, which can connect to king suites. All are decorated in standard long-term stay apartment style and include sleeper sofas (should you need to pack in extra family members), full kitchens, dining room tables that can double as workspaces, and decent-size bathrooms. What sets this place apart are the extras: The hotel provides a complimentary hot breakfast buffet as well as beverages and hors d'oeuvres on weekday evenings; there are also a free grocery-shopping service and free access to the Crunch gym next door.

40 E. Grand Ave. (at Wabash Ave.), Chicago, IL 60611. ℂ **800/CALL-HOME** or 800/2-255-4663, or 312/644-2222. Fax 312/644-7777. www.homewoodsuiteschicago.com. 233 units. $169–$389 2-room suite. AE, DC, DISC, MC, V. Valet parking $35 with in-out privileges. Subway/El: Red Line to Grand. **Amenities:** Fitness room w/small indoor pool and nice views of the city. *In room:* TV, hair dryer, high-speed Internet access, kitchen.

Hotel Cass ★ A hidden gem, the Hotel Cass is tucked just 2 blocks off the Magnificent Mile, within easy walking distance of shopping, restaurants, and far-more-expensive luxury hotels. Space may be at a premium here—the check-in area and lobby lounge are fairly compact—but everything is bright and stylish. The rooms are quite small (in some, there's barely room for the flatscreen TVs, which are mounted on mechanical arms that reach over the bed), and some only have views of the building next door. But the beds are soft and comfortable, with masses of pillows (helpfully labeled "soft" and "firm"), and bathrooms tuck stylish amenities like rectangular sinks into a compact space. A bonus for budget-conscious travelers: The complimentary buffet breakfast, which includes eggs, bacon, and decadently delicious cinnamon rolls.

640 N. Wabash Ave. (btw. Erie and Ontario sts.), Chicago, IL 60611. ℂ **800/799-4030** or 312/787-4030. Fax 312/787-8544. www.casshotel.com. 175 units. $145–$259 double. AE, DC, DISC, MC, V. Valet parking $45 with in-out privileges; self parking $32 with no in-out privileges. Subway/El: Red Line to Grand. Small pets accepted for a $25 fee. **Amenities:** Access to nearby health club for $10/day. *In room:* High-definition TV, hair dryer, free Wi-Fi.

Millennium Knickerbocker Hotel ★ The epitome of Jazz Age indulgence when built in 1927, this hotel was rumored to have shady underworld connections during the Capone era. Although its glamour has been long since superseded by newer, splashier properties, it regained some of its past shimmer after a major renovation in 2008. The Knickerbocker's real draw is its superb location, a block from Oak Street Beach and the lakefront and across the street from the more-expensive Drake Hotel. Although the standard rooms are quite small, they're decorated in cheery tones of deep yellow and red, and the compact bathrooms are immaculate. (Book a Superior Room if you need more space.) Views are often rather dismal, but you can catch a glimpse of the lake in all rooms ending in 14, and corner rooms (ending in 28) look onto Michigan Avenue.

163 E. Walton Place (half-block east of Michigan Ave.), Chicago, IL 60611. © **800/621-8140** or 312/751-8100. Fax 312/751-9663. www.millenniumhotels.com. 305 units. $169–$299 double; $285–$1,000 suite. AE, DC, DISC, MC, V. Valet parking $50 with in-out privileges. Subway/El: Red Line to Chicago. **Amenities:** Restaurant; bar; concierge; exercise room; room service. *In room:* High-definition TV, hair dryer, minibar, Wi-Fi ($9.95/day).

Tremont Hotel The Tremont won't dazzle you with style or amenities, but it fits the bill for anyone looking for a small, European-style hotel. The guest rooms aren't too big—in most, there's space for a bed, a desk, and either a sofa or two chairs—but they are bright, with yellow walls and large windows. Ask for a room facing Delaware Street if you crave natural light (rooms in other parts of the hotel look into neighboring buildings). The hotel also has 12 studio apartments with full kitchens in an annex next door. The furniture shows signs of wear, and the bathrooms are fairly basic, but the Tremont will appeal to anyone who likes his or her hotels homey rather than slick. The steak-and-chops restaurant off the lobby, the memorabilia-filled Mike Ditka's Restaurant (p. 116), is co-owned by the Chicago Bears' legendary former football coach.

100 E. Chestnut St. (1 block west of Michigan Ave.), Chicago, IL 60611. © **800/621-8133** or 312/751-1900. Fax 312/751-8650. www.tremontchicago.com. 130 units. $119–$279 double; $199–$350 suite. AE, DC, DISC, MC, V. Valet parking $49. Subway/El: Red Line to Chicago. **Amenities:** Restaurant; concierge; small exercise room. *In room:* TV, hair dryer, free Wi-Fi.

INEXPENSIVE

Red Roof Inn ★ (Value) This is your best bet for low-price lodgings in downtown Chicago. The location is the main selling point: Right off the Magnificent Mile (and within blocks of the Ritz-Carlton and the Peninsula, where rooms will cost you about four times as much). The guest rooms are stark and small, but the linens and carpeting are clean and relatively new. Ask for a room facing Ontario Street, where at least you'll get western exposure and some natural light (rooms in other parts of the hotel look right into neighboring office buildings). The bathrooms are tiny but spotless. Upgraded rooms are larger and come with mini-fridges and free Wi-Fi; there are also a few two-room suites that are good for families. You're not going to find much in the way of style or amenities, other than the free coffee available in the lobby, but at these prices, what do you expect?

162 E. Ontario St. (half-block east of Michigan Ave.), Chicago, IL 60611. © **800/733-7663** or 312/787-3580. Fax 312/787-1299. www.redroof-chicago-downtown.com. 195 units. $90–$140 double. AE, DC, DISC, MC, V. Valet parking $36 with in-out privileges. Subway/El: Red Line to Grand. *In room:* TV, hair dryer, free Wi-Fi.

5 RIVER NORTH

EXPENSIVE

Dana Hotel and Spa ★★ This boutique hotel draws younger travelers with its blend of sleek style (a glowing glass elevator tower) and earthy warmth (wood floors in the guest rooms; shower stalls lined with natural stone). You'll feel like you're staying at a friend's downtown loft, complete with floor-to-ceiling windows overlooking the bustle outside. That said, the Dana is definitely an urban experience: If you want to enjoy the views, you'll have to accept that residents of the surrounding high-rises can stare right back at you. (Heavy shades can be pulled down for nighttime privacy.) Befitting a hotel that highlights its spa services, the bathrooms are stylishly modern, with raised basin sinks and oversized shower stalls (sorry—no tubs). The lobby restaurant, **Ajasteak** (p. 120), serves steak and seafood with an Asian twist, while the top-floor **Vertigo Sky Lounge** (p. 275) is more nightclub than hotel bar, with a live DJ.

660 N. State St. (at Erie St.), Chicago, IL 60610. ℂ **888/301-3262** or 312/202-6000. Fax 312/202-6033. www.danahotelandspa.com. 216 units. $179–$279 double; suites from $349. AE, DC, DISC, MC, V. Valet parking $38 with in-out privileges. Subway/El: Red Line to Chicago. **Amenities:** Restaurant; lounge; concierge; exercise room and spa; room service. *In room:* TV, hair dryer, minibar, MP3 docking station, free Wi-Fi.

Hotel Felix ★★ (**Finds**)   The city's ultimate eco-chic retreat, the Felix was built with environmental consciousness in mind. Its mix of green credibility and modern style has made it a favorite with travelers in their 20s and 30s, who hang out with their laptops in the small but airy lobby bar. All the materials used in the neutral-toned guest rooms were chosen for their earth-friendly properties, from the carpeting made of recycled plastic bottles to the energy-efficient showerheads (bathrooms come with showers only—no tubs). Rooms are average-sized, with built-in drawers under the beds to free up space that would otherwise be filled by a dresser. The compact but tranquil on-site spa—unusual in a property of this size—offers massages and facials. If you can, snag a room facing east or north; rooms on the south side look onto the wall of an adjacent building and tend to be gloomy.

111 W. Huron St. (at Clark St.), Chicago, IL 60654. ℂ **877/848-4040** or 312/447-3440. Fax 312/787-6133. www.hotelfelixchicago.com. 225 units. $169–$250 double. AE, DC, DISC, MC, V. Valet parking $42 with in-out privileges (free for hybrid cars). Subway/El: Red Line to Chicago. **Amenities:** Restaurant; bar; concierge; exercise room; room service. *In room:* TV, hair dryer, MP3 docking station, free Wi-Fi.

Hotel Sax Chicago ★★   If you're looking for a hotel that combines unique style with high-tech perks, head for the Hotel Sax. The all-white lobby has a Miami Beach–like feel, but the adjoining lounge, Crimson, goes for a sultry, jewel-toned vibe, with screens and mirrors creating pockets of privacy. The eclectic sensibility carries over to the guest rooms, which feature wingback chairs covered in snakeskin and side tables constructed entirely of mirrored panels. Despite the eye-catching decor, one of the hotel's biggest selling points remains its location. It's in the entertainment-packed Marina Towers complex; steps away, you've got a bowling alley, the restaurants Bin 36 (p. 122) and A Mano (p. 126), and the House of Blues theater (p. 267). Designated "technology" rooms come with Xbox videogame consoles and MP3 players; you can also try out games like Rock Band in the nightclublike Studio, a cozy lounge stocked with refreshments, couches, and laptops.

333 N. Dearborn St. (at the river), Chicago, IL 60610. ℂ **877/569-3742** or 312/245-0333. Fax 312/923-2444. www.hotelsaxchicago.com. 353 units. $230–$450 double; suites from $350. AE, DC, DISC, MC, V. Valet parking $42 with in-out privileges. Subway/El: Brown Line to Clark/Lake, or Red Line to Grand. Pets accepted. **Amenities:** Lounge; concierge; exercise room; room service. *In room:* High-definition TV; hair dryer, minibar, free Wi-Fi.

The James Chicago   A boutique hotel of the sleek, minimalist variety, the James is aimed at younger travelers who prefer luxury with a contemporary spin. Guest rooms are neutral-toned and modern, with private dining niches, reproductions of Mies Van der Rohe chairs and Saaranen tables, dark wood floors and walls, and installations by up-and-coming Chicago artists. Studio rooms include a separate sitting area, and lofts include a private media room with projection DVD player. Although interior-view rooms have a

Chicago Hotels Go Green

With their large-scale heating and cooling costs—not to mention all those loads of laundry—Chicago's hotels suck up a considerable amount of energy. Now, the city's hospitality industry is taking a leading role in lessening that environmental footprint. About two dozen local hotels have signed up for a city-wide Green Hotels Initiative, signaling their commitment to recycling and energy conservation.

Hotel Allegro (p. 74), **Hotel Burnham** (p. 70), and **Hotel Monaco** (p. 72)—all part of the Kimpton hotel chain—print all material on recycled paper using soy-based inks. Though all three hotels are located in historic buildings, they've been fitted with energy-efficient lighting and air-conditioning systems.

At the **Talbott Hotel** (p. 80), automatic sensors adjust the lighting, heating, and air-conditioning in low-traffic areas when they're not in use, and unused in-room soaps and shampoos are donated to a charity that recycles them for the needy. The hotel also purchases wind energy credits to offset 100% of the property's carbon footprint.

The **InterContinental Chicago** (p. 79) was the first hotel in the city to receive an Energy Star rating from the Environmental Protection Agency, thanks to its use of water-conserving toilets and sinks and motion-sensitive thermostats in the guest rooms (which lower the heat or air-conditioning when there's no one inside).

Then there's the **Hotel Felix** (p. 84), the first hotel in the city to be built from the ground up with environmentally sensitive practices in mind. Sustainable or recycled materials were used throughout the property, from the flooring to the bedding. Guests who arrive in a hybrid car can even park for free.

fairly dismal view of a neighboring building during the day, it livens up at night, when the wall becomes the backdrop for a black-and-white animated film. The lobby lounge, J Bar (p. 277), is a dimly lit, clubby hangout that's popular with locals who live and work in the neighborhood.

55 E. Ontario St. (at Rush St.), Chicago, IL 60611. ℂ **877/526-3755** or 312/337-1000. www.jameshotels. com. 297 units (including 52 studios). $199–$329 double; studios from $259; lofts from $359. AE, DISC, MC, V. Valet parking $42. Subway/El: Red Line to Grand. Pets welcome. **Amenities:** Restaurant; bar; concierge; large exercise room; room service; spa. *In room:* TV, hair dryer, minibar, MP3 docking station, free Wi-Fi.

Westin Chicago River North ★★ ⒦ⓘⓓⓢ   The Westin Chicago River North has an understated feel that appeals to those looking for a quiet retreat. The hotel still retains traces of its previous incarnation as the Japanese-owned Hotel Nikko, with a Zen rock garden and bamboo in the lobby; the Hana Lounge also offers a sushi menu. Rooms are understated, with furniture and artwork that give them a residential look. For the best view, get a room facing south, overlooking the Chicago River. If you like to sleep in, the Westin chain is known for its "Heavenly Beds" and piles of pillows. (Believe me, it's more than just a marketing ploy—the beds are *really* comfortable.) Even though it has the personality of a business hotel, the Westin has made an effort to be family-friendly. Many baby and toddler accessories are available, and older kids can while away the hours with an in-room PlayStation.

320 N. Dearborn St. (on the river), Chicago, IL 60610. ✆ **800/WESTIN1** or 800/937-8461, or 312/744-1900. Fax 312/527-2650. www.westinchicago.com. 424 units. $129–$359 double; suites from $400. AE, DC, DISC, MC, V. Valet parking $39 with in-out privileges. Subway/El: Brown, Orange, or Green line to State/Lake. **Amenities:** Restaurant; lounge; concierge; executive-level rooms; large exercise room; room service; sauna. In room: TV, hair dryer, high-speed Internet access, minibar.

MODERATE

Best Western River North Hotel (Value) (Kids) This former motor lodge isn't going to win any design prizes, but it's got some of the most affordable rates to be found in this busy neighborhood, within easy walking distance of Chicago's art gallery district and numerous restaurants. Rooms are generic but spacious (with comfortable bedding and down pillows); the bathrooms, though no-frills, are spotless. One-room suites have a separate sitting area, while other suites have a separate bedroom; all suites come with a sleeper sofa and fridge. A big selling point for families is the indoor pool, with an adjoining outdoor roof deck (a smallish fitness room looks out onto the pool, for parents who want to work out while the kids splash around). The almost unheard-of free parking in the hotel's parking lot can add up to significant savings for anyone who drives here for a visit.

125 W. Ohio St. (at LaSalle St.), Chicago, IL 60610. ✆ **800/528-1234** or 312/467-0800. Fax 312/467-1665. www.rivernorthhotel.com. 150 units. $159–$199 double; $225–$350 suite. AE, DC, DISC, MC, V. Free parking for guests (1 car per room) with in-out privileges. Subway/El: Red Line to Grand. **Amenities:** Restaurant; exercise room; indoor pool; room service. In room: TV, hair dryer, high-speed Internet access.

Embassy Suites Chicago–Downtown ★★ (Kids) Although this hotel does a healthy convention business, its vaguely Floridian ambience—with a gushing waterfall and palm-lined ponds at the bottom of a huge central atrium—makes the place very family-friendly (there's plenty of room for the kids to run around). The guest rooms (all suites) have a generic chain-hotel feel but are spacious enough for both parents and kids. Each suite has two rooms consisting of a living room with a sleeper sofa, a round table, and four chairs; and a bedroom with either a king-size bed or two double beds; the rooms also have a minifridge and a microwave. The hotel serves a complimentary cooked-to-order breakfast in the morning and, in the other end of the atrium, complimentary cocktails and snacks in the evening. Off the lobby is an excellent Italian restaurant, Osteria Via Stato (p. 125), and next door is a Starbucks with outdoor seating.

600 N. State St. (at West Ohio St.), Chicago, IL 60610. ✆ **800/EMBASSY** or 800/362-2779, or 312/943-3800. Fax 312/943-7629. www.embassysuiteschicago.com. 366 units. $139–$279 king suite; $169–$319 double suite. AE, DC, DISC, MC, V. Valet parking $44 with in-out privileges. Subway/El: Red Line to Grand. **Amenities:** Restaurant (Italian); concierge; exercise room w/whirlpool; indoor pool; limited room service. In room: TV, hair dryer, kitchenette, Wi-Fi ($9.95/day).

Hampton Inn & Suites Chicago Downtown ★ (Value) (Kids) This family-friendly hotel manages to appeal to both adults and kids—the Prairie-style lobby and breakfast lounge add a touch of sophistication, while the indoor pool and free hot breakfast are a plus for families. The rooms have an urban look, with dark wood furniture and plush duvets. You can book a standard room, which includes a desk, armchair, and ottoman; a studio, which has a microwave, sink, and minifridge along one wall; or a suite, which includes a kitchenette with a separate bedroom. Request a room overlooking Illinois or Dearborn streets if you crave natural light. The complimentary continental breakfast with two hot items per day, served in an attractive second-floor lounge, can save families money on food; you won't need much lunch if you fill up here each morning.

33 W. Illinois St. (at Dearborn St.), Chicago, IL 60610. ✆ **800/HAMPTON** or 800/426-7866, or 312/832-
0330. Fax 312/832-0333. www.hamptoninn.com. 230 units. $159–$209 double; suites from $209. AE, DC,
DISC, MC, V. Valet parking $42 with in-out privileges. Subway/El: Red Line to Grand. **Amenities:** Restaurant; exercise room w/sauna; indoor pool w/Jacuzzi and sun deck. *In room:* TV, hair dryer, high-speed
Internet access.

6 THE GOLD COAST

MODERATE

Ambassador East ★   Although it's gotten a little shabby since its 1930s and '40s
heyday—when it hosted celebs including Frank Sinatra and Humphrey Bogart—the
Ambassador East retains a trace of its former elegance, from the large floral arrangements
in the lobby to the mahogany four-poster beds in the king-size rooms. Executive suites
have separate sitting areas; celebrity suites (named for the stars who've crashed in them)
come with a separate bedroom, two bathrooms, a small kitchen, and a dining room. The
Ambassador East has the usual drawbacks of a vintage building—small bathrooms, worn
carpets, and relatively thin walls—but its residential location makes it feel like a real
getaway spot, and the surrounding neighborhood of elegant town houses makes a great
place for a stroll. Best of all, you're still within easy walking distance of restaurants,
Michigan Avenue, and the lakefront.

1301 N. State Pkwy. (1 block north of Division St.), Chicago, IL 60610. ✆ **888/506-3471** or 312/787-7200.
Fax 312/787-4760. www.theambassadoreasthotel.com. 285 units. $139–$259 double; suites from $219.
AE, DC, DISC, MC, V. Valet parking $41 with in-out privileges. Subway/El: Red Line to Clark/Division. **Amenities:** Restaurant; concierge; small fitness room; room service. *In room:* TV, hair dryer, minibar, Wi-Fi
($9.95/day).

Flemish House of Chicago ★★ (**Finds**)   Want to pretend you live in a grand historic
mansion? Book a room at this B&B, tucked away on one of the Gold Coast's most picturesque (and expensive) streets. The entire building—including the Flemish Revival
facade that inspired its name—was renovated in the late 1990s by innkeepers Tom
Warnke (an architect) and Mike Maczka (a real estate appraiser). Their architecture
experience is evident in the rooms' tasteful decor: A mix of Victorian and Arts and Crafts
furniture and decorative details that respect the home's late-19th-century design—along
with all the necessary modern amenities. The rooms include spacious studios and one-
bedroom suites, all with full kitchens. This isn't the kind of B&B that promotes social-
izing; there are no common rooms, and breakfast is strictly self-serve (all the fixings are
stocked in the fridge). But for independent travelers looking for a quiet getaway, the
location and setting are truly unique.

68 E. Cedar St. (at Lake Shore Dr.), Chicago, IL 60611. ✆ **312/664-9981.** Fax 312/664-0387. www.inn
chicago.com. 7 units. $155–$225 double. AE, MC, V. Valet parking in nearby lot $25/day. Subway/El: Red
Line to Clark/Division. *In room:* TV/VCR, hair dryer, kitchen, free Wi-Fi.

Hotel Indigo ★   The Indigo is perfect for anyone looking for a cool (but not too
edgy) alternative to the cookie-cutter business hotel. The bright rooms have blonde
hardwood floors and white wood furniture; walls have splashes of vibrant color and giant
photomurals of seashells, fruit, and other "relaxing" images. King rooms on the north
side of the building tend to be larger, but they also look out on neighboring buildings
(and, in some cases, the fire escape). The queen rooms (on the south side of the building)
are small but have lovely views of downtown and plenty of natural light. Bathrooms have

glass-walled shower stalls (no tubs) and spa-style showerheads. Hotel Indigo won't overwhelm you with facilities; the hotel's restaurant and bar are both quite small, but there's a decent-size fitness room and—very unusual in a hotel of this size—a salon/spa with separate facial and massage treatment rooms.

1244 N. Dearborn St. (1 block north of Division St.), Chicago, IL 60610. © **866/521-6950** or 312/787-4980. Fax 312/787-4069. www.goldcoastchicagohotel.com. 165 units. $169–$249 double. AE, DC, DISC, MC, V. Valet parking $35 with in-out privileges. Subway/El: Red Line to Clark/Division. Pets accepted. **Amenities:** Restaurant; lounge; concierge; exercise room; room service; spa services. *In room:* TV, CD player, hair dryer, free Wi-Fi.

7 LINCOLN PARK & THE NORTH SIDE

MODERATE

Windy City Urban Inn ★★ (Finds) This grand 1886 home is located blocks away from busy Clark Street and Lincoln Avenue—both full of shops, restaurants, and bars. While the inn is charming enough, the true selling point is its hosts, Andy and Mary Shaw. He's a well-known local television reporter, while she has more than 20 years of experience in the Chicago bed-and-breakfast business. Together, they are excellent resources for anyone who wants to get beyond the usual tourist sites. The remodeled Victorian home has five rooms in the main house and three apartment suites in a coach house. Two of the coach-house apartments can sleep four: Two in an upstairs bedroom and two on a bed that folds up against the wall. In good weather, guests are invited to eat breakfast on the back porch or in the garden between the main house and the coach house.

607 W. Deming Place, Chicago, IL 60614. © **877/897-7091** or 773/248-7091. Fax 773/529-4183. www.windycityinn.com. 8 units. $115–$225 double; $225–$325 coach-house apts. Rates include buffet breakfast. AE, DISC, MC, V. Parking $6 in nearby lot with in-out privileges. Subway/El: Red Line to Fullerton. **Amenities:** Laundry machines. *In room:* TV, hair dryer (upon request), kitchenettes, free Wi-Fi.

INEXPENSIVE

Best Western Hawthorne Terrace ★ (Value) Located within walking distance of Wrigley Field, Lake Michigan, and the Lincoln Park walking and bike paths, this neighborhood spot is set back from busy Broadway Avenue, thanks to a charmingly landscaped terrace (a good spot to enjoy your complimentary continental breakfast when the weather's nice). Inside, the relatively large rooms—decorated in standard motel decor—won't win extra style points, but most are bright and cheery, with spotless bathrooms (another plus: Many rooms have two windows, a bonus if you crave natural light). The ground-level exercise room is especially welcoming, with large windows and a glass-enclosed hot tub. The hotel's extremely varied clientele—from business travelers in search of a homey environment, to diehard baseball fans, to gay travelers in town for the annual Gay Pride Parade—is part of its charm.

3434 N. Broadway Ave. (at Hawthorne Place), Chicago, IL 60657. © **888/401-8781** or 773/244-3434. Fax 773/244-3435. www.hawthorneterrace.com. 59 units. $149–$229 double and suites. Rates include continental breakfast. AE, DC, DISC, MC, V. Valet parking $20 with in-out privileges. Subway/El: Red Line to Addison. **Amenities:** Concierge; exercise room w/hot tub and sauna. *In room:* A/C, TV, fridge, hair dryer, free Wi-Fi.

City Suites Hotel ★ (Value) Steps from the El stop on Belmont Avenue, this former transient dive has been transformed into a charming small hotel. Most rooms are suites, with separate sitting rooms and bedrooms, all decorated in a homey and comfortable style. The overall feel is that of a bed-and-breakfast, with added amenities such as plush robes and complimentary continental breakfast. A bonus—or drawback, depending on your point of view—is the hotel's neighborhood setting. Most rooms can be fairly noisy; those facing north overlook Belmont Avenue, where the nightlife continues into the early morning hours, and those facing west look right out over the rumbling El tracks. On your way in and out of the hotel, you'll be able to mingle with plenty of locals, everybody from young professional families to gay couples to punks in full regalia. Room service is available from Ann Sather, a neighborhood institution (p. 142).

933 W. Belmont Ave. (at Sheffield Ave.), Chicago, IL 60657. *C* **800/248-9108** or 773/404-3400. Fax 773/404-3405. www.cityinns.com. 45 units. $139–$199 double; suites from $189. Rates include continental breakfast. AE, DC, DISC, MC, V. Parking $25 in nearby lot with in-out privileges. Subway/El: Red Line to Belmont. **Amenities:** Concierge; free access to nearby health club; limited room service. *In room:* TV, fridge, hair dryer, free Wi-Fi.

Majestic Hotel ★★ (Finds) Owned by the same group as the City Suites Hotel (above), the Majestic blends seamlessly into its residential neighborhood. Located on a charming tree-lined street—but convenient to the many restaurants and shops of Lincoln Park—this is a good choice for anyone who wants a quiet retreat rather than a see-and-be-seen spot. Guests receive a complimentary continental breakfast, 24-hour coffee and tea service, and afternoon cookies in the lobby. Some of the larger suites—the most appealing are those with sun porches—offer butler's pantries with a fridge, microwave, and wet bar. Most of the other rooms are fairly dark (since you're surrounded by apartment buildings on almost all sides), and you should avoid the claustrophobic single rooms with alley views. Ideally suited for enjoying the North Side, the Majestic is only a short walk from both Wrigley Field and the lake.

528 W. Brompton St. (at Lake Shore Dr.), Chicago, IL 60657. *C* **800/727-5108** or 773/404-3499. Fax 773/404-3495. www.cityinns.com. 52 units. $139–$199 double; suites from $189. Rates include continental breakfast. AE, DC, DISC, MC, V. Self-parking $25 in nearby garage with no in-out privileges. Subway/El: Red Line to Addison; walk several blocks east to Lake Shore Dr. and then 1 block south. **Amenities:** Free access to nearby health club; limited room service. *In room:* TV, fridge, hair dryer, free Wi-Fi.

8 NEAR MCCORMICK PLACE

MODERATE

Hyatt Regency McCormick Place ★ Rising 33 stories from Chicago's sprawling convention center, the Hyatt Regency is often solidly booked during trade shows and meetings. But it can be a good place to snag bargain rooms during convention lulls in the winter and summer. The trade-off? You'll be a bit isolated from the life of the city; although the hotel is relatively close to the Museum Campus, the lakefront, and the Loop, none are easy walks. However, cabs are plentiful, and the hotel offers a complimentary shuttle to downtown shopping areas, the main museums, and Navy Pier. The average-size rooms are decorated in standard business-hotel style; if you can, request one on the north side, which features scenic views of the city skyline and Lake Michigan.

2233 S. Martin Luther King Dr. (at 22nd St.), Chicago, IL 60616. *C* **800/233-1234** or 312/567-1234. Fax 312/528-4000. www.hyattregencymccormickplace.com. 800 units. $149–$329 double; suites from $650. AE, DC, DISC, MC, V. Valet parking $40 with in-out privileges. Bus: 3 or 4. **Amenities:** Restaurant; bar; concierge; exercise room; indoor lap pool; room service; sauna. *In room:* TV, hair dryer, high-speed Internet access, MP3 docking station.

Where to Dine

It's not easy to narrow down the list of impressive restaurants in this city. The competition among high-end establishments is especially intense. A few well-regarded chefs—Jean Joho at Everest, Arun Sampanthavivat at Arun's, Charlie Trotter at his namesake place—still reign after decades on the job, but newer spots have upped the stakes (and the average check price) considerably. The biggest splash has come from spots such as Alinea and Moto, where food comes in forms and combinations you've likely never experienced before. Other spots dazzle with decor, from the *Arabian Nights*-themed Tizi Melloul and colorful Carnivale to the Miami-cool De La Costa and luxe-lodge style of ZED 451.

If one-of-a-kind meals and splashy settings aren't your style, Chicago is still a meat-and-potatoes kind of town. There are dozens of steakhouses; although I've highlighted some of the best, I couldn't include them all. Comfort food remains a staple of many local restaurant menus, from the beyond-tender ribs at Carson's to the Southern catfish at Wishbone and the satisfyingly rich cinnamon rolls at Ann Sather.

Chicago's many ethnic restaurants—in all price ranges—are highlights of the city's dining scene. Funky fusion concepts include the Japan-meets-South America theme at SushiSamba Rio and the Indian/ Latin American combos at Vermilion. You'll find upscale versions of ethnic cuisine at places such as Frontera Grill (Mexican), Arun's (Thai), and Spiaggia (which might be the country's most elegant Italian restaurant). But affordable (and attitude-free) restaurants still thrive in the city's original immigrant neighborhoods— Greektown, Little Italy, and Chinatown. For suggestions on where to go, see the "Ethnic Dining near the Loop" box on p. 110.

Unfortunately, Chicago is no longer the budget-dining destination it once was. Hipness doesn't come cheap, and places like Alinea have upped the average check price considerably. But just because prices have risen doesn't mean that attitudes have. Restaurants in Chicago might have become trendy, but they're still friendly.

I've divided restaurants into four price categories: "Very Expensive" means most entrees cost $25 to $30 (and up); "Expensive" indicates most entrees run from $18 to $25; "Moderate" means most entrees are $20 or less; and at an "Inexpensive" place, they cost $15 or less.

Whether you're looking for a restaurant to impress a business colleague or simply a no-frills spot to dig in, these are the places the locals go when they want to eat well. To find out more about restaurants that have opened since this book went to press, check out the *Chicago Tribune*'s entertainment website (**www.metromix.com**), the websites for the monthly magazine *Chicago* (**www.chicagomag.com**) and the weekly *Time Out Chicago* (**www.timeout chicago.com**), and the local foodie website LTH Forum (**www.lthforum.com/ bb/index.php**).

Note to smokers: Smoking is against the law in restaurants; those with a separate bar area can choose to allow smoking there, but only if they have installed an air filtration system. If you want to light up when you go out, call first to see if smoking is permitted.

1 THE BEST DINING BETS

- **Best View:** Forty stories above Chicago, **Everest,** 440 S. LaSalle St. (☎ **312/663-8920**), astounds with a spectacular view—and food to match. Closer to earth, diners on the patio at Greektown's **Athena,** 212 S. Halsted St., between Adams and Jackson streets (☎ **312/655-0000**), get a panoramic view of the city skyline. See p. 98 and 130, respectively.

- **Best Spot for a Romantic Dinner:** Secluded **North Pond,** 2610 N. Cannon Dr. (☎ **773/477-5845**), is an Arts and Crafts–style retreat with a postcard-perfect setting in Lincoln Park. Not only does it boast a dramatic vista of the Gold Coast skyline, but the restaurant's out-of-the-way locale also requires diners to begin and end their meals with an idyllic stroll through the park. For charm at a much more affordable price, try **Cyrano's Bistrot & Wine Bar,** 526 N. Wells St. (☎ **312/467-0546**), a cozy spot with warm, personal service and an eclectic Parisian bistro decor that will make you feel like you've jetted off to the romantic City of Love. See p. 137 and 127, respectively.

- **Best Spot for a Business Lunch:** A sleek reinvention of the classic American steakhouse, stylish **N9NE Steakhouse,** 440 W. Randolph St. (☎ **312/575-9900**), offers superslick environs, prime steaks, fresh seafood, a champagne-and-caviar bar, and—most importantly—tiny TV sets above the men's-room urinals for those who can't bear to miss the latest from CNBC. See p. 101.

- **Best Spot for a Celebration:** Not only does **Nacional 27,** 325 W. Huron St. (☎ **312/664-2727**), offer a grand setting and a menu of creative Latin American dishes, but it also turns into a party on Friday and Saturday nights, when a DJ spins salsa tunes and center tables are cleared for dancing. See p. 124.

- **Best Value:** You'll have to head off the standard tourist path to find great food at affordable prices. Charming **RoseAngelis,** 1314 W. Wrightwood Ave. (☎ **773/296-0081**), tucked away on a residential side street in Lincoln Park, has built a devoted fan base thanks to its combination of relaxed charm and affordable, well-crafted dishes. For about $20 you can get a glass of wine, a generous serving of pasta, and slice of the city's best bread pudding. See p. 141.

- **Best Cheap Eats:** It's hard to find a dining bargain downtown, so **foodlife,** inside the Water Tower Place shopping center, 835 N. Michigan Ave. (☎ **312/335-3663**), is my top recommendation for an affordable lunch or dinner. Yes, it's a food court, but there are no chain fast-food stalls here: Instead you'll find a variety of made-to-order choices, from stir fry and burgers to fresh salads and pastas. In Lincoln Park and Wicker Park, cash-strapped 20-somethings and families head to **Penny's Noodle Shop,** 950 W. Diversey Ave. (☎ **773/281-8448**), and 1542 N. Damen Ave. (☎ **773/394-0100**), for delicious, cheap Asian noodles and soups. See p. 119 and 143, respectively.

- **Best for Kids:** Visiting families often limit themselves to the many chain restaurants in the River North neighborhood (Rainforest Cafe, Hard Rock Cafe, and the like), but for something different, try **Wishbone,** 1001 Washington St. (☎ **312/850-2663**), a family-owned spot specializing in Southern food with a casual vibe and plenty of mix-and-match menu options for fussy eaters. See p. 112.

- **Best American Cuisine:** It's no longer the see-and-be-seen spot it was when it first opened, but **mk,** 868 N. Franklin St. (☎ **312/482-9179**), is actually better now that the crowds have moved on, serving up accessible twists on classic American dishes in a space that is both comfortable and sophisticated. **Crofton on Wells,** 535 N. Wells

Farmers' Markets

If you're lucky enough to be here during good weather, celebrate by enjoying at least one picnic. Peruse the city's farmers' markets and then carry your lunch off to Grant Park or a spot along the lakefront.

The city-sponsored farmers' markets operate from late May through October. Two locations in the Loop are easy for visitors to get to: Daley Plaza (at Washington and Dearborn sts.; open on Thurs) and Federal Plaza (at Adams and Dearborn sts.; open on Tues), both open from 7am to 3pm. Both are good places to pick up fresh fruit or bakery treats. For more information, call the Mayor's Office of Special Events at © **312/744-3315.**

In Lincoln Park, local chefs head to the **Green City Market** (© **773/425-0280**) for seasonal produce. Pick up some fresh bread, locally produced cheese, and in-season fruit, and enjoy an alfresco picnic; Lincoln Park Zoo is just steps away. The market is open Wednesdays and Saturdays from 7am to 1:30pm, from mid-May through October.

St. (© **312/755-1790**), is a true labor of love for Chef Suzy Crofton—and her devoted local fans keep coming back for more. See p. 121 and 123, respectively.

- **Best French Cuisine:** For the intimate feel of a Parisian bistro, few places delight quite like Bucktown's charming **Le Bouchon,** 1958 N. Damen Ave. (© **773/862-6600**). Convivial **Mon Ami Gabi,** 2300 N. Lincoln Park West (© **773/348-8886**), re-creates the look and feel of a Parisian cafe, just steps from Lincoln Park Zoo. See p. 146 and 137, respectively.
- **Best Italian Cuisine:** Even without the glamorous view of the Magnificent Mile, **Spiaggia,** 980 N. Michigan Ave. (© **312/280-2750**), would draw diners with its gourmet takes on classic Italian cuisine. For a more casual, convivial atmosphere, it's hard to beat **Mia Francesca,** 3311 N. Clark St. (© **773/281-3310**), a bustling, Americanized version of a classic trattoria, where the fresh, seasonal pastas are the main draw. See p. 114 and 142, respectively.
- **Best Steakhouse:** Legendary Chicago restaurateur Arnie Morton no longer prowls the dining room, but **Morton's,** 1050 N. State St. (© **312/266-4820**), remains the king of the city's old-guard steakhouses, serving up gargantuan wet-aged steaks and baked potatoes. See p. 114.
- **Best Pizza:** In the town where deep-dish pies were born, Chicagoans take their out-of-town relatives to either **Gino's East,** 633 N. Wells St. (© **312/943-1124**), or **Lou Malnati's,** 439 N. Wells St. (© **312/828-9800**), to taste the real thing: Mouthwatering slabs of pizza loaded with fresh ingredients atop delectably sweet crusts. See p. 127 and 118, respectively.
- **Best Pre-theater Dinner:** A longtime local favorite in the Loop, the **Italian Village,** 71 W. Monroe St. (© **312/332-7005**)—three restaurants run by one family under one roof—knows how to get its clientele seated and (well) fed in time for a show. For Chicago Symphony Orchestra audiences, **Rhapsody,** 65 E. Adams St. (© **312/786-9911**), is conveniently located in the Symphony Center building. If you're seeing a

play in Lincoln Park, go for tasty tapas at **Café Ba-Ba-Reeba!,** 2024 N. Halsted St.
(© **773/935-5000**). See p. 104, 102, and 139, respectively.

- **Best Wine List:** Two spots take their food and drink pairings especially seriously: Try **Zealous,** 419 W. Superior St. (© **312/475-9112**), if money is no object, and **Bin 36,** 339 N. Dearborn St. (© **312/755-9463**), if you're looking for a more casual vibe. See p. 121 and 122, respectively.
- **Best Brunch:** The luxury hotels along Michigan Avenue offer all-you-can-eat gourmet spreads, but the locals prefer the longtime local hangout **Ann Sather,** 929 W. Belmont Ave. (© **773/348-2378**). See p. 142.

---

2 RESTAURANTS BY CUISINE

Alsatian

Brasserie Jo ★ (River North, $$$, p. 122)

Everest ★★★ (the Loop, $$$$, p. 98)

American

Ann Sather ★★ (Wrigleyville/North Side, $, p. 142)

Atwood Café ★★ (the Loop, $$$, p. 100)

The Berghoff ★ (the Loop, $$, p. 104)

Bin 36 ★★ (River North, $$$, p. 122)

Boka ★ (Lincoln Park, $$$, p. 137)

Bongo Room (Wicker Park/Bucktown, $, p. 129)

Carson's ★ (River North, $$, p. 127)

Charlie's Ale House (Lincoln Park, $, p. 131)

Charlie's Ale House at Navy Pier (Magnificent Mile/Gold Coast, $, p. 130)

Crofton on Wells ★★ (River North, $$$, p. 123)

Custom House ★★ (the Loop, $$$$, p. 98)

Dave & Buster's (Magnificent Mile/Gold Coast, $, p. 105)

ESPN Zone (Magnificent Mile/Gold Coast, $, p. 105)

The Gage ★ (the Loop, $$$, p. 100)

Goose Island Brewing Company (Lincoln Park, $, p. 139)

Graham Elliot ★★ (River North, $$$, p. 124)

Harry Caray's Italian Steakhouse (River North, $$, p. 128)

Hot Chocolate ★ (Wicker Park/Bucktown, $$, p. 146)

Hot Doug's (Wrigleyville, $, p. 119)

Jane's ★ (Wicker Park/Bucktown, $$, p. 146)

Lou Mitchell's (the Loop, $, p. 128)

Mike Ditka's Restaurant ★ (Magnificent Mile/Gold Coast, $$$, p. 116)

mk ★★★ (River North, $$$$, p. 121)

Moody's (Wrigleyville, $, p. 131)

Naha ★★ (River North, $$$$, p. 121)

N9NE Steakhouse ★★ (the Loop, $$$, p. 101)

North Pond ★★★ (Lincoln Park, $$$$, p. 137)

Northside Café (Wicker Park/Bucktown, $, p. 146)

Oak Street Beachstro (Magnificent Mile/Gold Coast, $$, p. 130)

Oak Tree ★ (Magnificent Mile/Gold Coast, $, p. 120)

O'Brien's Restaurant (Lincoln Park, $, p. 131)

Key to Abbreviations: $$$$ = Very Expensive $$$ = Expensive $$ = Moderate $ = Inexpensive one sixtyblue ★★ (West Loop, $$$$, p. 107)

Orange (Lincoln Park, $, p. 129)

Park Grill ★★ (the Loop, $$$, p. 102)

Perennial ★★ (Lincoln Park, $$$, p. 138)

Petterino's ★★ (the Loop, $$$, p. 102)

Piece ★ (Wicker Park/Bucktown, $, p. 148)

Portillo's ★★ (River North, $, p. 133)

Rainforest Cafe (River North, $$, p. 105)

Rhapsody ★★ (the Loop, $$$, p. 102)

Rockit Bar & Grill ★ (River North, $$, p. 132)

Silver Cloud ★★ (Wicker Park/ Bucktown, $, p. 148)

South Water Kitchen ★ (the Loop, $$$, p. 103)

Spring ★★★ (Wicker Park/ Bucktown, $$$, p. 143)

Superdawg Drive-In (Northwest Side, $, p. 119)

Table Fifty-Two ★ (Magnificent Mile/ Gold Coast, $$$, p. 116)

Tavern at the Park ★ (the Loop, $$$, p. 103)

Toast (Lincoln Park, $, p. 105)

ZED 451 ★★ (River North, $$$, p. 126)

Asian

Ajasteak ★ (River North, $$$$, p. 120)

Opera ★★ (the Loop, $$$, p. 101)

Penny's Noodle Shop ★ (Wrigleyville/ North Side, $, p. 143)

Red Light ★ (West Loop, $$$, p. 108)

Barbecue

Carson's ★ (River North, $$, p. 127)

Twin Anchors ★ (Lincoln Park, $$, p. 139)

Bistro

Bistrot Margot ★★ (Lincoln Park, $$, p. 138)

Cyrano's Bistrot & Wine Bar ★ (River North, $$, p. 127)

La Sardine ★ (West Loop, $$, p. 109)

Le Bouchon ★★ (Wicker Park/ Bucktown, $$, p. 146)

Mon Ami Gabi ★ (Lincoln Park, $$$, p. 137)

Yoshi's Café (Wrigleyville/North Side, $$$, p. 142)

Breakfast/Brunch

Ann Sather ★★ (Wrigleyville/North Side, $, p. 142)

Bongo Room (Wicker Park/Bucktown, $, p. 129)

The Café, Four Seasons Hotel (Magnificent Mile/Gold Coast, $$$, p. 128)

Drake Bros. Restaurant, The Drake Hotel (Magnificent Mile/Gold Coast, $$, p. 128)

House of Blues (River North, $$, p. 267)

Lou Mitchell's (the Loop, $, p. 128)

Nookies (Lincoln Park, $, p. 128)

Orange (Lincoln Park, $, p. 129)

Room 12 (the Loop, $$, p. 129)

Toast (Lincoln Park, $, p. 105)

Wishbone ★★ (West Loop, $, p. 112)

Cajun & Creole

Heaven on Seven ★★ (the Loop, $, p. 106)

House of Blues (River North, $$, p. 267)

Californian

Puck's at the MCA (Magnificent Mile/ Gold Coast, $, p. 130)

Chinese

Phoenix (Chinatown, $$, p. 110)

Saint's Alp Teahouse (Chinatown, $, p. 110)

Won Kow (Chinatown, $, p. 110)

Diner

Ed Debevic's (River North, $, p. 105)
Heaven on Seven ★★ (the Loop, $, p. 106)
Lou Mitchell's (the Loop, $, p. 128)
Nookies (Lincoln Park, $, p. 128)

Fast Food

Billy Goat Tavern ★ (Magnificent Mile/Gold Coast, $, p. 118)
Fluky's (Magnificent Mile/Gold Coast, $, p. 119)
foodlife ★★ (Magnificent Mile/Gold Coast, $, p. 119)
Gold Coast Dogs (Magnificent Mile/Gold Coast, $, p. 119)
Mr. Beef ★ (River North, $, p. 132)
Murphy's Red Hots (Wrigleyville, $, p. 119)
Portillo's (River North, $, p. 133)
Potbelly Sandwich Works (Lincoln Park, $, p. 140)
Superdawg Drive-In (Northwest Side, $, p. 119)
The Wieners Circle (Lincoln Park, $, p. 119)

Fondue

Geja's Cafe ★ (Lincoln Park, $$$$, p. 136)

French

Bistro 110 (Magnificent Mile/Gold Coast, $$$, p. 115)
Bistrot Margot ★★ (Lincoln Park, $$, p. 138)
Brasserie Jo ★ (River North, $$$, p. 122)
Cyrano's Bistrot & Wine Bar ★ (River North, $$, p. 127)
Everest ★★★ (the Loop, $$$$, p. 98)
La Creperie ★★ (Lincoln Park, $, p. 139)
La Sardine ★ (West Loop, $$, p. 109)
Le Bouchon ★★ (Wicker Park/Bucktown, $$, p. 146)

Le Colonial ★★ (Magnificent Mile/Gold Coast, $$, p. 117)
Marché ★ (West Loop, $$$, p. 108)
Mon Ami Gabi ★ (Lincoln Park, $$$, p. 137)
Tru ★★★ (Magnificent Mile/Gold Coast, $$$$, p. 115)
Yoshi's Café (Wrigleyville/North Side, $$$, p. 142)

German

The Berghoff ★ (the Loop, $$, p. 104)

Greek

Artopolis (Greektown, $, p. 111)
Athena ★ (Greektown, $$, p. 111)
Costas (Greektown, $$, p. 111)
Greek Islands (Greektown, $$, p. 111)
Parthenon (Greektown, $$, p. 111)
Pegasus (Greektown, $$, p. 111)
Santorini (Greektown, $$, p. 111)

Indian

Vermilion ★ (River North, $$$, p. 126)

Irish

The Gage ★ (the Loop, $$$, p. 100)

Italian

A Mano ★ (River North, $$, p. 126)
Buca di Beppo (Magnificent Mile/Gold Coast, $$, p. 105)
Club Lucky ★ (Wicker Park/Bucktown, $$, p. 144)
Francesca's Forno ★ (Wicker Park/Bucktown, $$, p. 144)
Francesca's on Taylor (Little Italy, $$, p. 110)
Gene & Georgetti ★ (River North, $$$, p. 124)
Gioco ★ (the Loop, $$$, p. 100)
Harry Caray's Italian Steakhouse (River North, $$, p. 128)
The Italian Village ★ (the Loop, $$, p. 104)
Maggiano's (River North, $, p. 105)

Mia Francesca ★★ (Wrigleyville/
North Side, $$, p. 142)

Osteria Via Stato ★★ (River North,
$$$, p. 125)

RoseAngelis ★★ (Lincoln Park, $,
p. 141)

Rosebud on Taylor ★ (Little Italy, $$,
p. 110)

Spiaggia ★★★ (Magnificent Mile/
Gold Coast, $$$$, p. 114)

312 Chicago ★ (the Loop, $$$,
p. 103)

Trattoria No. 10 (the Loop, $$$,
p. 104)

Tuscany (Little Italy, $$, p. 111)

Japanese

Mirai Sushi ★★ (Wicker Park/
Bucktown, $$$, p. 143)

Sushi Wabi ★ (West Loop, $$$,
p. 108)

Malaysian

Penang (near the Loop, $$, p. 110)

Mediterranean

Avec ★ (West Loop, $$, p. 109)

Tizi Melloul ★ (River North, $$$,
p. 125)

Mexican

Adobo Grill (Lincoln Park, $$, p. 138)

Café Jumping Bean (Pilsen, $, p. 111)

Café Mestizo (Pilsen, $, p. 111)

Frontera Grill & Topolobampo ★★★
(River North, $$$, p. 123)

Nuevo Leon (Pilsen, $, p. 111)

Playa Azul (Pilsen, $, p. 111)

Middle Eastern

Reza's ★★ (River North, $$, p. 129)

New American

Alinea ★★★ (Lincoln Park, $$$$,
p. 136)

Blackbird ★★★ (West Loop, $$$$,
p. 106)

Charlie Trotter's ★★★ (Lincoln Park,
$$$$, p. 136)

Moto ★★★ (West Loop, $$$$,
p. 107)

Tru ★★★ (Magnificent Mile/Gold
Coast, $$$$, p. 115)

Zealous ★★★ (River North, $$$$,
p. 121)

Pizza

Chicago Pizza & Oven Grinder
(Lincoln Park, $, p. 118)

Edwardo's (Magnificent Mile/Gold
Coast, South Loop, and Lincoln
Park, $, p. 118)

Gino's East ★★ (River North, $$,
p. 127)

Piece ★ (Wicker Park/Bucktown, $,
p. 148)

Pizzeria Due (River North, $, p. 133)

Pizzeria Uno ★ (River North, $,
p. 133)

Polish

Red Apple (Northwest Side, $, p. 109)

Russian

Russian Tea Time ★★ (the Loop,
$$$, p. 103)

Seafood

Cape Cod Room (Magnificent Mile/
Gold Coast, $$$$, p. 112)

La Cantina Enoteca (the Loop, $$,
p. 106)

Nick's Fishmarket ★★ (the Loop,
$$$$, p. 98)

Shaw's Crab House ★★ (Magnificent
Mile/Gold Coast, $$, p. 117)

South American

Carnivale ★ (West Loop, $$$, p. 107)

DeLaCosta ★ (Magnificent Mile/Gold
Coast, $$$, p. 115)

Nacional 27 ★★ (River North, $$$,
p. 124)

SushiSamba Rio ★★ (River North,
$$$, p. 125)

Vermilion ★ (River North, $$$,
p. 126)

Southern

House of Blues (River North, $$, p. 267)

Wishbone ★★ (West Loop, $, p. 112)

Spanish & Tapas

Arco de Cuchilleros ★ (Wrigleyville, $$, p. 131)

Café Ba-Ba-Reeba! ★ (Lincoln Park, $$, p. 139)

Café Iberico ★★ (River North, $, p. 132)

Mercat a la Planxa ★★ (the Loop, $$$, p. 101)

Steak

Ajasteak ★ (River North, $$$$, p. 120)

Gene & Georgetti ★ (River North, $$$, p. 124)

Gibsons Bar & Steakhouse ★★ (Magnificent Mile/Gold Coast, $$$$, p. 114)

Harry Caray's Italian Steakhouse (River North, $$, p. 128)

Mike Ditka's Restaurant ★ (Magnificent Mile/Gold Coast, $$$, p. 116)

Morton's ★★ (Magnificent Mile/Gold Coast, $$$$, p. 114)

N9NE Steakhouse ★★ (the Loop, $$$, p. 101)

Petterino's ★★ (the Loop, $$$, p. 102)

Sushi

Mirai Sushi ★★ (Wicker Park/Bucktown, $$$, p. 143)

Sushi Wabi ★ (West Loop, $$$, p. 108)

SushiSamba Rio ★★ (River North, $$$, p. 125)

Swedish

Ann Sather ★★ (Wrigleyville/North Side, $, p. 142)

Tea

The Greenhouse, Ritz-Carlton Hotel (Magnificent Mile/Gold Coast, $$$, p. 115)

Palm Court, The Drake Hotel (Magnificent Mile/Gold Coast, $$$, p. 115)

Russian Tea Time ★★ (the Loop, $$$, p. 103)

Seasons Lounge, Four Seasons Hotel (Magnificent Mile/Gold Coast, $$$, p. 115)

Thai

Arun's ★★★ (Wrigleyville/North Side, $$$$, p. 141)

Bamee Noodle Shop (Wrigleyville, $, p. 140)

Penny's Noodle Shop ★ (Wrigleyville/North Side, $, p. 143)

Star of Siam (River North, $, p. 140)

Thai Classic (Wrigleyville, $, p. 140)

Tiparos (Lincoln Park, $, p. 140)

VTK—Vong's Thai Kitchen ★ (River North, $$, p. 132)

Vegetarian

Green Zebra ★ (River North, $$$, p. 124)

Vietnamese

Le Colonial ★★ (Magnificent Mile/Gold Coast, $$, p. 117)

---

3 THE LOOP

In keeping with their proximity to the towers of power, many of the restaurants in the Loop and its environs feature expense-account-style prices, but it's still possible to dine here for less than the cost of your hotel room. The South Loop—a neighborhood just west of the lake and south of Congress Parkway—has seen a miniboom in restaurants in the past few years, accompanying a rash of condo conversions and new construction in the area. *Note:* Keep in mind that several of the best downtown spots are closed on Sunday.

VERY EXPENSIVE

Custom House ★★ AMERICAN   Chef Shawn McClain won raves for his seafood at Spring (p. 144), then followed up with the off-the-beaten-path, mostly vegetarian, Green Zebra (p. 124). At Custom House, McClain proved he does pretty well with red meat, too. The highlights here are mostly carnivore, from the rich, almost buttery short rib (served with horseradish-flavored cream puffs) to the pork chop accompanied by pork-stuffed cannelloni and wild mushrooms. You won't be dazzled with flavored foams or other fashionable culinary tricks, but McClain has a knack for mixing unexpected flavors. (Take, for example, the seemingly straightforward spinach salad, which is livened up with thick chunks of salty bacon, roasted shiitake mushrooms, and hazelnuts). The prices strike me as high for such simplicity, but the service is top-notch and the setting sophisticated, with velvet-upholstered booths that allow for quiet conversation and large windows looking out onto the surrounding cityscape.

500 S. Dearborn St. (at Congress Pkwy.), in the Hotel Blake. ℂ **312/523-0200.** www.customhouse.cc. Reservations recommended on weekends. Main courses $12–$18 lunch, $24–$38 dinner. AE, DC, DISC, MC, V. Mon–Fri 11:30am–2pm, and 5–10pm; Sat 5–10pm; Sun 5–9pm. Subway/El: Brown Line to Library.

Everest ★★★ ALSATIAN/FRENCH   Towering high above the Chicago Stock Exchange, Everest is an oasis of fine-dining civility, a place where you can taste the creations of one of Chicago's top chefs while enjoying one of the city's top views. The decor looks like a high-end corporate dining room, but the focus here is the view, the food, and you. Chef Jean Joho draws inspiration from the earthy cuisine of his native Alsace, and mixes what he calls "noble" and "simple" ingredients, such as caviar or foie gras, with potatoes or turnips. While the menu changes frequently, the salmon soufflé and cream-of-Alsace-cabbage soup with smoked sturgeon and caviar are popular appetizers; signature entrees include roasted Maine lobster in Alsace Gewürztraminer butter and ginger, and poached tenderloin of beef cooked *pot-au-feu* style and served with horseradish cream. Befitting a restaurant that's been in business for a few decades, service is smooth and polished.

440 S. LaSalle St., 40th floor (at Congress Pkwy.). ℂ **312/663-8920.** www.everestrestaurant.com. Reservations required. Main courses $27–$46; menu degustation $89; 3-course pre-theater dinner $49. AE, DC, DISC, MC, V. Tues–Thurs 5:30–9pm; Fri 5:30–9:30pm; Sat 5–10pm. Complimentary valet parking. Subway/El: Brown Line to LaSalle/Van Buren, or Red Line to Adams.

Nick's Fishmarket ★★ SEAFOOD   The most elegant seafood restaurant in town, Nick's is a special-occasion spot that attracts an older, power-elite crowd, as well as business travelers with generous expense accounts (jackets are recommended, and shorts are a no-no). Plush booths and loveseats (with individual light dimmers, no less) attract cuddly couples, while the generous space between tables allows you to whisper sweet nothings—or hammer out a business contract—without being overheard. Fresh seafood is the focus of the menu, which highlights the specials that are flown in daily. Most of the preparations are straightforward, although some dishes include French or Asian accents (citrus-ginger salmon served with black-sesame-seed-dotted rice). The menu also offers a decent selection for non-seafood eaters, including steak, veal marsala, and roasted free-range chicken.

Artopolis **14**
Athena **18**
Atwood Café **25**
Avec **10**
The Berghoff **32**
Blackbird **9**
Carnivale **8**
Costas **16**
Custom House **35**
Edwardo's **36**
Everest **34**
The Gage **30**
Gioco **39**
Greek Islands **13**
Heaven on Seven **24**
The Italian Village **29**
La Sardine **3**
Lou Mitchell's **19**
Marché **6**
Mercat a la Planxa **37**
Moto **1**
Nick's Fishmarket **28**
N9NE Steakhouse **11**
one sixtyblue **2**
Opera **38**
Park Grill **27**
Parthenon **15**
Pegasus **17**
Petterino's **22**
Red Light **7**
Rhapsody **33**
Russian Tea Time **31**
Santorini **12**
South Water Kitchen **20**
Sushi Wabi **5**
Tavern at the Park **23**
312 Chicago **21**
Trattoria No. 10 **26**
Wishbone **4**

The street-level **Nick's Grill** serves more casual fare, including sandwiches and flat-bread pizzas, and makes a good pre-theater option.

Bank One Plaza at Monroe and Clark sts. (C) 312/621-0200. www.nicksfishmarketchicago.com. Reservations recommended. Main courses $28–$48. AE, DC, DISC, MC, V. Mon–Thurs 11:30am–2pm and 5–10pm; Fri 11:30am–2pm and 5–11pm; Sat 5–11pm. Subway/El: Blue or Red line to Monroe.

EXPENSIVE

Atwood Café ★★ (Finds) AMERICAN   Located in the historic Hotel Burnham, this place combines a gracious, 1900-era feel with a fresh take on American comfort food. The dining room—one of my favorites in the city—mixes elegance and humor with soaring ceilings; lush velvet curtains; and whimsical, colorful china and silverware. Executive Chef Heather Terhune dabbles in global influences (most notably Asian and Southwestern), but the vast majority of the dishes are straightforward American. Recent entree selections included maple-grilled pork chops with three-cheese macaroni; roasted duck breast with wild mushroom risotto and sour cherries; and pan-seared scallops with crawfish flan. In the winter, try one of the signature potpies. Terhune began as a pastry chef, so desserts are a high point of the menu, from seasonal fruit cobblers to the rich banana-and-white-chocolate bread pudding.

Because Atwood Café is located inside a hotel, the restaurant also serves breakfast and lunch, as well as brunch on weekends.

1 W. Washington St. (at State St.). (C) 312/368-1900. www.atwoodcafe.com. Main courses $14–$27 lunch, $19–$35 dinner. AE, DC, DISC, MC, V. Mon–Thurs 7–10am, 11:30am–3:45pm and 5–10pm; Fri 7–10am, 11:30am–3:45pm, and 5–11pm; Sat 8–10am, 11:30am–3:45pm, and 5–11pm; Sun 8am–3pm and 5–10pm. Subway/El: Red Line to Washington.

The Gage ★ IRISH/AMERICAN   Downtown's first gastropub feels as if it's been here forever, thanks to an impeccable remodeling of a historic space. The owners, originally from Ireland, have created a place where the food deserves equal billing with the drinks. (This is one of the few places in the Loop that serves decent late-night food.) The menu leans toward appetizer-size portions, which you can order in any combination. Entree choices run the gamut from roasted Amish chicken to an exotic roast saddle of elk (for which you'll pay an eye-popping $42). The wide range of food is impressive—I can't think of many places downtown that offer duck leg confit, mussels with spicy Indian vindaloo sauce, and ricotta-and-semolina dumplings on the same menu. My only disappointment—surprisingly—was the bland fish and chips.

On weekends, the Gage serves brunch, including a traditional Irish breakfast of eggs, rashers, sausages, and beans on toast.

24 S. Michigan Ave. (btw. Madison and Monroe sts.). (C) 312/372-4243. www.thegagechicago.com. Reservations recommended on weekends. Main courses $12–$18 lunch, $20–$38 dinner. AE, DC, MC, V. Mon–Fri 11am–2am; Sat 10am–3am; Sun 10am–midnight. Subway/El: Red Line to Monroe or Brown or Orange line to Madison.

Gioco ★ ITALIAN   The South Loop was officially gentrified with the opening of this funky Italian restaurant. The cozy, lively ambience—with exposed brick, mahogany accents, an open kitchen, stacks of wine bottles, and hip music—is par for the course in other restaurant-rich neighborhoods, but it's a welcome addition to this area. The fine selection of pastas includes ricotta and spinach tortelloni, mushroom-stuffed ravioli, and pappardelle with braised wild boar. Seafood shows up in various preparations, along with heartier dishes such as filet of beef in Barolo wine sauce, or the massive *Bistecca alla Fiorentina*, a porterhouse steak served in a portion for two. Even if you're loath to order

tiramisu for the umpteenth time, try this heavenly version—light as air and easy on the
rum. The lunch menu also has a few panini and pizza selections.

1312 S. Wabash Ave. (at 13th St.). (**C** 312/939-3870. www.gioco-chicago.com. Main courses $13–$22 lunch, $17–$35 dinner. AE, DC, DISC, MC, V. Mon–Thurs 11:30am–2pm and 5–10pm; Fri 11:30am–2pm and 5–11:30pm; Sat 5–11:30pm; Sun 9:30am–2pm and 5–10pm. Subway/El: Red Line to Roosevelt.

Mercat a la Planxa ★★ SPANISH & TAPAS   South Michigan Avenue, a stretch of offices and venerable old buildings such as the Hilton Chicago and Symphony Center, isn't exactly hip. Which is why Mercat has been such a welcome addition to the neighborhood: Its bright, vivacious atmosphere has brought some much-needed culinary diversity to this rather staid neighborhood. The bi-level, loftlike space and laid-back dance-music soundtrack gives Mercat a younger vibe, and the eclectic drink menu sets the party mood (the Bolero, with tequila, orange liqueur, lime, and fresh avocado sounds odd, but gets raves). The extensive menu includes the usual tapas favorites, from traditional *chacuteria* (cured meats) to bacon-wrapped dates, garlic shrimp, and Spanish omelets. But executive chef Jose Garces (best known for Philadelphia's Amada) also gets creative with heartier options such as slow-cooked pork belly in a cider glaze, duck breast with duck confit, and a foie gras crepe.

638 S. Michigan Ave. (at Balbo Dr.), in the Blackstone Hotel. (**C** 312/765-0524. www.mercatchicago.com. Reservations recommended on weekends. Tapas $6–$12, entrees $16–$26. AE, DC, MC, V. Mon–Thurs 11am–11pm; Fri–Sat 11am–midnight; Sun 11am–10pm. Subway/El: Red Line to Harrison.

N9NE Steakhouse ★★ AMERICAN/STEAKS   The sizzle isn't all on the grill at this contemporary steakhouse. You'll feel like you're making a grand entrance as you step down an open staircase into the airy, white and silver dining room, with its dramatic central champagne-and-caviar bar. (The owners have since opened another N9NE in Las Vegas, a city deserving of this glam decor.) For a splurge, try the Kobe beef burger or the prime, dry-aged steaks, particularly the 24-ounce bone-in rib-eye and 22-ounce porterhouse. You can also sample selections from the extensive Raw Bar (including expense-account-busting caviar). The menu wisely accommodates a variety of tastes; non-red-meat options include a generous veggie chopped salad, roast chicken with chipotle marinade, and seafood selections such as the delicious miso-marinated black cod. If you want to keep hanging with the beautiful people after dinner, head upstairs to the sleek ghostbar.

440 W. Randolph St. (at Canal St.). (**C** 312/575-9900. www.n9ne.com. Reservations recommended. Main courses $9–$22 lunch, $21–$43 dinner. AE, DC, MC, V. Mon–Thurs 11:30am–2pm and 5:30–10pm; Fri 11:30am–2pm and 5–11pm; Sat 5–11pm. Subway/El: Blue, Orange, Brown, or Green line to Clark/Lake.

Opera ★★ ASIAN   This restaurant has nothing to do with *Aida* or *La Bohème*, but the mood is certainly theatrical at the South Loop's most eye-catching restaurant, thanks to the dramatic velvet curtains at the entrance and bold red-and-orange decor. Signature East-meets-West dishes include a spicy crab cake served with "chopsticks" (skinny crab-stuffed spring rolls) and peppered filet mignon served over a brandied beurre blanc with a side of broccoli in black bean sauce. If you want to go all out, try the signature Peking duck service: A tray with three different preparations (pulled duck tossed with noodles; sliced duck breast served mu shu-style with pancakes; and roasted duck leg). For a romantic night out, reserve one of the cozy dining nooks. (They used to be storage vaults in the building's previous life as a film warehouse.) *Note:* If you've sworn off meat and dairy, there's a special menu of vegan entrees.

1301 S. Wabash Ave. (at 13th St.). (**C** 312/461-0161. www.opera-chicago.com. Reservations recommended. Main courses $17–$36. AE, DC, MC, V. Mon–Thurs 11:30am–2pm and 5–10pm; Fri–Mon 11:30am–2pm and 5–11:30pm; Sat 5–11:30pm; Sun 5–10pm. Subway/El: Red Line to Roosevelt.

Park Grill ★★ AMERICAN   Location, location, location—it's what sets Park Grill apart from all the other upscale comfort-food restaurants around. Set in the middle of Millennium Park, it makes a great stop after a late-afternoon stroll or before a summer concert at the Pritzker Music Pavilion. (You can order from a special pre-theatre menu, but be sure to reserve in advance.) The dining room itself is simple but welcoming, with floor-to-ceiling windows that look out onto the Michigan Avenue skyline. (You won't, alas, get a panoramic view of the park.) The menu highlights American favorites, some prepared simply (grilled leg of lamb and rotisserie chicken), others featuring a more international twist, such as pappardelle pasta with littleneck clams, chorizo sausage, and basil; and braised rabbit. For lighter appetites, there are a number of fish dishes, salads, and some thin-crust pizzas. Lunch selections include a mix of sandwiches, and there's also a kids' menu.

11 N. Michigan Ave. (at Madison St.). © **312/521-PARK** [7275]. www.parkgrillchicago.com. Reservations recommended. Main courses $10–$21 lunch, $18–$26 dinner. AE, DC, MC, V. Sun–Thurs 11am–9:30pm; Fri–Sat 11am–10:30pm. Subway/El: Red Line to Washington or Brown, Orange, Purple, or Green line to Madison.

Petterino's ★★ AMERICAN/STEAK   Self-consciously retro, this restaurant re-creates the feeling of downtown dining in the 1940s and '50s. Located in the Goodman Theatre building, Petterino's is a popular pre-theater option, so book a table in advance if you have to catch a show. The dimly lit dining room is decorated in dark wood with red leather booths, and the overall feel is relaxed rather than hyped-up. The straightforward menu is filled with classic American big-night-out favorites: Veal chops, New York strip steak, slow-cooked beef brisket, and some fresh fish selections. Among the old-time appetizers, you'll find shrimp *de jonghe,* coated with garlic and bread crumbs, and an excellent tomato bisque soup. In keeping with the restaurant's entertainment connection, some dishes are named after local celebrities—a nicely done salad of chopped mixed greens and blue cheese is named for longtime *Chicago Sun-Times* columnist Irv Kupcinet.

150 N. Dearborn St. (at Randolph St.). © **312/422-0150.** www.petterinos.com. Reservations recommended. Main courses $8.95–$25 lunch, $10–$40 dinner. AE, DC, DISC, MC, V. Mon–Thurs 11am–10pm; Fri 11am–11pm; Sat 11:30am–11pm; Sun 11am–7:30pm. Subway/El: Red Line to Washington, or Brown Line to State/Lake.

Rhapsody ★★ AMERICAN   This fine-dining restaurant inside Symphony Center (with floor-to-ceiling windows overlooking an outdoor dining area and a small park) is a hit with the concert-going crowd, as much for the setting as for the food. In the summer the restaurant's outdoor garden is a mini oasis of flowers and greenery, definitely the most charming outdoor dining spot in the Loop. (*A note to the noise-sensitive:* You still have to contend with the squealing wheels of El trains passing overhead.) The menu emphasizes contemporary American dining with European influences. Recent entrees include roasted pork loin with kale, raisins, and capers; mahi mahi with spinach-curry sauce; and a beef filet with truffle spaetzle. The lunch menu features lighter choices such as salads and upscale sandwiches (for example, a truffle-and-goat-cheese club). Pre-concert dinners are Rhapsody's specialty, so be sure to make a reservation if you plan to catch a show.

65 E. Adams St. (at Wabash Ave.). © **312/786-9911.** www.rhapsodychicago.com. Reservations recommended before symphony concerts. Main courses $11–$15 lunch, $19–$40 dinner. AE, DC, DISC, MC, V. Mon–Thurs 11:30am–2pm and 5–9pm; Fri 11:30am–2pm and 5–10pm; Sat 5–10pm. During symphony season, mid-Sept to mid-June, the restaurant is also open Sun 4:30–9pm; Thurs–Sat 4:30–10:30pm. Subway/El: Brown, Purple, Green, or Orange line to Adams; or Red Line to Monroe or Jackson.

Russian Tea Time ★★ (Finds) RUSSIAN/TEA Another spot popular with Chicago Symphony Orchestra patrons and musicians, Russian Tea Time is far from being the simple tea cafe that its name implies. Reading through this family-owned restaurant's extensive menu is like taking a tour through the cuisine of czarist Russia and the former Soviet republics (for Russian neophytes, all the dishes are well described). The atmosphere is old-world and cozy, with lots of woodwork and a friendly staff. Start off a meal with potato pancakes, blini with Russian caviar, or chilled smoked sturgeon, then move on to the beef stroganoff; *kulebiaka* (meat pie with ground beef, cabbage, and onions); or roast pheasant served with a brandy, walnut, and pomegranate sauce. If you want to extend your meal well into the night, order one of the "vodka flights," three 1-oz. shots of chilled, flavored vodka; the staff will even show you the authentic Russian way to down them.

77 E. Adams St. (btw. Michigan and Wabash aves.). ✆ **312/360-0000.** www.russianteatime.com. Reservations recommended. Main courses $15–$27. AE, DC, DISC, MC, V. Sun–Thurs 11am–9pm; Fri–Sat 11am–midnight (the restaurant sometimes closes earlier during the summer months). Tea service daily 2:30–4:30pm. Subway/El: Brown, Purple, Green, or Orange line to Adams; or Red Line to Monroe or Jackson.

South Water Kitchen ★ (Kids) AMERICAN Because restaurants in the Loop cater to office workers and business travelers, there aren't a lot of family-friendly options other than fast food. So while South Water Kitchen's upscale American-favorites menu doesn't break any new culinary ground, it deserves a mention as one of the few places in the area that welcomes kids—while featuring food sophisticated enough for discerning moms and dads. The dining room evokes the spirit of an old-fashioned city saloon, and the menu goes the retro route as well. Entrees include modern twists on familiar favorites, including pork chops served with white-cheddar macaroni and cheese; grilled salmon with a side of bacon-potato chowder; and oven-roasted chicken breast with herb gnocchi. The restaurant provides not only kids' menus, but also games to keep the little ones occupied.

In the Hotel Monaco, 225 N. Wabash Ave. (at Wacker Dr.). ✆ **312/236-9300.** www.southwaterkitchen. com. Main courses $9–$19 lunch, $19–$26 dinner. AE, DC, MC, V. Mon–Fri 7–10:30am and 11am–3pm; Sat–Sun 7am–2:30pm; daily 5–10pm. Subway/El: Red Line to State/Lake.

Tavern at the Park ★ AMERICAN The "Park" in question is Millennium Park, although—in the interest of full disclosure—the restaurant is actually located across the street. Still, this is a convenient spot for lunch or dinner during a day of sightseeing, even if most tables don't have much of a view (try to snag a seat by the windows, which look out over the rippling steel roof of Frank Gehry's Pritzker Music Pavilion). The staid brown color scheme calls to mind a generic chain-hotel restaurant, but the food itself is more sophisticated than the decor. Executive chef John Hogan is known around town for his skill at creating comfort food with flair, so entrees such as the chicken pot pie, double-cut pork chops with cherry cola barbecue sauce, and the prime rib sandwich are both hearty and tasty; the melt-in-your-mouth-tender braised beef short ribs in red-wine demi-glaze are my personal favorite.

130 E. Randolph St. (at Michigan Ave.). ✆ **312/552-0070.** www.tavernatthepark.com. Sandwiches $12–$18, entrees $22–$37. AE, DC, DISC, MC, V. Mon–Thurs 11am–10pm; Fri 11am–10:30pm; Sat 4–10:30pm. Subway/El: Red Line to Washington or Brown Line to Randolph.

312 Chicago ★ ITALIAN Although this is technically a hotel restaurant (connected to the Hotel Allegro), it has a homey-yet-sophisticated character all its own—and a clientele that goes beyond hotel guests. Downstairs, the restaurant's dark booths and wood accents give the space a clubby feel; upstairs, the mood is brighter and more contemporary, thanks

6

THE LOOP

to large windows that welcome in natural light. Italian-born chef Luca Corazzina focuses on fresh, seasonal ingredients and classic Italian preparations with entrees such as home-made spinach-and-ricotta tortellini in a brown butter sage sauce; roast chicken with peppers and polenta; and veal medallions with porcini mushrooms and squash puree. Appropriately enough for an Italian restaurant, there's an extensive wine list. The lunch menu includes a selection of panini sandwiches. Because the restaurant caters to hotel guests, it's also open for breakfast and Sunday brunch.

136 N. LaSalle St. (at Randolph St.). © **312/696-2420.** www.312chicago.com. Reservations recommended. Main courses $17–$32. AE, DC, DISC, MC, V. Mon–Fri 7–10am and 11am–10pm; Sat 8–11am and 4:30–10pm; Sun 8am–3pm and 4–9pm. Subway/El: Red Line to Washington.

Trattoria No. 10 ITALIAN   Elegant but not pretentious, Trattoria No. 10 is a long-time, dependable favorite with downtown office workers. The burnt-orange tones, ceramic floor tiles, and gracefully arched ceilings set a dining-in-Italy mood. The house specialty is ravioli, which can be ordered as an appetizer or main course (recent fillings included butternut and acorn squash topped with walnut sauce, and homemade Italian sausage and mozzarella served with a spicy arrabbiata sauce). There are plenty of other worthwhile pasta dishes to choose from, such as farfalle with duck confit, asparagus, caramelized onions, and pine nuts, or the linguine with roasted eggplant, grilled tomatoes, and smoked mozzarella; you'll also find the expected beef, veal, and seafood options. For a lighter (and cheaper) meal, stop by between 5 and 7:30pm on weekdays for an all-you-can-eat buffet at the bar; $12 (with a $6 drink minimum) gets you tastes of salads, antipasti, shrimp, and various pasta specials.

10 N. Dearborn St. (btw. Madison and Washington sts.). © **312/984-1718.** www.trattoriaten.com. Main courses $16–$22 lunch, $18–$31 dinner. AE, DC, DISC, MC, V. Mon–Thurs 11:30am–2pm and 5:30–9pm; Fri 11:30am–2pm and 5:30–10pm; Sat 5:30–10pm. Subway/El: Red line to Madison.

MODERATE

The Berghoff ★ GERMAN/AMERICAN   A Chicago landmark, the Berghoff is housed in one of the first buildings constructed in the Loop after the Great Chicago Fire. Opened in 1898, it also has the honor of holding the first liquor license granted after the repeal of Prohibition in 1933. Unfortunately, much of the city's German heritage has dissipated over the years, and even the Berghoff's menu has moved along with the times, adding multicultural entrees like Asian chicken salad and ancho-chili-marinated chicken breast. The good news is that you can still order Berghoff classics like Wiener schnitzel and sauerbraten, along with a side of chewy spaetzle (noodles). (For the full Berghoff experience, wash it all down with a glass of the house draft beer.) Downstairs from the main restaurant, the counter-service **Berghoff Café** serves up sandwiches, panini, and salads to neighborhood office workers. (It's open for lunch only on weekdays.)

17 W. Adams St. (btw. State and Dearborn sts.). © **312/427-3170.** www.theberghoff.com. Reservations accepted. Main courses $7.95–$15 lunch, $11–$20 dinner. AE, DC, DISC, MC, V. Mon–Thurs 11am–9pm; Fri 11am–10pm; Sat 11:30am–10pm. Subway/El: Red Line to Jackson.

The Italian Village ★ (**Finds**) ITALIAN   Open since 1927 (and run by the grandchildren of the original owner), this downtown dining landmark houses three separate Italian restaurants that are popular with pre- and post-theater crowds. Each has its own menu and ambience, but my favorite is the **Village** on the second floor, a charmingly retro interpretation of alfresco dining in a small Italian town, complete with a midnight-blue ceiling, twinkling stars, and banquettes tucked into private, cavelike rooms. The food is old-school Italian: Eggplant parmigiana, a heavy fettuccine Alfredo that would send your

Family-Friendly Restaurants

One of the city's first "theme" restaurants, **Ed Debevic's,** 640 N. Wells St., at Ontario Street (✆ **312/664-1707**), is a temple to America's hometown lunch counter culture. The burgers-and-milkshakes menu is kid-friendly, but it's the staff shtick that makes this place memorable. The waitresses play the parts of gum-chewing toughies who make wisecracks, toss out good-natured insults, and even sit right down at your table. It's all a performance—but it works.

Two national chain spots in River North that do big family business are **Rainforest Cafe,** 605 N. Clark St., at Ohio Street (✆ **312/787-1501**), and **ESPN Zone,** 43 E. Ohio St., at Wabash Avenue (✆ **312/644-3776**). Rainforest Cafe creates a jungle feel with the sounds of waterfalls, thunder, and wild animals. Sports-loving older kids will find plenty of entertainment at ESPN Zone, including a game room and an endless array of TVs flashing the latest scores.

If you're in the mood for something a little more funky, **Wishbone** ★★ (p. 112) is a popular option for local families. The food is diverse enough that both adults and kids can find something to their liking (you can mix and match side dishes, a big plus), and there's also a menu geared just toward children. Another all-American choice in the Loop is **South Water Kitchen** ★ (p. 103), which offers a kids' menu and coloring books.

A fun breakfast-and-lunch spot in Lincoln Park, **Toast,** 746 W. Webster St., at Halsted Street (✆ **773/935-5600**), serves up all-American favorites (pancakes, eggs, sandwiches). Toast employs an age-old restaurateur's device for keeping idle hands and minds occupied: Tables at this neighborhood spot are covered with blank canvases of butcher-block paper on which kids of all ages can doodle away with crayons. But be forewarned: This is a very popular spot for weekend brunch, so showing up with ravenous kids at 11am on Saturday— only to be told there's an hour wait—is not the best idea.

At **Gino's East** ★★ (p. 127), the famous Chicago pizzeria, long waits can also be an issue during the prime summer tourist season. But once you get your table, the kids can let loose: Patrons are invited to scrawl all over the graffiti-strewn walls and furniture. For fun and games of the coin-operated and basement-rec room variety, seek out **Dave & Buster's,** 1024 N. Clark St. (✆ **312/943-5151**), the Chicago location of the Dallas-based mega entertainment/dining chain.

With heaping plates of pasta served up family style, **Maggiano's,** 516 N. Clark St. (✆ **312/644-7700**), in River North, and **Buca di Beppo,** 521 N. Rush St., right off Michigan Avenue (✆ **312/396-0001**), are good choices for budget-conscious families. These Italian-American restaurants (both parts of national chains) serve up huge portions of pasta and meat to be passed and shared.

cardiologist into fits, veal scaloppini, and even calves' liver. The food is good rather than great, but the service is outstanding, from the Italian maitre d' who flirts with all the ladies to the ancient waiters who manage somehow to keep up with the nonstop flow.

Downstairs from the Village you'll find **Vivere,** a trendier (and more expensive) restaurant experience with a flashy, eye-catching interior (including spiraling bronze sculptures and multicolored, fragmented mosaic floors). Pasta dishes feature upscale ingredients, from the pappardelle with braised duck to the *agnolottini* filled with pheasant. In the basement of the building, **La Cantina Enoteca** has the feel of a casual wine cellar; the specialty here is seafood, although you can order basic pasta and meat dishes as well.

71 W. Monroe St. (btw. Clark and Dearborn sts.). © 312/332-7005. www.italianvillage-chicago.com. Reservations recommended (accepted for parties of 3 or more). Main courses (including salad) $9–$23 lunch, $13–$24 dinner. AE, DISC, MC, V. Mon–Thurs 11am–1am; Fri–Sat 11am–2am; Sun noon–midnight. Subway/El: Red Line to Monroe.

INEXPENSIVE

Heaven on Seven ★★ (Finds) CAJUN & CREOLE/DINER Hidden on the seventh floor of an office building opposite Macy's, this no-frills spot is truly an insider's hangout. Chef/owner Jimmy Bannos's Cajun and Creole specialties come with a cup of soup and include such Louisiana staples as red beans and rice, a catfish po' boy sandwich, and jambalaya. If you don't have a taste for Tabasco, the extensive coffee-shop-style menu covers all the traditional essentials: Grilled-cheese sandwiches, omelets, tuna—the works. Although Heaven on Seven is usually open only for breakfast and lunch, they do serve dinner on the third Friday of the month from 5:30 to 9pm.

Heaven also has another downtown location just off the Mag Mile at **600 N. Michigan Ave.** (© **312/280-7774**); unlike the original location, they accept reservations and credit cards and are open for dinner. The ambience is more lively than gritty, making it a popular spot for families.

111 N. Wabash Ave. (at Washington St.), 7th floor. © **312/263-6443**. www.heavenonseven.com. Reservations not accepted. Sandwiches $8–$12, main courses $10–$14. No credit cards. Mon–Fri 8:30am–5pm; Sat 10am–3pm; 3rd Fri of each month 5:30–9pm. Subway/El: Red Line to Washington.

4 THE WEST LOOP

For restaurants listed in this section, see the map "Where to Dine in the Loop & West Loop" on p. 99.

The stretch of Randolph Street just west of the Chicago River—once known as the Market District—used to be filled with produce trucks and warehouses that shut down tight after nightfall. In the 1990s, in an echo of New York's Meatpacking District, a few bold restaurant pioneers moved in, bringing their super-hip clientele with them. It wasn't long before industrial buildings began their transformation into condos, and now it seems like there's a construction zone on every corner. Despite the upheaval, the West Loop still feels like a neighborhood in transition; it's home to some of the city's coolest restaurants and clubs, but not much else.

Transportation to the West Loop is easy. It's about a $7 cab ride from Michigan Avenue or a slightly longer trek by bus (no. 8 or 9) or El, with stops at Halsted and Lake streets, a block from the Randolph Street's "restaurant row." The walk from the Loop is pleasant and secure in the daytime, but at night I'd take a taxi.

VERY EXPENSIVE

Blackbird ★★★ NEW AMERICAN Stylishly spare, Chef Paul Kahan's Blackbird looks like a contemporary art gallery, an appropriate image for a place that creates miniature masterpieces out of traditional American ingredients. The white, narrow room is dense with close-packed tables, and the floor-to-ceiling windows in front frame the urban landscape outside. Blackbird is fun for people who like a scene, but it can feel over-crowded and loud. (I'd recommend elsewhere for a romantic dinner.) Kahan is a big proponent of local, organic ingredients, so expect top-notch quality and beautifully prepared dishes. Entrees change seasonally, but recent examples of Kahan's approach include braised rack of lamb with beet spaetzle, burnt orange, candied red onion, and mint; and grilled sturgeon with peas, peanuts, bacon, and bourbon caramel. Desserts are similarly original and well worth a splurge; choices might include pear cider doughnuts topped with hazelnut ice cream or white chocolate mousse with a green tea streusel.

619 W. Randolph St. ✆ **312/715-0708.** www.blackbirdrestaurant.com. Reservations recommended. Main courses $11–$15 lunch, $25–$36 dinner. AE, DC, DISC, MC, V. Mon–Fri 11:30am–2pm and 5:30–10:30pm; Sat 5:30–11:30pm.

Moto ★★★ NEW AMERICAN   Chef Homaro Cantu calls his cuisine "avant-garde with Asian influences"—but his goal is to take dining beyond just eating. At Moto, you experience food with all the senses, making for some of the most jaw-droppingly original dishes in town. Herbs are entwined in corkscrew-handled spoons, allowing their scent to waft toward diners as they chew, while everyday ingredients show up in unexpected forms (such as a "pizza and salad" soup). Cantu's got a sense of humor, too—during a raw food course, he uses a "virtual aroma device" to emit a smoky scent, and sometimes the menu itself is edible. Dining here is strictly degustation; you choose between five courses, seven courses, and the 18-course "gastronomic tasting menu" (although be prepared to snack later if you pick the five-course option). The restaurant itself has a minimalist Zen look—here, all the drama is on your plate.

945 W. Fulton Market Ave. (at Sangamon St.). ✆ **312/491-0058.** www.motorestaurant.com. Reservations recommended. Prix-fixe dinners $75–$175. AE, DC, DISC, MC, V. Tues–Sat 5–11pm.

one sixtyblue ★★ AMERICAN   If you're looking for a dining experience that is refined without being stuffy—and you prefer reading menus that don't require a thesaurus—then you'll have a memorable meal here. (Basketball legend Michael Jordan, one of the owners, has been known to mix margaritas at the bar.) High ceilings, upholstered banquettes, and carpeting keep down the noise level, and there's plenty of space between tables, making this is a good spot for business discussions or romantic whispers. Service is attentive but unobtrusive. The internationally inspired menu includes dishes such as duck breast topped with Thai barbecue sauce; super-tender short ribs with grits and horseradish; and ravioli stuffed with crab, spinach, and ricotta. This is one place where it's well worth splurging on dessert; try the chocolate panna cotta paired with peanut crisp and coffee ice cream for a suitably decadent ending to your meal.

1400 W. Randolph St. (at Loomis St.). ✆ **312/850-0303.** www.onesixtyblue.com. Reservations recommended on weekends. Main courses $29–$38. AE, DC, MC, V. Mon–Thurs 5:30–9:30pm; Fri–Sat 5:30–10:30pm.

EXPENSIVE

Carnivale ★ SOUTH AMERICAN   This sprawling, Pan-Latin spot was formerly a nightclub, and judging from the dance music that thumps throughout the place, the stereo system remains intact. If you want to be at the center of the action, head for the two-story central dining room, where brightly colored walls and enormous red-and-yellow lanterns complete the party atmosphere. If you prefer not to shout through your meal, request a table in one of the more intimate side rooms, or try snagging one of the tables just off the central staircase, which give you the best view of the action below.

Carnivale's menu takes inspiration from Central and South America, covering everything from rum-glazed pork shoulder with Puerto Rican rice and beans to Argentine-style steaks. Befitting its clubby vibe, there's also an extensive selection of tropical drinks. Overall, the food is good rather than great; Carnivale's main selling point is its bright, buzzy atmosphere.

702 W. Fulton St. (btw. Clinton St. and the Kennedy Expwy./I-94). ☎ **312/850-5005.** www.carnivale chicago.com. Reservations recommended on weekends. Main courses $8–$15 lunch, $16–$38 dinner. AE, DISC, MC, V. Mon–Thurs 11:30am–2:30pm and 5–10:30pm; Fri 11:30am–2:30pm and 5–11:30pm; Sat 5–11:30pm; Sun 5–10pm. Bar Mon–Thurs 5pm–midnight; Fri–Sat 5pm–1:30am; Sun 5–10pm. Subway/El: Green Line to Clinton.

Marché ★ FRENCH   If you've ever longed to run away and join Cirque du Soleil, spend an evening at Marché. An Americanized, oversize take on the French bistro, Marché offers a convivial (though noisy) dining experience, enhanced by the phantasmagoric decor. Multilevel seating, brightly colored umbrellas that hang from the ceiling, and velvet seats in shades of red and yellow add to the circus atmosphere, as do the clang of the open kitchen and enticing scents from the rotisserie. The food—a mix of bistro favorites—is fine, but the decor is the real draw here. The spit-roasted chicken is quite popular, and you can't miss with the New York strip au poivre partnered with a mound of shoestring frites. Chops and creative seafood entrees round out the menu. Simple, classic desserts and a cheese plate provide a refreshingly light finale to the meal.

833 W. Randolph St. (1 block west of Halsted St.). ☎ **312/226-8399.** www.marche-chicago.com. Reservations accepted. Main courses $12–$18 lunch, $17–$35 dinner. AE, DC, MC, V. Mon–Thurs 11:30am–4pm and 5:30–10pm; Fri 11:30am–4pm and 5:30pm–midnight; Sat 5:30pm–midnight.

Red Light ★ ASIAN   Run by the same owners as Marché (above), Red Light puts a similar emphasis on one-of-a-kind decor. Here, the mood is sultry: The dining rooms have deep-red walls, colorful lanterns, gently waving palm fronds, sensuously curved windows and ceilings, and chairs that could be mistaken for metal sculptures. (They're not very comfortable, but they do look cool.) Chef Jackie Shen incorporates Chinese, French, Thai, and other Asian ingredients and cooking techniques. Curries and seafood entrees are the highlights, from a traditional Japanese *tatsu* curry to the crispy Shanghai-style whole catfish in red-vinegar-sweet-and-sour sauce. You can also dig into traditional dishes such as pad thai or a modern version of kung pao chicken. And as befits a restaurant that's big on style, there's a fine selection of (expensive) specialty cocktails.

820 W. Randolph St. ☎ **312/733-8880.** www.redlight-chicago.com. Reservations recommended on weekends. Main courses $13–$16 lunch, $19–$28 dinner; chef's tasting menu $70. AE, DC, MC, V. Mon–Thurs 11:30am–2pm and 5:30–10pm; Fri 11:30am–2pm and 5:30pm–midnight; Sat 5:30pm–midnight.

Sushi Wabi ★ JAPANESE/SUSHI   Artfully presented sushi and chic crowds are the order of the day at this stylish but attitude-free restaurant. The minimal-chic decor is industrial and raw, and the lighting is dark and seductive—giving the restaurant a downtown lounge feel (enhanced by the live DJ music on weekends). Sushi connoisseurs can request the chef's selection sashimi plate, or go for specialties such as the sea scallop roll with smelt roe, mayonnaise, avocado, and sesame seeds; the dragon roll of shrimp tempura, eel, and avocado; or the spiky, crunchy spider roll of soft-shell crab, smelt roe, mayonnaise, and pepper-vinegar sauce. Simple entrees such as seared tuna, grilled salmon, teriyaki beef, and sesame-crusted chicken breast will satisfy landlubbers who are accommodating their sushi-loving companions. Drinks include a selection of teas in cast-iron pots, both chilled and hot sakes, or try a martini with a ginger-stuffed olive.

Main courses $12–$30. AE, DC, DISC, MC, V. Mon–Thurs 11:30am–2pm and 5–11pm; Fri 11:30am–2pm and 5pm–midnight; Sat 5pm–midnight; Sun 5–11pm.

MODERATE

Avec ★ MEDITERRANEAN A casual wine bar owned by Chef Paul Kahan of neighboring Blackbird (p. 106), Avec keeps things simple: Top-quality ingredients in simple preparations that take inspiration from Italian, French, and Spanish cuisines. The menu focuses on a variety of "small plates" meant for sharing (although there are always five or six entree-size offerings as well). The long, narrow dining room, with its wood walls and floors, will strike you as either cramped or cozy. I know many people who love Avec's convivial spirit; others find it annoyingly crowded and loud. Small plates include salads and appetizer-style dishes such as smoked lamb and quail brochettes and dates stuffed with chorizo sausage; large plates feature seasonal ingredients and tend to be heartier (pork shoulder or pappardelle with wild mushrooms, for example). There's also a good selection of specialty cheeses and—of course—an extensive European-focused wine list.

615 W. Randolph St. ℰ **312/377-2002.** www.avecrestaurant.com. Reservations not accepted. Small plates $5–$12; large plates $15–$20. AE, DC, DISC, MC, V. Mon–Thurs 3:30pm–midnight; Fri–Sat 3:30pm–1am; Sun 3:30–10pm.

La Sardine ★ ⓕFinds BISTRO/FRENCH Sister to Jean-Claude Poilevey's popular Le Bouchon (and named after a critic's description of that tiny Bucktown bistro; p. 146), this is a more spacious and gracious destination, with an open, airy feel. Well-prepared versions of bistro standards include the delicate bouillabaisse in a lobster-saffron broth; ragout of super-tender rabbit, onions, and mashed potatoes; steak frites; sensational escargots bourguignon; onion soup; and *salade Lyonnaise* (greens, bacon lardons, croutons, and poached egg). The dessert menu boasts traditional soufflés, with your choice of Grand Marnier or chocolate. At lunch, choose from an abbreviated menu of appetizers and salads, soups, sandwiches, and entrees, or opt for a hearty *plat du jour,* perhaps tuna Niçoise on Monday, or duck legs braised in red wine with mushrooms and potato purée

---

A Taste of Poland

Chicago has long been a popular destination for Polish immigrants. (Currently, about one million Chicagoans claim Polish ancestry.) It's somewhat mystifying, then, why they haven't made much of an impact on the city's dining scene. There are Polish restaurants here, but they tend to be small, casual, family-run affairs in residential neighborhoods far removed from the usual tourist attractions. If you'd like to try some hearty, stick-to-your-ribs Polish food, the best-known restaurant is **Red Apple** (Czerwone Jabluszko), 3121 N. Milwaukee Ave. (ℰ **773/588-5781;** www.redapplebuffet.com). Dining here is strictly buffet, and the lineup includes Polish specialties such as pierogi (meat- or cheese-stuffed dumplings) and blintzes, as well as a huge selection of roast meats, salads, and bread (there's even fruit, should you feel nutrient-starved). Best of all is the price: $9.99 on weekdays and $10.95 on weekends for all you can eat.

Finds **Ethnic Dining near the Loop**

CHINATOWN

Chicago's Chinatown is about 20 blocks south of the Loop. The district is strung along two thoroughfares, Cermak Road and Wentworth Avenue as far south as 24th Place. Hailing a cab from the Loop is the easiest way to get here, but you can also drive and leave your car in the validated lot near the entrance to Chinatown, or take the Orange Line of the El to the Cermak stop, a well-lit station on the edge of the Chinatown commercial district.

The spacious, fairly elegant **Phoenix,** 2131 S. Archer Ave. (btw. Wentworth Ave. and Cermak Rd.; © **312/328-0848**), has plenty of room for big tables of family or friends to enjoy the Cantonese (and some Szechuan) cuisine. A good sign: The place attracts lots of Chinatown locals. It's especially popular for dim sum brunch, so come early to avoid the wait. Late night, stop by the more casual **Saint's Alp Teahouse** downstairs (© **312/842-1886**), an outpost of the Hong Kong chain, which is open until midnight daily.

Penang, 2201 S. Wentworth Ave. (at Cermak Rd.; © **312/326-6888**), serves mostly Malaysian dishes, but some lean toward Indian and Chinese. (They've even added a sushi bar to complete the Pan-Asian experience.) Sink your teeth into the *kambing rendang* (lamb curry in 11 spices) or the barbecued stingray wrapped in a banana leaf.

Open since 1927, **Won Kow,** 2237 S. Wentworth Ave. (btw. 22nd Place and Alexander St.; © **312/842-7500**), is the oldest continually operating restaurant in Chinatown. You can enjoy dim sum in the mezzanine-level dining room from 9am to 3pm daily. Most of the items cost around $2. Other house specialties include Mongolian chicken and duck with seafood.

LITTLE ITALY

Convenient to most downtown locations, a few blocks along Taylor Street are home to a host of time-honored, traditional, hearty Italian restaurants. If you're staying in the Loop (an easy cab ride away), the area makes a good destination for dinner. (I don't think it's worth a special trip if you're staying farther north—there are plenty of great Italian places elsewhere in the city.)

Regulars return for the straightforward Italian favorites livened up with some adventurous specials at **Francesca's on Taylor,** 1400 W. Taylor St. (at Loomis St.; © **312/829-2828**). I recommend the fish specials above the standard meat dishes. Other standouts include eggplant ravioli in a four-cheese sauce with a touch of tomato sauce and shaved parmigiano, as well as sautéed veal medallions with porcini mushrooms in cream sauce. (This is part of a local chain that includes the popular Mia Francesca, p. 142.)

Expect to wait even with a reservation at **Rosebud on Taylor** ★, 1500 W. Taylor St. (at Laflin St.; © **312/942-1117**), but fear not—your hunger will be satisfied. Rosebud is known for enormous helpings of pasta, most of which lean toward heavy Italian-American favorites: deep-dish lasagna and a fettuccine Alfredo that defines the word "rich." I highly recommend any of the pastas served with vodka sauce. Another location is near the Mag Mile at 720 N. Rush St. (© **312/266-6444**).

Tuscany, 1014 W. Taylor St. (btw. Morgan and Miller sts.; © **312/829-1990**), is one of the most reliable Italian restaurants on Taylor Street. In contrast to the city's more fashionable Italian spots, family-owned Tuscany has the comfortable feel of a neighborhood restaurant. The menu features large portions of Tuscan pastas, pizzas, veal, chicken, and a risotto of the day. Specialties include anything cooked on the wood-burning grill and Tuscan sausage dishes. A second location is across from Wrigley Field at 3700 N. Clark St. (at Waveland Ave.; © **773/404-7700**).

GREEKTOWN

A short cab ride across the south branch of the Chicago River will take you to the city's Greektown, a row of moderately priced and inexpensive Greek restaurants clustered on Halsted Street between Van Buren and Washington streets.

To be honest, there's not much here to distinguish one restaurant from the other: They're all standard Greek restaurants with similar looks and similar menus. That said, **Greek Islands,** 200 S. Halsted St. (at Adams St.; © **312/782-9855**); **Santorini,** 800 W. Adams St. (at Halsted St.; © **312/829-8820**); **Parthenon,** 314 S. Halsted St. (btw. Jackson and Van Buren sts.; © **312/726-2407**); and **Costas,** 340 S. Halsted St. (btw. Jackson and Van Buren sts.; © **312/263-0767**), are all good bets for gyros, Greek salads, shish kabobs, and the classic moussaka. On warm summer nights, opt for either **Athena** ★, 212 S. Halsted St. (btw. Adams and Jackson sts.; © **312/655-0000**), which has a huge outdoor seating area, or **Pegasus,** 130 S. Halsted St. (btw. Monroe and Adams sts.; © **312/226-3377**), with its rooftop patio serving drinks, appetizers, and desserts. Both have wonderful views of the Loop's skyline. **Artopolis,** 306 S. Halsted St. (at Jackson St.; © **312/559-9000**), a more recent addition to the neighborhood, is a casual option offering up Greek and Mediterranean specialties, wood-oven pizzas, breads, and French pastries, all of them tasty.

PILSEN

Just south of the Loop and convenient to McCormick Place and Chinatown, Pilsen is a colorful blend of Mexican culture, artists and bohemians, and pricey new residential developments. The area's nascent restaurant scene is showing signs of life, but for now, the local fare is decidedly casual.

Nuevo Leon, 1515 W. 18th St. (at Laflin St.; © **312/421-1517**), is a popular Mexican restaurant serving the standard offerings. Across the street, **Playa Azul,** 1514 W. 18th St. (at Laflin St.; © **312/421-2552**), serves authentic Mexican seafood dishes, salads, and soups.

On the more bohemian side, linger over a salad, sandwich, or refreshing fruit milkshake *(liquado)* at **Café Jumping Bean,** 1439 W. 18th St. (at Bishop St.; © **312/455-0019**), or kick back with a cup of coffee at artsy **Café Mestizo,** 2123 S. Ashland Ave. (btw. 21st St. and Cermak Rd.; © **312/942-0095**).

on Thursday. There's also a daily $22 three-course lunch featuring soup or salad and your choice of entree and dessert.

111 N. Carpenter St. ℂ **312/421-2800.** www.frenchrestaurantschicago.com. Reservations recommended. Main courses $13–$15 lunch, $16–$20 dinner. AE, DC, DISC, MC, V. Mon–Fri 11:30am–2:30pm and 5–10pm; Sat 5–11pm.

INEXPENSIVE

Wishbone ★★ **(Kids** BREAKFAST/BRUNCH/SOUTHERN   A down-home spot that inspires intense loyalty, Wishbone blends hearty, home-style choices with healthy and vegetarian items. It's best known for its popular Sunday brunch, but lunch and dinner tend to be less crowded. Seafood lovers will enjoy the blackened catfish or crawfish cakes; other offerings include a hearty jambalaya stew and hoppin' John, the classic Southern dish of brown rice, black-eyed peas, and ham. Entrees come with your choice of two side dishes, which range from healthy (fresh fruit) to heavy (macaroni and cheese; mashed sweet potatoes); there are also several vegetarian options. The tart Key lime pie is one of my favorite desserts in the city. This is a great pick for parents: The restaurant has a children's menu and welcomes families.

There's a newer location on the North Side, at 3300 N. Lincoln Ave. (at W. School St.; ℂ **773/549-2663**), but the original location has more character.

1001 Washington St. (at Morgan St.). ℂ **312/850-2663.** www.wishbonechicago.com. Reservations accepted, except for weekend brunch. Main courses $5–$10 breakfast and lunch, $8–$15 dinner. AE, DC, DISC, MC, V. Mon 7am–3pm; Tues–Thurs 7am–3pm and 5–9pm; Fri 7am–3pm and 5–10pm; Sat 8am–3pm and 5–10pm; Sun 8am–3pm.

5 THE MAGNIFICENT MILE & THE GOLD COAST

Many tourists who visit Chicago never stray far from the Magnificent Mile and the adjoining Gold Coast area. From the array of restaurants, shops, and pretty streets, it's not hard to see why. The Gold Coast is home to some of the city's wealthiest, most tradition-bound families, people who have been frequenting the same restaurants for years. But newer places, such as Tru, have carved out their own culinary niches here as well. Restaurants here are some of the best in the city—and their prices are right in line with Michigan Avenue's designer boutiques.

VERY EXPENSIVE

Cape Cod Room **(Overrated** SEAFOOD   There's nothing nouvelle about the Cape Cod Room, which is part of the draw for old-timers; the restaurant, located on the lower level of the Drake Hotel, is dimly lit and hasn't changed much since it opened in the 1930s. Although the food is fine, I think the prices are far too steep for what you get. But that doesn't stop Cape Cod loyalists—many of whom have been coming here for decades—from filling up the place. Main-course offerings include Chilean sea bass served with truffle mashed potatoes, red snapper, bouillabaisse, and Dover sole (boned tableside, naturally). If seafood's not your thing, you can order steaks and chops off the menu of Drake Bros., the hotel's steakhouse. I wouldn't call the Cape Cod Room a good value, but as with any vintage restaurant, it has a certain timeless charm, and the people-watching can be priceless.

Where to Dine in the Magnificent Mile, Gold Coast & River North

Ajasteak **28**
A Mano **40**
Billy Goat Tavern **49**
Bin 36 **40**
Bistro 110 **12**
Brasserie Jo **39**
Café Iberico **17**
Cape Cod Room **9**
Carson 's **24**
Charlie's Ale House
  at Navy Pier **55**
Crofton on Wells **30**
Cyrano's Bistrot
  & Wine Bar **33**
Dave & Buster's **5**
DeLaCosta **54**
Ed Debevic's **26**

Edwardo's **1**
ESPN Zone **52**
foodlife **13**
Frontera Grill &
  Topolobampo **38**
Gene & Georgetti **31**
Gibsons Bar &
  Steakhouse **4**
Gino's East **25**
Gold Coast Dogs **43**
Graham Elliot **20**
Green Zebra **56**
Harry Caray's Italian
  Steakhouse **42**
House of Blues **41**
Karyn's Cooked **16**
Le Colonial **6**

Lou Malnati's
  Pizzeria **35**
Maggiano's **36**
Mike Ditka's
  Restaurant **11**
mk **15**
Mr. Beef **22**
Morton's **3**
Nacional 27 **23**
Naha **37**
Oak Street
  Beachstro **10**
Oak Tree **7**
Osteria Via
  Stato **29**
Pizzeria Due **51**
Pizzeria Uno **50**
Portillo's **27**

Puck's at
  the MCA **14**
Reza's **21**
Rockit Bar
  & Grill **48**
Shaw's Crab
  House **45**
Spiaggia **8**
Star of Siam **47**
SushiSamba Rio **32**
Table Fifty-Two **2**
Tizi Melloul **34**
Tru **53**
Vermillion **44**
VTK–Vong's Thai
  Kitchen **46**
Zealous **19**
ZED 451 **18**

In the Drake Hotel, 140 E. Walton Place (at Michigan Ave.). © **312/932-4615.** Reservations recommended. Main courses $25–$42. AE, DC, DISC, MC, V. Daily 11:30am–2pm and 5:30–10pm. Subway/El: Red Line to Chicago.

Gibsons Bar & Steakhouse ★★ STEAK   Popular with its Gold Coast neighbors, Gibsons is the steakhouse you visit when you want to take in a scene. There are sporty cars idling at the valet stand, photos of celebs who've appeared here, and overdressed denizens mingling in the bar, which has a life all its own. The dining rooms evoke a more romantic feel, from the sleek Art Deco decor to the bow-tied bartenders. But Gibson's isn't coasting on atmosphere alone; the top-notch steaks deserve some credit, too. Portions are notoriously enormous, so Gibsons is best for groups who are happy to share dishes. (I wouldn't recommend it for a romantic dinner *a deux.*) The namesake martinis are served in 10-ounce glasses, and the entrees are outlandishly scaled, from the six-piece shrimp cocktail so huge you swore you downed a dozen, to the turtle pie that comes with a steak knife (and could easily serve eight people).

1028 N. Rush St. (at Bellevue Place). © **312/266-8999.** www.gibsonssteakhouse.com. Reservations strongly recommended. Main courses $25–$80. AE, DC, DISC, MC, V. Daily 11am–midnight (bar open later). Subway/El: Red Line to Clark/Division.

Morton's ★★ STEAK   Morton's is a well-known chain with locations nationwide, but it's Chicago born and bred, and many still consider it the king of Chicago-style steakhouses. Hidden on the lower level of an undistinguished high-rise, the place hasn't changed its look in decades, and most of the menu has stayed the same for years, too: double filet mignon with béarnaise sauce; classic porterhouse, New York strip, and rib eye steaks, with the usual a la carte sides. (There are a few nods to health-conscious diners: The sautéed fresh-spinach-and-mushrooms combo is a tasty alternative to creamed spinach.) Overall, Morton's steaks are dependable rather than awe-inspiring, but the place has a relaxed ambience that welcomes everyone from power-suited businessmen to 20-somethings in jeans.

Morton's has a Loop location at 65 E. Wacker Place, between Michigan and Wabash avenues (© **312/201-0410**), with a slightly more upscale, clubby decor; unlike the original location, it's open for lunch.

1050 N. State St. (at Rush St.). © **312/266-4820.** www.mortons.com. Reservations recommended. Main courses $26–$44. AE, DC, DISC, MC, V. Mon–Sat 5:30–11pm; Sun 5–10pm. Subway/El: Red Line to Chicago.

Spiaggia ★★★ ITALIAN   *Spiaggia* means "beach" in Italian, and the name is a tribute to its spectacular view of Lake Michigan and Oak Street Beach. Generally acknowledged as the best fine-dining Italian restaurant in the city, this elegant setting is far removed from your neighborhood trattoria—so dress to impress. (Jackets are required for men, and jeans are a no-no.) Chef Tony Mantuano mixes organic, locally grown produce with fresh-from-Italy ingredients. Standouts include spaghetti with squid ink; duck breast with Ligurian black olives, tomatoes, fennel, and baby artichokes; and the homemade potato gnocchi topped with black truffles. You're encouraged to order Italian-style (appetizer, pasta, meat), which means the bill adds up quickly. But if you're a cheese lover, this is the place to splurge: They'll roll out a cart filled with rare varieties and give you extensive descriptions of each one.

The adjacent, more informal **Café Spiaggia** (© **312/280-2755**) is also open for lunch.

980 N. Michigan Ave. (at Oak St.). © **312/280-2750.** www.spiaggiarestaurant.com. Reservations strongly suggested on weekends. Main courses $34–$41; menu degustation $165. AE, DC, DISC, MC, V. Sun–Thurs 6–9:30pm; Fri–Sat 5:30–10:30pm. Subway/El: Red Line to Chicago.

> ## (Tips) A Spot of Tea
>
> If you're shopping on the Magnificent Mile and feel like having an elegant after-noon tea complete with finger sandwiches, scones, and pastries, head for the stately **Palm Court** at The Drake Hotel, 140 E. Walton Place ((C) **312/787-2200**); the cozy **Seasons Lounge** of the Four Seasons Hotel, 120 E. Delaware Place ((C) **312/280-8800**); or the **Greenhouse** in the Ritz-Carlton, 160 E. Pearson St. ((C) **312/266-1000**), in the sunny 12th-floor lobby above the Water Tower Place mall. In the Loop, the appropriately named **Russian Tea Time** ★★, 77 E. Adams St. ((C) **312/360-0000**), serves tea from 2:30 to 4:30pm daily (p. 103).

Tru ★★★ NEW AMERICAN/FRENCH   Offering "progressive French cuisine," Tru gives traditional European culinary techniques a creative American twist. The dining room has the elegance of a fine-dining restaurant (and prices to match), but the overall atmosphere is welcoming rather than stiff. Dining is strictly prix-fixe, from three to nine courses; choices might include Maine lobster with saffron tagliatelle; Alaskan halibut topped with bacon vinaigrette; or venison paired with blood oranges. If your wallet and stomach permit, go for the nine-course Chef's Collection ($145), featuring selections inspired by that day's markets. For an over-the-top splurge, order the visually sensational caviar staircase (caviars and fixin's climbing a glass spiral staircase), which goes for $250. The expansive wine list is a treat for oenophiles, with 1,200 selections. The restaurant's comfortable lounge, where you can order dessert sampler plates, is a relaxed after-dinner hangout (and you're welcome to stop in even if you've eaten elsewhere).

676 N. St. Clair St. (at Huron St.). (C) **312/202-0001**. www.trurestaurant.com. Reservations required. Prix-fixe menu $95–$145. AE, DC, DISC, MC, V. Mon–Thurs 5:30–10pm; Fri–Sat 5–11pm. Subway/El: Red Line to Chicago.

EXPENSIVE

Bistro 110 FRENCH   Although it's too large and pricey to feel like an authentic bistro, this stalwart has a bustling energy I find invigorating. While other restaurants chase the latest foodie trends, Bistro 110 keeps certain dishes on the menu year after year—such as the decadently hearty beef Wellington with a rich port demi glaze—and that's just how the regulars like it. The menu also includes French classics such as escargots in puff pastry, mussels in white-wine sauce, onion soup, cassoulet, and steak au poivre. The wood-roasted items, including a savory half chicken and a bountiful roast vegetable plate, are consistently good. Although the restaurant touts what it calls its "famous crème brûlée," I prefer to save up for the *Gâteau Paradis au Chocolat,* a decadent mix of chocolate cake, caramel, and toffee. On Sunday the restaurant hosts a popular brunch with live jazz music.

110 E. Pearson St. (just west of Michigan Ave.). (C) **312/266-3110**. www.bistro110restaurant.com. Main courses $16–$30. AE, DC, DISC, MC, V. Mon–Sat 11:30am–10pm; Sun 10:30am–9pm. Subway/El: Red Line to Chicago.

DeLaCosta ★ SOUTH AMERICAN   According to executive chef Douglas Rodri-guez (of New York's Patria and Philadelphia's Alma de Cuba), this restaurant draws inspiration from the coastal cuisines of Spain, the Caribbean, and South America—which

> **(Finds) Dessert Tour**
>
> **Eli's** cheesecake is a Chicago icon—the rich, creamy cakes have been served at presidential inaugurations and numerous other high-profile events. For a behind-the-scenes peek at Chicago's most famous dessert, you can take a tour of Eli's bakery on the northwest side of the city. After watching the cooking and decorating processes, you get to enjoy a full-size slice of your favorite flavor. Tours are given Monday through Friday at 1pm. (Although reservations aren't necessary, call to make sure the bakery isn't closed for periodic maintenance.) The 40-minute tour costs $3 for adults and $2 for children 11 and under; special packages are available for groups of 10 or more. Eli's bakery is at 6701 Forest Preserve Dr., at the corner of Montrose Avenue (✆ **800/ELI-CAKE** [354-2253]; www.elischeesecake.com).

means plenty of fresh fish and some bold flavor combinations. The overall vibe is Miami-chic, with a long, gleaming white bar and a buzzing, boisterous clientele. (In the summer, you can sit on a floating deck out back.) The ceviches are an ideal start to your meal; the "Fire and Ice" mixes tuna, calamari, chiles, coconut, and lime. Tapas include specialty cheeses, mussels, empanadas stuffed with porcini mushrooms, and marlin tacos. Among the entrees, the Churrasco DeLaCosta—a tender beef tenderloin topped with a tasty, mildly spicy chimichurri sauce—lives up to its billing as a signature dish; the Brazilian-inspired Xim Xim (chicken and giant shrimp in a coconut sauce with roasted cashews) is less filling but very flavorful.

465 E. Illinois St. (btw. McClurg Court and Lake Shore Dr.). ✆ **312/464-1700.** www.delacostachicago.com. Reservations recommended. Main courses $21–$38. AE, DC, DISC, MC, V. Sun–Thurs 5–10pm; Fri–Sat 5–11pm; bar until 1am Fri–Sat. Subway/El: Red Line to Grand, then a short cab ride.

Mike Ditka's Restaurant ★ AMERICAN/STEAK   In this city, nobody refers to him by name. He is simply "Da Coach." Immortalized in the classic "Super Fans" sketch on *Saturday Night Live,* "Iron" Mike Ditka remains the quintessential cigar-chomping, hard-nosed Chicagoan—despite the fact that it's been more than 2 decades since he led the Chicago Bears to a Super Bowl victory. Filled with dark wood, leather banquettes, and walls lined with memorabilia, this is man country with a meat-heavy menu to match—but the food is a good step up from your average sports bar. The "Coach's Meat-loaf Stack" is served on a bed of jalapeño cornbread and drenched with barbecue sauce, while "Da Pork Chop" is surrounded by mashed sweet potatoes and Michigan cherry jus. You may just see Da Coach himself making the rounds of the dining room; he broadcasts a radio show from the restaurant on Thursday mornings during football season.

100 E. Chestnut St. (in the Tremont Hotel, btw. Michigan Ave. and Rush St.). ✆ **312/587-8989.** www.mikeditkaschicago.com. Main courses $10–$16 lunch, $18–$40 dinner. AE, DC, DISC, MC, V. Mon–Thurs 11am–10pm; Fri–Sat 11am–11pm; Sun 10am–10pm. Subway/El: Red Line to Chicago.

Table Fifty-Two ★ AMERICAN   How does a modest restaurant specializing in non-trendy Southern food become so high-profile that weekend reservations are mandatory weeks in advance? Call it the Oprah effect. The chef-owner of this unassuming, cozy spot is Art Smith, Oprah's former personal chef. His association with the talk-show titan was

enough to make Table Fifty-Two a hot spot the minute it opened. The fact that it's **117**
tiny—only 13 tables—has kept up the demand. You'll get a taste of Smith's Southern
heritage as soon as you're seated, when the server brings out warm goat cheese biscuits
and deviled eggs. Appetizers and entrees include upscale versions of down-home classics,
such as shrimp with stone-ground grits; pork chops with brussels sprouts and pickled
cherries; and fried chicken with garlic mashed potatoes (available only for Sunday dinner). The prices are high for what's essentially comfort food, but regulars find Table
Fifty-Two's charm worth the price.

52 W. Elm St. (at Division St.). ☏ **312/573-4000.** www.tablefifty-two.com. Main courses $12–$28 lunch,
$19–$34 dinner. AE, DISC, MC, V. Tues–Sat 5–10pm; Sun 4–9pm. Subway/El: Red Line to Clark/Division.

MODERATE

Le Colonial ★★ Ⓕinds FRENCH/VIETNAMESE   Appropriately enough for its tony
Oak Street environs, Le Colonial has one of the loveliest dining rooms in the city—and the
second-floor lounge is a sultry, seductive destination for cocktails. An escapist's paradise, the
restaurant is a cleverly crafted re-creation of 1920s Saigon, with bamboo shutters, rattan
chairs, potted palms and banana trees, fringed lampshades, and ceiling fans. While the
ambience certainly merits a visit, the flavorful cuisine is a draw on its own. Start with the
hearty oxtail soup or the light and refreshing beef-and-watercress salad. Entrees include
grilled lime-glazed sea scallops with garlic noodle salad; sautéed jumbo shrimp in curried
coconut sauce; and roasted chicken with lemongrass-and-lime dipping sauce. Le Colonial
offers outdoor seating in warm weather; try to reserve one of the coveted, romantic mezzanine terrace tables, which look out over the bustling street below.

937 N. Rush St. (just south of Oak St.). ☏ **312/255-0088.** www.lecolonialchicago.com. Reservations
recommended. Main courses $15–$22 lunch, $18–$29 dinner. AE, DC, MC, V. Mon–Wed 11:30am–2:30pm
and 5–11pm; Thurs–Sat 11:30am–2:30pm and 5pm–midnight; Sun 11:30am–2:30pm and 5–10pm. Sub-
way/El: Red Line to Chicago.

Shaw's Crab House ★★ SEAFOOD   Shaw's is a local institution—if you ask
average Chicagoans where to go for seafood, chances are they'll point you here. The dining room—with its red leather banquettes, 1930s-era soundtrack, and white-jacketed

---

Ⓣips   Kitchens Up Close

Serious food fans can get a firsthand look at how some of the city's culinary stars
work by booking a seat at a chef's table. You'll get a personal tour of the kitchen,
a special selection of dishes, and—best of all—a front-row seat for dinner-hour
drama. At **Tru** (☏ **312/202-0001**), four to six people can sit in a glass-enclosed
room off the kitchen, where they can check out the scene without feeling the
heat. The chef's table at **Charlie Trotter's** ★★★ (☏ **773/248-6228**) seats four
to six right in the kitchen, so diners can catch Trotter's legendary perfectionism
up close. At **Zealous** ★★★ (☏ **312/475-9112**), the chef's table seats 8 to 10 and
is in the main dining room—but bamboo trees surround it, so other diners won't
get jealous when chef Michael Taus stops by for some one-on-one taste tests.

Chef's tables don't come cheap ($100–$175 per person), but they're a special
splurge for die-hard foodies. Just remember to reserve well in advance because
these tables book fast.

Only in Chicago

PIZZA

We have three pizza styles in Chicago: Chicago style, also known as deep-dish, which is thick-crusted and often demands a knife and fork; stuffed, which is similar to a pie, with a crust on both top and bottom; and thin crust. Many pizzerias serve both thick and thin, and some make all three kinds.

Three of the best places to try the classic Chicago deep-dish are **Pizzeria Uno** ★ (p. 133), **Pizzeria Due** (p. 133), and **Gino's East** ★★ (p. 127). In River North, **Lou Malnati's Pizzeria** ★, 439 N. Wells St. (at Hubbard St.; ✆ 312/828-9800), bakes both deep-dish and thin-crust pizza and even has a low-fat-cheese option. **Edwardo's** is a local pizza chain that serves all three varieties, but with a wheat crust and all-natural ingredients (spinach pizza is the specialty here); locations are in the Gold Coast at 1212 N. Dearborn St. (at Division St.; ✆ 312/337-4490); in the South Loop at 521 S. Dearborn St. (btw. Congress Pkwy. and Harrison St.; ✆ 312/939-3366); and in Lincoln Park at 2622 N. Halsted St. (at Wrightwood Ave.; ✆ 773/871-3400). Another popular chain—known for its stuffed pizza—is **Giordano's**, with downtown locations off the Magnificent Mile at 730 N. Rush St. (at Superior St.; ✆ 312/951-0747) and at the Prudential Plaza, 135 E. Lake St. (just east of Michigan Ave.; ✆ 312/616-1200).

For a unique twist on the deep-dish phenomenon, head to **Chicago Pizza & Oven Grinder,** 2121 N. Clark St. (btw. Webster and Dickens aves.; ✆ 773/248-2570), a few blocks from Lincoln Park Zoo. Here, the "pizza potpie" is baked in a bowl and then turned over when served. This neighborhood spot stays popular year after year, so plan on showing up early for dinner to avoid a long wait.

HOT DOGS

The classic Chicago hot dog includes a frankfurter by Vienna Beef (a local food processor and hallowed institution), heaps of chopped onions and green relish,

waitstaff—has a dimly lit, retro feel, but the extensive menu isn't stuck in the past; choices run the gamut from fried calamari to crab cakes to sushi. Fresh, seasonal seafood (flown in daily) is the main draw, although you can also indulge in surf-and-turf combinations. Overall, you won't go wrong ordering one of the classics: Alaskan king crab; Texas stone-crab claws; or fresh oysters, which you can select according to their provenance (Nova Scotia, British Columbia, and so on). The adjacent Oyster Bar offers a more casual menu and has live music on Sunday, Tuesday, and Thursday nights. The restaurant's Sunday brunch is an excellent weekend option for seafood lovers.

21 E. Hubbard St. (btw. State St. and Wabash Ave.). ✆ 312/527-2722. www.shawscrabhouse.com. Reservations accepted only for the main dining room. Main courses $14–$35. AE, DC, DISC, MC, V. Mon–Thurs 11:30am–2pm and 5:30–10pm; Fri 11:30am–2pm and 5–11pm; Sat 5–11pm; Sun 10:30am–1:30pm and 5–10pm. Subway/El: Red Line to Grand.

INEXPENSIVE

Billy Goat Tavern ★ (**Value**) FAST FOOD   Viewers of the original *Saturday Night Live* will remember the classic routine "Cheezeborger, cheezeborger," with John Belushi a slather of yellow mustard, pickle spears, fresh tomato wedges, a dash of celery salt, and, for good measure, two or three "sport" peppers, those thumb-shaped holy terrors that turn your mouth into its own bonfire.

Chicago is home to many standout hot dog spots but one, **Hot Doug's,** 3324 N. California Ave. (at Roscoe St., ⓒ 773/279-9550), takes encased meats to a new level, featuring several gourmet sausages on a bun every day except Sunday. (Plan on standing in line no matter which day you show up—and it's always worth it.) Hot Doug's also serves a great classic Chicago dog just like many other stands in town, including **Gold Coast Dogs,** 159 N. Wabash Ave., at Randolph Street (ⓒ 312/917-1677), in the Loop just a block from Michigan Avenue. **Fluky's,** in The Shops at North Bridge mall, 520 N. Michigan Ave. (ⓒ 312/245-0702), is part of a local chain that has been serving great hot dogs since the Depression (Dan Aykroyd and Jay Leno are fans). **Portillo's** (p. 133) is another local chain that specializes in hot dogs but also serves tasty pastas and salads. **Murphy's Red Hots,** 1211 W. Belmont Ave. (at Racine Ave.; ⓒ 773/935-2882), is a neighborhood spot not too far from Wrigley Field, while **the Wieners Circle,** in Lincoln Park at 2622 N. Clark St. (btw. Wrightwood Ave. and Drummond Place; ⓒ 773/477-7444), is a late-night favorite where rude order-takers are part of the shtick.

If you've got a car, head up to **Superdawg Drive-In,** 6363 N. Milwaukee Ave. (at Devon Ave.; ⓒ 773/763-0660), on the northwest side of the city (look for the giant hot dogs dressed as Tarzan and Jane on the roof). This classic 1950s-style flashback has been run by the same family for three generations, and, yes, they still have carhops who bring out your order.

as a crabby Greek short-order cook. The comic got his material from the Billy Goat Tavern, located under North Michigan Avenue near the bridge that leads to the Loop (walk down the steps across the street from the Chicago Tribune building). This is a classic dive: Dark, seedy, and no-frills. But unlike the *Saturday Night Live* skit, the guys behind the counter are friendly and you'll feel like an insider at this hangout for local newspaper reporters. The menu is pretty basic, but yes—the cheeseburgers are pretty good. After work, this is a good place to watch a game, chitchat at the bar, and down a few beers.

For the same "cheezeborgers" in less grungy (and more kid-friendly) surroundings, head to the Billy Goat's outpost on Navy Pier (ⓒ 312/670-8789).

430 N. Michigan Ave. ⓒ 312/222-1525. www.billygoattavern.com. Reservations not accepted. Menu items $4–$7. No credit cards. Mon–Fri 6am–2am; Sat 10am–2am; Sun 11am–2am. Subway/El: Red Line to Chicago.

foodlife ★★ (Finds) FAST FOOD Taking the standard food court up a few notches, foodlife consists of a dozen or so kiosks offering both ordinary and exotic specialties on the mezzanine of Water Tower Place mall. A hostess seats you, gives you an electronic card, and then it's up to you to stroll around and get whatever food strikes your fancy. (Each purchase is recorded on your card, and you pay on the way out.) The beauty of a food court, of course, is that it offers something for everybody (making this a great stop for families with picky eaters). At foodlife, diners can choose from burgers, pizza, south-of-the-border dishes, an assortment of Asian fare, and veggie-oriented, low-fat offerings. A lunch or snack is basically inexpensive, but the payment method makes it easy to build up a big tab while holding a personal taste-testing session at each kiosk if you're not careful.

In Water Tower Place, 835 N. Michigan Ave. ✆ 312/335-3663. www.foodlifechicago.com. Reservations not accepted. Most items $8–$15. AE, DC, DISC, MC, V. Breakfast kiosk daily 8–11:30am. All other kiosks Mon–Thurs 11:30am–8pm; Fri–Sat 11:30am–8:30pm; Sun 11:30am–7pm. Subway/El: Red Line to Chicago.

Oak Tree ★ AMERICAN Though it's located on the sixth floor of the ritzy 900 N. Michigan Ave. indoor mall (home of Bloomingdale's, Gucci, and others), Oak Tree isn't exactly high profile. But it's popular with the ladies-who-lunch crowd and local office workers and makes a convenient stop during a day of downtown shopping. Airy and boutique-hotel sleek, it's a relaxing retreat from the Michigan Avenue madness outside. If you can, snag a table along the windows that overlook the John Hancock Center—but remember that everyone else coming to eat here wants those spots, too. The menu focuses on a wide selection of salads and sandwiches. On a cold day, try one of the upscale grilled cheese selections, which include combinations such as apple, brie, watercress, and fig preserves. You can also order breakfast all day. The only downside for family travelers: There's no kids' menu.

900 N. Michigan Ave. (at Delaware Place), 6th floor. ✆ 312/751-1988. www.shop900.com/restaurant/oak-tree-restaurant. Reservations not accepted. Main courses $8–$15. AE, DC, DISC, MC, V. Mon–Sat 7:30am–6pm; Sun 7:30am–4pm. Subway/El: Red Line to Chicago.

6 RIVER NORTH

For restaurants listed in this section, see the map "The Magnificent Mile, Gold Coast & River North Dining" on p. 113.

River North, the area north of the Loop and west of Michigan Avenue, is home to the city's most concentrated cluster of art galleries and a something-for-everyone array of restaurants—from fast food and themed restaurants to chains and some of our trendiest dining destinations. Whether you seek a quick dog or burger, contemporary American fine dining, exotic Moroccan, or world-class Mexican fare, River North has it all—within easy walking distance of many downtown hotels.

VERY EXPENSIVE

Ajasteak ★ ASIAN/STEAK If you like your steaks served in a decidedly non-steakhouse setting—and have a fondness for Asian flavors—head to Ajasteak, where giant cuts of beef coexist harmoniously with sushi and edamame salad. The dining room's urbancool, mostly black color scheme signals that this is a clear departure from your stereotypical white tablecloth steak joint, while floor-to-ceiling windows overlooking State Street make you part of the action outside. (In good weather, the sidewalk patio is a popular see-and-be-seen spot.) Japanese-inspired dishes include maki rolls prepared at the in-house sushi bar and a miso-glazed black cod; there's also a full lineup of sake drinks. Steaks come in classic American cuts as well as authentic Kobe flown in from

Japan (for which you'll pay—gulp!—$18 per ounce). Rather keep the price down? Try one of the specialty burgers at lunch, including a ground lamb version with Indian spices.

660 N. State St. (at Erie St.), in the Dana Hotel. ⓒ **312/202-6050.** www.danahotelandspa.com/restaurant. Reservations recommended on weekends. Main courses $21–$48 dinner, $13–$20 lunch. AE, DC, MC, V. Daily 11:30am–2:30pm and 5:30–10pm. Subway/El: Red Line to Chicago.

mk ★★★ AMERICAN   Even though foodies rank it one of the best American restaurants in the city, mk doesn't flaunt its pedigree. The loftlike dining room is as understated as the lowercase initials that give the restaurant its name. Chef/owner Michael Kornick keeps the menu focused on a seasonal mix of meat and seafood: Menu selections range from hearty (roasted duck with baby turnips and fava beans; rack of lamb with lamb-stuffed cannelloni and fig jam) to lighter offerings, such as grilled salmon with a Chinese mustard glaze and ginger-soy vinaigrette. The presentations are tasteful rather than dazzling; Kornick wants you to concentrate on the food, and that's just what the chic, mixed-aged crowd does. Service is disciplined yet agreeable, and fine table appointments signal this restaurant's commitment to quality. As for dessert, the Peanut Gallery (peanut butter mousse, crispy milk chocolate, warm brownies, pretzels, hot fudge and caramel) is worth the calories.

868 N. Franklin St. (1 block north of Chicago Ave.). ⓒ **312/482-9179.** www.mkchicago.com. Reservations recommended. Main courses $27–$46. AE, DC, MC, V. Sun–Thurs 5:30–10pm; Fri–Sat 5:30–11pm. Subway/El: Brown Line to Chicago.

Naha ★★ AMERICAN   Chef Carrie Nahabedian (who used her nickname for the restaurant's name) did time at four-star hotels in California before returning to her hometown, and a West Coast influence is clear in her use of organic, seasonal ingredients. But she adds Mediterranean flavors to the mix, including dishes that reflect her Armenian heritage. Hearty entrees might include roasted squab with foie gras, dates, cherries, and fennel; or salmon topped with a savory mix of mushrooms, fava beans, and celery root. The dessert menu features creative combinations of mini-dishes, such as a tarte of walnuts and maple syrup served with pear slices and walnut ice cream, or the sundae of raisin ice cream, roasted apples, butterscotch, streusel, and star anise shortbread cookies.

The front lounge offers a special menu of meze (Mediterranean "small dishes"), including feta cheese phyllo triangles made from the chef's mother's recipe.

500 N. Clark St. (at Illinois St.). ⓒ **312/321-6242.** www.naha-chicago.com. Reservations recommended. Main courses $13–$26 lunch, $26–$46 dinner. AE, DC, DISC, MC, V. Mon–Thurs 11:30am–2pm and 5:30–9:30pm; Fri 11:30am–2pm and 5:30–10pm; Sat 5:30–10pm. Subway/El: Red Line to Grand.

Zealous ★★★ NEW AMERICAN   One of the most stylish contemporary restaurants in town, Zealous also has one of the most eclectic menus. Chef Michael Taus's cooking combines American dishes with the subtle complexity of Chinese, Vietnamese, Korean, and Indian flavors. You can order a la carte or from one of three degustation

---

Ⓕun Facts   Chicago Treats

Deep-dish pizza may be Chicago's culinary claim to fame, but the city has added to the national waistline in other ways. Twinkies and Wonder Bread were invented here; Chicago businessman James L. Kraft created the first processed cheese; and Oscar Mayer got his start as a butcher in the Old Town neighborhood.

menus; recent entrees have ranged from Asian-inspired (sesame-crusted Chilean sea bass with red coconut-curry sauce) to heartland hearty (roasted pork rack stuffed with dried peaches and served with carrot pierogi). Zealous is especially welcoming to non–meat eaters; there is always a five-course vegetarian menu available, and the kitchen will prepare vegan entrees on request. The dining room is bright and airy (thanks to a central skylight), and the purple chairs, green banquettes, and silver accents add to the vibrant ambience. The 6,000-bottle wine collection and glass-enclosed wine cellar show that Zealous takes its libations as seriously as it takes its food.

419 W. Superior St. ✆ **312/475-9112.** www.zealousrestaurant.com. Reservations recommended. Main courses $19–$39; menu degustation $75–$125. AE, DISC, MC, V. Tues–Sat 5–11pm. Subway/El: Brown Line to Chicago.

EXPENSIVE

Bin 36 ★★ AMERICAN   In one lofty space, this River North hot spot combines wine, food, and retail in a successful, wine-centric concept. You can swirl, sniff, and snack in the Tavern wine bar; sample a tasting menu of artisanal cheeses at the Cheese Bar; or settle down in the main restaurant for a meal of American bistro fare. The menu includes suggested wines for every dish, all of which are available by the glass—and you won't go wrong by following the menu's suggestions. You can also have fun ordering creative "wine flights," small glasses organized around a theme (Italian, Australian, and so on). Entrees include a variety of seafood, along with heavier dishes such as stuffed pork loin or braised rabbit. The food-wine pairings continue on the dessert menu; a recommended sherry along with a slice of gingerbread-pear cake here one evening was a delight.

339 N. Dearborn St. ✆ **312/755-9463.** www.bin36.com. Reservations recommended. Main courses $9–$15 lunch, $17–$28 dinner. AE, DC, DISC, MC, V. Mon–Thurs 11am–midnight; Fri 11am–2am; Sat noon–2am; Sun noon–10pm. Subway/El: Red Line to Grand.

Brasserie Jo ★ ALSATIAN/FRENCH   Brasserie Jo showcases the casual side of chef Jean Joho, whose upscale Everest, p. 98, is one of the city's longtime gourmet destinations. The sprawling dining room with its high ceilings feels like a bustling Art Deco Parisian cafe. Just like the classic Alsatian *brasserie* (brewery), Brasserie Jo offers a malty house brew, along with a good selection of other craft beers. You can order a hearty Alsatian choucroute here, but the menu focuses more on French classics: Chicken coq au

---

> **(Fun Facts**   **McDonald's Gets Glitzy**
>
> I have mixed feelings about recommending a fast-food chain restaurant in this guide, but let's get real: Most visitors (especially if they're here with kids) stop for a greasy fix at some point during their stay. If you're going to go the fast-food route, head for the McDonald's at the corner of Grand Avenue and Clark Street, which was unveiled for the company's 50th anniversary in 2005. The gleaming, glass-enclosed building looks like something out of *The Jetsons,* and it's filled with stylish amenities that would look right at home in a luxury airport lounge. You can chow down while relaxing in a reproduction of Mies van der Rohe's famous Barcelona chair, check out the exhibit of collectible Happy Meal toys from inside a 1960s-style egg chair, or order a cappuccino and gelato at the upstairs cafe.

vin; pork tenderloin ratatouille; rack of lamb; and tartes, the Alsatians' version of thin-crust pizza. One house specialty that's worth a try is the "shrimp bag," a phyllo pastry filled with a rich blend of shrimp, peas, and herb rice garnished with lobster sauce. I also love the rich chocolate mousse, which is served tableside from a massive silver bowl, then topped with fresh cream and shaved chocolate—just like in Paris.

59 W. Hubbard St. (btw. Dearborn and Clark sts.). ✆ 312/595-0800. www.brasseriejo.com. Reservations recommended. Main courses $18–$30. AE, DC, DISC, MC, V. Mon–Thurs 5–10pm; Fri–Sat 5–11pm; Sun 4–9pm. Subway/El: Brown Line to Merchandise Mart or Red Line to Grand.

Crofton on Wells ★★ ⒡inds AMERICAN   This unassuming restaurant is the perfect reflection of chef-owner Suzy Crofton, a place that values substance over style. Though the food is considerably more ambitious than your average neighborhood restaurant, it's served in a no-attitude, laid-back setting. The menu is based on seasonally available ingredients: You might start with a chilled cucumber-and-Vidalia-onion soup in the summer, or a roasted squash soup in colder weather. Entree selections run the gamut from seafood to venison and beef; Crofton's signature dish is the barbecued pork tenderloin garnished with tasty apple chutney. (You can even buy a jar of the chutney to go.) Other chefs may wow the food critics with their spectacular presentations, but Crofton has built her reputation with accessible dishes that attract a low-key crowd of satisfied regulars. A three-course, prix-fixe meal is available Monday through Saturday from 5 to 6pm for $35 ($55 with wine).

535 N. Wells St. (btw. Grand Ave. and Ohio St.). ✆ 312/755-1790. www.croftononwells.com. Reservations recommended. Main courses $28–$35. AE, DC, MC, V. Mon–Sat 5–10pm. Subway/El: Brown Line to Merchandise Mart.

Frontera Grill & Topolobampo ★★★ MEXICAN   Owners Rick and Deann Bayless are widely credited with bringing authentic Mexican regional cuisine to a wider audience, emphasizing the importance of fresh, organic ingredients supplied by local artisanal farmers. Their restaurant actually houses two separate establishments: The casual Frontera Grill (plain wood tables, terra-cotta tile floor) and the fine-dining Topolobampo (white linen tablecloths, a more hushed environment).

At Frontera, it's worth starting with the signature *sopes surtidos* appetizer, corn tortilla "boats" with a sampler of fillings (chicken in red mole, black beans with homemade chorizo, and so on). The ever-changing entree list might include pork loin in a green mole sauce; smoked chicken breast smothered in a sauce of chiles, pumpkin seeds, and roasted garlic; or a classic *sopa de pan* ("bread soup" spiced up with almonds, grilled green onions, and zucchini). At adjacent Topolobampo, both the ingredients and presentation are more upscale.

It can be tough to snag a table at Frontera during prime dining hours, so do what the locals do: Put your name on the list and order a few margaritas in the lively, large bar area.

For an affordable taste of Frontera downtown, stop by **Frontera Fresco,** a counter-service lunch spot on the 7th floor of Macy's, 111 N. State St. (✆ 312/781-4884). You can sample authentic Mexican tortas, quesadillas, and tamales, all priced less than $8; it's open Monday through Saturday from 11am to 4pm.

445 N. Clark St. (btw. Illinois and Hubbard sts.). ✆ 312/661-1434. www.fronterakitchens.com. Reservations strongly recommended for Topolobampo; limited reservations accepted at Frontera Grill. Frontera Grill main courses $21–$28. Topolobampo main courses $32–$38; chef's 5-course tasting menu $75 ($120 with wine pairings). AE, DC, DISC, MC, V. Frontera Grill Tues–Fri 11:30am–2:30pm; Sat 10:30am–2:30pm; Tues–Thurs 5–10pm; Fri–Sat 5–11pm. Topolobampo Tues 11:45am–2pm; Wed–Fri 11:30am–2pm; Tues–Thurs 5:30–9:30pm; Fri–Sat 5:30–10:30pm. Subway/El: Red Line to Grand.

Gene & Georgetti ★ ITALIAN/STEAK A classic vestige of old Chicago, Gene & Georgetti is a family-run steakhouse that's been serving up steak and Italian fare in a wood-frame house in the shadow of the El since 1941. The restaurant is dark and clubby, and the (exclusively male) waiters seem to have worked here for decades—and they no doubt have been serving some of the same patrons all that time. Gene & Georgetti has a popular following, so expect a wait at the bar if you show up on the weekend without a reservation. Although the place is best known for steaks, classic Italian-American specialties are also part of the menu (mostaccioli, veal parmigiana, and the like). This is not the kind of place you come to make the scene, but fans of old-time restaurants will find plenty of local character—some of the regulars have been coming here for half a century.

500 N. Franklin St. (at Illinois St.). © **312/527-3718.** www.geneandgeorgetti.com. Reservations recommended. Main courses $11–$24 lunch, $24–$45 dinner. AE, DC, MC, V. Mon–Thurs 11am–11pm; Fri–Sat 11am–midnight. Subway/El: Brown Line to Merchandise Mart.

Graham Elliot ★★ AMERICAN The chef/owner of this self-named restaurant describes it as the city's first "bistronomic" dining spot. Translation: Creative food served in a down-to-earth setting. The space itself is warm and welcoming, with large windows and exposed-brick walls. Though pop-rock songs play in the dining room and the servers hang out in jeans, the prices are in line with far more elegant spots, making it more of a special-occasion destination than a regular-guy hangout. Entrees might be inspired by down-home American classics (cornbread-crusted scallops with black-eyed peas and ham hock vinaigrette) or showcase a new twist on the standard meat-and-starch combo (such as the rabbit ménage a trios, with chive spaetzle and apricot chutney). Elliot also has been known to toss in far less haute ingredients (such as risotto with crushed Cheez-Its) in a humorous nod to American snack habits.

217 W. Huron St. (btw. Wells and Franklin sts.). © **312/624-9975.** www.grahamelliot.com. Main courses $25–$35. AE, DC, MC, V. Mon–Sat 5–10:30pm. Subway/El: Brown Line to Chicago.

Green Zebra ★ VEGETARIAN Chicago's a red-meat town, but if you need a break from all the beef, it's worth tracking down Green Zebra, about a 10-minute drive west of the River North neighborhood. It's all very restrained, from the minimalist decor to the straightforward food presentation, but executive chef Shawn McClain's flair for flavor and emphasis on fresh ingredients make this an almost gourmet experience. My only complaint is the "small plates" menu: It's hard to know how much food you're getting, and the tab can add up quickly if you're hungry. Still, vegetarians will find a wealth of choices here: Curried potato potstickers with cilantro lime sauce; herbed goat cheese ravioli; and Hawaiian heart of palm with kaffir lime and Thai basil chile. The menu is not strictly vegetarian—you'll find a few chicken and fish dishes—making this a good compromise spot for groups with both meat and non-meat eaters.

1460 W. Chicago Ave. (at Greenview St.). © **312/243-7100.** www.greenzebrachicago.com. Reservations accepted. Appetizer-size courses $8–$17. AE, DC, DISC, MC, V. Mon–Thurs 5:30–10pm; Fri–Sat 5–11pm; Sun 10:30am–2pm and 5–9pm. Bus: 66 (Chicago Ave.), or take a cab.

Nacional 27 ★★ (Finds) SOUTH AMERICAN Part sleek restaurant, part nightclub, Nacional 27 showcases the cuisine of 27 Latin American nations, including Venezuela, Argentina, Costa Rica, and Brazil. Rich walnut and bamboo woods and gauzy curtains lend a tropical air to the grand dining room, which has cozy booth seating and tables arranged around a central dance floor. The innovative drink menu will get you in the mood: You'll find classic mojitos, sangrias, and trendy martini variations. For starters, there are a variety of skewers, ceviches, and empanadas; entrees are divided into steaks, seafood, and "Latin Comfort Foods," which include stick-to-your-ribs selections such as **125** smoked pork tenderloin with mashed Cuban sweet potatoes or tequila-marinated chicken. (Some of the food can be spicy, so ask before you order if you've got sensitive taste buds.) Nacional 27 heats up on Friday and Saturday nights after 10pm, when a DJ spins Latin tunes and couples hit the dance floor.

325 W. Huron St. (btw. Franklin and Orleans sts.). ✆ **312/664-2727.** www.nacional27.net. Reservations recommended. Main courses $15–$28. AE, DC, DISC, MC, V. Dining room Mon–Thurs 5:30–9:30pm; Fri–Sat 5:30–11pm. Bar Mon–Thurs 5–10pm; Fri–Sat 5pm–2am. Subway/El: Brown Line to Chicago.

Osteria Via Stato ★★ (Finds) ITALIAN   An American take on the classic Italian trattoria, Osteria Via Stato delivers top-quality, authentic dishes in a cozy setting. Where it really shines, I think, is with its "Italian Dinner Party" menu: A set price of $39 buys you a full, European-style meal, including a range of antipasto plates, two pastas, and a meat entree. (Recent choices included halibut Milanese with lemon-herb breadcrumbs and braised pork shank with white beans and bacon.) They'll bring you unlimited helpings of everything except the entrees, so come with an appetite. If you're not up for a gut-busting meal, you can also order appetizer-only or appetizer-and-pasta versions, or choose from the a la carte menu. To keep drinks simple, request the "Just Bring Me Wine" program, which matches a glass of wine to each course at three different price levels. The adjacent **Pizzeria Via Stato** serves thin-crust pizzas and is open for lunch.

620 N. State St. (at Ontario St.). ✆ **312/642-8450.** www.osteriaviastato.com. Reservations accepted. Fixed-price dinner $39; entrees $16–$29. AE, DC, DISC, MC, V. Mon–Thurs 5–10pm; Fri–Sat 5–11pm; Sun 5–9:30pm. Subway/El: Red Line to Grand.

SushiSamba Rio ★★ SOUTH AMERICAN/SUSHI   At first glimpse, the menu seems like a gimmick—Latin American ceviche paired with sushi? But it's based on a real culinary tradition: when Japanese immigrants moved to Peru and Brazil in the early 20th century, they combined their native cuisine with South American flavors. I highly recommend the creative "samba rolls": The El Topo (salmon, jalapeño pepper, mozzarella, and crispy onions wrapped in sticky rice) tastes much better than it sounds. A modern take on surf and turf matches seared rare tuna with tender beef filet on a bed of carrot-and-ginger purée, while red snapper (served whole) is livened up with an aromatic red curry sauce and coconut rice. Part of the fun of dining here is the flashy decor, from the colorful, multilevel dining room with its sunken red conversation pit to the Miami Beach–inspired rooftop patio (a great place to sample the creative cocktail menu).

504 N. Wells St. (at Illinois St.). ✆ **312/595-2300.** www.sushisamba.com. Reservations recommended. Main courses $8–$17 lunch, $12–$29 dinner. AE, MC, V. Sun–Tues 11:45am–11pm; Wed–Fri 11:45am–1am; Sat 11:45am–2am; Sun brunch 11:45am–3:30pm. Subway/El: Brown Line to Merchandise Mart or Red Line to Grand.

Tizi Melloul ★ MEDITERRANEAN   An exotic haven in a neighborhood rife with generic theme restaurants, Tizi Melloul creates an *Arabian Nights* fantasy world of rich reds, deep blues, and sparkling metallics. The food is fine, but the real draw here is the decor. In the vibrantly colored, circular Crescent Room, you'll be seated on low banquettes with floor pillows and encouraged to eat with your hands (although they'll bring silverware if you request it). The sultry, red-hued main dining room offers more traditional service, while the stark white lounge is a hangout for the hipster set. For the full experience, order the five-course Crescent Room menu ($35), which includes traditional Moroccan *tagines* (stews) along with tabbouleh and other familiar Mediterranean fare. Eclectic entrees include braised lamb shank with citrus couscous and crispy roast duck flavored with cardamom. For an added dose of exotica, catch a belly dancing performance on Sunday night.

531 N. Wells St. (at Grand St.). © **312/670-4338.** www.tizimelloul.com. Reservations recommended. Main courses $16–$25. AE, MC, V. Sun–Thurs 5–10pm; Fri–Sat 5–11pm. Subway/El: Brown Line to Merchandise Mart or Red Line to Grand.

Vermilion ★ INDIAN/SOUTH AMERICAN Another seemingly wacky fusion concept? The food here is more than just a novelty. Owner Rohini Dey and executive chef Maneet Chauhan—both women, both originally from India—have found a common thread between Indian and Latin American cooking: Both feature similar ingredients (rice and chiles), use some of the same seasonings (cumin and coriander), and even share similar preparations (Latin salsas versus Indian chutneys). The result is a menu that mixes flavors in new ways that still seem somewhat familiar, whether it's empanadas with mango-coconut chutney, ceviche with Indian spices, or tandoori skirt steak served on sautéed garlic spinach with fried plantain. This isn't your usual Taj Mahal–meets-Bollywood Indian decor, either—the sleek white dining room is brightened with red decorative accents and large black-and-white fashion photographs. The lounge is open late for drinks and dessert, served to a soundtrack of Indian and Latin American tunes.

10 W. Hubbard St. (at State St.). © **312/527-4060.** www.thevermilionrestaurant.com. Reservations recommended on weekends. Main courses $18–$33. AE, DC, DISC, MC, V. Mon–Fri 11:30am–2:30pm; Sun–Thurs 5–10pm; Fri–Sat 5–11pm. Lounge until 3am Fri–Sat. Subway/El: Red Line to Grand.

ZED 451 ★★ AMERICAN If you often find yourself staring indecisively at menus because *everything* sounds good, the ZED 451 concept is made for you. Pay a set price ($49 per person), and your meal starts with unlimited trips to the "Harvest Table," a trendy take on the salad bar, with homemade soups, breads, antipasti, and vegetables. Back at your table, and the main course comes to you: Chefs stroll throughout the restaurant, offering appetizer-sized portions of the day's specialties, which could be anything from glazed pork ribs to lamb chops to duck (there are usually at least 10 choices). The space itself is gorgeous, with soaring ceilings and sexy lighting; the extensive use of natural materials (from the stone pillars to the bar's rock garden) give this distinctly urban environment a warm, sultry vibe. Head to the outdoor rooftop deck for an after-dinner drink: The sparkling lights of the high-rises make for a magical setting.

739 N. Clark St. (one block south of Chicago Ave.). © **888/493-3451.** www.zed451.com. Prix-fixe meal $49 per person. AE, DC, DISC, MC, V. Mon–Fri 11:30am–2pm and 5–10pm; Sat 4:30–10pm; Sun Noon–8pm. Subway/El: Brown or Red line to Chicago.

MODERATE

A Mano ★ ITALIAN A Mano's basement location means you won't get great views, but this urban trattoria is spacious and welcoming, with a huge open kitchen as its focal point. The wide-ranging menu offers small plates for nibbling with a glass of wine at the bar, pizzas and salads for light eaters, and traditional Italian three-course dinners if you've got an appetite. The preparations and ingredients are straightforward Italian, but they're combined in creative ways (the rich wild mushroom and carmelized onion pizza, for example, topped with white truffle oil and hazelnuts). The handmade pastas—such as gnocchi served with braised rabbit and rapini—prove that you don't need fancy techniques when you combine the right high-quality ingredients. The high point of a meal here for me is the gelato: Savoring the *nocciola*—a mix of chocolate and hazelnut—was like taking a mini-trip back to Italy.

225 N. Dearborn St. (just south of the Chicago River). © **312/629-3500**. www.amanochicago.com.
Reservations accepted. Main courses $16–$24. AE, DC, MC, V. Mon–Fri 11:30am–2pm and 5–11pm; Sat–
Sun 5–11pm. Subway/El: Red Line to Grand.

Carson's ★ AMERICAN/BARBECUE   A true Chicago institution, Carson's calls itself "The Place for Ribs," but you won't go wrong if you order anything slathered in the restaurant's sweet-and-tangy barbecue sauce. You can get ribs by the full or half slab, or gorge on one of the signature combo plates, which pair ribs with barbecue chicken, pork chops, or shrimp. (There are also entree-sized salads and sandwiches for smaller appetites.) For dinner, there's often a wait, but don't despair: In the bar area, you'll find a heaping mound of some of the best chopped liver around and plenty of cocktail rye to go with it. When you're seated at your table, tie on your plastic bib and indulge. Carson's popularity has led to something of a factory mentality among management, which sometimes herds diners in and out, but the servers are responsive to requests not to be hurried through the meal.

612 N. Wells St. (at Ontario St.). © **312/280-9200**. www.ribs.com. Reservations accepted for groups of 6 or more. Main courses $13–$34. AE, DC, DISC, MC, V. Mon–Thurs 11:30am–10:30pm; Fri 11:30am–11:30pm; Sat noon–11:30pm; Sun noon–10:30pm. Subway/El: Red Line to Grand.

Cyrano's Bistrot & Wine Bar ★ (Value) BISTRO/FRENCH   Warm and welcoming, Cyrano's exudes authentic bistro charm, due in part to the friendly presence of chef Didier Durand and his wife, Jamie. The cheery blue-and-red wood exterior, eclectic artwork, and personal asides on the menu ("Use of cellular phones may interfere with the stability of our whipped cream") signal the owner's hands-on touch. Start with one of Durand's sensationally flavorful soups (the lobster bisque is a highlight) or the frites, served with Dijon mustard, homemade ketchup, and mayonnaise. The house specialties are the rotisserie duck and chicken served with your choice of sauce and classics such as roasted rabbit with mustard sauce and cassoulet. There are also salads and some vegetarian options, but overall this is a place to eat hearty. The restaurant's lower-level cabaret has live entertainment most nights of the week, and in warmer months, a sidewalk cafe is open all day.

546 N. Wells St. (btw. Ohio St. and Grand Ave.). © **312/467-0546**. www.cyranosbistrot.com. Main courses $14–$28. AE, DC, DISC, MC, V. Mon–Fri 11:30am–2:30pm and 5:30–10:30pm; Sat 5:30–10:30pm. Subway/El: Brown Line to Merchandise Mart.

Gino's East ★★ (Kids) PIZZA   Many Chicagoans consider Gino's the city's quintessential deep-dish pizza. (I know transplanted Midwesterners who come for a cheesy fix whenever they're back in town.) True to its reputation, the pizza is heavy (a small cheese pizza is enough for two), so work up an appetite before chowing down. Specialty pizzas include the supreme, stuffed with sausage, onions, green pepper, and mushrooms; and the vegetarian, with onions, peppers, asparagus, summer squash, zucchini, and eggplant. Gino's also offers salads, sandwiches, and pastas. A warning for hungry families: Pizzas are cooked to order, so you'll have to wait about 45 minutes for your food (I highly recommend calling ahead to preorder, which will save you about a half-hour of waiting time, but preorders aren't accepted on Friday or Saturday). If you want to take a pizza home, call a day in advance and Gino's will pack a special frozen pie for the trip.

633 N. Wells St. (at Ontario St.). © **312/943-1124**. www.ginoseast.com. Reservations not accepted. Pizza $12–$29. AE, DC, DISC, MC, V. Mon–Thurs 11am–10pm; Fri–Sat 11am–11pm; Sun noon–9pm. Subway/El: Red Line to Grand.

Breakfast & Brunch

NEAR THE LOOP & MAGNIFICENT MILE

You can get a good (and upscale) breakfast at one of the hotels near the Loop or Magnificent Mile. Favorite spots for business travelers looking to impress include **the Café** at the Four Seasons Hotel, 120 E. Delaware Place ((C) **312/280-8800**), and **Drake Bros. Restaurant** at The Drake Hotel, 140 E. Walton Place at Michigan Avenue ((C) **312/787-2200**).

A more informal choice in the Loop, overlooking the El tracks, is **Heaven on Seven** ★★ (p. 106), where the Cajun and Creole specialties supplement an enormous diner-style menu.

For brunch with some soul, head to **House of Blues,** 329 N. Dearborn St., at Kinzie Street ((C) **312/527-2583;** p. 267), for its popular Sunday gospel brunch. To guarantee seating, it's a good idea to book a spot 2 weeks in advance.

A local breakfast favorite since 1923 is **Lou Mitchell's,** 565 W. Jackson Blvd. ((C) **312/939-3111**), across the south branch of the Chicago River from the Loop, a block farther west than Union Station. You'll be greeted at the door with a basket of doughnut holes and Milk Duds so that you can nibble while waiting for a table.

For a Southern-style breakfast of spicy red eggs, cheese grits, or biscuits and gravy, head over to **Wishbone** ★★ (p. 112), a family-friendly, laid-back spot in a converted warehouse building in the West Loop.

LINCOLN PARK & THE NORTH SIDE

A perfect breakfast or brunch spot if you're heading up to Wrigleyville for a Cubs game or a walk through Lincoln Park is **Ann Sather** ★★ (p. 142), famous for its homemade cinnamon rolls.

The **Nookies** restaurants are Chicago favorites for all the standard morning fare. Locations include 2114 N. Halsted St., in Lincoln Park ((C) **773/327-1400**);

Harry Caray's Italian Steakhouse AMERICAN/ITALIAN/STEAKS   A shrine to the legendary Cubs play-by-play announcer, this landmark building is a repository for Harry's staggering collection of baseball memorabilia. The main dining room, with its high tin ceilings and brick walls, has a certain retro charm, and the food is better than you'd expect from a celebrity restaurant. The menu is a greatest hits list of Italian-American favorites: Mounds of pasta with red sauce; chicken Vesuvio; veal piccata; and a variety of seafood. Harry's is also a good place to order massive plates of meat: Dry-aged steaks, lamb, veal, and pork chops (the Vesuvio potatoes are my top pick as a side dish). If you don't want a full-service meal, the bar is a lively place for watching a game and grabbing some munchies—and, incidentally, the bar is 60 feet, 6 inches long, the same distance from the pitcher's mound to home plate.

33 W. Kinzie St. (at Dearborn St.). (C) **312/828-0966.** www.harrycarays.com. Main courses $15–$40. AE, DC, DISC, MC, V. Mon–Sat 11:30am–3pm; Mon–Thurs 5–10:30pm; Fri–Sat 5–11pm; Sun 11:30am–4pm (bar only) and 4–10pm. Subway/El: Brown Line to Merchandise Mart or Red Line to Grand.

1748 N. Wells St., in Old Town (☎ **312/337-2454**); and 3334 N. Halsted St., in Lakeview (☎ **773/248-9888**).

Go to **Orange,** 3231 N. Clark St., at Belmont (☎ **773/549-4400**), for a fun twist on breakfast foods. Try the Green Eggs and Ham—eggs scrambled with pesto, tomatoes, mozzarella, and pancetta. There's a kids' menu, too, making this a popular choice for families. But a warning to all those with hungry kids (and parents): Come early or late; the line for a table winds outside during prime weekend brunch hours.

Lincoln Park's **Toast,** 746 W. Webster St., at Halsted Street (☎ **773/935-5600**), is homey yet slightly funky, and kids are encouraged to scribble away on the butcher-block table coverings. Breakfast includes a twist on the usual diner fare. Pancakes come in all sorts of tempting varieties, from lemon/poppy seed drizzled with honey to the "pancake orgy," a strawberry, mango, and banana-pecan pancake topped with granola, yogurt, and honey. Come early on weekends, though; by 10:30am or so, there's guaranteed to be a lengthy wait.

WICKER PARK/BUCKTOWN

The brightly colored **Bongo Room,** 1470 N. Milwaukee Ave. (btw. Evergreen Ave. and Honore St.; ☎ **773/489-0690**), is a neighborhood gathering place for the hipsters of Wicker Park/Bucktown, but the restaurant's tasty, creative breakfasts have drawn partisans from all over the city who feel right at home stretching out the morning with a late breakfast. (*A caveat:* Don't bother trekking over here for weekend brunch, when you'll have to wait an hour or more for a table; it's much more pleasant eating here during the week.) The same owners also run **Room 12,** 1152 S. Wabash Ave. (btw. 11th St. and Roosevelt Rd.; ☎ **312/291-0100**), in the South Loop; the food is just as good as at the Wicker Park location, and it tends to be less crowded.

Reza's ★★ Value MIDDLE EASTERN   Reza's doesn't look like the typical Middle Eastern restaurant. Housed in a former microbrewery, it has high ceilings and expansive, loftlike dining rooms, but the Persian-inspired menu will soon make you forget all about beer. Specialties include a deliciously rich chicken in pomegranate sauce and a variety of kabobs with heaps of dill rice (although, in a nod to carb-conscious diners, they'll substitute a salad if you want). If you can't decide what to order, go for an appetizer combo: A generous sampler of Middle Eastern dishes including hummus, stuffed grape leaves, tabbouleh, and other standbys, nicely presented in a red-lacquer bento box. (Despite the menu's meat-heavy emphasis, there's a selection of vegetarian sampler plates, too). Reza's has another location in Andersonville, at 5255 N. Clark St. (☎ **773/561-1898**), but the River North spot is the most convenient for visitors staying downtown.

432 W. Ontario St. (at Orleans St.). ☎ **312/664-4500.** www.rezasrestaurant.com. Main courses $13–$20. AE, DC, DISC, MC, V. Daily 11am–midnight. Subway/El: Red Line to Grand.

Dining Alfresco

Cocooned for 6 months of the year, with furnaces and electric blankets blazing, Chicagoans revel in the warm months of late spring, summer, and early autumn. For locals and visitors alike, dining alfresco is an ideal way to experience the sights, sounds, smells, and social fabric of this multifaceted city. Just be prepared to wait on a nice night, because you'll be fighting a lot of other diners for a coveted outdoor table.

LOOP & VICINITY

Athena ★　This Greektown mainstay offers a stunning three-level outdoor seating area. It's paved with brick and landscaped with 30-foot trees, flower gardens, and even a waterfall. Best of all: An incredible view of the downtown skyline with the Sears Tower right in the middle.

212 S. Halsted St., between Adams and Jackson streets (✆ **312/655-0000**).

Park Grill ★★　Millennium Park's restaurant serves upscale versions of American comfort food with panoramic views of Michigan Avenue. In the summer, you can pick up a sandwich and grab a seat on the large patio (converted into an ice-skating rink come winter). For a review, see p. 102.

11 N. Michigan Ave., at Madison Street (✆ **312/521-PARK** [7275]).

Rhapsody ★★　A tranquil oasis amid the Loop high-rises, Rhapsody's outdoor garden is my top pick for a romantic meal downtown. For more info, see p. 102.

65 E. Adams St., at Wabash Avenue (✆ **312/786-9911**).

MAGNIFICENT MILE & GOLD COAST

Charlie's Ale House at Navy Pier　One of several outdoor dining options along Navy Pier, this outpost of the Lincoln Park restaurant has lip-smacking pub fare and a great location on the southern promenade overlooking the lakefront and Loop skyline.

700 E. Grand Ave., near the entrance to the Pier (✆ **312/595-1440**).

Le Colonial ★★　This lovely French-Vietnamese restaurant, located in a vintage Gold Coast town house and evocative of 1920s Saigon, *does* have a sidewalk cafe, but you'd do better to reserve a table on the tiny second-floor porch, overlooking the street. For a full review, see p. 117.

937 N. Rush St., just south of Oak Street (✆ **312/255-0088**).

Oak Street Beachstro　Suit up and head for this warm-weather-only beachfront cafe—literally on the sands of popular Oak Street Beach—which serves inventive cafe fare (fresh seafood, sandwiches, and pastas). Beer and wine are available.

1000 N. Lake Shore Dr., at Oak Street Beach (✆ **312/915-4100**).

Puck's at the MCA　This cafe—run by celebrity chef Wolfgang Puck—is tucked in the back of the Museum of Contemporary Art, where you'll get a view of the museum's sculpture garden from the terrace. Take in the art, the fresh air, and a shrimp club sandwich, Chinois salad, or wood-grilled pizza. (Restaurant-only patrons can bypass museum admission.)

220 E. Chicago Ave., at Fairbanks Court (✆ **312/397-4034**).

RIVER NORTH

SushiSamba Rio ★★   For stunning nighttime views of the skyline—accompanied by views of some pretty stunning people—head to the rooftop deck of this Latin-Asian fusion spot. Canopied banquettes and flickering tea lights create a sultry atmosphere, along with a menu of specialty cocktails. For a full review, see p. 125.

504 N. Wells St., at Illinois Street (☎ **312/595-2300**).

ZED 451 ★★   You'll find another great rooftop deck on top of this funky all-you-can-eat spot. Here, the mood is less nightclub and more relaxed hangout; the wood decor and laid-back vibe let you imagine you're kicking back at a rich friend's penthouse. See p. 126 for more information.

739 N. Clark St., 1 block south of Chicago Avenue (☎ **888/493-3451**).

LINCOLN PARK

Charlie's Ale House   A true neighborhood hangout, this Lincoln Park pub's wonderful beer garden—surrounded by tall, ivy-covered brick walls—is spacious and buzzing with activity and good vibes.

1224 W. Webster Ave., at Magnolia Avenue (☎ **773/871-1440**).

North Pond ★★★   Set on the banks of one of Lincoln Park's beautiful lagoons, the excellent North Pond serves upscale, fresh-as-can-be American cuisine in a romantic and sylvan setting. *One caveat:* Alcohol is not permitted on the outdoor patio. Also see p. 137.

2610 N. Cannon Dr., halfway between Diversey Parkway and Fullerton Avenue (☎ **773/477-5845**).

O'Brien's Restaurant   Wells Street in Old Town is lined with several alfresco options, but the best belongs to O'Brien's, the unofficial nucleus of neighborhood life. The outdoor patio has teakwood furniture, a gazebo bar, and a mural of the owners' country club on a brick wall. Order the dressed-up chips, a house specialty.

1528 N. Wells St., 2 blocks south of North Avenue (☎ **312/787-3131**).

WRIGLEYVILLE & VICINITY

Arco de Cuchilleros ★   The tapas and sangria at this cozy Wrigleyville restaurant can compete with other, better-known Spanish spots, and the intimate, leafy terrace out back glows with lantern light.

3445 N. Halsted St., at Newport Avenue (☎ **773/296-6046**).

Moody's   For 30 years, Moody's has been grilling some of the best burgers in Chicago. It's ideal in winter for its dark, cozy dining room (warmed by a fireplace), but Moody's is better still in summer for its awesome outdoor patio, a real hidden treasure.

5910 N. Broadway Ave., between Rosedale and Thorndale avenues (☎ **773/275-2696**).

WICKER PARK/BUCKTOWN

Northside Café   On a sunny summer day, Northside seems like Wicker Park's town square, packed with an eclectic mix of locals catching up and checking out the scene. The entire front of the restaurant opens onto the street, making it relatively easy to get an "outdoor" table. For more info, see p. 146.

Located at 1635 N. Damen Ave., just north of North Avenue (☎ **773/384-3555**).

Rockit Bar & Grill ★ AMERICAN   Take your standard American burger joint, give it an upscale makeover, and you've got Rockit. The dining room is a trendy take on traditional tavern decor, where exposed-brick walls and distressed-wood tables combine with metallic accents and chocolate-brown leather booths. The menu is fairly predictable, but a few notches above standard bar fare. The Rockit Burger is a mix of Kobe beef and foie gras, served with french fries cooked in truffle oil, while the wonderfully tender pork medallions have a satisfyingly crunchy crust (I only wish they were served with something more exciting than kale). The Chopped Salad—a signature dish—is a hearty mix of salami, tomatoes, provolone, hot cherry peppers, corn, and egg with balsamic dressing. Rockit is no gourmet destination, but if you're looking to chow down on better-than-decent food in a high-energy setting, Rockit fits the bill. (**_Bonus:_** The waitstaff range from good-looking to gorgeous.)

22 W. Hubbard St. (btw. Wabash and State sts.). ✆ **312/645-6000.** www.rockitbarandgrill.com. Reservations accepted for parties of 6 or more. Main courses $9–$19 lunch, $12–$29 dinner. AE, DC, DISC, MC, V. Sun–Fri 11:30am–1:30am; Sat 11:30am–2:30am. Subway/El: Red Line to Grand.

VTK—Vong's Thai Kitchen ★ THAI   A more casual, affordable version of Chef Jean-Georges Vongerichten's Vong concept, this restaurant highlights Thai specialties, along with a dash of other Asian cuisines. Traditional Thai curries get a kick from nontraditional ingredients (like salmon and scallops), and there's always at least one seafood dish that's been wok-seared for extra flavor and texture. If you've never tried pad thai, the Thai-restaurant staple noodle dish, this is a good place to start—you can even splurge on an upscale version with crab. My favorite option for groups is the three-course family-style meal offered for $25 per person, which lets you sample a little of everything, including mini-desserts (you can do the same thing at lunch for $14 apiece). The creative cocktail menu is heavy on tropical-inspired drinks, not all of them alcoholic. (Treat the kids to a "Pink Elephant," with Sprite, grenadine, and pineapple juice.)

6 W. Hubbard St. (at State St.). ✆ **312/644-8664.** www.vongsthaikitchen.com. Main courses $8–$15 lunch, $14–$20 dinner. AE, DC, DISC, MC, V. Mon–Thurs 11:30am–9:30pm; Fri 11:30am–11pm; Sat noon–11pm; Sun 5–9pm. Subway/El: Red Line to Grand.

INEXPENSIVE

Café Iberico ★★ SPANISH & TAPAS   This no-frills tapas spot won't win any points for style, but the consistently good food and festive atmosphere make it a longtime local favorite for singles in their 20s and 30s. Café Iberico gets very loud, especially on weekends, so it makes a fun group destination—but plan your romantic tête-à-tête elsewhere. Crowds begin pouring in at the end of the workday, so you'll probably have to wait for a table. Not to worry: Order a pitcher of fruit-filled sangria at the bar with everyone else. When you get a table, I'd suggest starting with the _queso de cabra_ (baked goat cheese with fresh tomato-basil sauce), then continue ordering rounds of hot and cold tapas as your hunger demands. A few standout dishes are the vegetarian Spanish omelet, spicy potatoes with tomato sauce, chicken brochette with caramelized onions and rice, and grilled octopus with potatoes and olive oil.

739 N. LaSalle St. (btw. Chicago Ave. and Superior St.). ✆ **312/573-1510.** www.cafeiberico.com. Reservations accepted for parties of 6 or more; no reservations for Fri–Sat dinner. Tapas $4–$7, main courses $7–$10. DC, DISC, MC, V. Mon–Thurs 11am–11:30pm; Fri 11am–1:30am; Sat noon–1:30am; Sun noon–11pm. Subway/El: Red Line to Chicago or Brown Line to Chicago.

Mr. Beef ★ (Finds) FAST FOOD   Calling Mr. Beef a restaurant may be a stretch: The place is basically a sandwich stand, without much atmosphere or room for seating. (The "dining room" has one long communal picnic table.) Despite these drawbacks, Mr. Beef is a much-loved Chicago institution. Its claim to fame is the classic Italian beef sandwich, the Chicago version of a Philly cheese steak. The Mr. Beef variety is made of sliced beef dipped in *jus,* piled high on a chewy bun, and topped with sweet or hot peppers. (You can also get slices of New York–style pizza.) Heavy, filling, and *very* Chicago, Mr. Beef really hops during lunchtime, when dusty construction workers and suit-clad businessmen crowd in for their meaty fix. While you're chowing, check out the celebrity photos and newspaper clippings covering the walls, and you'll see why this place is considered a local monument.

666 N. Orleans St. (at Erie St.). ✆ **312/337-8500.** Sandwiches $6–$8.50. No credit cards. Mon–Thurs 8am–9pm; Fri 8am–5am; Sat 10:30am–3:30pm and 10:30pm–5:30am. Subway/El: Red Line to Grand.

Pizzeria Uno ★ **(Value)** PIZZA   Pizzeria Uno invented Chicago-style pizza, and many deep-dish aficionados still refuse to accept any imitations. Uno's is now a chain of restaurants throughout the country, but come here if you want to taste the original. You can eat in the restaurant itself on the basement level or, weather permitting, on the outdoor patio right off the sidewalk. Salads, sandwiches, and a house minestrone are also available, but let's be honest—the main reason to come here is for the pizza. As with Gino's East (see above), pizzas take about 45 minutes to make, so if you're starving, order an appetizer or salad.

Uno was so successful that the owners opened **Pizzeria Due** in a lovely gray-brick Victorian town house nearby at 619 N. Wabash Ave., at Ontario Street (✆ **312/943-2400**). The menu is exactly the same; the atmosphere just a tad nicer (with more outdoor seating).

29 E. Ohio St. (at Wabash Ave.). ✆ **312/321-1000.** www.unos.com. Reservations not accepted Fri–Sat. Pizza $7–$22. AE, DC, DISC, MC, V. Mon–Fri 11am–1am; Sat 11am–2am; Sun 11am–11pm. Subway/El: Red Line to Grand.

Portillo's ★★ **(Kids)** AMERICAN/FAST FOOD   Although known mostly for its Chicago-style hot dogs, this local chain has a surprisingly well-rounded menu, making it a good, affordable stop for families with varied tastes. At the Portillo's counter you can order from the usual fast food favorites (hot dogs, hamburgers, fries, and the like), although I highly recommend the tasty grilled tuna sandwich. Across the room, the Barnelli's counter serves up a range of pastas and salads; my favorites are the Asian chicken salad and the heartier chicken pecan version, both served with a hunk of chewy, addictive homemade bread. If you're in the mood to indulge, I think the rich chocolate cake is the best in town. Portillo's can get crowded and loud (especially if you're unlucky enough to arrive at the same time as a high school tour group), but it's an authentic Chicago spot, and a major bargain compared to other River North restaurants.

100 W. Ontario St. (at Clark St.). ✆ **312/587-8930.** www.portillos.com. Reservations not accepted. Main courses $4–$9. AE, DC, DISC, MC, V. Sun–Thurs 10am–11pm; Fri–Sat 10am–midnight. Subway/El: Red Line to Grand.

7 LINCOLN PARK & OLD TOWN

Singles and upwardly mobile young families inhabit Lincoln Park, the neighborhood roughly defined by North Avenue on the south, Diversey Parkway on the north, the park on the east, and Clybourn Avenue on the west. In the southeast corner of this area is Old Town, a neighborhood of historic town houses that stretches out from the intersection

WHERE TO DINE

6

LINCOLN PARK & OLD TOWN

Adobo Grill **34**
Alinea **30**
Ann Sather **9**
Arco de Cuchilleros **2**
Arun's **1**
Bamee Noodle Shop **11**
Bistrot Margot **36**
Boka **29**
Café Ba-Ba-Reebal **23**
Charlie's Ale House **18**
Charlie Trotter's **24**
The Chicago Diner **3**
Chicago Pizza &
  Oven Grinder **25**
Edwardo's **15**
Geja's Cafe **26**
Goose Island Brewing
  Company **28**
Karyn's Raw **27**
La Creperie **12**
Mia Francesca **5**
Mon Ami Gabi **21**
Murphy's Red Hots **10**
Nookies **6, 22, 32**
North Pond **17**
O'Brien's Restaurant **35**
Orange **8**
Penny's Noodle Shop **13**
Perennial **31**
Potbelly Sandwich
  Works **20**

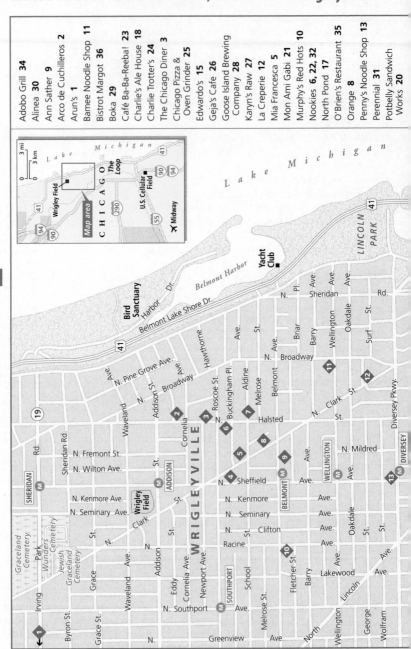

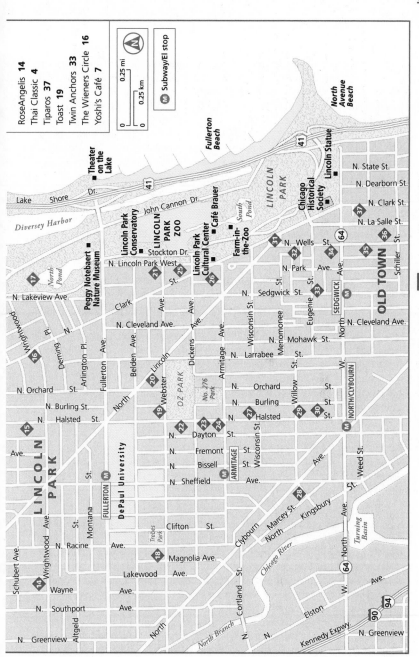

RoseAngelis **14**
Thai Classic **4**
Tiparos **37**
Toast **19**
Twin Anchors **33**
The Wieners Circle **16**
Yoshi's Café **7**

of North Avenue and Wells Street. You'll find a few fine-dining spots, but most restaurants here are more casual, with average prices lower than you'll find in River North or along the Magnificent Mile.

VERY EXPENSIVE

Alinea ★★★ NEW AMERICAN   Alinea—anointed the best restaurant in the country by no less than *Gourmet* magazine—is a place no serious foodie should miss. Like Homaro Cantu at Moto (p. 107), Chef Grant Achatz revolutionizes the way we eat, presenting familiar foods in new contexts and unexpected forms. (He's been known to serve dishes on lavender-scented pillows, so the aroma wafts up as you eat.) The 12- or 24-course fixed menus change constantly, but you're guaranteed to taste something new here, whether it's ravioli with a liquid-truffle filling; Wagyu beef with deconstructed A1 Steak Sauce; or lobster and popcorn served with a cube of enclosed, melted butter. Achatz says he wants diners to feel like they're taking a journey, "zigzagging between challenge and comfort." The restaurant itself is certainly comfortable, with shoulder-high chairs and soft, flattering lighting. Eat with an open mind (and a full wallet), and you'll be well rewarded.

1723 N. Halsted St. (btw. North Ave. and Willow St.). ⓒ **312/867-0110.** www.alinea-restaurant.com. Reservations strongly recommended. Fixed-price menus $145 and $225. AE, DC, DISC, MC, V. Wed–Sun 5:30–9:30pm. Subway/El: Red Line to North/Clybourn.

Charlie Trotter's ★★★ NEW AMERICAN   Charlie Trotter, Chicago's first celebrity chef, still draws foodies after more than 20 years in business by making his place a shrine to creative fine dining. Trotter delights in unfamiliar ingredients and presentations, and prides himself on using only organic or free-range products. There is no a la carte menu; your only choice is to decide between the vegetable ($135) or grand ($155) degustation menu. The entree descriptions signal Trotter's attention to detail; sample dishes include steamed Casco Bay cod with cockles, picholine olives, artichokes, and stinging nettles; and roasted saddle of rabbit with fingerling potatoes, turnips, and mustard greens. The dining room may be formal, but the overall attitude is attentive, not intimidating. A sommelier is on hand to help match wines with each course.

For a taste of Trotter's gourmet fare without the high price tag, check out **Trotter's to Go,** his gourmet food store in Lincoln Park at 1337 W. Fullerton Ave. (btw. Lakewood and Wayne aves.; ⓒ **773/868-6510**).

816 W. Armitage Ave. (at Halsted St.). ⓒ **773/248-6228.** www.charlietrotters.com. Reservations required. Jackets required, ties requested. Fixed-price menus $135 and $155. AE, DC, DISC, MC, V. Seatings Tues–Thurs at 6 and 9pm; Fri–Sat at 5:30 and 9pm. Subway/El: Brown Line to Armitage.

Geja's Cafe ★ FONDUE   A dark, subterranean hideaway, Geja's (pronounced gay-*haz*) regularly shows up on lists of the most romantic restaurants in Chicago. However, the interior might strike some as too gloomy, and the cook-it-yourself technique won't appeal to anyone who wants to be pampered. The best overall option is the Prince Geja's combination dinner, which starts with a Gruyère cheese fondue appetizer. Next, a huge platter arrives, brimming with squares of beef tenderloin, lobster tails, jumbo shrimp, chicken breast, and scallops—all raw—and a caldron of boiling oil to cook them in. These delicacies are accompanied by a variety of raw vegetables and eight different dipping sauces. When the flaming chocolate fondue arrives for dessert, with fresh fruit and pound cake for dipping and marshmallows for roasting, you'll want to beg for mercy. *Caution:* The aroma of cooking oil that fills the restaurant might bother some sensitive noses.

North Pond ★★★ (Finds) AMERICAN   Tucked away in Lincoln Park, north of the zoo, North Pond truly is a hidden treasure. The building's Arts and Crafts–inspired interior blends perfectly with the park outside, and a glass-enclosed addition lets you dine "outside" year-round. In keeping with the natural setting, chef Bruce Sherman emphasizes organic, locally grown ingredients and favors simple preparations—although the overall result is definitely upscale (at these prices, it better be). Examples of seasonal menu items include grass-fed beef with crispy polenta sticks and a garlic-parsley coulis; duck breast with star anise-roasted pineapple and bacon-wrapped broccolini; and grilled sea scallops with orange-Parmesan grain salad and spiced lobster sauce. For dessert, try a plate of artisanal cheeses or dark chocolate mousse with roasted apricots and a hazelnut biscuit. To enjoy the setting with a slightly lower price tag, try the three-course Sunday brunch ($32). The all-American wine list focuses on boutique vintners.

2610 N. Cannon Dr. (south of Diversey Pkwy.). ℂ 773/477-5845. www.northpondrestaurant.com. Reservations recommended. Main courses $32–$39. AE, DC, MC, V. Tues–Sat 5:30–10pm (closed Tues Jan–April); Sun 10:30am–1:30pm and 5:30–10pm. Lunch served June–Sept Tues–Fri 11:30am–2pm. Bus: 151.

EXPENSIVE

Boka ★ AMERICAN   In a neighborhood full of Irish pubs and casual sandwich joints, Boka is a sophisticated, grown-up alternative. The dimly lit dining room manages to be both romantic and dramatic, thanks to the white fabric "sculptures" stretched across the ceiling. The food—described by the owners as "progressive American"—combines upscale ingredients in creative ways, such as herbed salmon with passion fruit-basil vinaigrette or chicken breast topped with foie gras sauce. The desserts, which look like miniature modern art arrangements, offer a similar mix of flavors, such as a dark chocolate ice cream served with sesame cookies and roasted pineapple. Boka is a good place to grab dinner before a show at the nearby Steppenwolf Theatre, but make a reservation first. Aesthetically, Boka's main claim to fame is its cellphone booth, where diners are encouraged to make calls in private. Now that's an idea I hope catches on.

1729 N. Halsted St. (btw. North Ave. and Willow St.). ℂ 312/337-6070. www.bokachicago.com. Reservations recommended on weekends. Main courses $24–$32. AE, MC, V. Daily 5–11pm. Subway/El: Red Line to North/Clybourn.

Mon Ami Gabi ★ BISTRO/FRENCH   This "French steakhouse" concept seduces with its aromatic bistro atmosphere, tasty steak preparations, and rolling cart of wines by the glass ("Gabi" refers to executive chef Gabino Sotelino). There are numerous classic starters and hot seafood appetizers, such as plump mussels steamed in white ale, pâtés, and cheeses, and the simple-but-impeccably-executed entrees include chicken paillard (a crusty, pounded chicken breast in lemon butter) and trout Grenobloise (pan-seared trout in caper butter with a sprinkle of croutons). Steak frites can be customized with maître d'hotel butter, au poivre, Roquefort, or bordelaise (with caramelized onions in mushroom-and-red-wine sauce). Numerous seafood entrees, a section of seasonal specialties, and sides along the lines of whipped cauliflower and ratatouille round out the menu. For the full Gabi experience, don't skip dessert: The bananas foster crepe or profiteroles topped with warm fudge are the perfect ending to a French meal.

2300 N. Lincoln Park W. (at Belden Ave.). ✆ **773/348-8886.** www.monamigabi.com. Reservations recommended. Main courses $15–$30. AE, DC, DISC, MC, V. Mon–Thurs 5:30–10pm; Fri–Sat 5–11pm; Sun 5–9pm. Bus: 151.

Perennial ★★ AMERICAN   In a neighborhood stocked with bars and casual diners, this elegant charmer stands out for both its airy look and its fresh, seasonal preparations. The light-filled dining room juxtaposes sleek wood furniture and vibrant blue banquettes with rustic materials (from the flagstones lining the entryway to the "wall" of trees in the middle of the room). The result is a relaxed space that attracts young singles and couples from the neighborhood, many of whom fill the outdoor patio overlooking Lincoln Park (unfortunately, it also overlooks busy, traffic-filled Clark Street). The menu includes a range of meat, pastas, and seafood, from duck breast with herb bread pudding to grilled Amish chicken with cranberries and homemade cannelloni topped with a roasted red pepper sauce. In a nod to its urban-cool clientele, there's also an extensive list of specialty cocktails: The house version of a Bellini is jazzed up with passion fruit puree.

1800 N. Lincoln Ave. (at Clark St.). ✆ **312/981-7070.** www.perennialchicago.com. Main courses $14–$25. AE, DC, MC, V. Daily 5–11pm; Sat–Sun 10am–2pm. Bus: 22 (Clark St.)

MODERATE

Adobo Grill MEXICAN   A cut above the average taco joint, Adobo Grill showcases the flavors of Mexico in a bright, contemporary setting. Adobo Grill's signature dish is the fresh guacamole prepared tableside. (You choose the spice level, but be warned that even the "medium" will give your tongue a jolt.) Entrees include an achiote-marinated pork chop with black beans, pickled purple onions, and chiltomate salsa; and a hearty casserole of chile guajillo-braised beef tenderloin tips with potatoes. Before ordering a margarita or one of the 60 sipping tequilas, consider a refreshing Michelada (your choice of beer with lime juice in a chile- and salt-dusted glass). Although the busy bar is a singles' hangout, families are a regular part of the restaurant's clientele; there's even a kids' menu.

There's a second location in the up-and-coming West Division shopping district, at 2005 W. Division St. (at N. Damen Ave.; ✆ **773/252-9990**).

1610 N. Wells St. (at North Ave.). ✆ **312/266-7999.** www.adobogrill.com. Reservations recommended. Main courses $13–$20. AE, DC, MC, V. Mon–Thurs 5:30–10pm; Fri 5:30–11:30pm; Sat 11am–11:30pm; Sun 11am–9:30pm. Bus: 22, 36, or 156.

Bistrot Margot ★★ ⓕ Finds BISTRO/FRENCH   This family-owned-and-operated restaurant is not only one of the best in Old Town, it's also one of the top bistros in Chicago. The tables are quite close together, but, for many, the room's noisy bustle adds to its charm, giving the place the feel of an authentic Parisian cafe. Starters include out-of-this-world mussels in white wine with fresh herbs; escargots in garlic butter; and country-style pâté. The well-prepared French staples (roasted chicken with garlic and lemon; coq au vin; rack of lamb with Dijon mustard; steak frites) are proof that, when done right, it's hard to beat classic bistro cuisine. On warm nights, the restaurant sets about half a dozen tables on the sidewalk, which, on this busy stretch of Wells Street, makes for a truly memorable meal.

1437 N. Wells St. (at W. Schiller St.). ✆ **312/587-3660.** www.bistrotmargot.com. Reservations recommended. Main courses $16–$26. AE, DISC, MC, V. Mon 11:30am–9pm; Tues–Thurs 11:30am–10pm; Fri 11:30am–11pm; Sat 10:30am–11pm; Sun 10:30am–9pm. Subway/El: Red Line to Clark/Division, or Brown Line to Sedgwick.

Café Ba-Ba-Reeba! ★ SPANISH & TAPAS   One of the city's first tapas restaurants, Café Ba-Ba-Reeba! is still going strong decades later. The clientele at this vibrantly colored spot tends to be young and comes to the restaurant in groups, so be prepared: Loud conversations and tipsy toasts over pitchers of sangria may surround you. Café Ba-Ba-Reeba! isn't breaking any new ground with its menu, but tapas lovers will see plenty of favorites, including garlic potato salad, roasted eggplant salad with goat cheese, beef and chicken empanadas, and roasted dates wrapped in bacon (which have been a popular menu item for years). The menu has also been updated with miniversions of more upscale fare, including a spicy devil's lobster tail dish, a cured pork lomo with frisee salad, and a flavorful plate of seared Spanish sausages. Got a heartier appetite? Dig into an entree-size portion of paella.

2024 N. Halsted St. (at Armitage Ave.). ✆ **773/935-5000.** www.cafebabareeba.com. Reservations recommended on weekends. Tapas $4–$13, main courses $9–$30. AE, DC, DISC, MC, V. Mon–Thurs 5–10pm; Fri 5pm–midnight; Sat 11am–midnight; Sun 11am–10pm. Subway/El: Red or Brown line to Fullerton, or Brown Line to Armitage.

Twin Anchors ★ BARBECUE   A landmark in Old Town since 1932, Twin Anchors manages to maintain the flavor of old Chicago. It's a friendly, family-owned pub with Frank Sinatra songs on the jukebox and pictures of Ol' Blue Eyes on the walls (he apparently hung out here on swings through town in the 1960s). But rather than striking a self-consciously retro pose, this feels like the real deal, with a long mahogany bar up front and a modest dining room in back with red Formica-topped tables crowded close. Of course, you don't need anything fancy when the ribs—the fall-off-the-bone variety—come this good. The only downside to Twin Anchors' longtime success is that you'll probably have a long wait on weekends. Ribs and other entrees come with coleslaw and dark rye bread, plus your choice of baked potato, tasty fries, and the even-better crisp onion rings. For dessert, there's a daily cheesecake selection.

1655 N. Sedgwick St. (1 block north of North Ave.). ✆ **312/266-1616.** www.twinanchorsribs.com. Reservations not accepted. Sandwiches $6–$9; main courses $11–$24. AE, DC, DISC, MC, V. Mon–Thurs 5–11pm; Fri 5pm–midnight; Sat noon–midnight; Sun noon–10:30pm. Subway/El: Brown Line to Sedgwick.

INEXPENSIVE

Goose Island Brewing Company AMERICAN   Some of the best beer in Chicago is produced at this microbrewery on the western edge of Old Town. Goose Island produces about 100 varieties of lagers and ales, which means you're pretty much obligated to taste-test a few while you're here. (You can order 6-oz. samplers if you're not up for a full pint.) The food here is far more than an afterthought: Cut-above bar food includes an excellent burger topped with Stilton cheese; a tasty tilapia po' boy, and organic rotisserie chicken. Don't skip the side dishes, either; the homemade potato chips and doughy Bavarian pretzels are both deliciously addictive. While the loftlike, exposed-brick main room attracts mostly groups of 20- and 30-somethings, there's also a separate dining area that's a popular Sunday brunch spot for families. Goose Island also has a more sports-oriented location near Wrigley Field, at 3535 N. Clark St. (✆ **773/832-9040**).

1800 N. Clybourn Ave. (at Willow St.). ✆ **312/915-0071.** www.gooseisland.com. Reservations accepted. Sandwiches $9–$12; main courses $10–$14. AE, DC, DISC, MC, V. Sun–Thurs 11am–1am; Fri–Sat 11am–2am. Subway/El: Brown Line to Armitage.

La Creperie ★★ (Finds) FRENCH   Germain and Sara Roignant have run this intimate cafe since 1972, never straying from the reasonably priced crepes that have won them a loyal following. The decor is heavy on '70s-era brown, but if you find the main

---

ⓕ Finds   A Taste of Thai

Thai restaurants are to Chicago what Chinese restaurants are to many other American cities: Ubiquitous, affordable, and perfect for a quick meal that offers a taste of the exotic. If you've never tried Thai, Chicago is a great place to start. Good introductory dishes are pad thai noodles topped with minced peanuts or the coconut-based mild yellow curry.

Arun's (p. 141) is the city's reigning gourmet interpreter of Thai cuisine, but many other low-key places are scattered throughout the residential neighborhoods. Most entrees at these spots don't cost much more $10. A staple of the River North dining scene is the bright and airy **Star of Siam**, 11 E. Illinois St., at North State Street (ⓒ **312/670-0100**). In Old Town, **Tiparos**, 1540 N. Clark St. at North Avenue (ⓒ **312/712-9900**), is a very friendly place that features Thai textiles on its brick interior walls and serves delicious specialties such as mussaman curry. **Thai Classic**, 3332 N. Clark St., at Roscoe Street (ⓒ **773/404-2000**), conveniently located between the busy Belmont/Clark intersection and Wrigley Field, offers an excellent all-you-can-eat buffet on weekends. While wandering the Lakeview neighborhood, a good stop for a quick, no-frills meal is the **Bamee Noodle Shop**, 3120 N. Broadway Ave., at Wellington Street (ⓒ **773/281-2641**), which offers a wide selection of "Noodles on Plates" and "Noodles in Bowls," as well as a number of soups and fried-rice combinations.

---

dining room too dark, head to the back patio (enclosed in colder months), which sparkles with strings of white lights. Onion soup, pâté, and escargots are all good starters, but the highlights here are the whole-wheat crepes—prepared on a special grill that Germain imported from his native Brittany. Single-choice fillings include cheese, tomato, egg, or ham; tasty duets feature chicken and mushroom or broccoli and cheese. But I'd suggest going with the richer fillings, such as beef bourguignon, coq au vin, or curried chicken, for the best overall flavor. Don't leave without sharing one of the dessert crepes, which tuck anything from apples to ice cream within their warm folds.

2845 N. Clark St. (half-block north of Diversey Pkwy.). ⓒ **773/528-9050**. www.lacreperieusa.com. Reservations accepted for groups of 6 or more. Main courses $5–$14. AE, DC, DISC, MC, V. Tues–Fri 11:30am–11pm; Sat 11am–11pm; Sun 11am–9:30pm. Subway/El: Brown Line to Diversey.

Potbelly Sandwich Works Ⓥ Value FAST FOOD It doesn't matter what time I stop by Potbelly; there's invariably a line of 20- and 30-somethings waiting to get their fix. (Good thing the counter staff is so fast!) Yes, there's a potbelly stove inside, along with other Old West saloon-type memorabilia, but fans come here for the grilled sub sandwiches (that's all they serve). Prepared on homemade rolls stuffed with your choice of turkey, Italian meats, veggies, pizza ingredients, and more, they're warmed in a countertop toaster oven. Even with all the fixins, each is under $5 (unlike the massive subs found at other spots, Potbelly's are the size of normal sandwiches). Though this is the original, Potbelly has close to 30 locations throughout the city, including 190 N. State St. (ⓒ **312/683-1234**) and in the Westfield North Bridge shopping center, 520 N. Michigan Ave. (ⓒ **312/664-1008**), both of which are convenient to the Loop and Mag Mile.

tions not accepted. Sandwiches $3.50–$5.50. MC, V. Daily 11am–11pm. Subway/El: Brown or Red line to
Fullerton.

RoseAngelis ★★ Ⓥⁿⁱᵘᵉ ITALIAN What keeps me coming back to RoseAngelis
when there's not exactly a shortage of Italian restaurants in this city? The reliably good
food, warm ambience, and reasonable prices—this is neighborhood dining at its best.
Hidden on a Lincoln Park side street, the restaurant extends through a series of cozy
rooms and garden patio. The menu emphasizes pasta. (My favorites are the rich lasagna
and the ravioli al Luigi, served with a sun-dried-tomato cream sauce.) While RoseAngelis is not a vegetarian restaurant per se, there's no red meat on the menu, and many of
the pastas are served with vegetables rather than meat. Finish up with the deliciously
decadent bread pudding with warm caramel sauce, one of my favorite desserts in the city
(and big enough to share). I suggest stopping by on a weeknight to avoid the crowds
(who wait up to 2 hr. for a table on weekends).

1314 W. Wrightwood Ave. (at Lakewood Ave.). © **773/296-0081.** www.roseangelis.com. Reservations
accepted for parties of 8 or more. Main courses $10–$16. DISC, MC, V. Tues–Thurs 5–10pm; Fri–Sat
5–11pm; Sun 4:30–9pm. Subway/El: Brown or Red line to Fullerton.

---

8 WRIGLEYVILLE & THE NORTH SIDE

For restaurants listed in this section, see the map "Where to Dine in Lincoln Park, Old Town & Wrigleyville"
on p. 134.

The area surrounding Wrigley Field has a long history as a working-class neighborhood,
and although housing prices are now beyond the reach of most blue-collar workers, the
neighborhood still attracts hordes of recent college grads who prefer chicken wings to
truffles. Overall, restaurants here are more affordable and low-key than downtown,
though most aren't worth a special trip if you're staying elsewhere. Throughout the North
Side—a catchphrase encompassing the neighborhoods north of Lincoln Park—you'll
find mostly casual, neighborhood restaurants and a good range of ethnic eats.

VERY EXPENSIVE

Arun's ★★★ THAI Yes, Arun's is a Thai restaurant, but it's in a whole different
league from the noodle shops scattered around the city. Here, chef/owner Arun Sampanthavivat prepares a refined version of traditional Thai cuisine: Authentic, flavorful, and
beautifully presented. The 12-course chef's menu is your only option here, and the dishes
vary night to night. (If guests in your group have different tolerances to spicy food, they'll
customize each plate accordingly.) You might see courses of delicate dumplings accented
with edible, carved dough flowers; a salad of bitter greens and peanuts with green papaya,
tomatoes, chiles, and sticky rice; or a medley of clever curries, including a surprisingly
delightful sea-bass-and-cabbage sour curry. The service is as impeccable as the food. The
only downside to Arun's is its out-of-the-way location. You can get here by public transportation, but I recommend a taxi at night.

4156 N. Kedzie Ave. (at Irving Park Rd.). © **773/539-1909.** www.arunsthai.com. Reservations required
with credit card. 12-course chef's menu $85. AE, DC, DISC, MC, V. Tues–Thurs 5–10pm; Fri–Sat 5–10:30pm.
Subway/El and bus: Brown Line to Irving Park, and then transfer to westbound bus 80, or take a cab.

Yoshi's Café BISTRO   Yoshi Katsumura is a familiar name in the Chicago restaurant scene, and this casual bistro has been a neighborhood favorite for more than 2 decades (meaning you may wait for a table during prime weekend hours). The pastel decor brings to mind a hotel coffee shop, but the menu is an intriguing mix of Yoshi's native Japan and his French training. Spring rolls come filled with chicken, mushrooms, and goat cheese, while a leek-and-brie tart is livened up with shiitake mushrooms. Vegetable and shrimp tempura show up on the entree list side by side with steak frites au poivre and grilled duck breast. There are always a number of vegetarian options, from pasta to grilled tofu with brie and basil, topped with sweet-sesame paste and miso sauce. While the food is certainly a draw, it's the friendly, personal service that has turned many Wrigleyville residents into regulars.

3257 N. Halsted St. (at Aldine St.). *©* **773/248-6160.** www.yoshiscafe.com. Reservations recommended. Main courses $15–$27. AE, DC, MC, V. Tues–Thurs 5–10:30pm; Fri–Sat 5–11pm; Sun 11am–2:30pm and 5–9:30pm. Subway/El: Brown or Red line to Belmont.

MODERATE

Mia Francesca ★★ ITALIAN   Though it's been open since 1992, Mia Francesca remains a hot dining spot—with more than 10 sister restaurants throughout the city and suburbs. The restaurant's clean, modern take on the Italian trattoria concept attracts lots of local singles and couples, and the affordable prices keep them coming back. The food—unpretentious but never dull—includes a range of homemade pastas, thin-crust pizzas, chicken, and standout seafood (even if you don't usually order fish in an Italian restaurant). Tables are close together, so you can't help eavesdropping on your neighbors—and checking out their food. It gets loud, but the place has an undeniable energy.

Other Francesca's locations in the city include: **Francesca's on Taylor,** 1400 W. Taylor St., in Little Italy (*©* **312/829-2828**), and **Francesca's Bryn Mawr,** 1039 W. Bryn Mawr Ave., north of Wrigleyville (*©* **773/506-9261**). Another spin-off in Wicker Park, **Francesca's Forno** (p. 144) specializes in pizza and other grilled dishes.

3311 N. Clark St. (1½ blocks north of Belmont Ave.). *©* **773/281-3310.** www.miafrancesca.com. Reservations recommended. Main courses $13–$27. AE, MC, V. Sun–Thurs 5–10pm; Fri–Sat 5–11pm; Sat–Sun 11:30am–2pm. Subway/El: Brown or Red line to Belmont.

INEXPENSIVE

Ann Sather ★★ AMERICAN/BREAKFAST/BRUNCH/SWEDISH   This is a real Chicago institution, with an old-fashioned diner look to match. You can't go wrong ordering one of the Swedish specialties—such as meatballs with buttered noodles and brown gravy, or the Swedish sampler of duck breast with lingonberry glaze, meatball, potato-sausage dumpling, sauerkraut, and brown beans—but there are plenty of American choices, too, from catfish and crab cakes to pork chops and shepherd's pie. Sather's popular (and very affordable) weekend brunch can get frenzied, but you should be okay if you arrive before 11am. The restaurant's sticky cinnamon rolls are definitely a highlight. (If you crave more—and I always do—you can buy them at a counter up front on your way out.) Sather's attracts a truly diverse crowd, and the people-watching at brunch is especially priceless: A cross section of gay and straight, young and old, from club kids to elderly couples and families.

There are smaller cafes with similar menus at 3411 N. Broadway Ave. (*©* **773/305-0024**) and 3416 N. Southport Ave. (*©* **773/404-4475**).

929 W. Belmont Ave. (btw. Clark St. and Sheffield Ave.). © **773/348-2378.** www.annsather.com. Reservations accepted for parties of 6 or more. Main courses $6–$12. AE, DC, MC, V. Mon–Fri 7am–3pm; Sat–Sun 7am–4pm. Free parking with validation. Subway/El: Brown or Red line to Belmont.

Penny's Noodle Shop ★ Value ASIAN/THAI   Penny Chiamopoulous, a Thai native, has assembled a concise menu of delectable dishes, all of them fresh and made to order—and all at great prices. The two dining rooms are clean and spare; single diners can usually find a seat along the bar that wraps around the grill. The Thai spring roll, filled with seasoned tofu, cucumber, bean sprouts, and strips of cooked egg, makes a refreshing starter. Of course, noodles unite everything on the menu, so your main decision is choosing among the options (crispy wide rice, rice vermicelli, Japanese udon, and so on) served in a soup or spread out on a plate. There are several barbecued pork and beef entrees, and plenty of vegetarian options.

The original Penny's, under the El tracks at 3400 N. Sheffield Ave., near Wrigley Field (© **773/281-8222**), is smaller and often has long waits. You stand a better chance of scoring a table at the Diversey Avenue location or the one in Wicker Park at 1542 N. Damen Ave. (at W. Pierce Ave.; © **773/394-0100**).

950 W. Diversey Ave. (at Sheffield St.). © **773/281-8448.** Reservations not accepted. Main courses $5.50–$8.50. MC, V. Sun–Thurs 11am–10pm; Fri–Sat 11am–10:30pm. Subway/El: Brown Line to Diversey.

9 WICKER PARK/BUCKTOWN

The booming Wicker Park/Bucktown area followed closely on the heels of Lincoln Park and Wrigleyville in the race to gentrification. First came the artists and musicians, followed by armies of yuppies and young families—all attracted by cheap rents and real estate. The result is a well-established, happening scene, which includes some of the city's hippest restaurants and clubs. Get yourself to the nexus of activity at the intersection of North, Damen, and Milwaukee avenues, and you won't have to walk more than a couple of blocks in any direction to find a hot spot. Cab fares from downtown are reasonable, or you can take the El's Blue Line to Damen.

EXPENSIVE

Mirai Sushi ★★ JAPANESE/SUSHI   Blending a serious devotion to sushi and sake with a decidedly youthful, funky-chic ambience, Mirai is a hot destination for cold raw fish (though it serves other Japanese fare as well). The futuristic second-floor sake lounge is the hippest place in town to slurp down sushi, chilled sakes, and "red ones," the house cocktail of vodka with passion fruit, lime, and cranberry juices. The bright main-floor dining room offers a comparatively traditional environment. Fish is flown in daily for the sushi bar, where several chefs are hard at work master-crafting a lovely list of offerings— from the beginner sushi standards such as California rolls and *ebi* (boiled shrimp) to escalating classifications of tuna, three additional shrimp varieties, five types of salmon, a half-dozen varieties of fresh oysters, and a tantalizing list of four caviars (in addition to the four roes offered).

2020 W. Division St. (at Damen Ave.). © **773/862-8500.** www.miraisushi.com. Reservations recommended on weekends. Sushi $2–$6 per piece. AE, DC, DISC, MC, V. Mon–Wed 5–10pm; Thurs–Sat 5–11pm. Upstairs lounge until 2am. Subway/El: Blue Line to Division.

Spring ★★★ AMERICAN   Chef Shawn McClain is one of Chicago's culinary celebrities, and Spring—his first restaurant—is an oasis of Zen tranquillity in soothing, neutral colors. Diners step down into a dining room hidden from the street, sink into the banquettes that zigzag across the center of the room, and concentrate on the food. Unlike other chefs who feel pressured to keep outdoing themselves, McClain sticks to a focused menu with a heavy emphasis on seafood and Pan-Asian preparations. Choices change seasonally but might include New Zealand snapper with lemon couscous and fennel salad; or braised baby monkfish and escargots with roasted eggplant in smoked tomato bouillon. Beef short-rib pot stickers spiced up with Korean seasonings stand out among the non-fish options. Desserts also go the Asian route, focusing on seasonal fruits, although the coconut mochi brûlée with warm pineapple puts a whole new twist on rice pudding.

2039 W. North Ave. (at Milwaukee Ave.). ☏ **773/395-7100**. www.springrestaurant.net. Reservations recommended. Main courses $22–$36. AE, DC, DISC, MC, V. Tues–Thurs 5:30–9:30pm; Fri–Sat 5:30–10:30pm; Sun 5:30–9pm. Subway/El: Blue Line to Damen.

MODERATE

Club Lucky ★ (Value) ITALIAN   Club Lucky is the 21st century recreation of a '50s-era corner tavern, with an Italian mamma cooking up family recipes in the back. The Naugahyde banquettes and Formica-topped bar and tables give the place a fun retro flair. The scene here changes throughout the evening: Young families gradually give way to stylish couples posing with glasses of the restaurant's signature martinis. (Be prepared to wait on weekends.) The giant calamari appetizer will almost certainly keep you in leftover land for a day or two. The menu offers real Italian home-style cooking such as *pasta e fagioli* (thick macaroni-and-bean soup—really a kind of stew); rigatoni with veal meatballs, served with steamed escarole and melted slabs of mozzarella; or the spicy grilled boneless pork chops served with peppers and roasted potatoes. The lunch menu includes about a dozen Italian sandwiches, such as scrambled eggs and pesto, meatball, and Italian sausage.

1824 W. Wabansia Ave. (1 block north of North Ave., btw. Damen and Ashland aves.). ☏ **773/227-2300**. www.clubluckychicago.com. Reservations accepted for parties of 6 or more. Sandwiches $8–$11; main courses $10–$36. AE, DC, DISC, MC, V. Mon–Tues 11:30am–10pm; Wed–Thurs 11:30am–11pm; Fri 11:30am–midnight; Sat 5pm–midnight; Sun 4–10pm; cocktail lounge later. Subway/El: Blue Line to Damen.

Francesca's Forno ★ ITALIAN   A spin-off of the popular local Francesca's chain (see **Mia Francesca,** p. 142), this Wicker Park spot has the relaxed vibe of a neighborhood hangout, with rustic wood tables and large windows overlooking the action outside. The "Forno" refers to the many grilled dishes on the menu, from an appetizer of roasted red beets with Gorgonzola and toasted walnuts to the roasted half chicken with Italian sausage, onions, peppers, and garlic. The pizzas are standouts, with crispy, not-quite-charred crusts and straightforward-but-tasty toppings. Pastas are mostly traditional (spaghetti carbonara; ricotta-filled ravioli topped with tomato-basil sauce), and meat dishes include a double-cut pork chop wrapped in bacon and pepper-crusted beef tenderloin served with mascarpone polenta. But diners can also take a small-plates approach, ordering a selection of antipasti, salumi, and cheese plates. There's also a children's menu—proof that Francesca's Forno is more about eating than posing.

1576 N. Milwaukee Ave. (at North Ave.). ☏ **773/770-0184**. www.miafrancesca.com/restaurants/forno. Reservations recommended on weekends. Main courses $14–$24. AE, DC, MC, V. Mon–Thurs 11:30am–10:30pm; Fri 11:30am–11:30pm; Sat 10am–3pm and 4–11:30pm; Sun 10am–3pm and 4–10:30pm. Subway/El: Blue Line to Damen.

Bongo Room **10**

Club Lucky **5**

Francesca's Forno **9**

Hot Chocolate **3**

Jane's **2**

Le Bouchon **1**

Mirai Sushi **11**

Northside Café **6**

Piece **8**

Silver Cloud **4**

Spring **7**

Hot Chocolate ★ AMERICAN   Owner Mindy Segal built her reputation as a pastry chef, so no matter what you order here, make sure you save room for dessert. Though it has the sleek, contemporary look of a late-night lounge, the menu focuses on comfort food prepared with upscale, seasonal ingredients. The tuna melt, for example, comes with wild capers, havarti cheese, and homemade ciabatta bread, while the rich short rib is served with bleu cheese spaetzle and spiced carrot puree. There's also a wide selection of specialty ales, lagers, and wines aimed at late-night diners. However, desserts are the main event here. Many use seasonal fruit (like the apple cider potpie, or the napoleon of cara-melized bananas and graham crackers), but chocoholics can get their fill, too, with dishes such as the rich chocolate soufflé with caramel ice cream. In the winter, finish up with a flight of mini hot chocolates served with homemade marshmallows.

1747 N. Damen Ave. (at Willow St.). ✆ **773/489-1747.** www.hotchocolatechicago.com. Reservations not accepted. Main courses $10–$13 lunch, $16–$30 dinner. AE, MC, V. Tues 5:30–10pm; Wed 11:30am–2pm and 5:30–10pm; Thurs 11:30am–2pm and 5:30–11pm; Fri 11:30am–2pm and 5:30pm–midnight; Sat 10am–2pm and 5:30pm–midnight; Sun 10am–2pm and 5:30–10pm. Subway/El: Blue Line to Damen.

Jane's ★ (Finds) AMERICAN   Jane's may be overlooked by dining critics, but that does not mean snagging a table at this cozy charmer is easy. On the contrary: This is a hugely popular destination among Wicker Park/Bucktown locals, who'd prefer to keep it a secret. (Wait for your table at Bucktown Pub across the street.) Ensconced in an old house, Jane's encompasses two distinct dining rooms—the first with simple wood tables running parallel to the front bar; and a brighter back room, where the white furniture and floors create the feel of an elegant ice-cream parlor. (In the summer, a few tables are set up on an outside patio.) The dinner menu offers upscale comfort food, including both meat (duck breast pan-seared with turnips and peaches; Mediterranean seafood risotto) and vegetarian options (goat cheese, tofu, and veggie burrito). Creative sandwich options are offered at lunch, such as seared halibut topped with tarragon aioli.

1655 W. Cortland St. (1 block west of Ashland Ave.). ✆ **773/862-5263.** www.janesrestaurant.com. Res-ervations recommended, but only a small number are accepted for each evening. Main courses $14–$25. MC, V. Mon–Thurs 11am–3pm and 5–10pm; Fri 11am–3pm and 5–11pm; Sat 10am–11pm; Sun 10am–10pm. Subway/El: Blue Line to Damen.

Le Bouchon ★★ (Finds) BISTRO/FRENCH   Jean-Claude Poilevey's tiny storefront restaurant, Le Bouchon, is popular for both its intimate yet boisterous atmosphere and affordable authentic bistro fare. Whatever the season, the food here is fairly heavy, although specials are lighter in warmer months. Poilevey could pack this place every night with just regulars addicted to the house specialty of roast duck for two, bathed in Grand Marnier–orange marmalade sauce. The fare covers bistro basics, with authentic, tasty versions of steak frites, sautéed rabbit in white wine sauce, veal kidneys in mustard sauce, and bouillabaisse, most affordably priced at less than $20. The piped-in music and voices from the closely packed tables create an atmosphere that some perceive as conviv-ial, and others as claustrophobic and noisy. There's a small bar where you can wait—something you might have to do even if you have a reservation.

1958 N. Damen Ave. (at Armitage Ave.). ✆ **773/862-6600.** www.lebouchonofchicago.com. Reservations recommended. Main courses $17–$23. AE, DC, DISC, MC, V. Mon–Thurs 5:30–11pm; Fri–Sat 5pm–mid-night. Subway/El: Blue Line to Damen, and then a short cab ride.

INEXPENSIVE

Northside Café AMERICAN   Among the best cheap eats in the neighborhood, Northside cooks up great burgers, sandwiches, and salads—most for $10 or less. This is

Hold the Meat, Please

Yes, Chicago may have a reputation as a carnivore's paradise, but that doesn't mean vegetarians should stuff their bags with dried tofu before coming here. In recent years, more and more local restaurants have made an effort to accommodate non-meat eaters. While you can order a green salad or vegetable pasta almost anywhere, here are some places that treat veggie offerings as more than just an afterthought:

At **Green Zebra** (p. 124), the menu is almost exclusively meat-free, but the creative small-plates menu gives diners a wide range of flavors to sample. If you're in the mood for Asian, the stylish West Loop restaurant **Red Light** (p. 108) offers a selection of vegetarian entrees inspired by Thai and Chinese cuisine; the equally stylish **Opera** (p. 101), in the South Loop, has a separate menu of vegan Chinese dishes. At **Vong's Thai Kitchen** in River North (p. 132), many of the Thai specialties can be prepared with tofu instead of meat.

Going vegetarian doesn't mean giving up gourmet dining. Two of the city's best, most creative chefs—**Charlie Trotter** at his namesake restaurant (p. 136) and Michael Taus at **Zealous** (p. 121)—offer multi-course vegetarian degustation menus. At **Crofton on Wells** in River North (p. 123), chef Suzy Crofton always includes a few meat-free options on her nightly menu. (She'll customize them for vegans, too.) In Wrigleyville, chef Yoshi Katsumura of **Yoshi's Café** (p. 142) also offers a regular selection of vegetarian dishes featuring his signature blend of French and Asian flavors.

Reza's (p. 129), a sprawling Middle Eastern spot in River North, may specialize in giant mixed-meat kebabs, but their vegetarian plates are generous, flavorful mixes of hummus, tabbouleh, and other traditional dishes, nicely presented in red bento boxes. At the Southern spot **Wishbone** (p. 112), in the West Loop, veggie lovers can create their own sampler plates by selecting from a wide range of side dishes.

Vegans may find their options extremely limited on most menus, but local holistic health devotee Karyn Calabrese operates the two most vegan-friendly restaurants in town. **Karyn's Raw,** 1901 N. Halsted St. (℃ 312/255-1590), in Old Town, encompasses both a casual cafe and juice bar and a white-tablecloth restaurant specializing in raw food; **Karyn's Cooked,** 738 N. Wells St. (℃ 312/587-1050), in River North, offers globally inspired vegan dishes. You can check out both menus at www.karynraw.com. Farther north in Wrigleyville, **the Chicago Diner,** 3411 N. Halsted St. (℃ 773/935-6696; www.veggiediner.com), might sound like the kind of place you load up on greasy burgers, but it's actually one of the city's best and longest-lasting vegetarian restaurants. (Most dishes are vegan, too.) The wide-ranging menu includes salads, sandwiches (including a "California Reuben" with seitan instead of corned beef), tacos, and pastas; for dessert, try a peanut butter or vanilla chai vegan milk shake.

strictly neighborhood dining, without attitude and little in the way of decor; the back dining room looks like a rec room from 1973, complete with a fireplace, pinball machines, and a pool table. In nice weather, Northside opens up its large front patio for dining, and a sky-lit cover keeps it in use during the winter. You're always sure to be entertained by people-watching here, as Northside attracts all sorts. During the week, the cafe is more of a neighborhood hangout, while on weekends a more touristy crowd from Lincoln Park and the suburbs piles in. A limited late-night menu is available from 10pm to 1am.

1635 N. Damen Ave. (at North and Milwaukee aves.). ℂ **773/384-3555.** www.northsidechicago.com. Reservations not accepted. Menu items $6–$15. AE, DC, DISC, MC, V. Sun–Fri 11:30am–2am; Sat 11am–3am. Subway/El: Blue Line to Damen.

Piece ★ AMERICAN/PIZZA   Piece finally proved to deep-dish-loving Chicagoans that thin-crust pizza deserves respect. The large, airy dining room—a former garage that's been outfitted with dark wood tables and ceiling beams—is flooded with light from the expansive skylights overhead; even when it's crowded (as it gets on weekend evenings), the soaring space above keeps the place from feeling too crowded. Piece offers a selection of salads and sandwiches on satisfyingly crusty bread, but pizza in the style of New Haven, Connecticut (hometown of one of the owners), is the house specialty. Pick from three styles—plain (tomato sauce, Parmesan cheese, and garlic), red (tomato sauce and mozzarella), or white (olive oil, garlic, and mozzarella), then add on your favorite toppings. Sausage and/or spinach work well with the plain or red, but the adventurous should sample a more offbeat choice: Clam and bacon on white pizza.

1927 W. North Ave. (at Milwaukee Ave.). ℂ **773/772-4422.** www.piecechicago.com. Reservations accepted for groups of 10 or more. Pizza $11–$17. AE, DISC, MC, V. Mon–Thurs 11:30am–11pm; Fri–Sat 11:30am–12:30am; Sun 11am–10pm. Subway/El: Blue Line to Damen.

Silver Cloud ★★ AMERICAN   The motto of this casual cafe is "Food like Mom would make if she was gettin' paid." Indeed, Silver Cloud is comfort food-central, with a laid-back pub-meets-diner decor and suitably attitude-free clientele. If intimate conversation is your priority, try to snag one of the roomy red-leather booths. While the food isn't extraordinary, the restaurant does deliver consistently reliable home-style favorites: Chicken potpie, grilled-cheese sandwiches, pot roast, sloppy Joes with a side of tater tots, s'mores, and root beer floats. The Silver Cloud attracts a mix of families, couples, and groups of friends during the day and early evening hours, but it becomes more of a cocktail lounge at night. A warning for those with sensitive ears: The jukebox volume gets turned up at night, too. The Sunday brunch is especially popular; the "Hangover Helpers" attract a fair amount of hip young things recovering from nightly adventures.

1700 N. Damen Ave. (at Wabansia St.). ℂ **773/489-6212.** www.silvercloudchicago.com. Main courses $6–$10 lunch, $10–$16 dinner. AE, DC, MC, V. Mon–Thurs 11:30am–11pm; Fri 11:30am–midnight; Sat–Sun 10am–midnight. Bar stays open later every night except Sun. Subway/El: Blue Line to Damen.

Exploring Chicago

Whenever I get the chance to show visitors around my hometown, I find myself getting giddy with anticipation. With so much to do, so many places I want to show off . . . how will we fit it all in? That's the fun—and the challenge—of a visit to Chicago. You can put together a full itinerary each day and still have plenty left over for your next visit.

While what you see will depend on your interests (and stamina), some spots show up regularly on my own personal must-see list. The city's museums alone could keep you busy for at least a week. (If you don't have that much time, I'd have to pick the Impressionist masterpieces at the Art Institute of Chicago; Sue, the biggest *Tyrannosaurus rex* fossil ever discovered, at the Field Museum of Natural History; and the U-505 submarine at the Museum of Science and Industry, as my top three favorite exhibits.) Come summertime, my favorite way to spend an afternoon is with a stroll through picturesque Lincoln Park Zoo on the Near North Side; the setting makes it worth visiting even if you don't have kids along. (Added bonus: It's free!)

From a traveler's perspective, visiting Chicago is especially hassle-free because the majority of the places you'll want to see are in or near downtown, making it easy to plan your day and get from place to place. And because this is a town with a thriving tourist economy, you have plenty of guided sightseeing options: Walking tours of famous architecture; boat cruises on Lake Michigan; and even bus tours of notorious gangster sites. If you're lucky enough to visit when the weather's nice, you can join the locals at the parks and the beaches along Lake Michigan.

Extensive public transportation makes it simple to reach almost every tourist destination, but some of your best memories of Chicago may come from simply strolling along the sidewalks. Chicago's neighborhoods have their own distinct styles and looks, and you'll have a more memorable experience if you don't limit yourself solely to the prime tourist spots. And if you *really* want to talk about da Bears or da Cubs, chances are you'll find someone who's more than happy to join in.

1 IN & AROUND THE LOOP: THE ART INSTITUTE, THE SEARS TOWER & GRANT PARK

The heart of the Loop is Chicago's business center, where you'll find the Chicago Board of Trade (the world's largest commodities, futures, and options exchange), Sears Tower, and some of the city's most famous early skyscrapers. If you're looking for an authentic big-city experience, wander the area on a weekday, when commuters are rushing to catch trains and businesspeople are hustling to get to work. The Loop is also home to one of the city's top museums, the Art Institute of Chicago, as well as a number of cultural institutions including the Symphony Center (home of the Chicago Symphony Orchestra), the Auditorium Theatre, the Civic Opera House, the Goodman Theatre, and two fabulously restored historic theaters along Randolph Street. On the eastern edge of the

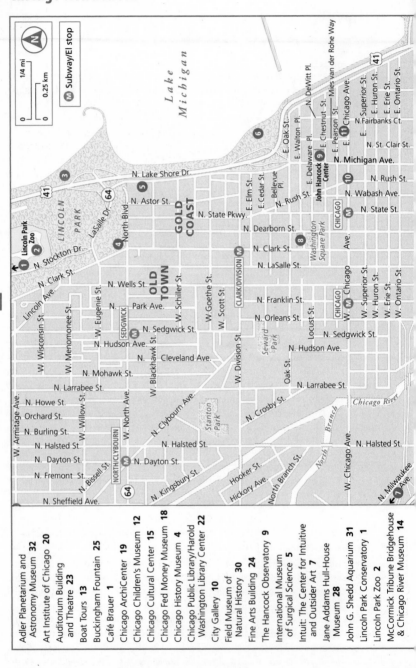

W Subway/El stop

Adler Planetarium and
Astronomy Museum **32**
Art Institute of Chicago **20**
Auditorium Building
and Theatre **23**
Boat Tours **13**
Buckingham Fountain **25**
Café Brauer **1**
Chicago ArchiCenter **19**
Chicago Children's Museum **12**
Chicago Cultural Center **15**
Chicago Fed Money Museum **18**
Chicago History Museum **4**
Chicago Public Library/Harold
Washington Library Center **22**
City Gallery **10**
Field Museum of
Natural History **30**
Fine Arts Building **24**
The Hancock Observatory **9**
International Museum
of Surgical Science **5**
Intuit: The Center for Intuitive
and Outsider Art **7**
Jane Addams Hull-House
Museum **28**
John G. Shedd Aquarium **31**
Lincoln Park Conservatory **1**
Lincoln Park Zoo **2**
McCormick Tribune Bridgehouse
& Chicago River Museum **14**

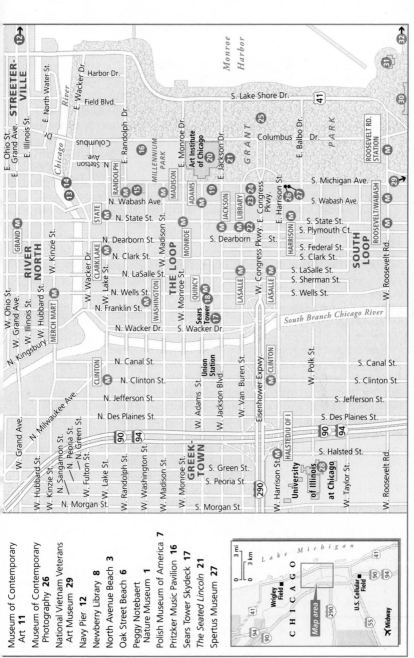

STREETER-VILLE

RIVER NORTH

THE LOOP

SOUTH LOOP

GREEK-TOWN

Harbor Dr.

Field Blvd.

E. Wacker Dr.

E. North Water St.

E. Illinois St.

E. Ohio St.

E. Grand Ave.

Chicago River

Columbus Ave.

N. Stetson Ave.

E. Randolph Dr.

MILLENNIUM PARK

E. Monroe Dr.

Art Institute of Chicago

E. Jackson Dr.

Monroe Harbor

GRANT PARK

S. Lake Shore Dr.

Columbus Dr.

E. Balbo Dr.

ROOSEVELT RD. STATION

41

RANDOLPH

N. Wabash Ave.

STATE

N. State St.

N. Dearborn St.

N. Clark St.

N. LaSalle St.

N. Wells St.

N. Franklin St.

N. Wacker Dr.

MADISON

ADAMS

JACKSON

LIBRARY

E. Congress Pkwy.

E. Harrison St.

S. Michigan Ave.

S. Wabash Ave.

S. State St.

S. Plymouth Ct.

S. Federal St.

S. Clark St.

S. LaSalle St.

S. Sherman St.

S. Wells St.

ROOSEVELT/WABASH

W. Congress Pkwy.

W. Wacker Dr.

W. Lake St.

W. Washington St.

W. Madison St.

W. Monroe St.

Sears Tower

S. Wacker Dr.

South Branch Chicago River

N. Canal St.

N. Clinton St.

N. Jefferson St.

N. Des Plaines St.

Union Station

W. Adams St.

W. Jackson Blvd.

W. Van Buren St.

Eisenhower Expwy.

HALSTED/U OF I

S. Canal St.

S. Clinton St.

S. Jefferson St.

S. Des Plaines St.

S. Halsted St.

W. Roosevelt Rd.

N. Grand Ave.

N. Kingsbury St.

N. Milwaukee Ave.

W. Hubbard St.

W. Kinzie St.

N. Sangamon St.

N. Peoria St.

N. Green St.

W. Grand Ave.

W. Hubbard St.

W. Illinois St.

W. Lake St.

W. Randolph St.

W. Washington St.

W. Madison St.

W. Monroe St.

S. Green St.

S. Peoria St.

S. Morgan St.

University of Illinois at Chicago

W. Harrison St.

W. Taylor St.

W. Roosevelt Rd.

290

90 94

Museum of Contemporary Art **11**

Museum of Contemporary Photography **26**

National Vietnam Veterans Art Museum **29**

Navy Pier **12**

Newberry Library **8**

North Avenue Beach **3**

Oak Street Beach **6**

Peggy Notebaert Nature Museum **1**

Polish Museum of America **7**

Pritzker Music Pavilion **16**

Sears Tower Skydeck **17**

The Seated Lincoln **21**

Spertus Museum **27**

Lake Michigan

3 mi

3 km

CHICAGO

Wrigley Field

Map area

U.S. Cellular Field

Midway

41

90 94

290

55

Loop in Grant Park, three popular museums are conveniently located within a quick stroll of each other on the landscaped Museum Campus. Busy Lake Shore Drive, which brings cars zipping past the Museum Campus, was actually rerouted a few years ago to make the area easier to navigate for pedestrians.

THE TOP ATTRACTIONS IN THE LOOP

For a map of these attractions (or this neighborhood), see p. 150.

Art Institute of Chicago ★★★ (**Kids**) You can't—and shouldn't—miss the Art Institute. (You really have no excuse, since it's conveniently located right on Michigan Ave. in the heart of downtown.) No matter what medium or century interests you, the Art Institute has something in its collection to fit the bill. Japanese *ukiyo-e* prints, ancient Egyptian bronzes, Greek vases, 19th-century British photography, masterpieces by most of the greatest names in 20th-century sculpture, and modern American textiles are just some of the works on display, but for a general overview of the museum's collection, take the free "Highlights of the Art Institute" tour, offered at 2pm on Tuesday, Saturday, and Sunday.

If time is limited, head straight to the museum's renowned galleries of **Impressionist art** ★★★, which include one of the world's largest collections of Monet paintings; this is one of the most popular areas of the museum, so arriving early pays off. Among the treasures, you'll find Seurat's pointillist masterpiece *Sunday Afternoon on the Island of La Grande Jatte.* The **Modern Wing** ★★, a light-filled addition opened in 2009, houses works by modern masters such as Picasso, Matisse, de Kooning, and Pollock, as well as rotating exhibits of contemporary art. Confusingly, American modern art from before 1950 is tucked into a separate gallery in the main building, but it's well worth making a detour to see the icons that hang there (Grant Wood's *American Gothic;* Edward Hopper's *Nighthawks*).

Often overlooked but worth seeing are the Arthur Rubloff collection of delicate mid–19th-century **glass paperweights,** and the great hall of **European arms and armor** ★ dating from the 15th to the 19th centuries. Composed of more than 1,500 objects, including armor, horse equipment, swords and daggers, polearms, and maces, the collection is one of the most important assemblages of its kind in the country. (If you do head down here, you'll see Marc Chagall's stunning stained-glass windows at the end of the gallery.)

The **Ryan Education Center** on the first floor of the Modern Wing has workstations where children can create their own works of art or pick up a list of "gallery games" to make visiting the museum more fun. When I was a kid, I was entranced by the **Thorne Miniature Rooms** ★, filled with tiny reproductions of furnished interiors from European and American history (heaven for a dollhouse fanatic).

EXPLORING CHICAGO

7

IN & AROUND THE LOOP

| (**Tips** | **Walker's Warning** |

While Chicago is a great city to explore on foot, Lake Shore Drive is no place for pedestrians. People have been seriously injured and even killed attempting to dodge traffic on the busy road. Near Grant Park, cross only in crosswalks at Jackson Boulevard or Randolph, East Monroe, or East Balbo drives, or by using the underpass on the Museum Campus. North of the river, use underpasses or bridges at East Ohio Street, Chicago Avenue, Oak Street, and North Avenue.

If you want to enjoy your favorite masterpieces in something resembling peace and quiet, put some thought into the timing of your visit to the Art Institute, a museum so popular that it draws as much traffic as our jammed expressways.

Some tips for avoiding the rush hour: Many people don't realize the museum is open on Monday; keep this secret to yourself, and visit when the galleries are relatively subdued. Also, many visitors aren't aware that the museum stays open late on Thursdays, so consider stopping by after an early dinner. (Another bonus: Free admission.)

The museum has a cafeteria and an elegant full-service restaurant with Millennium Park views, a picturesque courtyard cafe (open June–Sept), and a large gift shop. It offers a busy schedule of lectures, films, and other special presentations, as well as guided tours. The museum also has a research library. Allow 3 hours.

111 S. Michigan Ave. (at Adams St.). ✆ **312/443-3600.** www.artic.edu. Admission $18 adults, $12 seniors and students with ID, free for children 13 and under. Free admission Thurs 5–8pm year-round; Fri 5–9pm Memorial Day–Labor Day. Mon–Fri 10:30am–5pm (Thurs until 8pm, until 9pm Thurs–Fri Memorial Day–Labor Day); Sat–Sun 10am–5pm. Closed Jan 1, Thanksgiving, and Dec 25. Bus: 3, 4, 60, 145, 147, or 151. Subway/El: Green, Brown, Purple, or Orange line to Adams, or Red Line to Monroe/State or Jackson/State.

Sears Tower Skydeck   First Sears sold the building and moved to cheaper suburban offices in 1992. Then the Petronas Towers in Kuala Lumpur, Malaysia, went up, laying claim to the title of world's tallest building. (The Sears Tower added a 22-ft. antenna in an attempt to win back the title Dubai's Bur; Dubai is currently the world's tallest.) Now the final blow: As of mid-2009, this iconic landmark has officially been re-named Willis Tower, after the international insurance company that has become its main tenant. Real-estate deals aside, we Chicagoans continue to call it the Sears Tower, so feel free to do so as well.

Despite the fact that this observation area on the 103rd floor is called a "skydeck," you can't actually walk outside, but thanks to some recent upgrades, the view is more impressive than ever. The most nerve-wracking addition is the Ledge, a series of observation boxes that jut out from the side of the building: Step out and there's nothing between you and the ground but a layer of see-through glass. On a clear day, visibility extends up to 50 miles, and you can catch glimpses of four surrounding states. Multimedia exhibits on Chicago history and *Knee High Chicago,* an exhibit for kids, are additional attractions. Be forewarned that in the summer you may be stuck in a very long, very noisy line, so by the time you make it to the top, your patience could be as thin as the atmosphere up there. (Come in the late afternoon or early evening to avoid most of the crowds.) The 70-second, high-speed elevator trip will feel like a thrill ride for some, but it's a nightmare for anyone with even mild claustrophobia. Allow 1 hour, more if there's a long line.

233 S. Wacker Dr. (enter on Jackson Blvd.). ✆ **312/875-9696.** www.the-skydeck.com. Admission $15 adults, $11 seniors and children 3–11, free for children 2 and under. Apr–Sept daily 10am–10pm; Oct–Mar daily 10am–8pm. Bus: 1, 7, 126, 146, 151, or 156. Subway/El: Brown, Purple, or Orange line to Quincy, or Red or Blue line to Jackson; and then walk a few blocks west.

THE LOOP SCULPTURE TOUR

Monuments, statues, and contemporary sculptures are on view throughout Chicago, but the concentration of public art within the Loop and nearby Grant Park is worth noting.

Oprah in Person

Oprah Winfrey tapes her phenomenally successful talk show at Harpo Studios, 1058 W. Washington Blvd., just west of the Loop. If you'd like to be in her studio audience, you'll have to plan ahead: Reservations are taken by phone only (📞 312/591-9222), at least 1 month in advance. For information on upcoming shows, check the website (www.oprah.com); if you've got a great personal story that relates to a show being planned, submit it online and you just might get booked as a guest. Remember that Oprah's on vacation all summer and for most of December and January. If all else fails, you can always browse the O-logo merchandise at the **Oprah Store,** across the street from the studio (p. 243).

The best known of these works are by 20th-century artists including Picasso, Chagall, Miró, Calder, Moore, and Oldenburg. The newest addition is the massive elliptical sculpture *Cloud Gate* (known as "The Bean" because it looks like a giant silver kidney bean) by British artist Anish Kapoor. The sculpture, in Millennium Park, was Kapoor's first public commission in the U.S.

A free brochure, *The Chicago Public Art Guide* (available at the Chicago Cultural Center, 78 E. Washington St.), can help steer you toward the best examples of monumental public art. You can also conduct a self-guided tour of the city's best public sculptures by following "The Loop Sculpture Tour" map.

The single most famous sculpture is **Pablo Picasso's** *Untitled,* located in Daley Plaza and constructed out of Cor-Ten steel, the same gracefully rusting material used on the exterior of the Daley Center behind it. Viewed from various perspectives, its enigmatic shape suggests a woman, bird, or dog. Perhaps because it was the button-down Loop's first monumental modern sculpture, its installation in 1967 was met with hoots and heckles, but today "The Picasso" enjoys semiofficial status as the logo of modern Chicago. It is by far the city's most popular photo opportunity among visiting tourists. At noon on weekdays during warm weather, you'll likely find a dance troupe, musical group, or visual-arts exhibition here as part of the city's long-running "Under the Picasso" multicultural program. Call 📞 312/346-3278 for event information.

GRANT PARK & MILLENNIUM PARK
For a map of these attractions (or this neighborhood), see p. 150.

Thanks to architect Daniel Burnham and his coterie of visionary civic planners—who drafted the revolutionary 1909 Plan of Chicago—the city boasts a wide-open lakefront park system unrivaled by most major metropolises. Modeled after the gardens at Versailles, **Grant Park** (📞 312/742-PLAY [7529]; www.chicagoparkdistrict.com) is Chicago's front yard, composed of giant lawns segmented by *allées* of trees, plantings, and paths, and pieced together by major roadways and a network of railroad tracks. Incredibly, the entire expanse was created from sandbars, landfill, and debris from the Great Chicago Fire; the original shoreline extended all the way to Michigan Avenue. A few museums are spread out inside the park, but most of the space is wide open (a legacy of mail-order magnate Aaron Montgomery Ward's late-19th-century campaign to limit municipal buildings).

1 *Untitled ("The Picasso"),* Pablo Picasso (1967)

2 *Chicago,* Joan Miro (1981)

3 *Monument with Standing Beast,* Jean Dubuffet (1984)

4 *Freeform,* Richard Hunt (1993)

5 *Flight of Daedalus and Icarus,* Roger Brown (1990)

6 *Dawn Shadows,* Louise Nevelson (1983)

7 *Loomings* and *Knights and Squires,* Frank Stella

8 *Batcolumn,* Claes Oldenburg (1977)

9 *The Universe,* Alexander Calder (1974)

10 *Gem of the Lakes,* Raymond Kaskey (1990)

11 *San Marco II,* Ludovico de Luigi (1986)

12 *The Town-Ho's Story,* Frank Stella (1993)

13 *Ruins III,* Nita K. Sutherland (1978)

14 *Flamingo,* Alexander Calder (1974)

15 *Lines in Four Directions,* Sol Lewitt (1985)

16 *The Four Seasons,* Marc Chagall (1974)

17 *Untitled Sounding Sculpture,* Harry Bertoia (1975)

18 *Cloud Gate,* Anish Kapoor (2004)

19 *Large Interior Form,* Henry Moore (1983)

20 *Celebration of the 200th Anniversary of the Founding of the Republic,* Isamu Noguchi (1976)

21 *The Fountain of the Great Lakes,* Lorado Taft (1913)

Fun Facts   Did You Know?

Yugoslavian sculptor Ivan Mestrovic titled his bronze sculpture of Indian warriors on horseback *The Bowman and the Spearman;* however, the warriors' bow and arrow and spear have been removed. Mestrovic intentionally omitted them to make an antiwar statement.

The northwest corner of Grant Park (bordered by Michigan Ave. and Randolph St.) is the site of **Millennium Park** ★★★, one of the city's grandest public-works projects. Who cares that the park cost hundreds of millions more than it was supposed to, or the fact that it finally opened a full 4 years *after* the actual millennium? It's a winning combination of beautiful landscaping, elegant architecture (the classically inspired peristyle), and public entertainment spaces (including an ice rink and theater). The park's centerpiece is the dramatic Frank Gehry–designed **Pritzker Music Pavilion,** featuring massive curved ribbons of steel. The Grant Park Symphony Orchestra and Chorus stages a popular series of free outdoor classical music concerts here most Wednesday through Sunday evenings in the summer. For a schedule of concert times and dates, contact the **Grant Park Music Festival** (📞 312/742-7638; www.grantparkmusicfestival.com). Two public artworks well worth checking out are the kidney bean–shaped sculpture *Cloud Gate* and the *Crown Fountain,* where children splash in the shallow water between giant faces projected on video screens. Free walking tours of the park are offered daily from Memorial Day through October at 11:30am and 1pm, starting at the park's Welcome Center, 201 E. Randolph St. (📞 312/742-1168; www.millenniumpark.org).

During the summer, a variety of music and food festivals take over central Grant Park. Annual events that draw big crowds include a blues music festival (in June) and a jazz festival (Labor Day). The **Taste of Chicago** (📞 312/744-3315; www.cityofchicago.org/specialevents), purportedly the largest food festival in the world (the city estimates its annual attendance at around 3.5 million), takes place every year for 10 days around the 4th of July. Local restaurants serve up more ribs, pizza, hot dogs, and beer than you'd ever want to see, let alone eat. (See chapter 3 for a comprehensive listing of summer events in Grant Park.)

Head south to the lake via Congress Parkway, and you'll find *Buckingham Fountain* ★, the baroque centerpiece of Grant Park, composed of pink Georgia marble and patterned after—but twice the size of—the *Latona Fountain* at Versailles, with adjoining esplanades beautified by rose gardens in season. From April through October, the fountain spurts columns of water up to 150 feet in the air every hour on the hour, and beginning at 4pm, a whirl of colored lights and dramatic music amps up the drama. The fountain shuts down at 11pm; concession areas and bathrooms are available on the plaza.

Sculptures and monuments stand throughout the park, including a sculpture of two Native Americans on horseback, *The Bowman and the Spearman* (at Congress Pkwy. and Michigan Ave.), which was installed in 1928 and has become the park's trademark. Also here are likenesses of Copernicus, Columbus, and Lincoln, the latter by the great American sculptor Augustus Saint-Gaudens, located on Congress Parkway between Michigan Avenue and Columbus Drive. On the western edge of the park, at Adams Street, is the **Art Institute** (see above), and at the southern tip, in the area known as the

Museum Campus, are the **Field Museum of Natural History,** the **Adler Planetarium,**
and the **Shedd Aquarium** (see below for all three).

To get to Grant Park, take bus no. 3, 4, 6, 146, or 151. If you want to take the subway or the El, get off at any stop in the Loop along State or Wabash streets, and walk east.

ALONG SOUTH MICHIGAN AVENUE
For a map of these attractions (or this neighborhood), see p. 150.

Fashion and glamour might have moved north to the Magnificent Mile, but Chicago's grandest stretch of boulevard is still Michigan Avenue, south of the river. From a little north of the Michigan Avenue Bridge all the way down to the Field Museum, South Michigan Avenue runs parallel to Grant Park on one side and the Loop on the other. A stroll along this boulevard in any season offers both visual and cultural treats. Particularly impressive is the great wall of buildings from Randolph Street south to Congress Parkway (beginning with the Chicago Cultural Center and terminating at the Auditorium Building) that architecture buffs refer to as the "Michigan Avenue Cliff."

The following attractions are listed from north to south.

McCormick Tribune Bridgehouse & Chicago River Museum (Finds)   Chicago has more moveable bridges than any other city in the world, and this modest museum provides a glimpse into the machinery that operates them. Although it's located on one of the busiest corners in town—at the southwest corner of the Michigan Avenue Bridge—the entrance is easy to miss. (You have to walk down a flight of stone steps to river level.) Inside, as you walk up the bridgehouse's five floors, historic engravings and photos trace the history of the city as it relates to the river (including the engineering feat that reversed the river's flow). The coolest part is the observation deck directly under the bridge, where you can gawk at the massive gears while listening to the pounding of traffic overhead. To see the gears in action, reserve a spot during one of the scheduled bridge lifts, which take place about six times a month; admission is $10 per person. (Check the museum's website for dates.)

376 N. Michigan Ave. (at the Chicago River). (C) **312/977-0227.** www.bridgehousemuseum.org/home. Admission $3, free for children 4 and under. May–Oct Thurs–Mon 10am–5pm. Bus: 3, 4, 20, 56, 145, 146, 147, 151, or 157. Subway/El: Brown, Green, Orange, or Purple line to Randolph, or Red Line to Washington/State.

Chicago Cultural Center ★ (Finds)   The Chicago Cultural Center was built in 1897 as the city's public library, and in 1991, it was transformed into a showplace for visual and performing arts. Today, it's an overlooked civic treasure with a basic Beaux Arts exterior and a sumptuous interior of rare marble, fine hardwood, stained glass, and mosaics of Favrile glass, colored stone, and mother-of-pearl inlaid in white marble. The crowning centerpiece is Preston Bradley Hall's majestic **Tiffany dome** ★, said to be the largest of its kind in the world.

The building also houses a **Chicago Office of Tourism** visitor center, which makes it an ideal place to kick-start your visit. If you stop in to pick up tourist information and take a quick look around, your visit won't take longer than 15 minutes, but the Cultural Center also schedules an array of art exhibitions, concerts, films, lectures, and other special events (many free), which might convince you to extend your time here. A long-standing tradition is the 12:15pm Dame Myra Hess Memorial classical concert every Wednesday in the Preston Bradley Hall.

Guided architectural tours of the Cultural Center run at 1:15pm on Wednesday, and Saturday.

7

IN & AROUND THE LOOP

Moments **Photo Op**

For a great photo op, walk on Randolph Street toward the lake in the morning when the sun, rising in the east over the lake, hits the cliff of buildings along South Michigan Avenue, giving you the perfect backdrop for an only-in-Chicago picture.

78 E. Washington St. © **312/FINE-ART** [744-6630] for weekly events. www.explorechicago.org. Free admission. Mon–Thurs 9am–7pm; Fri 8am–6pm; Sat 9am–6pm; Sun 10am–6pm. Closed major holidays. Bus: 3, 4, 20, 56, 145, 146, 147, 151, or 157. Subway/El: Brown, Green, Orange, or Purple line to Randolph, or Red Line to Washington/State.

Chicago ArchiCenter   Chicago's architecture is one of the city's main claims to fame, and a quick swing through this center, run by the well-regarded **Chicago Architecture Foundation** (conveniently located across the street from the Art Institute), will help you understand why. Exhibits include a scale model of downtown Chicago, profiles of the people and buildings that shaped the city's look, and a searchable database with pictures of and information on many of Chicago's best-known skyscrapers. "Architecture ambassadors" are on hand to provide information on tours run by the foundation (see "Sightseeing Tours," p. 193). Two galleries feature changing exhibits about ongoing Chicago design projects, so you can see firsthand how local architecture continues to evolve. There's also an excellent gift shop filled with architecture-focused books, decorative accessories, and gifts. Allow a half-hour, more if you want to browse in the store.

224 S. Michigan Ave. © **312/922-3432,** ext. 241. www.architecture.org. Free admission. Exhibits daily 9:30am–5pm. Shop and tour desk daily 9am–6:30pm. Bus: 3, 4, 145, 147, or 151. Subway/El: Brown, Green, Purple, or Orange line to Adams, or Red Line to Jackson.

Fine Arts Building   A worthwhile brief stop for architecture and history buffs, this 1885 building was originally a showroom for Studebaker carriages. In 1917 it became an arts center, with offices, shops, two theaters, and studios for musicians, artists, and writers. Its upper stories sheltered a number of well-known publications (*The Saturday Evening Post, Dial*) and provided offices for such luminaries as Frank Lloyd Wright, sculptor Lorado Taft, and L. Frank Baum, author of *The Wonderful Wizard of Oz.* Harriet Monroe published her magazine, *Poetry,* here and introduced American readers to Carl Sandburg, T. S. Eliot, and Ezra Pound. Before the literary lions prowled its halls, the building served as a rallying base for suffragettes. Located throughout the building are a number of interesting studios and musical-instrument shops. Take at least a quick walk through the marble-and-wood lobby, and ride the vintage elevator to the top floor to see the **Art Nouveau–era murals.** Allow a half-hour.

410 S. Michigan Ave. © **312/566-9800.** www.fineartsbuilding.com. Free admission. Mon–Fri 7am–10p—; Sun 9am–5pm. Bus: 3, 4, 145, 147, or 151. Subway/El: Brown, Green, Purple, or, or Red Line to Jackson.

…lding and Theatre ★★   A truly grand theater with historic-… …e Auditorium gives visitors a taste of late-19th-century Chicago …s still a working theater—not a museum—it's not always open to the …y; to make sure you'll get in, schedule a guided tour, which are

(Value) Museum Free Days

If you time your visit right, you can save yourself some admission fees—but not during prime tourist season. While some major museums offer free admission at specific times year-round, others schedule free days only during the slowest times of the year (usually late fall and the dead of winter); keep in mind that you will still have to pay for special exhibitions and films on free days. The good news? Some smaller museums never charge admission.

Monday: Chicago History Museum; Field Museum of Natural History (2nd Monday of every month); and Shedd Aquarium (mid-Sept–Nov and Jan–Feb; Oceanarium admission extra).

Tuesday: Adler Planetarium (Jan–Mar and Sept–Dec); Museum of Contemporary Art; and Shedd Aquarium (mid-Sept–Nov and Jan–Feb; Oceanarium admission extra).

Wednesday: Spertus Museum (10am–noon).

Thursday: Art Institute of Chicago (5–8pm only, until 9pm Memorial Day–Labor Day); Chicago Children's Museum (5–8pm only); and Spertus Museum (2–6pm).

Sunday: DuSable Museum of African-American History.

Always Free: Chicago Cultural Center, Garfield Park Conservatory, David and Alfred Smart Museum of Art, Jane Addams Hull-House Museum, Lincoln Park Conservatory, Lincoln Park Zoo, National Museum of Mexican Art, Museum of Contemporary Photography, and Newberry Library.

offered on Mondays at 10:30am and noon and Thursday at 10:30am. (Call ✆ **312/431-2389** to confirm the date and time.) Tours cost $10 per person.

Designed and built in 1889 by Louis Sullivan and Dankmar Adler, the 4,000-seat Auditorium was a wonder of the world: The heaviest (110,000 tons) and most massive modern edifice on earth, the most fireproof building ever constructed, and the tallest building in Chicago. It was also the first large-scale building to be lit by electricity, and its theater was the first in the country to install air-conditioning. Originally the home of the Chicago Opera Company, Sullivan and Adler's masterpiece is defined by powerful arches lit by thousands of bulbs and features Sullivan's trademark ornamentation—in this case, elaborate golden stenciling and gold plaster medallions. It's equally renowned for otherworldly acoustics and unobstructed sightlines.

During World War II, the building sheltered GIs, and its theater stage was turned into a bowling alley. The theater reopened in 1967 following a $3-million renovation made possible through the fundraising efforts of the nonprofit Auditorium Theatre Council. Remnants of the building's halcyon days remain in the Michigan Avenue lobby, with its faux-marble ornamental columns, molded ceilings, mosaic floors, and Mexican onyx walls.

An insider tip: If you can't get in for a tour, you can still get a glimpse of the building's historic past. Around the corner on Michigan Avenue, walk in the entrance that now houses Roosevelt University, and you'll get a sense of the building's grand public spaces.

Take the elevator to the school's 10th-floor library reading room to see the theater's original dining room, with a barrel-vaulted ceiling and marvelous views of Grant Park.

Allow 1 hour for the guided tour.

50 E. Congress Pkwy. ℰ **312/922-2110.** www.auditoriumtheatre.org. For tickets to a performance at the Auditorium, call Ticketmaster at ℰ **312/902-1500.** Bus: 145, 147, or 151. Subway/El: Brown, Green, Orange, or Purple line to Library/Van Buren, or Red Line to Jackson.

Museum of Contemporary Photography   Ensconced in a ground-floor space at Columbia College—a progressive arts- and media-oriented institution that boasts the country's largest undergraduate film department and a highly respected photojournalism-slanted photography department—the Museum of Contemporary Photography is the only museum in the Midwest of its kind. As the name indicates, it exhibits, collects, and promotes modern photography, with a special focus on American works from 1959 to the present. Rotating exhibitions showcase images by both nationally recognized and "undiscovered" regional artists. Related lectures and special programs take place during the year. Allow 1 hour.

600 S. Michigan Ave. ℰ **312/663-5554.** www.mocp.org. Free admission. Mon–Sat 10am–5pm (Thurs until 8pm); Sun noon–5pm. Bus: 6, 146, or 151. Subway/El: Red Line to Harrison.

Spertus Museum   The Spertus Museum, an extension of the Spertus Institute of Jewish Studies, collects and preserves historic Jewish ceremonial objects, textiles, and sculpture, but its stunning, modern building is firmly ensconced in the present. A glass facade fills the airy, white interior with light (even on cloudy days), and an outdoor terrace off the 10th floor exhibition space lets you gaze out over Grant Park and the lake beyond. The museum's core collection of Judaica is beautifully showcased in a large semicircular display that allows viewers to trace the cross-cultural influences between the objects; other temporary exhibits examine the Jewish experience through contemporary art. The building also includes a 400-seat theater for lectures and films; an interactive exhibit space designed for kids; and a kosher cafe operated by Chef Wolfgang Puck's catering company. Researchers can register to visit the Asher Library or study the Chicago Jewish Archives collection. The museum shop carries a large selection of art, books, music, videos, and contemporary and traditional Jewish ceremonial gifts. Allow 1 hour.

610 S. Michigan Ave. ℰ **312/322-1747.** www.spertus.edu. Admission $7 adults; $5 seniors, students, and children 5 and older; free for children 4 and under. Free admission Weds 10am–noon and Thurs 2–6pm. Sun and Weds 10am–5pm; Thurs 10am–6pm. Bus: 3, 4, 6, 145, 147, or 151. Subway/El: Red Line to Harrison, or Brown, Purple, Orange, or Green line to Adams. Validated parking in nearby lots.

ELSEWHERE IN THE LOOP

For a map of these attractions (or this neighborhood), see p. 150.

Chicago Fed Money Museum   It's not worth a special trip (unless you're a monetary-policy megageek), but the visitor center at the Federal Reserve Bank of Chicago is worth a quick stop if you're wandering around the Loop. More than just the standard history-of-banking displays, the center has kid-friendly features such as a giant cube that holds a million dollars and an exhibit that lets you try detecting counterfeit bills. There's even a section where visitors can play Fed chairman, showing how changes in interest rates affect the economy. Free guided tours begin at 1pm on weekdays. Allow a half-hour.

230 S. LaSalle St. (at Quincy St.). ℰ **312/322-2400.** www.chicagofed.org. Free admission. Mon–Fri 9am–4pm. Closed federal holidays. Bus: 134, 135, 136, or 156. Subway/El: Brown Line to Quincy/Wells.

Chicago Public Library/Harold Washington Library Center A massive, hulking building that looks like an Italian Renaissance fortress, Chicago's main public library is
the largest in the world. Named for the city's first and only African-American mayor, who
died of a heart attack in 1987 at the beginning of his second term in office, the building
fills an entire city block at State Street and Congress Parkway. The interior design has been
criticized for feeling cold (you have to go up a few floors before you even see any books),
but the stunning, 52-foot glass-domed **Winter Garden** ★ on the top floor is worth a visit.
On the second floor is another treasure: The vast Thomas Hughes Children's Library, which
makes an excellent resting spot for families traveling with kids. The library also offers an
interesting array of events and art exhibitions that are worth checking out. A 385-seat
auditorium is the setting for a unique mix of dance and music performances, author talks,
and children's programs. Want to check your e-mail? Stop by the third-floor Computer
Commons, which has about 75 terminals available for public use. Allow a half-hour.

400 S. State St. ℂ **312/747-4300.** www.chipublib.org. Free admission. Mon–Thurs 9am–7pm; Fri–Sat
9am–5pm; Sun 1–5pm. Closed major holidays. Bus: 2, 6, 11, 29, 36, 62, 145, 146, 147, or 151. Subway/El:
Red Line to Jackson/State, or Brown Line to Van Buren/Library.

2 THE EARTH, THE SKY & THE SEA: THE BIG THREE IN THE GRANT PARK MUSEUM CAMPUS

For a map of these attractions (or this neighborhood), see p. 150.

With terraced gardens and broad walkways, the Museum Campus at the southern end of
Grant Park makes it easy for pedestrians to visit three of the city's most beloved institutions: The natural history museum, aquarium, and planetarium. To get to the Museum
Campus from the Loop, head east across Grant Park on East Balbo Drive from South
Michigan Avenue, and then trek south along the lakeshore path to the museums (about
a 15-minute walk). Or, follow 11th Street east from South Michigan Avenue to the
walkway that spans the Metra tracks. Cross Columbus Drive, and then pick up the path
that will take you under Lake Shore Drive and into the Museum Campus. The CTA no.
146 bus will take you from downtown to all three of these attractions; it also stops at the
Roosevelt El stop on the Red Line. Call ℂ **312/836-7000** (from any city or suburban
area code) for the stop locations and schedule.

Ⓥalue Museums for Less

If you're planning on visiting lots of Chicago museums, you should invest in a
CityPass, a pre-paid ticket that gets you into the biggest attractions (the Art Institute, Field Museum of Natural History, Shedd Aquarium, Adler Planetarium,
Museum of Science and Industry, and Hancock Observatory). The cost at press
time was $69 for adults and $59 for children, which is about 50% cheaper than
paying all the museums' individual admission fees. You can buy a CityPass at any
of the museums listed above, or purchase one online before you get to town
(www.citypass.com).

(Tips) **Website Extras**

Scanning the websites of museums and other attractions before you visit can enhance your trip when you get here. At the **Field Museum of Natural History** website (www.fieldmuseum.org), you can download an MP3 audio tour of the museum's permanent collection; you can also print out a Family Adventure Tour, which sends kids on a scavenger hunt throughout the museum. The **Millennium Park** MP3 audio tour (available at www.millenniumpark.org) includes interviews with the artists who created the park's eye-catching artwork. And if you're intimidated by the massive size of the **Museum of Science and Industry,** check out the website's Personal Planner, which will put together a customized itinerary based your family's interests (www.msichicago.org).

A large indoor parking lot is accessible from Lake Shore Drive southbound; you can park there for $16 for up to 4 hours, $19 all day. Be aware that there is no public parking during Chicago Bears games in the fall; Soldier Field is next to the Museum Campus, and football fans get first dibs on all the surrounding parking spaces.

Adler Planetarium and Astronomy Museum ★★   The building may be historic (it was the first planetarium in the Western Hemisphere), but some of the attractions here will captivate the most jaded video-game addict.

Your first stop should be the modern Sky Pavilion, where the don't-miss experience is the **StarRider Theater** ★★. Settle down under the massive dome, and you'll take a half-hour interactive virtual-reality trip through the Milky Way and into deep space, featuring a computer-generated 3-D-graphics projection system and controls in the armrest of each seat. Six high-resolution video projectors form a seamless image above your head—you'll feel as if you're literally floating in space. If you're looking for more entertainment, the **Sky Theater** shows movies with an astronomical bent; recent shows have included *Secrets of Saturn* and *Mars Now!*

The planetarium's exhibition galleries feature a variety of displays and interactive activities. If you're only going to see one exhibit (and have kids in tow), check out *Shoot For the Moon* ★★, an exhibit on lunar exploration that's full of interactive stations. (It also showcases the personal collection of astronaut Jim Lovell, captain of the infamous Apollo 13 mission, who now lives in the Chicago suburbs.) Other exhibits include *Bringing the Heavens to Earth* ★, which traces the ways different cultures have tried to make sense of astronomical phenomena, and *From the Night Sky to the Big Bang,* which includes artifacts from the planetarium's extensive collection of astronomical instruments. (Although suitable for older children, these can get a bit boring for little ones unless they're real astronomy nuts.)

The museum's cafe provides views of the lakefront and skyline. On the first Friday evening of the month, the museum stays open until 10pm, and visitors can view dramatic close-ups of the moon, the planets, and distant galaxies through a closed-circuit monitor connected to the planetarium's Doane Observatory telescope.

Allow 2 hours, more if you want to see more than one show.

1300 S. Lake Shore Dr. (©) **312/922-STAR** [7827]. www.adlerplanetarium.org. Admission $10 adults, $6 children 4–17, free for children 3 and under; admission including 1 show and audio tour $19 adults, $15 children. Free admission Tues Jan–Mar and Sept–Dec. Memorial Day–Labor Day daily 9:30am–6pm; early

Field Museum of Natural History ★★★ (Kids) Is it any wonder that Steven Spielberg thought the Field Museum of Natural History was a suitable home turf for the intrepid archaeologist and adventurer hero of his Indiana Jones movies? Spread over the museum's 9 acres of floor space are scores of permanent and temporary exhibitions—some interactive, but most requiring the old-fashion skills of observation and imagination.

Navigating all the exhibits can be daunting (I live here and I still haven't seen everything!), so pace yourself and prioritize what you want to see. Start in the grand Stanley Field Hall, where you'll stand face-to-face with **Sue** ★★★, the largest, most complete *Tyrannosaurus rex* fossil ever unearthed. The museum acquired the specimen—named for the paleontologist who discovered it in South Dakota in 1990—for a cool $8.4 million after a high-stakes bidding war. The real skull is so heavy that a lighter copy had to be mounted on the skeleton; the actual one is on display nearby.

Families should head downstairs for the most popular kid-friendly exhibits. Walking through *Inside Ancient Egypt* ★★, visitors explore scenes and rituals of everyday life, viewing actual mummies and realistic burial scenes, a living marsh environment and canal works, the ancient royal barge, a religious shrine, and a reproduction of a typical marketplace of the period. Next door, you'll find *Underground Adventure* ★★, a "total immersion environment" populated by giant robotic earwigs, centipedes, wolf spiders, and other subterranean critters. The Disneyesque exhibit is a big hit with kids, but—annoyingly—carries an extra admission charge ($7 on top of regular admission).

You might be tempted to skip the "peoples of the world" exhibits, but trust me—some are not only mind-opening but also great fun. *Traveling the Pacific* ★, hidden up on the second floor, is definitely worth a stop. Hundreds of artifacts from the museum's oceanic collection re-create scenes of island life in the South Pacific. (There's even a full-scale model of a Maori Meeting House.) *Africa* ★, an assemblage of African artifacts and provocative interactive multimedia presentations, takes viewers to Senegal, a Cameroon palace, the wildlife-rich savanna, and on a "virtual" journey aboard a slave ship to the Americas. Native Chicagoans will quickly name two more signature highlights: The taxidermies of *Bushman* (a legendary lowland gorilla that made international headlines while at the city's Lincoln Park Zoo) and the *Man-Eating Lions of Tsavo* (the pair of male lions that munched nearly 140 British railway workers constructing a bridge in East Africa in 1898; their story is featured in the film *The Ghost and the Darkness*).

If you've got little kids along (ages 7 and under), don't miss the **Crown Family Play-Lab,** which is full of hands-on activities, including an art room and a soundproofed space filled with drums and other percussion instruments.

The museum books special traveling exhibits (recent blockbusters included shows on King Tut and ancient Pompeii), but be forewarned: The high-profile exhibits are usually crowded and—again—have an additional admission charge. A much better deal is a free tour of the museum highlights; tours begin daily at 11am and 2pm.

When you're ready to take a break, the Corner Bakery cafe, just off the main hall, serves food a cut above the usual museum food court—although there's also a McDonald's on the lower level. Allow 3 hours (although you could easily spend all day).

Roosevelt Rd. and Lake Shore Dr. ℂ **312/922-9410.** www.fieldmuseum.org. Admission $15 adults, $12 seniors and students with ID, $10 children 3–11, free for children 2 and under. Extra fee applies for special exhibits. Free admission the second Mon of every month. Daily 9am–5pm. Closed Dec 25. Bus: 146.

EXPLORING CHICAGO

7

THE EARTH, THE SKY & THE SEA

(Tips) Getting the Most from Your Field Museum Visit

You could easily spend a day at the Field Museum—although sometimes it feels as if you've waited almost that long in the admission line. The Field is one of my must-see destinations for families, but it can get crowded, especially during school vacations in the winter and summer. Remember that the museum opens earlier than most people realize—at 9 in the morning—and you'll get a jump on the crowds as long as you arrive by 10am. Head for two of the most popular exhibits first: **Inside Ancient Egypt** (on the ground floor) and the **Dinosaur Hall** (on the upper level). It also pays to take an early lunch break: The Field has two on-site restaurants (McDonald's and Corner Bakery), but no cafeteria, and both places are often full by noon. If you plan ahead and bring your own food, you can eat in relative peace and quiet at the **Siragusa Center** on the lower level, a large, bright room with benches, tables, and vending machines.

John G. Shedd Aquarium ★★★ The Shedd is one of the world's largest indoor aquariums, and houses thousands of river, lake, and sea denizens in standard aquarium tanks and elaborate new habitats within its octagon-shaped marble building. The only problem with the Shedd is its relatively steep admission price. You can keep your costs down by buying "Aquarium Only" tickets; the tradeoff is that you'll miss some of the most stunning exhibits. A CityPass (see "Museums for Less," above) can save you money if you visit enough of the other included attractions.

The first thing you'll see as you enter is the **Caribbean Coral Reef** ★. This 90,000-gallon circular tank occupies the Beaux Arts–style central rotunda, entertaining spectators who press up against the glass to ogle divers feeding nurse sharks, barracudas, stingrays, and a hawksbill sea turtle. A roving camera connected to video monitors on the tank's periphery gives visitors close-ups of the animals inside, but I'd recommend sticking around to catch one of the daily feedings, when a diver swims around the tank and (thanks to a microphone) talks about the species and their eating habits.

The exhibits surrounding the Caribbean coral reef re-create marine habitats around the world. The best is *Amazon Rising: Seasons of the River* ★, a rendering of the Amazon basin that showcases frogs and other animals as well as fish (although the sharp-toothed piranhas are pretty cool).

You'll pay extra to see the other Shedd highlights, but they're quite impressive, so I'd suggest shelling out for them if you plan to spend more than an hour here. The ***Ocean-arium*** ★★★, with a wall of windows revealing the lake outside, replicates a Pacific Northwest coastal environment and creates the illusion of one uninterrupted expanse of sea. On a fixed performance schedule in a large pool flanked by an amphitheater, a crew of friendly trainers puts dolphins through their paces of leaping dives, breaches, and tail walking. Check out the Oceanarium schedule as soon as you get to the Shedd; seating can fill up quickly, so you'll want to get here early. If you're visiting during a summer weekend, you may also want to buy your Oceanarium ticket in advance to make sure you can catch a show that day.

Wild Reef—Sharks at Shedd ★★ is a series of 26 connected habitats that house a Philippine coral reef patrolled by sharks and other predators. The floor-to-ceiling windows bring the toothy swimmers up close and personal (they even swim over your head

The Pride of Prairie Avenue

Prairie Avenue, south of the Loop, was the city's first "Gold Coast," and its most famous address is **Glessner House,** 1800 S. Prairie Ave. (✆ **312/326-1480; www.glessnerhouse.org).** A must-see for anyone interested in architectural history and the only surviving Chicago building designed by Boston architect Henry Hobson Richardson, the 1886 structure represented a dramatic shift from traditional Victorian architecture (and inspired a young Frank Lloyd Wright).

The imposing granite exterior gives the home a forbidding air. (Railway magnate George Pullman, who lived nearby, complained, "I do not know what I have ever done to have that thing staring me in the face every time I go out my door.") But step inside, and the home turns out to be a welcoming, cozy retreat, filled with Arts and Crafts furnishings. Visits are by guided tour only; tours begin at 1 and 3pm Wednesday through Sunday (except major holidays) on a first-come, first-served basis (advance reservations are only taken for groups of 10 or more). Tours cost $10 for adults, $9 for students and seniors, and $6 for children 5 to 12.

A visit to Glessner House can also be combined with a tour of the nearby **Clarke House Museum,** a Greek Revival home that's the oldest surviving house in the city; tours are given at noon and 2pm. Combination tickets for both Glessner House and Clarke House cost $15 for adults, $12 student and seniors, and $8 for children. Admission for all tours is free on Wednesday.

To get to Prairie Avenue, catch the no. 1, 3, or 4 bus from Michigan Avenue at Jackson Boulevard, get off at 18th Street and walk 2 blocks east.

at certain spots). And if you're here with kids, you'll want to stop by the **Polar Play Zone,** where little ones can pet a starfish, try on a penguin suit, or get a good look at the real thing—the Play Zone is home to a dozen rockhopper penguins.

If you want a quality sit-down meal in a restaurant with a spectacular view of Lake Michigan, check out Soundings. There's also a family-friendly cafeteria.

Allow 2 to 3 hours.

1200 S. Lake Shore Dr. ✆ **312/939-2438.** www.sheddaquarium.org. Day Pass (for all exhibits) $25 adults, $18 seniors and children 3–11, free for children 2 and under; aquarium only $8 adults, $6 seniors and children. Free admission to aquarium only Mon–Tues mid-Sept–Nov and Jan–Feb. Memorial Day–Labor Day daily 9am–6pm; early Sept–late May Mon–Fri 9am–5pm, Sat–Sun 9am–6pm. Bus: 146.

3 NORTH OF THE LOOP: THE MAGNIFICENT MILE & BEYOND

For a map of these attractions (or this neighborhood), see p. 150.

Most of these sights are either on the Magnificent Mile (North Michigan Ave.) and its surrounding blocks or close by on the Near North Side.

(Fun Facts)   **A River Runs Through It**

The Chicago River remains one of the most visible of the city's major physical features. It's spanned by more movable bridges within the city limits (52 at last count) than any other city in the world. An almost-mystical moment occurs downtown when all the bridges spanning the main and south branches—connecting the Loop to both the Near West Side and the Near North Side—are raised, allowing for the passage of some ship, barge, or contingent of high-masted sailboats. The Chicago River has long outlived the critical commercial function that it once performed. Most of the remaining millworks that occupy its banks no longer depend on the river alone for the transport of their materials, raw and finished. The river's main function today is to serve as a fluvial conduit for sewage, which, owing to an engineering feat that reversed its flow inland in 1900, no longer pollutes the waters of Lake Michigan. Recently, Chicagoans have begun to discover other roles for the river, including water cruises, park areas, cafes, public art installations, and a riverside bike path that connects to the lakefront route near Wacker Drive. Actually, today's developers aren't the first to wonder why the river couldn't be Chicago's Seine. A look at the early-20th-century Beaux Arts balustrades lining the river along Wacker Drive, complete with comfortably spaced benches and Parisian-style bridge houses, shows that Chicago architect and urban planner Daniel Burnham knew full well what a treasure the city had.

The Hancock Observatory ★   The Hancock isn't as famous as the Sears Tower, but the view from the city's third-tallest building is as good as any in town. A high-speed elevator carries passengers to the observatory in 40 seconds, and on a clear day, you can see portions of the three states surrounding this corner of Illinois (Michigan, Indiana, and Wisconsin), for a radius of 40 to 50 miles. The view up the North Side is particularly dramatic, stretching from nearby Oak Street and North Avenue beaches, along the green strip of Lincoln Park, to the line of high-rises tracing the shoreline beyond. During your visit, you're given a handheld PDA that delivers a "**Sky Tour**," using audio and video to highlight features of interest across the skyline (kids get their own version). The Skywalk open-air viewing deck allows visitors to feel the rush of the wind at 1,000 feet through a "screened porch." There's also a cafe with an adjoining kids' play area if you want to linger over a cappuccino and snack. Allow 1 hour.

"Big John," as some locals call the building, also has a restaurant and adjoining lounge, the **Signature Room** (p. 276). For about the same cost as the observatory, you can take in the views with a libation in hand.

94th floor, John Hancock Center, 875 N. Michigan Ave. (enter on Delaware St.). (*) **888/875-VIEW** [8439], or 312/751-3681. www.hancock-observatory.com. Admission $15 adults, $14 seniors, $10 children 4–11, free for children 3 and under. Daily 9am–11pm. Bus: 145, 146, 147, or 151. Subway/El: Red Line to Chicago.

Museum of Contemporary Art (MCA) ★★   Although the MCA is one of the largest contemporary art museums in the country, theaters and hallways seem to take up much of the space, so seeing the actual art won't take you long. The gloomy, imposing

ⓘ Fun Facts   Rock Around the World

The impressive Gothic **Tribune Tower,** just north of the Chicago River on the east side of Michigan Avenue, is home to one of the country's media giants and the *Chicago Tribune* newspaper. It's also notable for an array of architectural fragments jutting out from the exterior. The newspaper's notoriously despotic publisher, Robert R. McCormick, started the collection shortly after the building's completion in 1925, gathering pieces during his world travels. *Tribune* correspondents then began supplying building fragments that they acquired on assignment. Each one now bears the name of the structure and country whence it came. There are 138 pieces in all, including chunks and shards from the Great Wall of China, the Taj Mahal, the White House, the Arc de Triomphe, the Berlin Wall, the Roman Colosseum, London's Houses of Parliament, the Great Pyramid of Cheops in Giza, Egypt, and the original tomb of Abraham Lincoln in Springfield, Illinois.

building, designed by Berlin's Josef Paul Kleihues, doesn't offer a warm welcome, but the interior spaces are more vibrant, with a sun-drenched two-story central corridor, elliptical staircases, and three floors of exhibition space. The MCA has tried to raise its national profile to the level of New York's Museum of Modern Art by booking major touring retrospectives of working artists such as Jeff Koons and Cindy Sherman; other exhibits emphasize experimentation in a variety of media, including painting, sculpture, photography, video and film, and performance.

You can see the MCA's highlights in about an hour, although art lovers will want more time to wander (especially if a high-profile exhibit is in town). Your first stop should be the handsome barrel-vaulted galleries on the top floor, dedicated to pieces from the permanent collection. Visitors who'd like a little guidance with making sense of the rather challenging works can rent an audio tour or take a free tour (1 and 6pm Tues; 1pm Wed–Fri; noon, 1, 2, and 3pm Sat–Sun). In addition to a range of special activities and educational programming, including films, performances, and a lecture series in a 300-seat theater, the museum features Puck's at the MCA, a cafe operated by Wolfgang Puck of Spago restaurant fame, with seating that overlooks a 1-acre terraced sculpture garden. The store, with one-of-a-kind gift items, is worth a stop even if you don't make it into the museum. The museum's First Friday program, featuring after-hours performances, live music, and food and drink, takes place on the first Friday of every month. Allow 1 to 2 hours.

220 E. Chicago Ave. (1 block east of Michigan Ave.). ⓒ **312/280-2660.** www.mcachicago.org. Admission $12 adults, $7 seniors and students with ID, free for children 12 and under. Free admission Tues. Tues 10am–8pm; Wed–Sun 10am–5pm. Closed Jan 1, Thanksgiving, and Dec 25. Bus: 3, 10, 66, 145, 146, or 151. Subway/El: Red Line to Chicago.

Navy Pier ★ ⓚ Kids   Built during World War I, this 3,000-foot-long pier was a Navy training center for pilots during World War II. The military aura is long gone, replaced with a combination of carnival attractions, a food court, and boat dock, making it a bustling tourist destination (whether or not that's a good thing depends on your tolerance for crowds). If you do make it all the way to the end of the pier, though, you'll be rewarded with great views of the city.

(Value) **Free Fireworks!**

Yes, Navy Pier can be chaotic, crowded, and loud, but come summer, it's also a prime gathering spot for visitors from around the world. From Memorial Day through Labor Day, the pier sponsors twice-weekly fireworks shows, where you can watch spectacular light displays reflected in the water of Lake Michigan below. It's a great way to appreciate the city at night (along with a few thousand of your fellow travelers). The shows start at 9:30pm on Wednesdays and 10:15pm on Saturdays.

Midway down the pier are the **Crystal Gardens** ★, with 70 full-size palm trees, dancing fountains, and other flora in a glass-enclosed atrium; a carousel and kiddie carnival rides; and a 15-story Ferris wheel, a replica of the original that made its debut at Chicago's 1893 World's Fair. The pier is also home to the **Chicago Children's Museum** (p. 192), a **3-D IMAX theater** (𝄐 **312/595-5629**), a small ice-skating rink, and the **Chicago Shakespeare Theatre** (p. 254). The shops tend to be bland and touristy, but there are a number of dining options. They include the white-tablecloth seafood restaurant Riva; a beer garden with live music; **Charlie's Ale House,** a casual pub with top-notch burgers; and Bubba Gump Shrimp Co. & Market, a family seafood joint. Summer is one long party at the pier, with fireworks on Wednesday and Saturday evenings.

The **Smith Museum of Stained Glass Windows** ★★ may sound dull, but decorative-art aficionados shouldn't miss this remarkable installation of more than 150 stained-glass windows set in illuminated display cases. Occupying an 800-foot-long expanse on the ground floor of Navy Pier, the free museum features works by Frank Lloyd Wright, Louis Sullivan, John LaFarge, and Louis Comfort Tiffany.

If the noise and commercialism get overwhelming, take the half-mile stroll to the end of the pier, where you can enjoy the wind, the waves, and the city view, which is the real delight of a place like this. Or, unwind in **Olive Park,** a small sylvan haven with a sliver of beach just north of Navy Pier.

You'll find more than half a dozen sailing vessels moored at the south dock, including a couple of dinner-cruise ships, the pristine white-masted tall ship *Windy,* and the 70-foot speedboats *Seadog I, II,* and *III.* In the summer months, water taxis speed between Navy Pier and other Chicago sights. For more specifics on sightseeing and dinner cruises, see "Lake & River Cruises," p. 194. Allow 1 hour.

600 E. Grand Ave. (at Lake Michigan). 𝄐 **800/595-PIER** [7437] (outside 312 area code), or 312/595-PIER [7437]. www.navypier.com. Free admission. Summer Sun–Thurs 10am–10pm, Fri–Sat 10am–midnight; fall–spring Mon–Thurs 10am–8pm, Fri–Sat 10am–10pm, Sun 10am–7pm. Parking: $20/day Mon–Thurs; $24/day Fri–Sun (lots fill quickly). Bus: 29, 65, 66, 120, or 121. Subway/El: Red Line to Grand/State; transfer to city bus 65 or board a free pier trolley bus.

Newberry Library   The Newberry Library is a bibliophile's dream. Established in 1887 thanks to a bequest by Chicago merchant and financier Walter Loomis Newberry, the noncirculating research library contains many rare books and manuscripts (such as Shakespeare's first folio and Jefferson's copy of *The Federalist Papers*), housed in a stately five-story granite building. The library is also a major destination for genealogists digging at their roots, with holdings that are free to the public (over the age of 16 with a photo ID). The collections include more than 1.5 million volumes and 75,000 maps, many of

a free 1-hour tour Thursday at 3pm or Saturday at 10:30am. The Newberry operates a
fine bookstore and also sponsors a series of concerts (including those by its resident early
music ensemble, the Newberry Consort), lectures, and children's story hours throughout
the year. One popular annual event is the **Bughouse Square debates** ★. Held across the
street in Washington Square Park in late July, the debates re-create the fiery soapbox ora-
tions of the left-wing agitators in the 1930s and 1940s. Allow a half-hour.

60 W. Walton St. (at Dearborn Pkwy.). 𝄐 **312/943-9090,** or 312/255-3700 for programs. www.newberry.
org. Reading room Tues–Thurs 10am–6pm; Fri–Sat 9am–5pm. Exhibit gallery Mon, Fri, and Sat 8:15am–
5:30pm; Tues–Thurs 8:15am–7:30pm. Bus: 22, 36, 125, 145, 146, 147, or 151. Subway/El: Red Line to Chi-
cago/State.

4 LINCOLN PARK ATTRACTIONS

For a map of these attractions (or this neighborhood), see p. 150.

Lincoln Park is the city's largest park, and certainly one of the longest. Straight and narrow, the park begins at North Avenue and follows the shoreline of Lake Michigan north
for several miles. Within its 1,200 acres are a world-class zoo, half a dozen beaches, a
botanical conservatory, two excellent museums, a golf course, and the meadows, formal
gardens, sporting fields, and tennis courts typical of urban parks. To get to the park, take
bus no. 22, 145, 146, 147, 151, or 156.

The park, named after Abraham Lincoln, is home to the **statue of the standing Abraham Lincoln** (just north of the North Ave. and State St. intersection), one of the city's
two Lincoln statues by Augustus Saint-Gaudens (the seated Lincoln is in Grant Park).
Saint-Gaudens also designed the *Bates Fountain* near the conservatory.

Cafe Brauer   This landmark 1900 building is not technically open to the public, aside
from an ice-cream parlor on the ground floor. (The lovely second-floor Great Hall, flanked
by two curving loggias, is one of the city's most popular wedding-reception spots; if you
stop by on a weekend, chances are you can sneak a peek while the caterers are setting up.)
Even if you don't make it inside, Cafe Brauer is a nice stopping-off point during a walk
around the park. Sit and sip a coffee, or rent a paddleboat at the edge of the lovely South
Pond ($10 per half-hour). Best of all, though, is the picture-postcard view from the adjacent
bridge spanning the pond of the John Hancock Center and neighboring skyscrapers
beyond Lincoln Park's treetops. Allow a quarter-hour, longer for a paddleboat ride.

2021 Stockton Dr. 𝄐 **312/742-2400.** Daily 10am–5pm. Bus: 151 or 156.

Chicago History Museum ★   The Chicago History Museum at the southwestern
tip of Lincoln Park is one of the city's oldest cultural institutions (founded in 1856), but
it's reinvented itself for the 21st century. The main, must-see exhibit is *Chicago: Cross-
roads of America* ★★, which fills the museum's second floor. A survey of the city's
history—from its founding as a frontier trading post to the riots at the 1968 Democratic
Convention—it's filled with photos, artifacts, and newsreels that make the past come
alive; surrounding galleries track the development of local sports teams, architecture,
music, and art. Although the exhibit is geared toward families with older children (you
can even download an MP3 audio tour for teenagers from the museum's website), little
ones love the re-creation of an 1890s El station, where they can run inside the city's first
elevated train. Another museum highlight is the hall of dioramas that re-create scenes

from Chicago's past. Although they've been around for decades (and are decidedly low-tech), they're a fun way to trace the city's progression from a few small cabins to the grand World's Columbian Exposition of 1893. The museum's Costume and Textile Gallery showcases pieces from the museum's renowned collection of historic clothing; recent exhibitions included couture gowns by French designer Christian Dior and a survey of American quilts. The Children's Gallery on the ground floor has interactive exhibits for kids, including my personal favorite, a giant table where you can experience the "Smells of Chicago."

There's a small cafe with sandwiches and salads that makes a convenient lunch stop. The History Museum also presents a wide range of lectures, seminars, and tours, including walking tours of the surrounding neighborhood; check the museum's website for details, as the schedules change frequently. Allow 1 to 2 hours.

1601 N. Clark St. (at North Ave.). ℰ **312/642-4600.** www.chicagohistory.org. Admission $14 adults, $12 seniors and students, free for children 12 and under. Free admission Mon. Mon–Sat 9:30am–4:30pm; Sun noon–5pm. Bus: 11, 22, 36, 72, 151, or 156.

Lincoln Park Conservatory ★

Just beyond the zoo's northeast border is a lovely botanical garden housed in a soaring glass-domed structure. Inside are four great halls filled with thousands of plants. If you're visiting Chicago in the wintertime, I can't think of a better prescription for mood elevation than this lush haven of greenery. The Palm House features giant palms and rubber trees (including a 50-ft. fiddle-leaf rubber tree dating back to 1891); the Fernery nurtures plants that grow close to the forest floor; and the Tropical House is a shiny symphony of flowering trees, vines, and bamboo. The fourth environment is the Show House, where seasonal flower shows take place.

Even better than the plants inside, however, might be what lies outside the front doors. The expansive lawn, with its French garden and lovely fountain on the conservatory's south side, is one of the best places in town for an informal picnic (especially nice if you're visiting the zoo and want to avoid the congestion at its food concession venues).

The Lincoln Park Conservatory has a sister facility on the city's West Side, in Garfield Park, that is even more impressive. In fact, the 2-acre **Garfield Park Conservatory,** 300 N. Central Park Ave. (ℰ **312/746-5100**), designed by the great landscape architect Jens Jensen in 1907, is one of the largest gardens under glass in the world. Unfortunately, it's surrounded by a rather blighted neighborhood with a high crime rate, so I recommend driving there rather than using public transportation. It's open 365 days a year from 9am to 5pm.

Allow a half-hour for the Lincoln Park Conservatory.

Fullerton Ave. (at Stockton Dr.). ℰ **312/742-7736.** Free admission. Daily 9am–5pm. Bus: 73, 151, or 156.

Lincoln Park Zoo ★★★ Ⓥalue

One of the city's treasures, this family-friendly attraction is not only open 365 days a year, but it's also free. Even if you don't have time for a complete tour of the various habitats, it's worth at least a quick stop during a stroll through Lincoln Park. The term "zoological gardens" truly fits here: Landmark Georgian Revival brick buildings and modern structures sit among gently rolling pathways, verdant lawns, and a kaleidoscopic profusion of flower gardens. The late Marlon Perkins, legendary host of the *Mutual of Omaha's Wild Kingdom* TV series, got his start here as the zoo's director, and filmed a pioneering TV show called *Zoo Parade* (*Wild Kingdom*'s predecessor) in the basement of the old Reptile House.

My favorite exhibit is the **Regenstein African Journey** ★★★, a series of linked indoor and outdoor habitats that's home to giraffes, rhinos, and other large mammals;

> **Moments**   **A Great View**
>
> After a visit to Lincoln Park Zoo or the Peggy Notebaert Nature Museum, take a quick stroll on Fullerton Avenue to the bridge that runs over the lagoon (just before you get to Lake Shore Dr.). Standing on the south side of Fullerton Avenue, you'll have a great view of the Chicago skyline and Lincoln Park—an excellent backdrop for family souvenir photos. This path can get very crowded on summer weekends, so I suggest trying this photo op during the week.

large glass-enclosed tanks allow visitors to go face-to-face with swimming pygmy hippos and (not for the faint of heart) a rocky ledge filled with Madagascar hissing cockroaches.

Your second stop should be the Regenstein Center for African Apes ★★. Lincoln Park Zoo has had remarkable success breeding gorillas and chimpanzees, and watching these ape families interact can be mesmerizing (and touching). *One caveat:* I've found the building incredibly noisy during weekend visits, so be prepared.

Other exhibits worth a visit are the **Small Mammal–Reptile House,** which features a glass-enclosed walk-through ecosystem simulating river, savanna, and forest habitats, and the popular **Sea Lion Pool** in the center of the zoo, which is home to harbor seals, gray seals, and California sea lions (walk down the ramp and take a look at the underwater viewing area). If you're here for a while and need nourishment, there's an indoor food court as well as the Big Cats Café, located on a terrace above the gift shop. Allow 3 hours. For the adjoining children's zoo, see "Kid Stuff," p. 192.

2200 N. Cannon Dr. (at Fullerton Pkwy.). ℂ 312/742-2000. www.lpzoo.com. Free admission. Buildings daily 10am–5pm (Memorial Day–Labor Day until 6:30pm Sat–Sun). Grounds Memorial Day–Labor Day daily 9am–7pm; Apr–late May and early Sept–Oct daily 9am–6pm; Nov–Mar daily 9am–5pm. Parking $14 for up to 3 hours in on-site lot. Bus: 77, 151, or 156.

Peggy Notebaert Nature Museum ★ (Kids)   Built into a slope that was once the site of an ancient sand dune—and part of the shoreline of Lake Michigan—this museum bills itself as "an environmental museum for the 21st century." Many of the exhibits are hands-on and designed for kids, making this a good stop for families.

Shaded by huge cottonwoods and maples, the sand-colored exterior, with its horizontal lines composed of interlocking trapezoids, resembles a sand dune. Rooftop-level walkways give strollers a view of birds and other urban wildlife below, and paths wind through gardens planted with native Midwestern wildflowers and grasses. Inside, large windows create a dialogue between the outdoor environment and the indoor exhibits designed to illuminate it. My favorite exhibit by far is the *Butterfly Haven* ★★, a greenhouse habitat where about 25 Midwestern species of butterflies and moths carry on their complex life cycles (wander through as a riot of color flutters all around you). If you're traveling with little ones, I'd also recommend the **Extreme Green House** ★, a bungalow where kids can play while learning how they can be environmentally friendly, and **RiverWorks,** a water play exhibit that gives children an excuse to splash around while building dams and maneuvering boats along a mini river. Allow 1 to 2 hours.

Fullerton Ave. and Cannon Dr. ℂ 773/755-5100. www.chias.org. Admission $9 adults, $7 seniors and students, $6 children 3–12, free for children 2 and under. Free admission Thurs. Mon–Fri 9am–4:30pm; Sat–Sun 10am–5pm. Closed Jan 1, Thanksgiving, and Dec 25. Bus: 77, 151, or 156.

5 EXPLORING HYDE PARK: THE MUSEUM OF SCIENCE AND INDUSTRY & MORE

Hyde Park, south of the loop, is the birthplace of atomic fission, home to the University of Chicago and the popular Museum of Science and Industry, and definitely worth a trip. It's gotten an added boost of publicity ever since a certain former resident, Barack Obama, came to national prominence. The Obamas are such fans of the area that they've kept their house here and return for regular visits. (For more about the Obama connection, see "Obama's Chicago" in Chapter 2, p. 27.) Allow at least half a day to explore the University of Chicago campus and surrounding neighborhood (one of Chicago's most successfully integrated). If you want to explore a museum or two as well, plan on a full day.

SOME HYDE PARK HISTORY   When Hyde Park was settled in 1850, it became Chicago's first suburb. A hundred years later, in the 1950s, it added another first to its impressive résumé, one that the current neighborhood is not particularly proud of: An urban-renewal plan. At the time, a certain amount of old commercial and housing stock— just the kind of buildings that would be prized today—was demolished rather than rehabilitated and replaced by projects and small shopping malls that actually make some corners of Hyde Park look more suburban, in the modern sense, than they really are.

What Hyde Park can be proud of is that, in racially divided Chicago, this neighborhood has found an alternative vision. As Southern blacks began to migrate to Chicago's South Side during World War I, many whites fled. But most whites here, especially those who wanted to stay near the university, chose integration as the only realistic strategy to preserve their neighborhood. The 2000 census proved that integration still works: About 40% of the residents are white and 37% are black; there is also a significant Asian population. Hyde Park is decidedly middle class, with pockets of affluence that reflect the early 20th-century period when the well-to-do moved here to escape the decline of Prairie Avenue. A well-known black resident from the area is the late Elijah Muhammad, and numerous Nation of Islam families continue to worship in a mosque, formerly a Greek Orthodox cathedral, that is one of the neighborhood's architectural landmarks. Surrounding this unusual enclave, however, are many marginal blocks where poverty and slum housing abound. For all its nobility, Hyde Park's achievement in integration merely emphasizes that even more unwieldy than racial differences are socioeconomic ones.

The University of Chicago is widely hailed as one of the more intellectually exciting institutions of higher learning in the country, and has been home to some 73 Nobel laureates, including physicist Enrico Fermi, novelist Saul Bellow, and economist Milton Friedman. (Almost one-third of all the Nobel Prizes in Economics have gone to University of Chicago professors, twice as many as any other institution.) Another long-time

---

Fun Facts   Did You Know?

The world's first Ferris wheel was built on Hyde Park's midway during the World's Columbian Exposition in 1893. It was eventually dynamited and sold for scrap metal.

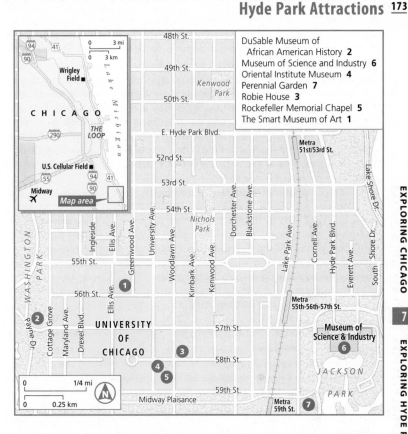

DuSable Museum of
   African American History **2**
Museum of Science and Industry **6**
Oriental Institute Museum **4**
Perennial Garden **7**
Robie House **3**
Rockefeller Memorial Chapel **5**
The Smart Museum of Art **1**

faculty member was English professor Norman Maclean, author of *A River Runs Through It*. Though they may joke about the school's staid social life, U of C undergrads take pride in their school's nerdy reputation.

The year the university opened its doors in 1892 was a big one for Hyde Park, but 1893 was even bigger. In that year, Chicago, chosen over other cities in a competitive international field, played host to the World's Columbian Exposition, commemorating the 400th anniversary of Columbus's arrival in America. To create a fairground, the landscape architect Frederick Law Olmsted was enlisted to fill in the marshlands along Hyde Park's lakefront and link what was to become Jackson Park to existing Washington Park on the neighborhood's western boundary with a narrow concourse called the Midway Plaisance. On the resulting 650 acres—at a cost of $30 million—12 exhibit palaces, 57 buildings devoted to U.S. states and foreign governments, and dozens of smaller structures were constructed under the supervision of architect Daniel Burnham. Most of the buildings followed Burnham's preference for the Classical Revival style and white stucco exteriors. With the innovation of outdoor electric lighting, the sparkling result was the "White City," which attracted 27 million visitors in a single season, from May 1 to October 31, 1893. The exposition sponsors, in that brief time, had remarkably recovered their investment, but within a few short years of the fair's closing, vandalism and fire destroyed most of its buildings. Only the Palace of Fine Arts, occupying the eastern tip of the midway, survives to this day, and it now houses the Museum of Science and Industry. (For more on the behind-the-scenes drama at the Exposition, read *The Devil in the White City* by Erik Larson, a nonfiction history book with the suspense of a thriller.)

GETTING THERE　From the Loop, the ride to Hyde Park on the **no. 6 Jeffrey Express bus** takes about 30 minutes. The bus originates on Wacker Drive, travels south along State Street, and ultimately follows Lake Shore Drive to Hyde Park. The bus runs daily from early morning to late evening, with departures about every 5 minutes on weekdays and every 10 minutes on weekends and holidays. The southbound express bus fare adds a surcharge of 25¢ to the normal fare of $2 (there's no surcharge if you use a CTA transit card). The **no. 1 local bus** originates at Union Station on Jackson Boulevard and Canal Street and takes about an hour.

For a faster trip, take the **Metra Electric train** on the South Chicago line, which goes from downtown to Hyde Park in about 15 minutes. Trains run every hour (more frequently during rush hour) Monday through Saturday from 5:15am to 12:50am, and every 30 to 90 minutes on Sunday and holidays from 5am to 12:55am. Downtown stations are at Randolph Street and Michigan Avenue, Van Buren Street and Michigan Avenue, and Roosevelt Road and Michigan Avenue (near the Museum Campus in Grant Park). Printed schedules are available at the stations. The fare is approximately $2 each way.

For CTA bus and Metra train information, call ✆ **312/836-7000**, or visit **www. transitchicago.com** or **www.metrarail.com**.

For taxis, dial ✆ **312/TAXI-CAB** (829-4222) for **Yellow Cab** or ✆ **312/CHECKER** (243-2537) for **Checker.** The one-way fare from downtown is around $15 to $20.

A SUGGESTED ITINERARY　A long 1-day itinerary for Hyde Park should include the following: A walk through the University of Chicago campus (including a stroll along the Midway Plaisance); a visit to the Museum of Science and Industry (for families); Frank Lloyd Wright's Robie House or one of the other local museums; and lunch or dinner in the neighborhood's commercial center.

THE TOP ATTRACTIONS

DuSable Museum of African-American History　The DuSable Museum is a repository of the history, art, and artifacts pertaining to the African-American experience and culture. Named for Chicago's first permanent settler, Jean Baptiste Point du Sable, a French-Canadian of Haitian descent, it was founded in 1961 in the home of Dr. Margaret Burroughs, an art teacher at the city's DuSable High School. In 1973, as a result of a community-based campaign, the museum took up residence in its present building (a former parks administration facility and police lockup) on the eastern edge of Washington Park. With no major endowment to speak of, the DuSable Museum has managed to accumulate a wide range of artifacts, including an excellent collection of paintings, drawings, and sculpture by African-American and African artists.

In 1993, the DuSable Museum added a 25,000-square-foot wing named in honor of the city's first and only African-American mayor, Harold Washington. The permanent exhibit on Washington contains memorabilia and personal effects, and surveys important episodes in his political career. Other recent exhibits included "Soul Soldiers," an examination of the Vietnam War through the perspective of African-American soldiers who served there. The museum also has a gift shop, a research library, and an extensive

---

(Tips) Hyde Park Bites

When you're ready to take a break, Hyde Park has an eclectic selection of restaurants. As in any university town, you'll find plenty of affordable, student-friendly hangouts. The most famous University of Chicago gathering spot is **Jimmy's Woodlawn Tap,** 1172 E. 55th St. (*(C)* **773/643-5516**). This 50-year-old bar and grill doesn't offer much in the way of atmosphere, but the hamburgers and sandwiches are cheap, and the person sitting next to you might just be a Nobel Prize–winning professor. Another casual spot near campus is **Medici,** 1327 E. 57th St. (*(C)* **773/667-7394;** www.medici57.com), where a few generations' worth of students have carved their names into the tables while chowing down on pizza, the house specialty. **Calypso Café,** 5211 S. Harper St., near the Metra train tracks (*(C)* **773/955-0229;** www.calypsocafechicago.com), serves conch chowder, jerk chicken, and other Caribbean favorites in a bright, funky setting. A few blocks south you'll find **La Petite Folie,** 1504 E. 55th St. (*(C)* **773/493-1394;** www.la petitefolie.com), a French bistro that offers a refined escape from student life.

---

program of community-related events, such as a jazz and blues music series, poetry readings, film screenings, and other cultural events, all presented in a 466-seat auditorium. Allow 1 to 2 hours.

740 E. 56th Place. *(C)* **773/947-0600.** www.dusablemuseum.org. Admission $3 adults, $2 students and seniors, $1 children 6–13, free for children 5 and under. Free admission Sun. Mon–Sat 10am–5pm, Sun noon–5pm. Closed major holidays. Bus: 6 or Metra Electric train to 57th St. and Lake Park Ave., and then a short cab ride.

Museum of Science and Industry ★★★ **(Kids)**   Even if you don't plan on spending the day in Hyde Park, you'll likely pass through the neighborhood on your way to one of Chicago's most popular tourist attractions. The massive Museum of Science and Industry is the granddaddy of interactive museums, with some 2,000 exhibits. Schedule at least 3 hours here; a comprehensive visit can take all day, especially if you catch an OMNIMAX movie.

While the museum is constantly adding new displays to cover the latest scientific breakthroughs, you shouldn't miss certain tried-and-true exhibits that have been here for years and epitomize the museum for Chicagoans. The **U-505** ★★★, a German submarine that was captured in 1944 and arrived at the museum 10 years later, brings home the claustrophobic reality of underwater naval life. The sub is displayed in a dramatic indoor arena with exhibits and newsreel footage that put the U-boat in historical context. (A guided tour of the sub's interior costs $5 extra, but the exhibit is worth visiting even if you don't go inside.) The full-scale **Coal Mine** ★★, which dates back to 1934, incorporates modern mining techniques into the exhibit—but the best part is the simulated trip down into a dark, mysterious mine. Get to these exhibits quickly after the museum opens because they attract amusement-park-length lines during the day.

Kids who love planes, trains, and automobiles shouldn't miss ***All Aboard the Silver Streak,*** a refurbished Burlington Pioneer Zephyr train with onboard interactive exhibits; the massive model-train exhibit that makes up ***The Great Train Story*** ★★; or ***Take Flight,*** an aviation exhibit featuring a full-size 727 airplane that revs up its engines and replays the voice recordings from a San Francisco–Chicago flight periodically throughout the day. *Networld* ★, which offers a flashy immersion in the Internet (with plenty of interactive screens), will entrance computer addicts. More low-tech—but fun for kids—are *The Farm* (where children can sit at the wheel of a giant combine) and the **chick hatchery** inside the exhibit *Genetics: Decoding Life,* where you can watch as tiny newborn chicks poke their way out of eggs. *Enterprise* ★ immerses mini-capitalists in the goings-on of a virtual company and includes an entire automated toy-making assembly line. If you have really little ones (under age 5), head for the *Idea Factory,* which is filled with hands-on play equipment (admission is limited to a set number of kids, so pick up a free timed ticket in advance).

I hate to indulge in gender stereotypes, but girls (myself included) love **Colleen Moore's Fairy Castle** ★★, a lavishly decorated miniature palace filled with priceless treasures (yes, those are real diamonds and pearls in the chandeliers). The castle is hidden on the lower level. Also tucked away in an inconspicuous spot—along the Blue stairwell between the Main Floor and the Balcony—are the *Human Body Slices,* actual slivers of human cadavers that are guaranteed to impress teenagers in search of something truly gross.

The **Henry Crown Space Center** ★★ is a museum-within-the-museum that documents the story of space exploration in copious detail, highlighted by a simulated space-shuttle experience through sight and sound at the center's five-story OMNIMAX Theater. The theater offers double features on the weekends; call for show times.

When you've worked up an appetite, you can visit the museum's large food court or the old-fashioned ice-cream parlor; there's also an excellent gift shop.

Although it's quite a distance from the rest of Chicago's tourist attractions, the museum is easy enough to reach without a car; your best options are the no. 6 Jeffrey Express bus and the Metra Electric train from downtown (the no. 10 bus runs from downtown to the museum's front entrance during the summer).

57th St. and Lake Shore Dr. © **800/468-6674** outside the Chicago area, 773/684-1414, or TTY 773/684-3323. www.msichicago.org. Admission to museum only: $13 adults, $12 seniors, $9 children 3–11, free for children 2 and under. Free admission weekdays in Oct and daily in Jan. Combination museum and OMNI-MAX Theater: $20 adults, $19 seniors, $14 children 3–11, free for children 2 and under on an adult's lap. Memorial Day–Labor Day Mon–Sat 9:30am–5:30pm, Sun 11am–5:30pm; early Sept–late May Mon–Sat 9:30am–4pm, Sun 11am–4pm. Closed Dec 25. Bus: 6 or Metra Electric train to 57th St. and Lake Park Ave.

Oriental Institute Museum ★   Near the midpoint of University of Chicago's campus, the Oriental Institute houses one of the world's major collections of Near Eastern art. Although most of the galleries have been renovated within the last few years, this is still a very traditional museum: Lots of glass cases and very few interactive exhibits (in other words, there's not much to interest young children). A few impressive pieces make it worth at least a brief stop, although history and art buffs should allow more time to linger.

Your first stop should be the **Egyptian Gallery** ★★, which showcases the finest objects among the museum's 35,000 Egyptian artifacts. At the center stands a monumental, 17-foot solid-quartzite statue of the boy king Tutankhamen; the largest Egyptian sculpture in the Western Hemisphere, it tips the scales at 6 tons. The surrounding exhibits have a wonderfully accessible approach that emphasizes themes, not chronology. Among them are mummification (there are 14 mummies on display—five people and nine animals), kingship, society, and writing (including a deed for the sale of a house, a copy of the *Book of the Dead,* and a schoolboy's homework).

The Oriental Institute also houses important collections of artifacts from civilizations that once flourished in what are now Iran and Iraq. The highlight of the **Mesopotamian**

| **Finds** | **More Frank Lloyd Wright Homes** |

In addition to Robie House, several of Wright's earlier works, still privately owned, dot the streets of Hyde Park. They include the **Heller House,** 5132 S. Woodlawn Ave. (1897); the **Blossom House,** 1332 E. 49th St. (1882); and the **McArthur House,** 4852 S. Kenwood Ave. (1892). *Note:* These houses are not open to the public, so they can only be admired from the outside.

Gallery ★ is a massive 16-foot-tall sculpture of a winged bull with a human head, which once stood in the palace of Assyrian king Sargon II. The gallery also contains some of the earliest man-made tools ever excavated, along with many other pieces that have become one-of-a-kind since the destruction and looting of the National Museum in Baghdad in 2003. Artifacts from Persia, ancient Palestine, Israel, Anatolia, and Nubia fill other galleries.

The small but eclectic gift shop, called the Suq, stocks many unique items, including reproductions of pieces in the museum's collection. Allow 1 hour.

1155 E. 58th St. (at University Ave.). ✆ **773/702-9514.** www.oi.uchicago.edu. Free admission; suggested donation $7 adults, $4 children. Tues–Sat 10am–6pm (Wed until 8:30pm); Sun noon–6pm. Bus: 6 or Metra Electric train to 57th St. and Lake Park Ave.

Robie House ★★ Frank Lloyd Wright designed this 20th-century American architectural masterpiece for Frederick Robie, a bicycle and motorcycle manufacturer. The home, which was completed in 1909, bears signs of Wright's Prairie School of design (an open layout and linear geometry of form), as well as exquisite leaded- and stained-glass doors and windows. It's also among the last of Wright's Prairie School–style homes: During its construction, he abandoned both his family and his Oak Park practice to follow other pursuits, most prominently the realization of his Taliesin home and studio in Spring Green, Wisconsin. Docents from Oak Park's Frank Lloyd Wright Home and Studio Foundation lead tours here, even though the house is undergoing a massive, 10-year restoration (the house is open throughout the process, but your photos may include some scaffolding). A **Wright specialty bookshop** is in the building's former three-car garage—which was highly unusual for the time in which it was built. Allow 1 hour per tour, plus time to browse the gift shop.

5757 S. Woodlawn Ave. (at 58th St.). ✆ **773/834-1847.** www.wrightplus.org. Admission $15 adults, $12 seniors and children 4–17, free for children 3 and under. Fri–Sun tours at 11am, noon, 1, 2 and 3pm. Bookshop daily 10am–5pm. Bus: 6 or Metra Electric train to 57th St. and Lake Park Ave.

Rockefeller Memorial Chapel To call the Rockefeller Memorial Chapel a chapel is false modesty, even for a Rockefeller. When the university first opened its doors, the students sang the following ditty:

> *John D. Rockefeller, wonderful man is he*
> *Gives all his spare change to the U of C.*

John D. was a generous patron, indeed. He founded the university (in cooperation with the American Baptist Society), built the magnificent minicathedral that now bears his name, and shelled out an additional $35 million in donations over the course of his lifetime. Memorial Chapel, designed by Bertram Goodhue, an architect known for his ecclesiastical buildings—including the Cadet Chapel at West Point and New York City's St. Thomas Church—was dedicated in 1928.

In keeping with the rest of the campus, which is patterned after Oxford, the chapel is reminiscent of English Gothic structures; however, it was built from limestone using modern construction techniques. Its most outstanding features are the circular stained-glass window high above the main altar (the windows, in general, are among the largest of any church or cathedral anywhere) and the world's second-largest carillon, which John D. Rockefeller, Jr., donated in 1932 in memory of his mother, Laura. The chapel's organ is nearly as impressive, with four manuals, 126 stops, and more than 10,000 pipes. Choir concerts, carillon performances, and other musical programs run throughout the year, usually for a small donation. Allow a half-hour.

5850 S. Woodlawn Ave. (✆ 773/702-2100. http://rockefeller.uchicago.edu. Free admission. Daily 8am–4pm (except during religious services). Bus: 6 or Metra Electric train to 57th St. and Lake Park Ave.

The Smart Museum of Art ★   The University of Chicago's fine-arts museum looks rather modest, but it packs a lot of talent into a compact space. Its permanent collection of more than 7,000 paintings and sculptures spans Western and Eastern civilizations, ranging from classical antiquity to the present day. Bona fide treasures include ancient Greek vases, Chinese bronzes, and Old Master paintings; Frank Lloyd Wright furniture; Tiffany glass; sculptures by Degas, Matisse, and Rodin; and 20th-century paintings and sculptures by Mark Rothko, Arthur Dove, Diego Rivera, Henry Moore, and Chicago sculptor Richard Hunt. Built in 1974, the contemporary building doesn't really fit in with the campus's Gothic architecture, but its sculpture garden and outdoor seating area make a nice place for quiet contemplation. The museum also has a gift shop and cafe. Allow 1 hour.

5550 S. Greenwood Ave. (at E. 55th St.). (✆ 773/702-0200. www.smartmuseum.uchicago.edu. Free admission. Tues–Fri 10am–4pm (Thurs until 8pm); Sat–Sun 11am–5pm. Closed major holidays. Bus: 6 or Metra Electric train to 57th St. and Lake Park Ave.

EXPLORING THE UNIVERSITY OF CHICAGO

Walking around the Gothic spires of the University of Chicago campus is bound to conjure up images of the cloistered academic life. Allow about an hour to stroll through the grassy quads and dramatic stone buildings. (If the weather's nice, do as the students do, and vegetate for a while on the grass.) If you're visiting on a weekday, your first stop should be the university's **Visitors Information Desk** (✆ 773/702-9739) on the first floor of Ida Noyes Hall, 1212 E. 59th St., where you can pick up campus maps and get information on university events. The center is open Monday through Friday from 10am to 7pm. If you stop by on a weekend when the Visitors Information Desk is closed, you can get the scoop on campus events at the **Reynolds Clubhouse** student center (✆ 773/702-8787).

Start your tour at the **Henry Moore statue,** *Nuclear Energy,* on South Ellis Avenue between 56th and 57th streets. It's next to the Regenstein Library, which marks the site of the old Stagg Field where, on December 2, 1942, the world's first sustained nuclear reaction was achieved in a basement laboratory below the field. Then turn left and follow 57th Street until you reach the grand stone Hull Gate; walk straight to reach the main quad, or turn left through the column-lined arcade to reach **Hutchinson Court** (designed by John Olmsted, son of revered landscape designer Frederick Law Olmsted). The Reynolds Clubhouse, the university's main student center, is here; you can take a break at the C-Shop cafe or settle down at a table at Hutchinson Commons. The dining

Oxford and Cambridge.

Other worthy spots on campus include the charming, intimate **Bond Chapel,** behind Swift Hall on the main quad, and the blocks-long **Midway Plaisance,** a wide stretch of green that was the site of carnival sideshow attractions during the World's Columbian Exposition in 1893. (Ever since, the term "midway" has referred to carnivals in general.)

The **Seminary Co-op Bookstore,** 5757 S. University Ave. (© **773/752-4381;** www. semcoop.com), is a treasure trove of academic and scholarly books. Its selection of more than 100,000 titles has won it an international reputation as "the best bookstore west of Blackwell's in Oxford." It's open Monday through Friday from 8:30am to 9pm, Saturday from 10am to 6pm, and Sunday from noon to 6pm.

ENJOYING THE OUTDOORS IN HYDE PARK

Hyde Park is not only a haven for book lovers and culture aficionados; the community also has open-air attractions. Worthy outdoor environments near Lake Michigan include **Lake Shore Drive,** where many stately apartment houses follow the contour of the shoreline. A suitable locale for a quiet stroll during the day is **Promontory Point,** at 55th Street and Lake Michigan, a bulb of land that juts into the lake and offers a good view of Chicago to the north and the seasonally active 57th Street beach to the south.

Farther south, just below the Museum of Science and Industry, is **Wooded Island** in Jackson Park, the site of the Japanese Pavilion during the Columbian Exposition and today a lovely garden of meandering paths. In the **Perennial Garden** at 59th Street and Stony Island Avenue in Jackson Park, more than 180 varieties of flowering plants display a palette of colors that changes with the seasons.

KENWOOD HISTORIC DISTRICT

A fun side trip for architecture and history buffs is the Kenwood Historic District, just north of Hyde Park. The area originally developed as a suburb of Chicago, when local captains of industry (including Sears founder Julius Rosenwald) began building lavish mansions in the mid-1850s. The neighborhood's large lots and eclectic mix of architecture (everything from elaborate Italianate to Prairie-style homes) make it unique in Chicago, especially compared to the closely packed buildings in Hyde Park. Although many of the fine homes here became dilapidated after the South Side's "white flight" of the 1950s and '60s, a new generation of black and white middle-class homeowners has been lovingly renovating the one-of-a-kind houses. Today, the blocks between 47th and 51st streets (north-south) and Blackstone and Drexel boulevards (east-west) make for a wonderful walking tour, with broad, shady streets full of newly restored mansions.

6 MORE MUSEUMS

City Gallery Along with the pumping station across the street, the **Chicago Water Tower** is one of only a handful of buildings to survive the Great Chicago Fire of 1871. It has long been a revered symbol of the city's resilience and fortitude, although today the building is dwarfed by the high-rise shopping centers and hotels of North Michigan Avenue. The Gothic-style limestone building is now an art gallery. The spiffed-up interior is intimate and sunny, and it's a convenient, quick pit stop of culture on your way to the Water Tower shopping center or the tourist information center across the street in the pumping station. Exhibits focus mostly on photography, usually featuring Chicago-based artists such as the fashion photographer Victor Skrebneski. Allow 15 minutes.

806 N. Michigan Ave. (btw. Chicago Ave. and Pearson St.). (C) **312/742-0808.** Free admission. Mon–Sat 10am–6:30pm; Sun 10am–5pm. Bus: 3, 145, 146, 147, or 151.

Historic Pullman ★★   Railway magnate George Pullman may have been a fabulously wealthy industrialist, but he fancied himself more enlightened than his 19th-century peers. So when it came time to build a new headquarters for his Pullman Palace Car Company, he dreamed of something more than the standard factory surrounded by tenements. Instead, he built a model community for his workers, a place where they could live in houses with indoor plumbing and abundant natural light—amenities almost unheard of for industrial workers in the 1880s. Pullman didn't do all this solely from the goodness of his heart: He hoped that the town, named after him, would attract the most skilled workers (who would be so happy that they wouldn't go on strike). As one of the first "factory towns," Pullman caused an international sensation and was seen as a model for other companies to follow. The happy workers that Pullman envisioned did go on strike in 1894, however, frustrated by the company's control of every aspect of their lives.

Today the Pullman district makes a fascinating stop for anyone with a historical or architectural bent. While most of the homes remain private residences, a number of public buildings (including the lavish Hotel Florence, the imposing Clock Tower, and the two-story colonnaded Market Hall) still stand. You can walk through the area on your own (stop by the visitor center for a map), or take a guided a tour at 1:30pm on the first Sunday of the month from May through October ($5 adults, $4 seniors, $3 students). Allow 1½ hours for the guided tour.

11141 S. Cottage Grove Ave. (C) **773/785-8901.** www.pullmanil.org. Visitor center Tues–Sun 11am–3pm. Free admission. Train: Metra Electric line to Pullman (111th St.), turn right on Cottage Grove Ave., and walk 1 block to the visitor center.

International Museum of Surgical Science ★ (Finds)   This unintentionally macabre shrine to medicine is my pick for the weirdest tourist attraction in town. Not for the faint of stomach, it occupies a historic 1917 Gold Coast mansion designed by the noted architect Howard Van Doren Shaw, who modeled it after Le Petit Trianon at Versailles. Displayed throughout its four floors are surgical instruments, paintings, and sculptures depicting the history of surgery and healing practices in Eastern and Western civilizations. (It's run by the International College of Surgeons.) The exhibits are old-fashioned (no interactive computer displays here), but that's part of the museum's odd appeal.

You'll look at your doctor in a whole new way after viewing the trepanned skulls excavated from an ancient tomb in Peru. The accompanying tools bored holes in patients' skulls, a horrific practice thought to release the evil spirits causing their illness. (Some skulls show signs of new bone growth, meaning that some lucky headache-sufferers actually survived the low-tech surgery.) There are also battlefield amputation kits, a working iron-lung machine in the polio exhibit, and oddities such as a stethoscope designed to be transported inside a top hat. Other attractions include an apothecary shop and dentist's office (ca. 1900) re-created in a historic street exhibit, and the hyperbolically titled *Hall of Immortals*, a sculpture gallery depicting 12 historic figures in medicine from Hippocrates to Madame Curie. Allow 1 hour.

1524 N. Lake Shore Dr. (btw. Burton Place and North Ave.). ✆ **312/642-6502.** www.imss.org. Admission **181**
$10 adults, $6 seniors and students. Tues–Sat 10am–4pm; May–Sept Sun 10am–4pm. Closed major holidays. Bus: 151.

Intuit: The Center for Intuitive and Outsider Art Chicago is home to an active
community of collectors of "outsider art," a term attached to a group of unknown,
unconventional artists who do their work without any formal training or connection to
the mainstream art world. Often called folk or self-taught artists, they produce highly
personal and idiosyncratic work using a range of media, from bottle caps to immense
canvases. Intuit was founded in 1991 to bring attention to these artists through exhibitions and educational lectures. It's in the warehouse district northwest of the Loop, and
has two galleries and a performance area. The museum offers a regular lecture series, and
if you time your visit right, you might be here for one of the center's tours of a private
local art collection. Allow 1 hour.

756 N. Milwaukee Ave. (at Chicago and Ogden aves.). ✆ **312/243-9088.** www.art.org. Free admission.
Tues–Sat 11am–5pm (Thurs until 7:30pm). Bus: 56 or 66. Subway/El: Blue Line to Chicago.

Jane Addams Hull-House Museum In 1889, a young woman named Jane
Addams bought a mansion on Halsted Street surrounded by the shanties of poor immigrants. Here, Addams and her co-worker, Ellen Gates Starr, launched the American settlement-house movement with the establishment of Hull-House, an institution that
endured on this site in Chicago until 1963. (It continues today as a decentralized social-
service agency known as Jane Addams Hull House Association.) In that year, all but two
of the settlement's 13 buildings, along with the entire residential neighborhood in its
immediate vicinity, were demolished to make room for the University of Illinois at Chicago campus, which now owns the museum buildings. Of the original settlement, what
remain today are the Hull-House Museum, the mansion itself, and the residents' dining
hall, snuggled among the ultramodern, poured-concrete buildings of the university campus. Inside are the original furnishings, Jane Addams' office, and numerous settlement
maps and photographs. Rotating exhibits re-create the history of the settlement and the
work of its residents, showing how Addams was able to help transform the dismal streets
around her into stable inner-city environments worth fighting over. Allow a half-hour.

University of Illinois at Chicago, 800 S. Halsted St. (at Polk St.). ✆ **312/413-5353.** www.uic.edu/jaddams/
hull. Free admission. Tues–Fri 10am–4pm; Sun noon–4pm. Closed university holidays. Bus: 8. Subway/El:
Blue Line to Halsted/University of Illinois.

National Museum of Mexican Art ★ Chicago's vibrant Pilsen neighborhood, just
southwest of the Loop, is home to one of the nation's largest Mexican-American communities. Ethnic pride emanates from every doorstep, *taqueria*, and bakery, and colorful
murals splash across building exteriors and alleyways. This institution—the only Latino
museum accredited by the American Association of Museums—may be the neighborhood's most prized possession. That's quite an accomplishment, given that it was
founded in 1987 by a passel of public-school teachers who pooled $900 to get it started.

Exhibits showcase Mexican and Mexican-American visual and performing artists,
often drawing on the permanent collection of more than 5,000 works, but the visiting
artists, festival programming, and community participation make the museum really
shine. Its Day of the Dead celebration, which runs for about 8 weeks beginning in September, is one of the most ambitious in the country. The Del Corazon Mexican Performing Arts Festival, held in the spring, features programs by local and international artists
here and around town, and the Sor Juana Festival, presented in the fall, honors Mexican

writer and pioneering feminist Sor Juana Ines de la Cruz with photography and painting exhibits, music and theater performances, and poetry readings by Latina women.

The museum is very family oriented, with educational workshops for kids and parents. It also has an excellent gift shop and stages a holiday market, featuring items from Mexico, on the first weekend in December. Allow 1 hour.

1852 W. 19th St. (a few blocks west of Ashland Ave.). ℂ **312/738-1503.** www.nationalmuseumofmexican art.org. Free admission. Tues–Sun 10am–5pm. Closed major holidays. Bus: 9. Subway/El: Blue Line to 18th St.

National Vietnam Veterans Art Museum ★ (Finds)   This museum houses a stirring collection of art by Vietnam veterans, and is the only one of its kind in the world. After the war, many veterans made art as personal therapy, never expecting to show it to anyone, but in 1981 a small group began showing their work together in Chicago and in touring exhibitions. The collection has grown to more than 1,500 paintings, drawings, photographs, and sculptures from all over the world, including Vietnam. (Recently, the museum has also started hosting exhibits of work by veterans who have returned from Iraq.) Titles such as *We Regret to Inform You, Blood Spots on a Rice Paddy,* and *The Wound* give you an idea of the power of the images. Housed in a former warehouse in the Prairie Avenue district south of the Loop, the museum is modern and well organized. An installation suspended from the ceiling, ***Above & Beyond*** ★, comprises more than 58,000 dog tags with the names of the men and women who died in the war—it creates an emotional effect similar to that of the Wall in Washington, D.C. The complex also houses a small theater, cafe (open for breakfast and lunch), gift shop, and an outdoor plaza with a flagpole that has deliberately been left leaning because that's how veterans saw them in combat. Allow 1 hour.

1801 S. Indiana Ave. (at 18th St.). ℂ **312/326-0270.** www.nvvam.org. Admission $10 adults, $7 seniors and students with ID. Tues–Fri 11am–6pm; Sat 10am–5pm. Closed major holidays. Bus: 3 or 4.

Polish Museum of America   One million people of Polish ancestry live in Chicago, giving the city the largest Polish population outside of Warsaw, so it's no surprise that the Polish Museum of America is here, in the neighborhood where many of the first immigrants settled. The museum has one of the most important collections of Polish art and historical materials outside Poland. (It is also the largest museum in the U.S. devoted exclusively to an ethnic group.) The museum's programs include rotating exhibitions, films, lectures, and concerts, and a permanent exhibit about Pope John Paul II. There's also a library with a large Polish-language collection, and archives where visitors can research genealogical history. (Call in advance if you want to look through those records.) Allow a half-hour.

984 N. Milwaukee Ave. (at Augusta Blvd.). ℂ **773/384-3352.** www.polishmuseumofamerica.org. Admission $5 adults, $4 students and seniors, $3 children 11 and under. Fri–Wed 11am–4pm. Subway/El: Blue Line to Division.

---

7 EXPLORING THE 'BURBS

OAK PARK

Architecture and literary buffs alike make pilgrimages to Oak Park, a nearby suburb on the western border of the city that is easily accessible by car or train. Bookworms flock here to see the town where Ernest Hemingway was born and grew up, while others come

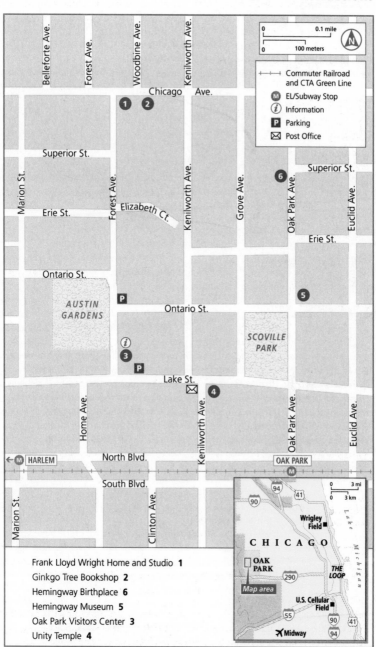

EXPLORING CHICAGO

7

EXPLORING THE 'BURBS

Frank Lloyd Wright Home and Studio **1**
Ginkgo Tree Bookshop **2**
Hemingway Birthplace **6**
Hemingway Museum **5**
Oak Park Visitors Center **3**
Unity Temple **4**

to catch a glimpse of the Frank Lloyd Wright–designed homes that line the well-maintained streets.

Getting There

BY CAR   Oak Park is 10 miles due west of downtown Chicago. By car, take the Eisenhower Expressway (I-290) west to Harlem Avenue (Ill. 43) and exit north. Continue on Harlem north to Lake Street. Take a right on Lake Street and continue to Forest Avenue. Turn left here, and immediately on your right you'll see the **Oak Park Visitor Center** (see below).

BY PUBLIC TRANSPORTATION   Take the Green Line west to the Harlem stop, roughly a 25-minute ride from downtown. Exit the station onto Harlem Avenue, and proceed north to Lake Street. Take a right on Lake Street, follow it to Forest Avenue, and then turn left to the **Oak Park Visitor Center** (see below).

BY TOUR   The **Chicago Architecture Foundation** regularly runs guided tours from downtown Chicago to Oak Park. For details, see "Sightseeing Tours," p. 193.

Visitor Information

The **Oak Park Visitor Center,** 158 Forest Ave. (© **888/OAK-PARK** [625-7275]; www.visitoakpark.com), is open daily from 10am to 5pm April through October, and from 10am to 4pm November through March. Stop here for orientation, maps, and guidebooks. There's a city-operated parking lot next door. The heart of the historic district and the Frank Lloyd Wright Home and Studio are only a few blocks away.

An extensive tour of Oak Park's historic district leaves from the **Ginkgo Tree Bookshop,** 951 Chicago Ave., on weekends from 11am to 3:30pm (exact departure times vary, depending on how many people show up). The tour lasts 1 hour and costs $15 for adults, $12 for seniors and children ages 4 to 17 (free for children 3 and under). If you can't make it to Oak Park on the weekend, you can follow a self-guided map and audiocassette tour of the historic district for the same price; the audio tour is available at the Ginkgo Tree Bookshop from 10am to 3:30pm. In addition to homes designed by Wright, you will see work by several of his disciples, as well as some charming examples of the Victorian styling that he so disdained. A more detailed map ($3 at the bookshop), *Architectural Guide Map of Oak Park and River Forest,* includes text and photos of all 80 sites of interest in Oak Park and neighboring River Forest.

The Wright Stuff

Frank Lloyd Wright Home and Studio ★★★   For the first 20 years of Wright's career, this remarkable complex served first and foremost as the sanctuary where he designed and executed more than 130 of an extraordinary output of 430 completed buildings. The home began as a simple shingled cottage that the 22-year-old Wright built for his bride in 1889, but it became a living laboratory for his revolutionary reinvention of interior spaces. Wright remodeled the house constantly until 1911, when he moved out permanently (in 1909, he left his wife and six children and went off to Europe with the wife of one of his clients). During Wright's fertile early period, the house was Wright's showcase, but it also embraces many idiosyncratic features molded to his own needs rather than those of a client. With many add-ons—including a barrel-vaulted children's playroom and a studio with an octagonal balcony suspended by chains—the place has a certain whimsy that others might have found less livable. This was not an architect's masterpiece but rather the master's home, and visitors can savor every room for the view it offers into the workings of a remarkable mind.

Wright's Oak Park

Oak Park has the highest concentration of Frank Lloyd Wright–designed and –built houses or buildings anywhere. People come here to marvel at the work of a man who saw his life as a twofold mission: To wage a single-handed battle against excessively ornamental architecture (Victorian, in particular), and to create in its place a new form that would be at the same time functional, appropriate to its natural setting, and stimulating to the imagination.

Not everyone who comes to Oak Park shares Wright's architectural philosophy, but scholars and enthusiasts admire him for being consistently true to his vision, out of which emerged a unique and genuinely American architectural statement. The reason for Wright's success could stem from the fact that he was a living exemplar of a quintessential American type. In a deep sense, he embodied the ideal of the self-made and self-sufficient individual who had survived, even thrived, in the frontier society—qualities that he expressed in his almost-puritanical insistence that each spatial or structural form in his buildings serve some useful purpose. He was also an aesthete in Emersonian fashion, deriving his idea of beauty from natural environments, where apparent simplicity often belies a subtle complexity.

The three principal ingredients of a tour of Wright-designed structures in Oak Park are the **Frank Lloyd Wright Home and Studio Tour,** the **Unity Temple Tour,** and a **walking tour**—guided or self-guided—to view the exteriors of homes throughout the neighborhood that were built by the architect. Oak Park has 25 homes and buildings by Wright, constructed between 1892 and 1913, which constitute the core output of his Prairie School period.

Tours cannot be booked in advance by phone, but a select number of tickets for each day can be reserved online. Allow 1 hour for the tour, more time if you want to browse in the bookshop.

951 Chicago Ave. ✆ **708/848-1976.** www.wrightplus.org. Admission $15 adults, $12 seniors and children 4–17, free for children 3 and under; combined admission for the home and studio tour and guided or self-guided historic district tour $25 adults, $20 seniors and students 4–17. Admission to the home and studio is by guided tour only; tours depart from bookshop Mon–Fri 11am, 1, and 3pm (every half-hour Memorial Day–Labor Day); Sat–Sun every 20 min year-round, 11am–3:30pm. Closed Jan 1, last week in Jan, Thanksgiving, and Dec 25. Facilities for people with disabilities are limited; please call in advance.

Unity Temple ★   After a fire destroyed its church around 1900, a Unitarian Universalist congregation asked one of its members, Frank Lloyd Wright, to design an affordable replacement. Using poured concrete with metal reinforcements—a necessity due to a small $40,000 budget—Wright created a building that on the outside seems as forbidding as a mausoleum but inside contains all the elements of the Prairie School that has made Wright's name immortal. Following the example of H. H. Richardson, Wright placed the building's main entrance on the side, behind an enclosure—a feature often employed in his houses as well—to create a sense of privacy and intimacy. Wright complained, furthermore, that the conventions of church architecture, such as the nave in the

---

> **(Tips) The Wright Plus Tour**
>
> Die-hard fans of the architect will want to be in town on the third Saturday in May for the annual Wright Plus Tour. The public can tour several Frank Lloyd Wright–designed homes and other notable Oak Park buildings, in both the Prairie School and Victorian styles, in addition to Wright's home, studio, and the Unity Temple. The tour includes 10 buildings in all. Tickets go on sale March 1 and can sell out by mid-April. Call the Frank Lloyd Wright Home and Studio (© **708/848-1976;** www.wrightplus.org) for details and ticket information.

Gothic-style cathedral across the street, were overpowering. Of that particular church, he commented that he didn't feel a part of it.

Yet his vision in this regard was somewhat confused and contradictory. He wanted Unity Temple to be "democratic," but perhaps Wright was unable to subdue his own personal hubris and hauteur in the creative process, for the ultimate effect of his chapel, and much of the building's interior, is grand and imperial. This is no simple meeting-house; instead, its principal chapel looks like the chamber of the Roman Senate. Even so, the interior, with its unpredictable geometric arrangements and its decor reminiscent of Native American art, is no less beautiful.

Wright was a true hands-on, can-do person; he knew his materials as intimately as the artisans who carried out his plans. He added pigment to the plaster (rather than the paint) to achieve a pale, natural effect. His use of wood trim and other decorative touches is still exciting to behold; his sensitivity to grain, tone, and placement was akin to that of an exceptionally gifted woodworker. His stunning, almost-minimalist use of form is what still sets him apart as a relevant and brilliant artist. Unity Temple still feels groundbreaking 100 years later—which Wright would consider the ultimate compliment. Allow a half-hour.

875 Lake St. © **708/383-8873.** www.unitytemple-utrf.org. Self-guided tours $8 adults; $6 seniors, children 6–12, and students with ID; free for children 5 and under. Free guided tours weekends at 1, 2 and 3pm. Mon–Fri 10:30am–4:30pm; Sat–Sun 1–4pm. Church events can alter schedule; call in advance.

On the Trail of Hemingway

Hemingway Museum   Frank Lloyd Wright might be Oak Park's favorite son, but the town's most famous native son is Ernest Hemingway. Hemingway had no great love for Oak Park; he moved away right after high school and later referred to his hometown as a place of "wide lawns and narrow minds." But that hasn't stopped Oak Park from laying claim to the great American writer. A portion of the ground floor of this former church, now the Oak Park Arts Center, holds a small but interesting display of Hemingway memorabilia. A 6-minute video sheds considerable light on Hemingway's time in Oak Park, where he spent the first 18 years of his life, and covers his high school experiences particularly well.

The **Ernest Hemingway Birthplace Home** is 2 blocks north, at 339 N. Oak Park Ave. The lovely Queen Anne house—complete with wraparound porch and turret—was the home of Hemingway's maternal grandparents, and it's where the writer was born on July 21, 1899. Its connection to Hemingway is actually pretty tenuous—he spent most of his boyhood and high school years at 600 N. Kenilworth Ave., a few blocks away (that house is still privately owned)—but the birthplace has been carefully restored to replicate its appearance at the end of the 19th century, making this an appealing stop for fans of historic house tours (whether they're Hemingway fans or not). The hours are the same as the Hemingway Museum's. Allow 1 hour.

200 N. Oak Park Ave. © **708/848-2222.** www.ehfop.org. Combined admission to Hemingway Museum and Ernest Hemingway Birthplace Home $8 adults, $6 seniors and children 6–12, free for children 5 and under. Sun–Fri 1–5pm; Sat 10am–5pm.

THE NORTH SHORE

Between Chicago and the state border of Wisconsin is one of the nation's most affluent residential areas, a swath of suburbia known as the North Shore. Although towns farther west like to co-opt the name for its prestige, the North Shore proper extends from Evanston, Chicago's nearest neighbor to the north, along the lakefront to tony Lake Forest, originally built as a resort for Chicago's aristocracy. Dotted with idyllic, picture-perfect towns such as Kenilworth, Glencoe, and Winnetka, this area has long attracted filmmakers such as Robert Redford, who filmed *Ordinary People* in Lake Forest, and the North Shore's own John Hughes, who shot most of his popular coming-of-age comedies (*Sixteen Candles, Ferris Bueller's Day Off, Home Alone,* and so on) here.

Although a Metra train line extends to Lake Forest and neighboring Lake Bluff, I highly recommend that you rent a car and drive north along **Sheridan Road,** which winds its leisurely way through many of these communities, past palatial homes and mansions designed in a startling array of architectural styles. Aside from Lake Shore Drive in Chicago, you won't find a more impressive stretch of roadway in the entire metropolitan area.

Exploring Evanston

Despite being frequented by Chicagoans, Evanston, the city's oldest suburb, retains an identity all its own. A unique hybrid of sensibilities, it manages to combine the tranquillity of suburban life with a highly cultured, urban charm. It's great fun to wander amid the shops and cafes in its downtown area or along funky Dempster Street at its southern end. The beautiful lakefront campus of **Northwestern University** (© **847/491-3741;** www.northwestern.edu) is here, and many of its buildings—such as Alice Millar Chapel, with its sublime stained-glass facade, and the Mary and Leigh Block Gallery, a fine-arts haven that offers a top-notch collection and intriguing temporary exhibitions—are well worth several hours of exploration.

Evanston was also the home of Frances Willard, founder of the Women's Christian Temperance Union (WCTU). **Willard House,** 1730 Chicago Ave. (© **847/328-7500;** www.franceswillardhouse.org), is open to visitors on the first and third Sundays of every month from 1 to 4pm ($5 adults, $3 children 12 and under). Nine of the 17 rooms in this old Victorian "Rest Cottage" (as Willard called it) have been converted into a museum of period furnishings and temperance memorabilia. Among her personal effects is the bicycle she affectionately called "Gladys" and learned to ride late in life, in the process spurring women across the country to do the same. The headquarters of the WCTU is still on-site.

Tucked away in north Evanston, a few miles from the Northwestern campus, is the unusual and informative **Mitchell Museum of the American Indian,** 2600 Central Park Ave. (© **847/475-1030;** www.mitchellmuseum.org). The collection ranges from stoneware tools and weapons to the work of contemporary Native-American artists. The museum is open Tuesday through Saturday from 10am to 5pm (Thurs until 8pm), and Sunday from noon to 4pm. It's closed on holidays and during the last 2 weeks of August.

> ## Moments A Suburban Respite
>
> If you've made it to the Bahá'í temple, take a stroll across Sheridan Road to the 60-acre **Gillson Park** for a taste of north suburban life. Check out the sailors prepping their boats for a day cruise, families picnicking and playing Frisbee, and kids frolicking on the sandy beach. (Boats are also available for rent if you'd like to explore Lake Michigan from the water.) Access to the beach is restricted to local residents in the summer, but in the fall and spring, you're welcome to wander (just don't expect to take a dip in the frigid water).

Admission is $5 for adults, $2.50 for seniors and children. Call in advance to arrange a volunteer-led tour.

For a bit of serenity, head to **Grosse Point Lighthouse and Maritime Museum,** 2601 Sheridan Rd. (© **847/328-6961;** www.grossepointlighthouse.net), a historic lighthouse built in 1873, when Lake Michigan still teemed with cargo-laden ships. Tours of the lighthouse, situated in a nature center, take place on weekends from June to September at 2, 3, and 4pm ($6 adults, $3 children 8–12; children 7 and under not admitted for safety reasons). The adjacent Lighthouse Beach is a favorite spot for local families during the summer. If you're here between Memorial Day and Labor Day, you'll have to pay to frolic on the sand ($7 adults, $5 children 1–11), but it's a great place for a (free) stroll on a sunny spring or fall day.

Other Area Attractions

Bahá'í House of Worship   Up the road from Evanston in Wilmette is the most visited of all the sights in the northern suburbs, the Bahá'í House of Worship, an ethereal edifice that seems not of this earth. The gleaming white stone temple, designed by the French-Canadian Louis Bourgeois and completed in 1953, is essentially a soaring nine-sided 135-foot dome, draped in a delicate lacelike facade, that reveals the Eastern influence of the Bahá'í faith's native Iran. Surrounded by formal gardens, it is one of seven Bahá'í temples in the world, and the only one in the Western Hemisphere. The dome's latticework is even more beautiful as you gaze upward from the floor of the sanctuary, which, during the day, is flooded with light. Downstairs, displays in the visitor center explain the Bahá'í faith. Temple members offer informal tours of the building and exhibits to anyone who inquires. Allow a half-hour.

100 Linden Ave. (at Sheridan Rd.), Wilmette. © **847/853-2300.** www.bahai.us/bahai-temple. Free admission. Daily 7am–10pm; visitor center 10am–5pm (until 8pm May–Sept). From Chicago, take the El Red Line north to Howard St. Change for the Evanston train and go to the end of the line, Linden Ave. (Or, take the Purple/Evanston Express and stay on the same train all the way.) Turn right on Linden, and walk 2 blocks east. If you're driving, go north on the Outer Dr. (Lake Shore Dr.), which feeds into Sheridan Rd.

Chicago Botanic Garden ★★ (Value)   Despite its name, the world-class Chicago Botanic Garden is 25 miles north of the city in the suburb of Glencoe. This 385-acre living preserve includes eight large lagoons and a variety of distinct botanical environments including the Illinois prairie, an English walled garden, and a three-island Japanese garden. Also on the grounds are a large fruit-and-vegetable garden, an "enabling garden" (which shows how gardening can be adapted for people with disabilities), and a 100-acre old-growth oak woodland. If you're here in the summer, don't miss the extensive rose gardens with more than 7,750 plants (just follow the bridal parties who flock here to get their pictures taken). The Botanic Garden also has an exhibit hall, auditorium, museum, library, education greenhouses, outdoor pavilion, carillon, cafe, designated bike path, and garden shop. Carillon concerts take place at 7pm Monday evenings from late June through August; tours of the carillon are offered beforehand.

Every summer the Botanic Garden stages a special outdoor exhibition. (One year giant animal-shaped topiaries stood in unexpected locations throughout the grounds; another year, model railroads wound through miniature versions of American national parks.) Check the website or call for event schedules. Allow 3 hours.

1000 Lake-Cook Rd. (just east of Edens Expwy./I-94), Glencoe. © 847/835-5440. www.chicago-botanic. org. Free admission. Daily 8am–sunset. Tram tours Apr–Oct. Closed Dec 25. From Chicago, take Sheridan Rd. north along Lake Michigan or the Edens Expwy. (I-94) to Lake-Cook Rd. Parking $15/day.

Ravinia Festival ★★ (Finds)   Want to know where the natives get away from it all? Come summertime, you'll find us chilling on the lawn at Ravinia, the summer home of the highly regarded Chicago Symphony Orchestra in suburban Highland Park. In operation since 1904, Ravinia started off as an amusement park. The Martin Theatre—build in the Prairie style—still remains, and is the only building still standing from the early days. Over the years, the festival has hosted an amazing array of performers, from Louis Armstrong, Duke Ellington, George Gershwin and Ella Fitzgerald to Janis Joplin, Frank Zappa, Luciano Pavarotti, and Steven Sondheim. The season runs from mid-June to Labor Day and includes far more than classical concerts: You can also catch pop acts, dance performances, operatic arias, and blues concerts. Tickets are available for the lawn and the covered pavilion, where you get a reserved seat and a view of the stage. The lawn is the real joy of Ravinia: Sitting under the stars and a canopy of leafy branches while listening to music and indulging in an elaborate picnic. (It's a local tradition to try to outdo everyone else by bringing candelabras and fine china.) I've been here for everything from Beethoven symphonies to folksy singer-songwriters, and the setting has been magical every time. The lawn to the left of the stage is a popular place for families to spread out, but I'm partial to the tree-filled area on the right. (The lights projected into the branches create a dramatic effect after the sun sets.)

Don't let the distance from downtown discourage you from visiting, because an extremely convenient public-transportation system serves Ravinia. On concert nights, a special Ravinia Metra commuter train leaves at 5:50pm from the North Western train station at Madison and Canal streets (just west of the Loop). The train stops at the festival at 6:30pm, allowing plenty of time to enjoy a picnic before an 8 o'clock show. After the concert, trains wait right outside the gates to take commuters back to the city. The round-trip train fare is $5, a real bargain considering that traffic around the park can be brutal.

Dining options at the park range from the fine-dining restaurant **Mirabelle** (© 847/ 432-7550 for reservations) to prepacked picnic spreads from the **Gatehouse,** featuring gourmet items to go. For $10, you can rent a pair of lawn chairs and a table from booths set up near the park entrance. In case you're wondering about the weather conditions at concert time, dial Ravinia's Weather Line (© 847/433-5010).

Green Bay and Lake-Cook rds., Highland Park. © 847/266-5100. www.ravinia.org. Tickets: Pavilion $20–$75; lawn $10–$20. Most concerts are in the evening.

The North Shore is only one slice of life north of Chicago. To its west lies a sprawling thicket of old and new suburbs, from the bucolic environs of equestrian-minded **Barrington** and its ring of smaller satellite communities in the far northwest, to near-northwest shopping mecca **Schaumburg,** home to the gigantic Woodfield Mall. While Woodfield attracts a steady stream of dedicated shoppers—allowing it to tout its status as one of the top tourist destinations in Illinois—it's not that distinctive; you'll find most of the same stores at your local megamall back home.

A more pastoral option for visitors with time on their hands might be a day trip to the **historic village of Long Grove,** about 30 miles northwest of Chicago. Settled in the 1840s by German immigrants and pioneers traveling west from New England, Long Grove has assiduously preserved its old-fashioned character. Set amid 500 acres of oak- and hickory-tree groves, the village maintains nearly 100 specialty stores, galleries, and restaurants, many of which are in former smithies, wheelwright barns, and century-old residences. (Don't skip the **Long Grove Confectionery Company,** a local institution.) By village ordinance, all new buildings constructed in the shopping district must conform to the architecture of the early 1900s. The village schedules several cultural and entertainment events, festivals, and art fairs throughout the year. The biggest and best is the annual **Strawberry Festival,** held during the last weekend in June. Call the village's information center or check the town's website (✆ **847/634-0888;** www.longgrove online.com) for updates on coming events. To get there from the Chicago Loop, take the I-94 tollway (also known as the Kennedy Expressway) north until it separates at I-90, another tollway that runs northwest. Follow I-90 until you reach Rte. 53, and drive north on 53 until it dead-ends at Lake-Cook Road. Take the west exit off 53, and follow Lake-Cook Road to Hicks Road. Turn right on Hicks Road and then left on Old McHenry Road, which will take you right into the center of town.

Arlington International Racecourse   With its gleaming-white, palatial, six-story grandstand and lush gardens, this racecourse is one of the most beautiful showcases for thoroughbred horse racing in the world. Its storied history stretches back to 1927, and such equine stars as Citation, Secretariat, and Cigar have graced the track. The annual Arlington Million (the sport's first million-dollar race, held in mid-August) attracts top jockeys, trainers, and horses and is part of the World Series Racing Championship, which includes the Breeders Cup races. Arlington's race days are thrilling to behold, with all of racing's time-honored pageantry on display—from the bugler in traditional dress to the parade of jockeys.

Arlington likes to say that it caters to families, and the ambience is more Disney than den of iniquity. "Family days" throughout the summer include live music and entertainment ranging from petting zoos to puppet shows.

2200 W. Euclid Ave., Arlington Heights. ✆ **847/385-7500.** www.arlingtonpark.com. May–Sept Wed–Sun gates open 11am, 1st post 1pm. No racing Oct–Apr. Admission $6 adults, $3–$6 for reserved seating. Take the Kennedy (I-94) Expwy. to the I-90 tollway, and exit north on Rte. 53. Follow 53 north to the Euclid exit. Or, take Metra train to Arlington Heights. Free parking.

THE WESTERN SUBURBS

So many corporations have taken to locating their offices beyond the city limits that today more people work in the suburbs than commute into Chicago. Much of the suburban sprawl in counties such as DuPage and Kane consists of seas of aluminum-sided houses that seem to sprout from cornfields overnight. But there are also some lovely older towns, such as upscale **Hinsdale** and, much farther west, the quaint tandem of **St. Charles** and **Geneva,** which lie across the Fox River from each other. Perhaps there is no more fitting symbol of this booming area than the city of **Naperville.** A historic, formerly rural community with a Main Street U.S.A. downtown district worthy of Norman Rockwell, Naperville has exploded from a population of about 30,000 residents in the early 1970s to approximately 140,000 today—which makes it the third-largest municipality in the state. Naperville maintains a collection of 19th-century buildings in an outdoor setting known as Naper Settlement, and its river walk is the envy of neighboring village councils. But much of its yesteryear charm seems to be disappearing bit by bit as new subdivisions and strip malls ooze forth across the prairie.

Brookfield Zoo ★★ (Kids)   In contrast to the more modest Lincoln Park Zoo, Brookfield is enormous, spreading out over 216 acres and housing thousands of animals—camels, dolphins, giraffes, baboons, wolves, tigers, green sea turtles, Siberian tigers, snow leopards, and more—in naturalistic environments that put them side by side with other inhabitants of their regions. These creative indoor and outdoor settings, filled with activities to keep kids interested, are what set Brookfield apart.

Start out at *Habitat Africa!* ★★, a multiple-ecosystem exhibit that encompasses 30 acres—about the size of the entire Lincoln Park Zoo. Then wander through some of the buildings that allow you to see animals close up; my personal favorites are *Tropic World* ★★, where you hang out at treetop level with monkeys, and *Australia House,* where fruit bats flit around your head. *The Living Coast* ★ explores the west coast of Chile and Peru, and includes everything from a tank of plate-size moon jellies to a rocky shore where Humboldt penguins swim and nest as Inca terns and gray gulls fly freely overhead. *The Swamp* re-creates the bioregions of a southern cypress swamp and an Illinois river scene and discusses what people can do to protect wetlands. The dolphins at the *Seven Seas Panorama* ★★ put on an amazing show that has been a Brookfield Zoo fixture for years. If you go on a weekend, buy tickets to the dolphin show at least a couple of hours before the one you plan to attend, because they tend to sell out quickly.

The **Hamill Family Play Zoo** is a wonderful stop for kids. They not only get to pet animals but can also build habitats, learn how to plant a garden, and even play animal dress-up. The only catch: The separate admission fee ($3.50 adults, $2.50 children). Allow 3 hours.

First Ave. and 31st St., Brookfield. ☏ **708/485-0263.** www.brookfieldzoo.org. Admission $12 adults, $8 seniors and children 3–11, free for children 2 and under. Parking $8. Free admission Tues and Thurs Oct– Feb. Memorial Day–Labor Day daily 9:30am–6pm (Sun until 7:30pm); fall–spring daily 10am–5pm. Bus: 304 or 311. Take the Stevenson (I-55) and Eisenhower (I-290) expressways 14 miles west of the Loop.

Morton Arboretum   Feel like getting away from it all? This suburban oasis, covering almost 2,000 acres, is dedicated to preserving an amazing variety of trees and shrubs in a peaceful, welcoming setting. You can follow walking trails through solemn forests, explore a re-creation of an original Illinois prairie, or wander the twisting pathways of the **Maze Garden.** (If you'd rather watch others wander, climb up to the viewing platform built around the trunk of a 60-foot tall sycamore tree.) Covering the arboretum's vast acreage requires some driving—and you'll need a car to get here, since it's not accessible by public transportation.

The arboretum's modestly named **Children's Garden** is more like a family wonderland, with dozens of nature-friendly attractions. Highlights include streams built for splashing, hidden grottoes, and a wooden walkway suspended between evergreen trees.

Morton Arboretum also offers regular nature talks, as well as special exhibits at the Sterling Morton Library. The Visitor Center has an attractive gift shop and restaurant.

4100 Illinois Rte. 53, Lisle. ℂ **630/968-0074.** www.mortonarb.org. Daily year-round 7am–7pm (or sunset, whichever comes soonest). Visitor Center 8am–5pm Nov–Feb; 8am–6pm March–Oct. Admission $11 adults, $10 seniors, $8 children 2–17. Take the Stevenson (I-290) Expwy. west from downtown Chicago to I-88. Exit north onto Rte. 53 and follow the signs for a ¹/₂ mile to the entrance.

8 KID STUFF

Chicago Children's Museum ★★ (Kids) Located on tourist-filled Navy Pier, this museum is one of the most popular family attractions in the city. The building has areas especially for preschoolers as well as for children up to age 10, and several permanent exhibits allow kids a maximum of hands-on fun. *Dinosaur Expedition* re-creates an expedition to the Sahara, allowing kids to experience camp life, conduct scientific research, and dig for the bones of Suchomimus, a Saharan dinosaur discovered by Chicago paleontologist Paul Sereno (a full-scale model stands nearby).

The *Inventing Lab* will appeal to budding scientists—here kids can take the Alarm Clock Challenge and wake up the sleeping bear or slide down the musical Grand Piano Slide. The *BIG Backyard* is an urban garden filled with enormous insects, giggling flowers, and giant toadstools.

There's also a **three-level schooner** that children can board for a little climbing, from the crow's nest to the gangplank; *PlayMaze,* a toddler-scale cityscape with everything from a gas station to a city bus that children 4 and under can touch and explore; and an **arts-and-crafts area** where visitors can create original artwork to take home. Allow 2 to 3 hours.

Navy Pier, 700 E. Grand Ave. ℂ **312/527-1000.** www.chichildrensmuseum.org. Admission $10 adults and children, $9 seniors. Free admission Thurs 5–8pm; free for ages 15 and under the first Sun of every month. Daily 10am–5pm (Thurs until 8pm). Closed Thanksgiving and Dec 25. Bus: 29, 65, or 66. Subway/El: Red Line to Grand; transfer to city bus or Navy Pier's free trolley bus.

Lincoln Park Pritzker Children's Zoo & Farm-in-the-Zoo ★ (Value (Kids) After hours of looking at animals from afar in the rest of Lincoln Park Zoo, kids can come here to get up close and personal. Unlike many other children's zoos, there are no baby animals at the **Pritzker Children's Zoo;** instead, the outdoor habitats feature wildlife of the North American woods, including wolves, beavers, and otters. Although there are a few interactive displays outside, most kids head inside to the Treetop Canopy Climbing Adventure, a 20-foot high wood-and-fabric tree (encased in soft safety netting) that kids can scramble up and down. There are also a few small padded play areas for little ones.

The **Farm-in-the-Zoo** ★ is a working reproduction of a Midwestern farm, complete with a white-picket-fenced barnyard, chicken coops, and demonstrations of butter churning and weaving. You'll also spot plenty of livestock, including cows, sheep, and pigs. Inside the Main Barn (filled with interactive exhibits), the main attraction is the huge John Deere tractor that kids can climb up into and pretend to drive. (Can you say "photo opportunity"?) Allow 1 hour.

2200 N. Cannon Dr. ℂ **312/742-2000.** www.lpzoo.com. Free admission. Daily 9am–5pm. Bus: 151 or 156.

Six Flags Great America ★ (Kids) One of the Midwest's biggest theme and amusement parks, Six Flags is midway between Chicago and Milwaukee on I-94 in Gurnee, Illinois. The park has more than 100 rides and attractions and is a favorite of roller

(Kids) Downtown Playgrounds

As anyone who's traveled with little kids well knows, children can only take so much museum-going. Sometimes they have to let loose and run around—but finding good places to play in the middle of downtown Chicago can be a challenge. Luckily, there are playgrounds tucked away in unassuming spots, as long as you know where to look. The **Seneca Playlot,** 228 E. Chicago Ave., is directly east of the Chicago Water Works Visitor Center and across the street from Water Tower Place mall. The play structures are mostly low-to-the-ground, making it a good choice for toddlers. Walk a few blocks east and you'll come to **Lake Shore Park,** 808 N. Lake Shore Dr., which has a good assortment of slides and climbing equipment. As an added bonus, you'll enjoy views of the lake. (Unfortunately, you'll also get to hear the steady drone of traffic on busy Lake Shore Drive.) An adjoining athletic field has a running track and plenty of space for impromptu soccer or football games. Occupying a large corner lot on the ritzy Gold Coast, **Goudy Square Park,** at the corner of Astor and Goethe streets, is a tranquil oasis surrounded by high-rises. There are three separate play areas, along with plenty of benches for parents to lounge.

coaster devotees. There are a whopping 10 of them here, including the nausea-inducing Déjà Vu, where riders fly forward and backward over a twisting, looping inverted steel track, and Superman, where you speed along hanging headfirst (with your legs dangling). Other don't-miss rides for the strong of stomach include the Iron Wolf, where you do corkscrew turns and 360-degree loops while standing up, and the American Eagle, a classic wooden coaster. Because this place caters to families, you'll also find plenty to appeal to smaller visitors. The Looney Tunes National Park is full of kiddie rides with a cartoon theme; other worthwhile stops include the double-decker carousel and bumper cars. Hurricane Harbor, a massive water park with a giant wave pool, is fun on a hot day, but you risk heatstroke waiting in the long lines. Six Flags also has live shows, IMAX movies, and restaurants. If you take the trouble to get out here, allow a full day.

I-94 at Rte. 132 E., Gurnee. ✆ **847/249-4636.** www.sixflags.com. Admission (including unlimited rides, shows, and attractions) $55 adults, $35 children under 54 in. tall, free for children 3 and under. May daily 10am–7pm; June–Aug daily 10am–10pm; Sept Sat–Sun 10am–7pm. Parking $10. Take I-94 or I-294 W. to Rte. 132 (Grand Ave.). Approximate driving time from Chicago city limits: 45 min.

9 SIGHTSEEING TOURS

If you're in town for a limited time, an organized tour may be the best way to get a quick overview of the city's highlights. Some tours—such as the boat cruises on Lake Michigan and the Chicago River—can give you a whole new perspective on the city's landscape. Because Chicago caters to sophisticated travelers from all over the world, many tours go beyond sightseeing to explore important historical and architectural landmarks in depth. These specialized tours can help you appreciate buildings or neighborhoods that you might otherwise have passed by without a second glance.

For information about touring Eli's bakery, which manufactures Chicago's most famous cheesecake, see the "Dessert Tour" box on p. 116.

CARRIAGE RIDES

Noble Horse (© 312/266-7878; www.noblehorsechicago.com/carriages.html) maintains the largest fleet of antique horse carriages in Chicago, stationed around the old Water Tower Square at the northwest corner of Chicago and Michigan avenues. Each of the drivers, outfitted in a black tie and top hat, has his or her own variation on the basic Magnificent Mile itinerary (you can also do tours of the lakefront, river, Lincoln Park, and Buckingham Fountain). The charge is $35 for each half-hour for up to four people. The coaches run year-round, with convertible coaches in the warm months and enclosed carriages furnished with wool blankets on bone-chilling nights. There are several other carriage operators, all of whom pick up riders in the vicinity.

ORIENTATION TOURS

Chicago Trolley Company   Chicago Trolley Company offers guided tours on a fleet of rubber-wheeled "San Francisco–style" trolleys that stop at a number of popular spots around the city, including Navy Pier, the Grant Park museums, the historic Water Tower, and the Sears Tower. You can stay on for the full 2-hour ride, or get on and off at each stop. During the summer, the trolleys also offer trips to residential neighborhoods, including Hyde Park, the West Loop (with a drive-by of Oprah's studio) and Wrigleyville. The trolleys operate year-round, but winter visitors won't need to wear a snowsuit: The vehicles are enclosed and heated during the chilliest months. The same company also operates the **Chicago Double Decker Company,** which has a fleet of London-style red buses. The two-level buses follow the same route as the trolleys; if you buy an all-day pass, you can hop from bus to trolley at any point. An added bonus: You'll get a free T-shirt, a Hershey's chocolate bar, and a sample of Garrett's popcorn (a local favorite) with each ticket.

615 W. 41st St. © 773/648-5000. www.chicagotrolley.com. All-day hop-on, hop-off pass $29 adults, $24 seniors, $15 children 3–11; family package (2 adults, 2 children) $64 (tickets are 10% cheaper if purchased in advance online). Apr–Oct daily 9am–6:30pm; Nov–Mar daily 9am–5pm. No tours Thanksgiving, Christmas, or New Year's Day.

Gray Line   Part of a worldwide bus-tour company, Gray Line Chicago offers professional tours in well-appointed buses. Excursions run 2 to 5 hours and feature highlights of downtown or various neighborhoods. For an additional fee, some tours include a cruise on Lake Michigan or a visit to the Sears Tower Skydeck.

27 E. Monroe St., Ste. 515. © 800/621-4153 or 312/251-3107. www.grayline.com. Tours $20–$50.

LAKE & RIVER CRUISES

Chicago Line Cruises   This company runs two types of 90-minute cruises: A tour of architecture along the Chicago River, and excursions that travel on the lake and river to explore the development of the city. The atmosphere is more upscale-educational than party-hearty, with knowledgeable guides who make no attempt to double as stand-up comedians. The price includes coffee (Starbucks, no less), soft drinks, cookies, and muffins. During the summer, "cocktail" cruises run daily at 6 and 8pm. For tickets, call or stop by the company's ticket office on the lower level on the east end of River East Plaza. Advance reservations are recommended.

adults, $31 seniors, $21 children 7–18, free for children 6 and under. May–Oct daily. Tours depart hourly 9am–4pm Memorial Day to Labor Day; every 2 hr. 10am–4pm May, Sept, and Oct.

Mystic Blue Cruises A more casual alternative to fancy dinner cruises, this is promoted as more of a "fun" ship (that means DJs at night, although you'll have to put up with some kind of "live entertainment" no matter when you sail). Daily lunch and dinner excursions are available, as are midnight voyages on weekends. The same company offers more formal (and expensive) cruises aboard the *Odyssey* (www.odysseycruises.com) and motorboat rides on the 70-passenger *Seadog* (www.seadogcruises.com), if you really want to feel the water in your face.

Departing from Navy Pier. ℂ **877/299-7783.** www.mysticbluecruises.com. Lunch cruise $36; dinner cruise $68–$77; midday cruise $29; moonlight cruise $35. Cruises run year-round.

Shoreline Sightseeing ★ Shoreline launches 30-minute lake cruises every half-hour from its two dock locations at the Shedd Aquarium and Navy Pier. Shoreline has also gotten in on the popularity of architecture tours. Narrated by architectural guides, they cost more than regular tours. A **water taxi** also runs every half-hour between Navy Pier and the Sears Tower, Michigan Avenue, and the Shedd Aquarium. Tickets for the water taxi cost $3 to $13, depending how far you travel.

Departing from Navy Pier, Shedd Aquarium, and Buckingham Fountain in Grant Park. ℂ **312/222-9328.** www.shorelinesightseeing.com. Tickets weekdays $14 adults, $13 seniors, $6 children 11 and under ($1 more per ticket on weekends); architectural tours $24 adults, $21 seniors, $12 children 11 and under ($2 more per ticket on weekends). May–Sept daily. Tours depart hourly 10am–5:30pm Memorial Day to Labor Day; every 30 min. 10am–4pm May and Sept.

The Spirit of Chicago This luxury yacht offers a variety of wining-and-dining harbor cruises, from a lunch buffet to the "Moonlight Dance Party." This can be a fairly pricey night out if you go for the dinner package; the late-night moonlight cruises are a more affordable option for insomniacs.

Departing from Navy Pier. ℂ **866/211-3804.** www.spiritcruises.com. Lunch cruise $40–$50; dinner cruise (seated) $80–$110; sunset and midnight cruises $32. Ask about children's rates. Year-round daily.

Wendella Sightseeing Boats ★ Started in 1935, Wendella is the granddaddy of Chicago sightseeing operators (it's now run by the original owner's grandsons). The company operates a 1-hour tour along the Chicago River and a 1½-hour tour along the river and out onto Lake Michigan. (One of the most dramatic events during the boat tours is passing through the locks that separate the river from the lake.) Boats run from late April to early October. The 2-hour sunset tour runs Memorial Day to Labor Day starting at 7:45pm. Scheduling depends on the season and the weather, but cruises usually leave every hour during the summer.

Departing from Michigan Ave. and Wacker Dr. (north side of the river, at the Wrigley Building). ℂ **312/337-1446.** www.wendellaboats.com. Tickets $22 adults, $20 seniors, $11 children 3–11, free for children 2 and under. Apr–Oct daily.

Windy ★★ One of the more breathtaking scenes on the lake is this tall ship approaching the docks at Navy Pier. The 148-foot four-masted schooner (and its new sister ship, the *Windy II*) sets sail for 90-minute cruises two to five times a day, both day and evening. (Because the boats are sometimes booked by groups, the schedule changes each week; check their website or call first to confirm sailing times). The boats are at the whims of the wind, so every cruise charts a different course. Passengers are welcome to help raise and trim the sails and occasionally take turns at the ship's helm (with the captain standing close by). The boats are not accessible for people with disabilities.

Departing from Navy Pier. ℂ 312/595-5555. www.tallshipwindy.com. Tickets $24 adults, $20 seniors and students, $10 children 3–12. Tickets may be purchased online in advance or bought in person 1 hr. before the 1st sail of the day at the ticket office, on the dock at Navy Pier.

SPECIAL-INTEREST TOURS

Chicago Architecture Foundation (CAF) ★★★   Chicago's architecture is world famous. Luckily, the Chicago Architecture Foundation offers first-rate guided tours to help visitors understand what makes this city's skyline so special. The foundation offers walking, bike, boat, and bus tours to more than 60 architectural sites and environments in and around Chicago, led by nearly 400 trained and enthusiastic docents (all volunteers). I highly recommend taking at least one CAF tour while you're in town—they help you look at (and appreciate) the city in a new way. Tours are available year-round but are scheduled less frequently in winter.

One of the CAF's most popular tours is the 1½-hour **Architecture River Cruise,** which glides along both the north and the south branches of the Chicago River. Although you can see the same 50 or so buildings by foot, traveling by water lets you enjoy the buildings from a unique perspective. The excellent docents also provide interesting historical details, as well as some fun facts. (David Letterman once called the busts of the nation's retailing legends that face the Merchandise Mart the "Pez Hall of Fame".) The docents generally do a good job of making the cruise enjoyable for visitors with all levels of architectural knowledge. In addition to pointing out buildings—Marina City, the Civic Opera House, the Sears Tower—they approach the sites thematically, explaining, for example, how Chicagoans' use of and attitudes toward the river have changed over time.

Tours are $28 per person weekdays, $32 on weekends and holidays. In the summer (June-Sept), cruises run hourly from 10am to 3pm weekdays and from 9am to 5pm weekends (with more limited schedules in May, Oct, and Nov). The trips are extremely popular, so purchase tickets in advance through **Ticketmaster** (ℂ 312/902-1500; www. ticketmaster.com), or avoid the service charge and buy tickets at one of the foundation's tour centers or from the boat launch on the southeast corner of Michigan Avenue and Wacker Drive.

If you want to squeeze a lot of sightseeing into a limited time, try **Highlights by Bus,** a 3½-hour overview tour that covers the Loop, Hyde Park—including a visit to the interior of Frank Lloyd Wright's Robie House—and the Gold Coast, plus several other historic districts. Tours start at 9:30am on Friday and Saturday April through October; tickets are $40 per person.

A 4-hour bus tour of Frank Lloyd Wright sights in **Oak Park** ($40) is available on the first Saturday of the month from May to October. The tour includes walks through three neighborhoods and commentary on more than 25 houses—but does not take visitors inside Wright's home and studio. A separate 4-hour bus tour ($52), on Tuesday at 9:30am (June–Oct), takes Wright fans inside the master's home and Oak Park's Unity Temple.

If you prefer exploring on your own, the CAF offers a variety of guided walking tours. For first-time visitors, I highly recommend two tours for an excellent introduction to the dramatic architecture of the Loop. **Historic Downtown: Rise of the Skyscraper** (daily 10am) covers buildings built between 1880 and 1940, including the Rookery and the Chicago Board of Trade; **Modern Skyscrapers** (daily 1pm) includes modern masterpieces

Finds The Wright Stuff in the Gold Coast

Architecture junkies may want to visit the **Charnley-Persky House,** 1365 N. Astor St., in the Gold Coast (② **312/915-0105** or 312/573-1365; www.charnley house.org), designed by Frank Lloyd Wright and Louis Sullivan in 1891. Sullivan was Frank Lloyd Wright's architectural mentor, and although Wright was a junior draftsman on this project, Sullivan allowed him to become involved in the design process. The result is an important landmark in modern architecture that rejected Victorian details and embraced symmetry and simplicity. Free 45-minute tours of the interior are given on Wednesday at noon. A 90-minute tour of the home and the surrounding neighborhood is offered Saturdays at 10am year-round ($10); an additional tour is given at 1pm April through November. Reservations are not accepted.

by Mies van der Rohe and postmodern works by contemporary architects. The 2-hour tours cost $15 each for adults and $12 each for seniors and students.

The CAF also offers more than 50 **neighborhood tours,** visiting the Gold Coast, River North, Grant Park, Old Town, the Jackson Boulevard Historic District, and even Lincoln Park Zoo. Most cost $10 and last a couple of hours.

Departing from the Chicago ArchiCenter, 224 S. Michigan Ave.; a few tours leave from the John Hancock Center, 875 N. Michigan Ave. ② **312/922-3432,** or 312/922-TOUR [8687] for recorded information. www. architecture.org. Tickets for most walking tours $12–$15. Subway/El: Brown, Green, Purple, or Orange line to Adams, or Red Line to Jackson.

Chicago Supernatural Tours An offbeat way to experience the real "spirit" of Chicago is to take a narrated bus tour of cemeteries, murder sites, Indian burial grounds, haunted pubs, and other spooky places. Richard Crowe, who bills himself as a "professional ghost hunter," spins ghost stories, legends, and lore on the 4-hour trip. Yes, there's plenty of shtick, but Crowe really knows his stuff, so you'll get an informative history lesson along the way. Reservations are required; Crowe's tours get especially popular around Halloween, so you'll definitely want to call ahead.

Crowe also leads 2-hour **supernatural boat excursions** from July through Labor Day weekend; the tour costs $27 per person and boards at 9:30pm at the Mercury boat dock at Michigan Avenue and Wacker Drive.

Departs from Goose Island Restaurant, 1800 N. Clybourn Ave. ② **708/499-0300.** www.ghosttours.com. $44 per person. Tours offered once or twice a month Fri–Sat nights; call for exact schedule. Subway/El: Red Line to North/Clybourn and short walk.

Untouchable Tours The days of Al Capone are long gone, but Chicago's notorious past is still good for business, it seems, given the popularity of these "Gangster Tours." The 2-hour bus trip takes you to all of the city's old hoodlum hangouts from the Prohibition era, including O'Bannion's flower shop and the site of the St. Valentine's Day massacre. The focus is definitely more on entertainment than history (guides with names such as "Al Dente" and "Ice Pick" appear in costume and role-play their way through the tour), but the trip does give you a pretty thorough overview of the city.

Departs from the southeast corner of Clark and Ohio sts. ② **773/881-1195.** www.gangstertour.com. $28 adults, $20 children. Tours depart Mon–Wed 10am; Thurs 10am and 1pm; Fri 10am, 1 and 7:30pm; Sat 10am, 1, 3 and 5pm; Sun 10am and 1pm.

It's a bit of a cliché to say that Chicago is a city of neighborhoods, but if you want to see what really makes the place special, that's where you have to go.

Sponsored by the city's Department of Cultural Affairs, **Chicago Neighborhood Tours** ★ (© 312/742-1190; www.chicagoneighborhoodtours.com) are 4- to 5-hour narrated bus excursions to about a dozen diverse communities throughout the city. Departing at 10am from the Chicago Cultural Center, 77 E. Randolph St., every Saturday, the tours visit different neighborhoods, from Chinatown and historic Bronzeville on the South Side to the ethnic enclaves of Devon Avenue and Uptown on the North Side. Neighborhood representatives serve as guides and greeters along the way as tour participants visit area landmarks, murals, museums, and shopping districts. Tickets (including a light snack) are $30 for adults and $25 for seniors, students, and children 8 to 18. Tours do not run on major holidays (call first) or, usually, in January. Regularly available specialty tours include Literary Chicago; the Great Chicago Fire; Roots of Blues, Gospel & Jazz; Irish Chicago; and Magnificent Churches. These tours, which generally run about 4 to 6 hours and include lunch, are more expensive ($50 adults, $45 seniors and children).

On Saturday mornings in the summer, the **Chicago History Museum** offers 2-hour walking tours of the neighborhoods surrounding the museum: The **Gold Coast, Old Town,** and **Lincoln Park.** Led by museum docents, they average about four per month June through August. Day and evening tours are available, and a few specialty walking tours are usually offered as well. Tours are $10 per person, and registration is recommended but not required. Tours depart from the museum at Clark Street and North Avenue, and light refreshments are served afterward. In the summer and fall, the museum also offers a few half-day trolley tours that cover unique themes or aspects of the metropolitan area's history. Led by historians and scholars, they take place in the city and surrounding areas ($40). Tours depart from the Chicago History Museum at Clark Street and North Avenue. Call © 312/642-4600, or visit the museum's website (www.chicago history.org) for schedules and to order tickets online.

Groups can arrange tours of Chicago's **"Black Metropolis,"** the name given to a South Side area of Bronzeville where African Americans created a flourishing business-and-artistic community after World War II. Contact **Tour Black Chicago** (© 773/684-9034; www.tourblackchicago.com) for more information. Another locally based company that specializes in black heritage tours, **Black Coutours** (© 773/233-8907; www.blackcoutours.com) offers a "Soul Side of the Windy City" tour, which has been expanded to include Obama-related sites.

Cemetery Tours

Don't be scared away by the creepy connotations. Some of Chicago's cemeteries are as pretty as parks, and they offer a variety of intriguing monuments that are a virtual road into the city's history.

One of the best area cemeteries is **Graceland,** stretching along Clark Street in the Swedish neighborhood of Andersonville, where you can view the tombs and monuments of many Chicago notables. When Graceland was laid out in 1860, public parks were rare. The elaborate burial grounds that were constructed in many large American cities around that time had the dual purpose of relieving the congestion of the municipal cemeteries closer to town and providing pastoral recreational settings for the Sunday outings of the living. Indeed, cemeteries like Graceland were the precursors of such great municipal green spaces as Lincoln Park. Much of Lincoln Park, in fact, had been a public cemetery since Chicago's earliest times. (Many who once rested there were re-interred in Graceland when the building of Lincoln Park went forward.)

The **Chicago Architecture Foundation** (✆ **312/922-TOUR** [8687]; www.architecture. org) offers walking tours of Graceland on select Sundays during August, September, and October. The tour costs $10 and lasts about 2 hours. Among the points of interest in these 121 beautifully landscaped acres are the Ryerson and Getty tombs, famous architectural monuments designed by Louis Sullivan. Sullivan himself rests here in the company of several of his distinguished colleagues: Daniel Burnham, Ludwig Mies van der Rohe, and Howard Van Doren Shaw. Chicago giants of industry and commerce buried at Graceland include Potter Palmer, Marshall Field, and George Pullman. The Chicago Architecture Foundation offers tours of other cemeteries including Rosehill Cemetery, suburban Lake Forest Cemetery, and Oak Woods Cemetery, the final resting place for many famous African-American figures, including Jesse Owens, Ida B. Wells, and Mayor Harold Washington.

10 STAYING ACTIVE

Perhaps because winters can be brutal, Chicagoans take their summers seriously. In the warmer months, with the wide blue lake and the ample green parks, it's easy to think that the city is one big grown-up playground. Whether you prefer your activity in the water or on dry ground, you'll probably find it here. For information, contact the city's park district (✆ **312/742-PLAY** [7529]; www.chicagoparkdistrict.com); for questions about the 29 miles of beaches and parks along Lake Michigan, call the park district's lakefront region office at ✆ **312/747-2474.**

Another handy resource is *Windy City Sports* (✆ **312/421-1551;** www.windycity sports.com), a free monthly publication available at many retail shops, grocery stores, bars, and cafes.

BEACHES

Public beaches line Lake Michigan all the way up north into the suburbs and Wisconsin, and southeast through Indiana and into Michigan. The best known is **Oak Street Beach.** Its location, at the northern tip of the Magnificent Mile, creates some interesting sights as sun worshippers sporting swimsuits and carting coolers make their way down Michigan Avenue. The most popular is **North Avenue Beach,** about 6 blocks farther north, which has developed into a volleyball hot spot and recently rebuilt its landmark steamship-shaped beach house and added a Venice Beach–style outdoor gym; this is where the Lincoln Park singles come to play, check each other out, and fly by on bikes and in-line skates. **Hollywood-Ardmore Beach** (officially Kathy Osterman Beach), at the northern end of Lake Shore Drive, is a lovely crescent that's less congested and has steadily become more popular with gays who've moved up the lakefront from the Belmont Rocks, a longtime hangout. For more seclusion, try **Ohio Street Beach,** an intimate sliver of sand in tiny Olive Park, just north of Navy Pier, which, incredibly enough, remains largely ignored despite its central location. If you have a car, head up to **Montrose Beach,** a beautiful unsung treasure about midway between North Avenue Beach and Hollywood-Ardmore Beach (with plenty of free parking). Long popular with the city's Hispanic community, it has an expanse of beach mostly uninterrupted by piers or jetties, and a huge adjacent park with soccer fields, one big hill that's great for kite flying, and even a small bait shop where anglers can go before heading to a nearby long pier designated for fishing.

If you've brought the pooch along, you might want to take him for a dip at the **doggie beach** south of Addison Street, at about Hawthorne and Lake Shore Drive (although this minute spot aggravates some dog owners because it's in a harbor where the water is somewhat fouled by gas and oil from nearby boats). *A tip:* Try the south end of North Avenue Beach in early morning, before it opens to the public for the day. (Also consider that, in the off season, all beaches are fair game for dogs. The police won't hassle you, I promise.)

Beaches officially open with a full retinue of lifeguards on duty around June 20, though swimmers can wade into the chilly water from Memorial Day to Labor Day. Only the bravest souls venture into the water before July, when the temperature creeps up enough to make swimming an attractive proposition. Please take note that the entire lakefront is not beach, and don't go do anything stupid such as dive off the rocks.

BIKING

Biking is a great way to see the city, particularly along the lakefront bike path that extends for more than 18 miles. The stretch between Navy Pier and North Avenue Beach gets extremely crowded in the summer (you're jostling for space with in-line skaters, joggers, and dawdling pedestrians). If you're looking to pick up some speed, I recommend biking south (once you're past the Museum Campus, the trail is relatively wide open, and you can zip all the way to Hyde Park). If you want a more leisurely tour with people-watching potential, head north (through the crowds). After you pass Belmont Harbor, the traffic lets up a bit. Ride all the way to Hollywood Beach (where the lakefront trail ends) for a good but not exhausting workout.

To rent bikes, try **Bike Chicago** (www.bikechicago.com), which has locations at Navy Pier (✆ 312/595-9600), North Avenue Beach (✆ 773/327-2706), and Millennium Park (✆ 888/BIKE-WAY [245-3929]). Open from 8am to 8pm May through October (weather permitting), Bike Chicago stocks mountain and touring bikes, kids' bikes, strollers, and—most fun of all—quadcycles, which are four-wheel contraptions equipped with a steering wheel and canopy that can accommodate four or five people. Rates for bikes start at $10 an hour, $30 a day, with helmets, pads, and locks included. If you'd like to cycle your way past some Chicago landmarks, guided tours are also available.

Both the park district (✆ 312/742-PLAY [7529]) and the **Chicagoland Bicycle Federation** (✆ 312/42-PEDAL [427-3325]; www.biketraffic.org) offer free maps that detail popular biking routes. The latter, which is the preeminent organization for cyclists in Chicago, sells a much larger, more extensive map ($6.95) that shows routes within a seven-county area. The federation sponsors a number of bike rides throughout the year, including the highly enjoyable **Boulevard Lakefront Tour,** held in September, which follows the historic circle of boulevards that had their genesis in the Chicago Plan of 1909. It starts in Hyde Park at the University of Chicago campus.

A word of caution: Never head anywhere on the city's streets without first strapping on a helmet. Chicago Mayor Richard M. Daley, an avid cyclist, has tirelessly promoted the addition of designated bike lanes along many main thoroughfares, but most cabbies and drivers tend to ignore them. Bike with extreme caution on city streets (you can get a ticket for biking on the sidewalk), and stick to the lakefront path if you're not an expert rider. Locking your bike anywhere you go is a no-brainer.

For a major metropolis, Chicago has an impressive number of golf options within the city limits (not to mention many plush and pricey suburban courses). The closest you'll get to golfing downtown is the **Green at Grant Park** (© 312/987-1818; www.thegreen online.com), an 18-hole putting course on Monroe Street between Columbus Avenue and Lake Shore Drive, just east of Millennium Park. It's not exactly tournament-level play, but it's more challenging than miniature golf—and the setting can't be beat. The course is open daily from May through October from 10am to 10pm, and putters and golf balls are provided. Rates are $9 per round for adults, $6 for children 12 and under.

To warm up your swing, head to the **Diversey Driving Range,** 141 W. Diversey Pkwy. (© 312/742-7929), in Lincoln Park just north of Diversey Harbor. This two-level range attracts all levels—from show-off heavy hitters to beginners—and is very popular on weekends with young singles who live in the surrounding apartment buildings. The price is right ($11 for a bucket of 100 balls), and the setting is pretty much perfect.

The Chicago Park District runs six golf courses in the city. One of the most popular is the 9-hole **Sydney Marovitz Course,** 3600 N. Lake Shore Dr. (at Waveland Ave.), which many Chicagoans simply call Waveland. Thanks to its picturesque lakefront location, it's always full on weekends, so make a reservation well in advance (and don't expect a quick game—this is where beginners come to practice). Another good bet—and usually less crowded—is the 18-hole course in **Jackson Park** on the South Side (63rd St. and Stoney Island Ave.). These city-run courses are open from mid-April through November; for information on greens fees, location, and hours, call the **Chicago Park District** golf office (© 312/245-0909; www.cpdgolf.com).

For information about suburban golf courses, visit the website of the **Chicago District Golf Association** (www.cdga.org).

ICE SKATING

The city's premier skating destination is the **McCormick-Tribune Ice Rink** at Millennium Park, 55 N. Michigan Ave. (© 312/742-5222). The location is pretty much perfect: You're skating in the shadows of grand skyscrapers and within view of the lake. The rink is open daily from 10am to 10pm November through March. Admission is free, and skate rentals are $7.

The park district runs dozens of other skating surfaces throughout the city, along the lakefront and in neighborhood parks. Call © 312/742-PLAY [7529] for locations. There's also a relatively small rink at **Navy Pier,** 600 E. Grand Ave. (© 312/595-PIER [7437]).

IN-LINE SKATING

The wheeled ones have been battling bikers over control of Chicago's lakefront paths since the early 1990s. If you want to join in the competition, **Londo Mondo,** 1100 N. Dearborn St. (© 312/751-2794), on the Gold Coast, rents blades for $7 an hour or $20 a day. The best route to skate is the lakefront trail that leads from Lincoln Park down to Oak Street Beach. Beware, though, that those same miles of trail are claimed by avid cyclists—I've seen plenty of collisions between 'bladers and bikers. Approach Chicago lakefront traffic as carefully as you would a major expressway.

SAILING

It seems a shame just to sit on the beach and watch all those beautiful sailboats gliding across the lake, so go on, get out there. **Chicago Sailing,** in Belmont Harbor (© 773/871-SAIL [7245]; www.chicagosailing.com), rents J-22 and J-30 boats from 9am to sunset, weather permitting, May through October. A J-22, which holds four or five adults, rents for $45 to $65 an hour; a J-30, which accommodates up to 10 people, costs $80 to $100 per hour. If you want to take the boat out without a skipper, you need to demonstrate your skills first (for an additional $15 fee). If you'd rather sit back and relax, you can charter a boat. Reservations are recommended.

SWIMMING

The Chicago Park District maintains about 30 indoor pools for lap swimming and general splashing around, but none is particularly convenient to downtown. The lakefront is open for swimming until 9:30pm Memorial Day to Labor Day in areas watched over by lifeguards (no swimming off the rocks, please). *But be forewarned:* The water is usually freezing. A good place for lake swimming is the water along the wall beginning at Ohio Street Beach, slightly northwest of Navy Pier. The Chicago Triathlon Club marks a course here each summer with a buoy at both the quarter- and half-mile distances. This popular swimming route follows the shoreline in a straight line. The water is fairly shallow. For more information, call the park district's beach and pool office (✆ **312/742-PLAY** [7529]).

---

11 IN THE GRANDSTAND: WATCHING CHICAGO'S ATHLETIC EVENTS

BASEBALL

Baseball is imprinted on the national consciousness as part of Chicago, not because of victorious dynasties but because of the opposite—the Black Sox scandal of 1919 and the perennially losing Cubs.

The **Chicago Cubs** haven't made a World Series appearance since 1945 and haven't been world champs since 1908, but that doesn't stop people from catching games at historic **Wrigley Field,** ★★ 1060 W. Addison St. (✆ **773/404-CUBS** [2827]; www.cubs.mlb.com), with its ivy-covered outfield walls, its hand-operated scoreboard, its view of the shimmering lake from the upper deck, and its "W" or "L" flag announcing the outcome of the game to the unfortunates who couldn't attend. After all the strikes, temper tantrums, and other nonsense, Wrigley has managed to hold on to something like purity. Yes, Wrigley finally installed lights (it was the last major-league park to do so), but by agreement with the residential neighborhood, the Cubs still play most games in the daylight, as they should. Because Wrigley is small, just about every seat is decent.

No matter how the Cubs are doing, tickets ($15–$50) go fast; most weekend and night games sell out by Memorial Day. Your best bet is to hit a weekday game, or try your luck buying a ticket on game day outside the park, when you'll often find some season-ticket holders looking to unload a few seats. And not that I would ever suggest doing something illegal, but if you're willing to pay above face value, scalpers usually lurk on street corners a block or two away.

Wrigley's easy to reach by El; take the Red Line to the Addison stop, and you're there. Or take the no. 22 bus, which runs up Clark Street. To buy tickets in person, stop by the ticket windows at Wrigley Field, Monday through Friday from 9am to 6pm, Saturday from 9am to 4pm, and on game days. Call ✆ **800/THE-CUBS** or 800/843-2827 for tickets through **Tickets.com** (✆ **866/652-2827** outside of Illinois); you can also order online through the team website.

> Wrigley Field is one of the last old-time baseball stadiums in the country (no luxury boxes here!). Built in 1914, Wrigley Field is the second-oldest major league ball park, after Boston's Fenway Park. Known as the "friendly confines," Wrigley Field was the site of Babe Ruth's "called shot," when Ruth allegedly pointed to a bleacher location in the 1932 World Series and then hit a home run to that exact spot. For an intimate look at the historic ballpark, take one of the tours offered on various Saturdays throughout the summer; stops include the visitors' and home-team locker rooms, press box, behind-the-scenes security headquarters, and, yes, a walk around the field itself (be sure to check out the original scoreboard, built in 1937). Tours sell out, so buy tickets ($20) as far in advance as possible. Call ✆ **800/THE-CUBS** [843-2827], or stop by the box office at 1060 W. Addison St.

Despite their stunning World Series win in 2005, the **Chicago White Sox** still struggle to attract the same kind of loyalty (despite the fact that they regularly win more games than the Cubs). Longtime fans rue the day owner Jerry Reinsdorf (who is also majority owner of the Chicago Bulls) replaced admittedly dilapidated Comiskey Park with a concrete behemoth that lacks the yesteryear charm of its predecessor. That said, the new stadium, **U.S. Cellular Field,** 333 W. 35th St. (✆ **312/674-1000;** www.whitesox.mlb.com), in the South Side neighborhood of Bridgeport, has spectacular sightlines from every seat (if you avoid the vertigo-inducing upper deck), and the park has every conceivable amenity, including above-average food concessions, shops, and plentiful restrooms. The White Sox's endearing quality is the blue-collar aura with which so many Cubs-loathing Southsiders identify. Games rarely sell out—an effect, presumably, of Reinsdorf's sterile stadium and the blighted neighborhood that surrounds it. All of this makes it a bargain for bona fide baseball fans. Tickets cost $12 to $45 and are half-price on Monday.

To get Sox tickets, call **Ticketmaster** (✆ **866/SOX-GAME** [769-4263]), or visit the ticket office, open Monday through Friday from 10am to 6pm, Saturday and Sunday from 10am to 4pm, with extended hours on game days. To get to the ballpark by El, take the Red Line to Sox/35th Street.

BASKETBALL

When it comes to basketball, Chicagoans still live in the past, associating the **Chicago Bulls** (✆ **312/455-4000**) with the glory days of Michael Jordan and the never-ending championships of the 1990s. The fact that Jordan chose to remain in town after his playing days were over—a decision almost unheard-of in professional sports—has only burnished his image here, and locals are still wowed by occasional Jordan sightings. The downside is that he's a constant reminder of our ever-more-distant winning past.

Although the Bulls have rebounded somewhat from the dismal seasons following Jordan's departure, the current players don't inspire the same city-wide excitement. The upside for visitors? The Bulls don't consistently sell out, which means you might be able to catch a game at the cavernous **United Center,** 1901 W. Madison St. (✆ **312/455-4500;** www.chicagosports.com). Yes, the space is massive and impersonal, but the pre-game buildup, with flashing lights and thumping music, is undeniably dramatic. Most tickets run $20 to $100 through **Ticketmaster** (ⓒ 312/559-1212), although be aware the cheap seats are practically in the rafters. If money is no object, you can usually score good seats through local ticket brokers without much advance notice.

FOOTBALL

The **Chicago Bears** play at **Soldier Field,** Lake Shore Drive and 16th Street (ⓒ 847/295-6600; www.chicagobears.com), site of a controversial renovation that added what looks like a giant space ship on top of the original stadium's elegant colonnade. Architecturally, it's a disaster, but from a comfort perspective, the place is much improved—although that doesn't impress longtime fans who prided themselves on surviving blistering-cold game days and horrifying bathrooms. The Bears themselves have been inspiring high hopes—most recently, winning a trip to the Super Bowl in 2007. But even during losing seasons, tickets are hard to come by. (Most are snapped up by season-ticket holders long before the season starts.) If you plan ahead, individual tickets run $45 to $300; expensive seats are usually available through ticket brokers or online sites.

The **Northwestern Wildcats** play Big Ten college ball at **Ryan Field,** 1501 Central St., in nearby Evanston (ⓒ 847/491-CATS [2287]). Full disclosure: As a Northwestern grad myself, I must admit we're not particularly loyal to our long-suffering team. In fact, fans of the visiting team often outnumber NU supporters in the stands.

HOCKEY

The **Chicago Blackhawks** have devoted, impassioned fans who work themselves into a frenzy with the first note of "The Star-Spangled Banner," but don't expect heroics that challenge the exploits of past Hawks legends such as Bobby Hull and Tony Esposito. The Blackhawks play at the **United Center,** 1901 W. Madison St. (ⓒ 312/455-7000; www.chicagoblackhawks.com). Tickets cost $15 to $100.

For a more affordable and family-friendly experience, catch the semipro **Chicago Wolves** at Allstate Arena, 6920 N. Mannheim Rd., Rosemont (ⓒ 847/724-GOAL [4625]; www.chicagowolves.com). The team has been consistently excellent over the past few years, and the games are geared toward all ages, with fireworks beforehand and plenty of on- and off-ice entertainment (tickets $13–$30).

HORSE RACING

Thoroughbreds race at **Arlington International Racecourse,** 2200 W. Euclid Ave., Arlington Heights (ⓒ 847/385-7500; www.arlingtonpark.com), in the northwest suburbs. Live local bands and DJs add to the party atmosphere on Fridays and Saturdays from Memorial Day weekend until Labor Day, starting at 2:30pm. For more details, see p. 190. The Chicago area's other major racetrack, **Hawthorne Race Course,** 3501 S. Laramie Ave., Stickney (ⓒ 708/780-3700; www.sportsmanspark.com), is located in the southwest suburbs, about a half-hour drive from downtown.

SOCCER

Chicago's Major League Soccer team, the **Chicago Fire,** plays at its own 20,000-seat stadium in suburban Bridgeview (about 12 miles southwest of downtown). The season runs from late May through October (ⓒ 888/MLS-FIRE [657-3473]; http://chicago.fire.mlsnet.com). Games have a family feel, with plenty of activities for kids and affordable ticket prices ($15–$60).

Chicago Strolls

Chicago is an October kind of city even in spring.

—Nelson Algren

Actually, October happens to be one of my favorite months to wander around town: The weather is cool but not freezing, most of the tourist hoards have moved on, and the crisp air is invigorating. But you can meander around Chicago in any season. With the right coat, scarf, and mittens, you can even brave the streets in January or February—then brag about it to friends back home. The following tours give a taste of Chicago's diversity, from the bustling downtown business center to a couple of distinctive residential neighborhoods.

WALKING TOUR 1   THE LOOP

START:	The Sears Tower.
FINISH:	Harold Washington Library Center.
TIME:	2 to 3 hours.
BEST TIME:	Daytime, particularly weekdays when downtown businesses are open.
WORST TIME:	Late evening, after shops and offices have closed.

Walk through the Loop's densely packed canyon of buildings, and you'll feel the buzzing pulse of downtown. While you'll pass plenty of modern high-rises, you'll also get a mini lesson in architectural history, as you survey the progression of the city's skyscrapers.

Start the tour at:

❶ The Sears Tower

Okay, so this 110-story megatower is no longer the world's tallest building. It's not even the Sears Tower any more, since the naming rights were bought by the London-based insurance broker Willis Group in early 2009. But "Willis Tower" (gulp) is still referred to as the Sears Tower by defiant Chicagoans and remains a bold symbol of the city. If it's a clear day (and you've got the time), take a trip up to the Skydeck (p. 153) before heading off on your tour: To the east you'll look out over the lake, to the northwest you can watch planes take off from O'Hare Airport, and to the north you'll be able to see all the way to Wisconsin.

Walk north along Wacker Drive until you arrive at:

❷ 333 W. Wacker Dr.

Proof that Chicago inspires architectural creativity, this 1983 office building was designed to fit a rather awkward triangular plot (previously thought suitable only for a parking lot). But architectural firm Kohn Pedersen Fox came up with a brilliant solution, designing a curved facade that echoes the bend of the Chicago River. Walk out to the Franklin Street Bridge to get the full effect of the building's mirrored surface, which reflects the surrounding cityscape in ever-changing shades of blue, green and gray.

Across the river you'll see:

❸ The Merchandise Mart

Touted as the world's largest commercial building, the Mart is a Chicago landmark as much for its place on the stage of

American merchandising as for its hulking institutional look. Completed in 1931, it's occupied mostly by furniture and interior-design businesses. Perched on top of the pillars that run the length of the building are oversized busts of American retail icons, including Julius Rosenwalk (Sears), Frank W. Woolworth, and Aaron Montgomery Ward.

Walk 2 blocks east along Wacker Drive. At LaSalle Street, turn right and continue 2 blocks to Randolph Street. Turn left (east), go half a block and you'll be standing in front of:

❹ The James R. Thompson Center

This postmodern cascade of glass and steel is—depending on your point of view—the pinnacle or the low point of architect Helmut Jahn's career. Home to offices of the Illinois state bureaucracy, it was designed to promote the idea of open government: The transparent glass walls inside allow citizens to see their tax dollars at work. Step into the atrium to check out the beehive-like atmosphere; you can even ride a glass elevator up to the 17th floor if you're not afraid of heights.

Cross Randolph Street and head south along Clark Street. On the left you'll come to an open space known as:

❺ Daley Plaza

Shadowed by the looming tower of the Richard J. Daley Center—a blocky dark monolith of government offices—this square was named for the legendary mayor (father of the current one) and longtime czar of Cook County politics. While you're here, go ahead and do what tourists do: Take a picture in front of the Picasso sculpture (p. 154).

Walk back up to Randolph Street and head east. At the corner of Randolph and State sts., you'll see two local landmarks: The marquee of the Chicago Theatre to your north, and the block-long Macy's (previously Marshall Field's) to the south. Continue south along State Street until you reach:

❻ The Reliance Building

Now known as the Burnham Hotel, this building may not look impressive, but it's famous in the world of architecture. Completed in 1895, it had a remarkably lighter look than its bulky predecessors, thanks to steel framing that allowed for the extensive use of glass on the facade. It also marked the first use of the "Chicago window": A large central pane of glass flanked by two smaller, double-hung windows used for ventilation. To get a glimpse of what it looked like when it was an office building, take one of the hotel elevators up to one of the guest room floors, which still have the original tile flooring and glass-windowed office doors.

Continue south along State Street until you reach Adams Street. Ready to pause for a bite or a drink? Then turn right (west), go half a block, and stop at:

 TAKE A BREAK
In a world of chain coffee shops and fast-food joints, the **Berghoff,** 17 W. Adams St. (ⓒ **312/427-3170;** p. 104), feels like a flashback to Old Chicago. The bar of this 100-year-old restaurant serves several different house brews on tap, along with sandwiches and appetizers. (For a non-alcoholic treat, try the homemade root beer.) If it's lunchtime, grab a table in the main dining room; although the menu has been modified for modern, lighter tastes, the Wiener schnitzel and spaetzle are always my first choice.

Go 2 blocks west along Adams Street until you reach LaSalle Street. Turn left (south) and you'll be at:

❼ The Rookery

Built between 1885 and 1888, the Rookery represents a dramatic transition in Chicago architecture. (It's also one of the only surviving buildings designed by noted architect Daniel Burnham, along with the Reliance Building, above.) The name refers to the previous building that sat on this site, Chicago's original City Hall, which was a favorite spot for nesting birds; today, it's an office building. The imposing Romanesque exterior has thick

1. The Sears Tower
2. 333 W. Wacker Dr.
3. The Merchandise Mart
4. The James R. Thompson Center
5. Daley Plaza
6. The Reliance Building
🍺 The Berghoff
7. The Rookery
8. Chicago Board of Trade
9. Monadnock Building
10. Manhattan Building
11. Harold Washington Library Center

Ⓜ Subway/El stop

MERCH MART Ⓜ W. Kinzie St.
North Branch Chicago River
RIVER NORTH
Chicago River
W. Wacker Dr.
W. Lake St.   CLARK/LAKE Ⓜ   STATE/LAKE Ⓜ
N. Franklin St.   N. Wells St.   N. LaSalle St.   N. Dearborn St.   N. State St.   N. Wabash Ave.   N. Michigan Ave.
W. Randolph Dr.   RANDOLPH Ⓜ
W. Washington St.   Ⓜ
WASHINGTON Ⓜ   WASHINGTON Ⓜ
W. Madison St.   MADISON Ⓜ
S. Wacker Dr.   South Branch Chicago River
THE LOOP
W. Monroe St.   MONROE Ⓜ
S. Clark St.   S. Dearborn St.   S. State St.
Union Station   Sears Tower ①   QUINCY Ⓜ   W. Adams St.   ADAMS Ⓜ
W. Jackson Blvd.   ★ start here   W. Jackson Blvd.   ⑦   JACKSON Ⓜ
S. Canal St.   S. Franklin St.   ⑧   ⑨   LIBRARY Ⓜ
W. Van Buren St.   ★ finish here
90 94   LASALLE Ⓜ   ⑪
Eisenhower Expwy.   290   W. Congress Pkwy.   ⑩   E. Congress Pkwy.
0   1/4 mi   LASALLE Ⓜ
0   0.25 km   Ⓝ   W. Harrison St.   E. Harrison St.
SOUTH LOOP   HARRISON Ⓜ

CHICAGO STROLLS

8

THE LOOP

masonry walls, but the inside is surprisingly open and airy, thanks to an innovative use of iron framing. The building is essentially a square built around an open interior court that rises the full height of the building's 11 stories. Walk upstairs and follow the staircase to get a glimpse of the Rookery's interior courtyard and the sublime stairway spiraling upward.

Continue south along LaSalle Street. At Jackson Boulevard, the street appears to dead-end at the:

⑧ Chicago Board of Trade

The city's temple to high finance, this building houses the city's commodities exchange, an echo of the days when corn and wheat from the prairie passed through

Chicago on its way east. Opened in 1930, the setbacks on the upper stories are typical of the Art Deco styling of the era, as are the geometric decorative elements over the entrance. Along the building's rear (southern) wall, a 24-story postmodern addition by Helmut Jahn repeats the original's pyramid-shaped roof, maintaining the symmetry between old and new. When it was built, the 45-story Board of Trade was considered so tall that the aluminum sculpture of Ceres, the Roman goddess of architecture who adorns the building's peak, was left faceless, because no one in neighboring buildings would ever be high enough to see it.

❾ Monadnock Building

This mass of stonework forms two office buildings that occupy this entire narrow block all the way to Van Buren Street. Only 2 years separate the construction of these architectural twins, but they are light years apart in design and engineering. (You'll need to step across Dearborn Street to fully appreciate the differences.)

Monadnock I, on the northern end, was built by the architectural firm of Burnham and Root between 1889 and 1891. To support a building of this size at the time, the masonry walls had to be built 6 to 8 feet thick (note the deeply recessed windows at street level). Monadnock II, on the southern wing, was built by Holabird & Roche in 1893. Here, steel framing was used, allowing the lower walls to be significantly narrower. The second building may have been an engineering marvel at the time, but the original Monadnock has a certain gravitas that the later addition lacks.

Walk south along Dearborn Street until you reach Congress Parkway. At 431 S. Dearborn St. you'll find the:

❿ Manhattan Building

Constructed in 1891 by William Le Baron Jenny, this broad structure was viewed as an architectural wonder by many who visited Chicago during the Columbian Exposition 2 years later. To some, the eclectic use of materials and varied design of the facade give the Manhattan Building an appearance of complete chaos; others see a dynamic rhythm in the architect's choices. Today, this former office building has been converted into condos.

From the corner of Dearborn and Van Buren streets, look a few blocks west along Van Buren until you spot a triangular tower, carved with slivers of window. That building is the Metropolitan Correctional Center, a 27-story jail for defendants preparing for trial in federal court downtown. The building's three-sided design derives from an attempt by the U.S. Bureau of Prisons to reform prison conditions: Cells were built along the edges surrounding a central lounge area. But it's still not a great place to hang out: To foil jailbreaks, the windows are only 5 inches wide (and have bars, to boot); although there's a recreation yard on the roof, it's enclosed on the sides and topped with wire mesh.

Walk 2 blocks east along Congress Parkway until you reach State Street. Turn left (north) to reach the entrance of the:

⓫ Harold Washington Library Center

This block-long behemoth, named for the city's first African-American mayor, is the world's largest municipal library (p. 161). Designed by a firm led by Thomas Beeby, then dean of Yale University's School of Architecture, and completed in 1991, it self-consciously echoes the city's original grand buildings, such as the Auditorium Theater a few blocks east. I find the whole place rather off-putting—it feels more like a fortress than a welcoming library. But judge for yourself.

Despite my distaste for the building as a whole, I do have a soft spot for the Winter Garden on the ninth floor, a lovely retreat drenched with natural light.

START: Oak Street Beach.

FINISH: Bellevue Place and Michigan Avenue.

TIME: 1 hour, more if you stop to eat along the way.

BEST TIME: Sunday is the ideal day for this walk at any time of the year. On weekdays, wait until after the morning rush before setting out.

WORST TIME: After dusk, when it's too dark to appreciate the buildings' decorative elements.

The Gold Coast—as its name implies—is Chicago's ritziest neighborhood, site of its most expensive and exclusive houses. Its reputation dates back to 1882, when Potter Palmer, one of the city's richest businessmen, built a lakeshore castle here, in what was then a relative wilderness north of the city. The mere presence of the Palmers served as an instant magnet, drawing other social climbers in their wake (and Palmer, who owned vast parcels of northside land, saw his holdings shoot up in value). This itinerary begins with a walk overlooking Lake Michigan before heading down charming tree-lined residential streets.

Begin the tour at:

① Oak Street Beach

This confluence of city and lakeshore epitomizes what Chicagoans love about our city: Facing downtown, you've got the ultimate urban vista; stare at the shoreline, and the seemingly endless expanse of water makes you feel like you've escaped the city completely. You can stroll along the sand or keep to the concrete path (but beware of speeding bikes and rollerbladers). As you head north, look across Lake Shore Drive to see a few remaining historic mansions scattered among the more modern high-rises.

The first mansion you'll pass, just north of Scott Street, is:

② The Carl C. Heissen House

Both the Heissen House (1250 N. Lake Shore Dr.), built in 1890, and its neighbor, the Starring House (1254 N. Lake Shore Dr.), built in 1889, show the popularity of the sturdy Romanesque style among wealthy Chicagoans.

A second cluster of former private mansions, all vaguely neoclassical in outline, faces Lake Michigan north of Burton Place. The first of these is:

③ 1516 N. Lake Shore Dr.

This building is home to the International College of Surgeons; its neighbor at 1524

N. Lake Shore Dr. is a museum belonging to the same institution. The International Museum of Surgical Science (p. 180) houses a fascinating collection of exhibits and artifacts that portray the evolution of medical surgery, but it's worth visiting for its elegant interior as well, designed by Chicago architect Howard Van Doren Shaw in 1917 as a private mansion (highlights include a massive stone staircase and the second-floor library, with fine wood paneling). A third structure, 1530 N. Lake Shore Dr., is today the Polish Consulate.

Follow the lakefront path to the Chess Pavilion on your left, and continue past the patch of green where the jetty leads out to a harbor light and into the parking lot. Straight ahead is:

④ North Avenue Beach

One of the city's prime summer spots, North Avenue Beach swarms with beach volleyball players and sun worshippers from June through August. But I think it's just as worth a visit—maybe more so—in spring and fall, when you can take in the view without the crowds. Check out the retro-style beach house, which was designed to look like an old ocean liner.

Double back and cross Lake Shore Drive by way of the North Avenue underpass, directly west of the Chess

Pavilion. From the cul-de-sac here, continue west on North Avenue 2 blocks to N. State Parkway. The imposing residence on your left, surrounded by spacious grounds, is the:

❺ Residence of the Roman Catholic Archbishop of Chicago

Catholicism has strong roots in Chicago, thanks to generations of German, Irish, and Polish immigrants who brought their faith along with them; our current archbishop, Francis Cardinal George, is a well-known local figure who receives regular press coverage. This Queen Anne–style mansion was built in 1885 for the first archbishop of Chicago, Patrick Feehan; it sits on the site of what used to be a cemetery that stretched between present-day North Avenue and Schiller Street. Of the 19 chimneys that march across the roofline, only three are still in use.

Across the street on the opposite corner of North Avenue is:

❻ 1550 N. State Pkwy.

Each apartment in this 1912 vintage luxury high-rise, known as the Benjamin Marshall Building, originally occupied a single floor and contained 15 rooms spread over 9,000 square feet. The architects were Marshall & Fox, highly regarded in their day as builders of fine hotels. There was once a garden entryway at the ground-floor level. Among the noteworthy architectural features adorning the exterior of this Beaux Arts classic are the many small balconies and the bowed windows at the corners of the building.

Continue west for 1 block on North Avenue and turn left, following Dearborn Street to Burton Place and the:

❼ Bullock Folsom House

As its mansard roof reveals, this landmark 1877 on the southwest corner, at 1454 N. Dearborn St., takes its inspiration from the French Second Empire. (That roof, incidentally, is shingled in slate, not asphalt.) Neighboring houses at nos. 1450 and 1434 have some of the same French-influenced ornamentation and styling.

Across Burton Place just to the north, at 1500 N. Dearborn St., is another example of a rival architectural fashion of the day, the Richardsonian or Romanesque Revival.

Return to the east along Burton, but before crossing North State Parkway, stop at:

❽ 4 W. Burton Place

Built as a private residence in 1902 by Richard E. Schmidt for a family named Madlener, this striking building today houses the Graham Foundation for Advanced Studies in the Fine Arts. There is something very modern about its appearance: The structure's clean lines and the ornamentation around the entrance were inspired by the work of architects Louis Sullivan and Frank Lloyd Wright. The Society of Architectural Historians offers tours of the home on Saturdays, along with the Charnley-Persky house (see stop no. 15, below).

Continue 1 block farther east to Astor Street. On the northwest corner, at 1500 N. Astor St., is the former:

❾ Cyrus McCormick Mansion

New York architect Stanford White designed this building, which was constructed for the Patterson family in 1893. Cyrus McCormick, Jr., bought it in 1914, and David Adler's north addition doubled the size of the building in 1927. The senior McCormick made his fortune by inventing the mechanical reaper, which made it possible to farm vast tracts of wheat on the prairie without depending on seasonal labor at harvest time. Cyrus Sr.'s heirs shared in the wealth, and eventually so many members of the family owned homes near Rush and Erie streets, just south of the Gold Coast, that the neighborhood was known as "McCormicksville."

Like the Fifth Avenue mansions White and his contemporaries built in New York, the McCormick palazzo is an essay in neoclassical detailing. Square and grand, like a temple of antiquity, the construction combines Roman bricks of burnt yellow

1 Oak Street Beach
2 The Carl C. Heissen House
3 1516 N. Lake Shore Drive
4 North Avenue Beach
5 Residence of the Roman Catholic Archbishop of Chicago
6 1550 N. State Pkwy.
7 Bullock Folsom House
8 4 W. Burton Place
9 Cyrus McCormick Mansion
10 1525 N. Astor St.
11 1451 & 1449 N. Astor St.
12 1444 N. Astor St.
13 Thomas W. Hinde House
14 Joseph T. Ryerson House
15 Charnley-Persky House
16 Playboy Mansion
17 1301 & 1260 N. Astor St.
☕ Third Coast
18 East Cedar St.
19 Bryan Lathrop House

Ⓜ Subway/El stop
— Pedestrian/bike path

0 ———— 1/4 mi
0 ———— 0.25 km

CHICAGO STROLLS

8

THE GOLD COAST

with touches of terra-cotta trim. The building now is divided into condominiums.

Head north briefly on Astor Street to check out a home with a connection to presidential history:

🔟 **1525 N. Astor St.**

This attractive town house was once the residence of Robert Todd Lincoln, the only surviving child of Abraham and Mary Todd Lincoln. The younger Lincoln started a private law practice after the Civil War. He remained in Chicago for much of his life, leaving twice during the 1880s and 1890s, to serve under presidents James Garfield and Chester Arthur as Secretary of War, and later under Benjamin Harrison as ambassador to Britain. On the death of George Pullman, one of his major

corporate clients, Lincoln became president of the Pullman Palace Car Company in 1897 (for more about the Pullman Company, see "Exploring Chicago," p. 180).

Reversing direction, walk south along Astor Street. Notice the houses at:

⓫ **1451 & 1449 N. Astor St.**

The former, occupying the corner lot, is the work of Howard Van Doren Shaw, built in 1910 according to the so-called "Jacobethan" fashion; a combination of Jacobean and Elizabethan, it revives certain 16th- and 17th-century English architectural features, including narrow, elongated windows, split-level roofs, and multiple chimney stacks. The house at no. 1449 was built around the turn of the century, but the architect of this glorious chateau remains a mystery. Guarding the home's entrance is a somewhat intimidating stone porch, seemingly out of scale. Among the home's other unique characteristics are the big front bay and frieze below the cornice, a scroll decorated with a pattern of shells.

Another neighboring home of interest across the street is:

⑫ 1444 N. Astor St.

While most of the homes in this area were built in the late 1800s and early decades of the 1900s—and most took their cues from architectural fashions from centuries before—this house was on the cutting edge of style when it was built in 1929. An Art Deco masterpiece, it was designed by Holabird & Roche, the same firm that designed Soldier Field football stadium a few years earlier.

Next, walk to 1412 N. Astor St., site of the:

⑬ Thomas W. Hinde House

This 1892 home, designed by Douglas S. Pentecost, is an homage to the Flemish architecture of the late Middle Ages. The facade has been altered, but some of the original stone ornamentation remains, as do such dominant features as the multi-paned, diamond-shaped windows.

On the same side of the street, at 1406 N. Astor St., is the:

⑭ Joseph T. Ryerson House

David Adler designed this 1922 landmark home in the manner of a Parisian hotel. Adler himself supervised the 1931 addition of the top floor and the mansard roof. Woven into the wrought-iron grillwork above the entrance are the initials of the original owners.

Walk to 1365 N. Astor St. to see the landmark:

⑮ Charnley-Persky House

Shortly before he left the firm of Adler & Sullivan, a then-obscure draftsman, Frank Lloyd Wright, played a major role in designing this 1892 home. The house's

streamlined structure gives it a far more contemporary look than its neighbors, making the case that there is something timeless in Wright's ideas. The building—appropriately enough—is now the headquarters of the Society of Architectural Historians, which gives tours of the house on Wednesdays and more extensive tours including the surrounding area on Saturdays. (Visit www.sah.org or call ② **312/ 915-0105** for details.)

Walk back to Schiller Street. Cross the street and turn left on North State Parkway, continuing south until the middle of the block to 1340 N. State Pkwy., the original:

⑯ Playboy Mansion

Little did the original owner of this building, an upright Calvinist named George S. Isham, know how his house would be transformed a mere half-century after it was built in 1899. Playboy founder Hugh Hefner lived here from 1959 to 1974, romping with his Bunnies and celebrities in the indoor pool and lounging in silk pajamas while perusing page layouts in his bedroom. Today, that hedonistic past has been erased, and the building has been converted into high-priced condos.

Continue south on State Parkway, then swing east on Goethe Street, back to Astor Street. On opposite corners diagonally across Goethe Street are apartment towers that represent the trend toward high-rise living that began in the 1930s:

⑰ 1301 & 1260 N. Astor St.

Constructed by architect Philip B. Maher in 1932 and 1931, respectively, these apartment buildings are classics of the sleek modernism that characterized American commercial architecture after World War I. Contrast their timeless style to the 1960s apartment tower at 1300 N. Astor St., by architect Bertrand Goldberg; avant-garde at the time, it has not aged as well.

If you're ready for a snack, turn back north to Goethe Street and head west 2 blocks to Dearborn Street. Turn left (south), and go halfway down the block until you reach:

> **TAKE A BREAK**
> The welcoming **Third Coast** coffeehouse, 1260 N. Dearborn St. (📞 **312/649-0730**), is more laid-back than the elegant neighborhood surrounding it. Tucked below street level, it has a shabby-cozy vibe and makes a good stop for mid-morning coffee or lunch (there's a full menu of sandwiches and salads).

Head south on Dearborn Street to Division Street. Walk 1 block east to State Street, then turn right (south), staying on the east side of the street where State and Rush streets merge, and proceed 2 blocks south to:

🔞 East Cedar Street

This long block between Rush Street and Lake Shore Drive deserves a look, because

much of its turn-of-the century scale has been so well-preserved, in particular the two clusters of "cottages," nos. 42-48 (built in 1896 by businessman Potter Palmer) and 50-54 (built in 1892).

Return to Rush Street, walk to the next block south, and turn left on Bellevue Place. At 120 E. Bellevue Place stands the:

🔞 Bryan Lathrop House

New York architect Charles F. McKim, partner of Stanford White, built this mansion for a local realtor and civic leader while staying in Chicago as a lead designer of the World's Columbian Exposition. It helped introduce the Georgian fashion in architecture that would replace the Romanesque Revival throughout the Gold Coast.

CHICAGO STROLLS

8

WICKER PARK

| WALKING TOUR 3 | **WICKER PARK** |

START AND FINISH:	The Damen El stop (Blue Line).
TIME:	1 hour, not including shopping or eating stops.
BEST TIME:	Any time during the day.
WORST TIME:	After dark, when you'll have trouble seeing homes' decorative details.

Wicker Park, along with adjacent Bucktown, is mostly known today as a place to shop at edgy clothing boutiques or try out the latest hip restaurant. This tour takes you along the residential side streets that many tourists overlook, but which testify to the rich history of this neighborhood. Middle-class artisans, mostly Germans and Scandinavians, began settling here around 1870. In the following decades, wealthy families whose foreign roots made them unwelcome along the Gold Coast built luxurious homes here as well. In the 20th century, the neighborhood's respectability gradually declined, and many of the grandest homes were converted into rooming houses. It was not until the 1980s that the distinctive homes here began to be rediscovered and renovated, just as the gritty main streets of Milwaukee and Damen avenues began sprouting new shops and cafes.

Walk south along Damen Avenue to:

① Wicker Park

Two brothers who were beginning to develop their extensive real estate holdings in the area donated this land to the city in 1870, hoping the green space would make the surrounding area more attractive to prospective builders. Unfortunately, little remains of the 19th-century landscaping,

which once included a pond spanned by a rustic bridge.

Cross the park to the corner of Damen Avenue and Schiller Street. Follow Schiller east, along the park, stopping first at:

② 1959-1961 W. Schiller St.

Built in 1886 for a ship's captain and a medical doctor, this double home reflects the fashionable Second Empire style. The building became a rooming house in the 1920s, but has been restored to its original style. Note the lively Victorian colors of the cornices, tower, and trim. Other distinctive features are the large mansard roof and the decorative sawtooth pattern in the brickwork.

Next move to:

❸ 1941 W. Schiller St.

Built for clothing manufacturer Harris Cohn in 1888, this home is also known as the Wicker Park Castle. Essentially Queen Anne in design, its limestone facade made it pricier and more luxurious than its neighbors. Granite columns were polished to look like marble, and a turret rests on a shell-shaped base.

At the end of the block, turn right on Evergreen Avenue until you come to:

❹ 1958 W. Evergreen Ave.

Novelist Nelson Algren lived in a third-floor apartment here from 1959 to 1975. After he was caught stealing a typewriter in 1933, Algren (1909-1981) spent 3 months in jail. This experience, which brought him in contact with criminals, outsiders, drug addicts, and prostitutes, was a strong influence on his work. Algren is best remembered for his two dark novels of the urban semiunderworld, *A Walk on the Wild Side* and *The Man with the Golden Arm* (which was set near here, around Division Street and Milwaukee Avenue), and for his tough but lyrical prose poem, *Chicago: City on the Make.*

Continue to Damen Avenue, then turn right (north) back to Schiller Street. Take Schiller west 1 block to Hoyne Avenue, then turn right (north) where you'll see:

❺ 1407 N. Hoyne Ave.

Built by German wine and beer merchant John H. Rapp in 1880, this was the largest single-family estate in Wicker Park at the time. The original coach house, behind the mansion, is now a separate residence. This was not a happy home. Mrs. Rapp went insane, a son was convicted of embezzlement, and Rapp was murdered by his female bookkeeper. The home itself is of Second Empire style, with a large, curved mansard roof. The original wrought-iron fence defines the boundaries of the original grounds.

Heading north, you'll pass other late 19th-century mansions, and, at 1426 N. Hoyne Ave., an example of a worker's cottage, a reminder that in these immigrant neighborhoods, artisans and their patrons often lived side by side. On the next corner, at Hoyne Avenue and Le Moyne Street, is the:

❻ Wicker Park Lutheran Church

The city's oldest Lutheran church, it was modeled from plans of Holy Trinity Church in Caen, France, dating from the 12th century. The stone for this Romanesque structure was recycled from a demolished brothel. When one of the scandalized parishioners protested, the pastor remarked that the building material "has served the devil long enough; now let it serve the Lord."

Walk on to:

❼ 1558 N. Hoyne St.

The building permit for this Queen Anne–style home was issued in 1877, making it one of the oldest homes in the area. It was built for C. Hermann Plautz, founder of the Chicago Drug and Chemical Company. Ever conscious of the Great Chicago Fire, the builders created all the decorative trim on both towers, the cornices, and the conservatory of the south side from ornamental pressed metal. The seemingly misplaced cannon in the front yard is a relic of the years (1927-72) when the building housed the local American Legion.

Return to Pierce Avenue and walk west to:

❽ 2137 W. Pierce Ave.

This well-preserved gem is one of the highlights of historic Wicker Park. Built for the German businessman Hermann Weinhardt in 1888, it's a fanciful combination of elements that defies categorization. Notable details include the elaborate

1. Wicker Park
2. 1959-1961 W. Schiller St.
3. 1941 W. Schiller St.
4. 1958 W. Evergreen Ave.
5. 1407 N. Hoyne Ave.
6. Wicker Park Lutheran Church
7. 1558 N. Hoyne Ave.
8. 2137 W. Pierce Ave.
9. 2138 W. Pierce Ave.
10. Caton Street
11. Luxor Baths
☕ Caffe de Luca

W. Bloomingdale Ave.
W. Willow St.
N. Hoyne Ave.
W. St. Paul Ave.
N. Milwaukee Ave.
W. Wabansia Ave.
Caton St.
W. Concord Pl.
N. Damen Ave.
N. Winchester Ave.
N. Wolcott Ave.
N. Honore St.
W. North Ave.
W. North Ave.
DAMEN
M start & finish here
W. Pierce Ave.
N. Elk Grove Ave.
N. Milwaukee Ave.
N. Claremont Ave.
N. Oakley Blvd.
N. Bell Ave.
N. Leavitt St.
W. Le Moyne St.
Wicker Park
W. Schiller St.
W. Hirsch St.
N. Hoyne Ave.
N. Leavitt Ave.
W. Evergreen Ave.
N. Damen Ave.
W. Evergreen Ave.
N. Wolcott Ave.
W. Ellen St.
M Subway/El stop
0 100 yds
0 100 m
N

CHICAGO STROLLS

8

WICKER PARK

carved-wood balcony and the unusual juxtaposition of green stone and redbrick limestone around the large front window. The large lot used to be flooded in the winter for ice-skating.

Across the street is another notable home:

⑨ 2138 W. Pierce Ave.

The original owner of this home, Hans D. Runge, was treasurer of a wood milling company, so it's no surprise that elaborate wood carvings characterize the home inside and out; among the unique designs are the Masonic symbols flanking the pair of dragon heads under the rounded arch. A well-heeled local banker and politician, John F. Smulski, acquired the house in

1902, about the time many Poles were moving into the neighborhood. Smulski committed suicide here after the stock market crash in 1929, and the house served for a time as the Polish consulate.

Continue west until you reach Leavitt Street. Turn right (north) and walk 3 blocks until you reach:

⑩ Caton Street

Many of the houses on this street were built in the early 1890s by the same architectural firm, each with its own style, including German Burgher (no. 2156) and Renaissance (no. 2152). The Classical Revival home at 2147 W. Caton St. was built by the owner of a metal company, hence the extensive metal ornamentation on the exterior. (If you peek at the porch, you'll see it has a tin ceiling.)

Retrace your steps along Caton Street and Leavitt Street to North Avenue and turn left (east). As you pass Hoyne Street, take a quick look at 1617-1619 N. Hoyne Ave.; the building used to house the neighborhood livery stables, where local families kept their horses and carriages. (It's now condos.) The final stop on the tour is at 2039 W. North Ave., an address that used to house the:

⓫ Luxor Baths

These public baths were built in the 1920s and were reportedly once a hangout for local politicians and wheeler-dealers. Today, the building has been transformed into—what else?—condos, and there's even an elegant Asian-fusion restaurant, Spring, on the ground floor. Still, it's a fitting end to the tour, a reminder of the days when this was a neighborhood of European immigrants trading news from home in the Luxor Baths steam room.

Head east to the three-way intersection of Milwaukee, Damen, and North avenues. From here, you can hop on the Blue Line El train, or walk a block and a half north on Damen toward a favorite local hangout:

TAKE A BREAK Long-time residents gripe about the encroaching suburbanization of Wicker Park, where sterile bank branches have replaced funky-divey coffeeshops and million-dollar houses no longer raise eyebrows. Still, many independently owned businesses remain, among them **Caffe de Luca,** 1721 N. Damen Ave. (✆ **773/342-6000**), an Italian-inspired hangout where you can grab a coffee and pastry in the morning, salad or panini at lunchtime, or a mid-afternoon dessert pick-me-up. Best of all, it's a place the locals come, where you can check out a cross-section of Wicker Park residents, from grungy wannabe artists to hip moms.

Shopping

Forget Rodeo Drive or Fifth Avenue—Chicago is the country's original shopping center. As the United States expanded westward, catalogs from Chicago-based Sears and Montgomery Ward made clothes, books, and housewares accessible to even the most remote frontier towns. Department store magnate Marshall Field operated his namesake department store here, which opened in 1852, under the motto "Give the lady what she wants." Field pioneered many customer-service policies that are now standard practice, such as hassle-free returns.

Today Montgomery Ward is no more (and Marshall Field's has been taken over by Macy's), but downtown Chicago still draws hordes of shoppers (as anyone who's tried to walk quickly down Michigan Ave. on a busy summer Saturday can attest to). From the fine furniture showrooms at the imposing Merchandise Mart to the who's who of designer boutiques lining Oak Street and Michigan Avenue, the quality of stores in Chicago is top-notch. Because so many of the best are concentrated in one easy-to-walk area, the convenience of shopping in Chicago is unmatched.

This chapter concentrates on the Magnificent Mile, State Street, and several trendy neighborhoods, where you'll find the sort of one-of-a-kind shops and boutiques that make shopping here such an adventure.

SHOPPING HOURS As a general rule, store hours are 10am to 6 or 7pm Monday through Saturday, and noon to 6pm Sunday. Neighborhood stores tend to keep later hours, as do some of the stores along Michigan Avenue, which cater to after-work shoppers as well as tourists. Almost all stores have extended hours during the holiday season. Nearly all of the stores in the Loop are open for daytime shopping only, generally from 9 or 10am to no later than 6pm, Monday through Saturday. (The few remaining big downtown department stores have some selected evening hours.) Many Loop stores not on State Street are closed Saturday; on Sunday the Loop—except for a few restaurants, theaters, and cultural attractions—shuts down.

SALES TAX You might do a double take after checking the total on your purchase: At 10.25%, the local sales tax on nonfood items is one of the steepest in the country.

1 SHOPPING THE MAGNIFICENT MILE

The nickname "Magnificent Mile"—hyperbole to some, an understatement to others—refers to the roughly mile-long stretch of North Michigan Avenue between Oak Street and the Chicago River.

In terms of density, the area's first-rate shopping is, quite simply, unmatched. Even jaded shoppers from other worldly capitals are delighted at the ease and convenience of the stores concentrated here. Taking into account that tony Oak Street (see below) is just around the corner, the overall area is a little like New York's Fifth Avenue and Beverly Hills's Rodeo Drive rolled into one. Whether your passion is Bulgari jewelry, Prada bags, or Salvatore Ferragamo footwear, you'll find it on this stretch of concrete. And don't think you're seeing everything by walking down the street: Michigan Avenue is home to several indoor, high-rise malls, where plenty more boutiques and restaurants are tucked away. Even if you're not the shop-till-you-drop type, it's worth a stroll because this stretch is, in many ways, the heart of the city, a place that bustles with life year-round (although it's especially crowded around Christmas and during the summer).

For the ultimate Mag Mile shopping adventure, start at one end of North Michigan Avenue and try to work your way to the other. Below I've listed some of the best-known shops on the avenue and nearby side streets.

A NORTH MICHIGAN AVENUE SHOPPER'S STROLL

This shopper's stroll begins at Oak Street at the northern end of the avenue and heads south toward the river. It just hits the highlights; you'll find much more to tempt your wallet as you meander from designer landmarks to well-known chain stores. (In general, this is not the place to pick up distinctive, one-of-a-kind items—other neighborhoods described later in this chapter cater more to shoppers searching for something unique.) North Michigan Avenue's four vertical malls—each a major shopping destination in its own right—are discussed below under "The Magnificent Malls."

The parade of designer names begins at the intersection of Michigan Avenue and Oak Street, including a couple housed in The Drake Hotel, such as the legendary Danish silversmith **Georg Jensen,** 959 N. Michigan Ave. (© **312/642-9160**), known for outstanding craftsmanship in sterling silver and gold, including earrings, brooches, watches, tie clips, and flatware; and **Chanel,** 935 N. Michigan Ave. (© **312/787-5500**). One block south is another luxury emporium, the spacious **Louis Vuitton** store at 919 N. Michigan Ave. (© **312/944-2010**), where you'll find trendy handbags and the company's distinctive monogrammed luggage.

On the other side of the street, opposite the dark, soaring Hancock Building, you'll find a quiet oasis that's worth a quick peek. The **Fourth Presbyterian Church,** 126 E. Chestnut St. (© **312/787-4570**), looks like something out of an English country village, with a Gothic stone exterior and a peaceful, flower-filled courtyard (perfect for escaping the Mag Mile crowds for a few moments).

One block south, you'll notice a steady stream of mothers and daughters toting distinctive red shopping bags from **American Girl Place,** on the ground floor of the Water Tower Place mall, 835 N. Michigan Ave. (© **877/AG-PLACE** [247-5223]). The multistory doll emporium is one of the most-visited attractions in town, thanks to the popularity of the company's historic character dolls. The store's cafe is a nice spot for a special mother-daughter lunch or afternoon tea (but be sure to book ahead during Christmas and summer break).

Across the street, overlooking a small park next to the historic Water Tower, is **Giorgio Armani**'s sleek boutique, 800 N. Michigan Ave., in the Park Hyatt Hotel (© **312/573-4220**). Offering an alternative to high-style minimalism is the **Hershey's Chicago** candy store, 822 N. Michigan Ave. (© **312/337-7711**), a multi-sensory overload of colors and chocolate.

The next block of Michigan Avenue has a New York vibe, thanks to the world's largest **Polo Ralph Lauren,** 750 N. Michigan Ave. (© **312/280-1655**), a four-floor, wood-paneled mini-mansion, and **Tiffany & Co.,** 730 N. Michigan Ave. (© **312/944-7500**), with its signature clock, jewels, and tabletop accessories. (To get your hands on one of the coveted robin's-egg blue shopping bags without spending a fortune, pick up one of the $80 sterling-silver key chains—the least expensive items in the store.)

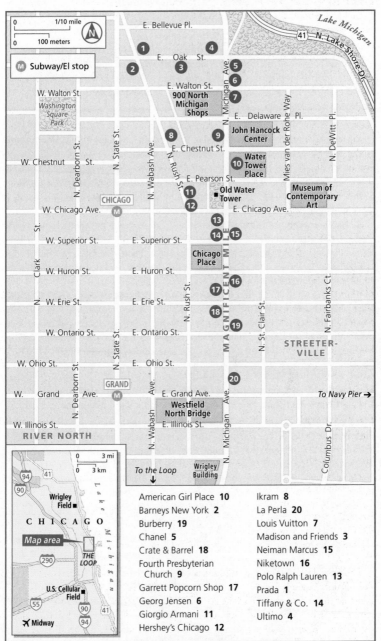

American Girl Place **10**
Barneys New York **2**
Burberry **19**
Chanel **5**
Crate & Barrel **18**
Fourth Presbyterian Church **9**
Garrett Popcorn Shop **17**
Georg Jensen **6**
Giorgio Armani **11**
Hershey's Chicago **12**

Ikram **8**
La Perla **20**
Louis Vuitton **7**
Madison and Friends **3**
Neiman Marcus **15**
Niketown **16**
Polo Ralph Lauren **13**
Prada **1**
Tiffany & Co. **14**
Ultimo **4**

SHOPPING

9

SHOPPING THE MAGNIFICENT MILE

Moments **Resting at Crate & Barrel**

Need a quick break during your shopping spree? The overstuffed couches on the third and fourth floors of Crate & Barrel practically beg to be tested out—and there are always at least a few weary shoppers slumped against the piles of pillows. Go ahead and rest awhile; the store's staff won't bug you. Make sure you stop by the terrace on the fourth floor for a bird's-eye view of Michigan Avenue, and enjoy a moment of contemplation before rejoining the hordes below.

A few doors south are **Neiman Marcus,** 737 N. Michigan Ave. (✆ **312/642-5900**), and at 669 N. Michigan Ave. (✆ **312/642-6363**), the hugely popular **Niketown,** a multilevel complex that helped pioneer the concept of retail as entertainment. Across the street, you'll probably see a line of people trailing out from the **Garrett Popcorn Shop,** 670 N. Michigan Ave. (✆ **312/944-2630**), a 50-year-old landmark. Join the locals in line and pick up some caramel corn for a quick sugar rush.

At the intersection of Michigan Avenue and Erie Street is the appropriately barrel-shaped **Crate & Barrel,** 646 N. Michigan Ave. (✆ **312/787-5900**). Crate & Barrel was started in Chicago, so this is the company's flagship location. Countless varieties of glassware, dishes, cookware, and kitchen gadgets for everyday use line the shelves. The top two floors are devoted to furniture.

Continuing south, you'll find **Burberry,** 633 N. Michigan Ave. (✆ **312/787-2500**), where the classic beige plaid shows up on chic purses, shoes, and bathing suits. (If you're looking for luxury souvenirs, check out the collection of baby clothes and dog accessories.) Beautifully made (but pricey) Italian lingerie is the draw at **La Perla,** 535 N. Michigan Ave. (✆ **312/494-0400**), a popular stop around Valentine's Day.

THE MAGNIFICENT MALLS

Many of the Magnificent Mile's shops are hidden inside high-rise malls, most of which take up a whole city block. Here's a quick guide to what you'll find inside.

Chicago Place   This mall's main claim to fame is as the home of upscale retailer **Saks Fifth Avenue** (p. 237). The rest of the stores here are not as exclusive; in fact, the mall as a whole lacks a clear identity. You'll find a few home decor and clothing stores here—but the main draw is the food court on the top floor (see box, "Lunch on the Mag Mile"). 700 N. Michigan Ave. (btw. Superior and Huron sts.). ✆ 312/642-4811. Subway/El: Red Line to Chicago.

900 North Michigan Shops   The most upscale of the Magnificent Mile's four vertical malls, 900 North Michigan (often called the Bloomingdale's building, for its most prominent tenant), avoids the tumult of Water Tower Place by appealing to a more well-heeled shopper. In addition to about 70 stores, there are a few good restaurants and a movie theater on the lower level.

The Chicago outpost of **Gucci** (ground floor; ✆ 312/664-5504) has the same hip attitude as the label's sexy clothing and much-in-demand purses. Also on the ground floor is **MaxMara** (✆ 312/475-9500), the Italian women's fashion house known for elegantly constructed coats and separates (some of which will cost you about as much as a flight to Italy). Other goodies worth checking out include funky European footwear at **Charles David** (second floor; ✆ 312/944-9013), amazingly intricate French glassware

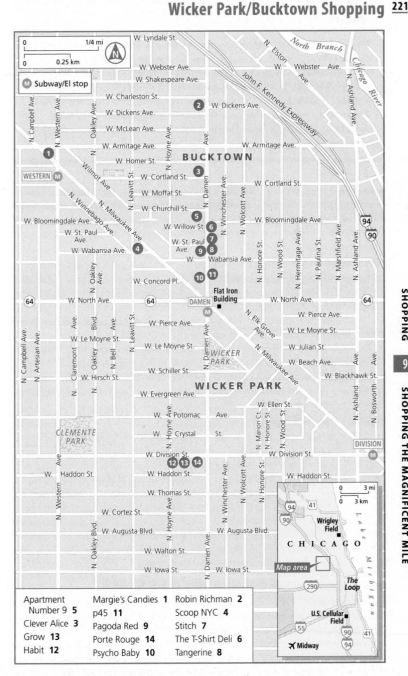

Apartment Number 9 **5**	Margie's Candies **1**	Robin Richman **2**
Clever Alice **3**	p45 **11**	Scoop NYC **4**
Grow **13**	Pagoda Red **9**	Stitch **7**
Habit **12**	Porte Rouge **14**	The T-Shirt Deli **6**
	Psycho Baby **10**	Tangerine **8**

> **Tips** **Lunch on the Mag Mile**
>
> When I worked just off Michigan Avenue, my favorite spot for lunch was the food court on the eighth floor of Chicago Place. A bright, airy space with a fountain and palm trees, it's my pick for the best cheap eats in the area, especially if you're traveling with kids. The cuisine may be uninspired—food choices include Subway, Taco Bell, McDonald's—but the setting makes this a few steps above the average mall food court. If you're lucky, you can even snag one of the tables overlooking Michigan Avenue, the kind of view that costs big bucks at the city's luxury hotels.

at **Lalique** (ground floor; ☎ 312/867-1787), and an eclectic selection of hats, mittens, scarves, and other accessories at **Glove Me Tender** (fifth floor; ☎ 312/664-4022), which should be your first stop if you're caught here during an unexpected cold spell. 900 N. Michigan Ave. (btw. Walton St. and Delaware Place). ☎ 312/915-3916. Subway/El: Red Line to Chicago.

Water Tower Place   Water Tower was the first big indoor mall to open downtown (in 1975), and 30 years ago its glass elevators and shiny gold trim gave the place a glamorous air. These days the mall remains popular but doesn't have much to distinguish it from any other upscale shopping center. Water Tower is a magnet for suburban teenagers (just like your mall back home) and can get quite crowded during prime summer tourist season. Most of its stores are part of national chains (Ann Taylor, Victoria's Secret, and so on). The mall is anchored on one end by the Mag Mile outpost of **Macy's** (see "Department Stores," in "Shopping A to Z," later in this chapter) and on the other by **American Girl Place** (p. 218). One of Water Tower's best features is its funky food court, **foodlife** (p. 119). 835 N. Michigan Ave. (btw. Pearson and Chestnut sts.). ☎ 312/440-3166. Subway/El: Red Line to Chicago.

Westfield North Bridge   The anchor of this development is a four-story **Nordstrom** (p. 237). The rest of the mall is bright and open, thanks to high ceilings and a wide central walkway—but it can also feel somewhat deserted compared to the bustling street outside. The stores are a mix of clothing, jewelry, and bath-and-body shops (in a mid-range to upscale price bracket). Distinctive stores that are worth checking out include the high-style chocolatier **Vosges Haut-Chocolat** on the second floor (p. 233) and the **LEGO** store on the third floor (☎ 312/494-0760), which features a mini re-creation of the Chicago skyline. The third-floor food court is a good stop for lunch, with a food station run by Tuscany, a local Italian restaurant, and other stands that offer Japanese tempura, grilled wraps, and Chicago-style hot dogs. 520 N. Michigan Ave. (btw. Grand Ave. and Illinois St.). ☎ 312/327-2300. Subway/El: Red Line to Grand.

CHIC SHOPPING ON NEARBY OAK STREET

Oak Street has long been a symbol of designer-label shopping; if a store has an Oak Street address, you can count on it being expensive. The shopping district itself is actually quite limited, taking up only 1 block at the northern tip of the Magnificent Mile (where Michigan Ave. ends and Lake Shore Dr. begins). While big-name designer boutiques such as Giorgio Armani and Louis Vuitton pride themselves on having a Michigan Avenue address, Oak Street features smaller, more personal shops (most of them high-priced). Since most

Oak Street is not the place to come shopping for bargains—with one exception—**Bravco,** 43 E. Oak St. (© **312/943-4305**). This crowded, narrow drugstore seems out of place among the luxury boutiques, but it's a popular spot among Chicago hairstylists and makeup artists. You'll find an excellent selection of professional hair and beauty products (including Aveda, Sebastian, and Bumble and bumble) here for much less than they cost at salons. Even if you haven't heard of some of the brands, trust me, if Bravco carries them, they're hot.

of the stores are tucked into converted town houses, it also has a more tranquil feel than Michigan Avenue. It's well worth a stroll for people-watching: This is Main Street for Chicago socialites. Most of Oak Street is closed on Sunday, except during the holiday season.

Chicago's most high-profile clothing boutique, **Ultimo,** is right around the corner from Michigan Avenue; upscale and exclusive, it caters to the seriously fashionable (p. 235). Footwear fans can browse Italian shoemaker **Tod's,** best known for its luxuriously soft (and pricey) driving shoes (p. 242). Shoes, stationery, and handbags are available at **kate spade,** 101 E. Oak St. (© **312/654-8853**), along with the Jack Spade line of men's accessories. The priciest accessories on this very pricey block can likely be found at French luxury house **Hermès of Paris,** 110 E. Oak St. (© **312/787-8175**). Thread-count fanatics swear by the sheets from **Pratesi,** 67 E. Oak St. (© **312/943-8422**), and **Frette,** 41 E. Oak St. (© **312/649-3744**), both of which supply linens to top hotels (and where sheet sets cost more than what some people pay in rent).

Anchoring the western end of the block are two haute heavyweights, hip Italian designer **Prada,** 30 E. Oak St. (© **312/951-1113**), which offers three floors of sleek, postmodern fashions for men and women and plenty of the designer's signature handbags; and equally style-conscious **Barneys New York** (p. 236).

2 MORE SHOPPING NEIGHBORHOODS

STATE STREET & THE LOOP

Shopping in the Loop is mostly concentrated along State Street, from Randolph Street south to Congress Parkway. (Although there are stores sprinkled elsewhere, they're mostly places that cater to office workers: drugstores, sandwich shops, and chain clothing stores.) State Street was Chicago's first great shopping district—by World War I, seven of the largest and most lavish department stores in the world were competing for shoppers' loyalties along this half-mile stretch. The area has been eclipsed by Michigan Avenue, but one grand old department store makes it worth a visit: **Macy's at State Street** (formerly Marshall Field's), 111 N. State St., at Randolph Street (© **312/781-1000**). A city landmark and one of the largest department stores in the world, it occupies an entire city block and features the largest Tiffany glass mosaic dome in the U.S. If you're in Chicago between Thanksgiving and New Year's, Macy's has maintained a long-time Marshall Field's tradition: Lavishly decorated holiday windows and lunch under the Great Tree in the store's restaurant, the Walnut Room.

Aside from Macy's, State Street has become a hot destination for bargain hunters in recent years, thanks to the opening of discount stores such as **Loehmann's,** 151 N. State St. (© **312/705-3810**), **Nordstrom Rack,** 24 N. State St. (© **312/377-5500**), **T.J. Maxx,** 11 N. State St. (© **312/553-0515**), and **Filene's Basement,** 1 N. State St. (© **312/553-1055**). If you've got the energy to hunt through racks of not-so-great stuff, you can sometimes find good designer-label deals.

State Street has a no-frills aura compared to Michigan Avenue—but it stays busy thanks to the thousands of office workers who stroll around during their lunch hour or after work. On weekends, the street is considerably more subdued.

RIVER NORTH

Since the 1960s, when the Chicago Imagists (painters Ed Paschke, Jim Nutt, and Roger Brown among them) attracted international attention with their shows at the Hyde Park Art Center, the city has been a fertile breeding ground for emerging artists and innovative art dealers. Today, the primary art-gallery district is concentrated in the River North neighborhood—the area west of the Magnificent Mile and north of the Chicago River— where century-old, redbrick warehouses have been converted into lofty exhibition spaces. More recently, a new generation of gallery owners has set up shop in the rapidly gentrifying West Loop neighborhood, where you'll tend to find more cutting-edge work. (For suggestions on the best places to visit, see "Art Galleries" under "Shopping A to Z," below.) The River North gallery district is an easy walk from many hotels; the West Loop may seem a little farther afield, but it's only a short cab ride from downtown. (You can also take the bus, but I'd recommend a taxi at night.)

The River North gallery season officially gets underway on the first Friday after Labor Day in September. Besides fall, another great time to visit the district is from mid-July through August, when the Chicago Art Dealers Association presents **Vision,** an annual lineup of programs tailored to the public. Early September also offers the annual **Around the Coyote** festival in Wicker Park/Bucktown (call © **773/342-6777** for information), when scores of artists open their studios to the public. The name of the festival refers to the now-departed Coyote Gallery, which used to stand at the corner of Damen and North avenues.

The *Chicago Reader,* a free weekly newspaper available at many stores, taverns, and cafes on the North Side, publishes a very comprehensive listing of current gallery exhibitions, as does the quarterly *Chicago Gallery News* (www.chicagogallerynews.com), which is available free at the city's visitor information centers. Another good resource is the Chicago Art Dealers Association (© **312/649-0065;** www.chicagoartdealers.org); the group's website has descriptions of all member galleries.

Along with its status as Chicago's primary art-gallery district, River North has attracted many interesting home-design shops, with many concentrated on Wells Street from Kinzie Street to Chicago Avenue. My favorites include **Manifesto,** 755 N. Wells

 Tips   **Point Zero**

If the quick change from north to south in the Loop confuses you, keep in mind that in Chicago, point zero for the purpose of address numbering is the intersection of State and Madison streets.

St., at Chicago Avenue (✆ **312/664-0733**), which offers custom-designed furniture, as well as imports from Italy and elsewhere in Europe; **Mig & Tig,** 540 N. Wells St., at Ohio Street (✆ **312/644-8277**), a charming furniture and decorative-accessories shop; and **Lightology,** 215 W. Chicago Ave., at Wells St. (✆ **312/944-1000**), a massive lighting store that carries a mind-boggling array of funky lamps, chandeliers, and glowing orbs from more than 400 manufacturers. (Even if you have no intention of flying home with a stack of lamps in your luggage, it's fun to browse.)

Looming above the Chicago River at the southern end of River North is the **Merchandise Mart,** the world's largest commercial building. The massive complex was built in 1930 by Marshall Field & Company and was bought in 1945 by Joseph P. Kennedy (JFK's dad). Although the Kennedys sold the Mart in the late 1990s, there's still a family connection: Christopher Kennedy (son of Robert and Ethel) is the president of the company that runs the complex. The Mart houses mostly interior design showrooms, which are open only to professional designers. One exception is Luxe Home, a collection of kitchen and bath showrooms on the first floor, all of which are open to the public (and worth a look for interior-design junkies). Public tours of the whole complex are offered once a week, usually on Fridays ($12 adults; ✆ **312/527-7762** for dates and reservations).

ARMITAGE AVENUE

Hovering between the North Side neighborhoods of Old Town and Lincoln Park, Armitage Avenue has emerged as a shopping destination in its own right, thanks to an influx of wealthy young professionals who have settled into historic town homes on the neighboring tree-lined streets. The main shopping district is concentrated between Halsted Street and Racine Avenue. I'd suggest starting at the Armitage El stop (Brown Line), working your way east to Halsted Street, and then wandering a few blocks north to Webster Street. As you stroll around, you'll get a good sense of the area's strong community spirit, with neighbors greeting each other and catching up on the street corners.

The shops and boutiques here are geared toward sophisticated, well-heeled, predominantly female shoppers (sorry, guys). You'll find trendy clothing boutiques, including that of Chicago-area native **Cynthia Rowley,** 808 W. Armitage Ave. (✆ **773/528-6160**); eclectic home-decor stores; beauty emporiums (see the box, "Pamper Yourself," below); and one of my favorite impossible-to-classify gift shops, **Art Effect** (p. 238). The upscale pet accessories shop **Barker & Meowsky,** 1003 W. Armitage Ave. (✆ **773/868-0200**),

SHOPPING

9

MORE SHOPPING NEIGHBORHOODS

(Finds)   Pamper Yourself

During your Armitage Avenue shopping spree, you'll pass a trio of bath-and-beauty product stores that are good places to pick up quick gifts for gal pals (or yourself). You'll find all-natural cleansers, creams, and bubble baths at the very fragrant **Lush** store, 859 W. Armitage Ave. (*©* **773/281-LUSH** [5874]), where custom-made soaps are sold by the slice. Skin-care products are the specialty at iconic New York apothecary **Kiehl's,** 907 W. Armitage Ave. (*©* **773/665-2515**); if you're here in the winter, their lip balm is a lifesaver. Want makeup that's guaranteed to blend with your skin tone? The technicians at **Colorlab Custom Cosmetics,** 857 W. Armitage Ave. (*©* **773/525-9086**), mix up personalized foundation, lipstick, and blush; they'll even store your formula so you can order more later. To get really creative, visit the cozy **Aroma Workshop,** 2050 N. Halsted St. (*©* **773/871-1985**), where you can concoct your own custom-scented body lotions and perfumes.

has everything you need to spoil furry family members, including catnip cigars, doggy "sushi," and designer-inspired outfits.

Despite the area's upscale feel, you can snag bargains at some top-notch discount and consignment shops, including **Lori's Designer Shoes, McShane's Exchange, Fox's,** and **the Second Child** (see "Vintage Fashion/Resale Shops" under "Shopping A to Z," below).

LINCOLN PARK & LAKEVIEW

A few major north-south thoroughfares—Lincoln Avenue, Clark Street, and Broadway Avenue—are the main shopping streets in both Lincoln Park (south of Diversey Pkwy.) and Lakeview (north of Diversey). Most of the shops cater to young singles who live in the surrounding apartment buildings; you'll find plenty of mini-mart groceries, some clothing and shoe boutiques, and the occasional used bookstore, but not much that's worth a special trip.

Radiating from the intersection of Belmont Avenue and Clark Street is a string of shops catering to rebellious kids on tour from their homes in the 'burbs. (The Dunkin' Donuts on the corner is often referred to as "Punkin' Donuts" in their honor.) One constant in the ever-changing youth culture has been the **Alley,** 3228 N. Clark St., at Belmont Avenue (*©* **773/883-1800**), an "alternative shopping complex" selling everything from plaster gargoyles to racks of leather jackets. It has separate shops specializing in condoms, cigars, and bondage wear. **Tragically Hip,** a storefront women's boutique, 931 W. Belmont Ave. (*©* **773/549-1500**), next to the Belmont El train stop, has outlasted many other similar purveyors of cutting-edge women's apparel.

You can get plugged into what the kids are reading at **Chicago Comics,** 3244 N. Clark St. (*©* **773/528-1983**), considered one of the best comics shops in the country. Besides the usual superhero titles, you'll find lots of European and Japanese comics, along with underground books and zines.

SOUTHPORT AVENUE

West of Lakeview, a few blocks from Wrigley Field, this commercial strip houses a mix of restaurants, cool (but not *too* cool) clothing boutiques, and cafes appealing to the upscale urban families who live in the surrounding area (watch out for strollers hogging more laid-back than the Gold Coast or Wicker Park, and the surrounding tree-lined residential streets are a pleasant place to stroll. Start at the Southport El stop on the Brown Line, and work your way north to Grace Street. (Round-trip, the walk will take you about a half-hour—but allow more if you're doing some serious shopping or want to stop for lunch.) Along the way you'll pass the historic **Music Box Theater** at 3733 N. Southport Ave. (© **773/871-6604**), north of Addison Street, which shows independent films from around the world. Two clothing shops catering to hip young women with plenty of disposable income are **Krista K,** 3458 N. Southport Ave. (© **773/248-1967**), and **Red Head Boutique,** 3450 N. Southport Ave. (© **773/325-9898**), which both stock up-and-coming designers that aren't widely available in Chicago.

WICKER PARK/BUCKTOWN

The gentrification of the Wicker Park/Bucktown area was followed by not only a rash of restaurants and bars but also retailers with an artsy bent that reflect the neighborhood's bohemian spirit. Mixed in with old neighborhood businesses, such as discount furniture stores and religious icon purveyors, is a proliferation of antique furniture shops, edgy clothing boutiques, and eclectic galleries and gift emporiums. Despite the hefty price tags in many of these shops, the neighborhood still feels gritty—so come here if you want to feel like you've gotten a real urban fix.

Start at the Damen El stop on the Blue Line, and walk north along Damen Avenue to Armitage Avenue to scope out the trendiest shops. If you've got time, some stores are also scattered along Milwaukee Avenue south of North Avenue.

The friendly modern-day Marco Polos at **Pagoda Red,** 1714 N. Damen Ave., second floor (© **773/235-1188**), have imported beautiful (and expensive) antique furniture and art objects, including Chinese concubine beds, painted Tibetan cabinets, Burmese rolling water vessels, cast-iron lotus bowls, bronze Buddhas, and Chinese inspiration stones. Design-conscious shoppers head to **Stitch** (p. 239) for one-of-a-kind, stylish gifts—the kind of thing you won't find at the mall back home. Damen Avenue is also known for its concentration of independent clothing boutiques, which range from body-conscious, urban looks at **p45** (p. 234) to flirty dresses and skirts at **Tangerine** (p. 235). Glance at the not-so-affordable price tags and you'll soon see that Wicker Park has come a long way from its grimy, starving-artist past.

(**Moments**) **Taking a Break in Wicker Park**

When you're ready to rest your weary self, settle down at a local coffeehouse and soak in Wicker Park's artsy vibe. **Earwax Café,** 1564 N. Milwaukee Ave. (© **773/772-4019**), attracts the jaded and pierced set with a no-frills, slightly edgy atmosphere. At **Gallery Café,** 1760 W. North Ave., 4 blocks east of Milwaukee Ave. (© **773/252-8228**), the atmosphere isn't quite as memorable, but the laid-back hangout roasts its own coffee and offers a full menu of breakfast and lunch dishes. Both cafes are near the bustling intersection of North, Milwaukee, and Damen avenues—the heart of Wicker Park—and draw a steady stream of locals. It's here you'll realize that Wicker Park is really just a small town—with cooler hair and funkier shoes.

Once home to just a few pioneering restaurants, Division Street is quickly being transformed from a desolate urban landscape to a hot shopping destination. It's a work in progress (you'll still find some boarded-up buildings among the cool boutiques), but for now this is what Wicker Park used to be: A place where rents are still cheap enough for eager young entrepreneurs. Start at the Division El stop on the Blue Line, and head west along Division Street; most stores are concentrated between Milwaukee Avenue and Damen Avenue (a round-trip walk will take about a half-hour). Along the way, you'll stroll past eclectic clothing and home boutiques, including **Habit** (p. 234), which stocks fashions from independent labels, and the hip kids' shop **Grow** (p. 244), where eco-conscious urban parents stock up on organic-cotton baby clothes and sustainable-wood furniture. The gorgeously eclectic **Porte Rouge,** 1911 W. Division St. (© **773/269-2800**), is filled with French antiques and housewares. (They'll even offer you a complimentary cup of tea.) The mix of people living here—from working-class Latino families to self-consciously edgy young singles—makes the local cafes great for people-watching.

3 SHOPPING A TO Z

Chicago has shops selling just about anything you could want or need, be it functional or ornamental, whimsical or exotic. Although the following list only scratches the surface, it gives you an idea of the range of merchandise available. You'll find more shops in many of these categories, such as clothing and home accessories, covered in the earlier sections of this chapter.

ANTIQUES

If you think half the fun of antiquing is sorting through piles of junk to discover hidden treasures, you'll probably enjoy browsing the series of independently owned antiques stores along Belmont Avenue west of Southport Avenue. (Since it's a haul from the El, I'd only recommend shopping here if you have a car.) Chicago's best-organized and best-stocked antique shops are scattered throughout the city, but if you're willing to venture beyond the usual tourist neighborhoods, you'll be well rewarded.

Architectural Artifacts, Inc. ★★ (**Finds**) Chicago has a handful of salvage specialists who cater to the design trades and retail customers seeking an unusual architectural piece for their homes, and this is the best of them. Although it's a fair distance from downtown, it's easy enough to reach by public transportation (about a 30-minute ride from the Loop on the Brown Line). Its brightly lit, well-organized, cavernous showroom features everything from original mantels and garden ornaments to vintage bathroom hardware and American and French Art Deco lighting fixtures. The store also has a museum on the lower level to display portions of historically significant buildings. 4325 N. Ravenswood Ave. (east of Damen Ave. and south of Montrose Ave.). © **773/348-0622.** www. architecturalartifacts.com. Subway/El: Brown Line to Montrose.

Broadway Antique Market ★ Visiting Hollywood prop stylists and local interior designers flock here to find 20th-century antiques in near-perfect condition. In this two-level, 20,000-square-foot vintage mega-mart, you'll spot both pricey pieces (for example, an Arne Jacobsen egg chair) and affordable collectibles for less than $100 (Roseville pottery, Art Deco barware, Peter Max scarves). 6130 N. Broadway Ave. (half-mile north of

Hollywood Ave. and Lake Shore Dr.). © 773/743-5444. www.bamchicago.com. Subway/El: Red
Line to Granville.

Jay Robert's Antique Warehouse   This mammoth River North space is within walking distance of downtown hotels, but you'll need comfortable shoes to explore all 25,000 square feet. The selection is wildly eclectic: Fine furniture that includes fireplaces, stained glass, statues, tapestries, and an impressive selection of antique clocks in a variety of styles ranging from elaborate Victorian to sophisticated Art Deco. 149 W. Kinzie St. (at LaSalle St.). © 312/222-0167. www.jayroberts.com. Subway/El: Brown Line to Merchandise Mart.

Modern Times   This shop specializes in the major designers of home furnishings from the 1930s to the 1960s—the sort of pieces that style-conscious shoppers buy to furnish their newly renovated lofts. You'll also find lighting fixtures of all types, tabletop accessories, and some jewelry. *Note:* The store is open only Friday through Sunday from noon to 6pm, although you can request an appointment to visit on other days if you call ahead. 2100 W. Grand Ave. (at Damen Ave.). © 312/243-5706. www.moderntimeschicago.com. Subway/El: Blue Line to Division, then about a half-mile walk; or take a cab.

Salvage One ★   Like Architectural Artifacts Inc. (above), this sprawling space stocks everything and the kitchen sink—literally: There's an entire room filled with vintage sinks. You'll find hundreds of one-of-a-kind pieces for the home handyperson, including doors, mantels, tubs, stained glass, and antique chandeliers. Don't worry about fitting your new purchase in your suitcase for the trip home: The store regularly ships items cross-country and even internationally. 1840 W. Hubbard St. (at Damen Ave.). © 312/733-0098. www.salvageone.com. Bus: 65 (Grand Ave.).

ART GALLERIES

Most of the city's major art galleries are concentrated in two neighborhoods. The city's original gallery district is in River North, within easy walking distance of most downtown hotels. More recently, galleries have been opening in the converted loft buildings of the West Loop, which is best reached by taxi.

Alan Koppel Gallery   This expansive gallery showcases modern and contemporary works of art as well as French and Italian furniture from the '20s through the '60s (in a separate area). Koppel also specializes in 20th-century photography, so if you're hankering for something by Diane Arbus, Man Ray, or Walker Evans, this is the place to look. 210 W. Chicago Ave. (at Wells St.). © 312/640-0730. www.alankoppel.com. Subway/El: Brown or Red line to Chicago.

Aldo Castillo Gallery   Aldo Castillo left his native Nicaragua in 1976, shortly after the Sandinistas began their revolution against the Somoza regime. He arrived in Chicago in 1985 and, 8 years later, appalled at the lack of attention given to Latin American art, opened his eponymous gallery in Lakeview, moving to his present River North location in 1993. Castillo continues to promote a range of work by emerging artists and established masters from Latin America, Spain, and Portugal. 675 N. Franklin St. (btw. Huron and Erie sts.). © 312/337-2536. www.artaldo.com. Subway/El: Brown or Red line to Chicago.

Ann Nathan Gallery ★★   Ann Nathan, who started out as a collector, shows exciting (and sometimes outrageous) pieces in clay, wood, and metal—along with paintings, photographs, and "functional art" (pieces that blur the line between furniture and sculpture). Nathan's space in the center of the River North district is one of the most beautiful in the city. 212 W. Superior St. (at Wells St.). © 312/664-6622. www.annnathangallery.com. Subway/El: Brown or Red line to Chicago.

Carl Hammer Gallery   A former schoolteacher and one of the most venerated dealers in Chicago, Carl Hammer touts his wares as "contemporary art and selected historical masterworks by American and European self-taught artists"—but it's the "self-taught" part that warrants emphasis. Hammer helped pioneer the field known as "outsider art," which has since become a white-hot commodity in the international art world. **740 N. Wells St. (at Superior St.). ⓒ 312/266-8512. www.hammergallery.com. Subway/El: Brown or Red line to Chicago.**

Catherine Edelman Gallery   One of Chicago's leading galleries in contemporary photography, Catherine Edelman represents a range of mostly American artists; she is also a proud booster of up-and-coming Chicago photographers. Across the street, **Stephen Daiter Gallery,** 311 W. Superior St. (ⓒ **312/787-3350**), also specializes in photography, with a strong selection of vintage 20th-century work. **300 W. Superior St. (at Franklin St.). ⓒ 312/266-2350. www.edelmangallery.com. Subway/El: Brown or Red line to Chicago.**

Donald Young Gallery ★   Renowned on the contemporary-art scene since the late 1970s, Donald Young is one of Chicago's most high-profile art dealers. His Michigan Avenue gallery is a haven for critically acclaimed artists working in video, sculpture, photography, painting, and installation, including Anne Chu, Gary Hill, Martin Puryear, Bruce Nauman, Cristina Iglesias, Robert Mangold, and Charles Ray. **224 S. Michigan Ave. (btw. Adams St. and Jackson Blvd.). ⓒ 312/322-3600. www.donaldyoung.com. Subway/El: Red Line to Jackson.**

Douglas Dawson Gallery ★   Offering a unique perspective to the Chicago art scene, Douglas Dawson specializes in ancient and historic ethnographic art—everything from tribal textiles to furniture, although a principal focus is African ceramics. The gallery's spectacular loft space in the West Loop looks like a museum. **400 N. Morgan St. (at Kinzie St.). ⓒ 312/226-7975. www.douglasdawson.com. Bus: 65 (Grand).**

G.R. N'Namdi Gallery   George N'Namdi founded his gallery, which specializes in African-American artists, 2 decades ago in the Detroit area. His son Jumaane operates this location (there's also another in New York). Artists they've helped bring to the attention of museums and art collectors include James Vanderzee, Al Loving, Edward Clark, and Robert Colescott. **110 N. Peoria St. (at Washington St.). ⓒ 312/563-9240. www.grnnamdigallery.com. Bus: 20 (Madison).**

Kavi Gupta Gallery   Owner Kavi Gupta is widely credited with kicking off the West Loop art scene when he developed this property as a home for new galleries. Gupta specializes in contemporary art by national and international emerging artists, so you never quite know what you're going to see here. Also worth checking out in the same building are the **Carrie Secrist Gallery** (ⓒ 312/491-0917; www.secristgallery.com) and **Thomas McCormick Gallery** (ⓒ 312/226-6800; www.thomasmccormick.com). **835 W. Washington St. (at Green St.). ⓒ 312/432-0708. www.kavigupta.com. Bus: 20 (Madison).**

Marx-Saunders Gallery   Chicago is home to two world-class galleries dealing in contemporary glass-art sculpture, conveniently located within steps of one another along Superior Street in River North. Marx-Saunders Gallery houses the city's largest showcase of glass art and features world-famous artists, past and present (William Morris, Mark Fowler, Therman Statom, and Hiroshi Yamano), as well as newcomers. Also worth a look for art-glass lovers is the nearby **Habatat Galleries Chicago,** 222 W. Superior St. (ⓒ 312/440-0288; www.habatatchicago.com). **230 W. Superior St. (btw. Franklin and Wells sts.). ⓒ 312/573-1400. www.marxsaunders.com. Subway/El: Brown or Red line to Chicago.**

Maya Polsky Gallery   Gallery owner Maya Polsky deals in international contempo- rary art and also represents some leading local artists, but she's best known for showcasing the contemporary and postrevolutionary art of Russia, including the work of such masters as Valery Koshliakov and Sergei Sherstiuk. 215 W. Superior St. (at Wells St.). ✆ **312/440-0055.** www.mayapolskygallery.com. Subway/El: Brown or Red line to Chicago.

Rhona Hoffman Gallery   The New York–born Rhona Hoffman maintains a high profile on the international contemporary-art scene. She launched her gallery in 1983 and, from the start, sought national and international artists, typically young and cutting-edge artists who weren't represented elsewhere in Chicago. Today she is the purveyor of such blue-chip players as Sol LeWitt as well as younger up-and-comers such as Dawoud Bey. 118 N. Peoria St. (btw. Randolph and Washington sts.). ✆ **312/455-1990.** www.rhoffmangallery.com. Bus: 20 (Madison).

Richard Gray Gallery ★   Richard Gray—whose gallery opened in 1963—is widely considered the dean of art dealers in Chicago. (He's served as president of the Art Dealers Association of America and been a longtime board member of the Art Institute of Chicago.) The gallery specializes in paintings, sculpture, and drawings by leading artists from the major movements in 20th-century American and European art. (He also has a second location in New York.) Gray and his son, Paul, who now runs the Chicago gallery, have shown the work of such luminaries as Pablo Picasso, Jean Dubuffet, Willem de Kooning, Alexander Calder, Claes Oldenburg, Joan Miró, and Henri Matisse. John Hancock Center, 875 N. Michigan Ave., Ste. 2503 (btw. Delaware and Chestnut sts.). ✆ **312/642-8877.** www.richardgraygallery.com. Subway/El: Red Line to Chicago.

Zolla/Lieberman Gallery ★★   Bob Zolla and Roberta Lieberman kicked off the River North revival when they opened their gallery (considered the grande dame of the area) here in 1976. Today, Zolla/Lieberman, directed by Roberta's son, William Lieberman, represents a wide range of artists, including sculptor Deborah Butterfield, installation artist Vernon Fisher, and painter Terence LaNoue. 325 W. Huron St. (at Orleans St.). ✆ **312/944-1990.** www.zollaliebermangallery.com. Subway/El: Brown Line to Chicago.

BOOKS

Abraham Lincoln Book Shop ★   This bookstore boasts one of the country's most outstanding collections of Lincolniana, from rare and antique books about the 16th president to collectible signatures, letters, and other documents illuminating the lives of other U.S. presidents and historical figures. The shop carries new historical and academic works, too. 357 W. Chicago Ave. (btw. Orleans and Sedgwick sts.). ✆ **312/944-3085.** www.alincolnbookshop.com. Subway/El: Brown Line to Chicago.

Barnes & Noble   This two-level Gold Coast store comes complete with a cafe in case you get the munchies while perusing the miles of books. There's another store in Lincoln Park, at 659 W. Diversey Ave., 1 block west of Clark Street (✆ **773/871-9004**), and one at 1441 W. Webster Ave., at Clybourn Avenue (✆ **773/871-3610**). 1130 N. State St. (at Elm St.). ✆ **312/280-8155.** Subway/El: Red Line to Clark/Division.

Borders   You couldn't ask for a better location, right across from Water Tower Place. This place is like a mini department store, with books, magazines, CDs, and computer software spread over four floors, and a cafe with a view overlooking the Mag Mile. There's also a Borders in the Loop at 150 N. State St., at Randolph Street (✆ **312/606-0750**), and one in Lincoln Park at 2817 N. Clark St., at Diversey Avenue (✆ **773/935-3909**). 830 N. Michigan Ave. (at Pearson St.). ✆ **312/573-0564.** Subway/El: Red Line to Chicago.

Powell's Bookstore Used books, especially from scholarly and small Chicago presses, dog-eared paperbacks, and hardcover classics fill the shelves at this book lover's haven. There are also outlets in Lakeview at 2850 N. Lincoln Ave. (✆ 773/248-1444), and Hyde Park at 1501 E. 57th St. (✆ 773/955-7780). 828 S. Wabash Ave. (btw. 8th and 9th sts.). ✆ 312/341-0748. www.powellschicago.com. Subway/El: Red Line to Harrison.

Prairie Avenue Bookshop ★★ This South Loop store does Chicago's architectural tradition proud with the city's finest stock of architecture, design, and technical books. 418 S. Wabash Ave. (btw. Congress Pkwy. and Van Buren St.). ✆ 312/922-8311. www.pabook. com. Subway/El: Red Line to Jackson.

Seminary Co-op Bookstore A classic campus bookstore located near the University of Chicago, this shop has extensive philosophy and theology sections and is one of the premier academic bookstores in the country. 5757 S. University Ave. (btw. 57th and 58th sts.). ✆ 773/752-4381. http://semcoop.booksense.com. Bus: 69 (Jeffrey Express).

Unabridged Books This quintessential neighborhood bookseller in the area known as Boys Town has strong sections in gay and lesbian literature, travel, film, and sci-fi; there's also a well-stocked children's area. Handwritten recommendations by the book-loving staff are posted throughout the store. 3251 N. Broadway Ave. (btw. Belmont Ave. and Addison St.). ✆ 773/883-9119. www.unabridgedbookstore.com. Subway/El: Red Line to Addison.

Women & Children First (Kids) This feminist and children's bookstore—located in the far North Side neighborhood of Andersonville—holds the best selection in the city of titles for, by, and about women. But the shop is far from a male-free zone; the owners promote great independent fiction by authors of both genders, making this a good place to discover books that have been overlooked by the bestseller lists. There's a section devoted to lesbian and gay books, and the store has a busy schedule of author appearances. 5233 N. Clark St. (btw. Foster and Bryn Mawr aves.). ✆ 773/769-9299. www.womenand childrenfirst.com. Subway/El: Red Line to Berwyn.

CANDY, CHOCOLATES & PASTRIES

Bittersweet ★★ Run by Judy Contino, one of the city's top pastry chefs and bakers, this Lakeview cafe and shop is sought out by brides-to-be and trained palates who have a yen for gourmet cakes, cookies, tarts, and ladyfingers. The rich chocolate mousse cake, a specialty of the house, is out of this world. 1114 W. Belmont Ave. (btw. Seminary and Clifton aves.). ✆ 773/929-1100. www.bittersweetpastry.com. Subway/El: Red Line to Belmont.

Ghirardelli Chocolate Shop & Soda Fountain This Midwest outpost of the famed San Francisco chocolatier, just a half-block off the Mag Mile, gets swamped in the summer, so good thing they've got their soda fountain assembly line down to a science. Besides the incredible hot-fudge sundaes, there's a veritable mudslide of chocolate bars, hot-cocoa drink mixes, and chocolate-covered espresso beans to tempt your sweet tooth. Hit with a late-night craving? They're open until midnight on Friday and Saturday nights. 830 N. Michigan Ave. (btw. Michigan Ave. and Rush St.). ✆ 312/337-9330. Subway/El: Red Line to Chicago.

Margie's Candies (Value) This family-run candy and ice-cream shop hasn't changed much since it opened in 1921. It still offers some of the city's finest handmade fudge, whether it comes in a box or melted over a banana split served in a clamshell dish. The store is known for its turtles—chocolate-covered pecan and caramel clusters—and might be the only place in the city still selling rock candy on wooden sticks. Although it's out of the way for most visitors, near a busy commercial intersection with little else to recommend it, it's worth a stop for dessert-lovers if you're in the Wicker Park area. 1960 N. Western Ave. (just south of Armitage Ave.). ✆ 773/384-1035. www.margiescandies.nv.switchboard.com. Subway/El: Blue Line to Western.

Vosges Haut-Chocolat ★ (Finds   Chocolatier Katrina Markoff's exotic gourmet truffles—with fabulous names such as absinthe, mint julep, wink of the rabbit, woolloomooloo, and ambrosia—are made from premium Belgian chocolate and infused with rare spices, seasonings, and flowers from around the world. The store—which looks more like a modern art gallery than a chocolatier—includes a gourmet hot-chocolate bar, where you're welcome to sit and sip. Vosges also has a small store on trendy Armitage Avenue (951 W. Armitage Ave.; ✆ 773/296-9866). 520 N. Michigan Ave. (in the Westfield North Bridge shopping center). ✆ 312/644-9450. www.vosgeschocolate.com. Subway/El: Red Line to Grand.

CLOTHING BOUTIQUES

In the not-so-distant past, local fashion addicts fled to the coasts to shop for cutting-edge designer duds. Those days are over. While over-the-top outrageousness doesn't sell here—this is the practical Midwest, after all—stylish Chicagoans now turn to local independent boutiques when they want to stay on top of the latest trends (without looking like fashion victims). Here are some of the best:

Apartment Number 9   Chicago men aren't renowned for their sense of style; most get by just fine with a wardrobe of baseball hats and sports-team T-shirts. But a few stores cater to hip young dudes, and this is the most stylish of the bunch. The clothing selection is trendy but not outrageous, with a good selection from menswear designers such as John Varvatos, Nicole Farhi, and Paul Smith, among other up-and-coming names. 1804 N. Damen Ave. (at Willow St.). ✆ 773/395-2999. www.apartmentnumber9.com. Subway/El: Blue Line to Damen.

Chasalla   More low-key than many of its Oak Street neighbors, this cozy, minimalist boutique specializes in men's and women's clothing from designers' younger, slightly more affordable labels, including D&G and Just Cavalli. 70 E. Oak St. (btw. Rush St. and Michigan Ave.). ✆ 312/640-1940. Subway/El: Red Line to Chicago.

(Finds   Shopping with the Pros

Want to stay on top of the trends, but have limited time to scout out hip boutiques? A guided tour of Chicago's coolest clothing shops is a great way to fit some concentrated shopping into a busy schedule. (Plus, you'll hit the insider places only the locals know about and get discounts along the way.) **Urban Shop Guide** (✆ 312/533-1256; www.urbanshopguide.com) offers tours to Lincoln Park or Bucktown, visiting smaller, independent boutiques; tours cost $40 to $125 per person. **Shop Walk Chicago** (✆ 773/255-7866; www.chicagoshopwalk.com) offers a number of different neighborhood tours (let them know the kinds of clothes you like, and they'll suggest where to go); there's also a "Made in Chicago" tour that focuses on local designers. Tours range from $40 to $70 per person. Both companies can also arrange custom tours on request.

Clever Alice   This Bucktown shop attracts a clientele of stylish women in search of creative-yet-polished looks. While the clothes here are body-conscious (including a good selection of hard-to-find European lines), the staff takes the time to help shoppers find pieces that fit and flatter. The store's eponymous clothing line features softly draped shirts and dresses. 1920 N. Damen Ave. (at Courtland St.). ✆ **773/276-2444.** www.cleveralice.com. Subway/El: Blue Line to Damen.

Habit ★★ (Finds)   On the southwestern fringe of Wicker Park, oh-so-hip West Division Street is the latest destination of choice for independent-minded shoppers. This cool-but-welcoming clothing boutique is emblematic of the neighborhood, mixing edgy looks with a laid-back attitude. Come here to find one-of-a-kind pieces from emerging designers (about half of them Chicago-based); styles range from pretty, work-appropriate dresses to funky, deconstructed leather vests. 1951 W. Division St. (at Damen Ave.). ✆ **773/342-0093.** www.habitchicago.com. Subway/El: Blue Line to Division.

Ikram ★★★   As a behind-the-scenes fashion advisor to Michelle Obama, owner Ikram Goldman helped craft the First Lady's stylish image. But Goldman has long been the go-to person for many of Chicago's most powerful (and wealthiest) women, the fashion expert they trust to match them with the perfect couture gown. Her shop has the subdued look and aura of a fine-art gallery, where the racks are filled with whichever designers *Vogue* has declared "hot" for the season. Tucked among the high-priced pieces are jewelry, stationery, and decorative accessories that give the place a personal touch. 873 Rush St. (btw. Delaware and Chestnut sts.). ✆ **312/587-1000.** www.ikram.com. Subway/El: Red Line to Chicago.

Maria Pinto (Finds)   Another local fashion fixture who got a boost from her Michelle Obama connection, designer Maria Pinto capitalized on her success by opening her first boutique in 2009. Known for her sophisticated, tailored evening gowns and luxurious coats, Pinto is a favorite with local socialites, who flock to her for special-occasion outfits. (Those glamorous dresses come with special-occasion, four-figure price tags, too.) The store, located in the formerly industrial West Loop, is minimalist and airy, a suitable backdrop for Pinto's understated version of glamour. 135 N. Jefferson St. (btw. Randolph and Washington sts.). ✆ **312/648-1350.** www.mariapinto.com. Bus: 20 (Madison) or a short cab ride from the Loop.

p45 ★   You'll find a number of cool boutiques aimed at the younger crowd clustered along Damen Avenue in Bucktown, but this is the most cutting-edge, with a vibe that's funky rather than girly. A gold mine of urbane women's fashion, the spare space is filled with a unique mix of hip national labels (3.1 Philip Lim, Michelle Mason, Susana Monaco) and local designers you've never heard of. If you're looking for something no one else at home will be wearing, this is the place to shop. 1643 N. Damen Ave. (btw. North and Wabansia aves.). ✆ **773/862-4523.** www.p45.com. Subway/El: Blue Line to Damen.

Robin Richman   You'll feel like you're poking through a big, antiques-filled closet as you browse around this airy Bucktown storefront. The walls are adorned with balls of string, vintage diaries, and artful handmade wire hangers. While Richman carries an assortment of men's and women's separates (mostly loose, unstructured pieces)—as well as a great, funky jewelry selection—the big draw here is her exquisite sweaters. 2108 N. Damen Ave. (at Dickens St.). ✆ **773/278-6150.** www.robinrichman.com. Subway/El: Blue Line to Damen, and then a long walk (10 blocks) or a short cab ride.

Scoop NYC   A hot spot for trendy young things with plenty of spending money, this loft-life space in Bucktown was the first Midwest outpost of the popular New York clothing boutique Scoop NYC. You'll find a mix of major fashion names (Marc Jacobs bags, Jimmy Choo shoes) along with the requisite selection of designer denim, flirty dresses, and seemingly simple T-shirts that will make you do a double take when you check out the price tags. (The store stocks men's and kids' clothing, too.) Even if you're not planning on blowing your paycheck on a pair of artfully distressed jeans, it's fun to browse for a quick overview of the hot looks of the season, and the in-store cafe is a good place to people-watch while sipping a latte. 1702 N. Milwaukee Ave. (at Wabansia Ave.). ✆ 773/227-9930. www.scoopnyc.com. Subway/El: Blue Line to Damen.

Tangerine   You can't help but smile when you enter this cheery Bucktown shop. Huge windows fill the place with light, and the colorful clothing selection—from designers such as Tocca, Nanette Lepore, and Trina Turk—is feminine and fun. (You will, however, pay a fair amount for these cute looks—most pieces start at $100 and up.) The sales staff has an upbeat attitude to match. 1719 N. Damen Ave. (at Wabansia Ave.). ✆ 773/772-0505. www.chicagotangerine.com. Subway/El: Blue Line to Damen.

The T-Shirt Deli ★★ (Finds)   For a new twist on custom clothing, stop by this cozy Bucktown storefront, where you can order up your own personalized T-shirt creation. Browse through the entertaining books of vintage iron-on patches, and you'll find everything from '80s icons such as Mr. T to '70s-style "Foxy Lady" logos. Choose a design (or create your own message), and your shirt will be printed up while you wait. When it's done, the shirt is packaged in a paper bag with a side of potato chips—just like a real deli. 1739 N. Damen Ave. (btw. Willow St. and St. Paul Ave.). ✆ 773/276-6266. www.tshirtdeli.com. Subway/El: Blue Line to Damen.

Ultimo ★★   The grande dame of local boutiques, Ultimo is known for carrying high-profile (and high-priced) designers, as well as up-and-coming names that have yet to show up in department stores. The store's warren of rooms, decked out in luxurious dark wood and red velvet, feels more like a spectacularly well-stocked private collection than a shop. Ultimo carries both women's and men's clothing, making it one of the rare spots fashion hounds of both genders can shop together. 114 E. Oak St. (btw. Michigan Ave. and Rush St.). ✆ 312/787-1171. www.ultimo.com. Subway/El: Red Line to Chicago.

COLLECTIBLES

Quake Collectibles   Off the beaten tourist path in the Lincoln Square neighborhood (northwest of downtown), this temple to all things kitschy includes an impressive vintage lunch-box collection and ample stacks of old fan magazines a la *Teen Beat,* with Shaun Cassidy tossing his feathered tresses. 4628 N. Lincoln Ave. (north of Wilson Ave.). ✆ 773/878-4288. www.quakechicago.com. Subway/El: Brown Line to Western.

Quimby's   The ultimate alternative newsstand, Quimby's stocks every kind of obscure periodical, from cutting-edge comics to zines "published" in some teenager's basement. Their book selection is also decadently different from your local Barnes & Noble; categories include "Conspiracy," "Politics & Revolution," and "Lowbrow Art." 1854 W. North Ave. (just east of Damen Ave.). ✆ 773/342-0910. www.quimbys.com. Subway/El: Blue Line to Damen.

Uncle Fun ★★ (Finds)   Whenever I'm looking for a quirky Christmas stocking stuffer or the perfect gag gift, I know Uncle Fun will come through for me. (1950s-era toy robots for a sci-fi-geek friend? Check. And how about some 3-D Jesus postcards for a Catholic-school grad?) Bins and cubbyholes are stuffed full of the standard joke toys (rubber-chicken key chains and chattering wind-up teeth), but you'll also find every conceivable modern pop-culture artifact, from Jackson Five buttons to Speed Racer's Mach-Five model car. 1338 W. Belmont Ave. (1 block east of Southport Ave.). ✆ **773/477-8223.** www.unclefunchicago.com. Subway/El: Red or Brown line to Belmont.

DEPARTMENT STORES

Barneys New York   This Midwest satellite has the same look and feel as the New York original: Minimalist-chic decor, high-priced, cutting-edge fashion, and a fair amount of attitude from the sales staff if you walk through the door in no-name shorts and sneakers. That said, the store has a stellar—if high-priced—shoe selection, along with a fun-to-browse accessories section on the ground floor (cosmetics are relegated to the basement). The top-floor cafe, **Fred's,** is a favorite hangout for the younger ladies-who-lunch crowd. In Lincoln Park, not far from the Armitage Avenue shopping district, you'll find **Barneys Co-Op,** 2209–11 N. Halsted St., at Webster Street (✆ **773/248-0426**), which features collections from younger, up-and-coming designers—and lots of specialty denim. 15 E. Oak St. (at Rush St.). ✆ **312/587-1700.** www.barneys.com. Subway/El: Red Line to Chicago.

Bloomingdale's   Though not as large as the New York flagship, Chicago's Blooming-dale's appeals to stylish shoppers looking for just a bit of urban edge. The shoe department has a good range (with serious markdowns during semiannual sales), and a special section is devoted to souvenir Bloomingdale's logo merchandise. 900 N. Michigan Ave. (at Walton St.). ✆ **312/440-4460.** www.bloomingdales.com. Subway/El: Red Line to Chicago.

Macy's ★★★   When Macy's took over Marshall Field's—Chicago's best-known "hometown" department store—in 2006, there was much local hand-wringing about what the buyout meant for Field's grand State Street headquarters. Although Field's iconic green awnings and shopping bags have been replaced by Macy's more dreary black, the good news is that the store itself remains impressive—a testament to the days when shopping downtown was an eagerly anticipated event rather than a chore. The impressive breadth of merchandise in this block-long store and its historically significant interior make it a must-see for serious shoppers. A number of exclusive "miniboutiques" are scattered throughout the overwhelming space, including the **28 Shop,** which stocks the latest from hot young designers; beauty stations where you can get a manicure and pick up exclusive products; and a gourmet food department developed by celebrity chef Charlie Trotter. The enormous shoe department is another highlight, with everything from killer high heels (at killer prices) and boots to sneakers and casual sandals.

If you're interested in the history of the store itself, you can download an audio tour from the website **www.visitmacyschicago.com** before your trip. (You can also print out discount coupons to use while you're here.)

The Water Tower store, 835 N. Michigan Ave. (✆ **312/335-7700**), is a scaled-down but respectable version of the State Street store. Its eight floors are actually much more manageable than the enormous flagship, and its merchandise selection is still vast (although this branch tends to focus on the more expensive brands). 111 N. State St. (at Randolph St.). ✆ **312/781-1000.** www.macys.com. Subway/El: Red Line to Washington.

Neiman Marcus   Yes, you'll pay top dollar for designer names here—the store does, after all, need to live up to its Needless Markup moniker—but Neiman's has a broader price range than many of its critics care to admit. It also has some mighty good sales. The four-story store, a beautiful environment in its own right, sells cosmetics, shoes, furs, fine and fashion jewelry, and clothing. The top floor has a fun gourmet food department as well as a pretty home accessories area. Neiman's has two restaurants: One relaxed, the other a little more formal. 737 N. Michigan Ave. (btw. Superior St. and Chicago Ave.). (C) **312/642-5900.** www.neimanmarcus.com. Subway/El: Red Line to Chicago.

Nordstrom   Nordstrom's spacious, airy design and trendy touches (wheatgrass growing by the escalators, funky music playing on the stereo system) gives it the feel of an upscale boutique rather than an overcrowded department store. The company's famed shoe department is large but not overwhelming; more impressive is the cosmetics department, where you'll find a wide array of smaller labels and an "open sell" environment (meaning you're encouraged to try on makeup without a salesperson hovering over you). In keeping with the store's famed focus on service, a concierge can check your coat, call a cab, or make restaurant reservations for you. 520 N. Michigan Ave., inside Westfield North Bridge mall, 55 E. Grand Ave. (at Rush St.). (C) **312/379-4300.** www.nordstrom.com. Subway/El: Red Line to Grand.

Saks Fifth Avenue   Saks Fifth Avenue might be best known for its designer collections—Valentino, Chloe, and Giorgio Armani, to name a few—but the store also does a decent job of buying more casual and less expensive merchandise. Still, the mood here can be somewhat chilly, and the high-fashion clothes on display seem geared toward the super-skinny. The men's department is located in a separate building across Michigan Avenue. Don't forget to visit the cosmetics department, where Saks is known, in particular, for its fragrance selection. Chicago Place, 700 N. Michigan Ave. (at Superior St.). (C) **312/944-6500.** www.saksfifthavenue.com. Subway/El: Red Line to Chicago.

GOURMET FOOD

Fox & Obel ★★   The city's top gourmet market is a foodie paradise: From the wide selection of specialty cheeses to the mouthwatering display of desserts. Browsing the shelves is like taking a mini-tour through the best specialty foods from around the world (and I dare you to walk through the bakery section without buying a loaf of freshly baked bread). An easy walk to Navy Pier and the lakefront, it's a great place to pick up a picnic lunch or a bottle of wine and some chocolates to enjoy late-night in your hotel room. There's also an in-store cafe if you want to take a break while strolling around the Michigan Avenue area. 401 E. Illinois St. (at McClurg Court). (C) **312/410-7301.** www.foxandobel. com. Subway/El: Red Line to Grand, and then 65 Grand bus.

Goddess & Grocer   This upscale version of a neighborhood deli stocks everything you need for a mouthwatering lunch or dinner on the go—from specialty sandwiches to chicken and pasta dishes to freshly baked cookies and brownies. The prepared foods are a few notches above the standard takeout spot (wild Alaskan salmon; wild mushroom risotto), and the staff can put together meals for any occasion, from a catered business lunch to a romantic evening picnic at Millennium Park. There are also good selections of wine and prepackaged snacks. The same owners run another, smaller, outpost in Bucktown, 1646 N. Damen Ave, at North Avenue ((C) **773/342-3200**). 25 E. Delaware St. (at Rush St.). (C) **312/896-2600.** www.goddessandgrocer.com. Subway/El: Red Line to Chicago.

The Spice House ★ (Finds)   Okay, so the Spice House isn't exactly a food store, but this aromatic, beautifully designed specialty shop is a must-see for serious home chefs (and anyone else hoping to add some oomph to their cooking). Spices and herbs from around the world are displayed in racks of glass jars—a modern take on the classic general

(Finds)   **In Search of Specialty Foods**

Chicago's got a huge variety of ethnic grocery stores, where you can sample authentic specialties from around the world and stock up on unusual cooking-related gifts. Because most of the shops are in residential neighborhoods far from the usual tourist haunts, the best way to get an overview of them is by taking a culinary tour, led by a guide who knows the cuisine (and, best of all, can organize tastings along the way). **Ethnic Grocery Tours** (© **773/465-8064;** www.ethnic-grocery-tours.com), run by Evelyn Thompson, organizes half-day excursions for up to four people that stop at a variety of shops, from Russian to Jamaican to Middle Eastern. Chef Rebecca Wheeler takes visitors to Southeast Asian and Indian stores and bakeries for her **Ethnic Market Tours** (© **773/368-1336;** www.rebeccawheeler.com). She'll even share cooking tips, so you can arrive home with a few new recipes to try out.

store. The friendly staff members are happy to provide tips on how to use everything, and most packages come with recipes. Looking for a Chicago-themed gift? Pick up one of the "Ethnic Chicago" sets, which include custom-designed spice mixes inspired by different Chicago neighborhoods. 1512 N. Wells St. (btw. North Ave. and Schiller St.). © **312/274-0378.** www.thespicehouse.com. Subway/El: Brown Line to Sedgwick.

HOME DECOR & GIFTS

Art Effect ★★   Classifying this wonderfully eclectic Armitage Avenue shop is no easy task. (The owners refer to it as a "modern day general store".) It's got everything from aromatherapy oils and kitchen mixing bowls designed by cookbook author Nigella Lawson to handcrafted jewelry and gag gifts, not to mention a whole room devoted to hippie-chic women's clothing. The merchandise has a definite female slant, with a vibe that's young and irreverent rather than fussy, but the laid-back, friendly sales staff makes everyone feel welcome. The wide, unpredictable selection makes this one of my favorite browsing spots in town. 934 W. Armitage Ave. (at Bissell St.). © **773/929-3600.** www.arteffectchicago. com. Subway/El: Brown Line to Armitage.

Flight 001   Wish you were traveling in the golden age of jumbo jets and stylish stewardesses? This streamlined travel shop—whose curved walls recall the interior of an airplane—carries luggage, maps, retro-inspired toiletry bags, and travel-sized amenities. The Red Eye Pack, packaged in an FAA-approved plastic bag, includes an eye mask, earplugs, lip balm, a moisturizing towelette, and other long-haul flight necessities—the perfect gift for frequent fliers. 1133 N. State St. (at Elm St.). © **312/944-1001.** www.flight001.com. Subway/El: Red Line to Clark/Division.

Orange Skin ★   It may look like an ultracool loft catering only to trendier-than-thou style experts, but don't be intimidated: Orange Skin is one of my favorite places to check out what's new in the world of modern interior design (and the staff is friendlier than you might expect). From colored clear-plastic dining chairs to bowls made of welded steel wires, checking out the store's selections will give you an overview of the latest in the world of design. Visit the shop's lower level for smaller tabletop items that make good, one-of-a-kind gifts. 223 W. Erie St. (at Franklin St.). © **312/335-1033.** www.orangeskin.com. Subway/El: Brown Line to Chicago.

P.O.S.H. Love pieces with a past but can't afford fine antiques? This fun shop sells discontinued china patterns from a more elegant time gone by; recent selections included dishes used for first-class service on American Airlines and a tea service once used in an English country inn. If you're looking for a one-of-a-kind souvenir, they also produce a line of Chicago skyline dinnerware. 613 N. State St. (btw. Ontario and Ohio sts.). ℭ 312/280-1602. www.poshchicago.com. Subway/El: Red Line to Grand.

Sawbridge Studios Craftsmanship is the driving force behind this inviting River North shop. Exquisitely handcrafted furniture, tabletop accessories, lamps, mirrors, and paintings have a timeless quality; the pieces here are original enough to feel special but classic enough to look like family heirlooms rather than of-the-moment fads. 153 W. Ohio St. (btw. LaSalle and Wells sts.). ℭ 312/828-0055. www.sawbridge.com. Subway/El: Red Line to Grand, or Brown Line to Merchandise Mart.

Stitch ★ (Finds) A favorite gift-shopping spot for savvy local fashion experts, Stitch stocks an almost unclassifiable mix of merchandise including candles, luggage, flatware, serving dishes, and bed linens. Unlike the stereotypical, overly cutesy "gift shoppe," the selection here is fresh and contemporary; whatever you buy here is pretty much guaranteed to be cool. 1723 N. Damen Ave. (at Wabansia St.). ℭ 773/782-1570. www.stitchchicago.com. Subway/El: Blue Line to Damen.

MUSIC

Dusty Groove America In 1996, using a rickety old PC, Rick Wojcik and John Schauer founded an online record store at **www.dustygroove.com**. Since then, the operation has expanded in both cyberspace and the real world. Dusty Groove covers a lot of ground, selling soul, funk, jazz, Brazilian, lounge, Latin, and hip-hop music on new and used vinyl and CDs. For the most part, selections are either rare, imported, or both. 1120 N. Ashland Ave. (1 block south of Division St.). ℭ 773/342-5800. www.dustygroove.com. Subway/El: Blue Line to Division.

Jazz Record Mart ★★ This is possibly the best jazz record store in the country. For novices, the "Killers Rack" displays albums that the store's owners consider essential to any jazz collection. Besides jazz, there are bins filled with blues, Latin, and "New Music." The albums are filed alphabetically and by category (vocals, big band, and so on), and there are a couple of turntables to help you spend wisely. Jazz Record Mart also features a stage and seating for 50, where local and national artists coming through town entertain with in-store performances. 27 E. Illinois St. (btw. Wabash Ave. and State St.). ℭ 312/222-1467. www.jazzrecordmart.com. Subway/El: Red Line to Grand.

New Sound Gospel Chicago is the birthplace of gospel music, and now, thanks to artists such as Kirk Franklin, it's also become big business. All the major labels have gospel music divisions, and this store on the city's far South Side is the best place in town to browse the full range of what's available. Not sure where to start? Ask the store's expert staff for advice—here, you'll find everything from gospel's greatest to groups with names such as Gospel Gangstaz. 10723 S. Halsted St. (at 107th St.). ℭ 773/785-8001. Subway/El: Red Line to 95th/Dan Ryan, then 108 Halsted bus to 107th St.

Reckless Records The best all-round local record store for music that the cool kids listen to, Reckless Records wins brownie points for its friendly and helpful staff. You'll find new and used CDs and albums in a variety of genres (psychedelic and progressive rock, punk, soul, and jazz) here, along with magazines and a small collection of DVDs. There are also locations in Lincoln Park at 3126 N. Broadway Ave. (ℭ 773/404-5080), and Wicker Park at 1532 N. Milwaukee Ave. (© **773/235-3727**). 26 E. Madison St. (btw. State and Wabash sts.). © **312/795-0878**. www.reckless.com. Subway/El: Red Line to Monroe or Brown Line to Madison.

PAPER & STATIONERY

All She Wrote   One of the many owner-operated specialty shops along Armitage Avenue, All She Wrote stocks a fun mix of cards and notepaper, all with a lighthearted, whimsical feel. 825 W. Armitage Ave. (1 block west of Halsted St.). © **773/529-0100**. www.all shewrote.com. Subway/El: Red Line to North/Clybourn.

Paper Boy ★ (Finds)   Run by the same owners as the novelty shop Uncle Fun (see "Collectibles," above), this stationary shop has one of the most offbeat and artsy selections of greeting cards in the city—with messages ranging from sweet to R-rated. You can also browse an eclectic assortment of knickknacks, wind-up toys, fridge magnets, and other impulse-buy items. 1351 W. Belmont Ave. (at Southport Ave.). © **773/388-8811**. www. unclefunchicago.com/pboy.html. Subway/El: Brown Line to Southport.

Paper Source ★★★   The acknowledged leader of stationery stores in Chicago, Paper Source has now expanded throughout the country (with locations from Boston to Beverly Hills), but this shop in River North is the chain's home base. Paper Source's claim to fame is its collection of handmade paper in a variety of colors and textures. You'll also find one-of-a-kind greeting cards and a large collection of rubber stamps for personalizing your own paper at home. There's also a location in the trendy Armitage shopping district at 919 W. Armitage Ave. (© **773/525-7300**). 232 W. Chicago Ave. (at Franklin St.). © **312/337-0798**. www.paper-source.com. Subway/El: Red or Brown line to Chicago.

The Watermark   Chicago socialites come here to order their engraved invitations, but you don't need to wait for a special occasion to visit: This stationery store also carries a fine selection of unique handmade greeting cards. Yes, they'll set you back considerably more than Hallmark, but just think of them as miniature works of art. 109 E. Oak St. (1 block from Michigan Ave.). © **312/337-5353**. Subway/El: Red Line to Clark/Division.

SALONS & SPAS

Art + Science   This Lincoln Park spot, just steps from the Armitage Avenue shopping strip, may look a little intimidating from the outside, but the ambience inside is welcoming, no matter what your look. Stylists can get as creative as you want, but most clients here are young professional women who want the same basic cut as everyone else. There's also another location in Wicker Park at 1552 N. Milwaukee Ave. (© **773/227-HAIR** [4247]). 1971 N. Halsted St. (at Armitage Ave.). © **312/787-HAIR** (4247). www.artandscience salon.com. Subway/El: Brown Line to Armitage.

Charles Ifergan   Charles Ifergan, one of the city's top salons, caters to an affluent Gold Coast crowd, and his rates, which vary according to the seniority of the stylist, are relatively high. But if you're a little daring, you can get a cut for the price of the tip on Tuesday and Wednesday evenings when junior stylists do their thing gratis—under the watchful eye of Monsieur Ifergan. (Call © **312/640-7444** btw. 10am and 4pm to make an appointment for that night.) 106 E. Oak St. (btw. Michigan Ave. and Rush St.). © **312/642-4484**. www.charlesifergan.com. Subway/El: Red Line to Chicago.

Kiva Day Spa ★★   Kiva is the city's reigning "super spa," and is named for the round ceremonial space used by Native Americans seeking to quiet, cleanse, and relax the spirit. The two-floor, 6,000-square-foot space offers spa, salon, nutrition, and apothecary services, and a nutritional-juice-and-snack bar in a setting that evokes its namesake inspiration. The round first-floor salon is equipped with a massive granite circular counter surrounded by hair-care, facial, and aromatherapy products and body massage oils. Water Tower Place, entrance at 196 E. Pearson St. (at Mies van der Rohe Way). ℂ **312/840-8120.** www. premierspacollection.com. Subway/El: Red Line to Chicago.

Mon Ami Coiffeur   Sure, you can get a haircut at this popular Gold Coast salon, but Mon Ami also has some of the very best colorists in town. Resident makeup artist Diane Ayala is known for her magic touch with eyebrow shaping (as well as her custom cosmetics line). 65 E. Oak St. (btw. Rush St. and Michigan Ave.). ℂ **312/943-4555.** Subway/El: Red Line to Clark/Division.

Salon Buzz   This hip hair parlor, operated by wizardly stylist Andreas Zafiriadis (who has wielded his scissors in Paris, Greece, New York, and California), is popular with women in creative professions. But it's far from a girls-only hangout: Among the regulars are a number of local professional athletes. 1 E. Delaware Place (at State St.). ℂ **312/943-5454.** Subway/El: Red Line to Chicago.

Spa Space ★★ (Finds)   Located in the up-and-coming West Loop, this trendy spa offers the latest skin-care treatments in a stylishly modern building that feels like a boutique hotel. The gender-neutral decor and specialized menu of guy-friendly treatments (including a massage designed for golfers) has given this spa a far larger male clientele than other local spots. 161 N. Canal St. (at Randolph St.). ℂ **312/943-5454.** www.spaspace.com. Subway/El: Green Line to Clinton.

Tiffani Kim Institute   Occupying a modern three-story building in the heart of River North's art-gallery district, the Tiffani Kim Institute is a virtual mini-mall of beauty treatments. Here, you can get a haircut, schedule a massage or facial, or book a cosmetic surgery procedure. Wellness treatments include a detox seaweed body wrap, Asian ear candling, acupuncture and Chinese herbal medicine, and the "Serenity Stone Massage," a Tiffani Kim specialty in which smooth stones are warmed in a thermal unit to 135°F (57°C) and then used as tools in a Swedish-style massage. 310 W. Superior St. (btw. Franklin and Orleans sts.). ℂ **312/943-8777.** www.tiffanikiminstitute.com. Subway/El: Red or Brown line to Chicago.

Truefitt & Hill ★ (Finds)   Women have their pick of hair and beauty salons, but men don't often come across a place like Truefitt & Hill, the local outpost of a British barbershop listed in the *Guinness Book of World Records* as the oldest barbershop in the world. You'll pay a steep price for a haircut here (about $50), but the old-world atmosphere is dead-on, from the bow-tied barbers to the antique chairs. Services include lather shaves, manicures, massages, and shoeshines. Up front, the apothecary sells imported English shaving implements and toiletries. 900 N. Michigan Ave. shopping center (btw. Walton St. and Delaware Place), 6th floor. ℂ **312/337-2525.** www.truefittandhill.com. Subway/El: Red Line to Chicago.

Urban Oasis (Finds)   After a long day of sightseeing, try a soothing massage in this spa's subdued, Zen-like atmosphere. The ritual begins with a steam or rain shower in a private changing room followed by the spa treatment you elect—various forms of massage (including a couples' massage, in which you learn to do it yourself), an aromatherapy wrap, or an exfoliating treatment. Fruit, juices, or herbal teas are offered on completion. There's also another location in a burgeoning retail district a few blocks south of the Armitage Avenue shopping strip at 939 W. North Ave. (ℂ **773/640-0001**). 12 W. Maple St., 3rd floor (btw. Dearborn and State sts.). ℂ **312/587-3500.** www.urbanoasis.biz. Subway/El: Red Line to Clark/Division.

Alternatives Yes, many of the shoes you see in the window may be black, but this locally owned chain offers far more than Doc Marten wannabe designs; you'll find cutting-edge shoes for men and women that are more affordable than you'd find in designer boutiques. 900 N. Michigan Ave. (btw. Walton St. and Delaware Place), 5th floor. ☎ **312/266-1545.** www.altshoes.com. Subway/El: Red Line to Chicago.

1154 Lill Studio ★ (Finds) Purse-a-holics and wannabe designers will find fashion heaven at this custom-handbag shop. Pick a style (which includes everything from evening purses to diaper bags), and then browse the huge selection of fabrics to create your own custom interior and exterior. Your finished creation can be picked up in a few weeks or shipped to your home. Not feeling particularly creative? There's also a selection of premade bags. Personal handbag parties can be arranged for groups of five or more. 904 W. Armitage Ave. (at Fremont St.). ☎ **773/477-LILL** (5455). www.1154lill.com. Subway/El: Brown line to Armitage.

Lori's Designer Shoes ★★ (Value) Lori's looks like a local version of Payless Shoes (shoeboxes stacked on the floor and women surrounded by piles of heels and boots), but the designer names on most of those shoes prove that this is a step above your typical discount store. A mecca for the shoe-obsessed, Lori's stocks all the latest styles, at prices that average 10% to 30% below department-store rates. 824 W. Armitage Ave. (btw. Sheffield Ave. and Halsted St.). ☎ **773/281-5655.** www.lorisdesignershoes.com. Subway/El: Brown Line to Armitage.

Pump (Finds) Located in the up-and-coming Division Street shopping corridor, Pump may be off the usual tourist route, but it's a worthy stop for footwear fanatics in search of something unique. This independently owned shoe boutique stocks fun, eye-catching heels, boots, and flats from lesser-known labels, but what really sets it apart is the friendly, personal service. 1659 W. Division St. (at Paulina St.). ☎ **773/384-6750.** www.pumpshoes chicago.com. Subway/El: Blue Line to Division.

Stuart Weitzman Head to Stuart Weitzman for shoes that make a dramatic impression—on your feet and on your wallet. Strappy high-heeled sandals from this shoe seller make regular appearances on the red carpet at the Academy Awards and other A-list celebrity events. You'll find lots of special-occasion heels here, as well as some lovely knee-high boots. 900 N. Michigan Ave. (btw. Walton St. and Delaware Place), 1st floor. ☎ **312/943-5760.** www.stuartweitzman.com. Subway/El: Red Line to Chicago.

Tod's Characterized by detailed workmanship and top-quality materials, this upscale Italian footwear line is known for its moccasin-style driving shoes, but the shop also stocks high-heeled sandals, ballerina-style flats, mules in various colors, plus their glamorous trademark handbags. Just remember: The ritzy Oak Street location is a tip-off that such luxury doesn't come cheap. 121 E. Oak St. (btw. Michigan Ave. and Rush St.). ☎ **312/943-0070.** www.tods.com. Subway/El: Red Line to Chicago.

SOUVENIRS & MAPS

ArchiCenter Shop ★★★ Stop here for the coolest gifts in town. This bright, sleek shop is part of the Chicago Architecture Foundation, so everything in stock—including photography books, tour guides, stationery, and kids' toys—has a definite sense of style. Whether you're in the market for a $900 reproduction of a vase from Frank Lloyd Wright's Robie House or more affordable black-and-white photos of the city skyline, it's well worth

Chicago Tribune Store   Yes, you'll find plenty of newspaper-logo T-shirts and Cubs
hats here (the Tribune Company owns the team), but this shop, located on the ground
floor of the newspaper offices, also has a great collection of books. You can also order
reproductions of past *Tribune* front pages or color prints of photos from the newspaper's
archives. 435 N. Michigan Ave. (at Hubbard St.). ☏ **312/222-3080.** Subway/El: Red Line to Grand.

City of Chicago Store   Located in the Water Works Visitor Center right off Michigan Avenue, this is a convenient stop for Chicago-related souvenirs and gifts, including
truly one-of-a-kind pieces of retired municipal equipment. (Although the parking meters
I've seen for sale here might be a little hard to stuff in your suitcase.) 163 E. Pearson St. (at
Michigan Ave.). ☏ **312/742-8811.** Subway/El: Red Line to Chicago.

The Oprah Store   Can't snag a coveted ticket to the most popular show in town?
Across the street from Harpo Studios—where *The Oprah Winfrey Show* tapes—you'll find
this celebration of all things Oprah. If you've got a mom or aunt who tunes into the show
faithfully, this is a good place to pick up O-logo gifts, from T-shirts and hoodies to tea-
pots and baby clothes. There's also a nice selection of handcrafted home accessories made
in South Africa (site of Oprah's school for girls), as well as books by Oprah-approved
authors including Dr. Oz and Maya Angelou. Tucked discretely toward the back is a
closet where a small selection of designer outfits and shoes worn by Oprah herself are
offered for sale at far less than retail. (Although you can still plan on shelling out hundreds of dollars for these special items.) Even if you're a bit put off by the overwhelming
"O"s that fill the store, try to stifle your inner Scrooge: All profits go to the nonprofit
Angel Network. 37 N. Carpenter St. (at Washington St.). ☏ **312/633-2100.** Bus: 20 Madison.

SPORTING GOODS

Niketown (Overrated)   When Niketown first opened, it was truly something new: A
store that felt more like a funky sports museum than a place hawking running shoes.
These days, however, Niketown is no longer unique to Chicago (it's sprung up in cities
from Atlanta to Honolulu), and the store's celebration of athletes can't cover up the fact
that the ultimate goal is to sell expensive shoes. But the crowds keep streaming in to
snatch up products pitched by Niketown's patron saints Michael Jordan, Tiger Woods,
and Lance Armstrong. 669 N. Michigan Ave. (btw. Huron and Erie sts.). ☏ **312/642-6363.** http://
niketown.nike.com. Subway/El: Red Line to Grand.

Fleet Feet Sports ★ (Finds)   If you're serious about running, jog over to this Old
Town shop, where the knowledgeable staff takes the time to find the shoes that work best
for you. (They'll even check out the wear patterns on your old shoes to diagnose trouble
spots.) You can also stock up on stylish athletic gear and accessories such as heart rate
monitors and watches. 1620 N. Wells St. (at North Ave.). ☏ **312/587-3338.** www.fleetfeet
chicago.com. Subway/El: Brown Line to Sedgwick.

Sports Authority   The largest sporting-goods store in the city, Sports Authority
offers seven floors of merchandise, from running apparel to camping gear. Sports fans will
be in heaven in the first- and fifth-floor team merchandise departments, where Cubs, Bulls,
and Sox jerseys abound. Cement handprints of local sports celebs dot the outside of the
building; step inside to check out the prints from Michael Jordan and White Sox slugger
Frank Thomas. 620 N. LaSalle St. (at Ontario St.). ☏ **312/337-6151.** www.sportsauthority.
com. Subway/El: Red Line to Grand.

Fantasy Costumes (Finds)   Not exactly a toy store, this sprawling costume shop (covering an entire city block) is nonetheless devoted to make-believe and is just as fun. The store stocks more than a million items, including 800 styles of masks (priced $1–$200) and all the accessories and makeup needed to complete any costume. There's also a full-service wig salon here. 4065 N. Milwaukee Ave. (west of Cicero Ave.). © 773/777-0222. www.fantasycostumes.com. Subway/El: Blue Line to Irving Park.

Grow   For a look at the future of baby style, trek out to this trendy boutique in the rapidly gentrifying West Division Street neighborhood. The bright, open space showcases streamlined, ultramodern kids' furniture (such as bubble-shaped high chairs that would look right at home on *The Jetsons*), as well as clothing made of organic fabrics. Sure, many of the environmentally friendly products on display are out of most parents' price range, but families that have had their fill of plastic kiddy gear will have fun browsing here. 1943 W. Division St. (at Damen Ave.). © 773/489-0009. www.grow-kids.com. Subway/El: Blue Line to Division.

Little Strummer ★   This compact store is located in the Old Town School of Folk Music, which offers music classes for children, and stocks every kind of mini-instrument imaginable, from accordions and guitars to wind chimes and music boxes. There's also a good selection of music-related games and kid-friendly CDs. 909 W. Armitage Ave. (at Halsted St.). © 773/751-3410. Subway/El: Brown Line to Armitage.

Madison & Friends   Clothing for kids that's both cute and fashion-conscious is the specialty here, from baby-size leather bomber jackets to yoga pants for toddlers. A separate back room caters to older kids and tweens—including a staggering array of jeans. 43 E. Oak St. (btw. Rush St. and Michigan Ave.). © 312/642-6403. www.madisonandfriends.com. Subway/El: Red Line to Chicago.

Psycho Baby   A hangout for cool moms and their equally cool offspring, this Bucktown shop stocks baby and kids' clothes that are refreshingly free of either pastel animals or cartoon characters. The prices may sometimes cause a double take ($60 for shoes that your kid will outgrow in 3 months), but the creative selection and happy vibe make it fun for browsing. (There are even toys scattered around to entertain the kids while you shop.) If you need to pick up a gift for a little one, the store also carries a selection of creative toys. 1630 N. Damen Ave. (1 block north of North Ave.). © 773/772-2815. www.psychobabyonline.com. Subway/El: Blue Line to Damen.

VINTAGE FASHION/RESALE SHOPS

Beatnix   This massive, over-the-top vintage store crams together pretty much every dress-up option in one overstuffed space, from fluorescent-colored wigs to campy '70s tuxes to used wedding gowns. Expect crowds in the weeks before Halloween; this is also a popular stop for local drag queens year-round. 3400 N. Halsted St. (at Roscoe St.). © 773/281-6933. Subway/El: Red Line to Addison.

The Daisy Shop ★   A significant step up from your standard vintage store, the Daisy Shop specializes in couture fashions. These designer duds come from the closets of the city's most stylish socialites and carry appropriately hefty price tags. Even so, paying hundreds of dollars for a pristine Chanel suit or Louis Vuitton bag can still be considered a bargain, and well-dressed women from around the world stop by here in search of the perfect one-of-a-kind item. 67 E. Oak St. (btw. Michigan Ave. and Rush St.). © 312/943-8880. Subway/El: Brown Line to Sedgwick.

Fox's   This no-frills shop near Armitage Avenue offers designer clothing at a steep discount. The downside: Most clothing labels are cut out, so you might not know exactly which A-list name you're buying, but the last time I was here, I heard a woman telling a friend that she'd seen the same clothes in Saks, a sure sign that Fox's stays up-to-date with the fashion pulse. A note for the modest: Be prepared to strip in front of your fellow shoppers in the no-frills, open dressing room. 2150 N. Halsted St. (at Dickens St.). 🕐 773/281-0700. Subway/El: Brown Line to Armitage.

McShane's Exchange ★★ (Finds)   This consignment shop has a selection that's a few steps above the standard thrift store, and for designer and name-brand bargains, it can't be beat. The store expands back through a series of cramped rooms, with clothes organized by color, making it easy to scope out the perfect black dress. The longer a piece stays in stock, the lower the price drops—and I've done plenty of double takes at the price tags here: Calvin Klein coats, Prada sweaters, and Armani jackets all going for well under $100. If that's not tempting enough, you'll also find barely used shoes and purses. McShane's has another location with a similar selection at 1141 W. Webster St. (🕐 773/525-0211). 815 W. Armitage Ave. (at Halsted St.). 🕐 773/525-0282. www.mcshanes exchange.com. Subway/El: Brown Line to Armitage.

The Second Child (Kids)   This self-described "upscale children's resale boutique" may not look all that upscale—it's basically one long, dark room on the second floor of an Armitage Avenue town house—but take a look at the labels on these kids' clothes (Ralph Lauren, Lilly Pulitzer, and the like), and you'll see that they come from very fashionable closets. There's also a nice—if limited—selection of maternity clothes. 954 W. Armitage Ave. (btw. Bissell St. and Sheffield Ave.). 🕐 773/883-0880. www.2ndchild.com. Subway/El: Brown Line to Armitage.

WINE & LIQUOR

Binny's Beverage Depot (Value)   This River North purveyor of fermented libations is housed in a delightfully no-frills warehouse space and offers an enormous selection of wine, beer, and spirits—often at discounted prices. Binny's has a second, smaller location at 3000 N. Clark St. (🕐 773/935-9400). 213 W. Grand Ave. (at Wells St.). 🕐 312/332-0012. www.binnys.com. Subway/El: Red Line to Grand.

House of Glunz ★★ (Finds)   Not only is this Chicago's oldest wine shop, but it's also the oldest in the Midwest, with an inventory of 1,500 wines dating back to 1811. The shop periodically cracks open a few of its vintage wines for special wine-tasting events, but not all the selections here are rare or expensive. There's a stock of modern wines from California and Europe, and the knowledgeable owners are able to steer you to the right bottle to fit your budget. 1206 N. Wells St. (at Division St.). 🕐 312/642-3000. www.thehouseof glunz.com. Subway/El: Brown Line to Sedgwick.

Sam's Wines & Spirits   Believe it or not, this football-field-size warehouse store evolved from a modest packaged-goods store. Today, the family-owned operation is the best-stocked wine and spirits merchant in the city and offers pleasant, friendly service. It also features a superb cheese selection in the on-site Epicurean shop. 1720 N. Marcey St. (near Sheffield and Clybourn aves.). 🕐 800/777-9137 or 312/664-4394. www.samswine.com. Subway/El: Red Line to North/Clybourn.

Chicago After Dark

Chicago's bustling energy isn't confined to daylight hours. The city offers loads of after-hours entertainment, including Broadway musicals, world-class classical music, and a theater scene that rivals New York's.

The inviting atmosphere at both the Chicago Symphony Orchestra and the Lyric Opera of Chicago is appealing to culture vultures, while theater buffs can choose between high-profile companies such as Steppenwolf and Goodman and the scrappy groups that spring up in storefronts around the city. The theater scene here was built by performers who valued gritty realism and a communal work ethic, and that down-to-earth energy is still very much present. Music and nightclub haunts are scattered throughout the city, but Chicago's thriving music scene is concentrated in Lincoln Park, Lakeview, and Wicker Park, where clubs are devoted to everything from jazz and blues to alternative rock and reggae.

While the city has its share of see-and-be-seen spots, Chicagoans in general are not obsessed with getting into the latest hot club; we'd much rather chill out with our buddies at a neighborhood bar. To join us, you only have to pick a residential area and wander. You don't have to go far to find a tavern filled with neighborhood regulars and friendly bartenders.

For up-to-date entertainment listings, check the local newspapers and magazines, particularly the "At Play" (Thurs) and "On the Town" (Fri) sections of the *Chicago Tribune* and the "Weekend Plus" (Fri) section of the *Chicago Sun-Times;* the weekly magazine *Time Out Chicago,* which has excellent comprehensive listings; and the *Chicago Reader* or *New City,* two free weekly tabloids with extensive listings. The *Tribune's* entertainment-oriented website, **www.chicago. metromix.com**; the *Reader's* website, **www. chicagoreader.com**; and *Time Out Chicago's* website, **www.timeout.com/chicago**, are also excellent sources of information, with lots of opinionated reviews.

1 THE PERFORMING ARTS

Chicago is a regular stop on the big-name entertainment circuit, whether it's Broadway shows such as *Wicked* or pop music acts such as U2 or the Dave Matthews Band. (Both of whom sell out multiple nights at stadiums when they come to town.) High-profile shows, including Monty Python's *Spamalot* and Mel Brooks's stage version of *The Producers,* had their first runs here before moving on to New York.

Thanks to extensive renovation efforts, performers have some impressive venues where they can strut their stuff. The **Auditorium Theatre,** 50 E. Congress Pkwy., between Michigan and Wabash avenues (© **312/922-2110;** www.auditoriumtheatre.org), is my pick for the most beautiful theater in Chicago—and it's also a certified national landmark. Built in 1889 by Louis Sullivan and Dankmar Adler, this grand hall schedules mostly musicals and dance performances. Even if you don't catch a show here, stop by for a tour. (For more details, see p. 158.)

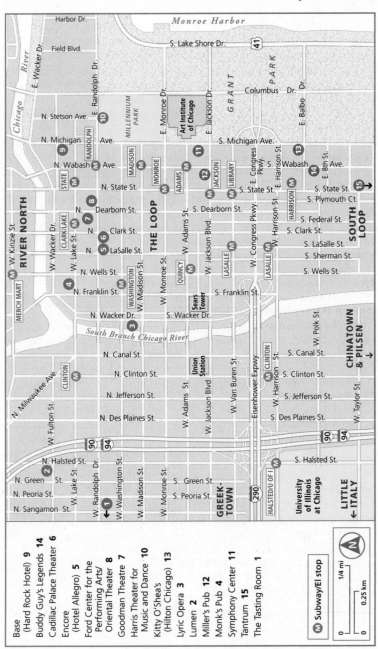

CHICAGO AFTER DARK

10

THE PERFORMING ARTS

Base
(Hard Rock Hotel) **9**
Buddy Guy's Legends **14**
Cadillac Palace Theater **6**
Encore
(Hotel Allegro) **5**
Ford Center for the
Performing Arts/
Oriental Theater **8**
Goodman Theatre **7**
Harris Theater for
Music and Dance **10**
Kitty O'Shea's
(Hilton Chicago) **13**
Lyric Opera **3**
Lumen **2**
Miller's Pub **12**
Monk's Pub **4**
Symphony Center **11**
Tantrum **15**
The Tasting Room **1**

Ⓜ Subway/El stop

0   1/4 mi
0   0.25 km

Tips **Finding a Better Seat**

Most of Chicago's grand old theaters have balconies that go way, way up toward the ceiling—and if you're stuck in the cheap seats, you'll be straining to see what's happening onstage. While theaters are very strict about checking tickets when you arrive, the ushers relax during intermission, so scope out empty seats during the first act, and then move down to better (and much pricier) spots for the rest of the show.

The city's other great historic theaters are concentrated in the North Loop. The **Ford Center for the Performing Arts/Oriental Theater,** 24 W. Randolph St., and the **Cadillac Palace Theater,** 151 W. Randolph St., book major touring shows and are well worth a visit for arts buffs. The Oriental's fantastical Asian look includes elaborate carvings almost everywhere you look; dragons, elephants, and griffins peer down at the audience from the gilded ceiling. The Palace features a profusion of Italian marble surfaces and columns, gold-leaf accents a la Versailles, huge decorative mirrors, and crystal chandeliers. (If you'd like to get a look at these historic theaters for a fraction of the standard ticket price, guided tours of both start at 11am Sat and cost $10 per person; meet in the Oriental lobby.) The **Bank of America Theatre** (formerly the Schubert Theatre), 18 W. Monroe St., was built in 1906 as a home for vaudeville; today it books mostly big-name musicals and sometimes comedy performers. For show schedules at all three theaters, call © 312/977-1700, or visit www.broadwayinchicago.com.

The **Chicago Theatre,** 175 N. State St., at Lake Street (© 312/443-1130), is a 1920s music palace reborn as an all-purpose entertainment venue, playing host to pop acts, magicians, stand-up comedians, and more. (Both the Chicago Theatre and the Bank of America Theatre, above, are quite large, so be forewarned that the cheaper seats are in nosebleed territory.) **Arie Crown Theater,** in the McCormick Place convention center at 23rd Street and Lake Shore Drive (© 312/791-6190), books musicals and pop acts, but compared to the venues listed above, the massive hall feels somewhat impersonal.

Symphony Center, 220 S. Michigan Ave., between Adams Street and Jackson Boulevard (© 312/294-3000), is the building that encompasses Orchestra Hall, home of the Chicago Symphony Orchestra (CSO). The building holds a six-story sky-lit arcade, recital spaces, and the fine-dining restaurant Rhapsody (p. 102). While the CSO is the main attraction, the Symphony Center schedules a series of piano recitals, classical and chamber music concerts, a family matinee series, and the occasional jazz or pop artist.

Chicago has a few other major venues for traveling shows, but they are not as convenient for visitors. The **Rosemont Theatre,** 5400 River Rd. in Rosemont, near O'Hare Airport (© 847/671-5100), is a top suburban stop for family-friendly musicals and concerts. The **North Shore Center for the Performing Arts in Skokie,** 9501 Skokie Blvd. in the northern suburb of Skokie (© 847/673-6300), is home to the well-respected Northlight Theater troupe, the Skokie Valley Symphony Orchestra, and a series of nationally known touring acts, including comics, dance troupes, and children's programs.

CLASSICAL MUSIC

Not surprisingly, the world-class talent of the Chicago Symphony Orchestra—considered one of the best in the country—dominates the classical music calendar. However, many

orchestra members play in smaller ensembles around town on a semi-regular basis; a few
independent musical groups have also built loyal followings with eclectic programming.

To find out what's playing when you're in town, check out the **Chicago Classical Music** website (www.chicagoclassicalmusic.org), maintained by a consortium of the city's leading music groups.

Chicago Symphony Orchestra ★★   The Chicago Symphony Orchestra is considered among the best in the world; a legacy of the late maestro Sir Georg Solti, who captured a record-breaking 31 Grammy awards for his CSO recordings and showcased the orchestra at other major musical capitals during frequent overseas tours. Come fall 2010, the arrival of superstar conductor Riccardo Muti as musical director should further entrench its international reputation. The symphony's schedule includes regular visits from internationally known guest artists, and although the repertoire has been expanded to include more modern works, crowd-pleasing favorites by Beethoven or Brahms are performed regularly as well.

Like many other orchestras around the country, the CSO has diversified its programming to attract younger audiences. The "Symphony Center Presents" series has included some of the top jazz, world beat, Latin, and cabaret artists in the world. Although concerts sell out when there's a high-profile performer, good seats sometimes become available on the day of the show, turned in by subscribers who can't make it. Call Symphony Center, or stop by the box office to check availability.

Summertime visitors have an opportunity to hear a CSO performance at the delightful **Ravinia Festival ★★** (✆ **847/266-5100**) in suburban Highland Park, led by music director Christoph Eschenbach. (For more information, see p. 189.)

The highly regarded **Civic Orchestra of Chicago,** the CSO's training orchestra since 1919, presents free programs at Orchestra Hall. The **Chicago Symphony Chorus** also performs there. Orchestra Hall in Symphony Center, 220 S. Michigan Ave. ✆ **312/294-3000.** www.cso.org. Tickets $25–$110; box seats $185. Subway/El: Red Line to Jackson.

Grant Park Symphony and Chorus (Value)   One of the city's best cultural bargains, this music festival offers a series of free outdoor classical music concerts from June through August. The symphony, along with visiting musicians and singers, performs in the Frank Gehry–designed Pritzker Music Pavilion in Millennium Park. Featuring Gehry's signature sinuous lines, the pavilion is surrounded by dramatic ribbons of curved steel. The Grant Park Symphony not only looks better than ever, but it sounds great, too—thanks to a state-of-the-art sound system. Concerts are held Wednesday, Friday, and Saturday, with most performances beginning at 6:30pm (7:30pm on Sat). Seats in the front of the pavilion are reserved for subscribers, but the back rows are available on a first-come, first-served basis. There's also plenty of lawn seating, so bring a blanket and enjoy a picnic dinner with a view of the skyline as a backdrop. Pritzker Music Pavilion, Michigan Ave. and Randolph St. ✆ **312/742-7638.** www.grantparkmusicfestival.com. Subway/El: Red Line to Washington/State; or Brown, Orange, or Green line to Randolph/Wabash.

Additional Offerings

The oldest all-volunteer civic chorus in the country, **Apollo Chorus of Chicago** (✆ **312/427-5620;** www.apollochorus.org), was founded in 1872, 1 year after the Great Chicago Fire. Today, it's best known for its annual holiday-season performances of Handel's *Messiah* at Orchestra Hall. The group also presents at least two other concerts during the year at various downtown venues.

The **Chicago Chamber Musicians (CCM)** (© 312/819-5800; www.chicagochamber music.org), a 15-member ensemble drawn from performers from the CSO and Northwestern and DePaul universities, presents chamber music concerts at various locales around the city. The season runs September through May, and you can always find the CCM performing free noontime concerts on the first Monday of the month (except Sept and Mar) at the Chicago Cultural Center. The **Chicago String Quartet** is affiliated with the group.

The **Chicago Sinfonietta** (© 312/236-3681; www.chicagosinfonietta.org), with its racially diverse 45-member orchestra and a wide-ranging repertoire, seeks to broaden the audience for classical music. In the past the group has followed a Beethoven piano concerto with a piece featuring a steel drum. Playing about 10 times a year at Orchestra Hall and other venues, the group often takes a multimedia approach to its multicultural mission, collaborating with dance troupes, visual artists, museums (such as slide shows depicting art from the Art Institute and the National Museum of Mexican Art), rock bands, and gospel choirs.

Music of the Baroque (© 312/551-1414; www.baroque.org) is a small orchestra and chorus that pulls members from both the CSO and the Lyric Opera orchestra, and features professional singers from across the country. The ensemble performs the music of the 16th, 17th, and 18th centuries, in (appropriately) Gothic church settings in various neighborhoods. The group has made several recordings and has introduced works by Mozart and Monteverdi to Chicago audiences.

OPERA

Lyric Opera of Chicago ★★

One of the top American opera companies, the Lyric attracts the very best singers in the world for its lavish productions. Opening night in September remains the quasi-official kickoff of the Chicago social season, but don't be scared off by the snooty factor; audiences here are relatively casual (to the dismay of all those opera snobs). Talented musicians and performers satisfy opera devotees, while newcomers are often swept away by all the grandeur. (English supertitles make it easy to follow the action.) Another plus for both opera newbies and veterans: An hour before each performance, audience members are invited to hear a lecture about that night's show. (It's free, but you'll have to show your ticket to get in.)

The Lyric Opera performs in the handsome, massive 3,563-seat Art Deco Civic Opera House, the second-largest opera house in the country, built in 1929. If you're sitting in one of the upper balconies, you'll definitely want to bring binoculars. (If you're nice, the regulars sitting nearby may lend you theirs.) There's only one problem with catching a show at the Lyric: The season, which runs through early March, usually sells out, although single tickets are sometimes available a few months in advance. Your other option is to call the day of a performance, when you can sometimes buy tickets that subscribers have turned in.

If you're in town in February or March, you can check out the theater by taking a tour (offered only during those months; call © **312/827-5685**). The opera has an adjunct, the Lyric Opera Center for American Artists, which in spring and summer performs in smaller venues around town. Civic Opera House, Madison St. and Wacker Dr. © **312/332-2244.** www.lyricopera.org. Tickets $31–$187. Subway/El: Brown Line to Washington.

Chicago Opera Theater

The "other" opera company in town, Chicago Opera Theater, doesn't get all the big names, but it offers an alternative to the more traditional Lyric by focusing on often-neglected works. (To make them accessible to a wider audience, English supertitles are used during performances.) It also helps that tickets are less expensive and more plentiful than the Lyric Opera's. The company performs three operas each spring (Mar–May), which usually run the gamut from classical tragedies by Handel to 20th-century satirical works. No matter what the bill, the talent and production values are top-notch. On certain evenings during the season, ticket holders are invited to a pre-performance lecture and Q&A session with the director, conductor, or other members of the artistic staff. Harris Theater for Music and Dance, 205 E. Randolph Dr. © 312/704-8414. www.chicagooperatheater.org. Tickets $35–$120 adults, half-price for children and students. Subway/El: Red Line to Washington/State.

DANCE

Chicago's dance scene is lively, but unfortunately it doesn't attract the same crowds as our theaters or music performances. Some resident dance troupes have international reputations, but they spend much of their time touring to support themselves. Dance performances in Chicago tend to occur in spurts throughout the year, with visiting companies such as the American Ballet Theatre and the Dance Theater of Harlem stopping in Chicago for limited engagements. Depending on the timing of your visit, you may have a choice of dance performances—or there may be none at all.

Dance lovers should schedule their visit for November, when the annual **"Dance Chicago"** festival (© 773/989-0698; www.dancechicago.com) is held at various locations around town. Featuring performances and workshops from the city's best-known dance companies and countless smaller groups, it's a great chance to check out the range of local dance talent. Another phenomenon that has enlivened the local scene is the scintillating **Chicago Human Rhythm Project** (© 773/281-1825; www.chicagotap.com), an annual tap-dance festival and nonprofit foundation created in 1990. The organization brings together tap and percussive dancers from around the world for a series of workshops and performances in the summer and fall at locations throughout the city and suburbs.

To find out what's going on at other times of the year, visit the website for **See Chicago Dance** (www.seechicagodance.com), which gives a comprehensive roundup of local performances.

The major Chicago dance troupes listed below perform at the **Harris Theater for Music and Dance,** 205 E. Randolph St. (© 312/334-7777), in Millennium Park. The 1,500-seat theater feels fairly stark and impersonal—the gray concrete lobby could be mistaken for a parking garage—but the sightlines are great, thanks to the stadium-style seating.

The Dance Center–Columbia College Chicago (Finds) Columbia College, a liberal arts institution specializing in the arts and media, has nurtured a new generation of creative talent. Its Dance Center—the hub of Chicago's modern-dance milieu—features an intimate "black box" 275-seat performance space with stadium seating and marvelous sightlines. The center schedules at least a dozen performances a year by both international and national touring groups and homegrown choreographers. 1306 S. Michigan Ave. © 312/344-8300. www.colum.edu/dance_center. Tickets $18–$26. Bus: 151. Subway/El: Red Line to Roosevelt.

Hubbard Street Dance Chicago ★ If you're going to see just one dance performance while you're in town, make it a Hubbard Street one. Chicago's best-known dance troupe mixes jazz, modern, ballet, and theater dance into an exhilarating experience.

Sometimes whimsical, sometimes romantic, the crowd-pleasing 22-member ensemble incorporates a range of dance traditions, from Kevin O'Day to Twyla Tharp (who has choreographed pieces exclusively for Hubbard Street). Although the troupe spends most of the year touring, it has regular 2- to 3-week Chicago engagements in the fall and spring. In the summer, the dancers often perform at Ravinia, the Chicago Symphony Orchestra's lovely outdoor pavilion in suburban Highland Park (p. 189). Office: 1147 W. Jackson Blvd. ℰ 312/850-9744. www.hubbardstreetdance.com. Tickets $20–$75.

Joffrey Ballet of Chicago ★ While this major classical company concentrates on touring, the Joffrey schedules about 6 weeks of performances a year in its hometown. Its repertoire extends from the ballets of founder Robert Joffrey, George Balanchine, and Jerome Robbins to the cutting-edge works of Alonzo King and Chicago choreographer Randy Duncan. The company is usually in town in the spring (Mar or Apr), fall (Sept or Oct), and December, when it stages a popular rendition of the holiday favorite *The Nutcracker.*

A bonus for dance lovers: The Joffrey offers free tours of its beautiful, light-filled administrative and rehearsal building in the Loop. Tours are given at noon on the 2nd and 4th Wednesday of each month; call ℰ **312/386-8912** to reserve a spot. Even if you can't make a tour, you can often catch a glimpse of dancers warming up through the floor-to-ceiling windows overlooking Randolph Street. Office: 10 E. Randolph St. ℰ **312/ 739-0120.** www.joffrey.com. Tickets $25–$130.

Muntu Dance Theatre of Chicago The tribal costumes, drumming, and energetic moves of this widely touring group, which focuses on both traditional and contemporary African and African-American dance, are always a hit with audiences. The company performs at the Harris Theater for Music and Dance in December and the spring (Apr or May). Office: 6800 S. Wentworth Ave. ℰ 773/602-1135. www.muntu.com. Tickets $25–$50.

River North Dance Company Chicago can be a brutal testing ground for start-up dance companies, which have to struggle to find performance space and grab publicity. But the odds didn't buckle the well-oiled knees of the River North Dance Company. This talented jazz dance ensemble performs programs of short, Broadway-style numbers by established and emerging choreographers. They perform periodically at the Harris Theater for Music and Dance, but you never know where they'll pop up next; check their website or call for information on upcoming shows. Office: 1016 N. Dearborn St. ℰ 312/944-2888. www.rivernorthchicago.com. Tickets $25–$30.

THEATER

Ever since the Steppenwolf Theatre Company burst onto the national radar in the late '70s and early '80s with in-your-face productions of Sam Shepard's *True West* and Lanford Wilson's *Balm in Gilead,* Chicago has been known as a theater town. As Broadway produced bloated, big-budget musicals with plenty of special effects but little soul, Chicago theater troupes gained respect for their risk-taking and no-holds-barred emotional style. Some of Broadway's most acclaimed dramas in recent years (the Goodman Theatre's revival of *Death of a Salesman* and Steppenwolf's *August: Osage County,* to name a couple) hatched on Chicago stages. With more than 200 theaters, Chicago might have dozens of productions playing on any given weekend—and seeing a show here is on my must-do list for all visitors.

The city's theaters have produced a number of legendary comedic actors, including comic-turned-director Mike Nichols (*The Graduate, Postcards from the Edge, Primary Colors*), as well as fine dramatic actors and playwrights. David Mamet, one of America's

greatest playwrights and an acclaimed film director and screenwriter, grew up in Chica- **253**
go's South Shore steel-mill neighborhood and honed his craft with the former St. Nicholas Players, which included actor William H. Macy (*Fargo, Boogie Nights*).

The thespian soil here must be fertile. Tinseltown and TV have lured away such talents
as John Malkovich, Joan Allen, Dennis Franz, George Wendt, John and Joan Cusack,
Aidan Quinn, Anne Heche, and Lili Taylor. But even as emerging talents leave for higher
paychecks, a new pool of fresh faces is always waiting to take over. This constant renewal
keeps the city's theatrical scene invigorated with new ideas and energy. Many of the
smaller theater companies place great emphasis on communal work: Everyone takes part
in putting on a production, from writing the script to building the sets. These companies
perform in tiny, none-too-impressive venues, but their enthusiasm and commitment are
inspiring. Who knows, the group you see performing in some storefront theater today
could be the Steppenwolf of tomorrow.

The listings below represent only a fraction of the city's theater offerings. For a complete listing of current productions playing, check the comprehensive listings in the two
free weeklies, the *Reader* (which reviews just about every show in town) and *New City;*
the weekly *Time Out Chicago;* or the Friday sections of the two dailies. The website of
the **League of Chicago Theatres** (www.chicagoplays.com) also lists all theater productions playing in the area.

Getting Tickets

To order tickets for many plays and events, call the **Ticketmaster Arts Line** (📞 312/
902-1500), a centralized phone-reservation system that allows you to charge full-price
tickets (with an additional service charge) for productions at more than 50 Chicago
theaters. Individual box offices also take credit card orders by phone, and many of the
smaller theaters will reserve seats for you with a simple request under your name left on
the answering machine. For hard-to-get tickets, try **Chicago Ticket Exchange** (📞 312/
902-1888; www.chicagoticketexchange.com) or **Gold Coast Tickets** (📞 800/889-
9100; www.goldcoasttickets.com).

About Face Theatre   About Face Theatre takes its mission seriously: To promote the
creation of new works that examine gay and lesbian themes and experiences. While that
often makes for a night of thought-provoking theater, the fare isn't always heavy with social-
justice issues. One of the group's big hits was a very campy musical version of *Xena: Warrior
Princess.* Performances are in the upstairs studio at Steppenwolf Theatre (see below). Office:
1222 W. Wilson Ave. 📞 773/784-8565. www.aboutfacetheatre.com. Tickets $20–$40.

American Theater Company   Its mission is to produce stories that ask the question:
"What does it mean to be an American?" With that broad mandate, the company generally focuses on serious American dramas (Mamet's *American Buffalo,* for instance, and
works by Sam Shepherd and Thornton Wilder), but comical and even musical fare shows
up on the schedule from time to time. Recent literary adaptations have included *Catch-
22* and *Working,* based on the book by veteran Chicago writer Studs Terkel. 1909 W. Byron
St. (2 blocks south of Irving Park Rd. at Lincoln Ave.). 📞 773/929-1031. www.atcweb.org. Tickets
$20–$35. Subway/El: Brown Line to Irving Park.

Briar Street Theatre (**Kids**)   The Briar Street Theatre has been the "Blue Man Theater" since the fall of 1997. The avant-garde New York City performance phenomenon
known as **Blue Man Group** has transformed the 625-seat theater, beginning with the
lobby, which is now a jumble of tubes, wires, and things approximating computer
innards. The show—which mixes percussion, performance art, mime, and rock 'n'

CHICAGO AFTER DARK

10

THE PERFORMING ARTS

(Value) Half-Price Theater Tickets

For half-price tickets on the day of the show, drop by one of the **Hot Tix** ticket centers ((C) **312/977-1755;** www.hottix.org), located in the Loop at 72 E. Randolph St. (btw. Wabash and Michigan aves.), and the Water Works Visitor Center, 163 E. Pearson St. Branches are open Tuesday through Saturday 10am to 6pm, Sunday 11am to 4pm; on Friday you can also purchase tickets for weekend performances. Hot Tix also offers advance-purchase tickets at full price. Tickets are not sold over the phone. The website lists what's on sale for that day beginning at 10am.

In addition, a few theaters offer last-minute discounts on leftover seats. **Steppenwolf Theatre Company** often has $20 tickets available beginning at 11am on the day of a performance; stop by Audience Services at the theater. Also, half-price tickets become available 1 hr. before the show; call or stop by the box office, or visit www.steppenwolf.org. The "Tix at Six" program at the **Goodman Theatre** offers half-price day-of-show tickets; many of them are excellent seats returned by subscribers. Tickets go on sale at the box office at 6pm for evening performances, noon for matinees.

roll—has become an immensely popular permanent fixture on the Chicago theater scene. (*Note to those with sensitive ears:* It can also get pretty loud.) The three strangely endearing performers, whose faces and heads are covered in latex and blue paint, know how to get the audience involved. Your first decision: Do you want the "splatter" or the "nonsplatter" seats? (The former necessitates the donning of a plastic sheet.) Although the show is a great pick for older children, it's not recommended for kids 4 and under. 3133 N. Halsted St. (at Briar St.). (C) **773/348-4000.** www.blueman.com. Tickets $49–$64. Subway/El: Red or Brown line to Belmont.

Chicago Shakespeare Theatre ★ This group's home on Navy Pier is a visually stunning, state-of-the-art jewel. The centerpiece of the glass-box complex, which rises seven stories, is a 525-seat courtyard-style theater patterned loosely after the Swan Theater in Stratford-upon-Avon. The complex also houses a 180-seat studio theater, an English-style pub, and lobbies with commanding views of Lake Michigan and the Chicago skyline. But what keeps subscribers coming back is the talented company of actors, including some of the finest Shakespeare performers in the country.

The main theater presents three Shakespeare plays a year; founder and artistic director Barbara Gaines usually directs one show. Chicago Shakespeare also books special short-run performances and events, such as a recent production of *Hamlet* by acclaimed British director Peter Brook. Shakespeare Theatre subscribers are loyal, so snagging tickets can be a challenge; reserve in advance if possible for weekend shows. If you have a choice of seats, avoid the upper balcony; the tall chairs are uncomfortable, and you have to lean way over the railing to see all the action onstage—definitely not recommended for anyone with a fear of heights. 800 E. Grand Ave. (C) **312/595-5600.** www.chicagoshakes.com. Tickets $50–$70. Subway/El: Red Line to Grand, and then bus 29 to Navy Pier. Discounted parking in attached garage.

Court Theatre (Finds)   Given its affiliation with the University of Chicago, it should 255 come as no surprise that this theater knows its way around the classics, from Molière to Ibsen. The productions here, however, are far from stuffy academic exercises: The vibrant, energetic takes on well-known works draw some of the finest actors in the city. In recent years, Court's seasons have included at least one musical (Tony Kushner's *Caroline, or Change* and *Raisin,* based on Lorraine Hansberry's *A Raisin in the Sun*), as well as plays by modern masters such as August Wilson and Tom Stoppard. It's a bit of trek to get here from downtown (I'd recommend a cab at night), but no matter what show is playing when you're in town, it's well worth the trip for theater lovers. 5535 S. Ellis Ave. (at 55th St.). ℂ 773/753-4472. www.courttheatre.org. Tickets $38–$54. Metra train: 57th St.

ETA Creative Arts Foundation   Since 1971, this theater has been staging original or seldom-seen dramatic works by African-American writers from Chicago and beyond. Along with **Black Ensemble Theater** (which performs at the Uptown Center Hull House, 4520 N. Beacon St.; ℂ 773/769-4451; www.blackensembletheater.org), this is one of the best African-American theater troupes in the city. The company stages six plays a year in its 200-seat theater, including works geared toward children that are performed on Saturday afternoons. 7558 S. Chicago Ave. (at 76th St.). ℂ 773/752-3955. www. etacreativearts.org. Tickets $30. Subway/El: Red Line to 69th St., transfer to bus 30.

Factory Theater   This irreverent young troupe offers the quintessential low-budget Chicago theater experience. The group specializes in original works written by the ensemble, many of which aim at a young, nontheatrical crowd. (You're encouraged to bring your own beer and drink it during the late-night shows.) The company's biggest hit was the raunchy trailer-park potboiler *White Trash Wedding and a Funeral,* and other recent productions (such as the Renaissance-Fair–inspired *RenFair: A Fistful of Ducats*) continue the cheeky fun. But the Factory also makes room for serious dramatic works written by members of its ensemble. 3504 N. Elston Ave. ℂ 312/409-3247. www.thefactory theater.com. Tickets $15–$20. Subway/El: Red Line to Addison, then bus 152 (Addison St.).

Goodman Theatre ★★   The Goodman, under artistic director Robert Falls, is the dean of legitimate theaters in Chicago. The theater produces both original shows and familiar standards, including everything from Shakespeare to musicals. (Some of its high-profile productions, including acclaimed revivals of Arthur Miller's *Death of a Salesman* and *Desire Under the Elms,* both starring Brian Dennehy, have gone on to Broadway). Productions at the Goodman are always solid; you may not see anything revolutionary, but you'll get some of the best actors in the city and top-notch production values.

The Goodman's custom-designed home in the North Loop is a rehab of the historic Harris and Selwyn theaters, a pair of rococo former movie houses. The renovation retained none of the historic bric-a-brac, and the new structure has a modern, minimalist feel. (The side of the building glows with different colors in the evenings.) The centerpiece is the 830-seat limestone-and-glass Albert Ivar Goodman Theatre. Connected to the main theater is a cylindrical, glass-walled building that houses retail operations, the 400-seat Owen Theatre, and the restaurant Petterino's (p. 102).

Every December, the Goodman stages a production of *A Christmas Carol,* which draws families from throughout the Chicago area and beyond. If you're in town then, it's great fun, but buy your tickets in advance, because many performances sell out. 170 N. Dearborn St. ℂ 312/443-3800. www.goodman-theatre.org. Tickets $10–$68. Subway/El: Red Line to Washington/State or Lake/State; Brown or Orange line to Clark/Lake.

The House Theatre (Finds) If you're looking for the up-and-coming stars of Chicago theater, keep your eyes on the House. This group of young actors takes on big themes (Harry Houdini and his obsession with death; the space-age tales of Ray Bradbury) and turns them into nonstop spectacles of drama, music, and comedy. Despite the usual budget constraints, the sets and special effects are impressive—as are the troupe's energy, imagination, and humor. Come see them while their tickets remain ultra-affordable. Office: 4611 N. Ravenswood Ave. (C) 773/769-3832. www.thehousetheatre.com. Tickets $17–$22. Performances: The Chopin Theatre, 1543 W. Division St. Subway/El: Blue Line to Division.

Lookingglass Theatre Company ★ One of the most visually oriented companies on the Chicago theatrical scene, Lookingglass produces original shows and unusual literary adaptations in a highly physical, imaginative style. (Its location in the Water Tower Pumping Station—just off Michigan Ave. and within walking distance of many downtown hotels—makes it especially visitor-friendly.) The company, founded more than a decade ago by graduates of Northwestern University (including *Friend* David Schwimmer), stages several shows each year. Recent offerings included *Metamorphoses,* a sublime and humorous modern recasting of Ovid's myths that became a hit in New York, and *Lookingglass Alice,* an acrobatic retelling of *Alice in Wonderland.* Ensemble member Mary Zimmerman—who directed *Metamorphoses*—has built a national reputation for her creative interpretations of literature, so if she's directing a show while you're in town, don't miss it. Schwimmer also appears here occasionally, as either an actor or director. Lookingglass shows emphasize visual effects as much as they do acting, whether it's having performers wade through a giant shallow pool or take to the sky on trapeze. 821 N. Michigan Ave. (at Chicago Ave.). (C) 312/337-0665. www.lookingglasstheatre.org. Tickets $25–$55. Subway/El: Red Line to Chicago.

Neo-Futurists (Finds) A fixture on Chicago's late-night theater scene, the Neo-Futurists have been doing their hit *Too Much Light Makes the Baby Go Blind* since 1988. (It's now the longest-running show in Chicago.) The setting—a cramped room above a funeral home—isn't much, but the gimmick is irresistible: Every night the performers stage a new collection of "30 plays in 60 minutes." The "plays" vary from a 3-minute comedy sketch to a lightning-quick wordless tableau; the mood veers from laugh-out-loud silly to emotionally touching. The show starts at 11:30pm on weekends; get there about an hour ahead, because seats are first-come, first-served, and they do sell out. The late-night curtain attracts a younger crowd, but I've taken 60-something relatives who have had a great time. (Unlike many improv comedy troupes, the Neo-Futurists don't rely on raunchy or gross-out humor.) Admission is random: Theatergoers pay $7 plus the roll of a six-sided die. If you want to feel that you've experienced edgy, low-budget theater—but still want to be entertained—this is the place to go. 5153 N. Ashland Ave. (at Foster Ave.). (C) 773/275-5255. www.neofuturists.org. Tickets $8–$13. Subway/El: Red Line to Berwyn.

Pegasus Players Performing in a rented college auditorium in the gritty North Side neighborhood of Uptown, Pegasus Players specializes in the kind of intellectually demanding fare that bigger mainstream theaters are afraid to risk. The group prides itself on picking shows that highlight social issues, such as the recent premiere *Heat Wave,* a dramatization of the tragic summer of 1995, when extreme weather led to the death of more than 700 Chicagoans, most of them elderly and poor. O'Rourke Performing Arts Center, Truman College, 1145 W. Wilson Ave. (C) 773/878-9761. www.pegasusplayers.org. Tickets $15–$25. Subway/El: Red Line to Wilson.

Redmoon Theater (Finds) Redmoon Theater might well be the most intriguing and visionary theater company in Chicago. Founded in 1990, the company produces "spectacle theater" involving masks, objects, and an international range of puppetry styles in indoor and outdoor venues around town. Utterly hypnotic, highly acrobatic and visceral, and using minimal narration, Redmoon's adaptations of Melville's *Moby Dick,* Mary Shelley's *Frankenstein,* Victor Hugo's *The Hunchback of Notre Dame,* and *Rachel's Love,* an original work based on Jewish folktales, were revelations that earned the company an ardent and burgeoning following. Every September, Redmoon presents an annual "spectacle," transforming a public park into a site for performance art, larger-than-life puppet shows, and dramatic visual effects. Office: 1438 W. Kinzie St. ℂ 312/850-8440. www.redmoon. org. Tickets $20–$30.

Steppenwolf Theatre Company Once a pioneer of bare-bones guerilla theater, Steppenwolf has moved firmly into the mainstream with a state-of-the-art theater and production budgets to rival those in any big city. The company has garnered many national awards and has launched the careers of several respected and well-known actors, including John Malkovich, Gary Sinise, Joan Allen, John Mahoney (of *Frasier*), and Laurie Metcalf (of *Roseanne*). Famous for pioneering the edgy, "rock-'n'-roll," spleen-venting style of Chicago acting in the 1970s and '80s—characterized by such incendiary tours de force as Sam Shepard's *True West* and Lanford Wilson's *Balm in Gilead*—Steppenwolf was reinvigorated with the triumph of *August: Osage County,* a harrowing-but-hilarious drama that got raves when it moved to New York and won multiple Tony Awards in 2008. While shows here can be hit or miss, the acting is never less than powerful; Steppenwolf's ensemble of performers is the best in the city.

Under artistic director Martha Lavey, Steppenwolf has drawn upon its star power, bringing back big names to perform or direct from time to time. But don't come here expecting to see John Malkovich or Joan Allen on stage; most of the big-name actors are too busy with their movie careers. Smaller theater troupes often perform at Steppenwolf's smaller studio theater, which stages more experimental fare.

For shows that aren't sold out, a limited number of discounted tickets ($20) go on sale at Audience Services at 11am the day of a performance; rush tickets (subject to availability; main stage half-price, studio $10) go on sale an hour before the performance. 1650 N. Halsted St. (at North Ave.). ℂ 312/335-1650. www.steppenwolf.org. Tickets $25–$68. Subway/El: Red Line to North/Clybourn.

Theater Wit Befitting its name, this up-and-coming troupe specializes in lighthearted productions filled with clever banter; it's best known for an annual December production of David Sedaris's The Santaland Diaries. While it started as a vagabond company that performed in various venues around town, its move to a permanent home in Lincoln Park has revitalized the group and raised its profile considerably. 1229 W. Belmont Ave. (at Racine Ave.). ℂ 773/327-5252. www.theaterwit.org. Tickets $20–$40. Subway/El: Red or Brown line to Belmont.

Theater on the Lake (Value) What a great way to see two of the city's signature strengths: A sublime skyline view from the water's edge, and an evening of off-Loop Chicago theater. The Prairie School–style building, built in 1920 as a sanitarium for babies and children suffering from tuberculosis, has hosted theatrical productions along the lake for half a century, but in recent years, the park district has hit upon a perfect programming gimmick. Each week a different independent theater company gets to strut its stuff, usually restaging a play they performed earlier in the year. Performances run from June into August on Wednesday to Sunday evenings, and some shows do sell out, so it pays to reserve in advance. At intermission, you can walk out the back door and look south to the city lights. If it's a cool night, bring a sweater, because the screened-in theater is open to the night air (allowing the noise of traffic on Lake Shore Dr. to intrude somewhat). And a warning for those hot summer nights: The building is not air-conditioned. Fullerton Ave. and Lake Shore Dr. ☎ **312/742-7994.** Tickets $18. Bus: 151 (Sheridan).

Trap Door Theatre   Trap Door is emblematic of the streetwise, no-holds-barred brand of off-Loop theater. A risk-taking, emotionally high-voltage company that has somehow stayed afloat (despite performing in a converted garage hidden behind a Bucktown restaurant), Trap Door concentrates on plays with a social or political bent. Many tend to be original works or decidedly noncommercial, provocative pieces by rarely produced cerebral artists, many of them European. (A few years ago, the show *AmeriKafka*, inspired by writer Franz Kafka and his visit to a performance by a Yiddish theater troupe, even featured a brief X-rated puppet show.) Prepare to be challenged: Theater doesn't get any more up close and personal than this. 1655 W. Cortland St. (1 block west of Ashland Ave.). ☎ **773/384-0494.** www.trapdoortheatre.com. Tickets $15–$20. Subway/El: Blue Line to Division.

Victory Gardens Theater (Finds)   Victory Gardens is one of the few pioneers of off-Loop theater that has survived from the 1970s. The company was rewarded for its unswerving commitment to developing playwrights with a Tony Award for regional theater in 2001—a real coup for a relatively small theater. The five or six productions presented each season are new works, many developed through a series of workshops. The plays tend to be accessible stories about real people and real situations—nothing too experimental. Even though most shows don't feature nationally known actors, the casts are always first-rate, and the plays usually leave you with something to think about (or passionately discuss) on the way home.

Victory Gardens stages shows at its main stage inside the former Biograph movie theater (known in Chicago lore as the place where the FBI gunned down bank robber John Dillinger in 1934). Smaller independent companies such as Shattered Globe and Remy Bumppo play on four smaller stages at the Victory Gardens Greenhouse Theater, 2257 N. Lincoln Ave., a few blocks south. 2433 N. Lincoln Ave. (1 block north of Fullerton Ave.). ☎ **773/871-3000.** www.victorygardens.org. Tickets $30–$45. Subway/El: Red or Brown line to Fullerton.

(Tips)   Theater for All

Visitors with disabilities will find that some local theaters go the extra mile to make their performances accessible. The Steppenwolf, Goodman, and Lookingglass theaters offer sign-language interpretation for deaf patrons and audiodescribed performances for visually impaired audiences. Victory Gardens Theater, which has a long-standing commitment to accessible theater, schedules special performances customized for audiences with different disabilities throughout the year. The theater even offers deaf patrons special glasses that project captions of dialogue onto the frame of the glasses.

2 COMEDY & IMPROV

In the mid-1970s, the nation was introduced to Chicago's brand of comedy through the skit-comedy show *Saturday Night Live*. Back then, John Belushi and Bill Murray were among the latest brood to hatch from the number-one incubator of Chicago-style humor, Second City. Generations of American comics, from Mike Nichols and Robert Klein to Mike Myers and Tina Fey, have honed their skills in Chicago before making it big in film and TV. Chicago continues to nurture young comics, affording them the chance to learn the tricks of improvisational comedy at Second City, the ImprovOlympic, and numerous other comedy and improv outlets.

ComedySportz (Kids) Most improv-comedy shows aren't exactly family-friendly, but ComedySportz does away with the barlike atmosphere and R-rated topics to deliver shows that are funny for the whole family. Chicago's only all-ages professional improv troupe sets two groups of five comedians against each other to compete for audience applause. "It isn't *about* sports—it *is* a sport," is the tagline here. Shows are held Thursdays at 8pm, Fridays at 8 and 10pm, and Saturdays at 6, 8, and 10pm; kids 10 and older are welcome at the early evening shows. 929 W. Belmont Ave. (℃ 773/549-8080. www.comedysportzchicago.com. Tickets $19. Subway/El: Red or Brown line to Belmont.

iO (Finds) The iO improv troupe was founded in 1981 by the late, great, and inexplicably unsung Del Close, an improv pioneer who branched off from his more mainstream counterparts at Second City to pursue an unorthodox methodology (the letters "iO" stand for "ImprovOlympic," the group's original name). A legendary iconoclast, the colorful Close developed a long-form improv technique known as "The Harold." It eschewed the traditional sketch format in favor of more conceptual comedy scenes: The audience suggests a theme for the evening, then a series of skits, monologues, and songs are built around it. Second City, whose vignette-blackout-vignette format had grown weary, has since co-opted the method.

iO offers a nightclub setting for a variety of unscripted nightly performances, from free-form pieces to shows loosely based on concepts such as *Star Trek* or dating. Like all improv, it's a gamble: It could be a big laugh, or the amateur performers could go down in flames. Monday is an off night for most other clubs in town, and iO takes advantage with a show called the Armando Diaz Experience, an all-star improv night that teams up some of the best improvisers in Chicago, from Second City and elsewhere. Besides Mike Myers, successful alums include Tim Meadows, Andy Dick, Amy Poehler, and the late Chris Farley. 3541 N. Clark St. (at Addison St.). (℃ 773/880-0199. http://chicago.ioimprov.com. Tickets $5–$14. Subway/El: Red Line to Addison.

Second City For nearly 50 years, Second City has been the top comedy club in Chicago and the most famous of its kind in the country. Photos of famous graduates line the lobby walls and include Elaine May, John Belushi, Stephen Colbert, Steve Carell, and Tina Fey.

Today's Second City is a veritable factory of improv, with shows on two stages (the storied main stage and the smaller Second City ETC) and a hugely popular training school. The main-stage ensembles change frequently, and the shows can swing wildly back and forth on the hilarity meter. In recent years, the club has adopted the long-form improvisational program pioneered by iO (ImprovOlympic; see above listing), which has

An Escape from the Multiplex

Chicago has a fine selection of movie theaters, but even the so-called art houses show mostly the same films that you'd be able to catch back home (or eventually on cable). But three local movie houses cater to cinema buffs with original programming. The **Gene Siskel Film Center,** 164 N. State St. ((©**312/ 846-2600;** www.siskelfilmcenter.org; subway/El: Red Line to Washington or Brown Line to Randolph), named after the well-known *Chicago Tribune* film critic who died in 1999, is part of the School of the Art Institute of Chicago. The center schedules a selection of films in two theaters, including lectures and discussions with filmmakers. The Film Center often shows foreign films that are not released commercially in the U.S.

The **Music Box Theatre,** 3733 N. Southport Ave. ((© **773/871-6604;** www. musicboxtheatre.com; subway/El: Brown Line to Southport), is a movie palace on a human scale. Opened in 1929, it was meant to re-create the feeling of an Italian courtyard; a faux-marble loggia and towers cover the walls. The Music Box books a selection of foreign and independent American films—everything from Polish filmmaker Krzysztof Kieslowski's epic *Decalogue* to a sing-along version of *The Sound of Music.* (I saw the Vincent Price cult favorite, *House of Wax,* complete with 3-D glasses, here.)

Facets MultiMedia, 1517 W. Fullerton Ave. ((© **773/281-4114;** www.facets. org; subway/El: Red or Brown line to Fullerton), a nonprofit group that screens independent film and video from around the world, is for the die-hard cinematic thrill-seeker. The group also mounts a Children's Film Festival (Oct–Nov) and the Chicago Latino Film Festival (Apr–May), and rents its impressive collection of classic, hard-to-find films on video and DVD by mail.

brought much better reviews. Check the theater reviews in the *Reader,* a free local weekly, for an opinion on the current offering. To sample the Second City experience, catch the free postshow improv session (it gets going around 10:30pm); no ticket is necessary if you skip the main show (except Fri). 1616 N. Wells St. (in the Pipers Alley complex at North Ave.). (© **877/778-4707** or 312/337-3992. www.secondcity.com. Tickets $8–$25. Subway/El: Brown Line to Sedgwick.

Zanie's Comedy Club Just down the street from Second City in Old Town is Zanie's, one of the few traditional comedy clubs left in Chicago. Zanie's often draws its headliners straight off *The Late Show with David Letterman* and *The Tonight Show,* and it's a regular stop for nationally known comedians. (Recent headliners have included Craig Ferguson and Chelsea Handler.) Stand-up routines are the usual fare, played to packed, appreciative houses. Patrons must be 21 or older. 1548 N. Wells St. (btw. North Ave. and Schiller St.). (© **312/337-4027.** www.chicago.zanies.com. Tickets $25 plus 2-drink minimum, more for big-name performers. Subway/El: Brown Line to Sedgwick.

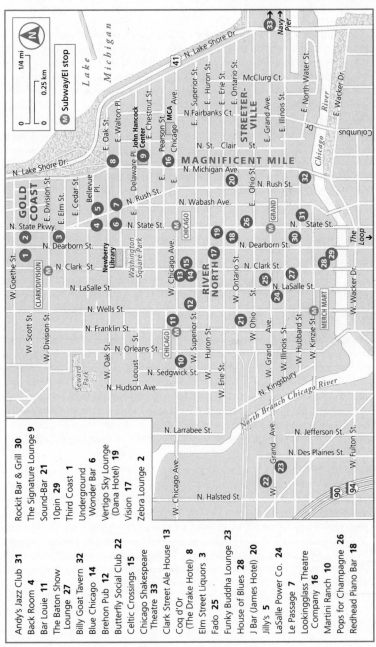

3 THE MUSIC SCENE

JAZZ

In the first great wave of black migration from the South just after World War I, jazz journeyed from the Storyville section of New Orleans to Chicago. Jelly Roll Morton and Louis Armstrong made Chicago a jazz hot spot in the 1920s, and their music lives on in a whole new generation of talent. Chicago jazz is known for its collaborative spirit and a certain degree of risk-taking—which you can experience at a number of lively clubs.

Andy's Jazz Club   Casual and comfortable, Andy's, a full restaurant and bar, is popular with both the hard-core and the neophyte jazz enthusiast. The club has one of the busiest schedules in town, with sets starting at 5 and 9pm every day of the week. (If you're catching the late show, the kitchen stays open until 1am). Families are welcome on Sundays, when the club is open to all ages, as long as they're seated in the dining room area. 11 E. Hubbard St. (btw. State St. and Wabash Ave.). © **312/642-6805.** www.andysjazzclub.com. Cover $5–$15. Subway/El: Red Line to Grand.

Back Room   One of the vestiges of the celebrated old Rush Street, the Back Room still packs a well-dressed crowd into an intimate candlelit spot at the back of a long gangway. The tuxedoed doorman offers patrons a seat on the main floor or in the balcony overlooking the stage. Shows start at 9:15pm, 10:45pm, and 12:15am Sundays through Fridays; Saturdays cater to night owls, with sets at 9:30pm, 11pm, 12:30am, and 1:45am. Rather than booking traditional jazz quartets and trios, Back Room features acts that mix jazz with Motown, R&B, and funk. 1007 N. Rush St. (btw. Oak St. and Bellevue Place). © **312/751-2433.** www.backroomchicago.com. Cover $8–$12 plus 2-drink minimum. Subway/El: Red Line to Chicago.

Green Dolphin Street ★   An old garage on the north branch of the Chicago River was transformed, Cinderella-like, into this sexy, retro, 1940s-style nightclub and restaurant. The beautiful, well-appointed crowd shows up here to smoke stogies from the humidor, lap up martinis, and take in the scene. (There's also a fine-dining restaurant whose patrons can move on to jazz after dinner without paying the cover charge.) Green Dolphin books jazz in all its permutations, from big band to Latin, with shows Tuesday through Saturday. 2200 N. Ashland Ave. (at Webster Ave.). © **773/395-0066.** www.jazzitup.com. Cover $10–$20. Subway/El: Brown Line to Armitage or Red Line to Fullerton, and then a 10-min. cab ride.

Green Mill ★ Finds   Green Mill, in the heart of Uptown, is "Old Chicago" down to its rafters. It became a popular watering hole during the 1920s and 1930s, when regulars included Al Capone, Sophie Tucker (the Last of the Red Hot Mamas), and Al Jolson, and today it retains its speakeasy flavor. On Sunday night, the Green Mill plays host to the **Uptown Poetry Slam,** when poets vie for the open mic to roast and ridicule each other's work. Most nights, however, jazz is on the menu, beginning around 9pm and winding down just before closing at 4am (5am Sat). Regular performers include vocalist Kurt Elling, who performs standards and some of his own songs with a quartet, and chanteuse Patricia Barber. (They're both worth seeing.) The Green Mill is a Chicago treasure and not to be missed. Get there early to claim one of the plush velvet booths. 4802 N. Broadway Ave. (at Lawrence Ave.). © **773/878-5552.** www.greenmilljazz.com. Cover $6–$15. Subway/El: Red Line to Lawrence.

Pops for Champagne (Finds) A civilized, elegant way to enjoy jazz, the Pops champagne bar is one of the prettiest rooms in the city, and its River North location makes it
a convenient walk from most downtown hotels. Live jazz—mostly small-combo music—
is presented Thursday through Saturday, starting at 9pm. While you're here, it's pretty
much required that you sample one of the club's 100 varieties of bubbly. 601 N. State St.
(at Ohio St.). ℭ **312/266-7677.** www.popsforchampagne.com. Cover $8–15. Subway/El: Red Line
to Grand.

BLUES

Blue Chicago Blue Chicago pays homage to female blues belters with a strong lineup
of the best women vocalists around. The 1940s-style brick-walled room, decorated with
original artwork of Chicago blues vignettes, is open Monday through Saturday, with
music beginning at 9pm. Admission allows you to club-hop between this venue and a
second location, open Tuesday through Sunday, at 536 N. Clark St. Next door, at 534
N. Clark St., is the Blue Chicago Store, which sells blues-related clothing, merchandise,
and artwork. 736 N. Clark St. (btw. Chicago Ave. and Superior St.). ℭ **312/642-6261.** www.
bluechicago.com. Cover $8–$10. Subway/El: Red or Brown line to Chicago.

B.L.U.E.S. On the Halsted strip, look for B.L.U.E.S.—the name says it all. This is a
small joint for the serious aficionado—if you've got claustrophobia, this isn't the place for
you. On the upside, the cozy space makes every performance personal; you won't miss a
single move of the musicians standing onstage only yards away. Shows start at 9:30pm
nightly. 2519 N. Halsted St. (btw. Wrightwood and Fullerton aves.). ℭ **773/528-1012.** www.
chicagobluesbar.com. Cover $5–$10. Subway/El: Red or Brown line to Fullerton.

Buddy Guy's Legends ★★ (Finds) A legend himself, gifted guitarist Buddy Guy
runs one of the most popular and comfortable clubs in town. Blues paraphernalia, from
a Koko Taylor dress to a Muddy Waters tour jacket, decorates the walls of this club near
the South Loop. Buddy himself plays a series of shows every January. (Reason enough to
brave Chicago in the dead of winter!). The kitchen serves good Louisiana-style soul food
and barbecue. 754 S. Wabash Ave. (btw. Balbo Dr. and Eighth St.). ℭ **312/427-0333.** www.buddy
guys.com. Cover $10–$15. Subway/El: Red Line to Harrison.

Kingston Mines ★ Chicago's premier blues bar, Kingston Mines, is where musicians
congregate after their own gigs to jam and socialize. Celebs have been known to drop by
when they're in town shooting movies, but most nights the crowd includes a big contingent of conventioneers looking for a rockin' night on the town. But don't worry about
the tourist factor—everyone's here to have a good time, and the energy is infectious. The
nightly show begins at 9:30pm, with bands on two stages, and goes until 4am (5am Sat).
The late-night kitchen serves up burgers and ribs. 2548 N. Halsted St. (btw. Wrightwood and
Fullerton aves.). ℭ **773/477-4646.** www.kingstonmines.com. Cover $10–$15. Subway/El: Red or
Brown line to Fullerton.

Rosa's Lounge ★ Rosa's is strictly a neighborhood hangout, but it has all the atmosphere required to fuel its heartfelt lamentations. Mama Rosa and her son, Tony Mangi-
ullo, run a homey, lovable spot that, despite its somewhat distant location, is decidedly
one of the best joints in town for spirited, authentic Chicago blues. (Because of its off-
the-beaten-track location, it attracts local fans rather than tourists.) Rosa's also sponsors
a blues cruise on Lake Michigan every summer. Shows start at 9:30pm Tuesday through
Saturday. 3420 W. Armitage Ave. (at Kimball Ave.). ℭ **773/342-0452.** www.rosaslounge.com.
Cover $5–$15. Subway/El: Blue Line to Logan Sq., and then a short cab ride.

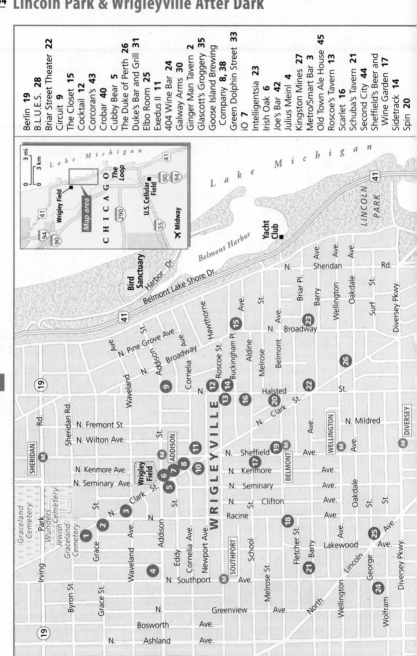

Berlin **19**
B.L.U.E.S. **28**
Briar Street Theater **22**
Circuit **9**
The Closet **15**
Cocktail **12**
Corcoran's **43**
Crobar **40**
Cubby Bear **5**
The Duke of Perth **26**
Duke's Bar and Grill **31**
Elbo Room **25**
Exedus II **11**
404 Wine Bar **24**
Galway Arms **30**
Ginger Man Tavern **2**
Glascott's Groggery **35**
Goose Island Brewing Company **8, 38**
Green Dolphin Street **33**
iO **7**
Intelligentsia **23**
Irish Oak **6**
Joe's Bar **42**
Julius Meinl **4**
Kingston Mines **27**
Metro/Smart Bar **3**
Old Town Ale House **45**
Roscoe's Tavern **13**
Scarlet **16**
Schuba's Tavern **21**
Second City **44**
Sheffield's Beer and Wine Garden **17**
Sidetrack **14**
Spin **20**

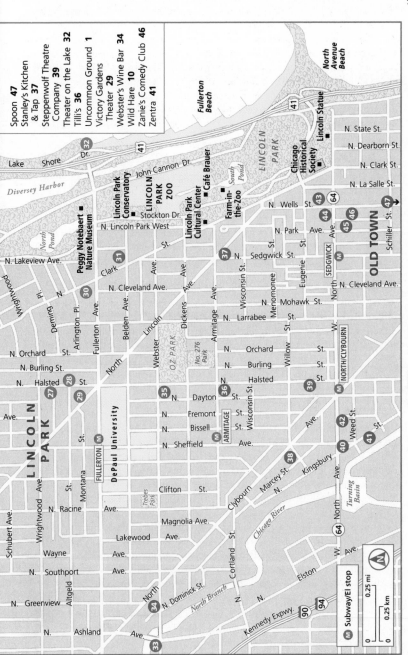

Spoon **47**
Stanley's Kitchen
& Tap **37**
Steppenwolf Theatre
Company **39**
Theater on the Lake **32**
Tilli's **36**
Uncommon Ground **1**
Victory Gardens
Theater **29**
Webster's Wine Bar **34**
Wild Hare **10**
Zanie's Comedy Club **46**
Zentra **41**

Lake Shore Dr.

Diversey Harbor

John Cannon Dr.

Café Brauer

Farm-in-
the-Zoo

South
Pond

LINCOLN PARK

Chicago
Historical
Society

Lincoln Statue

N. State St.

N. Dearborn St.

N. Clark St.

N. La Salle St.

N. Wells St.

N. Park Ave.

Lincoln Park
Conservatory

Stockton Dr.

N. Lincoln Park West

LINCOLN
PARK
ZOO

Lincoln Park
Cultural Center

Peggy Notebaert
Nature Museum

North
Pond

N. Lakeview Ave.

Clark St.

Ave.

Ave.

St.

N. Cleveland Ave.

Belden Ave.

Lincoln

Dickens

Ave.

Ave.

Armitage

N. Sedgwick St.

Wisconsin St.

St.

Eugenie

N. Menomonee St.

N. Mohawk St.

N. Larrabee St.

SEDGWICK

North

OLD TOWN

N. Cleveland Ave.

Schiller St.

Wrightwood

Pl.

N.

Deming

Arlington Pl.

Fullerton

Webster

OZ PARK

No. 276
Park

Ave.

N. Orchard St.

N. Burling St.

N. Halsted St.

LINCOLN
PARK

Ave.

St.

N.

DePaul University

FULLERTON

N. Dayton St.

N. Fremont St.

N. Bissell St.

N. Sheffield Ave.

ARMITAGE

Wisconsin St.

N. Orchard

N. Burling

N. Halsted

Willow St.

St.

St.

St.

NORTH/CLYBOURN

W.

Ave.

Weed St.

St.

Montana St.

Trebes
Park

N. Racine Ave.

Wrightwood Ave.

St.

Clifton St.

Magnolia Ave.

Lakewood Ave.

Wayne Ave.

N. Southport Ave.

N. Greenview

N. Ashland Ave.

N. Dominick St.

North Branch

North

Clybourn

Marcey St.

Kingsbury

N.

Chicago River

Cortland St.

Ave.

Ave.

Turning
Basin

W. North Ave.

64

Elston Ave.

Kennedy Expwy.

90

94

Schubert Ave.

Altgeld

N. Greenview

N. Ashland Ave.

M Subway/El stop

0   0.25 mi

0   0.25 km

Fullerton Beach

North
Avenue
Beach

LINCOLN PARK

CHICAGO AFTER DARK

10

THE MUSIC SCENE

Underground Wonder Bar   This intimate club on the Near North Side only gets better as the night wears on. (It's open until 4am Sun–Fri, until 5am Sat.) Although I've listed it under blues clubs, it's one of the most vibrant, eclectic live-music spots in town; you'll hear jazz trios, folk singers, and R&B vocalists playing the quirky, compact, and, yep, below-street-level room early in the evening. Things really heat up when co-owner Lonie Walker and her Big Bad Ass Company Band take the stage at 11pm on Friday and Saturday, playing a raucous blues-rock mix. Stick around until the wee hours, which is when the fun really begins—musicians stop by after gigs at other clubs to improvise a final set. The kitchen serves Tex-Mex and other chow late into the night. 10 E. Walton St. (at State St.). ✆ 312/266-7761. www.underground wonderbar.com. Cover $8–$15. Subway/El: Red Line to Chicago.

ROCK (BASICALLY)

In the early 1990s, Chicago's burgeoning alternative rock scene produced such national names as the Smashing Pumpkins, Liz Phair, Veruca Salt, Urge Overkill, and Material Issue. Although the city's moment of pop hipness quickly faded (as did most of the aforementioned artists), the live music scene has continued to thrive. Although local groups still occasionally hit it big (Wilco, Fall Out Boy), most Chicago bands concentrate on keeping it real, happy to perform at small local clubs and not obsessing (at least openly) about getting a record contract. The city is also a regular stop for touring bands, from big stadium acts to smaller up-and-coming groups. Scan the *Reader, New City,* or *Time Out Chicago* to see who's playing where.

The biggest rock acts tend to play at the local indoor stadiums: The **United Center** (✆ 312/455-4500; www.unitedcenter.com), home of the Bulls and Blackhawks, and **Allstate Arena** (✆ 847/635-6601; www.allstatearena.com), in Rosemont near O'Hare Airport. These venues are about what you expect: The overpriced seats nearest the stage are fine, but you'd better bring binoculars if you're stuck in the more affordable upper decks. During the summer, you'll also find the big names at the outdoor **First Midwest Bank Amphitheatre** (✆ 708/614-1616; www.livenation.com/venue/getVenue/venueId/785), inconveniently located in the suburb of Tinley Park, about an hour outside the city, and cursed with pretty bad acoustics.

The good news: You can catch mid-level rock acts at local venues with a lot more character. The **Riviera Theatre,** 4746 N. Racine Ave. (✆ 773/275-6800), is a relic of the Uptown neighborhood's swinging days in the 1920s, '30s, and '40s. A former movie palace, it retains the original ornate ceiling, balcony, and lighting fixtures, but it has definitely gotten grimy with age. (Head upstairs to the balcony seats if you'd rather avoid the crowd that rushes toward the stage during shows.) The **Aragon Ballroom,** a few blocks away at 1106 W. Lawrence Ave. (✆ 773/561-9500; www.aragon.com; subway/El: Red Line to Lawrence), was once an elegant big-band dance hall; the worn Moorish-castle decor and twinkling-star ceiling now give the place a seedy charm. A former vaudeville house is now the **Vic Theatre,** 3145 N. Sheffield Ave. (✆ 773/472-0366; www.victheatre.com; subway/El: Red or Brown line to Fullerton), a midsize venue that features up-and-coming acts. (Get there early to snag one of the lower balcony rows.)

More sedate audiences love the **Park West,** 322 W. Armitage Ave. (✆ 773/929-5959; www.parkwestchicago.com; subway/El: Brown Line to Armitage, or bus no. 22 [Clark St.]), both for its excellent sound system and its cabaret-style seating (no mosh pit here). For tickets to most shows at all these venues, you're stuck going through the service-fee-grabbing **Ticketmaster** (✆ 312/559-1212).

Here are some bars and clubs that book live music most nights of the week.

Abbey Pub   Irish brogues abound at this barnlike gathering place for indie rock, folk
pop, and other hard-to-classify acts. It's tucked away in a residential neighborhood—far
from the usual tourist haunts—so you're pretty much guaranteed to be surrounded by
locals. Besides Guinness and other Emerald Isle beers on tap, there's a full menu. Traditional Irish music sessions are held Sunday night. 3420 W. Grace St. (at Elston Ave.). ✆ 773/
478-4408. www.abbeypub.com. Cover $7–$20. Subway/El: Brown Line to Irving Park, and then
a 10-min. cab ride.

Cubby Bear   Across from Wrigley Field, Cubby Bear is a showcase for new rock bands
and an occasional offbeat act. (One recent example: The all-female cover band Lez Zeppelin.) It draws in a scrub-faced postcollegiate crowd and gets especially packed after
Cubs games during the summer. Concerts are staged on weekends and many Thursday
nights. Wednesday night is rock band karaoke, when you can strut your stuff onstage,
backed by live musicians. Otherwise, there are always billiards, darts, and other distrac-
tions. 1059 W. Addison St. (at Clark St.). ✆ 773/327-1662. www.cubbybear.com. Cover $5–$10
on band nights, more for special shows. Subway/El: Red Line to Addison.

Double Door (Finds)   This club has capitalized on the Wicker Park/Bucktown neighborhood's ascendance as a breeding ground for rock and alternative music. Owned by the
proprietors of Metro (see below), the club has some of the better acoustics and sightlines
in the city and attracts buzz bands and unknowns to its stage. When you need to escape
the noise, there's a lounge-type area with pool tables in the basement. 1572 N. Milwaukee
Ave. (at North Ave.). ✆ 773/489-3160. www.doubledoor.com. Tickets $5–$20. Subway/El: Blue
Line to Damen.

Elbo Room (Value)   Upstairs, Elbo Room looks like any other low-key Lincoln Park
watering hole, but in the basement you'll find delightfully schizophrenic live music:
rockabilly, hip-hop, soul, funk, and more. The subterranean setting is cozy and brings
the bands up close and personal, but when the place gets packed, you might not see
much of the onstage action. 2871 N. Lincoln Ave. (at George St.). ✆ 773/549-5549. www.elbo
roomchicago.com. Cover $5–$10. Subway/El: Brown Line to Diversey.

The Empty Bottle   This alternative-rock club in the Ukrainian Village neighborhood
is a haven for young arty scenesters drawn here for camaraderie, obscure bands, and
cheap beer. Offerings are diverse, with experimental jazz on Wednesday, and other nights
given over to a DJ's underground improvisations. 1035 N. Western Ave. (btw. Division St.
and Augusta Blvd.). ✆ 773/276-3600. www.emptybottle.com. Cover $8–$20. Subway/El: Blue
Line to Western, and then bus 49.

House of Blues   The largest location in a national chain of music venues, the House
of Blues could more appropriately be called the House of Pop. Although it's decorated
with Mississippi Delta folk art, the bands that play here tend to be rock groups, '80s
novelty acts, and the occasional hip-hop or reggae performer. This is a great place to see
a show—concerts are in a theater that re-creates a gilded European opera house (minus
the seats), and the stage views are pretty good no matter where you stand. A restaurant
also serves lunch and dinner with hometown blues accompaniment. The popular **Sunday gospel brunch,** offering a Southern-style buffet, brings a different Chicago gospel
choir to the stage each week; the three weekly "services" often sell out, so get tickets in
advance. 329 N. Dearborn St. (at Kinzie St.). ✆ 312/923-2000 for general information, or
312/923-2020 for concert information. www.hob.com. Tickets usually $15–$45. Subway/El:
Red Line to Grand.

Joe's Bar   Part sports bar, part music venue, Joe's Bar is a vast, warehouse-size space with the spirit of a quirky neighborhood tavern. There's live music Fridays and Saturdays, with local and national bands playing everything from rock to reggae. Gimmicks abound, such as the popular summer "Doggy Happy Hour" on the patio. Joe's can get crowded, but the scenery—lots of attractive people in their 20s—makes up for it. *Another bonus:* Because there are so many bar areas, you won't have to wait long to get a drink. 940 W. Weed St. (at North Ave.). ✆ 312/337-3486. www.joesbar.com. Live music cover $3–$20. Subway/El: Red Line to North/Clybourn.

Martyrs' (Finds)   Dedicated to the memories of such late great rock and blues performers as Jimi Hendrix and Janis Joplin (who are immortalized on the mural facing the stage), Martyrs' presents a variety of local bands and the occasional performance by national touring acts. On the first Wednesday of the month, catch the popular Tributasaurus, a note-perfect rock tribute band that "becomes" a different rock legend every month. The low tables, high ceiling, and huge windows make Martyrs' one of the best places to catch a rock-'n'-roll show. 3855 N. Lincoln Ave. (btw. Berenice Ave. and Irving Park Rd.). ✆ 773/404-9494. www.martyrslive.com. Cover $5–$15. Subway/El: Brown Line to Addison.

Metro ★   Metro is located in an old auditorium and is Chicago's premier venue for live alternative and rock acts on the verge of breaking into the big time. There's not much in the way of atmosphere—it's basically a big black room with a stage—but the place has an impressive history. Everybody who is anybody played here when they were starting out, including REM, Pearl Jam, and local heroes the Smashing Pumpkins. Newer "alternative" bands that are getting attention from MTV and radio stations show up at Metro eventually. The subterranean Smart Bar—at the same location—is a dance club open 7 nights a week. (You can get in free if you've seen a concert that night at Metro.) Some shows are all-ages, but most require concertgoers to be at least 21. Tickets are sold in person through the adjoining **Metro Store** (sans service charges), or by phone through Ticketmaster. 3730 N. Clark St. (at Racine Ave.). ✆ 773/549-0203 or 312/559-1212 for Ticketmaster orders. www.metrochicago.com. Tickets $8–$25. Subway/El: Red Line to Sheridan.

Phyllis' Musical Inn   Typical of the borderline dive-y neighborhood bars that used to be scattered around Wicker Park—before rampant gentrification brought hip lounges and overpriced martinis—Phyllis' is a small, generally uncrowded hangout that books live rock music (sometimes jazz and blues) on weekends. Depending on the night, you could be surrounded by a crowd of hipsters, or find yourself chatting with a far-from-busy bartender. Either way, Phyllis' will whisk you back to the days of blue-collar Chicago. 1800 W. Division St. (at Wood St.). ✆ 773/486-9862. Cover $3–$5. Subway/El: Blue Line to Division.

COUNTRY, FOLK & ETHNIC MUSIC

Exedus II   Like its flashier neighbor, the Wild Hare (see below), Exedus offers shows Thursday through Saturday; the specialty here is Jamaican dancehall, performed live or by DJs. Although this small storefront tavern gets crowded, the music's good and the attitude of the international crowd is laid-back. In general, it's more authentic than the competition, which tends to draw more of the frat-party element. 3477 N. Clark St. (btw. Newport Ave. and Roscoe St.). ✆ 773/348-3998. www.exeduslounge.com. Cover usually under $10. Subway/El: Red Line to Addison.

The Hideout (Value)   This friendly tavern's OLD STYLE BEER sign shines like a beacon, guiding roots-music fans through the grimy industrial neighborhood that surrounds it.

The owners' beer-can collection and some "celebrity" memorabilia are on display in the front room. In back, local musicians play country, rock, and bluesy tunes on a small stage backed by an impressive stuffed sailfish. It's no-frills, all right, but the Hideout also books some of the best lineups of folk and "alt country" bands in the city, including Jeff Tweedy (of Wilco), Kelly Hogan, and the New Duncan Imperials. 1354 W. Wabansia Ave. (btw. Elston Ave. and Throop St.). © 773/227-4433. www.hideoutchicago.com. Cover usually $5–$10. Subway/El: Blue Line to Damen.

Old Town School of Folk Music ★ (Finds)   Country, folk, bluegrass, Latin, Celtic— the Old Town School of Folk Music covers a spectrum of indigenous musical forms. Best known as a training center offering a slate of music classes, the school also plays host to everyone from the legendary Pete Seeger to bluegrass phenom Alison Krauss. The school's home, in a former 1930s library, is the world's largest facility dedicated to the preservation and presentation of traditional and contemporary folk music. The Old Town School also houses an art gallery showcasing exhibitions of works by local, national, and international artists; a music store offering an exquisite selection of instruments, sheet music, and hard-to-find recordings; and a cafe. In midsummer it sponsors the popular Folk and Roots outdoor music festival. The school maintains another retail store and offers children's classes at its first location, 909 W. Armitage Ave. 4544 N. Lincoln Ave. (btw. Wilson and Montrose aves.). © 773/728-6000. www.oldtownschool.org. Tickets $10–$25. Subway/El: Brown Line to Western.

Schubas Tavern (Finds)   Country and folk singer-songwriters have found a home in this divine little concert hall in a former Schlitz tavern. It's a friendly and intimate place, best experienced from one of the wooden booths ringing the room. There's music 7 nights a week, and Schubas occasionally books big-name performers such as John Hiatt and Train. You'll also find a bar up front and an attached restaurant, Harmony Grill, where you can grab a pretty good burger and fries after the show. 3159 N. Southport Ave. (at Belmont Ave.). © 773/525-2508. www.schubas.com. Tickets $10–$25. Subway/El: Red or Brown line to Belmont.

Wild Hare   Number one on Chicago's reggae charts is the Wild Hare, in the shadow of Wrigley Field. After 20 years in business (an eternity in the nightclub world), this spot has kept up with the times by adding state-of-the-art sound and video systems and booking dancehall and occasional hip-hop artists. Owner Zeleke Gessesse, who has toured with Ziggy Marley and the Melody Makers, books top acts such as Burning Spear and Yellow Man; he also nurtures local talent. With a Red Stripe in hand, you might even forget that it's 20 degrees outside. 3530 N. Clark St. (btw. Addison and Roscoe sts.). © 773/327-4273. www.wildharemusic.com. Cover $5–$12. Subway/El: Red Line to Addison.

CABARETS & PIANO BARS

The Baton Show Lounge   Catch the city's long-running revue of female impersonators at this River North lounge, which has been showcasing fabulous "gals" in outrageous getups for 40 years. Shows are Wednesday through Sunday at 8:30 and 10:30pm, and 12:30am. This is a very popular spot for bachelorette outings, so be prepared for groups of rowdy women. 436 N. Clark St. (btw. Hubbard and Illinois sts.). © 312/644-5269. www.thebatonshowlounge.com. Cover $10–$14 plus 2-drink minimum. Subway/El: Red Line to Grand.

Coq d'Or   Whether you're huddled close around the piano or hanging back on the red Naugahyde banquettes, this old-time, clubby haunt in The Drake Hotel offers an intimate evening of song stylings. (It's one of the few downtown hotel lounges that still offers live music.) The Coq d'Or claims to be the second bar in Chicago to serve drinks after the repeal of Prohibition in 1933—and the place hasn't changed much since then. In The Drake Hotel, 140 E. Walton St. (at Michigan Ave.). ✆ 312/787-2200. Subway/El: Red Line to Chicago/State.

Davenport's Piano Bar & Cabaret (Finds)   The youthful hipster haunt of Wicker Park isn't the first place you'd expect to find a tried-and-true piano bar and cabaret venue, but Davenport's does its best to revive a fading art form. Owner Bill Davenport and his partners transformed a single-story storefront into an intimate, chic gem that provides a much-needed showcase for Chicago-bred talent, with a sprinkling of visiting performers from New York and L.A. The piano bar in front is flashier than the subdued cabaret in back, featuring a singing waitstaff, blue velvet banquettes, funky lighting fixtures, and a hand-painted mural-topped bar. The cabaret's sound equipment is first-rate. 1383 N. Milwaukee Ave. (just south of North Ave.). ✆ 773/278-1830. www.davenportspianobar.com. Cover $10–$20. Subway/El: Blue Line to Damen.

Jilly's   Named for Frank Sinatra's former manager, Jilly's has a retro feel that's timeless, not dated. Music and a lively buzz from the patrons spill into the street during warm weather, and pianists and trios play the dark room decorated with photos of the Rat Pack, Steve and Eydie, and the like. The crowd includes everyone from wealthy Gold Coast residents to young singles catching up after work. 1007 N. Rush St. (at Oak St.). ✆ 312/664-1001. www.jillyschicago.com. Subway/El: Red Line to Chicago.

Redhead Piano Bar   The Redhead attracts a well-heeled, sharp-dressed Gold Coast clientele with its classic, old-time lounge vibe. Yesteryear memorabilia—movie-star glamour shots, playbills, and old sheet music—covers the walls, and the drink list focuses on single-malt scotch and other premium liquors rather than flavored martinis. (The crowd teeming around the piano is a throwback as well.) Suggested attire is "business casual," so don't show up wearing shorts and gym shoes. 16 W. Ontario St. ✆ 312/640-1000. www.redheadpianobar.com. Subway/El: Red Line to Grand.

Zebra Lounge (Finds)   The most quirky piano bar in town, Zebra Lounge has a loyal following despite (or maybe because of) the campy decor. Just as you would expect, black-and-white stripes are the unifying element at this dark, shoebox-size Gold Coast spot, furnished with black vinyl booths, a small mirrored bar, and zebra kitsch galore. Bar lore has it that the Zebra Lounge opened December 5, 1933—the day Prohibition ended. Since then, it has passed through numerous owners, but the name, a tribute to a long-forgotten tavern in New York, has remained. For the past quarter-century, it has been a raucous piano bar, attracting a multigenerational crowd of regulars. The place is relatively mellow early in the evening, though it can get packed late into the night on weekends. 1220 N. State Pkwy. (btw. Division and Goethe sts.). ✆ 312/642-5140. Subway/El: Red Line to Clark/Division.

4 THE CLUB SCENE

Chicago is the hallowed ground where house music was hatched in the 1980s, so it's no surprise to find that it's also home to several vast, industrial-style dance clubs with pounding music and a mostly under-30 crowd. Some spots specialize in a single type of music, while others offer an ever-changing mix of rhythms and beats that follow the latest DJ-driven trend. Many clubs attract a different clientele on each day of the week

(Sunday night, for example, is gay-friendly at many of the clubs listed below), so check **271** the club's website to get an idea of each night's vibe. Given the fickle nature of clubgoers, some places listed below might have disappeared by the time you read this, but there is an impressive list of longtime survivors—clubs that have lasted more than a decade but continue to draw crowds.

Berlin One of the more enduring dance floors in Chicago, Berlin is primarily gay during the week but draws dance hounds of all stripes on weekends and for special theme nights (disco the last Wednesday of every month, Prince music the last Sunday of the month). It has a reputation for outrageousness and creativity, making it prime ground for people-watching. The space isn't much—basically a square room with a bar along one side—but the no-frills dance floor is packed late into the evening. The owners are no dummies: The cover charge applies only on Friday and Saturday after midnight, which is about an hour earlier than you ought to show up. (For more, see "The Gay & Lesbian Scene," p. 285.) 954 W. Belmont Ave. (at Sheffield Ave.). ✆ 773/348-4975. www.berlinchicago. com. Cover $3–$5. Subway/El: Red or Brown line to Belmont.

Crobar A veteran of Chicago's late-night scene, Crobar has managed to stay hip since 1991; it's even expanded to locations in New York City and Miami. The warehouse-gone-glam look and thumping sound system give the space a quintessential dance-club feel, and the booth-lined balcony overlooking the huge dance floor is a good spot for people-watching. If you're especially gorgeous—or free-spending—you might make it into the glass-encased VIP room. The soundtrack is mostly hip-hop and house, and the weekend DJs have a strong local following, so you might be fighting for prime dance space. The crowd is fairly mixed racially and age-wise and mostly attitude-free. 1543 N. Kingsbury St. (at North Ave.). ✆ 312/266-1900. www.crobar.com. Cover $20 on weekends. Subway/El: Red Line to North/Clybourn.

Funky Buddha Lounge A bit off the beaten path, west of the River North gallery district, this club blends in with its industrial surroundings—even the whimsical Buddha sculpture on the heavy steel front door is a rusted husk. Inside is a different scene altogether: Low red lighting, seductive dens with black-leather and faux leopard-skin sofas, lots of candles, and antique light fixtures salvaged from an old church. The DJs are among the best in the city, flooding the nice-size dance floor with everything from hip-hop, bhangra, and funk to African, soul, and underground house. The crowd is just as diverse as the music—everything from yuppies and after-dinner hipsters to die-hard clubhoppers and barely legal wannabes. Hugely popular Thursday nights pack in the young, mostly white club kids; Friday and Saturday feature a cool, urban crowd decked out in funky gear. The bus runs to this area, but take a cab at night. 728 W. Grand Ave. ✆ 312/666-1695. www.funkybuddha.com. Cover $10–$30. Bus: 65 (Grand Ave.).

Le Passage The Gold Coast's swankiest nightclub fits all the prerequisites for chic exclusivity, starting with the semi-hidden entrance at the end of a narrow (but well-lit) alleyway just steps from Oak Street's Prada and Barneys New York stores. You descend a long flight of stairs into a dimly lit, sultry lounge; to gain access, you must pass muster with the gatekeepers staffing the velvet rope. The beautiful, the rich, and the designer-suited come here for the front room's loungy aesthetic and the accessible soundtrack of hip-hop and dance mash-ups in the Discotheque. If you'd rather focus on cocktails and conversation, head for the elegant Dining Room, with its menu of upscale small plates and pricey custom drinks. 1 Oak Place (btw. Rush and State sts). ✆ 312/255-0022. www.lepassage. tv. Cover $20. Subway/El: Red Line to Chicago.

Rednofive Taking its name from the ubiquitous dye used in food products, Rednofive is no fake, thanks to its sleek design and tight lineup of local DJs spinning a sonic deluge of progressive and abstract house music, hip-hop, and pop, sometimes accompanied by a percussionist on drums. The glittering space—with antique crystal chandeliers and red velvet banquettes—attracts a well-dressed crowd; you probably won't make it past the doorman in shorts and sneakers. That said, the club prides itself on keeping the crowd diverse, so you don't have to be draped in the latest designer label to get inside. The bi-level space offers booth seating—with an elevated VIP area—but devoted dance fans will throw down just about anywhere. 440 N. Halsted St. (at Hubbard St.). (℃) **312/733-6699**. www.rednofive.com. Cover $10–$20. Subway/El: Green Line to Clinton.

Smart Bar A long-established name on the dance circuit, Smart Bar, tucked in the basement below the rock club Metro (p. 268), spins the latest musical forms from underground house and punk to ethereal and gothic. The scene starts late, and the dancing denizens vary widely depending on which bands are playing upstairs (concertgoers get free admission to the Smart Bar). The no-frills club, which has stayed in business (amazingly) since 1982, attracts a diverse and edgy crowd, and that's part of the appeal. This is an established Chicago spot where clubbers can come as they are, and you'll see a range of fashion. Smart Bar stays open until 5am on weekends. No cover before 11pm during the week. 3730 N. Clark St. (at Racine Ave.). (℃) **773/549-4140**. www.smartbarchicago.com. Cover $10–$15 (free with show at Metro). Subway/El: Red Line to Addison.

Sonothèque A lounge/club hybrid, Sonothèque is a bright, minimalist-chic alternative to the standard industrial-style megaclub. With white walls and banquettes, dark wood floors and neon-blue lighting, it looks like a hipster art gallery that just happens to have a killer sound system. The soundtrack is one of the most eclectic in the city—everything from African beats to jazz-soul to '80s new wave—and DJs are showcased doing their thing from a glass-enclosed booth in the middle of the dance floor. That dance floor, unfortunately, is narrow and crowded, so don't come here expecting to throw down your best moves. 1444 W. Chicago Ave. (two blocks east of Milwaukee Ave.). (℃) **312/226-7600**. www.sonotheque.net. Cover $5–$15. Subway/El: Blue Line to Division.

Sound-Bar DJs are the stars at this multilevel, high-tech dance club, which prides itself on booking top international nightlife names. The look is industrial chic, with silver banquettes, frosted-glass walls, and stainless-steel accents; holographic images and laser lights flash across the massive central dance floor. The crowd tends to be young and club-savvy on weeknights, with a little more diversity on weekends. (Dress well if you want to make it past the bouncers.) While there's a fair amount of posing, overall this crowd comes for the music, which includes electronic dance, trance, and house. Saturday night resident DJ John Curley is a longtime local club fixture with an encyclopedic house repertoire; if you want a primer on Chicago house, this is a good place to start. 226 W. Ontario St. (at Franklin St.). (℃) **312/787-4480**. www.sound-bar.com. Cover $10–$20. Subway/El: Red Line to Grand, or Brown Line to Merchandise Mart.

Transit Carved out of a warehouse space beneath the elevated train tracks just west of the hip Randolph Street restaurant row, Transit is a no-nonsense dance club that doesn't trick itself out with a wacky theme. Its 10,000 square feet feature a sleek, boldly colored geometric interior with modern, minimalist furniture. The postindustrial metal staircases surrounding the large dance-floor area lead to a VIP room, the tiny Light Bar, and the Mezzanine, where DJs spin Latin dance tunes on Saturday nights. The bone-rattling, state-of-the-art sound system and DJs—spinning progressive dance, remixed hip-hop,

Tips   Late-Night Bites

Chicago's not much of a late-night dining town; most restaurants shut down by 10 or 11pm, leaving night owls with the munchies out of luck. But if you know where to go, you can still get a decent meal past midnight. Here are a few spots that serve real food until real late:

In the Loop, your best—and practically only—choice is **Miller's Pub** (p.274), 134 S. Wabash Ave. (© **312/645-5377**), which offers hearty American comfort food until 2am daily. Many late-night visitors to this historic watering hole and restaurant are out-of-towners staying at neighboring hotels.

In River North, food is available until 4am at **Bar Louie** (p. 276), 226 W. Chicago Ave. (© **312/337-3313**). The menu is a step above mozzarella sticks and other standard bar food: Focaccia sandwiches, vegetarian wraps, and salads are among the highlights.

After a night out, Wicker Park and Bucktown residents stop by **Northside Café** (p. 146), 1635 N. Damen Ave. (© **773/384-3555**), for sandwiches and salads served until 2am (3am Sat). In nice weather, the front patio is the place to be for prime people-watching.

The bright, welcoming atmosphere at **Clarke's Pancake House,** 2441 N. Lincoln Ave. (© **773/472-3505**), is a dose of fresh air after an evening spent in dark Lincoln Park bars. Yes, there are pancakes on the menu, as well as plenty of other creative breakfast choices, including mixed skillets of veggies, meat, and potatoes. If you need to satisfy a *really* late-night craving, Clarke's is open 24 hours.

When the Lincoln Park bars shut down at 2am, the action moves to the **Wieners Circle,** 2622 N. Clark St. (© **773/477-7444**). This hot-dog stand is strictly no-frills: You shout your order across the drunken crowd, and the only spots to sit are a few picnic tables out front. Open until 4am during the week and 6am on weekends, the Wieners Circle is the center of predawn life in Lincoln Park—and I know people who swear that the greasy cheese-topped fries are the perfect hangover prevention.

and R&B—don't disappoint the die-hard dance fans. Come wearing your best club attire. 1431 W. Lake St. © **312/491-8600.** www.transitnightclubchicago.com. Cover $15–$20. Subway/El: Green Line to Ashland.

Vision   The spot now known as Vision has been through several name and decor changes, but it keeps plugging away, taking advantage of a tourist-friendly location not far from Michigan Avenue. Stretching over four levels, Vision caters to the current club trend of providing different environments in different spaces. The dance floor—thumping with house, trance, progressive, and hip-hop—fills the first floor; upper floors offer plenty of nooks and crannies for groups to sit and chat. Vision prides itself on offering some of the best turntable talent in the city—the club's owners even bring in internationally known DJs. 640 N. Dearborn St. (at Ontario St.). © **312/266-2114.** www.visionnightclub.com. Cover $10–$25. Subway/El: Red Line to Grand/State.

Zentra Club-hoppers often make Middle Eastern and Moroccan-flavored Zentra, which stays open into the wee hours, their last stop of the night. A large four-room space, Zentra goes for an East meets West vibe, with exotic Moroccan textiles, thick drapes, Indian silks, red lanterns, and funky chrome fixtures. There are two floors, each catering to different sounds of resident and guest DJs. Upstairs entertains those who want to move to progressive dance and techno sounds, while downstairs has DJs spinning mostly house and hip-hop. Zentra attracts a mix of patrons who come to soak in the exotic vibes, do some people-watching, and simply have fun dancing. In the summer, an outdoor deck puts a funky spin on the beer-garden concept. There is no dress code, but feel free to dress up—you'll see a bit of everything here. 923 W. Weed St. (just south of North Ave. at Clybourn Ave.). ⓒ 312/787-0400. www.zentranightclub.com. Cover $15–$20. Subway/El: Red Line to North/Clybourn.

5 THE BAR & CAFE SCENE

If you want to soak up the atmosphere of a neighborhood tavern or sports bar, it's best to venture beyond downtown into the surrounding neighborhoods. Lincoln Park, Wrigleyville, and Bucktown/Wicker Park have well-established nightlife zones that abound with bright, upscale neighborhood bars. You'll also find numerous dives and no-frills "corner taps" in the blue-collar neighborhoods.

As for hotel nightlife, virtually every hotel in Chicago has some kind of bar, which range from undistinguished scatterings of tables and chairs in the lobby to trendy club-like hotspots. If you're looking for an old-school, cocktail-lounge vibe, the piano bar at The Drake Hotel, Coq d'Or (p. 79, earlier), is a standout. Some of the other top hotel lounges are highlighted in the box "Hotel Hopping," p. 275.

BARS
The Loop & Vicinity

Lumen The gimmick at this newer spot, which occupies a former meat-packing facility in the West Loop, is light, particularly the overhead LED display, which changes color throughout the night. The 5,000-square-foot space features concrete, stainless steel, and bamboo in its design, along with the aforementioned light spectacle, which is coordinated with its powerful sound system. There's no VIP list, which gives it an everyman kind of feel, and means minimal line-waiting out front. 839 W. Fulton Market, at Halsted St. ⓒ 312/733-2222. www.lumen-chicago.com. Subway/El: Green Line to Clinton.

Miller's Pub ★ A true Loop landmark, Miller's has been serving up after-work cocktails to downtown office workers since 1935; it's one of the few places in the area that offers bar service until the early morning hours. There's also a full dinner menu. Autographed photos of movie stars and sports figures cover the walls; while some might be unrecognizable to younger patrons, they testify to the pub's long-standing tradition of friendly hospitality. 134 S. Wabash Ave. (btw. Jackson Blvd. and Adams St.). ⓒ 312/645-5377. www.millerspub.com. Subway/El: Red Line to Jackson.

Monk's Pub (Finds) A no-nonsense, peanut-shells-on-the-floor hangout for downtown workers, this is the kind of joint you'd walk by without even knowing it's there. But once inside, you'll discover a one-of-a-kind, German–Old English hodgepodge of a place, where shelves stocked with vintage books line one wall and wooden barrels are tucked in the

(Finds) Hotel Hopping

Forget the stereotypical bland hotel bar filled with drunken conventioneers. In downtown Chicago, some of the most distinctive watering holes are in hotel lobbies. In the Loop, the coolest happy-hour spot is **Encore** in the Hotel Allegro, 171 W. Randolph St. (© **312/236-0123**), with a black-and-white color scheme and urban lounge feel; for late-night drinks, head to **Base,** the bar in the Hard Rock Hotel, 230 N. Michigan Ave. (© **312/345-1000**). The look is sleek—lots of black and gray—and the music (live acts or a DJ) is always good. If you prefer to stick to tradition, **Kitty O'Shea's,** 720 S. Michigan Ave. (© **312/294-6860**), is an authentically appointed Irish pub inside the Hilton Chicago—a genuine Irish bartender will even pour your Guinness. Further north, in the blocks surrounding the Magnificent Mile, you'll find style-conscious spots such as **Le Bar,** in the Sofitel Chicago Water Tower, 20 E. Chestnut St. (© **312/324-4000**), a popular after-work hangout with a low-lit, intimate vibe. At **Whiskey Sky,** on the top floor of the W. Chicago Lakeshore hotel, 644 N. Lakeshore Dr. (© **312/943-9200**), there's not much seating and the decor is minimal, but the views—of both the surrounding skyline and the gorgeous staff—are terrific. **Vertigo Sky Lounge,** atop the Dana Hotel and Spa, 660 N. State St. (© **312/202-6060**), is a dark, clublike space with live DJs, but expansive floor-to-ceiling windows make you feel like you're floating amid the high-rises. An added bonus is the outdoor deck, a great spot to take in the views when the weather's nice.

rafters overhead. In business since 1969, Monk's has a decent lineup of beer on tap, as well as a full lunch and dinner menu. (A burger is your best bet—they've got more than 20 varieties.) 205 W. Lake St. (btw. Randolph St. and the Chicago River). © 312/357-6665. www.mmonks.com. Subway/El: Brown Line to Clark/Lake.

The Tasting Room Step into this sophisticated wine bar, with its exposed-brick walls, high ceilings, and contemporary, stainless-steel accents, and you'll feel like you've walked into a stylish friend's downtown loft. (Adding to the insider-y feeling is the remote far West Loop location, where few other tourists venture.) Located upstairs from Randolph Wine Cellars, a well-stocked wine shop, the Tasting Room caters to wine lovers with a variety of themed flights, as well as cheese and charcuterie plates. But even better than the vintages are the views, thanks to the large windows that look out over the Loop. 1415 W. Randolph St., at Loomis St. © 312/942-1313. Subway/El: Green Line to Ashland, but I'd recommend a cab at night.

Near the Magnificent Mile

Billy Goat Tavern (Value) Hidden below the Wrigley Building is this storied Chicago hole-in-the-wall, a longtime hangout for newspaper reporters over the years, evidenced by the yellowed clippings and memorabilia papering the walls. The "cheezeborger, cheezeborger" served at the grill inspired the famous *Saturday Night Live* sketch. Despite all the press, the Goat has endured the hype without sacrificing a thing (including its vintage decor, which pretty much epitomizes the term "dive bar"). 430 N. Michigan Ave. © 312/222-1525. www.billygoattavern.com. Subway/El: Red Line to Grand/State.

Elm Street Liquors   In a neighborhood often teeming with tourists, this lounge for locals exudes an urban but laid-back style with its anything-goes attitude. Dressing to impress here means an old-school T-shirt and Chuck Taylors (leave the striped button-down at home, boys). The music is familiar, and the drinks are forward-thinking, boasting champagne cocktails rather than the ubiquitous martinis found at every other nightspot in Chicago. I especially like that you don't have to pay a cover charge to enjoy the party. 12 W. Elm St. (at State St.). ✆ **312/337-3200**. www.elmstreetliquors.com. Subway/El: Red Line to Clark/Division.

Signature Lounge   For the price of a trip to the John Hancock tower observatory (two floors below), you can drink in the view and a cocktail at this lofty lounge. Yes, the drinks may be somewhat overpriced and you'll probably be surrounded by other tourists, but the views are fabulous (especially at sunset), making this an only-in-Chicago experience. You can also order from a limited menu of appetizers and desserts. This makes an especially appealing after-dinner stop; it's open until 1am Sunday through Thursday and until 2am on the weekends. 96th floor, John Hancock Center, 875 N. Michigan Ave. ✆ **312/787-7230**. www.signatureroom.com. Subway/El: Red Line to Chicago.

River North & Vicinity

Bar Louie   A slightly more upscale take on the neighborhood-bar concept, Bar Louie has built its reputation on better-than-average bar food and a creative selection of beers and cocktails. (The concept was so successful here that it's since expanded to cities across the country.) Professionals gather here after work; their restaurant and club equivalents stop by between 1 and 3am. Bar Louie isn't doing anything revolutionary, but its friendly service and approachable atmosphere make it a popular spot for locals who want a casual night out. Other downtown locations include one in the Printer's Row neighborhood of the South Loop (47 W. Polk St.; ✆ **312/347-0000**); the West Loop (741 W. Randolph St.; ✆ **312/474-0700**); and Wrigleyville (3545 N. Clark St.; ✆ **773/296-2500**). 226 W. Chicago Ave. (btw. Franklin and Wells sts.). ✆ **312/337-3313**. www.restaurants-america.com/barlouie. Subway/El: Red or Brown line to Chicago.

Brehon Pub   Big front windows, a high tin ceiling, and a great antique back bar lend charm to this little neighborhood bar in (often) tourist-packed River North. Brehon regulars hang out weeknights after work and even at lunchtime, when the tavern serves sandwiches and soup. In the 1970s, the *Sun-Times* newspaper set up this spot as a phony bar (appropriately named the Mirage) and used it in a sting operation to expose city corruption. 731 N. Wells St. (at Superior St.). ✆ **312/642-1071**. www.brehonpub.com. Subway/El: Red or Brown line to Chicago.

Butterfly Social Club   At last, a lounge that Al Gore can appreciate. This eco-chic sister property to the Funky Buddha nightclub (p. 271, earlier) incorporates recycled and natural materials into its design, such as "trees" made from mud, sand, clay, and straw. Sip your drink (made with organic juice, of course) and curl up in one of the tree house-like nooks, or groove to the upbeat world music thumping through speakers made of recycled wood. 722 W. Grand Ave. (btw. Union Ave. and Halsted St.). ✆ **312/666-1695**. www.funkybuddha.com. Bus: 65 (Grand Ave.).

Celtic Crossings   Drop in on a Sunday evening for the bar's weekly traditional Irish jam session, and you're sure to hear an authentic brogue. There's no television in this quaint pub, just a decent jukebox stocked with Irish and American favorites, delicious pints of Guinness (the best in Chicago, claim many Irish expats), and a cozy fireplace.

Clark Street Ale House (Finds)   A handsome, convivial tavern and a popular after-work spot for white- and blue-collar types alike, Clark Street Ale House features a large open space filled with high tables and a long cherrywood bar along one wall. Better than the atmosphere are the 95 varieties of beer, a large majority of them from American microbreweries. The bar also offers a wide selection of scotches and cognacs. 742 N. Clark St. 🕐 312/642-9253. Subway/El: Red or Brown line to Chicago.

Fado   This sprawling, multilevel theme-park facsimile of an Irish pub still lures the masses on weekends, despite grumblings from some that it's all looks, with little authentic pub soul. Bursting with woodwork, stone, and double-barreled Guinness taps (all of it imported from Ireland), Fado has several themed rooms, each designed to evoke a particular Irish pub style—country cottage and Victorian Dublin, for instance. The pub fare is above par. 100 W. Grand Ave. 🕐 312/836-0066. Subway/El: Red Line to Grand.

J Bar   Yes, this lounge is just off the lobby of the James Hotel, but it's no conventioneer hangout. The low-slung leather couches, seating cubes, and flickering votive candles give it the look of an upscale urban club, and its laid-back vibe has made it a gathering place for stylish locals in their 20s and 30s. The drinks also have a sense of style. (The house martini blends blue raspberry vodka and elderflower cordial and is served in a glass coated with a raspberry-candy shell.) One drawback: You have to call and reserve a table if you want to be guaranteed a place to sit into the late-night hours. 610 N. Rush St. (at Wabash Ave.) 🕐 312/660-7200. Subway/El: Red Line to Grand.

LaSalle Power Co.   With a little something for everyone, this three-level nightspot opened in 2009, but has the semi-grungy vibe of a place that's been around far longer. The ground floor is the main bar area, where the cocktails lean toward the classics rather than original concoctions. Upstairs, you'll find a diner-style restaurant where you can chow down on everything from burgers to waffles, while the top floor is a live-music club, which books mostly indie bands. With its black tables, booths, and red-lit ceilings, LaSalle Power Co. recreates the look of a lost-in-time rock club, but the crowd is more clean-cut-Midwest than edgy-alternative. 500 N. LaSalle Blvd. (at Illinois St.). 🕐 312/661-1122. www.lasallepowerco.com. Subway/El: Red Line to Grand.

Martini Ranch   Staying in a Magnificent Mile hotel and looking for a late-night libation? Martini Ranch serves 40 different versions of its namesake cocktail until 4am during the week, attracting bar and nightlife insiders—and a fair share of insomniacs. The Western theme is subtle (paintings of Roy Rogers and other cowpoke art) and the seating is minimal (come early to snag one of the four red booths), but fans swear by the chocolate martini, and the pop-rock soundtrack keeps the energy level high. If the crowded bar scene is too much, chill out at the pool table in the back room, or settle down at one of the tables in the heated beer garden. 311 W. Chicago Ave. (at Orleans St.). 🕐 312/335-9500. Subway/El: Red or Brown line to Chicago.

Rockit Bar & Grill   This roadhouse-chic restaurant and late-night hangout was designed by Oprah's sidekick, Nate Berkus (see restaurant listing on p. 132). The buzzing upstairs bar area is where clean-cut professionals in their 20s and 30s go to flirt or catch up with friends—there are some pool tables, but posing attractively seems to be the main recreational activity here. Expect to be among the nose-pressers cooling your heels outside if you don't arrive early enough. 22 W. Hubbard St. (btw. State and Dearborn sts.). 🕐 312/645-6000. Subway/El: Red Line to Grand.

CHICAGO AFTER DARK

10

THE BAR & CAFE SCENE

10pin   A modern interpretation of the classic bowling alley, this lounge is tucked away under the Marina Towers complex on the Chicago River. Everything feels bright and new (even the rental shoes), and there's a full menu of designer beers and upscale snacks (gourmet pizzas, smoked salmon, specialty martinis). A giant video screen overlooks the 24 bowling lanes, and a top-notch sound system gives the place a nightclubby vibe. You don't *have* to bowl—the bar area is a casual, welcoming place to hang out—but I'd certainly recommend giving it a try. 330 N. State St. (btw. Kinzie St. and the Chicago River). © 312/644-0300. www.10pinchicago.com. Subway/El: Red Line to Grand or Brown Line to Merchandise Mart.

Rush & Division Streets

Around Rush Street are what a bygone era called singles bars—although the only singles that tend to head here now are suburbanites, out-of-towners, and barely legal partiers. Rush Street's glory days may be long gone, but there are still a few vestiges of the old times on nearby Division Street, which overflows with party-hearty spots that attract a loud, frat-party element. They include **Shenanigan's House of Beer,** 16 W. Division St. (© **312/642-2344**); **Butch McGuire's,** 20 W. Division St. (© **312/337-9080**); the **Lodge,** 21 W. Division St. (© **312/642-4406**); and **Mother's,** 26 W. Division St. (© **312/ 642-7251**). Many of these bars offer discounts for women, as loud pitchmen in front of each establishment will be happy to tell any attractive ladies who pass by.

Old Town

The center of nightlife in Old Town is Wells Street, home to Second City and Zanies Comedy Club, as well as a string of reliable restaurants and bars, many of which have been in business for decades. You're not going to find many trendy spots in Old Town; the nightlife here tends toward neighborhood pubs and casual restaurants, filled mostly with a late-20s and 30-something crowd.

Corcoran's   Owned by the same family for more than 30 years, this is one of Old Town's favorite local hangouts, and it makes a good stop before or after a show at Second City, which is located right across the street. The cozy, wood-lined interior and hearty pub food (bangers and mash, shepherd's pie, fish and chips) will put you right at ease. In nice weather, check out the beer garden in back, which offers a tranquil retreat from the city traffic. 1615 N. Wells St. (at North Ave.). © 312/440-0885. Subway/El: Brown Line to Sedgwick.

Goose Island Brewing Company (Finds)   The city's best-known brewpub is somewhat hidden on the western fringes of Old Town, but it's well worth the trip for beer lovers. The attractive, high-ceilinged space—with exposed-brick walls and a large central bar—is a welcoming place to linger while sampling Goose's ever-changing lineup of drinks. Their basic lager, Honker's Ale, is the most popular, but you can also order porters, stouts, and pilsners; try a tasting sampler if you can't make up your mind. The attached restaurant serves comfort food dishes that are quite a few notches up from standard bar food (p. 139). Goose Island also has an outpost in Wrigleyville, at 3535 N. Clark St. (© **773/832-9040**). 1800 N. Clybourrn Ave. © 312/915-0071. www.gooseisland. com. Subway/El: Brown Line to Armitage.

Old Town Ale House   This was one of Old Town's legendary saloons until the ironic college kids discovered it. A dingy neighborhood hangout since the late 1950s with a fading mural that captures the likenesses of a class of regulars from the early 1970s, the place was cleaned up in 2006 and lost much of its old charm. Gone are the days when John Belushi commandeered the pinball machines or old-timers outnumbered kids in their 20s. If drinking with kids doesn't bother you, put some quarters in the jukebox, which is filled with a selection of crooner tunes, and just hang out. 219 W. North Ave. (at Wells St.). ✆ 312/944-7020. Subway/El: Brown Line to Sedgwick.

Spoon   The closest Old Town has to a trendy nightspot, this bar and restaurant pulls in an attractive, professional crowd on weekend evenings. The modern, loftlike space would be right at home in the River North neighborhood, but it's a novelty in tradition-bound Old Town. Although Spoon attracts loud groups of singles on weekends, weeknights are a little less frenzied, and locals are able to sip their Mucho Mango martinis in peace. 1240 N. Wells St. (at Division St.). ✆ 312/642-5522. www.spoonchicago.com. Subway/El: Red Line to Clark/Division.

Stanley's Kitchen & Tap   Staying true to the neighborhood bar formula, Stanley's has built its long-standing reputation on providing a comfortable atmosphere and good food for its loyal patrons. Stanley's has a Southern-roadhouse-inspired vibe and home-style cooking, and is a great place to catch a game (and don't forget the free mashed potatoes offered every night at midnight). Sunday nights are live-band karaoke, which often attracts musicians passing through town and a host of athletes such as the Chicago Blackhawks hockey team. If you need to recover from a big night out, Stanley's also has a popular Sunday buffet, with Bloody Mary bar. 1970 N. Lincoln Avenue (at Armitage Ave.). ✆ 312/642-0007. www.stanleyskitchenandtap.com. Bus: 22 (Clark St.).

Lincoln Park

Lincoln Park, with its high concentration of apartment-dwelling singles, is one of the busiest nightlife destinations in Chicago. Prime real estate is at a premium in this residential neighborhood, so you won't find many warehouse-size dance clubs here; most of the action is at pubs and bars. Concentrations of in-spots run along Halsted Street and Lincoln Avenue.

The Duke of Perth   This traditional Scottish pub serves one of the city's best selections of single-malt whiskey, along with cross-cultural specialties such as the Scotch Egg Burger (topped with a fried egg and roasted red pepper). You can also dig in to more traditional pub food, such as the baskets of fish and chips (on Wednesdays and Friday, get all you can eat for $9.50). The outdoor beer garden is especially inviting on warm summer nights. 2913 N. Clark St. (at Wellington Ave.). ✆ 773/477-1741. www.dukeofperth.com. Subway/El: Brown Line to Diversey.

Duke's Bar and Grill ⟨Finds⟩   Sophisticated yet unpretentious, Duke's looks like a cross between a mountain lodge and an urban cocktail lounge, with broad-plank wood walls, cream-colored leather banquettes, and a large flatscreen TV showing nature scenes behind the bar. It's attractive enough to feel like a step up from a neighborhood bar, but the vibe never gets snooty. If you're hungry, try one of the burgers: There are always at least 20 varieties on the menu. It's a good bet you'll be surrounded by locals who think of Duke's as their own special discovery. 2616 N. Clark St. (at Belden Ave.). ✆ 773/248-0250. www.dukeschicago.com. Bus: 22 (Clark).

Galway Arms   The large heated front patio, which is open from St. Patrick's Day through late fall, sets this Irish bar apart from all the other pubs in town. Indoors, the quaint, cozy dining rooms with fireplaces attract a slightly more upscale crowd than other neighboring watering holes. Every Sunday night, the pub hosts a traditional Irish music session, where a rotating group of musicians jam from 8pm on. 2442 N. Clark St. (at Arlington). ✆ 773/472-5555. www.galwayarms.com. Subway/El: Red or Brown line to Fullerton.

Glascott's Groggery   A favorite meeting spot for young Lincoln Park professionals, Glascott's has been in the same family since it opened in 1937. It attracts an eclectic mix of neighborhood regulars of all ages: Groups of guys stopping in after their weekly basketball game, couples coming in after dinner to catch up with their friends, and singles discretely checking each other out. 2158 N. Halsted St. (at Webster Ave.). ☎ 773/281-1205. www.glascotts.com. Subway/El: Brown Line to Armitage.

Tilli's   A favorite gathering spot for good-looking 20- and 30-somethings, Tilli's is an upscale version of the neighborhood bar. In nice weather, the entire front opens to the street; when it's chilly, try to snag a table near the brick fireplace in the main dining room. You can snack on appetizers or order dinner, but the main attraction is the front room, where everyone people-watches around the bar. 1952 N. Halsted St. (at Armitage St.). ☎ 773/325-0044. www.tillischicago.com. Subway/El: Brown Line to Armitage.

Webster's Wine Bar   It's a bit off the beaten track—on the western fringe of Lincoln Park—but the low-lit, sophisticated decor makes Webster's a good alternative to the usual beer blast. The waitstaff can help you choose from a list of dozens of wines by the bottle or glass, or you can hone your taste buds with a flight of several wines. There's also a tapas-style menu for noshing. Step back into the library area to light up a cigar and recline on the couch. 1480 W. Webster Ave. (btw. Clybourn and Ashland aves.). ☎ 773/868-0608. www.websterwinebar.com. Subway/El: Red or Brown line to Fullerton, and then a short cab ride.

Wrigleyville, Lakeview & the North Side

Real estate in Wrigleyville and Lakeview is a tad less expensive than in Lincoln Park, so the nightlife scene here skews a little younger. You'll find a mostly postcollegiate crowd partying on Clark Street across from Wrigley Field (especially after games in the summer). But head away from the ball field, and you'll discover some more exotic choices.

Chicago Brauhaus   Lincoln Square—a few miles northwest of Wrigley Field—used to be the heart of Chicago's German community. Although not much of that tradition remains, a few old world-style delis and European shops (including a terrific old-fashioned apothecary) dot Lincoln Avenue from Wilson to Lawrence avenues. For a dose of Oktoberfest at any time of year, stop into the Brauhaus. German bands perform on weekends, when the older crowd puts the youngsters to shame on the dance floor. The Erdinger, Spaten, and BBK flow freely, and the kitchen serves up big plates of 'wurst, schnitzel, and sauerkraut. 4732 N. Lincoln Ave. (btw. Leland and Lawrence aves.). ☎ 773/784-4444. www.chicagobrauhaus.com. Subway/El: Brown Line to Western.

404 Wine Bar   One of the most inviting bars in the city, 404 Wine Bar makes you feel as if you've been invited to a party in a private home (it adjoins Jack's, a standard sports-and-beer spot; make sure you go in the entrance on the left side of the building). Tables and soft leather couches fill a series of cozy, low-lit rooms; the laid-back vibe attracts groups of friends and couples rather than on-the-prowl singles. The wine list features more than 100 labels from around the world, all fairly reasonably priced. Order by the bottle, glass, or flight. (The selection changes every 2 weeks.) In the summer, tables are set up in an outdoor courtyard; in the winter, fireplaces fill the rooms with a warm glow. 2852 N. Southport Ave. (at George St.). ☎ 773/404-5886. www.jacks404.com. Subway/El: Brown Line to Wellington.

Ginger Man Tavern   Ginger Man definitely plays against type in a row of predictable sports bars across the street from Wrigley Field. On game days the earthy bar has been known to crank classical music in an attempt to calm drunken fans—or at least shoo them away. Pool tables (free on Sun) are always busy with slightly bohemian neighborhood 20-somethings, who have more than 80 beers to choose from. 3740 N. Clark St. (at Racine Ave.). ☎ 773/549-2050. Subway/El: Red Line to Addison.

Irish Oak (Finds) Owned and staffed by folks from the Old Sod, this is one of the city's nicest Irish bars. It may only be 10 years old, but the handsome woodwork, copper canopy over the bar, and eclectic collection of antiques give the tavern a timeless feel. Overall, the mood here is laid-back and mellow—except when the post-Cubs-game crowds invade. There are plenty of whiskeys, stouts, and ales to sip, and the kitchen offers shepherd's pie and other Irish fare. Live bands perform on Friday and Saturday nights. 3511 N. Clark St. (btw. Cornelia Ave. and Addison St.). ☎ 773/935-6669. www.irishoak.com. Subway/El: Red Line to Addison.

Sheffield's Beer and Wine Garden A popular neighborhood gathering spot for years, the main claim to fame at Sheffield's is the large beer garden, where you can order off an extensive menu of BBQ dishes. The bar boasts a selection of more than 80 beers, including a number of specialty craft beers and one featured "bad beer" of the month. Sheffield's can get jammed with a young, loud crowd, but the attitude is welcoming—there always seems to be room to squeeze in one more person. 3258 N. Sheffield Ave. (btw. Belmont Ave. and Roscoe St.). ☎ 773/281-4989. www.sheffieldschicago.com. Subway/El: Red or Brown line to Belmont.

Wicker Park & Bucktown

The closest Chicago has to an alternative scene is Wicker Park and Bucktown, where both slackers and adventurous suburbanites populate bars dotting the streets leading out from the intersection of North, Damen, and Milwaukee avenues. Don't dress up if you want to blend in: A casually bohemian getup and low-key attitude are all you need. While you can reach most of these places relatively easily by public transportation, I recommend taking a cab at night—the surrounding neighborhoods are what I'd call "transitional."

Betty's Blue Star Lounge Just south of Wicker Park in Ukrainian Village, what was once an unpretentious neighborhood tavern has been transformed into a pseudo-trendy late-night destination. The action is in the back room, equipped with a stellar sound system and lots of mirrors. This wannabe club enforces a dress code on the weekends (no sneakers or shorts), as well as an annoying $10 cover. But it's one of the only places in the area with live DJs and a dance floor, so if you're looking to get your groove on, you may well end up here. Betty's has a 5am license on weekends; the early morning people-watching can be priceless. 1600 W. Grand Ave. ☎ 312/243-8778. www.bettysbluestarlounge.com. Bus: 65 (Grand Ave.), but I'd recommend a cab at night.

The Bucktown Pub (Value) The owners' collection of groovy 1960s and '70s rock-'n'-roll posters and cartoon art is phenomenal. However, most Bucktown patrons are more interested in nursing their pints of imported and domestic microbrews than in gawking at the walls. Other Wicker Park/Bucktown bars try to come off as low-key; this is the real thing, where attitude is firmly discouraged at the door. The psychedelic- and glam-rock-filled jukebox keeps toes tapping, and competition on the skittle-bowling machine can get quite fierce. Credit cards not accepted. 1658 W. Cortland St. (at Hermitage Ave.). ☎ 773/394-9898. www.bucktownpub.com. Subway/El: Blue Line to Damen.

The California Clipper   Located in Humboldt Park (southwest of Wicker Park), the Clipper is a bit removed from the main drag, but it's well worth seeking out. For the past couple of years, this beautifully restored 1940s tavern, with its gorgeous Art Deco bar and red walls bathed in dim light, has been colonized on the weekends by the young and terminally restless. Friday and Saturday nights feature live music, mostly rockabilly and "country swing." 1002 N. California Ave. © 773/384-2547. www.californiaclipper.com. Subway/El: Blue Line to Division, then a short cab ride.

Cortland's Garage   This cozy spot in Bucktown is unpretentious and cleanly designed, with a retractable garage door in front and exposed brick walls inside featuring black-and-white photos of garage scenes. DJs spin records from an elevated booth in the corner Thursday through Saturday nights. Although there's music other nights of the week, it's mostly a place to hang out rather than catch the latest hip band. 1645 W. Cortland St. (btw. Ashland and Hermitage aves.). © 773/862-7877. www.cortlandsgarage.com. Subway/El: Blue Line to Damen.

Danny's Tavern   Located off the beaten Milwaukee/Damen path, Danny's has become the neighborhood hangout of choice for Bucktown's original angry young men and women, the ones who complain that an influx of yuppies is ruining the area. Just finding Danny's takes insider knowledge: The only sign out front flashes SCHLITZ in neon red. Inside, votive candles on the tables provide dim lighting; head to the back room to grab a seat on the leather couches and chairs. Once there, you can revel in the fact that you're hanging with the cool kids—just don't let them know you're a tourist. And bring cash—Danny's doesn't accept credit cards. 1951 W. Dickens Ave. (at Damen Ave.). © 773/489-6457. Subway/El: Blue Line to Damen.

EvilOlive   That's right, it's a palindrome, and the palindromes don't end with the name of this 4am bar (5am on Sat); they're also scribbled on the wall ("If I had a hi-fi") and printed on the drink menu (try a "Dr. Awkward"). Hand-stuffed olives are a specialty here, too, both in drinks and on plates. The place has an upscale rock club feel, with oversize booths, a pool table, a photo booth, and projected movies. A DJ is perched on the second floor spinning rock and hip-hop well into the wee hours. 15551 W. Division St. (at Ashland Ave.). © 773/235-9100. www.evil-olive.com. Subway/El: Blue Line to Division.

The Map Room ★ (Finds)   Hundreds of travel books and guides line the shelves of this globe-trotter's tavern. Peruse that tome on Fuji or Antarctica while sipping a pint of one of the 20-odd draft beers. The Map Room's equally impressive selection of bottled brews makes this place popular with beer geeks as well as the tattered-passport crew. Tuesday is theme night, featuring the food, music, and spirits of a certain country, accompanied by a slide show and tales from a recent visitor. 1949 N. Hoyne Ave. (at Armitage Ave.). © 773/252-7636. www.maproom.com. Subway/El: Blue Line to Damen.

Marie's Riptide Lounge   Nothing here looks as though it has been updated since the 1960s (owner Marie is long past retirement age), but personal touches and the retro cool of the place have made it a hip stop on the late-night circuit. A jukebox stocked with campy oldies, a curious low-tech duck-hunting "video" game, and the occasional blast of black light make Marie's a hoot. The owner takes great pains to decorate the interior of the little bar for each holiday season. (The wintertime "snow-covered" bar is not to be missed.) 1745 W. Armitage Ave. (at Hermitage Ave.). © 773/278-7317. Subway/El: Blue Line to Damen.

The Violet Hour   The Violet Hour has a retro ambiance that's unique in the Chicago nightlife scene, especially in verging-on-gritty Wicker Park. The interior feels like an English or French country manor, with blue walls and white crown molding; glittering

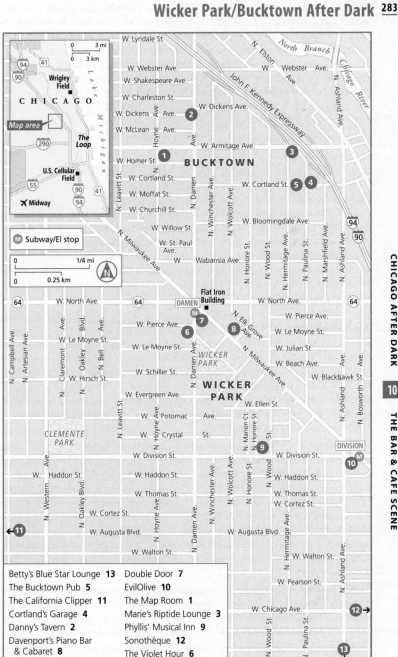

Betty's Blue Star Lounge **13**
The Bucktown Pub **5**
The California Clipper **11**
Cortland's Garage **4**
Danny's Tavern **2**
Davenport's Piano Bar
  & Cabaret **8**

Double Door **7**
EvilOlive **10**
The Map Room **1**
Marie's Riptide Lounge **3**
Phyllis' Musical Inn **9**
Sonothèque **12**
The Violet Hour **6**

chandeliers; extra-high wingback chairs; and dramatic floor-length curtains. The door policy maintains the civilized mood: Customers aren't admitted until there's room for them to sit (and no, they don't take reservations, so you might be waiting a while on weekends). The specialties here are cocktails served up by expert "mixologists" (don't call them bartenders!), such as the Juliet & Romeo, a mix of gin, mint, cucumber, and rose water. One annoyance: The bar is too cool to put a sign out front; you'll find it on the corner of Damen Avenue and Pierce Street, marked only by a series of abstract, multicolored murals. 1520 N. Damen Ave. (at Pierce St.). ✆ 773/252-1500. www.thevioplethour.com. Subway/El: Blue Line to Damen.

CAFES

Café Jumping Bean   A great little cafe in the heart of Pilsen, just southwest of the Loop, the Jumping Bean is ideal for taking in this vibrant Mexican-American neighborhood. It serves the usual espresso drinks, muffins, and pastries, but it also offers decent salads, cheesecakes, natural vegetable and fruit juices, and—best of all—a tantalizing selection of *liquados,* Mexican drinks made with milk, sugar, ice, and fresh fruit (try the mango). The artistic doings outside, characterized by colorful outdoor murals, spill over into the cafe, which features rotating exhibitions of paintings and hand-painted tables by local artists. The place even schedules live flamenco music and poetry readings in Spanish. Everyone is welcome, from families with little kids to the loft-dwelling artists who've lately infiltrated Pilsen. 1439 W. 18th St. (2 blocks east of Ashland Ave.). ✆ 312/455-0019. Subway/El: Blue Line to 18th St.

Intelligentsia   A down-to-earth San Francisco married couple set up this coffee-roasting operation in the heart of Lakeview, and their brew has become one of the most popular in town. (You'll see it on the menus of some of the city's top restaurants.) A French roaster dominates the cafe, and the owners also make their own herbal and black teas. Warm drinks are served in handsome cups nearly too big to get your hands around, and tea sippers receive their own pots and brew timers. Sit at the window or in an Adirondack chair on the sidewalk, or decamp to the homey back seating area. 3123 N. Broadway Ave. (btw. Belmont Ave. and Diversey Pkwy.). ✆ 773/348-8058. www.intelligentsia coffee.com. Subway/El: Red Line to Addison.

Julius Meinl ★   Austria's premier coffee roaster chose Chicago—and, even more mysteriously, a location near Wrigley Field—for its first U.S. outpost. The result is a mix of Austrian style (upholstered banquettes, white marble tables, newspapers hanging on wicker frames) and American cheeriness (lots of natural light, smiling waitstaff, smoke-free air). The excellent coffee and hot chocolate are served European-style on small silver platters with a glass of water on the side, but it's the desserts that keep the regulars coming back. Try the apple strudel or millennium torte (glazed with apricot jam and chocolate ganache), and for a moment you'll swear you're in Vienna. 3601 N. Southport Ave. (at Addison St.). ✆ 773/868-1857. www.meinl.com/northamerica/home.html. Subway/El: Brown Line to Southport.

Third Coast ★   Just steps from the raucous frat-boy atmosphere of Division Street is this laid-back, classic, independent coffeehouse. The below-ground space is no-frills but comfortable, attracting a mix of office workers, students, and neighborhood regulars. The full menu is available late, and the drinks run the gamut from lattes to cocktails. There's often some kind of folk music on weekends. 1260 N. Dearborn St. (north of Division St.). ✆ 312/649-0730. www.3rdcoastcafe.com. Subway/El: Red Line to Clark/Division.

Uncommon Ground ★★ When you're looking for refuge from Cubs game days **285** and party nights in Wrigleyville, Uncommon Ground offers a dose of laid-back, vaguely bohemian civility. Just off busy Clark Street, the cafe has a fireplace in winter (when the cafe's bowl—yes, bowl—of hot chocolate is a sight for cold eyes) and a spacious sidewalk operation in more temperate months. Breakfast is served all day, plus there's a full lunch and dinner menu. Music figures strongly, with live performances from singer-songwriters on weekends. Open until 2am daily. There's also another location, in Rogers Park on the far North Side of the city, at 1401 W. Devon Ave. (✆ **773/465-9801**). 1214 W. Grace St. (at Clark St.). ✆ **773/929-3680**. www.uncommonground.com. Subway/El: Red Line to Addison.

---

6 THE GAY & LESBIAN SCENE

Most of Chicago's gay bars are conveniently clustered on a stretch of North Halsted Street in Lakeview (in what's known as Boys Town), making it easy to sample many of them in a breezy walk. Men's bars predominate—few places in town cater exclusively to lesbians—but a few gay bars get a mix of men and women. A couple of helpful free resources are the weekly entertainment guide *Nightspots* and the club rag *Gab*. The bars and clubs recommended below don't charge a cover unless otherwise noted.

Berlin Step into this frenetic Lakeview danceteria, and you're immediately swept into the mood. The disco tunes pulse, the clubby crowd chatters, and the lighting bathes everyone in a cool reddish glow. Special nights are dedicated to disco, amateur drag, and 1980s new wave; male dancers perform some nights. Don't bother showing up before midnight; the club stays open until 4am Friday and 5am Saturday. 954 W. Belmont Ave. (east of Sheffield Ave.). ✆ **773/348-4975**. www.berlinchicago.com. Cover after midnight Fri–Sat $5. Subway/El: Red or Brown line to Belmont.

Big Chicks ⟮**Finds**⟯ One of the more bohemian bars in the city, Big Chicks is a magnet for the artsy goateed set (perhaps a bit weary of the bars on Halsted Street), lesbians, a smattering of straights, and random locals from the surrounding rough-hewn neighborhood. (The bar's motto is "Never a Cover, Never an Attitude".) They come for owner Michelle Fire's superb art collection, the midnight shots, and the free buffet on Sunday afternoon. There is also dancing on weekends. The same owner also runs the restaurant next door, **Tweet**, 5020 N. Sheridan Rd. (✆ **773/728-5576**), which offers a menu of mostly organic American comfort food; it has become a popular gay-friendly weekend brunch spot. 5024 N. Sheridan Rd. (btw. Argyle St. and Foster Ave.). ✆ **773/728-5511**. www.bigchicks.com. Subway/El: Red Line to Berwyn.

Circuit It has all the necessary nightclub elements: Flashing lights, a killer sound system, the biggest dance floor in Boys Town, and plenty of eye candy. Open 'til 4am on weekends, Circuit attracts a hard-partying, minimally dressed crowd after all the other local bars have closed. Friday is "girls' night." 3641 N. Halsted St. (at Addison St.). ✆ **773/325-2233**. www.circuitclub.com. $5–$10 cover. Subway/El: Red Line to Addison.

The Closet The Closet is an unpretentious neighborhood spot with a loud and constant loop of music videos (and sports, when the game matters) that draws mostly lesbian regulars, although gay men and straights also show up. The space is not much bigger than a closet, which makes it easy to get up close and personal with other partiers. There's also a small dance floor that's usually packed on weekends. Open until 4am every night, 5am

CHICAGO AFTER DARK

10

THE GAY & LESBIAN SCENE

on Saturday. 3325 N. Broadway Ave. (at Buckingham St.). ✆ **773/477-8533.** Subway/El: Red or Brown line to Belmont.

Cocktail   This corner spot is a friendly hangout in the afternoons and early evenings, when it's easy to converse and watch the passing parade from big picture windows (on Sunday afternoons, regulars even stop by with their dogs in tow). Things get a little more frenzied after 10pm on Thursdays through Sunday, when the club's lineup of go-go dancers hits the floor. 3359 N. Halsted St. (at Roscoe St.). ✆ **773/477-1420.** www.cocktailbarchicago. com. Subway/El: Red or Brown line to Belmont.

Crew   Crew is a gay-friendly sports bar, where local softball leagues stop by for a drink after the game. Up to eight pro games play on multiple TVs, and there's a full menu of sandwiches, salads, and shareable appetizer plates. Located in the residential neighborhood of Uptown, a few miles north of the main Halsted Street strip, Crew attracts a crowd that's more interested in hanging out than hooking up. The same owners have also opened a pub next door, **Wild Pug,** 4810 N. Broadway Ave. (✆ **773/784-4811**), which has DJs and dancing on the weekends. 4804 N. Broadway Ave. (at Lawrence St.). ✆ **773/784-CREW** (2739). www.worldsgreatestbar.com. Subway/El: Red Line to Lawrence.

Roscoe's Tavern (**Finds**)   The picture windows facing Halsted Street make Roscoe's, a gay neighborhood bar in business since 1987, an especially welcoming place. It has a large antiques-filled front bar, an outdoor patio, a pool table, and a large dance floor. The 20- and 30-something crowd is friendly and laid-back—except on weekends when the dance floor is hopping. The cafe serves sandwiches and salads. 3356 N. Halsted St. (at Roscoe St.). ✆ **773/281-3355.** www.roscoes.com. Cover after 10pm Sat $4. Subway/El: Red or Brown line to Belmont.

Scarlet   The name of this lounge is an homage to the semi-underground gay community of the 1920s, when members wore a piece of scarlet-colored clothing to signal their affiliation to others. Today, though you can wear whatever you want here, the attractively designed space might inspire you to take your wardrobe up a notch. From the glowing red-orange lights behind the bar to the red glass chandelier in the men's room, Scarlet has a more upscale vibe than most other places in Boys Town—and attracts an upscale clientele to match. 3320 N. Halsted St. (at Aldine St.). ✆ **773/348-1053.** www.scarletbar chicago.com. Subway/El: Red or Brown line to Belmont.

Sidetrack (**Finds**)   If you make it to Roscoe's (above), you'll no doubt end up at Sidetrack. The popular bars are across the street from each other, and there's a constant flow of feet between the two. Sidetrack is a sleek video bar where TV monitors are never out of your field of vision, nor are the preppy professional patrons. Don't miss Show Tunes Night on Sunday, Monday, and Friday, when the whole place sings along to Broadway and MGM musical favorites. 3349 N. Halsted St. (at Roscoe St.). ✆ **773/477-9189.** www.sidetrack chicago.com. Subway/El: Red or Brown line to Belmont.

Spin   This dance club attracts one of Halsted Street's most colorful crowds, a mix of pretty boys, nerds, tough guys, and the occasional drag queen. The video bar in front houses pool tables and plays a steady stream of dance-friendly music videos. The club thumps with house music. Spin keeps regulars coming back with daily theme parties, featuring everything from Friday-night shower contests to cheap drinks. 800 W. Belmont Ave. (at Halsted St.). ✆ **773/327-7711.** www.spin-nightclub.com. Cover $5 Sat. Subway/El: Red or Brown line to Belmont.

Fast Facts, Toll-Free Numbers & Websites

1 FAST FACTS: CHICAGO

AREA CODES The 312 area code applies to the Loop and the neighborhoods closest to it, including River North, North Michigan Avenue, and the Gold Coast. The code for the rest of the city is 773. Suburban area codes are 847 (north), 708 (west and southwest), and 630 (far west). You must dial "1" plus the area code for all telephone numbers, even if you are making a call within the same area code.

AUTOMOBILE ORGANIZATIONS Motor clubs will supply maps, suggested routes, guidebooks, accident and bail-bond insurance, and emergency road service. The **American Automobile Association (AAA)** is the major auto club in the United States. If you belong to a motor club in your home country, inquire about AAA reciprocity before you leave. You may be able to join AAA even if you're not a member of a reciprocal club; to inquire, call AAA (© **800/222-4357;** www.aaa.com). AAA has a nationwide emergency road service telephone number (© **800/AAA-HELP** [222-4357]).

BABYSITTERS Check with the concierge or desk staff at your hotel; they likely maintain a list of reliable sitters whom they have worked with in the past. Many of the top hotels work with **American ChildCare Service** (© **312/644-7300;** www.americanchildcare.com), a state-licensed and insured babysitting service that can match you with a sitter. The sitters are required to pass background checks, provide multiple child-care references, and be trained in infant and child CPR. It's best to make a reservation 24 hours in advance; the office is open from 9am to 5pm weekdays. Rates are $19 per hour, with a 4-hour minimum, and a $20 agency fee. (You're also expected to give the sitter a cash tip.)

BUSINESS HOURS Shops generally keep normal business hours, 10am to 6pm, Monday through Saturday. Most stores stay open late at least 1 evening a week. Certain businesses, such as bookstores, are almost always open during the evening hours all week. Most shops downtown are also open on Sundays, usually from noon to 6pm. Malls are generally open until 7pm and on Sunday as well. Banking hours in Chicago are normally from 9am (8am in some cases) to 5pm Monday through Friday, with select banks remaining open later on specified afternoons and evenings.

DRINKING LAWS The legal age for purchase and consumption of alcoholic beverages is 21; proof of age is required and often requested at bars, nightclubs, and restaurants, so it's always a good idea to bring ID when you go out.

In Chicago, beer, wine, and other alcoholic beverages are sold at liquor stores and supermarkets. Bars may sell alcohol until 2am, although some nightclubs have special licenses that allow alcohol sales until 4am.

Do not carry open containers of alcohol in your car or any public area that isn't zoned for alcohol consumption. The police can fine you on the spot. Don't even think about driving while intoxicated.

DRIVING RULES See "Getting There & Getting Around," p. 38.

ELECTRICITY Like Canada, the United States uses 110–120 volts AC (60 cycles), compared to 220–240 volts AC (50 cycles) in most of Europe, Australia, and New Zealand. Downward converters that change 220–240 volts to 110–120 volts are difficult to find in the United States, so bring one with you.

EMBASSIES & CONSULATES All embassies are located in the nation's capital, Washington, D.C. Some consulates are located in major U.S. cities, and most nations have a mission to the United Nations in New York City. If your country isn't listed below, call for directory information in Washington, D.C. (© 202/555-1212) or check **www.embassy.org/embassies**.

The embassy of **Australia** is at 1601 Massachusetts Ave. NW, Washington, DC 20036 (© 202/797-3000; www.usa.embassy.gov/au).

The embassy of **Canada** is at 501 Pennsylvania Ave. NW, Washington, DC 20001 (© 202/682-1740; www.canadianembassy.org). Other Canadian consulates are in Buffalo (New York), Detroit, Los Angeles, New York, and Seattle.

The embassy of **Ireland** is at 2234 Massachusetts Ave. NW, Washington, DC 20008 (© 202/462-3939; www.irelandemb.org). Irish consulates are in Boston, Chicago, New York, San Francisco, and other cities. See website for complete listing.

The embassy of **New Zealand** is at 37 Observatory Circle NW, Washington, DC 20008 (© 202/328-4800; www.nzembassy.com). New Zealand consulates are in Los Angeles, Salt Lake City, San Francisco, and Seattle.

The embassy of the **United Kingdom** is at 3100 Massachusetts Ave. NW, Washington, DC 20008 (© 202/588-7800; www.britainusa.com). Other British consulates are in Atlanta, Boston, Chicago, Cleveland, Houston, Los Angeles, New York, San Francisco, and Seattle.

EMERGENCIES For fire or police emergencies, call © 911. This is a free call. If it is a medical emergency, a city ambulance will take the patient to the nearest hospital emergency room. The nonemergency phone number for the Chicago Police Department is © 311.

GASOLINE (PETROL) In the past year, the price of gas in Chicago has fluctuated wildly, from $2 to $4 per gallon. Taxes are already included in the printed price. One U.S. gallon equals 3.8 liters or .85 imperial gallons. In general, you pay more within the Chicago city limits than you will in the suburbs (the city adds an extra tax into the price), so if you're planning a day trip, it pays to fill up once you're out of town.

HOLIDAYS Banks, government offices, post offices, and many stores, restaurants, and museums are closed on the following legal national holidays: January 1 (New Year's Day), the third Monday in January (Martin Luther King, Jr., Day), the third Monday in February (Presidents' Day), the last Monday in May (Memorial Day), July 4 (Independence Day), the first Monday in September (Labor Day), the second Monday in October (Columbus Day), November 11 (Veterans' Day/Armistice Day), the fourth Thursday in November (Thanksgiving Day), and December 25 (Christmas). The Tuesday after the first Monday in November is Election Day, a federal government holiday in presidential-election years (held every 4 years, and next in 2012).

For more information on holidays see "Chicago Calendar of Events," in chapter 3.

HOSPITALS The best hospital emergency room in downtown Chicago is at Northwestern Memorial Hospital, 251 E. Huron St. (© **312/926-2000;** www.nmh. org), a state-of-the-art medical center right off North Michigan Avenue. The emergency department (© **312/926-5188** or 312/944-2358 for TDD access) is located at 251 E. Erie St., near Fairbanks Court. For an ambulance, dial © **911,** which is a free call.

INSURANCE Although it's not required of travelers, **health insurance** is highly recommended. Most health insurance policies cover you if you get sick away from home—but check your coverage before you leave.

International visitors to the U.S. should note that unlike many European countries, the United States does not usually offer free or low-cost medical care to its citizens or visitors. Doctors and hospitals are expensive, and in most cases will require advance payment or proof of coverage before they render their services. Good policies will cover the costs of an accident, repatriation, or death. Packages such as **Europ Assistance's "Worldwide Healthcare Plan"** are sold by European automobile clubs and travel agencies at attractive rates. **Worldwide Assistance Services, Inc.** (© **800/777-8710;** www. worldwideassistance.com) is the agent for Europ Assistance in the United States.

Canadians should check with their provincial health plan offices or call **Health Canada** (© **866/225-0709;** www. hc-sc.gc.ca) to find out the extent of their coverage and what documentation and receipts they must take home in case they are treated in the United States.

Travelers from the U.K. should carry their European Health Insurance Card (EHIC), which replaced the E111 form as proof of entitlement to free/reduced cost medical treatment abroad (© **0845/606-2030;** www.ehic.org.uk). Note, however, that the EHIC only covers "necessary medical treatment," and for repatriation costs, lost money, baggage, or cancellation, travel insurance from a reputable company should always be sought (www.travelinsuranceweb. com).

The cost of **travel insurance** varies widely, depending on the destination, the cost and length of your trip, your age and health, and the type of trip you're taking, but expect to pay between 5% and 8% of the vacation itself. You can get estimates from various providers through **Insure-MyTrip.com**. Enter your trip cost and dates, your age, and other information, for prices from more than a dozen companies.

U.K. citizens and their families who make more than one trip abroad per year may find an annual travel insurance policy works out cheaper. Check **www.money supermarket.com**, which compares prices across a wide range of providers for single- and multi-trip policies.

Most big travel agents offer their own insurance and will probably try to sell you their package when you book a holiday. Think before you sign. **Britain's Consumers' Association** recommends that you insist on seeing the policy and reading the fine print before buying travel insurance. **The Association of British Insurers** (© **020/7600-3333;** www.abi.org.uk) gives advice by phone and publishes Holiday Insurance, a free guide to policy provisions and prices. You might also shop around for better deals: Try **Columbus Direct** (© **0870/033-9988;** www.columbus direct.net).

For information on traveler's insurance, trip cancellation insurance, and medical insurance while traveling please visit www. frommers.com/planning.

INTERNET ACCESS In Chicago, most hotels have business centers with Internet access for guests. (Be prepared to pay an hourly rate to use the computers, though.) The Harold Washington Public Library (p. 161) has computers available to the public. You can also pay per hour to use computers at FedEx Office (formerly Kinko's); centrally located stores include one at Illinois Center, 111 W. Wacker Dr., near Michigan Avenue and Chicago River (© 312/938-0650), and inside the John Hancock Center, 875 N. Michigan Ave. (© 312/664-5966).

In Lincoln Park, you'll find Screenz, 2717 N. Clark St., 1 block south of Diversey Ave. (© 773/348-9300; www. screenz.com), a computing center where you can check e-mail, burn CDs, and print out your digital photos. The only downside is that it's not within walking distance of downtown hotels. To find other cybercafes in the city, try www. cybercafe.com.

LAUNDROMATS The closest Laundromat to downtown is **Sudz Coin Laundry,** 1246 N. Ashland Ave. (© 773/218-9630; www.sudzlaundry.com), about a block north of Division Street. Rates are 95¢ per pound for drop-off service and $2.25 per wash at self-service machines. It's open daily from 5am to midnight (last wash at 10:30pm). You can also arrange to have your laundry picked up and delivered.

LEGAL AID If you are "pulled over" for a minor infraction (such as speeding), never attempt to pay the fine directly to a police officer; this could be construed as attempted bribery, a much more serious crime. Pay fines by mail, or directly into the hands of the clerk of the court. If accused of a more serious offense, say and do nothing before consulting a lawyer. Here the burden is on the state to prove a person's guilt beyond a reasonable doubt, and everyone has the right to remain silent, whether he or she is suspected of a crime or actually arrested. Once arrested, a person can make one telephone call to a party of his or her choice. International visitors should call your embassy or consulate.

MAIL At press time, domestic postage rates were 28¢ for a postcard and 44¢ for a letter. For international mail, a first-class letter of up to 1 ounce costs 98¢ (75¢ to Canada and 79¢ to Mexico); a first-class postcard costs the same as a letter. For more information go to **www.usps.com**.

If you aren't sure what your address will be in the United States, mail can be sent to you, in your name, c/o General Delivery at the main post office of the city or region where you expect to be. (Call © 800/275-8777 for information on the nearest post office.) The addressee must pick up mail in person and must produce proof of identity (driver's license, passport, and so forth). Most post offices will hold your mail for up to 1 month, and are open Monday to Friday from 8am to 6pm, and Saturday from 9am to 3pm.

Always include zip codes when mailing items in the U.S. If you don't know your zip code, visit www.usps.com/zip4.

NEWSPAPERS & MAGAZINES The *Chicago Tribune* (© 312/222-3232; www. chicagotribune.com) and the *Chicago Sun-Times* (© 312/321-3000; www.sun times.com) are the two major dailies. (The *Tribune* focuses on sober, just-the-facts reporting; the *Sun-Times* is a scrappier, attitude-filled tabloid). Both have cultural listings, including movies, theaters, and live music, not to mention reviews of the latest restaurants that have opened since this guidebook went to press. The Friday edition of both papers contains a special pullout section with more detailed, up-to-date information on special events happening over the weekend. The weekly magazine *Time Out Chicago* (© 312/924-9555; www.timeoutchicago.com) lists just about everything going on around town during the week, from art openings to theater performances; if you want to squeeze in as much culture as you can while you're here, I'd highly recommend picking up a copy. The *Chicago Reader* (© 312/828-0350; www.chicagoreader. com) is a free weekly that appears each Thursday, with all the current entertainment and cultural listings. *Chicago magazine* (www.chicagomag.com) is a monthly with an especially good restaurant-review section. The *Chicago Defender* covers local and national news of interest to the African-American community. The Spanish-language *La Raza* (www.laraza.com) reports on stories from a Latino point of view. The *Chicago Free Press* (www.chicagofreepress.com) and *Windy City Times* (www.windycitytimes.com) publish both news and feature articles about gay and lesbian issues.

PASSPORTS See "Embassies & Consulates," above, for whom to contact if you lose yours while traveling in the U.S. For other information, please contact the following agencies:

For Residents of Australia Contact the **Australian Passport Information Service** at © **131-232,** or visit the government website at www.passports.gov.au.

For Residents of Canada Contact the central **Passport Office,** Department of Foreign Affairs and International Trade, Ottawa, ON K1A 0G3 (© **800/567-6868;** www.ppt.gc.ca).

For Residents of Ireland Contact the **Passport Office,** Setanta Centre, Molesworth Street, Dublin 2 (© **01/671-1633;** www.irlgov.ie/iveagh).

For Residents of New Zealand Contact the **Passports Office** at © **0800/225-050** in New Zealand or 04/474-8100, or log on to www.passports.govt.nz.

For Residents of the United Kingdom Visit your nearest passport office, major post office, or travel agency or contact the **United Kingdom Passport Service** at © **0870/521-0410** or search its website at www.ukpa.gov.uk.

For Residents of the United States To find your regional passport office, either check the U.S. State Department website or call the **National Passport Information Center** toll-free number (© **877/487-2778**) for automated information.

POLICE For emergencies, call © **911.** This is a free call (no coins required). For nonemergencies, call © **311.**

SMOKING Smoking is banned in all public buildings in Chicago, including offices, restaurants, and bars. Hotels are still allowed to have smoking rooms available, though, so request one if you plan on lighting up.

TAXES The United States has no value-added tax (VAT) or other indirect tax at the national level. Every state, county, and city may levy its own local tax on all purchases, including hotel and restaurant checks and airline tickets. These taxes will not appear on price tags.

When visiting Chicago, be prepared to pay up: The city's 10.25% sales tax is the highest in the country, and the hotel room tax is a steep 14.9%.

TIME The continental United States is divided into four time zones: eastern standard time (EST), central standard time (CST), mountain standard time (MST), and Pacific standard time (PST); Chicago is in the central time zone. Alaska and Hawaii have their own zones. For example, when it's 9am in Los Angeles (PST), it's 7am in Honolulu (HST), 10am in Denver (MST), 11am in Chicago (CST), noon in New York City (EST), 5pm in London (GMT), and 2am the next day in Sydney.

Daylight saving time is in effect from 1am on the second Sunday in March to 1am on the first Sunday in November, except in Arizona, Hawaii, the U.S. Virgin Islands, and Puerto Rico. Daylight saving time moves the clock 1 hour ahead of standard time.

TIPPING Tips are a very important part of certain workers' income, and gratuities are the standard way of showing appreciation for services provided. (Tipping is certainly not compulsory if the service is poor!)

In hotels, tip **bellhops** at least $1 per bag ($2–$3 if you have a lot of luggage) and tip the **chamber staff** $1 to $2 per day (more if you've left a disaster area for him or her to clean up). Tip the **doorman** or **concierge** only if he or she has provided you with some specific service. (For example, calling a cab for you or obtaining difficult-to-get theater tickets.) Tip the **valet-parking attendant** $1 every time you get your car.

In restaurants, bars, and nightclubs, tip **service staff** and **bartenders** 15% to 20% of the check, tip **checkroom attendants** $1 per garment, and tip **valet-parking attendants** $1 per vehicle.

As for other service personnel, tip **cab drivers** 15% of the fare; tip **skycaps** at airports at least $1 per bag ($2–$3 if you have a lot of luggage); and tip **hairdressers** and **barbers** 15% to 20%.

TOILETS You won't find public toilets or "restrooms" on the streets in most U.S. cities but they can be found in hotel lobbies, bars, restaurants, museums, department stores, railway and bus stations, and service stations. Large hotels and fast-food restaurants are often the best bet for clean facilities. Restaurants and bars in resorts or heavily visited areas may reserve their restrooms for patrons.

VISAS For information about U.S. visas go to **http://travel.state.gov** and click on "Visas." Or go to one of the following websites:

Australian citizens can obtain up-to-date visa information from the **U.S. Embassy Canberra,** Moonah Place, Yarralumla, ACT 2600 (✆ **02/6214-5600**) or by checking the U.S. Diplomatic Mission's website at **http://usembassy-australia.state.gov/consular**.

British subjects can obtain up-to-date visa information by calling the **U.S. Embassy Visa Information Line** (✆ **0891/200-290**) or by visiting the "Visas to the U.S." section of the American Embassy London's website at **www.usembassy.org.uk**.

Irish citizens can obtain up-to-date visa information through the **Embassy of the USA Dublin,** 42 Elgin Rd., Dublin 4, Ireland (✆ **353/1-668-8777**) or by checking the "Visas to the U.S." section of the website at **http://dublin.usembassy.gov**.

Citizens of **New Zealand** can obtain up-to-date visa information by contacting the **U.S. Embassy New Zealand,** 29 Fitzherbert Terrace, Thorndon, Wellington (✆ **644/472-2068**), or get the information directly from the website at **http://wellington.usembassy.gov**.

VISITOR INFORMATION Before your trip, check in with the **Chicago Convention & Tourism Bureau** (✆ **877/CHICAGO** [244-2246]; www.choosechicago.com), to find out about upcoming events and travel packages. (They'll also mail you a packet of materials if you want.) Click the "Maps" link on the right-hand side of the home page for links to maps of Chicago neighborhoods. The **Illinois Bureau of Tourism** (✆ **800/2CONNECT** [226-6632], or TTY 800/406-6418; www.enjoyillinois.com) will also send you information about Chicago and other Illinois destinations.

Once you're here, you may want to stop by one of the city's two official visitors' centers. The **Chicago Cultural Center,** 77 E. Randolph St. (at Michigan Ave.), once the city's public library, is a beautiful, landmark building that's worth a look as you're passing through the Loop. Its visitors' center is open Monday through Friday from 8am to 6pm, Saturday from 9am to 6pm, and Sunday from 10am to 6pm; it's closed on holidays.

The **Chicago Water Works Visitor Center** is in the old pumping station at Michigan and Chicago avenues in the heart of the city's shopping district. The entrance is on the Pearson Street side of the building, across from the Water Tower

Place mall. It's open daily from 7:30am to 7pm. This location has the added draw of housing a location of **Hot Tix,** which offers both half-price day-of-performance and full-price tickets to many theater productions around the city, as well as a gift shop.

For more travel planning information, see chapter 1 for a list of the best Chicago websites.

2 AIRLINE, HOTEL & CAR RENTAL WEBSITES

The following is a list of airlines that serve Chicago. All international flights arrive at O'Hare's Terminal 5 (which is separate from the rest of the airport), but a few (Iberia, Lufthansa) depart from different terminals, so check before going to the airport.

MAJOR AIRLINES

Aeroméxico
www.aeromexico.com

Air France
www.airfrance.com

Air India
www.airindia.com

Air Jamaica
www.airjamaica.com

Alaska Airlines/Horizon Air
www.alaskaair.com

Alitalia
www.alitalia.com

American Airlines
www.aa.com

British Airways
www.british-airways.com

Continental Airlines
www.continental.com

Delta Air Lines
www.delta.com

El Al Airlines
www.elal.co.il

Frontier Airlines
www.frontierairlines.com

Iberia Airlines
www.iberia.com

Japan Airlines
www.jal.co.jp

Korean Air
www.koreanair.com

Lufthansa
www.lufthansa.com

Midwest Airlines
www.midwestairlines.com

Northwest Airlines
www.nwa.com

Swiss Air
www.swiss.com

TACA
www.taca.com

Turkish Airlines
www.thy.com

United Airlines
www.united.com

US Airways
www.usairways.com

Virgin Atlantic Airways
www.virgin-atlantic.com

BUDGET AIRLINES

Aer Lingus
www.aerlingus.com

AirTran Airways
www.airtran.com

Frontier Airlines
www.frontierairlines.com

JetBlue Airways
www.jetblue.com

Ryanair
www.ryanair.com

Ted (part of United Airlines)
www.flyted.com

Southwest Airlines
www.southwest.com

MAJOR HOTEL & MOTEL CHAINS

Best Western International
www.bestwestern.com

Clarion Hotels
www.choicehotels.com

Comfort Inns
www.ComfortInn.com

Courtyard by Marriott
www.marriott.com/courtyard

Crowne Plaza Hotels
www.ichotelsgroup.com/crowneplaza

Days Inn
www.daysinn.com

Doubletree Hotels
www.doubletree.com

Econo Lodges
www.choicehotels.com

Embassy Suites
www.embassysuites.com

Fairfield Inn by Marriott
www.fairfieldinn.com

Four Seasons
www.fourseasons.com

Hampton Inn
www.hamptoninn1.hilton.com

Hilton Hotels
www.hilton.com

Holiday Inn
www.holidayinn.com

Howard Johnson
www.hojo.com

Hyatt
www.hyatt.com

InterContinental Hotels & Resorts
www.ichotelsgroup.com

La Quinta Inns and Suites
www.lq.com

Loews Hotels
www.loewshotels.com

Marriott
www.marriott.com

Motel 6
www.motel6.com

Omni Hotels
www.omnihotels.com

Quality
www.QualityInn.ChoiceHotels.com

Radisson Hotels & Resorts
www.radisson.com

Ramada Worldwide
www.ramada.com

Red Carpet Inns
www.bookroomsnow.com

Red Lion Hotels
www.redlion.rdln.com

Red Roof Inns
www.redroof.com

Renaissance
www.renaissancehotels.com

Residence Inn by Marriott
www.marriott.com/residenceinn

Sheraton Hotels & Resorts
www.starwoodhotels.com/sheraton

Super 8 Motels
www.super8.com

Travelodge
www.travelodge.com

Westin Hotels & Resorts
www.starwoodhotels.com/westin

Wyndham Hotels & Resorts
www.wyndham.com

CAR RENTAL AGENCIES

Advantage
www.advantage.com

Alamo
www.alamo.com

Avis
www.avis.com

Budget
www.budget.com

Dollar
www.dollar.com

Enterprise
www.enterprise.com

Hertz
www.hertz.com

National
www.nationalcar.com

Thrifty
www.thrifty.com

FAST FACTS, TOLL-FREE NUMBERS & WEBSITES

11

AIRLINE, HOTEL & CAR RENTAL WEBSITES

INDEX

See also Accommodations and Restaurant indexes, below.